System Center 2012 Configuration Manager SP1

Mastering the Fundamentals, 2nd Edition

Kent Agerlund

PUBLISHED BY
Deployment Artist
http://www.deploymentartist.com

ISBN: 978-91-87445-01-9

Warning and Disclaimer

Every effort has been made to make this book as complete and as accurate as possible, but no warranty or fitness is implied. The information provided is on an "as is" basis. The authors and the publisher shall have neither liability nor responsibility to any person or entity with respect to any loss or damages arising from the information contained in this book.

Feedback Information

We'd like to hear from you! If you have any comments about how we could improve the quality of this book, please don't hesitate to contact us by visiting www.deploymentfundamentals.com, send an email to feedback@deploymentfundamentals.com or visit our Facebook site www.facebook.com/deploymentfundamentals.

Foreword

Are you new to System Center Configuration Manager, especially System Center 2012 Configuration Manager? If the answer is a 'yes', then this book may be exactly what you need to get your feet underneath you and help you get familiar with the product and its features. Configuration Manager is an application that can complete quite a few management tasks that you need to perform to effectively manage your client computer environment. It is not just a simple—throw in the DVD, run Setup, and away you go—product. Sure, if you have experience with previous versions of Microsoft's Systems Management Server or Configuration Manager, it may be fairly easy for you to install Configuration Manager 2012 and get your environment to work as you need. However, if you are new to Microsoft systems management, then this book should help you out immensely.

Configuration Manager interacts with a number of your infrastructure components, such as Active Directory Domain Services, SQL Server, Windows Server Update Services, Windows Deployment Services, Internet Information Services, network protocols and communications. With that background information, it is very important for you to effectively plan your environment before you do attempt to install Configuration Manager. This book will help you design and deploy your environment before you attempt to install it to use for client management.

I know Kent, and know that you are in for a treat. He is one of our Microsoft Most Valuable Professionals (MVP). He is very knowledgeable on Configuration Manager, having presented at a number of Microsoft events. I'm sure that you'll enjoy the book and learn a lot about Configuration Manager. No one book can teach you all there is to know about Configuration Manager; however, this book will be a great start to your adventure with System Center 2012 Configuration Manager. Enjoy the book and your experience with Configuration Manager.

With kind regards,

Wally Mead
Senior Program Manager
Configuration Manager product group

Acknowledgements

This book would not exist without the love and support from my (very) patient family. Thank you, Nanna, Julie and Susanne. You are always in my heart.

Thank you, Johan Arwidmark, for giving me the opportunity to write this book, a challenge that I just couldn't resist.

Thanks to the System Center product team at Microsoft, and my fellow MVP mates around the globe, especially to Mr. Brian Mason for bringing me to the best steak houses in the US, and for having time to discuss ConfigMgr 2012. As always, huge thanks to my colleagues at Coretech, whom I'm proud to be associated with. These guys are by far the best and most creative team I have ever worked with. Guys, you'll Never Work Alone. Thanks to Henrik Hoe for testing all the labs in the book.

One thing I have learned from working with Configuration Manager is that the knowledge is universal. Configuration Manager really rocks the world, and administrators all over the world are often facing the same challenges. Just for fun, I made a note of the places that I visited while writing this book. While working on the book, I have also done ConfigMgr-related work in Copenhagen, Stockholm, Oslo, Trondheim, Seattle, Boston, New York, Zürich, Minneapolis, Las Vegas, Atlanta, Orlando, Geneva, and finally London.

While I was writing the book, my good friend and colleague Michael Petersen sadly passed away. I have known and worked closely together with Michael for many years. Never before in my life have I met a guy as passionate about his work as Michael. Those thousands of readers who have been following Michael on twitter (@osdeploy) or thru his blog (blog.coretech.dk/mip) knows about his dedication and his ability to make complex challenges look easy. Working with Michael on a daily basis has been a blast.

@Michael, you will never be forgotten – thanks for everything.

Finally, a huge thanks to my Bose noise reduction headset, which has blessed my journey with tunes from Bruce Springsteen, AC/DC, John Denver, Volbeat, Toto, and the all mighty Mr. Frank "Blue Eyes" Sinatra. Trust me when I say, "a little Sinatra each day keeps the dark side away."

About the Authors

Kent Agerlund

Kent Agerlund is chief system management architect and System Center specialist working as certified trainer, consultant and event speaker. Kent started his computer endeavors back in the late 80s working with databases like dBase, Paradox, and FoxPro. Almost since the beginning of his professional computer career, Kent has worked as a certified trainer and consultant. Today Kent works for Coretech, a Danish System Center house where he also contributes by writing articles and sharing tips and tricks on http://blog.coretech.dk. In recent years, Kent has travelled the globe delivering his Mastering Configuration Manager classes and speaking at various conferences like MMS and TechEd. Through the years, Kent has attained various certifications and achievements such as Windows 2008 R2 Enterprise Administrator, MCSE+A, and MCT, and has been awarded Microsoft Most Valuable Professional (MVP) in Enterprise Client Management.

You can connect with Kent on Twitter @Agerlund and on Linkedin at http://www.linkedin.com/in/kentagerlund

Contributing Authors

Kaido Jarvemets

A special tribute to Kaido Jarvemets, a fellow Enterprise Client Management MVP. Kaido provided the PowerShell scripts used in the book. Kaido works as an IT expert at Coretech Denmark and is the president at System Center User Group Estonia. Kaido also writes articles and shares tips and tricks on blog.coretech.dk/author/kaj.

Peter Daalmans

Huge thanks to Peter for contributing good ideas and helping out with writing some of the chapters. Peter is a fellow Microsoft MVP in Enterprise Client Management and lives in Breda, Netherlands. Peter works at IT-Concern, a Microsoft Gold Partner, as a Senior Technical Consultant. Peter is one of the founders of the Windows Management User Group in the Netherlands.You can follow Peter from his blog at configmgrblog.com or on Twitter @pdaalmans.

Contents

Introduction

System Center 2012 Configuration Manager SP1: Mastering the Fundamentals, 2nd Edition is the ultimate source for the working IT Pro who wants to design and implement System Center 2012 Configuration Manager in a in a midsize or small business environment. Enterprise administrators also will find a lot inspiration by reading the book, as many of the features and scenarios discussed fit all three environments.

Configuration Manager (ConfigMgr) is by far the most complex Microsoft product. This book focuses on HOW TO GET IT DONE RIGHT THE FIRST TIME, based on years of experience with Configuration Manager and SMS. You will not find 1,000 pages describing all the possible ways to implement ConfigMgr, but rather learn the time-tested essentials for a successful implementation, saving you many hours and headaches. After reading this book, you will have a working Configuration Manager 2012 environment with all the major features implemented. Furthermore, you will have a solid understanding of how to configure the features according to best practices and know how to troubleshoot real-world scenarios.

Say Hello (Possibly Again) to ViaMonstra Inc.

In this book, you implement ConfigMgr 2012 SP1 for the fictive ViaMonstra Inc. organization. ViaMonstra is a midsized company with 6,500 users. There is one datacenter based in New York and several remote offices in the United States and Europe. Among the users, 3,500 work in the New York office; the remote sites all have fewer than 200 users except for Liverpool, which has 750 employees.

ViaMonstra currently doesn't use any standardized system management solution. Decisions have been made to standardize and automate the company's desktop and server management. The management solution is Microsoft System Center 2012, and Configuration Manager (also known as ConfigMgr) is the first product to be implemented. The focus of the book is ConfigMgr 2012 SP1, and I do anticipate that you already have knowledge about Windows Server Update Services (WSUS), Windows Deployment Services (WDS), Domain Name System (DNS), Dynamic Host Configuration Protocol (DHCP), and Microsoft Active Directory.

BTW, the name ViaMonstra comes from *Viam Monstra*, Latin, meaning "Show me the way."

Structure of the Book

The first chapter is a concept crash course, which explains the terminology and scenarios used in the book. The second chapter describes ViaMonstra Inc. in more detail, as well as the proof-of-concept environment I use.

Chapters 3–4 explain how to install and configure ConfigMgr 2012 site server and site system server. Chapters 5–11 focus on each of the primary features in ConfigMgr. Chapter 12 covers backup and restore, and Chapter 13 is a tribute to the ConfigMgr communities, blogs, and tools that I use on a daily basis.

Finally, I have the appendices, which include extra material on how to set up the related services.

How to Use This Book

I have packed this book with step-by-step guides, which means you can implement your solution as you read along.

In numbered steps, all names and paths are in bold typeface. I also have used a standard naming convention throughout the book when explaining what to do in each step. The steps normally are something like this:

- On the **Advanced Properties** page, select the **Confirm** check box, and then click **Next**.

Code and sample scripts are formatted like the following, on a grey background.

```
OSDMigrateMode=Advanced
```

The step-by-step guides in this book assume that you have configured the environment according to the information in Chapter 2, "ViaMonstra Inc. and the Datacenter."

This book is not intended as a reference volume, covering every deployment technology, acronym, or command-line switch known to man, but rather is designed to make sure you learn what you need to know to build a great deployment solution for your Windows servers.

Sample Files

All sample files used in this book can be downloaded from www.deploymentfundamentals.com.

Additional Resources

In addition to all the tips and tricks provided in this book, you will find extra resources like video recordings on the www.deploymentfundamentals.com site.

Topics Not Covered

I do not cover out of band management in this edition of the book.

Chapter 1

Crash Course

As promised earlier, I have a concept crash course in this book, and this is it. The shorthand story: When using ConfigMgr, there are terms and services you need to know. This is a ten-minute crash course in Microsoft System Center 2012 Configuration Manager SP1 terminology.

The System Center 2012 Suite

With the release of System Center 2012 on April 17 2012, Microsoft has reached a milestone in its effort to deliver a complete set of tools to manage all aspects of the datacenter and client devices. Configuration Manager is a crucial part of the suite, and you can implement it as a stand-alone solution or together with the other System Center products like Operations Manager, Orchestrator, and Service Manager.

The System Center 2012 Family

Product	**Short Description**
Configuration Manager	Configuration Manager, or ConfigMgr, is a systems management application providing application deployment, operating systems deployment, software update management, compliance management, and inventory management to servers, users, and their devices.
Operations Manager	Operations Manager, or OpsMgr, allows management across server operating systems and hypervisors through views that show state, health, and performance information. It also allows you to be proactive by generating alerts based on factors like performance, availability, configuration, security, and much more.
Service Manager	Service Manager provides built-in processes for change control and incident and problem resolution. Service Manager can be integrated with the other System Center products like Orchestrator, ConfigMgr, and OpsMgr. Together they form a powerful alliance in any datacenter.

Product	Short Description
Orchestrator	I often refer to Orchestrator as the glue that enables you to convert a manual process into a fully automated process. You can use Orchestrator to grab information from one System Center product, connect to any client (or server), and then perform one or a series of tasks based on the information. At any given point during this sequence of tasks, you can configure Orchestrator to interact and deliver information to the other System Center applications.
Data Protection Manager (DPM)	DPM delivers unified data protection for Windows servers and clients. In essence, this is the backup solution you should use across the board regardless of where you store data—on tape, disk, or cloud.
Virtual Machine Manager (VMM)	VMM enables centralized management of physical and virtual IT infrastructure. It is also a platform for planning, deploying, managing, and optimizing the virtual infrastructure.
App Controller	App Controller provides a self-service experience across private and public clouds. It enables application owners to build, configure, deploy, and manage new services in the private or public cloud.
Endpoint Protection	Endpoint Protection is the successor of Forefront Endpoint Protection, an antimalware application that can be deployed and managed through Configuration Manager 2012.

Site Servers

A site server is the server you install through the System Center Installation Wizard. Without a site server in your environment, you cannot have ConfigMgr installed. It's as simple as that. When installing the site server, you also automatically install a site that is represented with a site name and a three-digit site code. Once you have the site server, you start installing site system roles. A site system role can be hosted on the site server, or you can choose to install the role on another server; one site system can even be deployed on a client operating system.

Prior to installing your environment, you need to have some basic knowledge of the three different site servers that you can install and when you need to install them. I work with enterprise, midsize, and small business customers, and what I have learned is that there is no installation scenario that fits all; but there are some questions you can ask yourself to figure out how many sites and, by extension, how many site servers you need.

Central Administration Site

A central administration site (CAS) is the top site server in the hierarchy. Unlike the other site servers, you cannot assign any clients to the CAS, nor can you install any user-facing site systems roles except from the software update point. A CAS stores client data for all clients in the hierarchy in a SQL Server database called the ConfigMgr site database. The CAS can have multiple primary child sites, all of which send data to the CAS. At the CAS, you also have the Administrator console from which you can manage hierarchy.

Question: *Do I always need a central administration site?*

Answer: No, a CAS is needed only when you have more than one primary site in the hierarchy. As a matter of fact, most readers of this book may never need to implement a CAS.

Question: *If needed, when should I install the central administration site?*

Answer: With Service Pack 1, you can install a CAS after you have installed a primary site. Prior to Service Pack 1 you had to install the CAS first. With that in mind, there is really no reason to install a CAS upfront as a "just in case solution." I have seen that done by many customers, and so far none of them needs a CAS.

Primary Site

You always need at least one primary site in the hierarchy. If you do not, there is really no reason for you to finish reading this book or any other ConfigMgr-related book. It's very simple: without a primary site, you have no working ConfigMgr environment. Clients can be assigned only to a primary site. A primary site stores client data for all clients assigned to the site in a SQL Server database called the ConfigMgr site database. Primary sites have administrative tools, such as the Administrator console, that enable an administrator to manage the site directly. Primary sites can have multiple secondary sites, all of which send data to the primary site.

Question: When do I need more than one primary site?

Answer: That's a good question, and I'm so glad you asked it. Unlike previous versions of ConfigMgr (and SMS), there are not many reasons why you would implement more than one primary site when using ConfigMgr 2012. The main reasons for implementing more than one primary site are:

- You have more than 100,000 users, which is the recommended maximum number for a primary site.
- For political reasons, you are required to have a primary site in each data center.

Question: *I get the point; I need an additional primary site only if I scale beyond 100,000. I have no plans for that; however, fault tolerance is really important in my organization, and we will not tolerate downtime for too long. After all, we do plan to use ConfigMgr to deploy applications and new operating systems, and also to keep our operating systems and applications up-to-date with the latest security patches. Not to mention that we plan to implement Endpoint Protection and always must have the latest definition updates applied.*

Answer: Ouch! We are just in the first chapter, and you are already asking one of the most important questions in terms of designing ConfigMgr. Well, you need to understand that a ConfigMgr site consists of different site systems and those site systems do not have to be installed on the same server. As a matter of fact, in most midsized companies, I always recommend that you remove any user-facing site system roles from the site server. When you plan for fault tolerance, you need to look at the individual role because there are individual rules for the different site system roles. Some roles support clustering (like the site system database), whereas other site systems can be hosted on several servers (e.g. distribution points and management points) and finally other site systems also support network load balancing (NLB).

Question: *OK, I understand. So, what you are saying is that I should focus on implementing multiple site system roles instead of multiple primary site servers. But what are the consequences if my boss does not understand me and still requires two primary sites?*

Answer: Well, first off, you need to implement two new sites, a CAS and one additional site. That will give you a total of three sites that you need to manage, which in my opinion makes the environment too complex and you haven't achieved much in terms of fault tolerance compared to having a single site with multiple site systems. Also, remember that whenever you start to implement a site, you say "Hello" to site replication. Replication between sites is done through SQL replication, and the old-fashioned file-based replication. One of the things that, as a consultant, I have struggled with most in the past has been replication issues, and I will go a long way to avoid that in ConfigMgr 2012.

Secondary Site

Unlike previous versions of ConfigMgr and SMS, a secondary site now also requires a SQL Server database. It doesn't have to be a Standard or Enterprise version, as the SQL Server Express edition will do just fine. If you don't have a local database, the secondary site installation can take care of that and install a version of SQL Server Express. The secondary site is always a child site of the primary site and thus managed thru the ConfigMgr Administrator console connected to the primary site. The secondary site forwards the information it gathers from clients, such as computer inventory data and system status information, to its parent site. The primary site then stores the data of both the primary and secondary sites in the site database. Secondary sites are particularly useful for remote locations where you need links where you need to control the bandwidth.

Question: *Are there any rules of thumb for when I should implement a secondary site at a remote location?*

Answer: I only recommend installing a secondary site at remote locations and only if one of the following statements is true:

- The remote location has more than 500 clients.
- You need to compress traffic going to the site.
- You need to control the upward flowing traffic.
- You need a local management point.
- You need a local software update point.

Real World Note: Do not use a management point (covered in the next section) instead of a secondary site. I highly discourage configuring a management point in a remote location. It is not what I call a "site-aware site system" like a distribution point. Inevitably, some clients from the entire site will connect to and use the management point, which eventually will cause a backlog on the server.

Site Systems

As mentioned earlier in this chapter, a site is made up of a site server hosting the site *server* role and multiple site *system* roles. The site system roles can be hosted on several different servers, or you can choose to implement all site systems on the same server. I have seen several medium and small site installations where all the roles are hosted on the same server, and everything runs perfectly.

Management Point

The management point is the primary point of contact between clients and the site server. A ConfigMgr 2012 site can host ten management points, but you should not install them across a WAN link because a management point is not "site-aware." A management point provides specific client configuration details, also known as client *policies*. It receives inventory, software metering, and status information from clients and forwards it to the site server.

Software Update Point (SUP)

A software update point is a WSUS server controlled by Configuration Manager. Unlike a stand-alone WSUS solution, clients do not download or install updates directly from a software update point. The only data downloaded by the client from a software update point is the update metadata. In Service Pack 1, there is support for multiple software update points in a primary site. A client will toggle between software update points only when the assigned software update point is not responding. For that reason, you might want to configure multiple software update points before you start deploying clients. Otherwise, you will have one software update point servicing all clients and another software update point acting as a "hot standby server." If you need to plan for true network load balancing, the solution is to implement a Windows Network Load Balancing (NLB) solution. With Service Pack 1, that can be achieved either using the ConfigMgr SDK or PowerShell. It's outside the scope of this book to describe that configuration; however, you can find information about it in this TechNet article: http://technet.microsoft.com/en-us/library/hh237369.aspx.

Distribution Point

Whenever a client needs to install an application or a software update, the client will connect to a distribution point to fetch the software. With Service Pack 1, there are two different distribution points, on-premise and cloud based. There are no more branch distribution points or server shares. The distribution point stores packages in a new content library, which supports single instance storage for all content and thus minimizes the space required to host all packages. Another of the new cool features in this version is that you can control traffic going to the distribution point and also prestage content using any media. It's not uncommon for a distribution point to host several 100 GBs of content. So when setting up a new distribution point at a remote location, you will find the prestaging very convenient. No more sneaking along the walls when you are passing the network monitoring team office. No worries, you will not flood the network.

Distribution points can be grouped in state-based distribution point groups. The major benefit of distribution point groups is that all distribution points in the group will have the exact same content. Even if you add a new distribution point to the group, it automatically receives the same packages. (Yes, I did use the word "packages." I use that term to describe content regardless of whether it's an application, WIM file, or software update.)

Distribution Requirements

An on-premise distribution point is the only site system role that can be deployed to a client operating system and supports both x32 and x64. When you install a distribution point, you can configure the site server to install the needed IIS role and features. A cloud-based distribution point requires a Windows Azure subscription and a management certificate.

Application Catalog Web Service Point

An Application Catalog web service point provides software information to the Application Catalog website from the Software Library. This site system role is installed only on the primary site.

Application Catalog Website Point

A new end-user web portal allows end users to request and install software. Applications deployed to end users are presented in the Self-Service Portal.

Site Database Server

The ConfigMgr site database server is a computer running SQL Server that stores information such as discovery data, hardware and software inventory data, and configuration and status information for the ConfigMgr sites in the hierarchy.

Fallback Status Point (FSP)

The fallback status point is used by clients when they are unable to communicate with management points. There are a few scenarios in which that can happen, such as during the client installation and assignment phase, or when a client configured to communicate using HTTPS for some reason has a problem with the certificate. Before installing the FSP, you need to be aware of the fact the non-authenticated and non-encrypted traffic is accepted by the site system.

Reporting Services Point

The SQL Reporting Services point, or reporting services point, is the only supported reporting solution in ConfigMgr 2012. You can find SQL Server Reporting Services on your SQL Server DVD and install it along with the SQL Server database.

Asset Intelligence Synchronization Point

The Asset Intelligence synchronization point is always installed at the top-most site server in the hierarchy. The site system will connect to System Center Online and synchronize updates to the Assent Intelligence.

Endpoint Protection Point

The Endpoint Protection point is a required site system when you want to install and manage Endpoint Protection clients using ConfigMgr You need to install the site system at the CAS server. When installing the site system, you won't really do much, only accept the Endpoint Protection client license information and configure the relationship with Microsoft Active Protection Service (formerly known as Microsoft Spynet).

Enrollment Point

An enrollment point is used to complete mobile device enrollment, enroll Apple Macintosh OS X computers, and provision AMT-based computers using PKI certificates. The mobile devices that use enrollment points are often refered to as being legacy mobile devices with operating systems like Windows Mobile 6.x. Newer devices like Windows Phone 8 and Apple iOS are managed through Windows Intune.

Enrollment Proxy Point

An enrollment proxy point manages the enrollment requests from mobile devices and Apple Macintosh OS X computers.

Out of Band Service Point

An out of band service point provisions and configures AMT-based computers for out of band management. To better understand what out of band management is, think of in-band management, which is basically managing computers that are powered on and accessible. Out of band management is the opposite of that; it's managing computers that are not powered on.

Windows Intune Connector

This site system role is available only after you have created a Windows Intune subscription in the ConfigMgr console. The connector is a gateway that connects to the Windows Intune Service and enables ConfigMgr to manage mobile devices from within the ConfigMgr console Configuration Manager Related Services.

One of the real powers of ConfigMgr is that it often uses services already implemented in the network. For most organizations, no new network services have to be implemented in order to service ConfigMgr. Having said that, you still need to ensure that you have good knowledge of the following:

- Active Directory
- Dynamic Host Configuration Protocol (DHCP)
- Domain Name System (DNS)
- Internet Information Server (IIS)
- Key Management Service (KMS)
- Public key infrastructure (PKI)—if you choose to let site systems and clients communicate using HTTPS
- Windows Deployment Services (WDS)
- Windows Management Instrumentation (WMI)
- Windows Server Update Services (WSUS)

That wraps up the elementary school. Now you know what a site and a site system are and what services you rely on when implementing ConfigMgr 2012.

Chapter 2

ViaMonstra Inc. and the Datacenter

As you remember from the first chapter, ViaMonstra Inc. is the fictive company I use throughout this book. In this chapter, I describe the company in more detail, as well as the management solution I have built for that company. I also provide details about the proof-of-concept (datacenter) environment I use in the step-by-step guides.

In addition to the information in this chapter, you can find detailed instructions on how to install and configure the servers in Appendix A. If you want to follow all the step-by-step guides in this book, you need to have your environment set up as described in Appendix A. In the appendix, you use the sample files included with this book; all these files can be downloaded from www.deploymentfundamentals.com.

Note: The password for the accounts created by the hydration kit is Password01 (including the Administrator account).

ViaMonstra Inc.

ViaMonstra Inc. was invented for the very purpose of having a "real" company for which to build a deployment solution. In the real world, these deployment solutions come from multiple consulting engagements I have done. For purposes of this book, I have consolidated them into a single generic scenario. As mentioned in Chapter 1, ViaMonstra has a single datacenter, which is described in the following sections.

Hardware

ViaMonstra Inc. knows that the key factors involved in developing any good performing ConfigMgr site server is choosing the correct disk layout, combined with lots of memory for SQL Server and the appropriate CPUs. With that in mind, ViaMonstra has decided to install a storage area network (SAN) with the storage of five RAID 10 LUNs with separate spindles.

The site server (virtual machine) and disk layout for a midsized installation like ViaMonstra looks like this:

- **Host (to run the virtual machines).** HP ProLiant DL380p Gen8
- **Memory.** 32 GB RAM (You will do just fine with 16 GB RAM to finish all the exercises in this book.)
- **CPU.** 2 * Intel® Xeon® E5-2630 with six cores

Drive	Usage	Disk Size
C:\	Operating system	72 GB
D:\	Program files	100 GB
E:\	Content library	300 GB
F:\	SQL Server TempDB system database (TempDB)	50 GB (Estimated TempDB size is 35% of total database size.)
G:\	SQL Server database (.db) files	100 GB (Estimated database size is 30 GB.)
H:\	SQL Server transaction log files	75 GB (Estimated log size is 11 GB.)

Software

Like most companies, ViaMonstra has some core desktop applications and some custom-made lines of business applications. The following list describes ViaMonstra's deployed roles, features, and applications related to this ConfigMgr project:

- Domain controller
- DNS
- DHCP
- Exchange 2013
- Hyper-V
- SQL Server 2012
- Microsoft Office 2013
- 7-Zip
- WinRAR
- BGInfo

Servers

In the step-by-step guides, what I call Build-While-Reading, I use the following virtual machines.

Real World Note: In any production-like environment, make sure that at least one of the domain controllers runs on a physical machine. Please don't make the mistake of running all the domain controllers as virtual machines, at least not when your Hyper-V hosts are members of the domain they host.

- **DC01.** A **Windows Server 2012 Enterprise** machine, fully patched with the latest security updates, and configured as Active Directory Domain Controller, DNS Server, Certificate, and DHCP Server in the **corp.viamonstra.com** domain.
  - Server name: **DC01**
  - IP Address: **192.168.1.200**
  - Roles: **DNS, DHCP** and **Domain Controller**
- **CM01.** A **Windows Server 2012** machine, fully patched with the latest security updates, and configured as a member server in the **corp.viamonstra.com** domain. The server has been configured with the WDS and WSUS roles; it has SQL Server 2012 Standard installed.
  - Server name: **CM01**
  - IP Address: **192.168.1.214**
  - Roles: **Management Point**, **Software Update Point**, **Distribution Point**, **Application Catalog Web Service Point**, and **Application Catalog Website Point**
  - Software: **SQL Server 2012 Standard, Configuration Manager 2012 Site Server**, and **Microsoft Deployment Toolkit 2012 Update 1**

  For detailed, step-by-step guidance on how to configure the CM01 server, please review Appendix A, "Using the Hydration Kit to Build the POC Environment."
- **PC0001.** A **Windows 8 x64 client**, fully patched with the latest security updates, and configured as a member server in the **corp.viamonstra.com** domain.
  - Client name: **PC0001**
  - IP Address: **DHCP client**
  - Roles: **Client**
- **PC0002.** A **Windows 7 x64 client**, fully patched with the latest security updates, and configured as a member server in the **corp.viamonstra.com** domain.
  - Client name: **PC0002**
  - IP Address: **DHCP client**
  - Roles: **Client**
- **CM02.** A **Windows Server 2012** machine, fully patched with the latest security updates, and configured as a member server in the **corp.viamonstra.com** domain. This server represents the remote distribution point that ViaMonstra has in the Stockholm site. The site system roles are all installed as part of the book guides.
  - Server name: **CM02**
  - IP Address: **192.168.2.215**
  - Roles: **Remote PXE-enabled Distribution Point**

- **CM03.** A **Windows Server 2012** machine, fully patched with the latest security updates, and configured as a member server in the **corp.viamonstra.com** domain. This is the secondary site server in Liverpool. The site server and site system roles all are installed as part of the book.
    - Server name: **CM03**
    - IP Address: **192.168.3.214**
    - Roles: Secondary **Site Server with Management Point**, **Remote PXE-enabled Distribution Point**, and **State Migration Point**
- **EX01.** An optional **Windows Server 2012** machine, fully patched with the latest security updates, and configured as a mail server in the **corp.viamonstra.com** domain. This server is used only for email subscription configurations and is not required in order to complete the step-by-step guides. The Exchange Server setup itself is not covered in this book.
    - Server name: **EX01**
    - IP Address: **192.168.1.229**
    - Roles: **Exchange 2013**

Real World Note: For a stand-alone lab or test environment, two single disks are just fine. For production use, a distribution point should have two separate disk sets for OS and data (RAID 1 for the OS disk set, and RAID 5 for the data disk set).

Software Requirements

In addition to the configuration and software needed for servers CM01, CM02 and CM03 (see Appendix A), you need the following software to be able to perform all the step-by-step guides in this book:

- Windows Server 2012 media and product key (the product key is used differently depending on whether you use Multiple Activation Keys [MAKs] or Key Management Service [KMS] for activation).
- System Center 2012 Configuration Manager Service Pack 1
- Office 2013 Professional Plus x86 (volume license) and product key
- The following free software downloaded from microsoft.com:
    - System Center Updates Publisher (SCUP) 2011
    - Microsoft Deployment Toolkit (MDT) 2012 Update 1
    - Configuration Manager 2012 Toolkit Service Pack 1
    - Scriptomatic from Microsoft's Scripting Guys
    - BGInfo

- The following software downloaded from rarlabs.com:

  WinRAR

- The following software downloaded from 7-Zip.org:

  7-Zip

Chapter 3

Installing and Configuring ConfigMgr 2012

In this chapter, you learn to install ConfigMgr. As mentioned in Chapter 2, the step-by-step guides in this and the following chapters assume that you have installed and configured the servers as described in Appendix A.

Installing ConfigMgr 2012 is not in itself a difficult task, at least not if you know what you want to install and why. In ViaMonstra, I have decided to install the following ConfigMgr servers:

- In the datacenter, a primary site server
- In Liverpool, a secondary site server
- In each of the remote locations, a remote PXE-enabled distribution point

Before you start installing any site servers, you first need to prepare Active Directory and install SQL Server.

Real World Note: The reason for selecting a secondary site in Liverpool is due to the number of supported users in that location. The magic number is 500 users. Above that you should consider adding a site server in the location. This is not a fixed value, but one based purely on my experiences.

Active Directory Prerequisites

Before implementing ConfigMgr, you need to make a decision whether you want to extend the Active Directory schema. It is not a requirement, but it is a very good idea that will make your life as administrator somewhat easier. After you have extended the schema, clients will be able to query the global catalog and get information about site systems and command-line installation properties. As part of preparing Active Directory, you complete the tasks covered in the following sections.

Extend the Active Directory Schema

1. On **DC01**, log on as **VIAMONSTRA\Administrator**. The password, if you have been using the book hydration kit, is **Password01**.
2. Ensure that you have access to the **ConfigMgr 2012 SP1 DVD** (or other medium).

3. Open a command prompt as **Administrator**, navigate to **.\SMSSETUP\BIN\X64** on the **ConfigMgr 2012 SP1 DVD**, and run **extadsch.exe**.

4. Verify that the schema extension was successful by reviewing the **ExtADSch.log** located in the root of **C:**.

Real World Note: There have been no additional Active Directory schema changes since Configuration Manager 2007. For that reason, if the schema is already extended, you do not have to extend it again.

Create the System Management Container

The System Management container is a folder below the System folder in Active Directory used by the site server and the management points to store published data like boundaries and certificates. The site server can create the container during the installation, but that requires full administrator permissions for the site server computer account on the System Management container. For security reasons, I prefer to add all site servers and management points to a local security group and create the container manually using adsiedit.msc. That way I do not have to grant the site server computer account unnecessary permissions.

1. Create the **ConfigMgr_Servers** AD group:

   a. On **DC01**, log on as **VIAMONSTRA\Administrator** and open **Active Directory Users and Computers**.

   b. In the **Security Groups** OU, create a domain local security group named **ConfigMgr_Servers**.

   c. Add the **CM01, CM02** and **CM03** computers to the **ConfigMgr_Servers** group.

Note: As you learned in Appendix A, the CM02 and CM03 servers only need to be added if you want to configure the Stockholm and Liverpool remote sites. Most of the guides in this book can be completed with only the CM01 server.

   d. Restart the **CM01, CM02** and **CM03** servers. Restarting the servers is needed to update the group membership for a computer account.

2. On **DC01**, open a command prompt as **Administrator** and type **adsiedit.msc** to launch the **ADSI Edit MMC console**.

3. Right-click the **ADSI Edit** node, and then click **Connect to** and **OK**.

4. In the console pane, expand **Default naming context[DC01.corp.viamonstra.com]**, and then expand **DC=corp,DC=viamonstra,DC=com**.

5. Right-click **CN=System**, click **New** on the context menu, and then click **Object**.

6. In the **Create Object** dialog box, select **container** and click **Next**.

7. In the **Value** field, type **System Management** and click **Next**.

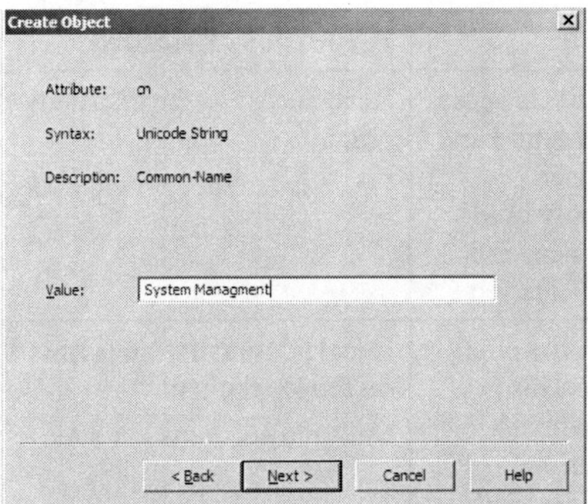

Creating the System Management container.

8. Click **Finish**.
9. Expand the **CN=System** container, right-click **CN=System Management**, and select **Properties**.
10. In the **CN=System Management Properties** dialog box, click the **Security** tab.
11. Click **Advanced**, and click **Add.** Click **Select a principal** and enter **ConfigMgr_Servers**; then click **OK.**
12. Grant the group **Full Control** permissions.
13. In the **Applies to** list, verify that **This object and all descendant objects** is selected.
14. Click **OK** three times, and then close the **ADSI Edit** console.

Users, Groups, and Group Policy Objects

Both ConfigMgr 2012 and SQL Server 2012 can run under the context of the local system account. However, for SQL Server, it is considered a security best practice to create a user account with limited permissions and use that as the service account. For ConfigMgr, the number of user accounts needed depends on the features you wish to implement. In order to use some features, you also need to configure some Group Policy objects (GPOs). You use the GPOs to configure the Windows firewall, add the client push account to the local Administrator group, and configure the local WSUS settings.

The following table includes the different accounts, short descriptions of their purposes, and required permissions.

Account	Description	Permissions Required
Network access	Used whenever a client needs access to the ConfigMgr infrastructure and can't use the logged on user credentials. Two commonly used scenarios are OS deployment and supporting workgroup clients.	Read access to the distribution point. One account per primary site.
Client push	Used in conjunction with the client push installation method. This account connects to the admin$ share on the client, copies the needed client bootstrap files, and creates the ccmsetup service.	Local administrative permissions on the local client. Multiple accounts per site.
Exchange connector	Used to synchronize information from Exchange Server 2013.	Read and modify access to Exchange Server 2013 active sync. One account per hierarchy.
Discovery	Used when the site server computer account does not have access to read information about user, computer, and group objects in Active Directory.	Read access to the needed objects in Active Directory. One account per discovery LDAP path.
Join domain	Used during a task sequence to join the computer account to a domain.	A domain user account with permissions to create and modify computer accounts in a specified OU. Multiple accounts per hierarchy.
SQL Reporting Services dataset authentication	Used whenever you access a SQL Reporting Services report. During the installation of the Reporting Services site system, ConfigMgr will automatically grant the account the needed permissions in SQLServer.	A domain user account. One account per Reporting Services site system.
SQL Server service	Used to start and run the required SQL Server services.	A local system account or a user account. One account per SQL installation.

For ViaMonstra, you need six service accounts: a Network Access Account, a client push account, a join domain account, a SQL Service account, a SQL Reporting Services dataset authentication account, and finally an Exchange connector account.

Review the Required Service Accounts

The hydration kit you used in Appendix A creates the required service accounts.

1. On **DC01**, open **Active Directory Users and Computers**.
2. Expand the **ViaMonstra** OU, and select the **Service Accounts** OU. You should see the following accounts:
    a. **CM_CP** (ConfigMgr 2012 Client Push Account)
    b. **CM_EX** (ConfigMgr 2012 Exchange Connector Account)
    c. **CM_JD** (ConfigMgr 2012 Join Domain Account)
    d. **CM_NAA** (ConfigMgr 2012 Network Access Account)
    e. **CM_SQ** (ConfigMgr 2012 SQL Service Account)
    f. **CM_SR** (ConfigMgr 2012 SQL Reporting Services Account)

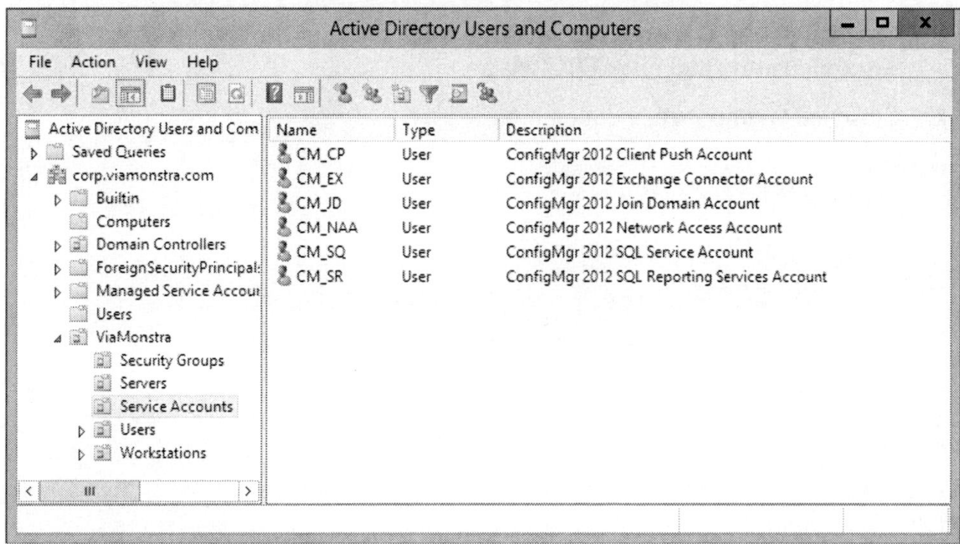

Reviewing the required service accounts.

Configure Group Policy Objects

1. On **DC01**, in the **Security Groups** OU, create a domain local group called **LocalCorpAdmins** and add **CM_CP** account to the group.

2. Create a GPO that adds the client push account **CM_CP** to the local administrators group on each machine in the domain :

   a. On **DC01**, open the **Group Policy Management console**.

   b. Expand **Forest: corp.viamonstra.com**.

   c. Expand **Domains**.

   d. Right-click the **corp.viamonstra.com** domain and select **Create a GPO in this domain, and Link it here**.

   e. Create a new Group Policy object called **Add Client Push to Local Admin** and click **OK**.

   f. Expand the **corp.viamonstra.com** domain, right-click **Add Client Push to Local Admin GPO**, and select **Edit**.

   g. Expand **Computer Configuration / Policies / Windows Settings / Security Settings**.

   h. Right-click **Restricted Groups** and select **Add Group**.

   i. Browse to the **LocalCorpAdmins** group you created, add it to **Restricted Groups**, and click **OK**.

   j. For **This group is a member of**, click **Add**. Then, in the **Group** box, type **Administrators** and click **OK** twice.

   k. Close the **Group Policy** dialog box.

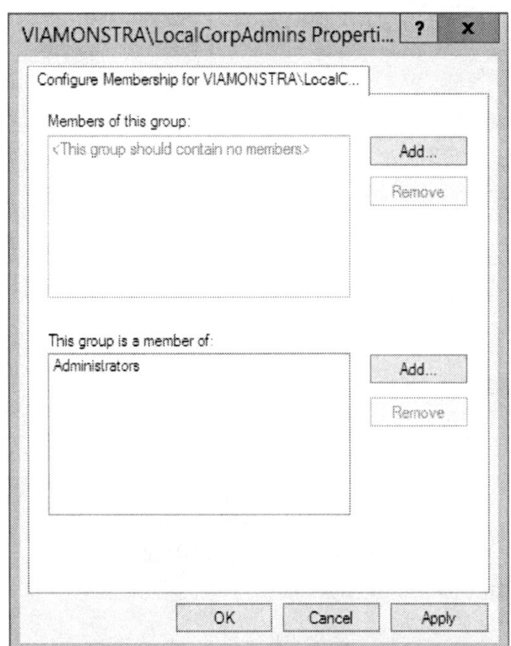

The final part of the GPO configuration for group membership.

3. Configure the Windows Firewall:
   a. In the **Group Policy Management console**, right-click the **corp.viamonstra.com** domain and select **Create a GPO in this domain, and Link it here**.
   b. Create a new **Group Policy object**, and name the object **Configure Firewall**.
   c. Right-click the **Configure Firewall** policy and select **Edit**.
   d. Expand **Computer Configuration / Policies / Administrative Templates / Network / Network Connections / Windows Firewall / Domain Profile**.
   e. Enable the **Windows Firewall: Allow inbound file and printer sharing exception** and **Windows Firewall: Allow inbound remote administration exception** policies.
   f. Close the **Group Policy** dialog box.
4. Configure local WSUS policies:
   a. In the **Group Policy Management console**, right-click the **corp.viamonstra.com** domain and select **Create a GPO in this domain, and Link it here**.
   b. Create a new **Group Policy object**, and name the object **Configure WSUS**.
   c. Right-click **Configure WSUS** and select **Edit**.
   d. Expand **Computer Configuration / Policies / Administrative Templates / Windows components / Windows Update**.
   e. Enable the **Allow signed updates from an Intranet Microsoft Update service location** policy.
   f. Disable the **Configure Automatic Updates** policy.
   g. Close the **Group Policy** dialog box.
5. Close the **Group Policy Management console**.

Configure Join Computer Permissions

1. On **DC01**, open **Active Directory User and Computers**.
2. In the **View** menu, select **Advanced Features**.
3. Expand the **ViaMonstra** OU, right-click the **Workstations** OU, select **Properties**, select the **Security** tab, and then click the **Advanced** button.
4. In the **Advanced Security Settings for Workstations** window, click **Add**, click **Select a principal**, type **CM_JD**, and click **OK**.
5. In the **Permissions Entry for Workstations** window, verify that **Applies to:** is set to **This object and all descendant objects**. Then select the following permissions:
   a. **Create Computer objects**
   b. **Delete Computer objects**

6. Click **OK**.
7. In the **Advanced Security Settings for Workstations** window, click **Add** once more, click **Select a principal**, type **CM_JD**, and click **OK**.
8. In the **Permissions Entry for Workstations** window, in **Applies to:**, select **Descendant Computer objects**, and select the following permissions (don't remove the default permissions):
    a. **Read All Properties**
    b. **Write All Properties**
    c. **Read Permissions**
    d. **Modify Permissions**
    e. **Change Password**
    f. **Reset Password**
    g. **Validated write to DNS host name**
    h. **Validated write to service principal name**
9. Click **OK** three times.

SQL Server

There are some facts that you need to be aware of before installing and some post configuration tasks you need to perform to ensure maximum performance. First, the table contains some facts you need know.

Setting	**Value**
Recommended SQL Server version	SQL Server 2012 with SP1 and the latest CU.
SQL Server edition	For a hierarchy with more than 50,000 clients, SQL Server Enterprise Edition at the CAS and Standard Edition at the primary sites. For hierarchies with fewer than 50,000, always SQL Server Standard Edition. SQL Server Standard is often included in the System Center license whereas Enterprise is not. SQL Server Standard edition supports 32 cores and 64 GB RAM.
Installation directory	Same drive as ConfigMgr 2012, e.g. D:\Program Files\.
Database directory	Dedicated drive.
Database files	Equal to the number of cores in the server but never more than eight files.
Log directory	Dedicated drive.

Setting	Value
Log files	One file per database.
TempDB directory	Dedicated drive.
TempDB files	Equal to half the number of CPUs.
TempDB log directory	Dedicated drive. (If this is not possible, place it on the same drive as TempDB.)
TempDB log file	One file.
Memory	A minimum of 8 GB RAM reserved for SQL on CAS and primary sites and 4 GB RAM on a secondary site server.
Collation	SQL_Latin1_General_CP1_CI_AS. (Notice that this, along with Chinese, is the only supported collation orders.)
Service account	Can be the local system or a user account. Using a domain user account is considered to be more secure, but it also requires more work, as you have to manually register the service principal names (SPN). When using a user account, you must register the SPN (service principal name) in Active Directory manually. Registering NetBIOS syntax: Setspn -A MSSQLSvc/<SQL Server name>:1433 <domain>\<user> Registering FQDN syntax: Setspn -A MSSQLSvc/<FQDN SQL Server name>:1433 <domain>\<user>

Real World Note: Often you'll find it easier to install SQL Server 2012 using a scripted installation. When doing that, remember to specify the collation order as it will default to the server's local settings.

Local vs. Remote SQL Installation

This must be one of the most commonly asked questions when starting a new project: shall I configure a local SQL Server or a remote SQL Server? I always go a very long way to argue for a local installation. *Why?* You might ask:

- **Saves time in the project.** Often I find that DBAs (database administrators) try to configure a ConfigMgr SQL Server database like any other SQL Server database, and it's not like any of the other databases.
- **Simplifies permissions.** The site server requires the installer to be a member of the local Administrator group on SQL Server and the person installing Configuration Manager must have sysadmin permissions.

One thing you should be aware off is the limitation on the number of clients you can have when using a local SQL Server. The supported number of clients is limited to 50,000. If you have more than that, you should consider a remote SQL Server installation.

When installing SQL Server, you are required to select only the Database Engine Services service. Even if you have multiple sites (which requires SQL Server replication), you're not required to install any replication services unless you plan to use management points with SQL Server database replicas. In this installation, you will install SQL Server, SQL Server Reporting Services, Business Intelligence Development Studio (BIDS), and the management tools. The installation properties are stored in a file called configurationfile.ini that you can find in the book sample files.

Install SQL Server 2012

Before you start the installation, make sure that you have installed all the required components described in Appendix A. In these steps, I assume you have downloaded and extracted SQL Server 2012 to D:\Setup\SQL2012; SQL Server 2012 SP1 to D:\Setup\SQL2012SP; Server 2012 SP1 CU2 to D:\Setup\SQL2012CU; and the book sample files to D:\Setup\Scripts on CM01.

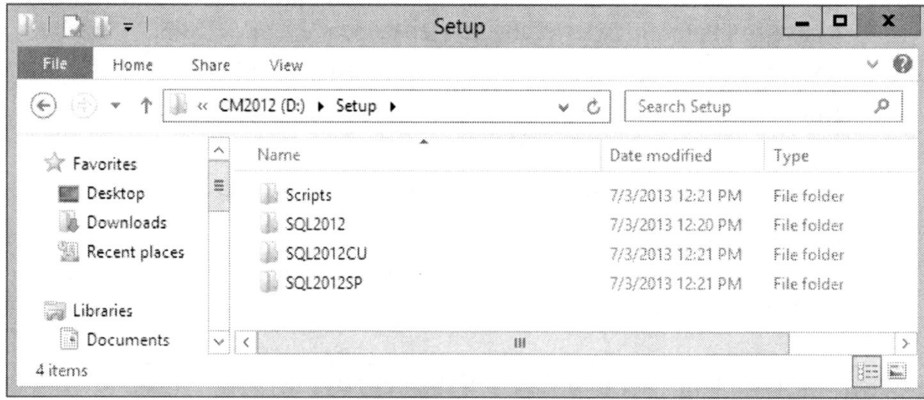

The D:\Setup folder on CM01 after adding the SQL 2012 installation files.

When installing SQL Server, you either can start by installing the SQL Server RTM version first and then applying service packs and CUs, or you can use a configuration file that installs everything for you. A configuration file also can include other information like where to place database files, log files, account information, and so forth.

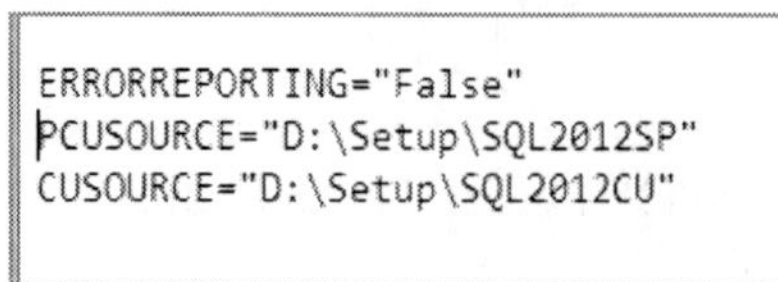

```
ERRORREPORTING="False"
PCUSOURCE="D:\Setup\SQL2012SP"
CUSOURCE="D:\Setup\SQL2012CU"
```

Inject service pack and CU into the SQL installation using a configuration file

1. On **CM01**, log on as **VIAMONSTRA\Administrator**.
2. Open a command prompt with administrative permissions.
3. Navigate to **D:\Setup\SQL 2012** and type the following:

   setup.exe /Configurationfile=D:\Setup\Scripts\SQLConfigurationfile.ini

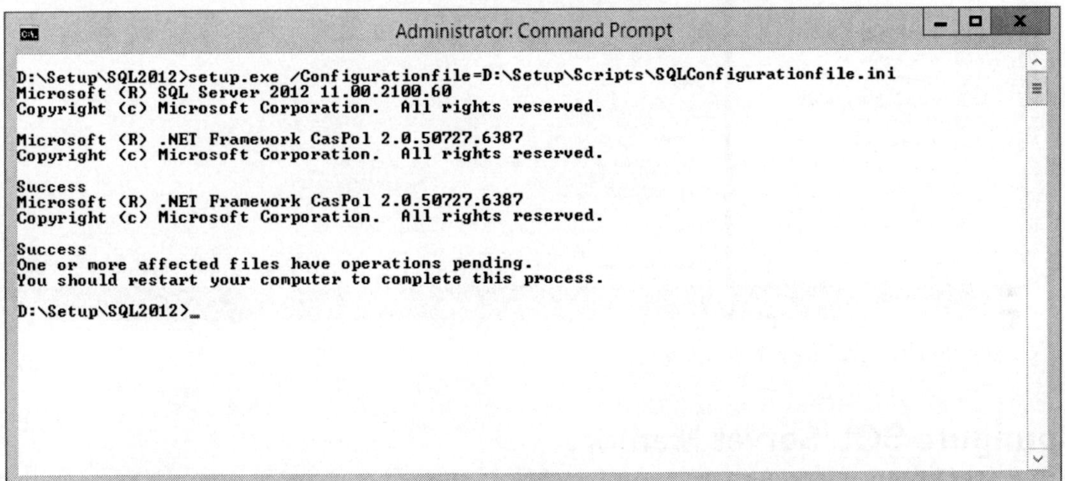

Installing SQL Server 2012.

4. After the setup has completed, restart **CM01**.

Verify SQL Server Installation Success

1. On **CM01**, open **SQL Server Management Studio**, and connect to CM01.
2. Click **New Query** and ensure that the **Master** database is selected.
3. Type the following statement and then press **F5**:

   SELECT SERVERPROPERTY('productversion'), SERVERPROPERTY ('productlevel'), SERVERPROPERTY ('edition')

   With SP1 and CU2 installed, you should have a product version of **11.0.3339.0** and product level of **SP1**.

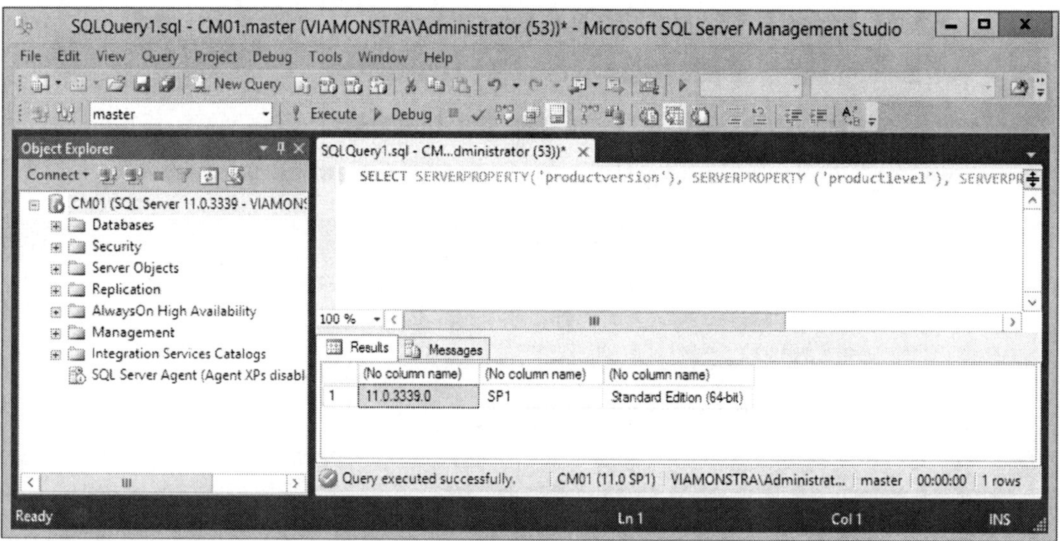

Checking the SQL Server version.

Configure SQL Server Memory

SQL Server likes memory. As a matter of fact, SQL Server likes memory so much that it will take all available memory, leaving very little to other applications and the operating system. For that reason, you should limit the amount of memory allocated to SQL Server. There are a lot of best practices when it comes to allocating SQL Server memory, my rule of thumb is:

- 2 GB for the operating system
- 2 GB for other applications running on the server
- 4 GB for ConfigMgr
- 8 GB or more for SQL Server 2012

Real World Note: The memory calculation assumes you have 16 GB of memory. ConfigMgr can run with less memory, however, and there is no fixed limit. Technically, if you have a small environment, like a lab environment or fewer than 500 users, then ConfigMgr will likely perform well with as little as 4–8 GB RAM. In those scenarios, you should limit the SQL memory to a maximum of 50 percent of the physical memory. Please note that you are on unsupported ground if assigning less than 8 GB of RAM to SQL Server 2012 (which means that you need to have at least 16 GB RAM on your CAS or primary site server to be supported when running SQL Server locally).

Perform the following steps to configure SQL Server memory:

1. On **CM01**, open **SQL Server Management Studio.**
2. Connect to the CM01 SQL Server.
3. Right-click **CM01 (SQL Server 11.0.3339 – VIAMONSTRA\Administrator)** and select **Properties.**
4. Select the **Memory** node and configure these settings (provided that you have 16 GB of RAM):
    a. Minimum server memory (in MB): **8192**
    b. Maximum server memory (in MB): **12228**

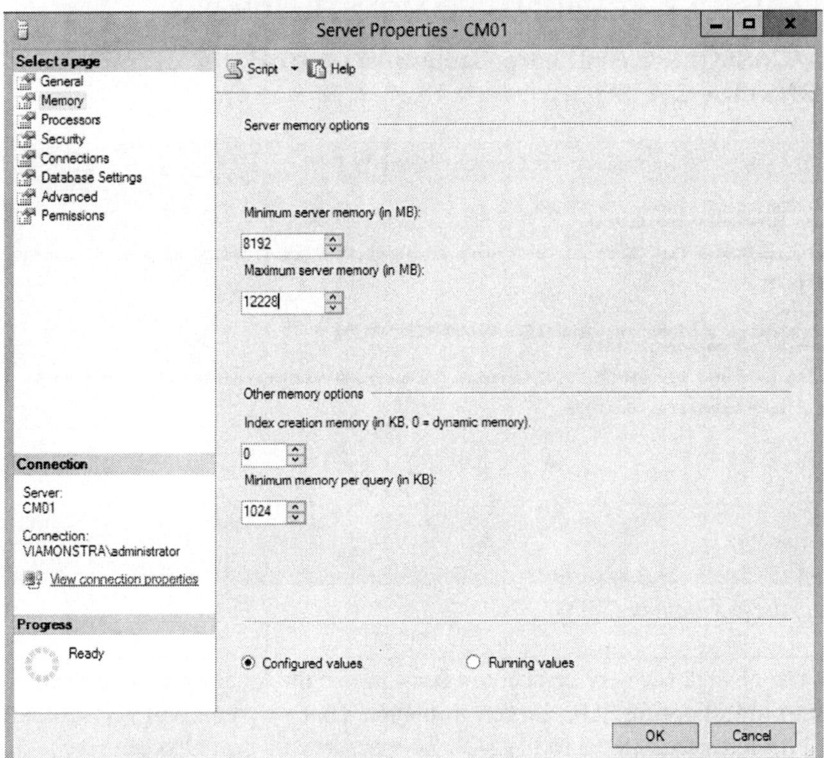

Configuring SQL Server memory.

5. Click **OK** to save the changes.

Configure the SQL Server Service Account

To follow best practices, ViaMonstra uses a domain user account for all of its SQL Server service accounts.

1. On **CM01**, start **Server Manager**.

2. From the **Server Manager Dashboard,** select **Tools / Services**.
3. Right-click **SQL Server (MSSQLSERVER)** and select **Properties**.
4. Select the **Log On** tab, click **This account**, click **Browse**, and find the **CM_SQ** account for the **VIAMONSTRA domain**.
5. Type the password (**Password01**) and click **OK**.
6. Notice the message in the two dialog boxes, and click **OK** for each.
7. Restart the **SQL Server (MSSQLSERVER)** service.
8. Open a command prompt with administrative permissions, and type and execute these two commands one at the time:
    a. **setspn -A MSSQLSvc/CM01:1433 VIAMONSTRA\CM_SQ**
    b. **setspn -A MSSQLSvc/cm01.corp.viamonstra.com:1433 VIAMONSTRA\CM_SQ**

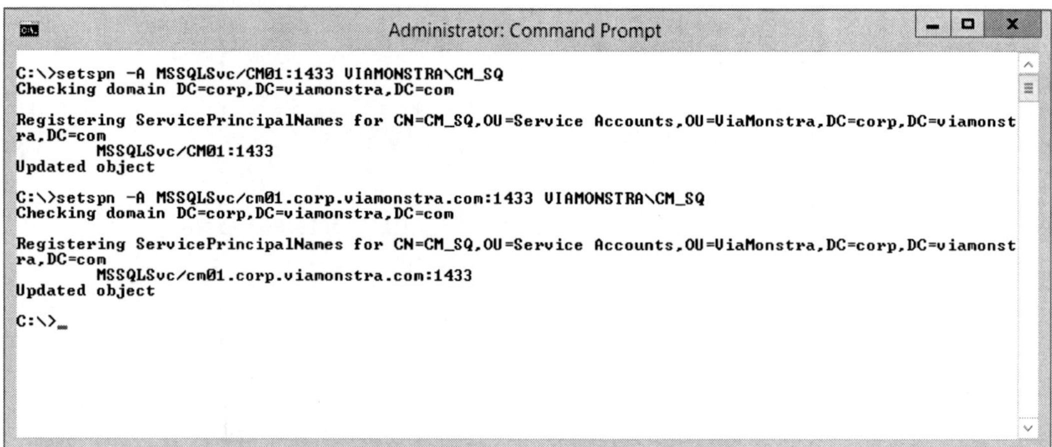

Registering service principal names (SPN).

Real World Note: You can change the service account back to use the local system account. This can be very useful when troubleshooting SQL Server problems. That way you will very quickly figure out whether your problems are related to the SQL Server service. You also can run setspn -L VIAMONSTRA\CM_SQ to verify that the principal names are correctly registered.

Configure the SQL Server Firewall Rules

By default, SQL Server uses port 1433 for normal SQL communication and port 4022 for the Service Broker. During the ConfigMgr installation, a prerequsites checker runs and warns you if these ports are not configured correctly in the firewall. This occurs whether you have the firewall enabled or not. For ViaMonstra, I have decided to create custom firewall rules.

1. On **CM01**, from the **Server Manager Dashboard,** select **Tools / Windows Firewall with Advanced Security**.

2. Select **Inbound Rules** and click **New rule.**
3. On the **Rule Type** page, select **Port** and click **Next**.
4. On the **Protocols and Ports** page, select **TCP**; then type **1433, 4022** in **Specific local ports** and click **Next**.

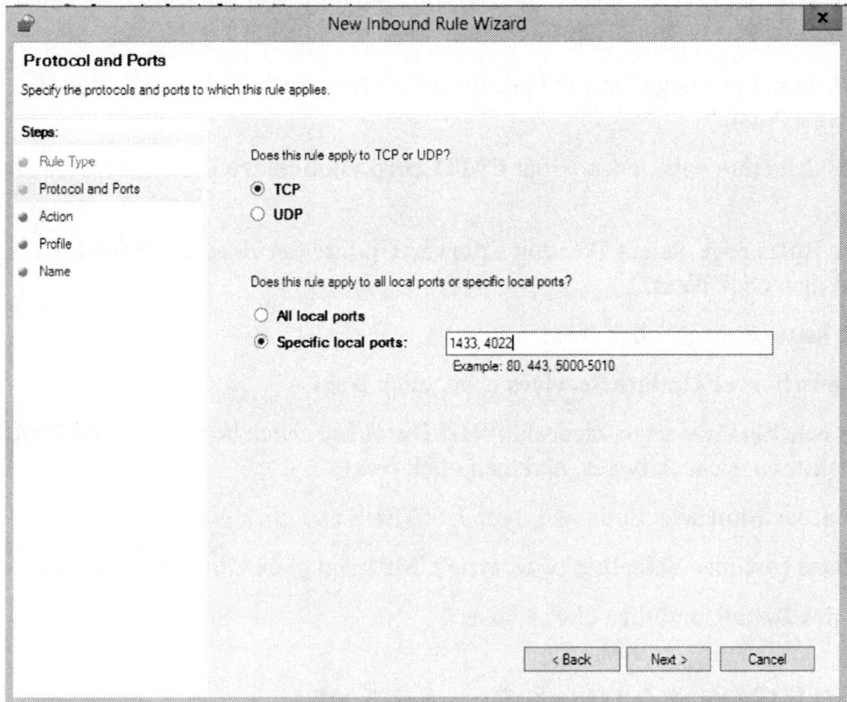

Configuring firewall rules for SQL Server 2012.

5. On the **Action** page, ensure **Allow the connection** is selected and click **Next**.
6. On the **Profile** page, clear the **Private** and **Public** check boxes, and click **Next**.
7. On the **Name** page, type **ConfigMgr SQL settings** and click **Finish**.

Installing and Configuring WSUS 4.0

Even though you configure and control all aspects of the software update process from within the ConfigMgr console, you still need to install a WSUS server in each primary site and in the CAS site. In this section, you install the core WSUS service using the GUI or PowerShell.

Option 1: Install WSUS 4.0 Using the GUI

To perform these steps, you need to have Internet access on CM01.

1. On **CM01**, using **Server Manager Dashboard,** click **Manage / Add Roles and Features**.
2. On the **Before You Begin** page, select the **Skip this page by default** check box, and click **Next**.
3. On the **Installation Type** page, ensure **Role-based or feature-based installation** is selected and click **Next.**
4. On the **Server Selection** page, ensure that **CM01.corp.viamonstra.com** is selected and click **Next.**
5. On the **Server Roles** page, select **Windows Server Update Services,** click **Add Features**, and then click **Next**.
6. On the **Select features** page, click **Next**.
7. On the **Windows Server Update Services** page, click **Next**.
8. On the **Select role Services** page, clear the **WID Database** check box, select the **WSUS Services** and **Database** check boxes, and then click **Next**.
9. On the **Content location selection** page, type **E:\WSUS** and click **Next**.
10. On the **Database Instance Selection** page, type **CM01** and click **Check connection**.
11. Click **Next**, click **Install**, and then click **Close.**

Option 2: Install WSUS 4.0 Using PowerShell

To perform these steps, you need to have Internet access on CM01.

1. On **CM01**, launch **PowerShell** as **Administrator**.
2. Type the following command:

   ```
   Set-ExecutionPolicy Unrestricted -Force
   ```

3. Type the following command:

   ```
   Install-WindowsFeature -Name UpdateServices-DB,
   UpdateServices-UI
   ```

4. Using **Server Manager Dashboard,** select **Tools / Windows Updates Service**.
5. In the **Complete WSUS Installation** wizard, in the **DB instance** text box, type **CM01** and click **Run**.
6. When the **Windows Server Update Services Configuration Wizard** starts, click **Cancel**, and then close the **Update Services** console.

Real World Note: Hosting the WSUS database on the site server database server is in full compliance with the System Center license terms.

Installing the Site Server

Installing the ConfigMgr primary site server is a fairly straightforward operation. But, before you start, you need to know what the final hierarchy will look like. After you have installed a primary site server, you are not able to move it to another hierarchy.

Install ADK on the Site Server

To install the site server, you need to install the Assessment and Deployment Kit (ADK) first. In this guide, I assume you have downloaded the full ADK for Windows 8 to D:\Setup\ADK on CM01. (To download the full ADK, you first download the adksetup.exe and then use it to download the rest.)

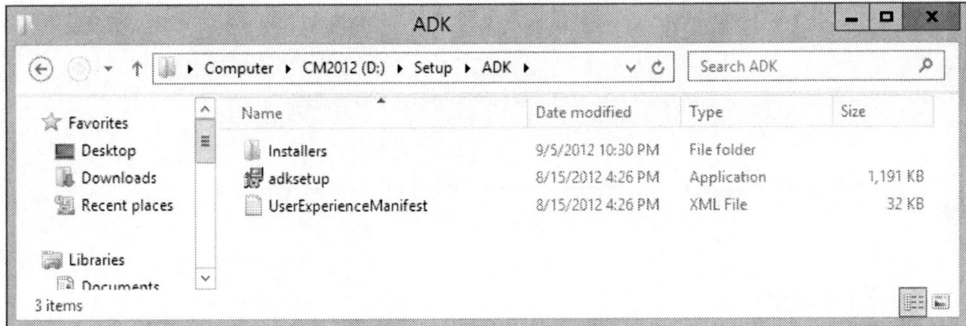

The D:\Setup\ADK folder, after running adksetup.exe and downloading the about 2.5 GB of installers (including the UserExperienceManifest.xml file).

1. On **CM01**, log on as **VIAMONSTRA\Administrator**.
2. Install **ADK (D:\Setup\ADK\adksetup.exe)** selecting only the following components:
    a. **Deployment Tools**
    b. **Windows Preinstallation Environment (Windows PE)**
    c. **User State Migration Tool (USMT)**

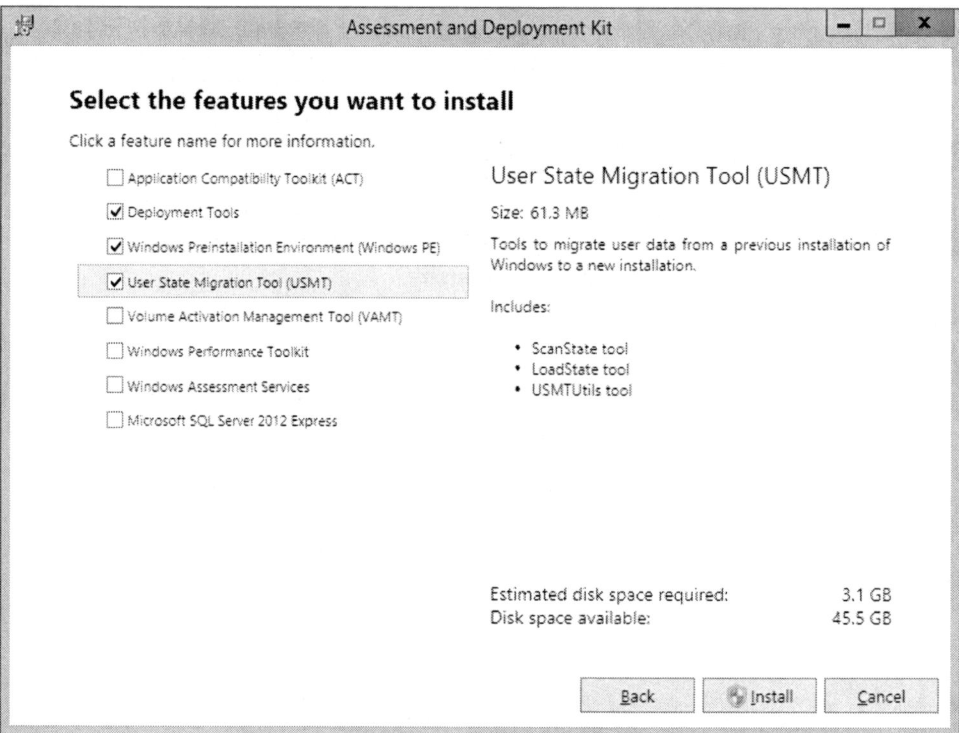

The ADK setup.

Install the Site Server

For ViaMonstra, you already know that you need only one primary site server. In this guide, I assume you have downloaded ConfigMgr 2012 SP1 to D:\Setup\CM2012 on CM01.

1. On **CM01**, open a **command prompt** with administrative privileges.
2. Navigate to **D:\Setup\CM2012** and type **splash.hta**. When prompted, select **Microsoft (R) HTLM Application Host**.
3. On the **Configuration Manager 2012 SP1 Setup** page, click **Install**.
4. On the **Before You Begin** page, read the notes and click **Next**.

5. On the **Getting Started** page, select **Install a Configuration Manager primary site** and click **Next**.

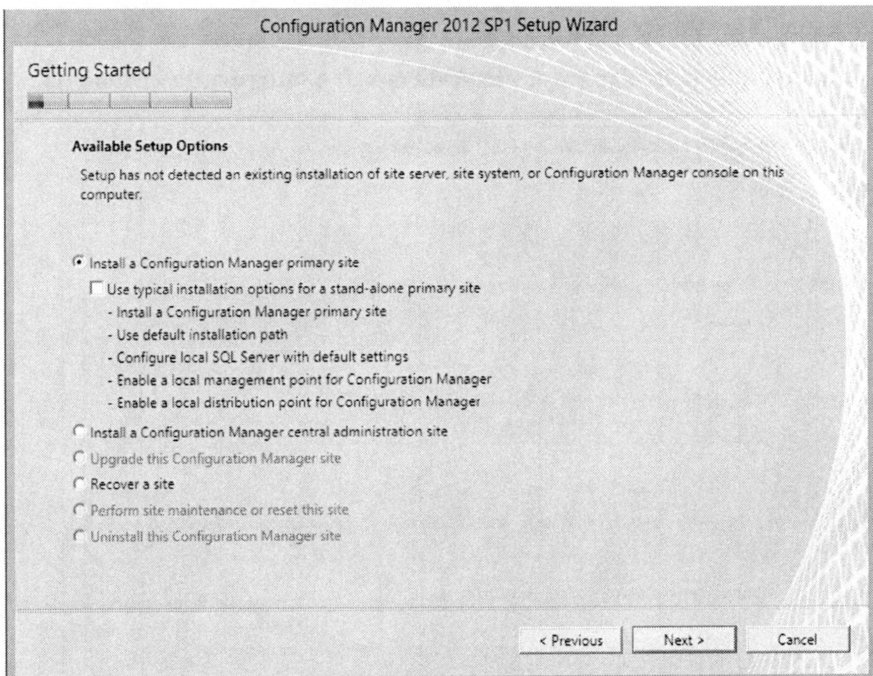

Installing a primary site server.

6. On the **Product Key** page, enter your 25-character product key, or select **Install the evaluation edition of this product** if you don't have the key at the present time, and click **Next**.
7. On the **Microsoft Software License Terms** page, select the **I accept these license terms** check box, and then click **Next**.
8. On the **Prerequisite Licenses** page, accept the prerequisite license terms and click **Next**.
9. On the **Prerequisite Download** page, click **Download required files**; use the **Browse** button to create the **D:\Setup\CM2012DL** folder, select it, and then click **Next**.
10. After the download is completed, on the **Server Language Selection** page, ensure that **English** is the only selected language and click **Next**.
11. On the **Client Language Selection** page, select the client languages you wish to support in your environment. In ViaMonstra, English is the only supported language.

Real World Note: You can always rerun setup and add additional client languages. The client will apply the language along with the client installation. For that reason, you have to reinstall the client to reflect any new language settings.

12. On the **Site and Installation Settings** page, enter the following settings and click **Next**:
    a. Site code: **PS1**
    b. Site name: **ViaMonstra HQ**
    c. Installation folder: **D:\Program Files\Microsoft Configuration Manager**

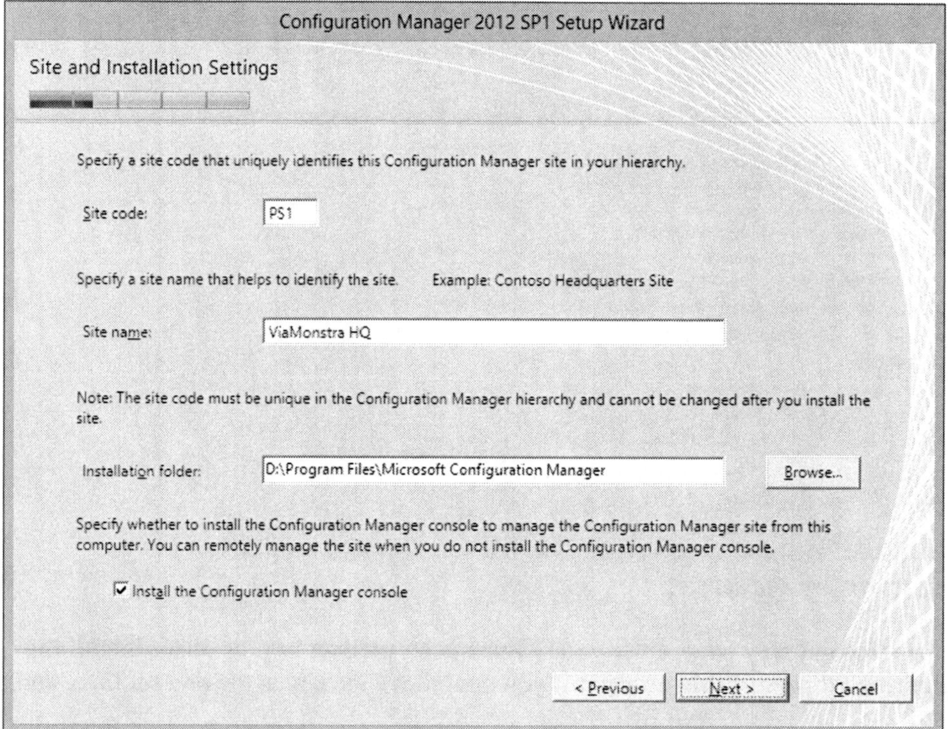

Specifying the site code.

13. On the **Primary Site Installation** page, select **Install the primary site as a stand-alone site** and click **Next**.
14. Click **Yes** in the information dialog box.

Real World Note: In ConfigMgr SP1, you are now able to join a CAS to an existing stand-alone primary site.

15. On the **Database Information** page, accept the default SQL Server information and click **Next**. This performs the installation as a default instance.
16. On the **SMS Provider Settings** page, click **Next**.
17. On the **Client Computer Communication Settings** page, select **Configure the communication method on each site system role** and click **Next**.

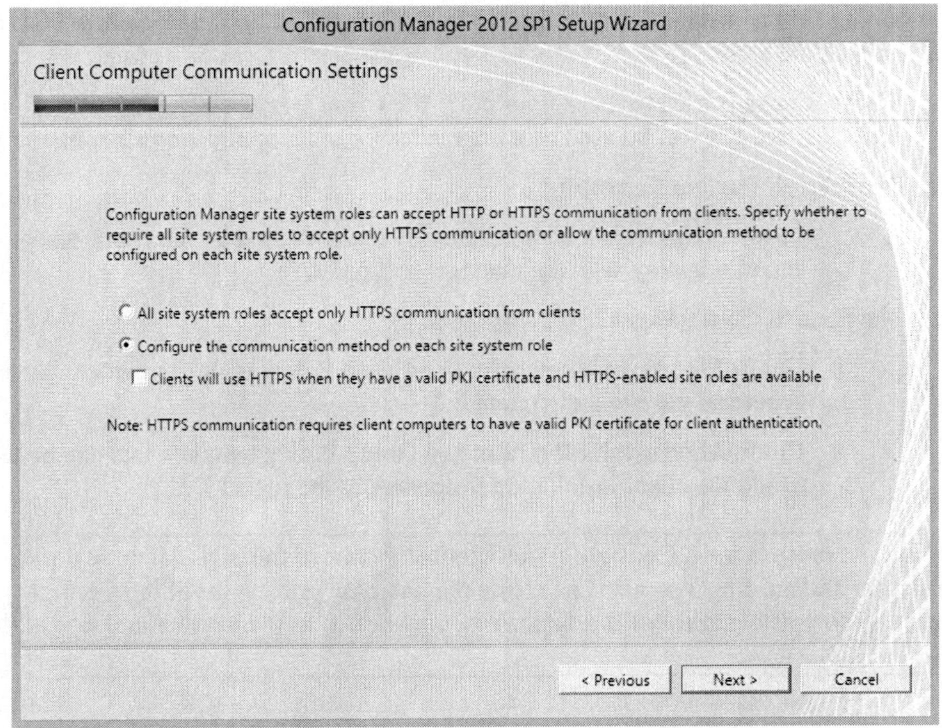

Configuring a client communication protocol.

18. On the **Site System Roles** page, ensure that both the management point and distribution point roles are selected and click **Next**.
19. On the **Customer Experience Improvement Program Configuration** page, select **Join the Customer Experience Improvement Program** and click **Next**.
20. On the **Settings Summary** page, review the summary and click **Next**.
21. On the **Prerequisite Checker** page, click **Begin Install** to start the installation. You might receive warning messages about Publishing to Active Directory. For now you can safely ignore those warnings.
22. Open **D:\Setup\CM2012\SMSSetup\Tools\CMTrace.exe** and accept it as the default log viewer.
23. Pin **CMTrace.exe** to the **Windows taskbar**.
24. Check **C:\ConfigMgrSetup.log** and monitor the installation.

25. While waiting for the installation to finish, open **D:\Setup\CM2012\SMSSetup\TOOLS** and investigate the tools:

   a. **CMtrace.exe** is used to make your daily life easier when reading log files. Notice that CMtrace.exe can be used as a log reader for other applications as well.

   b. Navigate to **Portconfiguration**:

      Portswitch.vbs is a script to modify the port used by the client when communicating with the management point.

   c. Navigate to **ConfigMgrADMTemplates**:

      - **ConfigMgrAssignment.adm** is a Group Policy template that can be used to control the site assignment.
      - **ConfigMgrInstallation.adm** is a Group Policy template that can be used to add the client installation properties to the registry.

Real World Note: In this example, ConfigMgr automatically created the SQL database during the install with a single database file. You also can create the database prior to installing ConfigMgr. That way you are in complete control of the database settings, such as the number and size of the database files.

Verify the ConfigMgr Installation

After the core ConfigMgr services installation is finished, you still have a lot going on in the background, like configuring, installing, and configuring components. I usually monitor the following two log files to verify that everything is all right. Both are server log files and found in D:\Program files\Microsoft Configuration Manager\Logs:

- **Sitecomp.log.** This log file is for the Site Component Manager, the component responsible for installing most of the ConfigMgr components.
- **hman.log.** This is the log file for the Hierarchy Manager who is responsible for updating Active Directory, handling certificates, the site control file(s) and much more.

Furthermore, I perform a simple check against the management point. To do that, open **Internet Explorer** and go to **http://cm01/SMS_MP/.sms_aut?MPLIST**. This should give you a list of the management points installed in the site.

```
http://cm01/SMS_MP/.sms_aut?MPLIST        cm01

- <MPList>
  - <MP Name="CM01.CORP.VIAMONSTRA.COM" FQDN="CM01.corp.viamonstra.com">
      <Version>7804</Version>
    - <Capabilities SchemaVersion="1.0">
        <Property Name="SSLState" Value="0" />
      </Capabilities>
    </MP>
  </MPList>
```

Verifying the management point.

Create a ConfigMgr Package Source Directory

A package source directory is used to store source files for all your packages. The term *packages* is used for all content like drivers, software updates, applications, and so forth. I usually recommend that you locate the package source directory on a remote server like a file server. That way you do not have to worry about the original source files in the event of a hardware failure on the site server.

You can use a PowerShell script like the example below to create the source folders. The PowerShell script Source_Folder_Structure.ps1 is found in the book's sample files. In the following example, I assume that you have copied the script to D:\Setup\Scripts on CM01.

1. On **CM01**, open **PowerShell** as **Administrator**.
2. Navigate to **D:\Setup\Scripts** and type the following command:

   ```
   .\Source_Folder_Structure.ps1
   ```

3. Share the **D:\Sources** folder as **Sources$**.
4. Allow the **Everyone** group **Full Control** permissions on the share.

The following code snippet shows the contents of the Source_Folder_Structure.ps1 script:

```
$Source = 'D:\Sources'

#Source Directory
New-Item -ItemType Directory -Path "$Source"

#software folders
New-Item -ItemType Directory -Path "$Source\Software"
New-Item -ItemType Directory -Path "$Source\Software\Adobe"
New-Item -ItemType Directory -Path "$Source\Software\Other"
New-Item -ItemType Directory -Path "$Source\Software\Microsoft"

#OSD folders
New-Item -ItemType Directory -Path "$Source\OSD"
New-Item -ItemType Directory -Path "$Source\OSD\Images"
New-Item -ItemType Directory -Path "$Source\OSD\OSInstall"
New-Item -ItemType Directory -Path "$Source\OSD\BootImages"
New-Item -ItemType Directory -Path "$Source\OSD\DriverPackages"
New-Item -ItemType Directory -Path
"$Source\OSD\DriverPackages\Win7x64\HP"
New-Item -ItemType Directory -Path
"$Source\OSD\DriverPackages\Win7x64\Lenovo"
New-Item -ItemType Directory -Path
"$Source\OSD\DriverPackages\Win8x64"
New-Item -ItemType Directory -Path
"$Source\OSD\DriverPackages\Win8x64\HP"
```

```
New-Item -ItemType Directory -Path
"$Source\OSD\DriverPackages\Win8x64\Lenovo"
New-Item -ItemType Directory -Path "$Source\OSD\DriverSources"
New-Item -ItemType Directory -Path
"$Source\OSD\DriverSources\Win7x86\HP"
New-Item -ItemType Directory -Path
"$Source\OSD\DriverSources\Win7x86\Lenovo"
New-Item -ItemType Directory -Path
"$Source\OSD\DriverSources\Win7x64"
New-Item -ItemType Directory -Path
"$Source\OSD\DriverSources\Win7x64\HP"
New-Item -ItemType Directory -Path
"$Source\OSD\DriverSources\Win7x64\Lenovo"
New-Item -ItemType Directory -Path
"$Source\OSD\DriverSources\Win8x64"
New-Item -ItemType Directory -Path
"$Source\OSD\DriverSources\Win8x64\HP"
New-Item -ItemType Directory -Path
"$Source\OSD\DriverSources\Win8x64\Lenovo"
New-Item -ItemType Directory -Path "$Source\OSD\SW"
New-Item -ItemType Directory -Path "$Source\OSD\SW\Settings"
New-Item -ItemType Directory -Path "$Source\OSD\SW\Toolkit"
New-Item -ItemType Directory -Path "$Source\OSD\SW\USMT"
New-Item -ItemType Directory -Path "$Source\OSD\Prestart"
New-Item -ItemType Directory -Path "$Source\OSD\Logs"

#Software Update folders
New-Item -ItemType Directory -Path "$Source\Updates"
New-Item -ItemType Directory -Path "$Source\Updates\2013-1"
New-Item -ItemType Directory -Path "$Source\Updates\2013-2"
New-Item -ItemType Directory -Path "$Source\Updates\Definitions"
```

Post SQL Configuration

One of the recommended post installation tasks is to create additional ConfigMgr database files. You most likely can find different best practices when searching the Internet, but ViaMonstra has decided to create one file per core (up to the maximum eight-file recommended limit). Since the server has two CPUs with six cores each, which totals 12 cores, you will create the maximum seven additional files (making eight files total). With 6,500 clients in the database, the estimated size of the database is 37 GB. When creating the files, you can configure them to the estimated size of the database, or configure a lower value and let them autogrow when needed. Since 37 GB is not that big of a database, ViaMonstra has decided to create seven additional database files of 4700 MB each. As needed, the files will autogrow 1 GB at the time. Those settings match ViaMonstra, but will not match a larger enterprise installation.

Before you create the additional files, a short introduction to the files might be in order. The ConfigMgr database is called CM_PS1 and was created automatically during the installation. The database consists of two files, a *database* file and a *transaction log* file:

- The database file *.mdf stores database objects, such as indexes, table, and stored procedures.
- The log file *.ldf is a transaction log file. Every single database transaction is written to the log file that is committed to the database.

Create Additional Files

You can configure the additional SQL files manually in SQL Server Management Studio, or by running the script below (also in SQL Server Management Studio) as described in the following steps:

1. Start **SQL Server Management Studio** and connect to the **local SQL Server**.
2. Click **New Query,** type the text below, and click **Execute**. (You also can copy and paste the query. You can find it in the Add SQL files.txt file in the book sample files.)

```
Use masterALTER DATABASE CM_PS1

ADD FILE (NAME = CM_PS1_2, FILENAME =
'G:\SQLdb\CM_PS1_2.mdf', SIZE = 4700MB, MAXSIZE=UNLIMITED,
FILEGROWTH = 1024MB)

ALTER DATABASE CM_PS1

ADD FILE (NAME = CM_PS1_3, FILENAME =
'G:\SQLdb\CM_PS1_3.mdf', SIZE = 4700MB, MAXSIZE=UNLIMITED,
FILEGROWTH = 1024MB)

ALTER DATABASE CM_PS1

ADD FILE (NAME = CM_PS1_4, FILENAME =
'G:\SQLdb\CM_PS1_4.mdf', SIZE = 4700MB, MAXSIZE=UNLIMITED,
FILEGROWTH = 1024MB)

ALTER DATABASE CM_PS1

ADD FILE (NAME = CM_PS1_5, FILENAME =
'G:\SQLdb\CM_PS1_5.mdf', SIZE = 4700MB, MAXSIZE=UNLIMITED,
FILEGROWTH = 1024MB)

ALTER DATABASE CM_PS1

ADD FILE (NAME = CM_PS1_6, FILENAME =
'G:\SQLdb\CM_PS1_6.mdf', SIZE = 4700MB, MAXSIZE=UNLIMITED,
FILEGROWTH = 1024MB)

ALTER DATABASE CM_PS1
```

```
ADD FILE (NAME = CM_PS1_7, FILENAME =
'G:\SQLdb\CM_PS1_7.mdf', SIZE = 4700MB, MAXSIZE=UNLIMITED,
FILEGROWTH = 1024MB)

ALTER DATABASE CM_PS1

ADD FILE (NAME = CM_PS1_8, FILENAME =
'G:\SQLdb\CM_PS1_8.mdf', SIZE = 4700MB, MAXSIZE=UNLIMITED,
FILEGROWTH = 1024MB)

GO
```

3. All additional files are now created with an autogrowth value of 1 GB. However, the initial database created during ConfigMgr setup is not yet configured with the same autogrowth settings. While still in SQL Server Studio Management, expand **Databases**, right-click the **CM_PS1** database, and select **Properties**.
4. Select the **Files** tab; notice all the files you just created. (If you didn't use the script, you can always create the files manually by clicking the **Add** button and completing the **Add File** dialog box.)
5. Look at the File Growth setting for the first file; it's configured to grow by 2 percent at the time. Click the **...** (ellipsis) button next to **By 2 percent, Unlimited**. (You may have to scroll to the right, or resize the window to see it.)

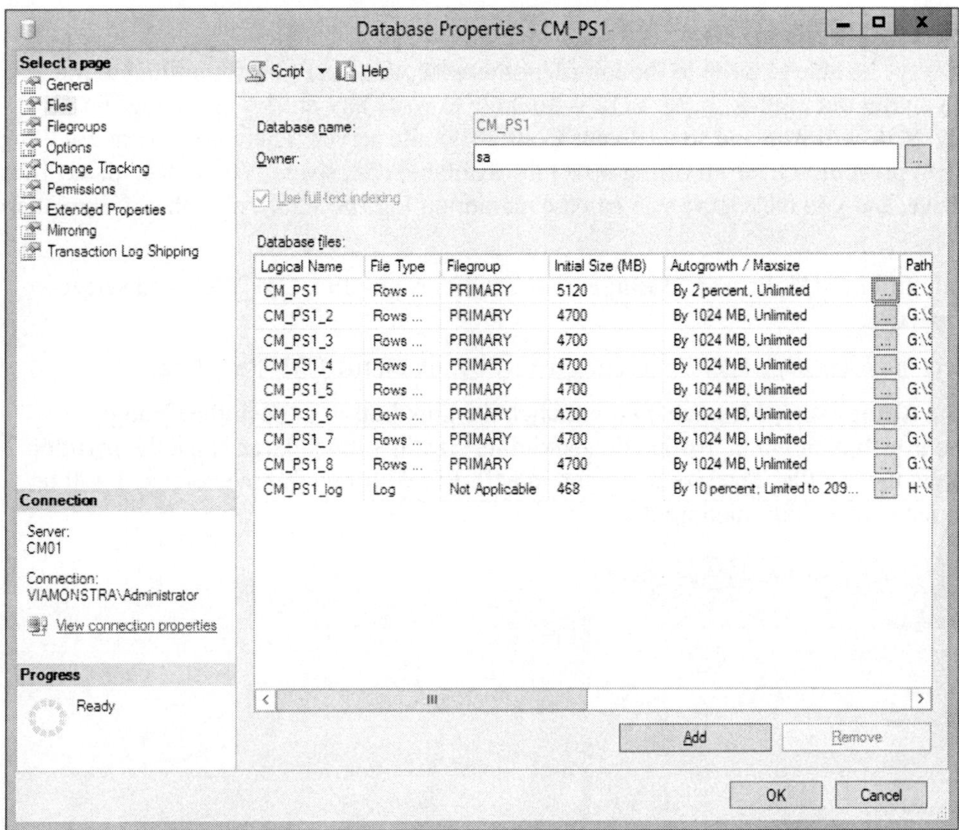

The CM_PS1 Database Properties, resized to display the ... button.

6. Change the setting from In Percent to **In Megabytes** and enter **1024**.

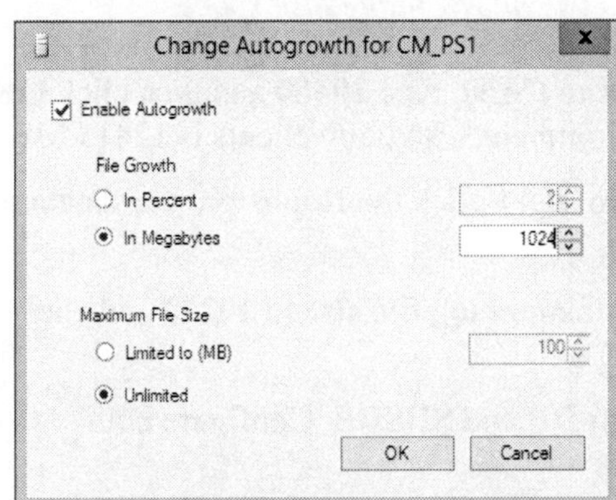

Configuring autogrowth for the SQL Server database.

7. Click **OK** and leave **SQL Management Studio** open.

Cap SQL Log File Size

SQL must always be able to write to the log file; otherwise, data can't be committed to the database. If you run out of disk space, SQL is not able to write any entries to the log files, and consequently, SQL will stop and so will your ConfigMgr site server. There are several easy steps you can take to prevent SQL from filling up all the available disk space. You create all log files on a separate drive, and you make sure you cap the maximum log file size. To do that, follow these steps:

1. While still in **SQL Server Management Studio**, right-click **CM_PS1**, and select **Properties**.
2. Select the **Files** page again, and click the **...** button on the **CM_PS1**_Log line.
3. In the **Autogrowth/Maxsize** column, click the grey button to open the Change Autogrowth dialog box. Notice the maximum size: it's much larger than the partition hosting the log file. The size is written in MB. For your own brain exercise, I will let you calculate the default maximum size.

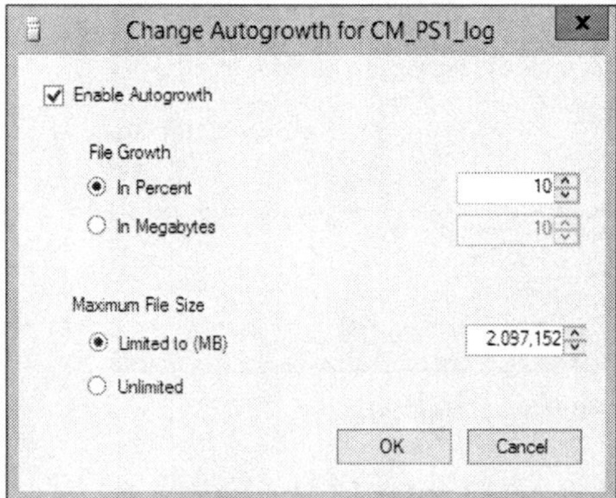

The default maximum log file size can cause SQL to use all available disk space.

4. In the **Maximum File Size** area, select **Limited to (MB)**, type **20480** and then click **OK** twice. The estimated size of the log file an environment with 6500 clients is 12415 MB.
5. While still in **SQL Server Management Studio**, right-click the **ReportServer** database and select **Properties**.
6. Select the **Files** page**,** and then configure the maximum log file size to **10240** and click **OK** twice.
7. Repeat steps 6 and 7 for the **ReportServerTempDB** and **SUSDB**. Configure both maximum sizes to **10240**
8. Click **OK** and leave **SQL Management Studio open**.

Real World Note: You might be wondering why you configure the maximum size for all databases. A WSUS database log file should never reach 10240 MB, but it's better to be safe than sorry, especially in our line of business.

Change the Database Recovery Model

The database recovery model controls whether transaction log files can be used in a database restore scenario. By default, many databases use the Full recovery model when log files are required to perform a restore. The benefit of a Full recovery model is that you can restore to almost any specific time provided that you have a valid backup of the log files. This scenario is very beneficial for an online payment system where being able to restore data to any point in time is a requirement. With ConfigMgr, we don't have to restore to a specific time, so performing a restore from the latest backup is sufficient. For that reason, the default recovery model is configured to Simple. A Simple recovery model instructs SQL to truncate the transactional log files each time the database reaches a checkpoint. This saves disk space and ensures your log files never grow out of proportion. The flipside is that log files can't be used in a restore scenario.

1. While still in **SQL Server Management Studio**, right-click **ReportServer**, and select **Properties**.
2. Select the **Options** page, and then configure the **Recovery Model** to **Simple** and click **OK**.
3. Close **Microsoft SQL Server Management Studio**.

Chapter 4

Configuring the Site Server

Installing a site server is the easy part. Configuring the server often requires a little more planning and thinking. There are some basic things you need to plan before you start working with each of the features:

- What features do you want to work with and what are the dependencies?
- Where do you want to install your site system roles?
- How are clients communicating with the site system roles, http or https?

Different features have specific site system role dependencies that you have to consider when deciding on which features you will use. In ViaMonstra, you start out with these features and site system roles:

- **Client Management**: Requires a management point.
- **Application Management**: Requires a distribution point, an application web service point, and an application web catalog point.
- **Software Updates**: Requires a distribution point and a software update point.
- **Operating System Deployment**: Requires a distribution point and perhaps a state migration point if user state migration is used.
- **Endpoint Protection**: Requires a distribution point, software update point, and Endpoint Protection point.
- **Inventory Management**: Requires a management point and Asset Intelligence synchronization point. The last role is not a requirement for inventory management, but it allows you to synchronize new Asset Intelligence software catalogs from Microsoft.

It's very common for midsize and enterprise installations to offload all user-facing site system roles from the primary site server for performance reasons. I also believe that's a very good idea but not necessarily a rule in every environment. ViaMonstra sees itself as a midsize business with average system management needs. You are not supporting 40,000–60,000 clients and will not upgrade 1,000 machines with new images every single week. For that reason, ViaMonstra decided to go ahead with all site systems on the same server.

However, if performance-related issues were to arise in the future, you would start by offloading the user-facing site system roles in this order:

- Distribution point
- State migration point
- Management point
- Software update point
- Reporting services point

Installing the Site System Roles

In this section, you walk through the installation of the needed site system roles. As mentioned earlier in this book, you do not have to install all site systems on the primary site server. For performance reasons, enterprise companies often choose to offload the site server and install "user-facing" site system roles on other servers.

Install the Roles

Use the steps below to install a software update point, Application Catalog web point, Application Catalog web service point, Asset Intelligence synchronization point, and reporting services point. You will install the Endpoint Protection point later after you have your software update point running.

1. On **CM01**, on the **Start screen**, click the **Configuration Manager Console**.
2. Select the **Administration** workspace.
3. Navigate to **Overview / Site Configuration / Servers and Site System Roles**.

4. Select **\\CM01.corp.viamonstra.com**; on the ribbon, click **Home**, and then click **Add Site System Roles**.

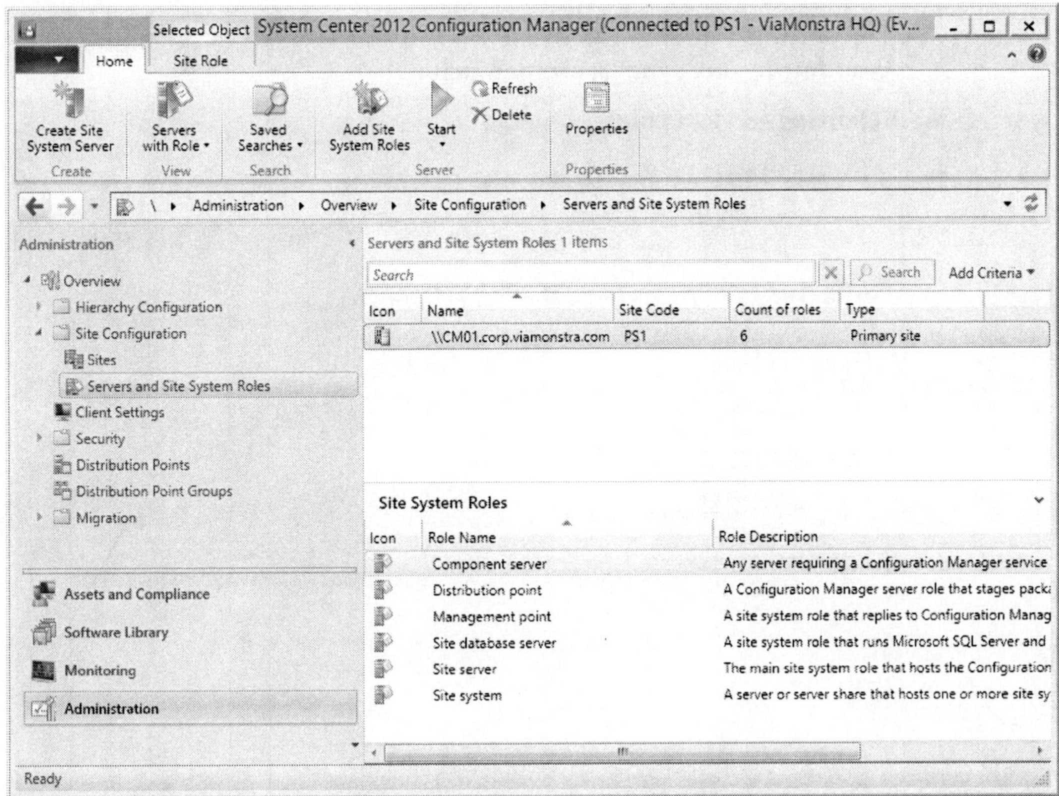

Adding site system roles.

5. On the **General** page, click **Next**.
6. On the **Proxy** page, click **Next**.

7. On the **System Role Selection** page, select the following site system roles and click **Next**:
   a. **Application Catalog Web Service Point**
   b. **Application Catalog Website Point**
   c. **Asset Intelligence synchronization point**
   d. **Reporting services point**
   e. **Software update point**

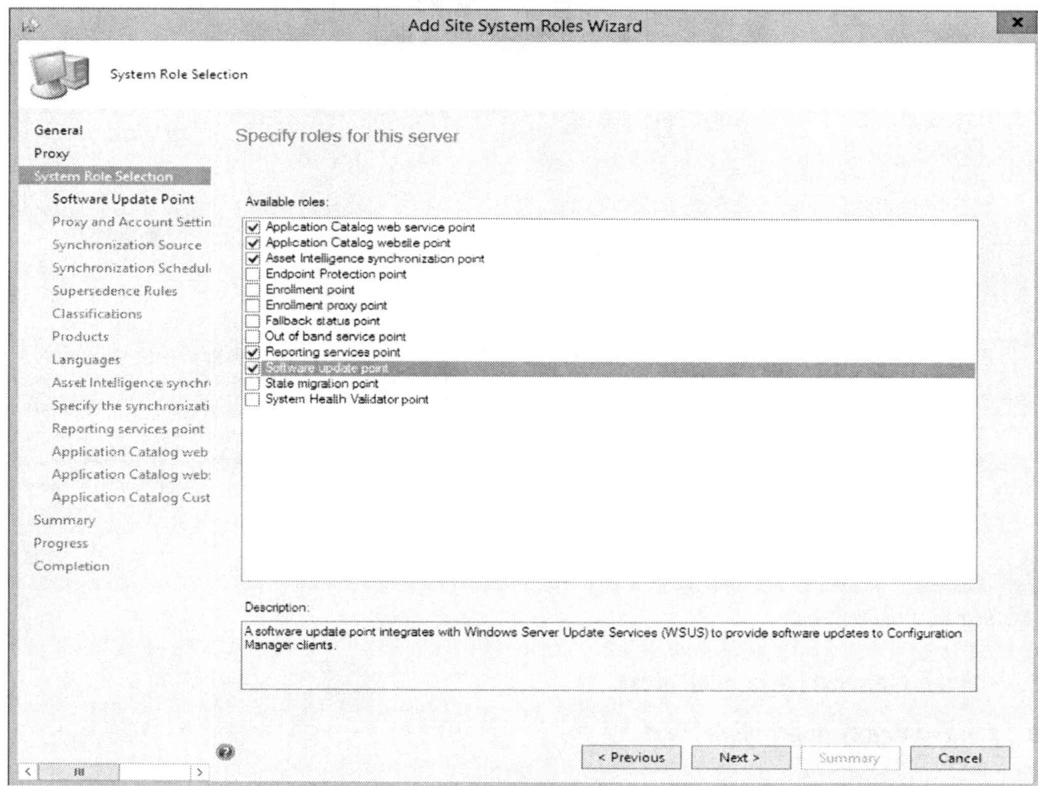

Selecting the site system roles.

8. On the **Software Updates Point** page, select **WSUS is configured to use ports 8530 and 8531 for client communications** and click **Next**.

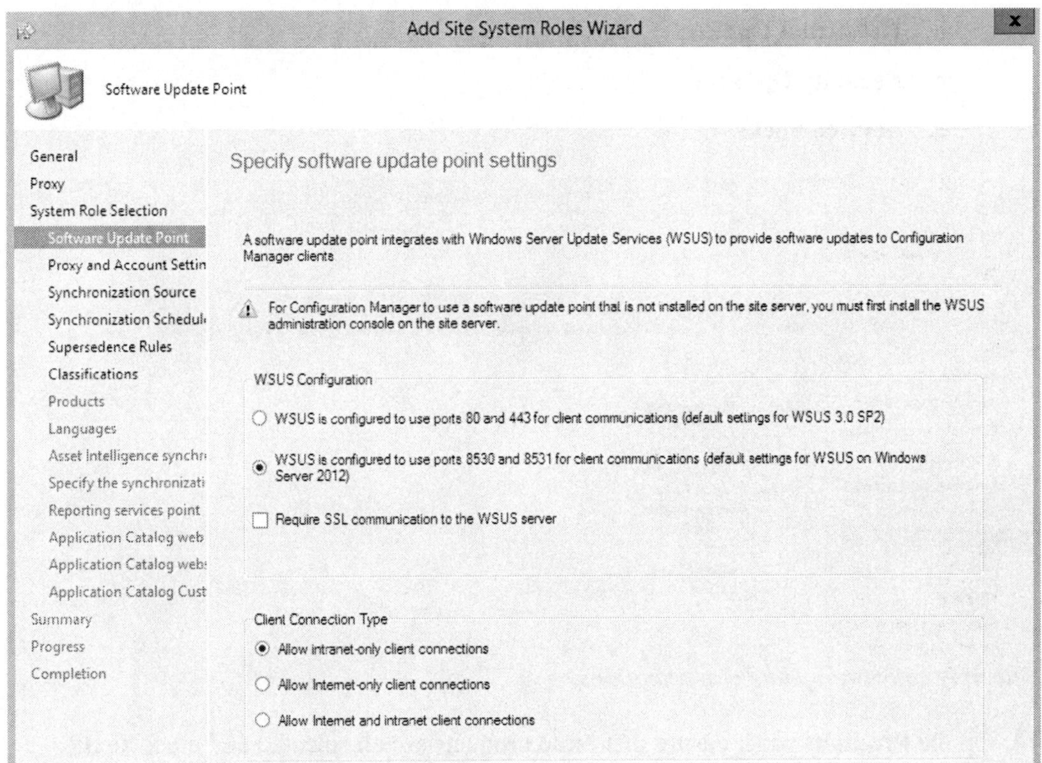

Configure ConfigMgr to use custom WSUS ports.

9. On the **Proxy and Account Setting** page, click **Next**.
10. On the **Synchronization Source** page, ensure **Synchronize from Microsoft Update** is selected and click **Next**. Note that this setting requires Internet access in order to connect to Windows Update and download the WSUS metadata.
11. On the **Synchronization Schedule** page:
    a. Select **Enable synchronization on a schedule**.
    b. Select **Simple schedule** and configure a synchronization schedule of every **8** hours.
    c. Select **Alert when synchronization fails on any site in the hierarchy**.
    d. Click **Next**.
12. On the **Supersedence Rules** page, select **Immediately expire a superseded software update** and click **Next**.

13. On the **Classifications** page, select these update classifications and click **Next**:
    a. **Critical Updates**
    b. **Definition Updates**
    c. **Security Updates**
    d. **Service Packs**

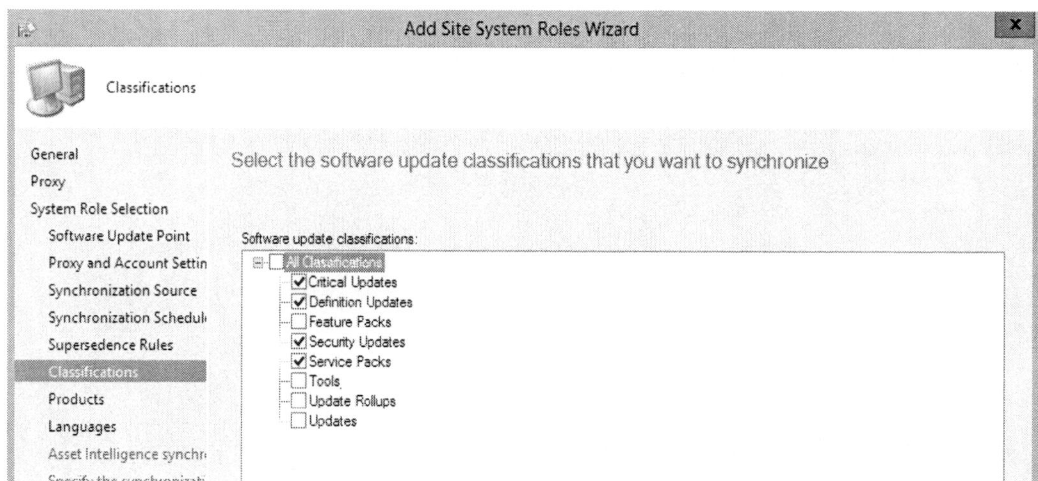

Selecting software update classifications.

14. On the **Products** page, ensure that these products are all selected and click **Next**:
    a. **Windows 7**
    b. **Forefront Endpoint Protection 2010**

Real World Note: You also will enable the Office 2013, Windows 8 and Windows Server 2012 products, but they are not available until after the initial synchronization between WSUS and Microsoft Update.

15. On the **Languages** page, deselect all languages except for **English** and click **Next.**
16. On the **Asset Intelligence Synchronization point Settings** page, click **Next** to accept the default settings. You will be asked about a certificate for System Center Online, proxy settings, and a synchronization schedule. There is no requirement for specifying a certificate, as one is already exists in ConfigMgr 2012.
17. On the **Specify the synchronization Schedule** page, accept the default settings and click **Next.**

18. On the **Reporting Services Point** page, do the following:

    a. Click **Verify** to verify your site database connection settings.

    b. In **Reporting Services Point Account**, click **Set** and **New Account**. Then click **Browse** and find the **CM_SR** account in the VIAMONSTRA domain. Assign the password (**Password01**), click **OK**, and then click **Next**.

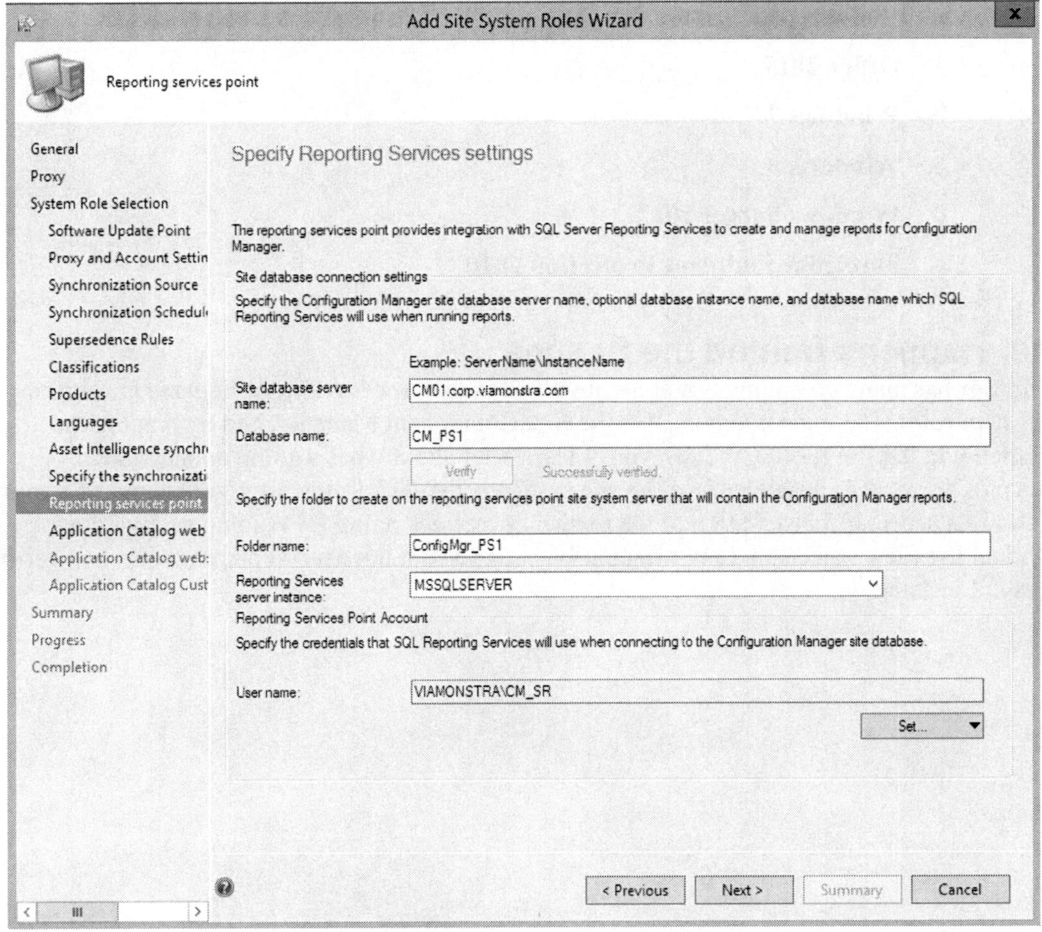

Configuring the reporting services point.

19. On the **Specify settings for Application Catalog Web Service Point** page, keep the default settings and click **Next**. This configures the web service to use HTTP and port 80.

20. On the **Specify settings to configure IIS for this Application Catalog Website Point** page, keep the default settings and click **Next**.

21. On the **Specify customized settings for the Application Catalog website point** page, type **ViaMonstra**, select a website theme, and click **Next**.

22. On the **Summary** page, verify that the all roles are listed and click **Next**.
23. Click **Close**.
24. Wait until WSUS has completed its first synchronization (review wsyncmgr.log).
25. In the **Administration** workspace, select **Site Configuration**, **Sites**, and then from the ribbon, select **Configure Site Components / Software Update Point**.
26. On the **Products** page, ensure that these products are all selected and click **OK**:
    a. **Office 2013**
    b. **Windows 7**
    c. **Windows 8**
    d. **Windows Server 2012**
    e. **Forefront Endpoint Protection 2010**

What Happens Behind the Scenes

ConfigMgr has many components that are involved in the process of installing and configuring site system roles. The main component is the Site Component Manager, and by reading the corresponding log file (sitecomp.log), you'll learn a lot about what's going on and which commands are used to install each of the site system roles. The following figure contains a snippet that shows a successful installation of the reporting services point. By reading each of the individual log files, you can get important information about the needed prerequisites and verify a successful installation.

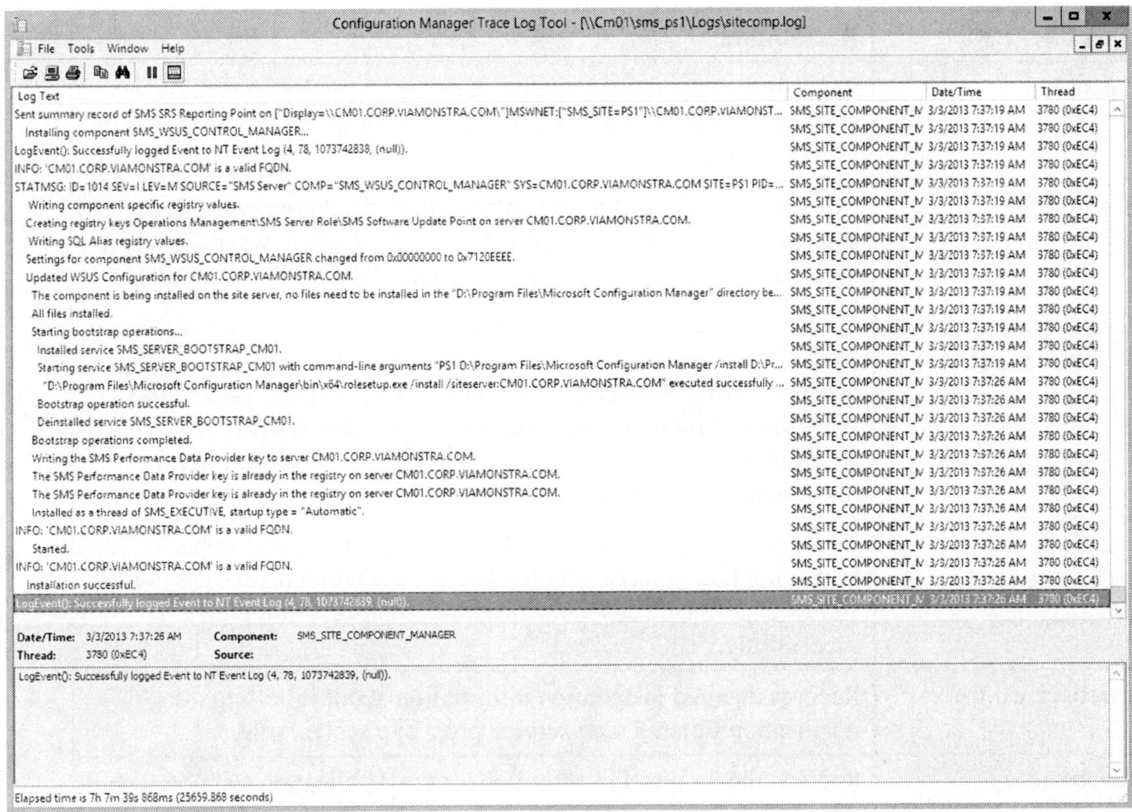

The sitecomp.log file.

Useful Log Files

The log files in the following table can be used to track your site system role installations.

Log File	Description
sitecomp.log	Records activity on the Site Component Manager.
srsrpsetup.log	Records activity on the SQL Reporting Services setup. In this log file, you see whether the needed prerequisites are present and whether the srsrpmsi installation process completes successfully.
srsrpmsi.log	Records activity on the SQL Reporting Services setup.
srsrp.log	Records activity on the SQL Reporting Services in terms of configuring security and copying reports. In this log file, you see information about the reports being imported, security being added, and the style being applied to the reports.
wcm.log	Records activity on WSUS configuration for subscribed update categories, classifications, and languages.

Log File	Description
hman.log	Records activity about changes made to the site like installing new site system roles and also information about publishing information to Active Directory.
wsusctrl.log	Records activity on WSUS configuration, database connectivity, and health of the WSUS server. If you see errors in wsyncmgr.log, most likely you will find an explanation to the problem in this log file.
wsyncmgr.log	Records activity on WSUS synchronization. The initial synchronization between WSUS and ConfigMgr can easily take more than 30 minutes. This log file is especially useful for monitoring detailed information about the synchronization process like duration, time left, and so forth.
smsawebsvcsetup.log	Records activity on installing the Application Catalog web service. In this log file, you see whether the needed prerequisites are present and whether the awebsvcmsi installation process completes successfully.
awebsvcmsi.log	Records detailed installation information about installing the Application Catalog web service point site system role.
awebsctl.log	Records the monitoring activities for the Application Catalog web service point site system role, including certificate maintenance.

The Basic Site Server Configuration

The next logical step is to perform the basic configuration of the site server. Basic configuration includes:

- Backup and other site maintenance tasks
- Discovery of resources from Active Directory

Configure Site Maintenance Tasks

ConfigMgr provides a graphical interface for managing site maintenance properties and maintaining the SQL Server database. The benefit of the site maintenance tasks is that administrators do not have to use any native SQL Server configuration tools to manage the database. There are many different tasks, but not all of them need to be configured. ViaMonstra requires a daily backup of ConfigMgr, a weekly update of the SQL Server indexes, and the cleanup of inactive and obsolete clients.

1. On **CM01**, open the **ConfigMgr console**.
2. Select the **Administration** workspace.

3. Navigate to **Overview / Site Configuration / Sites**.
4. From the ribbon, select **Settings / Site Maintenance**.
5. A list of predefined maintenance tasks is shown; select **Backup site server**, click **Edit**, and then click **Enable this task**.
6. Click **Set Paths** and configure the backup files to be stored in **D:\CM2012.BCK** and click **OK** (the folder is created automatically by the backup process). Make sure that you do not select a drive where you also store the site database. (We cover backup and recovery later in this book.)
7. Configure the backup process to generate an alert if the site backup task fails by selecting the **Enable alerts for backup task failures** check box and click **OK**.

Real World Note: Unlike with previous versions of ConfigMgr, you are no longer forced to perform a backup from the maintenance tasks. A "normal" SQL backup performed within SQL Server is supported, and more importantly, it will work in a restore scenario. If you don't have knowledge of SQL, I still recommend using the maintenance tasks to configure the backup.

8. Select **Delete Inactive Client Discovery Data**, click **Edit**, and select **Enable this task**.
9. Configure the task to delete all records **older than 60 days** and click **OK**.
10. Select **Delete Obsolete Client Discovery Data** and click **Edit**.
11. Configure the task to delete all records **older than 1 day** and **run the task daily**, and then click **OK**.
12. Select **Rebuild Indexes** and click **Edit** and then click **Enable this task**
13. Configure the task to start every **Sunday after 12:00 AM** and no later then **3:00 AM**, and then click **OK**.
14. Click **OK** to close the Site Maintenance dialog box.

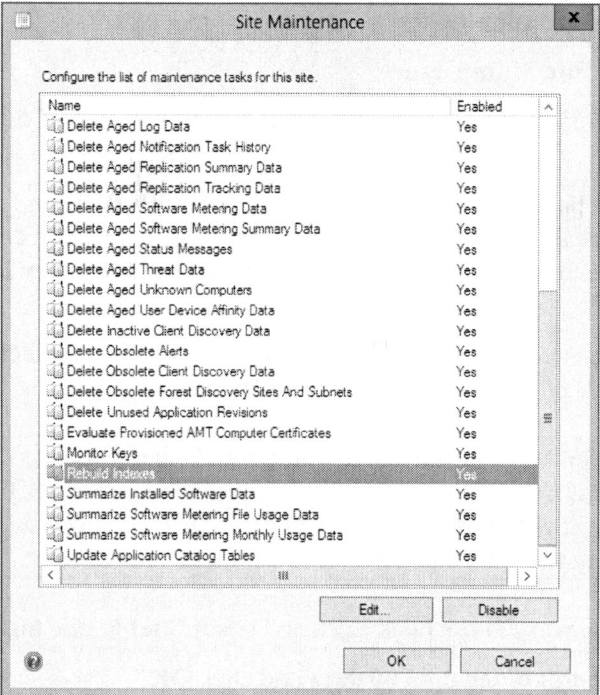

Configuring site maintenance tasks.

Configure Discovery

Discovery is a process by which ConfigMgr queries a predefined source and searches for basic information about a given object. The source and object are configured in the properties of each discovery method. Discovery comes in different "flavors." Different discovery methods are used for different purposes. For ViaMonstra, you will configure the Active Directory discovery methods in the following table.

Discovery Method	What the Method Does	Why You Use the Method
Active Directory Forest	Discovers Active Directory sites and IP ranges.	You use it to automate the creation of boundaries, thus minimizing your own manual work and eliminating typos.
Active Directory System	Discovers computer objects and adds information like basic computer information, information about the OU, and System group membership.	For ViaMonstra, you want to see all your computer objects before you start installing clients. That way you can create collections based on the operating system and location.
Active Directory	Discovers user objects.	You need the user information to support your user-centric

Discovery Method	What the Method Does	Why You Use the Method
User		application strategy.
Active Directory Group	Discovers Active Directory security groups.	You also need the security group information to support our user-centric application strategy.
Heartbeat	Discovers a variety of data that will be cover later in Chapter 6, "Inventory Management and Reporting." This is the only method enabled by default. This method also is the only one initiated by the client and thus works only for existing clients. The heartbeat discovery also is listed as the Discovery Data Collection Cycle when looking at the client properties. Data in this record includes computer name, domain name, operating system name, last logged on user, and so forth.	For ViaMonstra, you will be changing the default interval from 7 days to 1 day. The traffic generated by a data discovery cycle is about 8 KB per client. The benefit of running a more frequent discovery is getting more up-to-date information in the ConfigMgr console.

Even though it might be tempting to discover the entire domain, that's really not a good idea. It might work in a lab environment or in a small business installation. But for midsize and enterprise scenarios, it's really important that you specify the exact LDAP path to the location of the objects. For ViaMonstra, you want to use the discovery methods in the following list to discover resources in the indicated organizational units and paths:

- **Active Directory Forest** (OUs: N/A)

  DC=corp,DC=viamonstra,DC=com

- **Active Directory System** (OUs: Workstations, Domain Controllers, Servers)
  - LDAP://OU=Domain Controllers,DC=corp,DC=viamonstra,DC=com
  - LDAP://OU=Workstations,DC=corp,DC=viamonstra,DC=com
  - LDAP://OU=Servers,DC=corp,DC=viamonstra,DC=com
- **Active Directory User** (OUs: Users, VIM Users)
  - LDAP://CN=Users,DC=corp,DC=viamonstra,DC=com
  - LDAP://OU=VIM Users,DC=corp,DC=viamonstra,DC=com
- **Active Directory Security Group** (OU: Software Groups)

  LDAP://OU=Software Groups,DC=corp,DC=viamonstra,DC=com

Follow these steps to configure discovery:

1. On **DC01**, using **Active Directory Users and Computers**, in the **ViaMonstra** OU, create the **Software Groups** OU.
2. In the **ViaMonstra / Users** OU, create the following user accounts:
    - BOP, full name Bob Paisly
    - JAP, full name Julie Petersen
    - MAC, full name Mark Carragher
    - MLG, full name Michael L Gerrad
    - NEP, full name Nanna E Petersen
    - SAN, full name Suzanne Angelhart
    - SMA, full name Sofie M Andersen
    - WKO, full name Wally Konig
3. On **CM01**, log on as **VIAMONSTRA\Administrator**, and open the **ConfigMgr console**.
4. Select the **Administration** workspace.
5. Navigate to **Overview / Hierarchy Configuration / Discovery Methods**.
6. Right-click **Active Directory Forest Discovery** and select **Properties**.
7. Select **Enable Active Directory Forest Discovery, Automatically create Active Directory site boundaries when they are discovered**, and **Automatically create IP Ranges when they are discovered**.

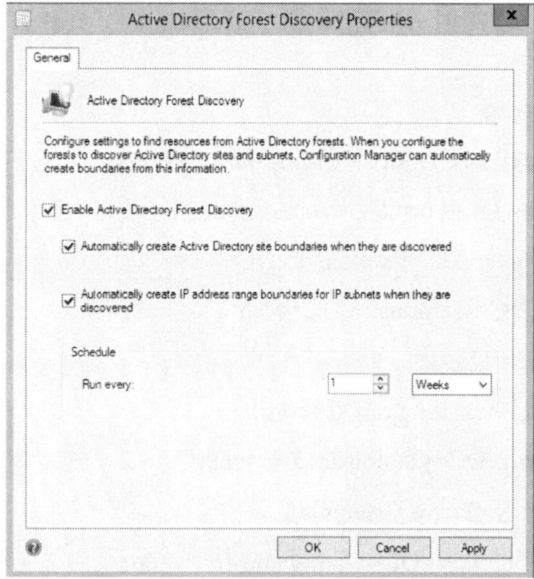

Configuring Active Directory Forest Discovery.

8. Click **OK** and **Yes** to close the dialog box and run the Active Directory Forest Discovery method.
9. Select **Active Directory System Discovery** and click **Properties**.
10. In the **General** tab:
    a. Select the **Enable Active Directory System Discovery** check box.
    b. Click **New**, click **Browse**, and then select this path: **LDAP://OU=Domain Controllers,DC=corp,DC=viamonstra,DC=com**.
    c. In the **Search options** area, ensure that **Recursively Search Active Directory child containers** is selected.
    d. Click **OK**.
    e. Repeat steps B–D for these two LDAP paths:
        i. **LDAP://OU=Workstations, OU=Viamonstra,DC=corp,DC=viamonstra,DC=com**
        ii. **LDAP://OU=Servers,OU=Viamonstra,DC=corp,DC=viamonstra,DC =com**

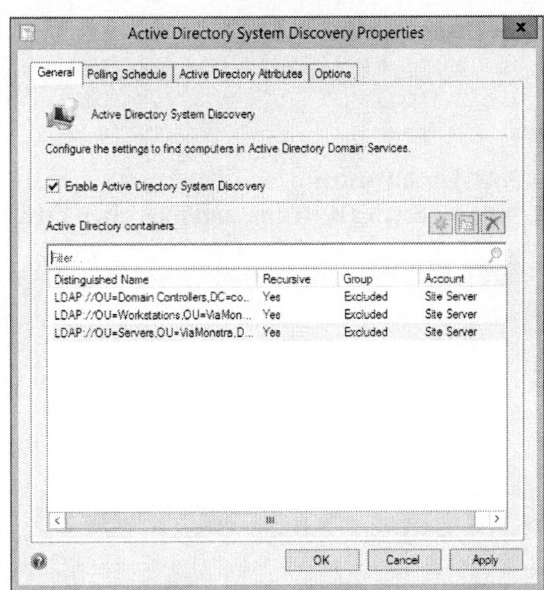

Active Directory System Discovery.

11. In the **Options** tab:
    a. Enable **Only discover computers that have logged on to a domain in a given period of time** and select **30**.
    b. Enable **Only discover computers that have updated their computer account password in a given period of time** and keep the default settings.

12. Click **OK** to save the settings and **Yes** to run a full discovery.
13. Right-click **Active Directory User Discovery** and click **Properties**.
14. In the **General** tab:
    a. Select the **Enable Active Directory User Discovery** check box.
    b. Click **New**, click **Browse**, and then select this path: **LDAP://CN=Users,DC=corp,DC=viamonstra,DC=com**.
    c. In the **Search options** area, ensure that **Recursively Search Active Directory child containers** is selected.
    d. Click **OK**.
    e. Click **New**, click **Browse**, and then select this path: **LDAP://OU=Users,OU=Viamonstra,DC=corp,DC=viamonstra,DC=com**.
    f. In the **Search options** area, ensure that **Recursively Search Active Directory child containers** is selected.
    g. Click **OK** twice and **Yes** to run a full discovery.
15. Right-click **Active Directory Group Discovery** and click **Properties**.
16. Select the **Enable Active Directory Group Discovery** check box.
17. Click **Add / Location**.
18. In the **Name** field, type **Software Groups**.
19. For **Location**, click **Browse**, select **LDAP://OU=Software Groups,OU=ViaMonstra,DC=corp,DC=viamonstra,DC=com**, and then click **OK**.

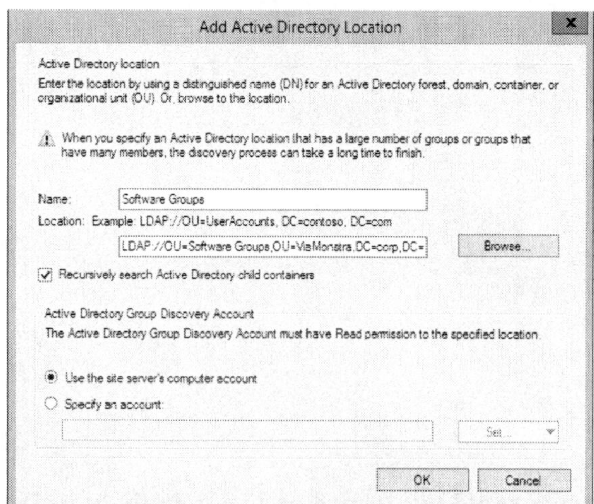

Specifying the LDAP path.

20. In the **Option** tab, configure these options:

a. Enable **Only discover computers that have logged on to a domain in a given period of time**. Time since last logon (days): **30**

b. Enable **Only discover computers that have updates their computer account password in a given period of time** and leave the default settings.

21. Click **OK** to save the settings and **Yes** to run a full discovery.

Verifying the Discovery Process

The discovery process runs in the background and should by now have generated multiple data discovery records in the ConfigMgr console. Go thru these checks to verify that the process ran successfully.

Verify Active Directory Forest Discovery

Navigate to the **Administration** workspace, and to **Overview / Hierarchy Configuration / Boundaries**. You should see three IP ranges and an Active Directory site. Unlike in previous versions of ConfigMgr, a boundary in ConfigMgr 2012 has no real value until it's added to a boundary group. By default, ConfigMgr queries only objects from Active Directory Sites and Services in the local forest. You can add additional forest support by creating a new forest object in **Hierarchy Configuration\Active Directory Forests**. From this view, you can verify the discovery and publishing status. From the publishing status, you can tell whether ConfigMgr can successfully write data to Active Directory (the system management container).

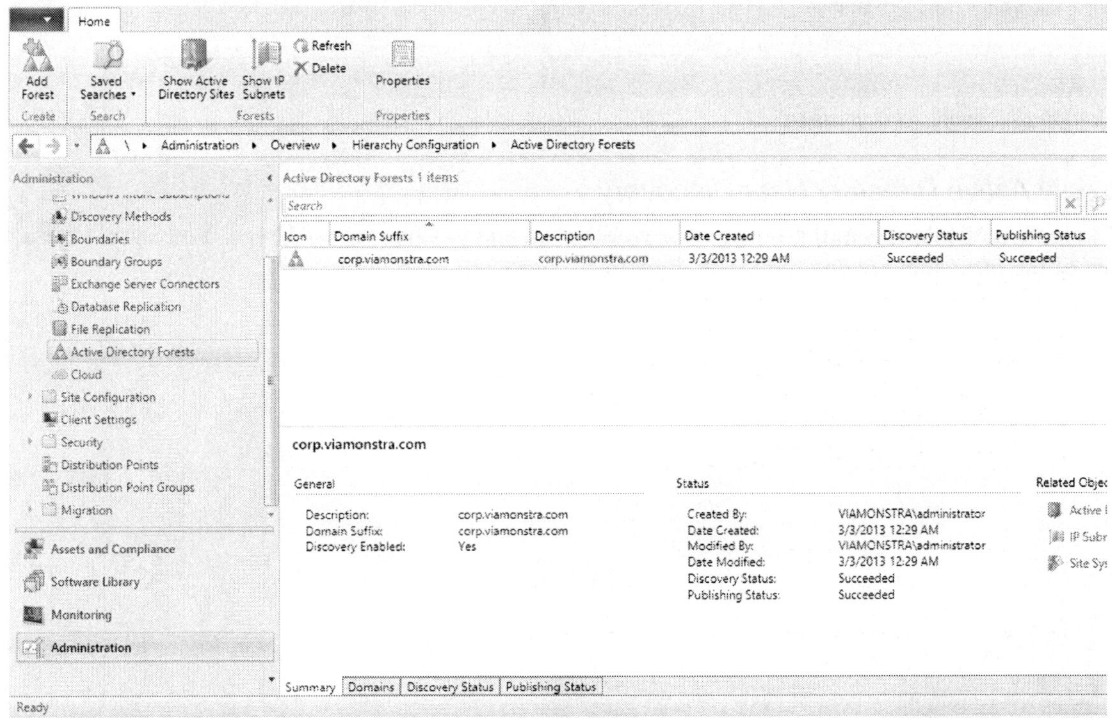

Verifying Forest discovery.

Verify Active Directory System Discovery

Navigate to the **Assets and Compliance** workspace, and to **Overview / Devices**. You should see a list of the devices that are created in the domain. You can right-click each of the computers to see the discovery information generated by the process. The discovery data is not as rich as the data produced by the hardware inventory process, but the data can still be used later when you want to create queries, reports, or collections.

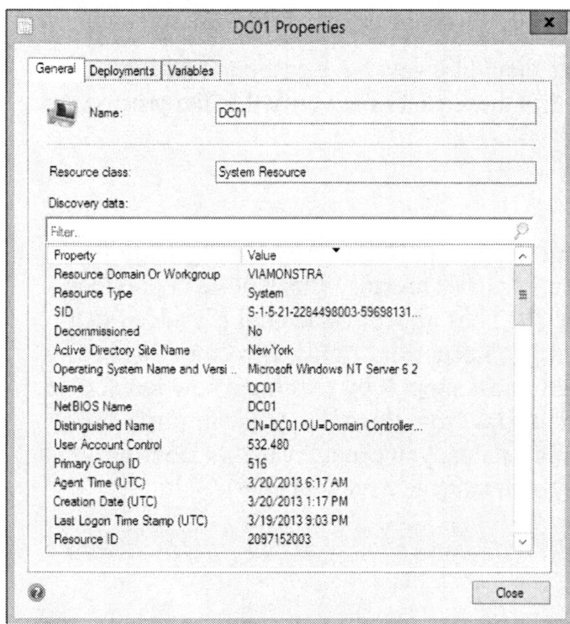

Device discovery information.

Verify Active Directory User Discovery

Navigate to the **Assets and Compliance** workspace, and to **Overview / Users**. You should see a list of the users that are created in the domain.

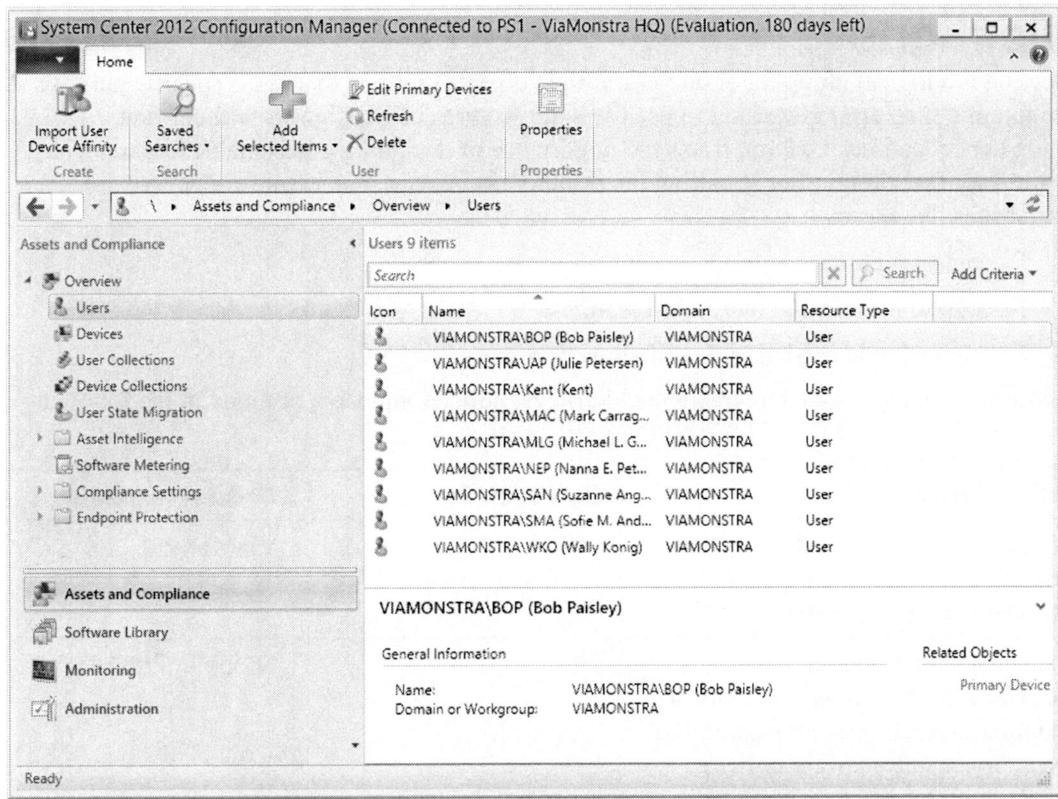

Viewing users in the domain.

Verify Active Directory Security Group Discovery

Navigate to the **Assets and Compliance** workspace, and to **Overview / User Collections**. Right-click the **All Users Group** collection and click **View Members**. As this point in the book you have not created any groups in the **Software Groups** OU so the member count should be 0.

What Happens Behind the Scenes

When you are initiating a discovery process, the site server automatically queries Active Directory for the resources that you have specified in the LDAP path. There are two different discovery schedules, a Full discovery and the Delta discovery process. The full will by default run once a week and do a complete scan for all objects unlike the delta process that will only find objects added, removed or modified since the last full cycle. This process by default runs every five minutes:

1. The site server queries Active Directory.
2. For each resource, a data discovery record (ddr) is created and written to D:\Program files\Microsoft Configuration Manager\Inboxes\Auth\ddm.box.
3. From there, the data are processed and added to the database by the data loader component.

Collections

A collection is a logical grouping of one or multiple objects grouped to serve a specific purpose. A very commonly seen error is starting to use the main features of ConfigMgr without first designing the collections. I cannot stress the importance of designing a reasonable hierarchy as one of the very first things after installing the primary site server. You create collections for several reasons like these:

- To control security
- To support the way to control you features
- To minimize the needed SQL code in your reports

In ViaMonstra, I have decided to create the high-level collection design outlined in the following table.

Collection Purpose	Collection Prefix	Created in Folder
Used to define the role-based security in ViaMonstra and reflect the physical infrastructure of the company.	VM	ViaMonstra
Used to control the Endpoint Protection feature. The collection is used to control the Endpoint Protection agent installation and the applying antimalware policies.	EP	Endpoint Protection
Used to control the application deployment. There will be two Software folders in ViaMonstra, one for Users and one for Devices. You create software collections for most applications and packages, one collection to control the install process, and one collection to control the uninstall process.	SWD (for software device collections) SWU (for software user collections)	Software
Used to control the compliance settings. There will be two Settings Management folders in ViaMonstra, one for Users and one for Devices. You create settings management collections to control deployment of the company baselines.	SM	Settings Management
Used to control the operating system deployment process. During the operating system installation, you are able to read data and variables from a collection.	OSD	Operating System Deployment
Used to control the software update patching process.	SUM	Software Updates

Create Folders

1. On **CM01**, open the **ConfigMgr console**.
2. Select the **Asset and Compliance** workspace.
3. Right-click **User Collections** and select **Folder / Create Folder**.
4. Type **ViaMonstra** as the folder name and click **OK**.
5. Repeat steps 3–4 and create the following folder:

   Settings Management
6. Right-click **Device Collections** and select **Folder / Create Folder**.
7. Type **Software Updates** as the folder name and click **OK**.
8. Repeat steps 6–7 and create the following folders:
   a. **Settings Management**
   b. **Software**
   c. **ViaMonstra**
   d. **Operating System Deployment**

> **Real World Note:** You might find it easier to use a scripted solution when building the initial collection design.

Automate Creating Folders Using PowerShell

The script used in this section creates two folders, a device folder called **Endpoint Protection** and a user folder called **Software**. (It's the -Type value that determines whether it's a device or user folder.) For this guide, I assume you have copied the book sample script to D:\Setup\Scripts on CM01.

1. On CM01. open **PowerShell** as **Administrator**.
2. Navigate to the folder containing the scripts.
3. Type the following command (note the space between the two dots):
   ```
   . .\CM12_Function_Library_SP1.ps1
   ```
4. Type the following command:
   ```
   Add-CMFolder -SiteCode PS1 -SiteServer CM01 -FolderName
   "Endpoint Protection" -Type 5000
   ```
5. Type the following command:
   ```
   Add-CMFolder -SiteCode PS1 -SiteServer CM01 -FolderName
   "Software" -Type 5001
   ```

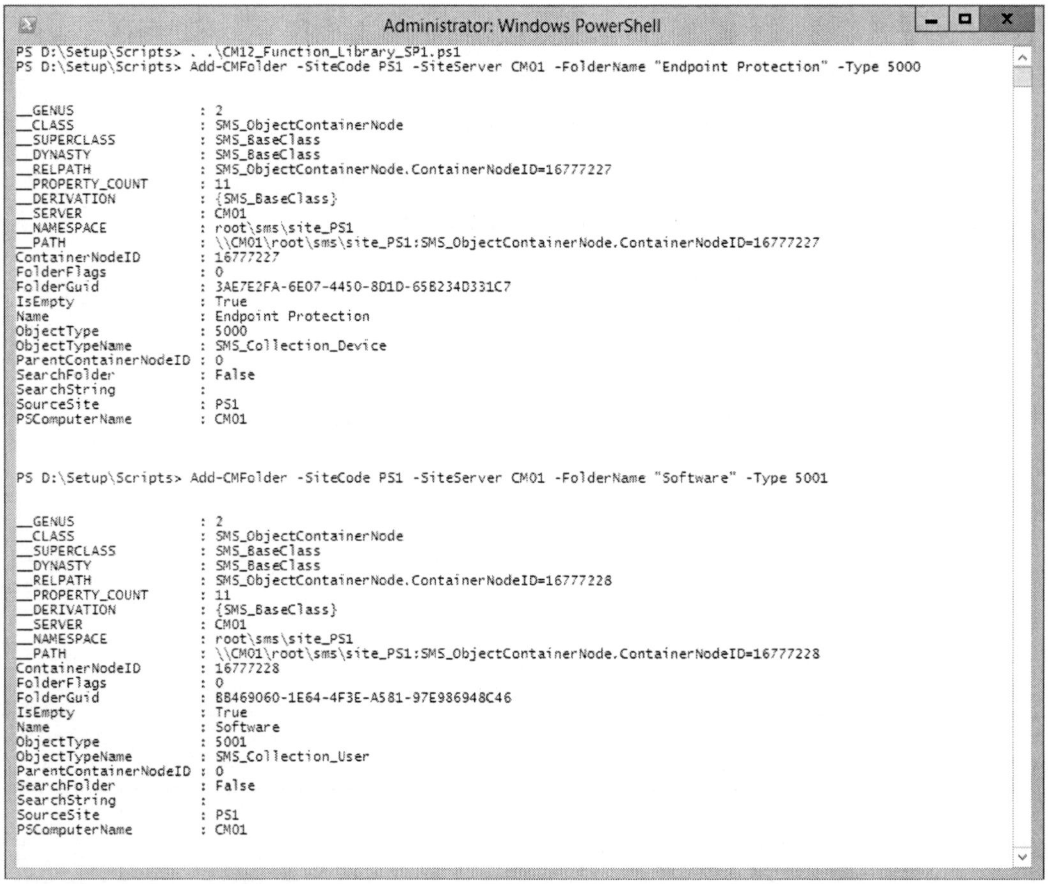

```
Administrator: Windows PowerShell
PS D:\Setup\Scripts> . .\CM12_Function_Library_SP1.ps1
PS D:\Setup\Scripts> Add-CMFolder -SiteCode PS1 -SiteServer CM01 -FolderName "Endpoint Protection" -Type 5000

__GENUS                 : 2
__CLASS                 : SMS_ObjectContainerNode
__SUPERCLASS            : SMS_BaseClass
__DYNASTY               : SMS_BaseClass
__RELPATH               : SMS_ObjectContainerNode.ContainerNodeID=16777227
__PROPERTY_COUNT        : 11
__DERIVATION            : {SMS_BaseClass}
__SERVER                : CM01
__NAMESPACE             : root\sms\site_PS1
__PATH                  : \\CM01\root\sms\site_PS1:SMS_ObjectContainerNode.ContainerNodeID=16777227
ContainerNodeID         : 16777227
FolderFlags             : 0
FolderGuid              : 3AE7E2FA-6E07-4450-8D1D-65B234D331C7
IsEmpty                 : True
Name                    : Endpoint Protection
ObjectType              : 5000
ObjectTypeName          : SMS_Collection_Device
ParentContainerNodeID   : 0
SearchFolder            : False
SearchString            :
SourceSite              : PS1
PSComputerName          : CM01


PS D:\Setup\Scripts> Add-CMFolder -SiteCode PS1 -SiteServer CM01 -FolderName "Software" -Type 5001

__GENUS                 : 2
__CLASS                 : SMS_ObjectContainerNode
__SUPERCLASS            : SMS_BaseClass
__DYNASTY               : SMS_BaseClass
__RELPATH               : SMS_ObjectContainerNode.ContainerNodeID=16777228
__PROPERTY_COUNT        : 11
__DERIVATION            : {SMS_BaseClass}
__SERVER                : CM01
__NAMESPACE             : root\sms\site_PS1
__PATH                  : \\CM01\root\sms\site_PS1:SMS_ObjectContainerNode.ContainerNodeID=16777228
ContainerNodeID         : 16777228
FolderFlags             : 0
FolderGuid              : BB469060-1E64-4F3E-A581-97E986948C46
IsEmpty                 : True
Name                    : Software
ObjectType              : 5001
ObjectTypeName          : SMS_Collection_User
ParentContainerNodeID   : 0
SearchFolder            : False
SearchString            :
SourceSite              : PS1
PSComputerName          : CM01
```

Creating user and device folders using PowerShell.

Role-Based Administration (RBA)

RBA goes hand in hand with defining collections. Before you start planning security, you need to know the basics and also have knowledge about the way you want to control your own environment. For ViaMonstra, you have several ConfigMgr administrators but all with different tasks to perform and responsibilities.

Defining the Support Model

ViaMonstra knows the importance of defining the support model that will maintain ConfigMgr. Even though ConfigMgr might only be a "single" application, it is by far the most complex application currently shipped out of Microsoft in Redmond. No other application requires that a single administrator is a master of software deployment, Active Directory, operating system deployment, security processes, update management, SQL Server, antimalware management, Mobile device management and on top of that know everything there is to know about the infrastructure. If you are tired after a hard day's work, it's fully understandable and, yes, you do deserve that big bowl of ice cream.

In ViaMonstra, I have decided to use security roles in the following table.

Security Role	**Responsibility**
Full Administrator	Overall responsible for ConfigMgr; must have full access to every single object in the ConfigMgr console.
Server operators	Must have full access to manage all server objects, including creating applications, operating system images, and applications.
Workstation operators	Must have full access to manage all workstation objects, including creating applications, operating system images, and applications.
Endpoint Protection manager	Responsible for managing everything related to Endpoint Protection.
Reporting users	Read-only access; for users who can only read reports and not access any object in the ConfigMgr console.

Security Objects in ConfigMgr

Before you start defining security there are a few objects you need to understand.

Object	**Purpose**
Security Role	A role defines the actions a user can perform in the ConfigMgr console. ConfigMgr ships with several built-in security roles and also enables you to create custom roles.
Scope	Most objects in the console can be configured to belong to one or more scopes. When importing users or groups, you can limit them to work only with objects from one or more scopes. For ViaMonstra, have applications and images that are meant to be used only by the server administrators and/or the workstation administrators. Those objects will be assigned to either the Server or the Workstation scope. Objects that can be shared between the two groups will be added to both scopes.

Object	Purpose
Collections	Look at a collection like a security boundary where you are limited to work only with those objects in that specific collection. For ViaMonstra, you will create specific collections containing servers only and workstations only. That way you ensure that server operators can't work with workstations and vice versa. All collections are limited to objects in a parent collection, and collections are always divided between users or devices. At the top of the hierarchy, you find the default collections All Systems and All Users. In ViaMonstra, only the Full Administrator group will have access to members in these collections. The other teams will get access only to a subset of devices and users.

Creating the Collections to Support Your Security Model

1. On **CM01**, open the **ConfigMgr console**.
2. Select the **Assets and Compliance** workspace.
3. Select **Device Collections**, right-click the **ViaMonstra** folder, and select **Create Device Collection**.

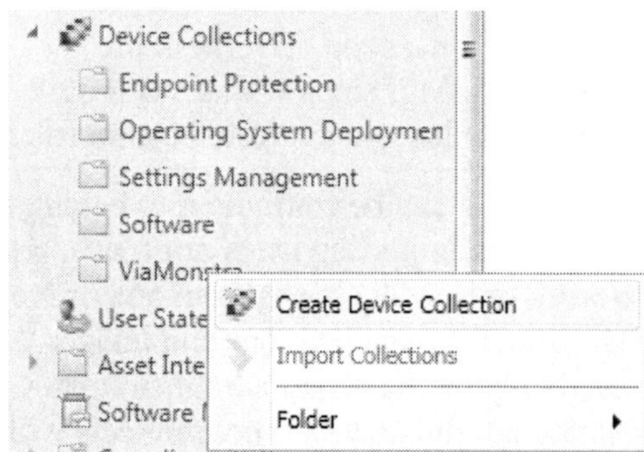

Creating a device collection.

4. On the **General** page, enter the following details:
    a. Name: **VM All Servers**
    b. Comment: **Top level collection for all company servers**
    c. Limiting Collection: Click **Browse** and select **All Systems**.

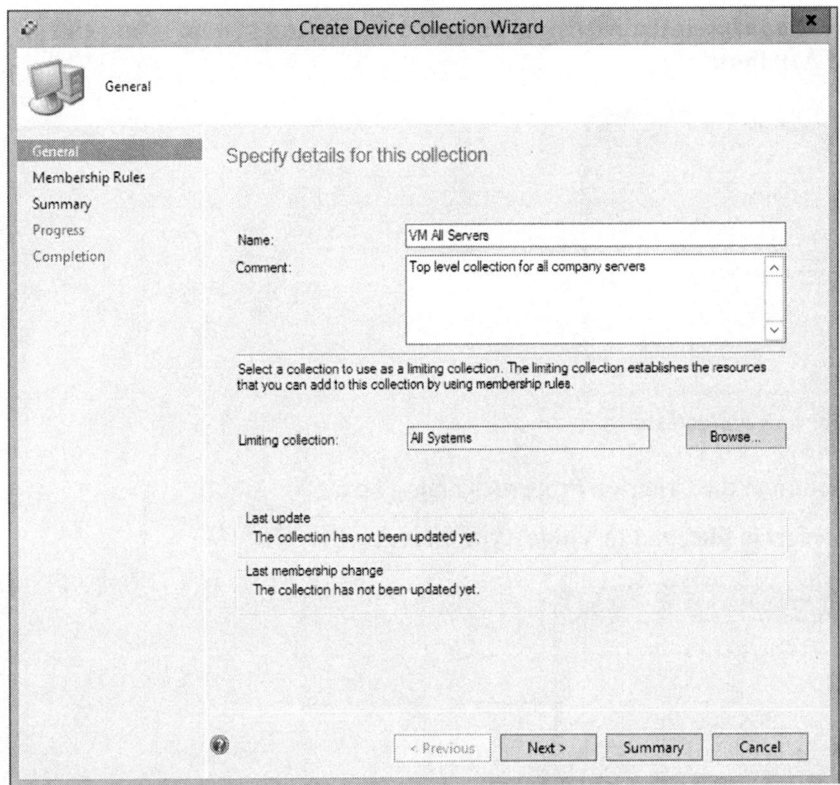

Creating a collection.

5. Click **Next**.
6. Click **Add Rule / Query Rule**.

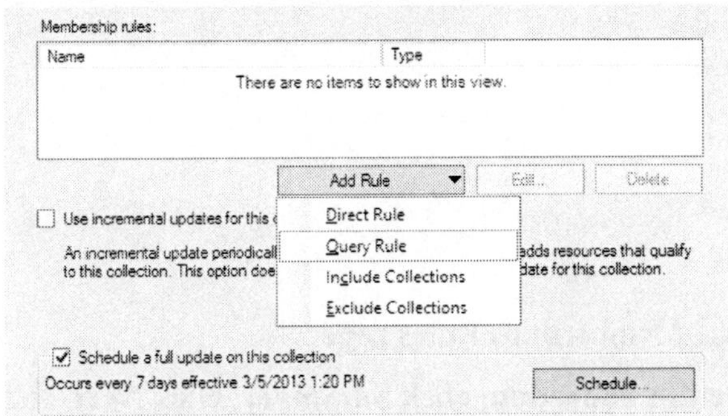

Adding a query rule.

7. Name the rule **All Servers** and click **Edit Query Statement**.
8. Select the **Criteria** tab.
9. Click the **yellow icon** and click **Select** to create the criteria.

10. Select **System Resource** as the **Attribute class** and **Operating system name and version** as the **Attribute**.

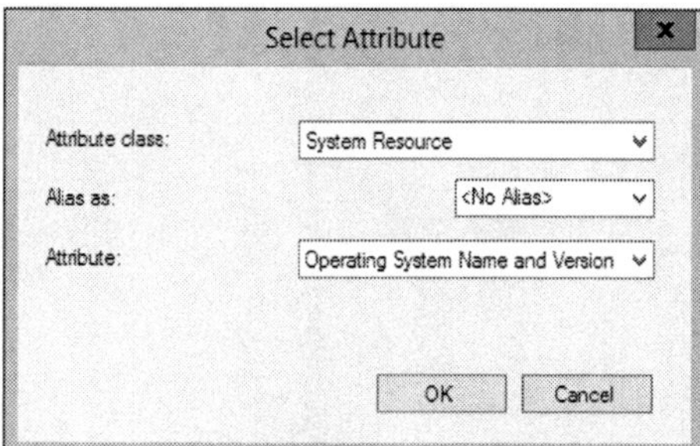

Creating the All Servers collection.

11. Click **OK** to return to the Criterion Properties dialog box.
12. In **Operator**, select **is like**, and in **Value**, type **%Server%**.

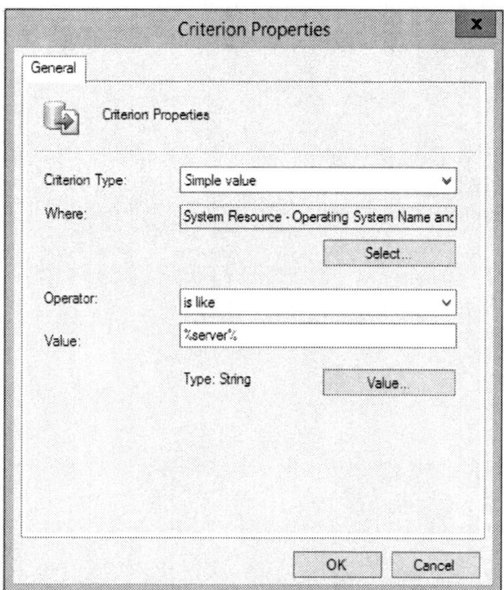

Creating a query using wildcards.

13. Click **OK** three times and return to the Memberships Rules page.
14. Enable **Use incremental updates for this collection**, click **Summary**, click **Next**, and then click **Close** to close the wizard.

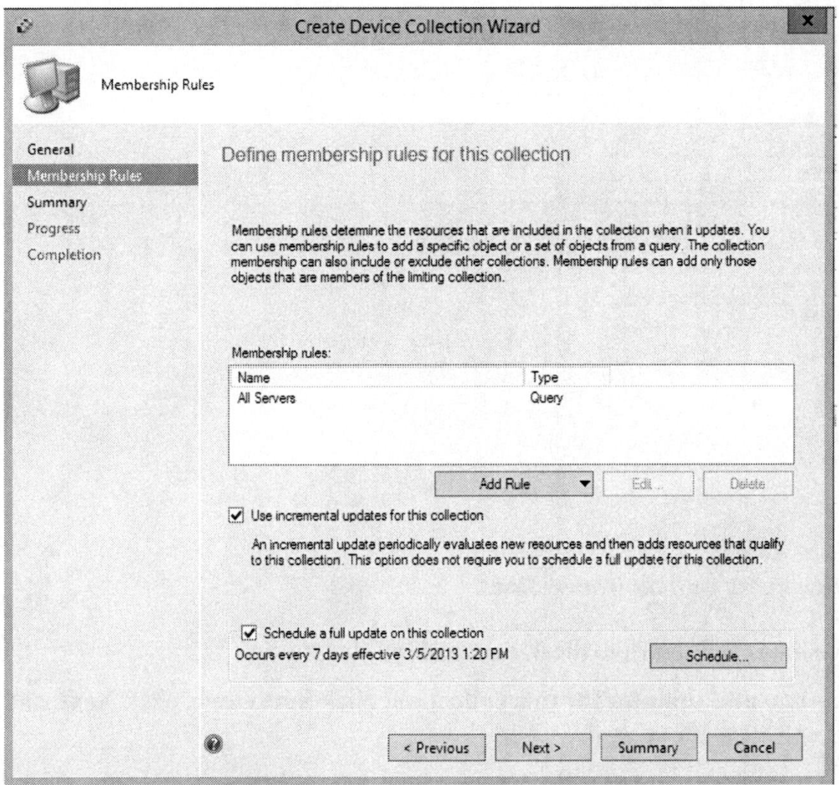

Using incremental updates for a query based collection

15. Create a new device collection called **VM All Workstations** using the same methodology as the VM All Servers collection (steps 3–13):

  a. For step 10, use the following criteria and then click **OK**:

    i. Attribute Class: **System Resource**

    ii. Attribute: **Operating system name and version**

  b. In **Operator**, select **is like**, and in **Value**, type **%Workstation%.**

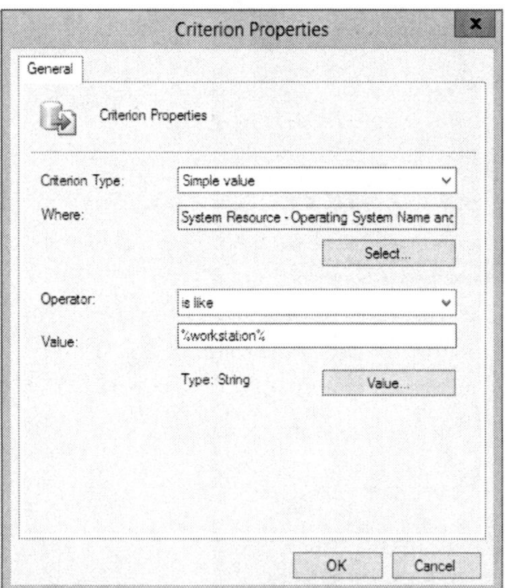

Creating a collection query with all workstations.

16. Click **OK** three times and return to the **Memberships Rules** page.
17. Enable **Use incremental updates for this collection**, click **Summary**, click **Next**, and then click **Close** to close the wizard.

Automate Creating Collections Using PowerShell

Below are a few examples showing you how to automate the process of creating collections. These are only command examples and none of the collections are required for any of the guides in this book. First few examples are using the custom cmdlet.

1. On CM01, open **PowerShell** as **Administrator**.
2. Navigate to the folder containing the scripts.
3. Type the following command:

```
. .\CM12_Function_Library_SP1.ps1
```

4. Create a user collection by typing the following command:

```
Add-CMCollection -SiteCode PS1 -SiteServer localhost -Name
"All HR Users" -Type User -LimitToCollectionID SMS00002
```

5. Create a user collection with full collection update schedule every second Saturday and incremental updates by typing the following command:

```
Add-CMCollection -SiteCode PS1 -SiteServer localhost -Name
"All Sales Users" -Type User -LimitToCollectionID SMS00002
-Day Saturday -NumberOfWeeks 2 -Incremental
```

6. Create a user collection in a folder called ViaMonstra with a comment by typing the following command:

```
Add-CMCollection -SiteCode PS1 -SiteServer localhost -Name
"All Marketing Users" -LimitToCollectionID SMS00002 -Folder
"ViaMonstra" -Type user -Comment "Mastering ConfigMgr 2012
Fundamentals"
```

The next example explains how you can use the ConfigMgr cmdlet to create collections.

1. From the **ConfigMgr console**, select the drop-down list next to the **Home** menu and click **Connect via Windows PowerShell**. Type **A** and press **Enter** to Always run.
2. Create a device collection by typing the following command:

```
New-CMDeviceCollection -Name "SWD Microsoft Office 2013
Project Install" -LimitingCollectionName "VM All
Workstations" -Comment "Mastering ConfigMgr 2012
Fundamentals"
```

3. Create a user collection by typing the following command:

```
New-CMUserCollection -Name "SWU Microsoft Office 2013
Project Install" -LimitingCollectionName "All Users"
-Comment "Mastering ConfigMgr 2012 Fundamentals"
```

Creating the Security Roles

Create the Administrative Groups in Active Directory

1. On **DC01**, log on as **Administrator**.
2. Start **Active Directory Users and Computers**.
3. Navigate to the **ViaMonstra / Security Groups** OU and create two domain local security groups:
   a. **Server Admins**
   b. **Workstation Admins**

4. In the **ViaMonstra / Users** OU, create two user accounts and add them to the corresponding groups:
    a. Account **SrvAdmin**: add to **Server Admins**.
    b. Account **WrkAdmin**, add to **Workstation Admins**.

Assign Security Roles

1. On **CM01**, open the **ConfigMgr console**.
2. Navigate to the **Administration** workspace, and expand **Security / Administrative Users**.
3. On the ribbon, click **Add User or Group**.
4. Click **Browse** and add the **Server Admins** group.
5. In **Assigned Security roles**, click **Add**, select these roles, and click **OK**:
    a. **Application Administrator**
    b. **Asset Manager**
    c. **Compliance Settings Manager**
    d. **Operating System Deployment Manager**
    e. **Remote Tools Operator**
    f. **Software Update Manager**

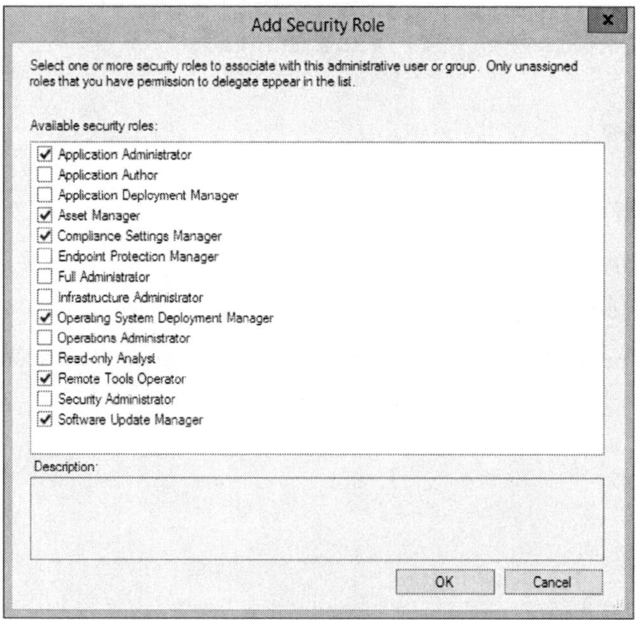

Adding security roles.

6. In **Assigned security scopes and collections**, select the **All Systems** collection and **All Users and User Groups** collection, and then click **Remove.**
7. Click **Add Collection.**
8. Select **Device collections.**
9. Select **ViaMonstra / VM All Servers** and click **OK.**
10. Click **OK** to close the **Add User or Group** window.
11. On the ribbon, click **Add User or Group.**
12. Click **Browse** and add the user to the **Workstation Admins** group.
13. In **Assigned roles**, click **Add**, select these roles, and click **OK**:
    a. **Application Administrator**
    b. **Asset Manager**
    c. **Compliance Settings Manager**
    d. **Operating System Deployment Manager**
    e. **Remote Tools Operator**
    f. **Software Update Manager**
14. In **Assigned security scopes and collections**, select the **All Systems** collection and **All Users and User Groups** collection, and then click **Remove.**
15. Click **Add Collection.**
16. Select **Device collections.**
17. Select **ViaMonstra / VM All Workstations** and click **OK.**
18. Click **OK** to close the **Add User or Group** window.

Test the New Server Administrator Role

Testing security roles is an important step. In this section, you verify that the SrvAdmin user (who is a server administrator) can see only objects related to security role. You can easily perform the test by creating a new collection containing one or more servers. The SrvAdmin should not be able to see or work with any workstation computers.

1. Open a new instance of the **ConfigMgr console.** (On the **Start screen**, right-click the **Configuration Manager Console**, and click **Run as a different user.**)
2. Start the console as **VIAMONSTRA\SrvAdmin** and navigate to the **Asset and Compliance** workspace.
3. Select **Device Collections** and the **ViaMonstra** folder.
4. On the ribbon, click **Create Device Collection.**

5. Create a new collection named **VM All Domain Controllers** limited to the **VM All Servers** collection.
6. Click **Next,** click **Add Rule**, and create a new **Direct Rule**.
7. Click **Next.**
8. Type **DC01** in the **Value** field and click **Next**.

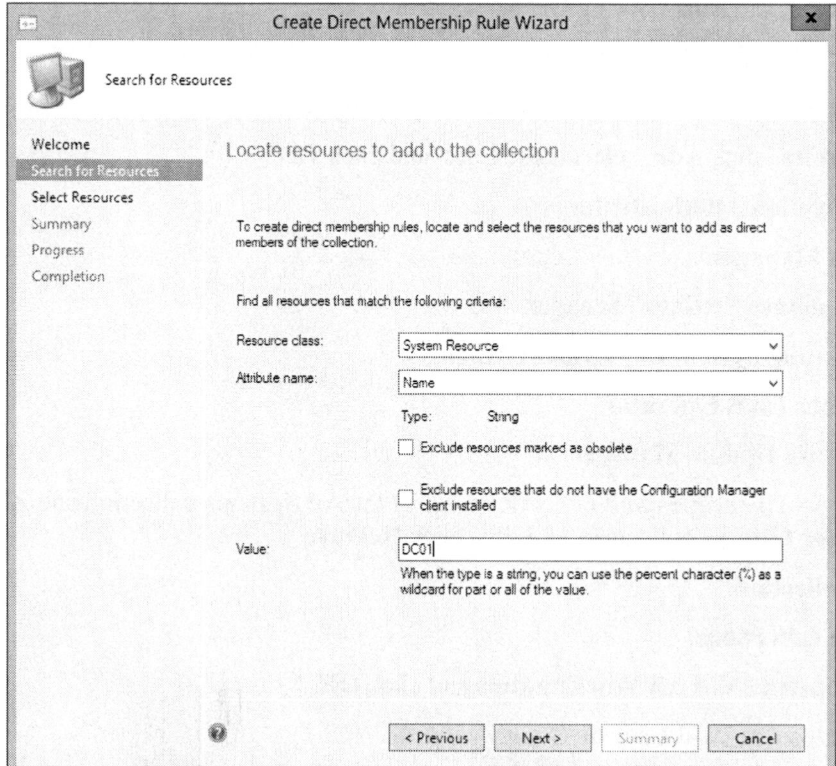

Creating a collection with a direct membership rule.

9. Select **DC01**, click **Summary**, click **Next**, and then click **Close**.
10. Finish the wizard, accepting the defaults for the remaining pages.
11. Close the **ConfigMgr console**.

Automate Creating Collection Direct Rules Using PowerShell

This is an optional example of how to create a direct collection rule using PowerShell:

1. On **CM01**, open **PowerShell** as **Administrator**.
2. Navigate to the folder containing the scripts.
3. Type the following command:

```
. .\CM12_Function_Library_SP1.ps1
```

4. Type the following command:

```
Set-CMCollectionDirectRule -SiteServer Localhost -SiteCode
PS1 -ResourceName DC01 -CollectionName "VM All Domain
Controllers"
```

The next optional example explains how you can use the Configmgr cmdlet to create collections.

1. From the ConfigMgr console, select the drop-down list next to the Home menu and click **Connect via Windows PowerShell**.
2. Create a direct membership rule:
   a. Type the following command:

```
New-CMDeviceCollection -Name "VM All DC"
-LimitingCollectionName "VM All Servers"
```

   b. Then type this command:

```
Add-CMDeviceCollectionDirectMembershipRule -CollectionName
"VM All DC" -ResourceId 2097152003
```

> **Note:** Each object in ConfigMgr has a unique resource ID. You can view the ID by opening the object properties or by selecting the Resource ID column. You can add and remove column names by right-clicking any existing column name.

Work with Scopes

1. Ensure that you are logged in to **ConfigMgr console** as **Full Administrator**.
2. Select the **Administration** workspace and navigate to **Security / Security Scopes**.
3. On the ribbon, click **Create Security Scope**.
4. Create these two scopes:
   a. **Servers**
   b. **Workstations**

5. Navigate to **Administrative Users**. Right-click **VIAMONSTRA\Server Admins** and select **Properties**.
6. In the **Security Scopes** tab, select **Default** and then click **Remove**.
7. Click **Add / Security Scope**. Then select **Servers** and click **OK** twice.

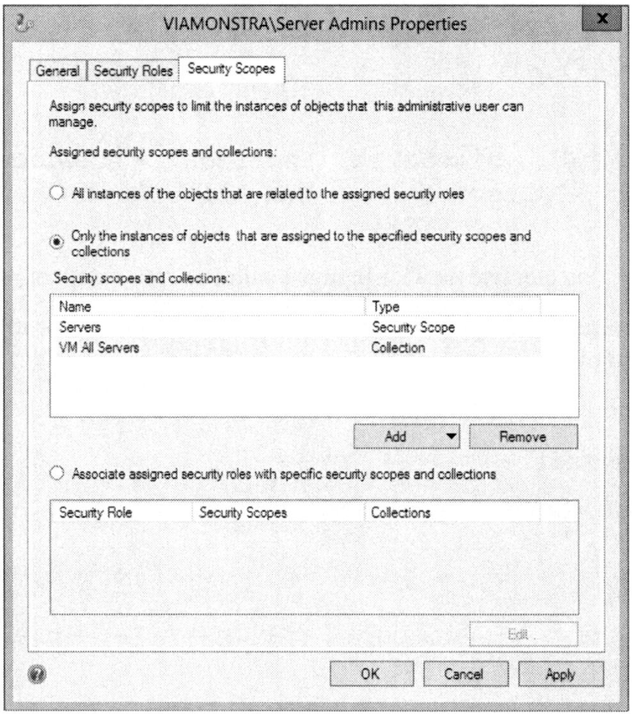

Creating a security scope.

8. Repeat the steps with **VIAMONSTRA\Workstation Admins** (limit the scopes to **Workstations**).

Audit Administrative Users

1. In the **ConfigMgr console**, running as **Full Administrator**, navigate to the **Monitoring** workspace.
2. Select **Reporting / Reports**, and type **Security** in the **Search** field.

3. Select the report **Administration Activity log**, and on the ribbon, click **Run**. Notice that all the administrative changes in the console are written to the report.

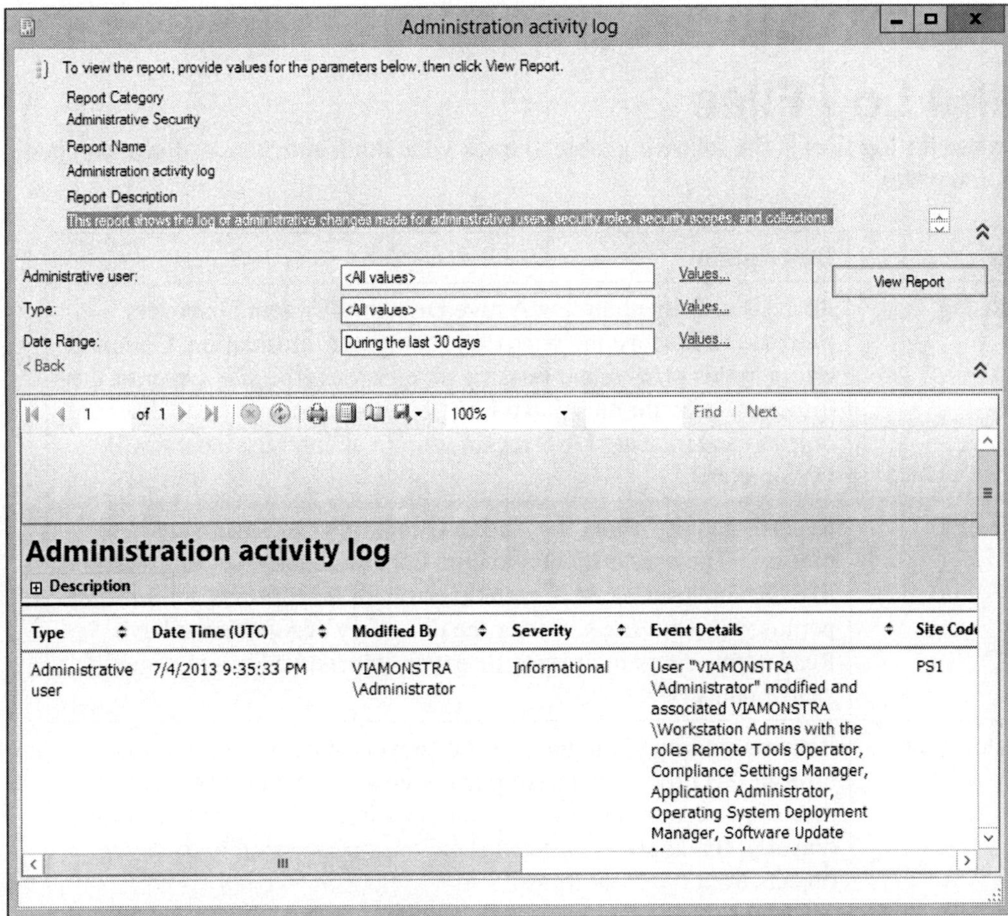

The Administration activity log report.

4. Close the report.
5. Run the report **Security roles summary**. This report will list all the security roles and any user or group associated with the role.
6. Close the report.
7. Run the report **Security for a specific or multiple Configuration Manager objects**.
8. In **Administrative User**, click **Values**, and then select **VIAMONSTRA\Server Admins** and click **View Report**.
9. Close the report.
10. Type **Audit** in the **Search** field (make sure to have the **Reports** node selected when searching) and run the report **All audit messages for a specific user**.

11. In **SMS User Name**, click **Values**, and then select **VIAMONSTRA\SrvAdmin** and click **View Report**.
12. Close the report.

Useful Log Files

You can use the log files in the following table to track your site maintenance, discovery, and collection updates.

Log File	Description
Adsysdis.log	Records activity about the Active Directory System Discovery process. The record includes basic computer information. Common errors in this process are missing permissions (the site server or the discovery account must have Read permissions in order to discover objects) and missing DNS registration (a client must have a valid DNS record).
Adusrdis.log	Records activity about the Active Directory User Discovery process. The user discovery record contains basic user information like OU and user name. Common errors in this process are missing permissions (the site server or the discovery account must have Read permissions in order to discover objects) and misconfigured LDAP paths.
Adforestdisc.log	Records activity about the forest discovery process. A common error in this process is missing permissions (the site server or the discovery account must have Read permissions in order to discover objects). By default, ConfigMgr only has permission to discover objects from the local forest.
Adsgdis.log	Records activity about the security group discovery process.
Colleval.log	Records activity about the collection updates process. This is a commonly used log file whenever you are troubleshooting why collections are not being refreshed.
InventoryAgent.log	Records activity about the local heartbeat discovery process. This log file is only on the client.
SMSdbmon.log	Records activity about processing the site maintenance tasks.
SMSprov.log	Records all WMI actions. This file is very useful when you want to translate WQL into SQL statements.

Chapter 5

Installing and Managing ConfigMgr Clients

The first requirement for managing a client is to install the ConfigMgr client. In most scenarios, that is a pretty straightforward process, and you will find that 95% of all your client deployments succeed with very little effort. Before deploying clients, however, you need to know which features you want to enable on the different clients. In ViaMonstra, I have decided to use the features in the following table.

Feature	Environment
Hardware Inventory	Servers and workstations
Software Inventory	Servers and workstations
Software Metering	Workstations
Power Management	Workstations
Remote Control	Servers and workstations but with different security settings
Endpoint Protection	Servers and workstations but with different policies

Configuring Client Settings

Client features and settings are controlled through an object called *Default Client Settings*. By default, all clients automatically download and apply all settings. Whenever you have to apply settings that differ from the default settings, you should create custom client settings and deploy those to a collection. In the event of a conflict, the client agent will apply the setting with the lowest priority.

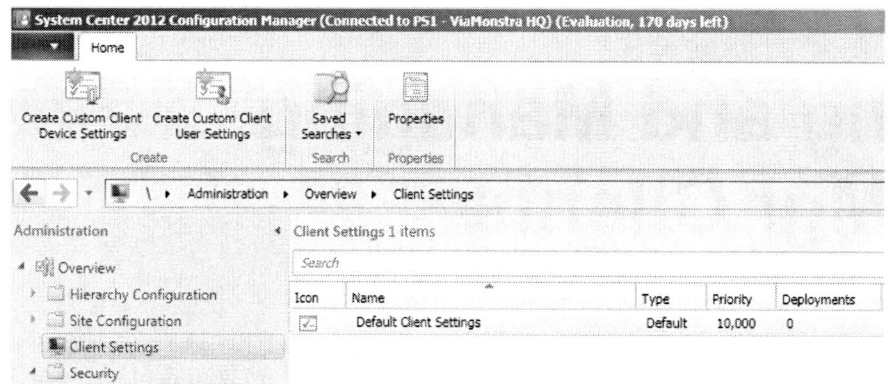

Default Client Settings.

Complete the following steps:

1. On **CM01**, open the **ConfigMgr console**.
2. In the **Administration** workspace, select **Client Settings**, select **Default Client Settings**, and on the ribbon, click **Properties**.
3. Modify these settings:
    a. Client Policy

        Client policy interval (in minutes): **30**
        (This setting will fit a midsized environment like ViaMonstra's.)

    b. Compliance Settings

        Schedule compliance evaluation: **Daily check**

    c. Computer Agent

        Organization Name displayed in Software Center: **ViaMonstra**

    d. Hardware Inventory

        Schedule hardware inventory: **Simple schedule daily**

    e. Power Management

        Allow power management of devices: **No.**

    f. Software Inventory

        i. Select **Inventory these file types** and click **Set Types**.
        ii. Click the **yellow icon**, type ***.EXE**, and click **OK** twice.

    g. Software Metering

        Enable software metering on clients: **No**

h. Software Updates

   i. Software update scan schedule: Click **Schedule** and configure a **Simple schedule daily check**.

   ii. When any software Update deployment deadline is reached...: **Yes**

i. User and Device Affinity

   Allow user to define their primary devices: **Yes**.

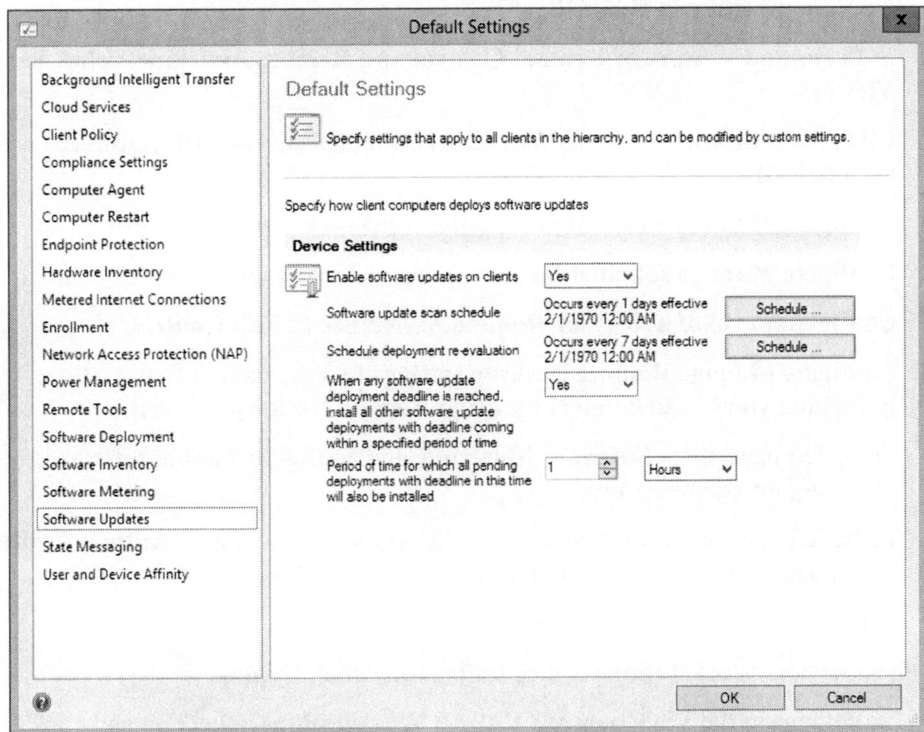

Configuring the default client settings.

4. Click **OK** to close the **Default Settings** dialog box.

Create Custom Settings for Workstations

1. On the ribbon, click **Create Custom Client Device Settings** and configure these device settings:

   a. Name: **Workstations**

   b. Select **Metered Internet Connections, Power Management, Remote Tools, Software Metering**, and **User and Device Affinity**.

   c. In the left pane, click **Metered Internet Connections**, and configure **Specify how clients communicate on metered network connections** to **Limit**.

d. In the left pane, click **Power Management**, and configure **Allow power management of devices** to **Yes**.
e. Configure **Enable wake-up proxy** to **Yes**, and click **OK** in the warning message.
f. Click **Configure** and configure the **Windows Firewall exception for wake-up proxy** to enable the **Firewall Settings for the Domain profile**, and click **OK**.
g. In the left pane, click **Remote Tools** and click **Configure**. Then click **Enable Remote Control on client computers**, enable the **Firewall Settings for the Domain profile**, and click **OK**.
h. In **Permitted viewers of Remote Control and Remote Assistance**, click **Set Viewers**.
i. Click the **yellow icon**, specify the **VIAMONSTRA\Workstation Admins** group, and click **OK**.
j. Configure **Manage unsolicited Remote Assistance settings** to **Yes**.
k. Configure **Manage solicited Remote Assistance settings** to **Yes**.
l. Configure **Level of access for Remote Assistance** to **Full Control**.
m. Configure **Manage Remote Desktop settings** to **Yes**, and configure **Allow permitted viewers to connect by using Remote Desktop connection** to **Yes**.
n. In the left pane, click **Software Metering**, and configure **Enable software metering on clients** to **Yes**.
o. In the left pane, click **User and Device Affinity**, and configure **Automatically configure user device affinity from usage data** to **Yes**.
p. Click **OK** to close the dialog box.

2. Right-click the new **Workstations** device settings and click **Deploy**.
3. Deploy the settings to the **ViaMonstra / VM All Workstations** collection and click **OK**.

Create Custom Settings for Servers

1. On the ribbon, click **Create Custom Client Device Settings**, and configure these device settings:

   a. Name: **Servers**
   b. Select **Computer Restart** and **Remote Tools**.
   c. In the left pane, click **Computer Restart**, and configure **Display a temporary notification to the user that indicates the interval before the user logged off or the computer restart (minutes)** to **3**.

d. Configure **Display a dialog box that the user cannot close, which displays the countdown interval before the user is logged off or the computer restarts (minutes)** to **2.**

e. In the left pane, click **Remote Tools**, and click **Configure**. Click **Enable Remote Control on client computers**, enable the **Firewall Settings for the Domain profile**, and click **OK**.

f. In **Permitted viewers of Remote Control and Remote Assistance**, click **Set Viewers**.

g. Click the **yellow icon**, specify the **VIAMONSTRA\Server Admins** group, and click **OK**.

h. Configure **Manage unsolicited Remote Assistance settings** to **Yes**.

i. Configure **Manage solicited Remote Assistance settings** to **Yes**.

j. Configure **Level of access for Remote Assistance** to **Full Control**.

k. Configure **Manage Remote Desktop settings** to **Yes**, and configure **Allow permitted viewers to connect by using Remote Desktop connection** to **Yes**.

l. Click **OK** to close the dialog box.

2. Right-click the new **Servers** settings and click **Deploy**.
3. Deploy the settings to the **VIAMONSTRA\VM All Servers** collection and click **OK**.

Client Installation Methods

As mentioned previously, ConfigMgr does support the use of different client installation methods. Not all environments are alike, and you need to know the different client deployment alternatives and their requirements before installing the first client. The table below is a list of the most commonly used deployment methods, along with short descriptions.

Regardless of the selected installation method, a client installation sequence always goes through these three phases:

1. Starting the client installation, deploying the needed bootstrap files to the client, and downloading the prerequisites.
2. Installing the client by running the client.msi file.
3. Approving and assigning the client to a site.

Method	Description and Requirements	Used in ViaMonstra
Client push	Client push is an often used deployment method and can be initiated manually or automatically from the ConfigMgr console. The Client Configuration Manager component on the site server connects to the local client, pushes the needed files (ccmsetup.exe and mobileclient.tcf), and starts the installation service (ccmsetup service). This method requires an account with local administrative privileges on the client. The local firewall must be configured to enable file and printer sharing and allow access to the administrative shares like IPC$ and Admin$.	Yes
Logon script	Welcome to the 90s and logon scripts! This requires that the end user is a local administrator on the client, and there is no way I would allow that in ViaMonstra.	No
Software update	This installation method will publish the ConfigMgr client as a required infrastructure update in WSUS. You can the leverage the existing WSUS infrastructure to deploy the client. This installation method will bypass any local firewall rules and will run in the context of the local system account.	No
Group policy	This method uses an Active Directory software group policy installation policy. ConfigMgr ships with a ccmsetup.msi file that you can use to create the package. The reason why I have chosen this as the primary installation method for workstations is that all workstations perform a daily restart and will then install the ConfigMgr client.	Yes
Manual	The manual installation method is often used when installing clients that reside in a workgroup, or when testing client installation command-line properties. In order to run a manual installation, you need to have local Administrator permissions on the server or workstation.	Yes
Startup script	Although not an official installation method, the startup script is still a very powerful way to control the client installation and perform a client health check. There are several very good community examples available for download. In ViaMonstra, it's been decided to pilot test the startup script developed by Jason Sandys, which you can download from http://blog.configmgrftw.com/?page_id=349.	Yes

Client Command-line Properties

The list of supported command-line properties is long, and I will not cover all the properties in this book. For a full list, open your favorite search engine and search for "Configuration Manager 2012 ccmsetup.exe" and open the link for "About Client installation properties in Configuration Manager." Notice that you can specify command lines for the CCMSetup.exe process and for the client.msi process. CCMSetup.exe will be processed first and then call Client.msi to finish the installation.

In ViaMonstra, you will use command lines to control the assigned site and the initial management point. For servers, you will also disable Silverlight (Silverlight is a required component when using the Application Web Catalog Point). The default command lines can be published to Active Directory and used by the client by running CCMSetup.exe without specifying any command lines.

The CCMSetup.exe process is able to use command lines from several places. Knowing how command lines are applied can help you tailor the different scenarios. The following sequence is the order used by the CCMSetup process:

1. Command line specified manually.
2. Registry specified by the ConfigMgrInstallation.adm and written to \HKLM\SOFTWARE\Policies\Microsoft\ccmsetup\SetupParameters.
3. Lookup in Active Directory and search for any command lines that are specified in the properties of the Client Push feature, as explained later in this chapter.

Boundaries and Boundary Groups

As explained previously, all client installation sequences go through three phases, in which the third phase is the site assignment phase. During that phase, the client either searches Active Directory for any site that has a boundary group configured for site assignment matching the local IP information or uses the hardcoded sitecode from the command line.

What Is a Boundary?

A boundary is an IP scope that you create manually, or that is discovered and created automatically using the Active Directory Forest Discovery method. Boundaries come in four flavors:

- IP ranges
- IP subnets
- AD sites
- IPV6

I always recommend that you use IP ranges, as they always work as intended. IP subnets and AD sites do not always work, especially if you are working with IP subnetting and IP supernetting in your environments. In ViaMonstra, I have decided to support the use of IP ranges and AD sites (since ViaMonstra is not using IP supernetting).

Automate Creating Boundaries Using PowerShell

In this optional example, you create Boundary AD HQ and the value is Active Directory Site name. Parameter Type can be AD, IPv6, IPSubnet, or IPRange. Again, this is just an optional example syntax; you have already created the following boundary since you configured Active Directory Forest Discovery previously in this book.

1. Launch **PowerShell** from the **ConfigMgr console**.

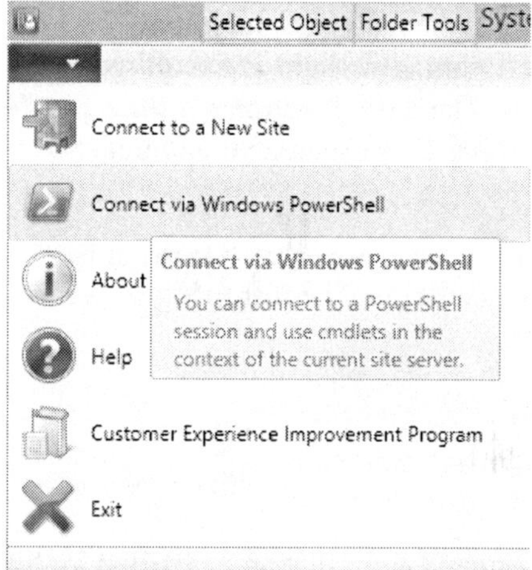

Launching PowerShell from the left menu.

2. Type the following command:

```
New-CMBoundary -Name "New York Office" -Value "NewYork"
-Type ADSite
```

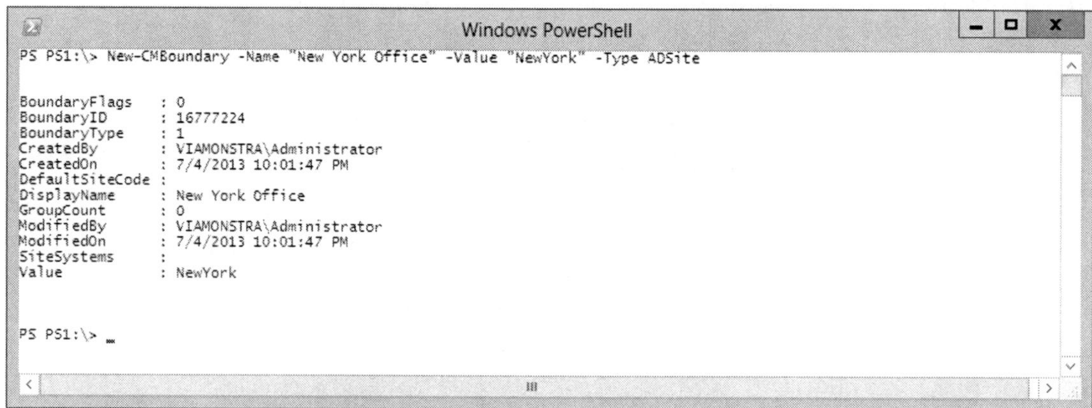

Creating a boundary using PowerShell.

What Is a Boundary Group?

A boundary group is essentially a group of boundaries created for the following purposes:

- To assign the client to a site during the client installation process.
- To locate distribution points when installing images, applications, packages, or software updates. In ViaMonstra, you do have several remote locations that will host a local distribution point. For each of those locations, you will create a unique *content location* boundary group.

Note: Site Assignment boundary groups are only required in environments with multiple primary sites where the commandline smssitecode=auto is used, or when using the Client Push installation method in a multi-primary site environment.

1. Create a Site Assignment Boundary Group: Navigate to the **Administration** workspace; select **Hierarchy Configuration / Boundary Groups**, and on the ribbon, click **Create Boundary Group**.
2. In the **Name** field, type **VM Assignment** and click the **References** tab.
3. In **Site assignment**, select **Use the boundary group for site assignment** and click **OK**.

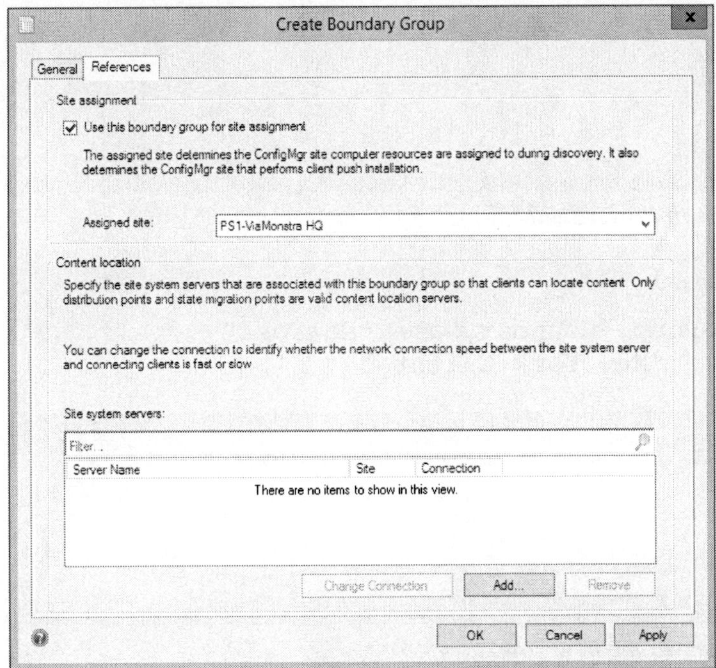

Creating a site assignment boundary group.

4. Select **Boundaries**.

5. Right-click the **NewYork** Active Directory site boundary and select **Add Selected Items / Add Selected Items to Existing Boundary Groups**.
6. Select the **VM Assignment** boundary group and click **OK**.

Automate Creating Boundary Groups Using PowerShell

In this optional example, you create a boundary group called **New York Clients**, add the New York boundary to the group, and add the site server to the New York Clients group. Again, these are just optional sample commands; you don't need to do this configuration for the setup in this book.

1. Launch **PowerShell** from the **ConfigMgr console**.
2. Type the following command:

```
New-CMBoundaryGroup -Name "New York Clients"
```

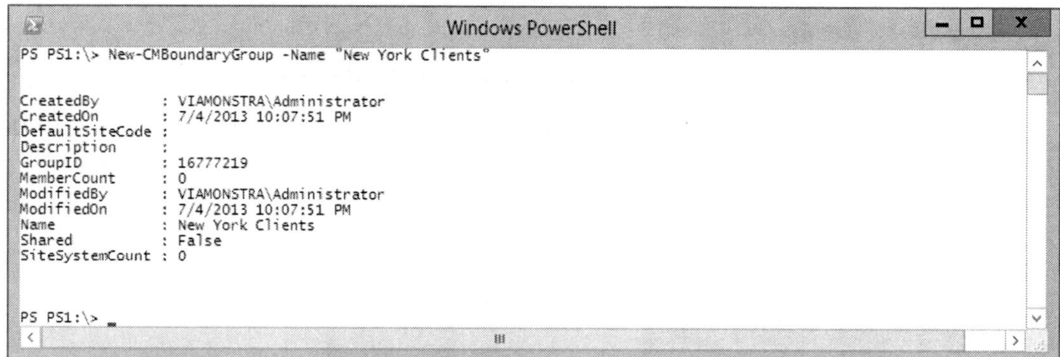

Creating a boundary group with PowerShell.

3. Type the following command:

```
Add-CMBoundaryToGroup -BoundaryName "NewYork"
-BoundaryGroupName "New York Clients"
```

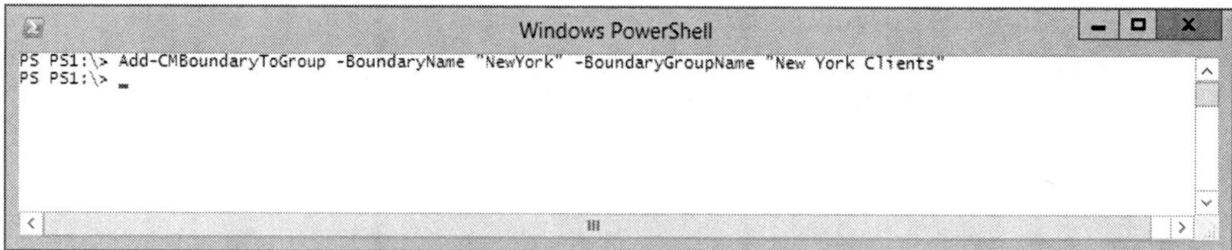

Adding the New York boundary to the new boundary group.

Configuring the Network Access Account

The Network Access Account is used in two scenarios: when working with operating system deployments and when you want to support client computers that are not in a trusted domain. The Network Access Account is used to establish a connection to a distribution point for downloading content like software updates, packages, applications, and images.

1. In the **Administration** workspace, navigate to **Site Configurations / Sites**.
2. Select the **PS1 – ViaMonstra HQ** site, and then from the ribbon, select **Settings / Configure Site Components / Software Distribution**.
3. Select the **Network Access Account** tab.
4. Select **Specify the account that accesses network locations**, and then select **Set / New Account**.
5. Click **Browse** and search for **CM_NAA**; then click **OK**.
6. Supply the password (**Password01**) twice and click **OK**.

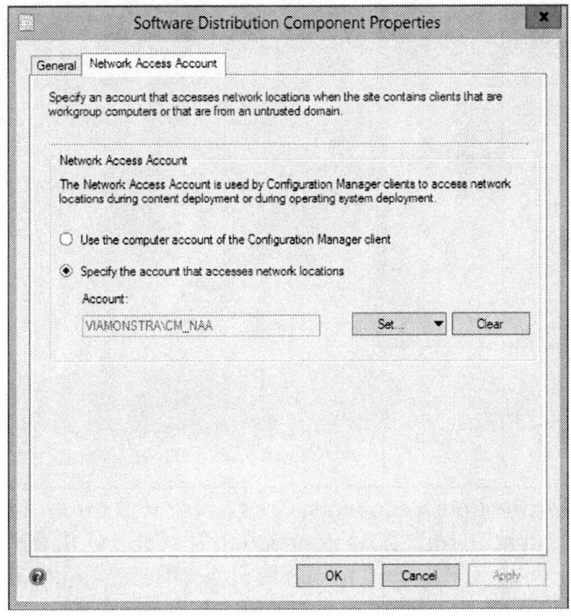

Configuring the Network Access Account.

7. Click **OK**.

Configuring Client Push Installation Properties

Before installing a client, you should start by configuring the client push installation properties. These properties are automatically replicated to Active Directory and will be used by different installation methods without specifying any command lines.

1. Start **PC0001**, and wait until it's fully started.

2. On **CM01**, open the **ConfigMgr** console, select the **Administration** workspace, and navigate to **Site Configuration / Sites**.
3. On the ribbon, click **Settings**, and select **Client Installation Settings / Client Push Installation**.
4. In the **Accounts** tab, click **New** and then **New Account**.
5. Click **Browse**, find the user **VIAMONSTRA\CM_CP**, and specify the password (**Password01**).
6. Click **Verify**; then in **Network share**, type **\\PC0001\Admin$** and click **Test Connection**. If the Test connection fails, you may need to run **gpupdate /force** on **PC0001** to force a group policy update.

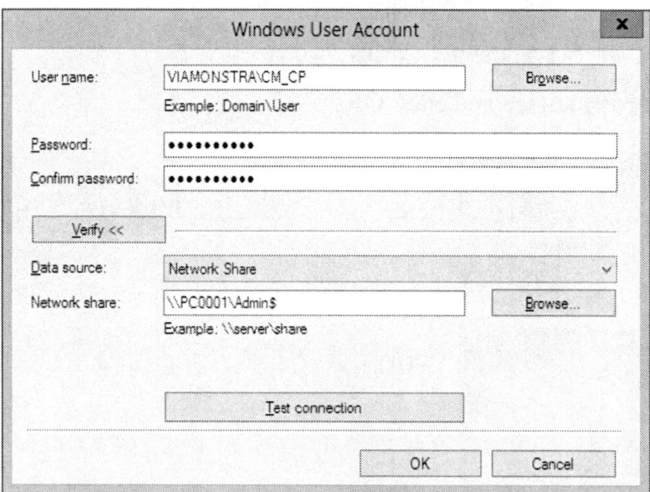

Verifying the client push account.

7. Click **OK**.

Real World Note: You can configure multiple client push accounts. ConfigMgr will try to connect to the client using each of the client push accounts. If no connection is successful, the site server computer account will be used. Usually you are required to create a specific account for servers and one for workstations.

8. In the **Installation Properties** tab, configure properties to **SMSSITECODE=PS1 SMSMP=CM01.corp.viamonstra.com** and click **OK**.
9. Start **CMTrace** and open **D:\Program Files\Microsoft Configuration Manager\Logs \CCM.log**.

   Notice that the values you have configured in the client push properties are written to the CCM.log file. When you start a client push installation, all activities are written to this log file.

Installing Clients Using Client Push

1. Start **CM02**, and wait until it's fully started.
2. On **CM01**, navigate to the **Assets and Compliance** workspace and select **Devices**.
3. Select **CM01, CM02**, and on the ribbon, click **Install Client**.
4. On the first page, read the information and click **Next**.
5. Select the following settings and click **Next**:
    a. **Always install the client software**
    b. **Install the client software from a specified site**

Note: The preceding settings are not required in this specific scenario but can be very useful when redeploying clients and/or controlling the site used to download the client installation files.

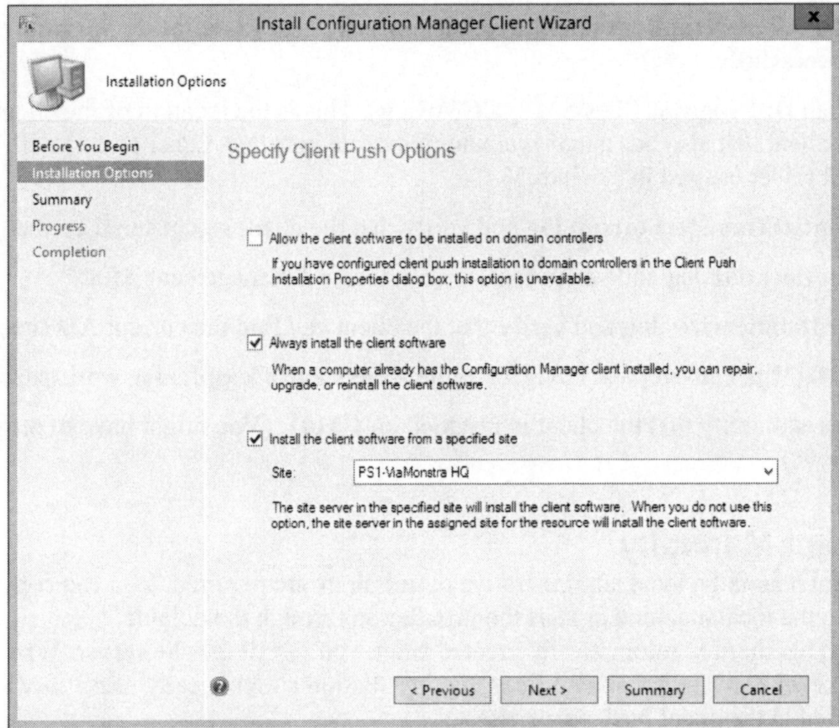

Starting the client push installation.

6. On the **Summary** page, read the summary and click **Next**.
7. On the **Completing the Client Push Installation** page, click **Close**.

You can monitor the client push process by reading the **ccm.log** with **CMtrace.exe** and by opening the folder **D:\Program Files\Microsoft Configuration Manager\inboxes \ccr.box\InProc** in **File Explorer**. When the client push process begins, you can see activity in the log file and also see an object created in the inproc folder. The object created in the folder will be processed quickly and removed from the folder.

Real World Note: The good thing about using the client push installation method is that you can control exactly when the installation starts. The downside is that the site server needs to connect to the Admin$ share on the client. If the client configuration manager component can't connect, then it will retry the attempt once an hour for a week. This can potentially generate a lot of warning and error messages in the ConfigMgr console.

Verify the Client Installation

1. On **CM01**, log on as **VIAMONSTRA\Administrator** and open the **%windir%\ccmsetup** folder.
2. In the folder, you will find several files; among those files is the **ccmsetup.cab** file, which contains a list of prerequisites along with other information.
3. Open **%windir%\ccmsetup\logs\client.msi.log** and search for **Installation operation completed successfully**.
4. On **CM01**, open **D:\Program Files\SMS_CCM\Logs**. This is the location of the client log files for a client that also has a management point role installed. Other clients will have the CCM folder created in %windir%.
5. Open the **ClientIDManagerStartup.log** and verify that the client is registered correctly.
6. Open the **Clientlocation.log** and verify that you can locate a management point.
7. Open the **LocationServices.log** and verify that the client can find the current AD site.
8. Open the **ConfigMgr console,** and navigate to the **Assets and Compliance** workspace.
9. Select **Devices** and verify that the client is installed on **CM01**. (You might have to refresh the console view.)

Installing a Client Manually

When installing a client manually, local administrative permissions are required. You can copy the entire .\Client folder to the local machine or start the installation through the default SMS_Sitecode share. This share is automatically created when you install the site server. When running CCMSetup.exe without any command lines, the installation automatically uses the MSI command lines specified in the client push properties.

1. On **DC01**, log on as **VIAMONSTRA\Administrator**.

2. Press the **Windows logo key + R,** type the following command, and accept the installation when prompted:

```
\\CM01\SMS_PS1\Client\ccmsetup.exe SMSSITECODE=PS1 /MP:CM01
/skipprereq:Silverlight.exe
```

3. The installation will run without any user intervention. You can monitor the process by opening **Task Manager** and monitoring the **CCMSetup.exe** process.

4. Open **C:\Windows\ccmsetup\logs\ccmsetup.log** and monitor the installation process using **CMTrace.exe**.

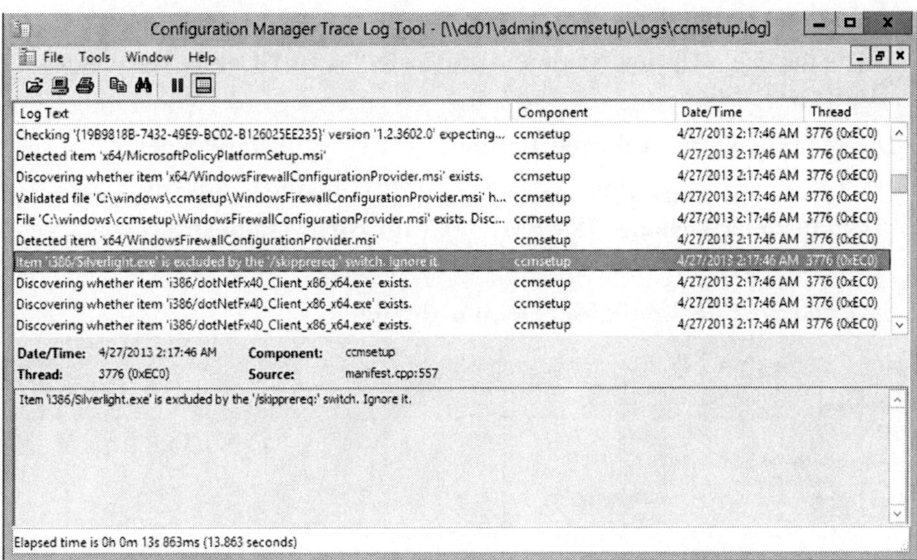

Excluding Silverlight from client installation.

Installing a Client Using a Startup Script

A computer startup script is a popular method for installing the ConfigMgr client. The startup script is applied to the computer using a group policy. Some of the advantages of using a startup script is that the installation runs under the context of the local computer's system account, you avoid firewall issues, and you also can add health checks in the script.

Jason Sandys, the creator of the script, kindly allowed me to include his script in the book sample files. For more information, check out this link: http://blog.configmgrftw.com/?page_id=349.

In these steps, I assume that you have downloaded the startup script, which is available as part of the book sample files, and copied it to D:\Setup\ConfigMgrStartup1.6.

1. On **CM01**, open **File Explorer** and create a subfolder called **ClientStartup** in **D:\Sources\Software**.

2. Navigate to **D:\Setup\ConfigMgrStartup1.6** and open the **ConfigMgrStartup.xml** file using **Notepad**.

3. Make the following changes to **ConfigMgrStartup.xml** and save the file:

   a. Delete the line **<Option Name="LocalAdmin" >lab1/dadmin</Option>**.

   b. Change the line **<Option Name="SiteCode" >Auto</Option>** to **<Option Name="SiteCode" >PS1</Option>**.

   c. Change the line **<Option Name="ClientLocation">\\cm1\ConfigMgr\Client \Install</Option>** to **<Option Name="ClientLocation"> \\CM01\Sources$\Software\ClientStartup</Option>**.

   d. Delete the line **<Option Name="ErrorLocation">\\cm1\ConfigMgr\Client \ErrorLogs</Option>**.

   e. Delete the line **<Option Name="AutoHotfix">\\cm1\ConfigMgr\Client \Hotfixes</Option>**.

   f. Delete the line **<InstallProperty Name="FSP"></InstallProperty>**.

   g. Change the line **<InstallProperty Name="SMSMP"></InstallProperty>** to **<InstallProperty Name="SMSMP">CM01.corp.viamonstra.com. </InstallProperty>**

   h. Save and close the **ConfigMgrStartup.xml** file.

```
ConfigMgrStartup.xml - Notepad
File Edit Format View Help
<?xml version="1.0"?>
<Startup>
        <Option Name="SiteCode" >PS1</Option>
        <Option Name="CacheSize">8120</Option>
        <Option Name="AgentVersion">5.00.7804.1000</Option>
        <Option Name="MinimumInterval">0</Option>
        <Option Name="ClientLocation">\\CM01\Sources$\Software\ClientStartup</Option>
        <Option Name="MaxLogFile">2048</Option>
        <Option Name="Delay" >5</Option>
        <InstallProperty Name="SMSMP">CM01.corp.viamonstra.com </InstallProperty>
        <CCMSetupParameter Name="BITSPriority">HIGH</CCMSetupParameter>
        <ServiceCheck Name="BITS" State="Running" StartMode="Auto" Enforce="True" />
        <ServiceCheck Name="winmgmt" State="Running" StartMode="Auto" Enforce="True" />
        <ServiceCheck Name="wuauserv" State="Running" StartMode="Auto" Enforce="True" />
        <ServiceCheck Name="lanmanserver" State="Running" StartMode="Auto" Enforce="True" />
        <ServiceCheck Name="RpcSs" State="Running" StartMode="Auto" Enforce="True" />
        <RegistryValueCheck Key="HKLM\SOFTWARE\Microsoft\Ole" Value="EnableDCOM" Expected="Y" Enforce="True" Type="REG_SZ"/>
        <RegistryValueCheck Key="HKLM\SOFTWARE\Microsoft\Ole" Value="EnableRemoteConnect" Expected="Y" Enforce="False"
Type="REG_SZ"/>
        <RegistryValueCheck Key="HKLM\SOFTWARE\Microsoft\Ole" Value="LegacyAuthenticationLevel" Expected="2" Enforce="False"
Type="REG_DWORD"/>
        <RegistryValueCheck Key="HKLM\SOFTWARE\Microsoft\Ole" Value="LegacyImpersonationLevel" Expected="2" Enforce="False"
Type="REG_DWORD"/>
</Startup>
```

The ConfigMgrStartup.xml file used in ViaMonstra.

4. Copy **D:\Program Files\Microsoft Configuration Manager\Client\ccmsetup.exe** to the newly created **D:\Sources\Software\ClientStartup** folder.

5. On **DC01**, log on as **VIAMONSTRA\Administrator** and open the **Group Policy Management console**:
   a. Expand **Forest: corp.viamonstra.com / Domains / corp.viamonstra.com / ViaMonstra**.
   b. Right-click the **Workstations** OU and select **Create a GPO in this domain, and Link it here**.
   c. Name the new group policy **Startup Script Install ConfigMgr 2012 Client Agent** and click **OK**.
   d. Expand the **Workstations** OU, right-click the **Startup Script Install ConfigMgr 2012 Client Agent** GPO, and select **Edit**.
   e. Select **Computer Configuration / Policies / Windows Settings / Scripts (Startup/Shutdown)**.
   f. Right-click **Startup** and select **Properties**.
   g. Click **Add**, and click **Browse**; then copy **ConfigMgrStartup.vbs** and **ConfigMgrStartup.xml** from **\\CM01\D$\Setup\ConfigMgrStartup1.6** to the **D:\Sources\Software\ClientStartup** folder and select the **ConfigMgrStartup.vbs** file.
   h. In **Script Parameters**, type **/Config:ConfigMgrStartup.xml** and click **OK** twice.
   i. Close the GPO.
6. Start or restart **PC0001** to apply the new computer-based GPO. After restarting, you can verify the client installation process by opening **Event Viewer** (View Event Logs on the Start screen), and select **Windows Logs / System**.

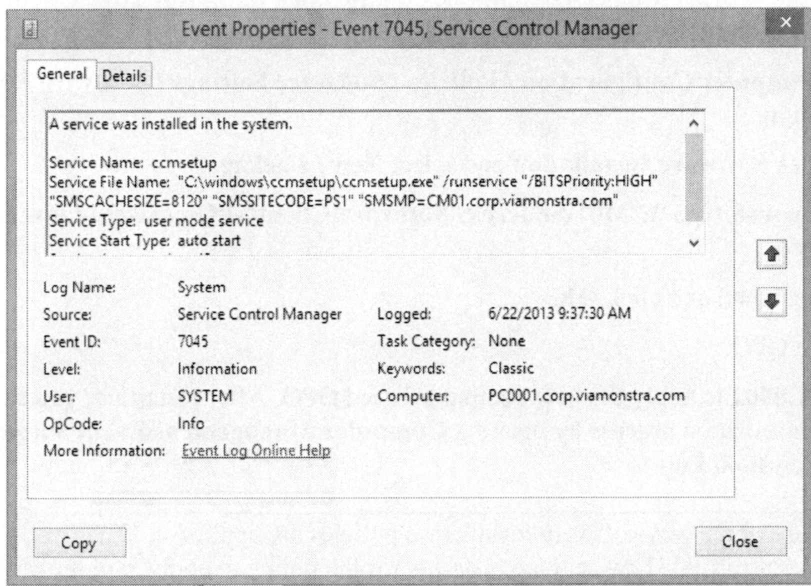

Information from the System log about the client installation.

Optional—Installing a Client Using a Software Group Policy

Installing clients manually is too time-consuming for any company and using the client push method will not guarantee that all clients will start an installation attempt. For that reason, you have to mix client push with another installation method like the startup script you learned in the previous section, or a software group policy.

By default ConfigMgr ships with an .msi version of ccmsetup.exe that is found in .\Program files\Microsoft Configuration Manager\bin\i386\ccmsetup.msi. The .msi file can be used in a software group policy to installation the client. This optional guide shows how to install the client using a software group policy. Since you already added a client deployment solution based on a startup script in the previous section, this information is for reference only.

1. On **CM01**, open **File Explorer** and create a subfolder called **ClientGPO** in **D:\Sources\Software**.
2. Copy **D:\Program files\Microsoft Configuration Manager\bin\i386\ccmsetup.msi** to the newly created **ClientGPO** folder.
3. On **DC01**, log on as **VIAMONSTRA\Administrator** and open the **Group Policy Management console**:
    a. Expand **Forest: corp.viamonstra.com / Domains / corp.viamonstra.com / ViaMonstra**.
    b. Right-click the **Workstations** OU and select **Create a GPO in this domain and Link it here**.
    c. Create a new Group Policy object called **Install ConfigMgr 2012 Client Agent** and click **OK**.
    d. Expand the **Workstations** OU, right-click the **Install ConfigMgr 2012 Client Agent** GPO and select **Edit**.
    e. Select **Computer Configuration / Policies / Software Settings / Software Installation**.
    f. Right-click **Software Installation** and select **New / Package**.
    g. For **File name**, type **\\CM01\Sources$\Software\ClientGPO\ccmsetup.msi** and click **Open**.
    h. Select **Assigned** and click **OK**.
    i. Close the GPO.
4. Start or restart **PC0001** to apply the new computer-based GPO. After restarting, you can verify the client installation process by opening **Computer Management\Event Viewer \Windows Logs\System Log**.

> **Real World Note:** Because of the way software installation policies are applied in Windows, you most likely will need to restart PC0001 twice. One restart is for the policy to apply, and the other is for the actual install.

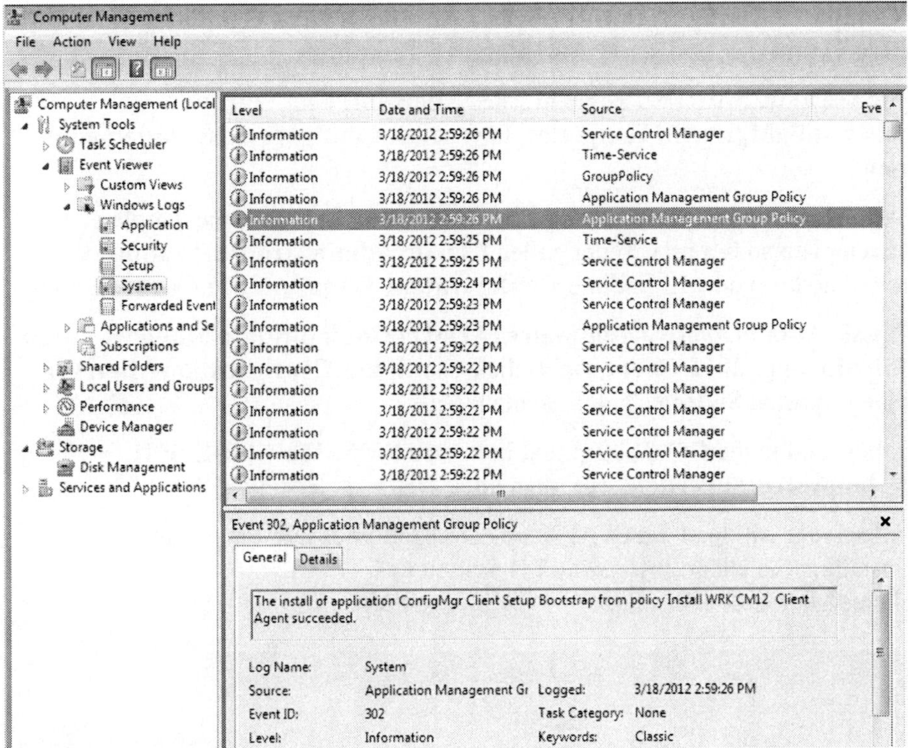

Verifying the GPO installation.

There will be scenarios in which you do not want to apply the published client command lines. In those scenarios, you can tattoo the CCMSetup command lines to the registry either manually or by applying the command lines in the group policy. ConfigMgr ships with two ADM files both found on the installation media in .\SMSSetup\Tools\ConfigADMTemplates. ConfigMgrAssignment.adm can be used to assign the client to a specific site, and ConfigMgrInstallation.adm will tattoo CCMSetup command lines to the registry.

> **Real World Note:** Using the ConfigMgrAssignment.adm template can be very useful when installing clients in a forest where you didn't extend the Active Directory schema.

Create a GPO to Tattoo CCMSetup Command Lines to the Registry

1. On **DC01**, log on as **VIAMONSTRA\Administrator** and open the **Group Policy Management console**.
2. Expand **Forest: corp.viamonstra.com / Domains / corp.viamonstra.com / ViaMonstra**.
3. Right-click the **Servers** OU and select **Create a GPO in this domain, and Link it here**.
4. Name the new group policy **ConfigMgr command lines** and click **OK**.
5. Expand the **Servers** OU, right-click the **ConfigMgr command lines** GPO, and select **Edit**.

6. Navigate to **Computer Configuration / Policies / Administrative Templates**, right-click **Administrative Templates**, and select **Add/Remove Templates**.
7. Click **Add**; browse to **\\CM01\D$\Program Files\Microsoft Configuration Manager\tools\ConfigMgrADMTemplates**; then select **ConfigMgrInstallation.adm** and click **Open**.
8. Back in the **Add/Remove templates** dialog box, click **Close** to import the template. Importing the template adds a new folder called **Classic Administrative Templates (ADM)**. As child nodes, you will find the **Configuration Manager 2012 Client** settings.
9. Browse to **Classic Administrative Templates (ADM) / Configuration Manager 2012 / Configuration Manager 2012 Client**, right-click **Configure Configuration Manager 2012 Client Deployment Settings**, and then click **Edit**.
10. Enable the policy, and in the **CCMSetup** text box, type **SMSSITECODE=PS1 /MP:CM01 /skipprereq:Silverlight.exe**; then click **OK** and close the GPO.

With the new GPO, all servers will load the CCMSetup command lines into the registry and use those settings when installing the client. Information is written to HKLM\Software\Policies\Microsoft\ccmsetup\.

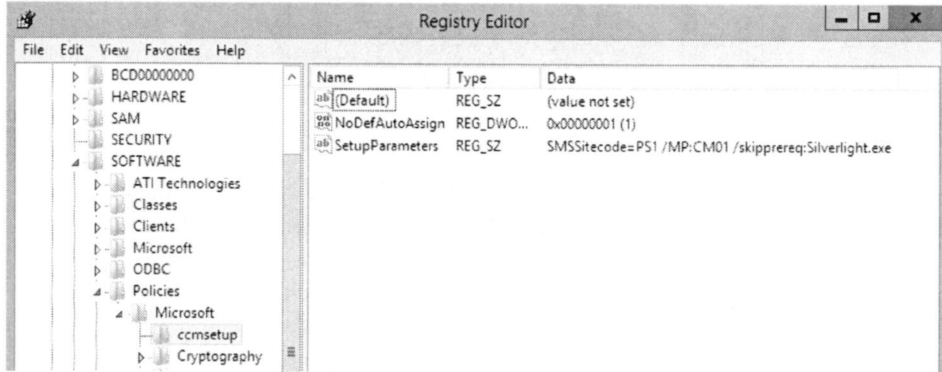

Client command lines in the registry.

The Client Interfaces

With the client installation you also get the Software Center installed. From the Software Center, the logged on client can easily see a status of installed applications along with information about upcoming installations. Software Center also allows the user to control settings like Working Hours, Power Management, and Remote Control. All of those settings can naturally be controlled by the ConfigMgr administrators, or left in the hands of the user.

The Configuration Manager Client properties can be launched from the Windows 8 Start screen (System and Security in the Control Panel in earlier versions of Windows). With the properties, a user can manually launch one of the enabled client agent actions like running the hardware inventory cycle or download new policies from the management point.

Modify the Local Working Hours in the Software Center

Business hours define when the user is working on the device. When software or updates are deployed to the user, the user can postpone the installation so it takes place outside the defined business hours. A deployment can be postponed only until the defined deadline for the deployment.

1. On **PC0001**, log on as **VIAMONSTRA\Administrator**.
2. From the **Start screen**, launch **Software Center**.
3. Click **Options** and customize the **Business hours** from **7:00 AM** through **6:00 PM**.
4. Click **Apply**.

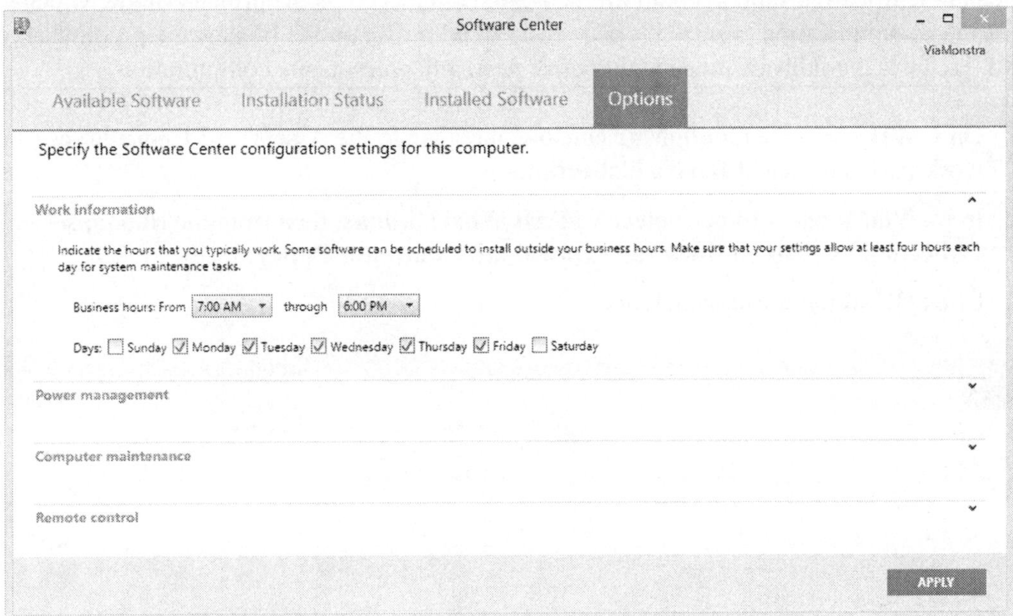

The client Software Center.

Manually Refresh the Machine Policies

1. On **PC0001**, log on as **VIAMONSTRA\Administrator**.
2. From the **Start screen** (Settings area), open the **Configuration Manager** applet.
3. Select the **Actions** tab, select **Machine Policy Retrieval & Evaluation Cycle,** and click **Run Now**.

Client Notification

A new feature in SP1 enables you to perform a machine refresh on all devices in a collection. The feature is called *Client Notification* and can be found in the ConfigMgr console when you work with collections. The feature has three components that work together: the Notification Manager on the site server, the Notification Server installed on management point(s), and a client Notification Agent. The components communicate using a predefined fast channel that bypasses normal ConfigMgr client traffic. This allows administrators to invoke machine policies to be downloaded on clients almost instantly. The communication port is TCP 10123, this can be changed in the properties for the site along with the other client communication ports. The feature requires that both client and server are running on SP1.

Note: Client notification supports both the TCP and HTTP. TCP is the primary mode, which requires the communication port to be open for inbound traffic on the Management Point server firewall. HTTP is the fallback mode and doesn't need any prerequisite configuration.

1. On **CM01**, open the **ConfigMgr console**, navigate to the **Assets and Compliance** workspace, and select **Device Collections**.
2. In the **ViaMonstra** folder, select **VM All Workstations**; then from the ribbon, select **Collection / Client Notification / Download Computer Policy**.
3. Click **OK** in the warning message.

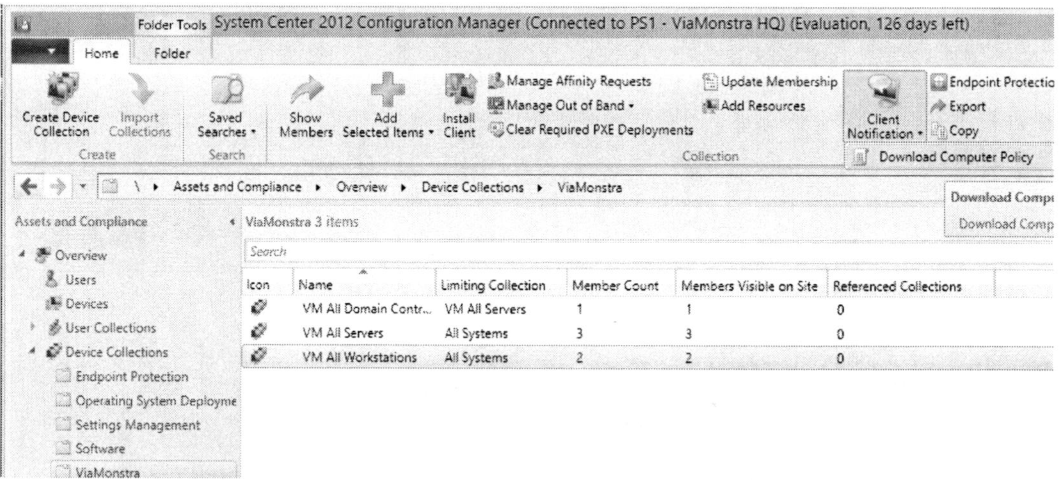

The new Client Notification feature in SP1.

4. You can monitor the notification process in the Monitoring workspace. Select **Client Operations**, and if needed, click **Run Summarization**.

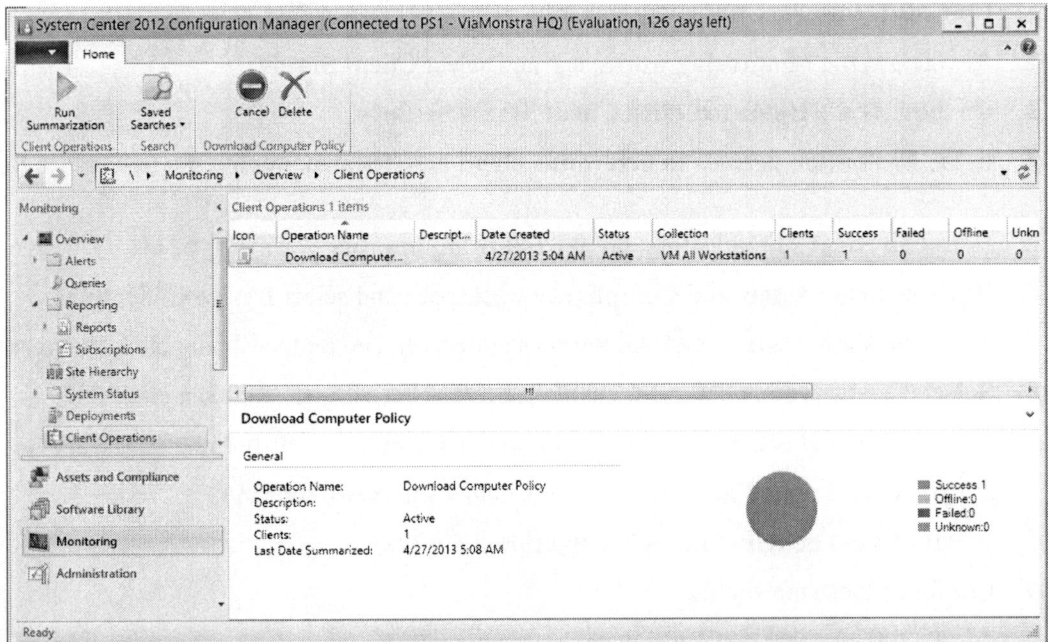

Monitoring the client notification process.

Note: The feature was formerly known as the Big Green Button. When searching for log files, look for files beginning with the letters "bgb".

Working with Client Health

It is one thing to install the client; it is another thing to ensure that all clients stay healthy. Unhealthy clients are unmanaged and can potentially harm your infrastructure. Client remediation is built into the client installation through a Windows task that performs a series of different checks and remediates if any of the checks fails. The process is called ccmeval and can be manually launched by running ccmeval.exe from C:\windows\ccm or running the Windows scheduled task.

Besides keeping the clients healthy, it's also beneficial to know how many of your clients are active on the network. In ViaMonstra, you support workstations, laptops, and servers clients. Those have different behaviors: for instance, the laptops can be disconnected from the office for days or even weeks, whereas desktops are always connected. In order not to receive too many alerts in the ConfigMgr console, ViaMonstra has decided to modify the client activity thresholds and create custom alert settings for servers.

Modify the Client Health and Activity Thresholds for Servers

In these steps, you modify the settings for the VM All Servers collection:

1. On **CM01**, start the **ConfigMgr console**.
2. Navigate to the **Monitoring** workspace and select **Client Status**.
3. On the ribbon's **Home** tab, click **Client Status Settings**.
4. In the **Evaluation periods to determine client activity** area, modify the five values from 7 to **21**.
5. In **Retain client status history for the following number of days**, type **60**.
6. Navigate to the **Assets and Compliance** workspace and select **Device Collections**.
7. Select the **ViaMonstra / VM All Servers** collection, and on the ribbon, click **Properties**.
8. Select the **Alerts** tab, click **Add**, enable the following settings, and then click **OK**:
    a. **Client check pass or no results for active clients falls below threshold (%)**
    b. **Client remediation success falls below the threshold (%)**
    c. **Client activity falls below the threshold (%)**
9. Configure these thresholds:
    a. Client check: **ALERT Severity, Critical 95%**
    b. Client remediation: **ALERT Severity, Critical 99%**
    c. Client activity: **ALERT Severity, Critical 95%**

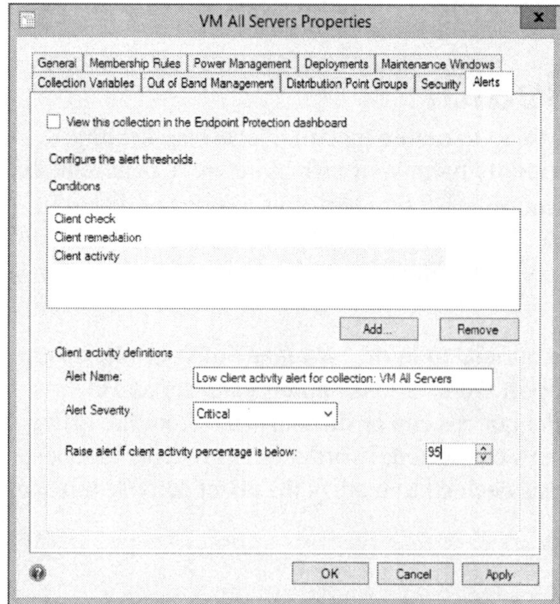

Client status settings.

10. Click **OK** to save the settings.
11. Navigate to the **Monitoring** workspace, and expand **Client Status**.
12. Click **Client Check** and monitor the dashboard. You might not have that much information yet, but you will in a few days when you have some more client history.

Modify the Client Health and Activity Thresholds for Clients

In these steps you modify the settings for the VM All Workstations collection:

1. Navigate to the **Assets and Compliance** workspace and select **Device Collections**.
2. Select the **ViaMonstra / VM All Workstations** collection, and on the ribbon, click **Properties**.
3. Select the **Alerts** tab, click **Add**, enable the following settings, and click **OK**:
    a. **Client check pass or no results for active clients falls below threshold (%)**
    b. **Client remediation success falls below the threshold (%)**
    c. **Client activity falls below the threshold (%)**
4. Configure these thresholds:
    a. Client check: **ALERT Severity, Critical 95%**
    b. Client remediation: **ALERT Severity, Critical 99%**
    c. Client activity: **ALERT Severity, Critical 95%**

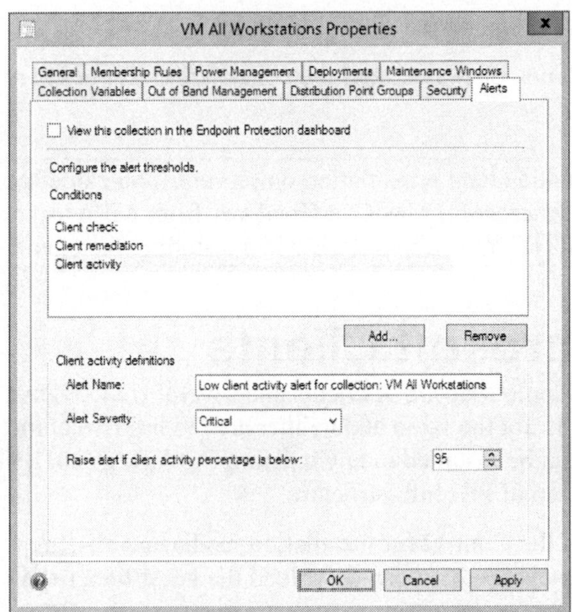

Defined client alert settings.

Manually Start the Client Health Check

1. On **PC0001**, log on as **VIAMONSTRA\Administrator**.
2. Open a command prompt with administrative privileges.
3. Navigate to **C:\Windows\CCM** and run **CcmEval.exe**.

Monitor Client Health

You can monitor client health information in at least three different places. In the ConfigMgr console, you have two options. You can either look at an individual client, or get the overview from the Client Status dashboard in the Monitoring workspace.

1. On **CM01**, start the **ConfigMgr console**.
2. To view the dashboard:

   In the **Monitoring** workspace, select **Client Status**. Client Activity presents you with the activity status, and Client Check provides you with remediation data.

3. To view individual client data:

   In the **Assets and Compliance** workspace, select **Overview / Devices.** Select any client and note the **Client Check Details** tab at the bottom of the console.

4. To view data in a report:
   a. In the **Monitoring** workspace, select **Reporting / Reports.** Then, in the search box, type **Client Status**.
   b. Select **Client Status Summary**, and on the ribbon, click **Run**.
   c. Click **Values**, select **All Systems**, click **OK**, and then click **View Report** to run the report.

Note: Not all organizations wish to run automatic client remediation on servers. You can disable the feature by changing the HKLM\Software\Microsoft\CCM\CCMEval key from False to True, or you can use the ccmsetup command line NOTIFYONLY=TRUE when installing the client.

Working with Non-Microsoft Clients

ConfigMgr 2012 SP1 introduces support for Apple Mac OS X clients and several UNIX/Linux versions. The support for the different clients is not the same and neither are the infrastructure requirements. Whereas UNIX/Linux clients can be installed in any existing ConfigMgr 2012 SP1 environment, Apple Mac OS X requires an internal PKI infrastructure.

The client install files are currently not part of the ConfigMgr installation media and also are updated outside the normal ConfigMgr update cycles. You can download the latest files from http://go.microsoft.com/fwlink/?LinkId=254684.

Apple Mac OS X Support and Requirements

Just like in the old SMS days, support for Apple Mac OS X is back. In SP1, there is support for these versions:

- Mac OS X 10.6 (Snow Leopard)
- Mac OS X 10.7 (Lion)
- Mac OS X 10.8 (Mountain Lion)

The supported features are:

- Discovery from Active Directory and Network discovery
- Hardware inventory including a list of installed software
- Application deployment via the application model
- Settings management, which allows you to configure and control preference lists

Supporting Mac OS requires that you implement PKI in your infrastructure. Mac OS clients use a certificate to authenticate themselves just like ConfigMgr clients that are configured to communicate using HTTPS. The primary site server can be configured to accept both HTTP and HTTPS traffic, but a site system role can only be configured to accept either HTTP or HTTPS. If you are working in a pure HTTP environment, I recommend installing a new server with the required site system roles.

Install the ConfigMgr Client on Mac OS X

Installing the ConfigMgr client on a Mac computer requires that you work through these steps. You are not required to install the Mac OS client in order to finish any other labs in the book.

> **Note:** As you learned in the previous section, supporting Mac OS requires a PKI infrastructure, and you find the instructions on how to configure the ViaMonstra environment for PKI in Appendix J. That being said, Appendix J is added only as a reference for the Mac OS support (and the cloud-based distribution point you learn about in Chapter 7). The other chapters and guides in this book do not require any PKI infrastructure.

1. Download the Apple Mac client install files from **http://go.microsoft.com/fwlink/?LinkId=254684**.
2. Add the enrollment point role and the enrollment proxy point role site system:
    a. On CM01, in the **Administration** workspace, select **Site Configuration / Servers and Site System Roles**.
    b. Select **\\CM01.corp.viamonstra.com**, and on the ribbon's **Home** tab, click **Add Site System Roles**.
    c. On the **General** page, click **Next**.
    d. On the **Proxy** page, click **Next**.

e. On the **System Role Selection** page, select the **Enrollment point** and **Enrollment proxy point** roles, and click **Next**.

f. On the **Enrollment Point** page, ensure **HTTPS** and **Port number 443** are selected, and click **Next**.

g. On the **Enrollment Proxy Point** page, ensure **HTTPS** and **Port number 443** are selected, and click **Next**.

h. On the **Summary** page, read the summary and click **Next**.

i. On the **Completion** page, click **Close**.

3. Create certificate templates for Mac client support, enrollment point, enrollment proxy point, distribution point, and management point. These steps are all described in Appendix J.

4. Enable Internet FQDN on the primary site server:

   a. In the **Administration** workspace, select **Site Configuration / Servers and Site System Roles**.

   b. Select **CM01.corp.viamonstra.com** and open the **Site system** properties.

   c. Enable **Specify an FQDN for this site system for use in the Internet**. Type **cm01.corp.viamonstra.com** as the **Internet FQDN** and click **OK**.

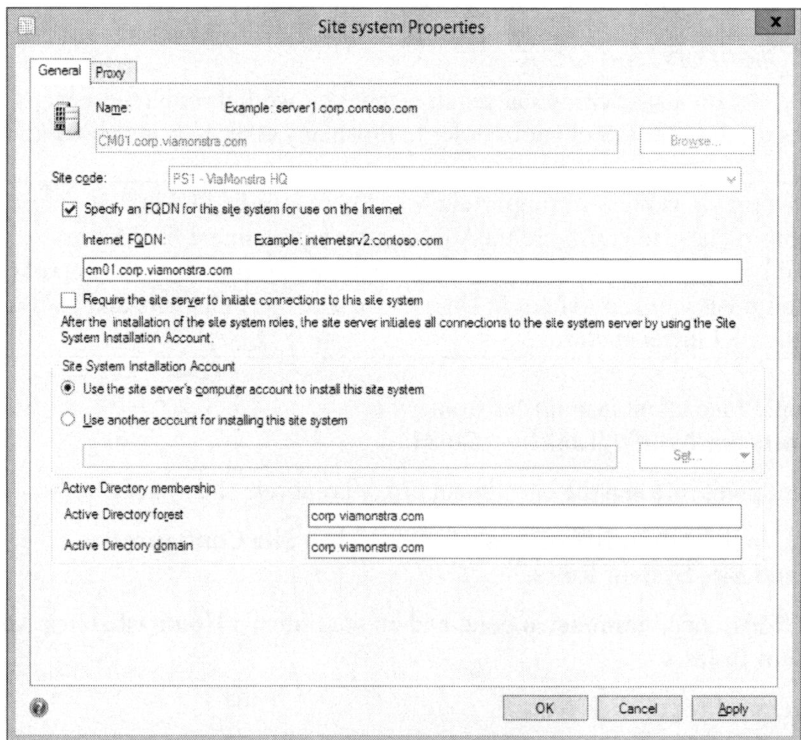

Specifying an Intranet FQDN to enable Mac OS support.

5. Enable **HTTPS** on the management point and the distribution point. These steps are all described in Appendix J.
6. Configure Mac enrollment in the **Default Client Settings**.
    a. In the **Administration** workspace, select **Client Settings**.
    b. Open the **Default Client Settings** properties and select **Enrollment**.
    c. In **Users Settings**, configure **Allow users to eroll mobile devices and Mac computers** to **Yes**.

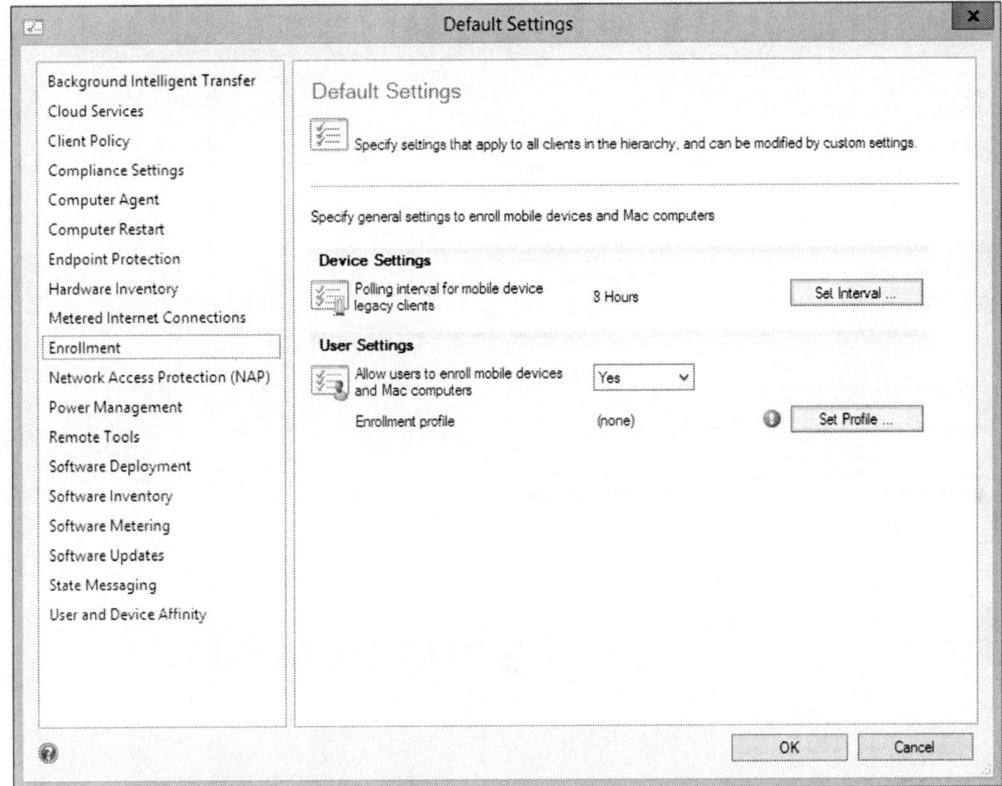

Allow users to enroll Mac computers,

    d. Click **Set Profile** and click **Create** in the Mobile Device Enrollment Profile dialog box.

e. Configure the enrollment profile and click **OK**.

   i. Name: **Mac Users**

   ii. Issuing certification authorities: Click **Add**, select **DC01.corp.viamonstra.com**, and click **OK**.

   iii. Certificate template for mobile device or Mac computer: Select **CM2012 MAC Client Certificate** and click **OK**.

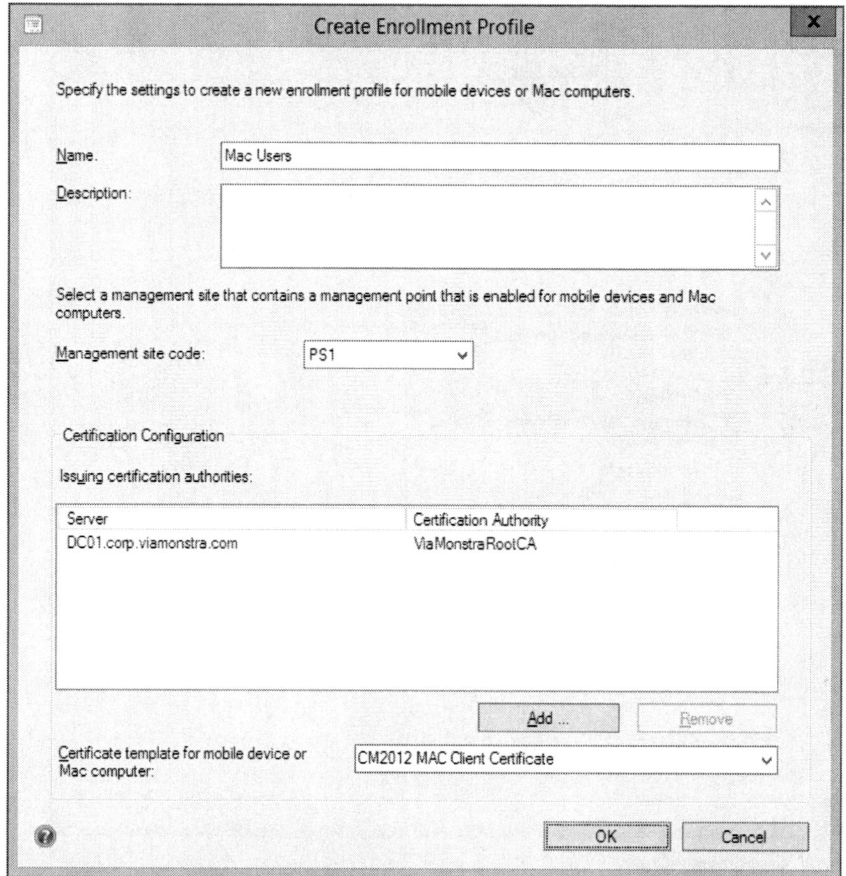

Creating the Mac enrollment profile.

f. Click **OK** twice to close the Default Client Settings.

7. Intstall the **ConfigMgr agent** on the Mac computer and enroll the device.

   a. On a Windows computer, download and install the **ConfigMgr client** by running **ConfigmgrMacClient.msi**. This extracts the Mac client package.

   b. Copy the Mac client package (**Macclient.dmg**) to the Mac computer.

c. Run the **Macclient.dmg** file on the Mac computer. This extracts several files, such as ccmsetup.exe and CMClient.pkg. The process also creates a folder named Tools where you will find the following files: CMDiagnostics, CMUninstall, CMAppUtil, and CMEnroll.

d. Open a terminal session, type **sudo ./ccmsetup**, and press **Enter**. If you are prompted for a restart, do not do that.

e. Navigate to the **Tools** folder and type the following command:

```
sudo ./CMEnroll -s cm01.corp.viamonstra.com
-ignorecertchainvalidation -u 'VIAMONSTRA\NEP
```

Note: You can monitor the enrollment process by reading the Enrollmentservice.log file.

UNIX Support and Requirements

ConfigMgr 2012 SP1 currently offers support for only certain UNIX variants and only servers. As of April 2013; these versions are supported:

- RHEL Version 6 (x86 & x64)
- RHEL Version 5 (x86 & x64)
- RHEL Version 4 (x86 & x64)
- Solaris Version 10 (x86 & SPARC)
- Solaris Version 9 (SPARC)
- SLES Version 11 (x86 & x64)
- SLES Version 10 SP1 (x86 & x64)
- SLES Version 9 (x86)

The supported features are:

- Hardware inventory including a list of installed software
- Software deployment via the traditional software package model

Install the ConfigMgr Client on SUSE 11

Installing the ConfigMgr client agent on the SUSE 11 server is not required in order to finish any later labs in this book.

1. Download the UNIX installation files (SC 2012 CM SP1 RTM client for SLES.EXE) and extract them by running the EXE file.
2. Copy the extracted files to your UNIX host. In ViaMonstra, you have only one SUSE 11 X64 server, and the only tar file you need is **ccm-SLES11x64.1.0.0.4014.tar**.

3. Open a terminal session and type **sudo ./install –mp cm01.corp.viamonstra.com –sitecode ps1 ccm-SLES11x64.1.0.0.4014.tar**.

```
suse:~/Documents/suse # dir
total 22752
-rwxr-xr-x 1 root root 23193600 Jan 21 12:40 ccm-SLES11x64.1.0.0.4014.tar
-rwxr-xr-x 1 root root    31706 Jan 21 12:40 install
-rw-r--r-- 1 root root    34724 Jan 21 12:13 License.rtf
-rw-r--r-- 1 root root      162 Apr 27 15:32 readme.txt
suse:~/Documents/suse # sudo ./install -mp cm01.corp.viamonstra.com -sitecode PS1 ccm-SLES11x64.1
.0.0.4014.tar

Checking Prerequisites...
Running preinstall validator
All pre-install tests succeeded!
Beginning installation of Config Manager in /opt/microsoft/configmgr
```

Installing the ConfigMgr client on a SUSE 11 X64 server.

4. After the installation, you should see the SUSE host in the ConfigMgr console. The client is not yet approved and, as such, will not accept any machine policies. Open the **ConfigMgr console**, select the **Asset and compliance** workspace, and navigate to devices.

5. Right-click **suse.corp.viamonstra.com**, and select **Approve**.

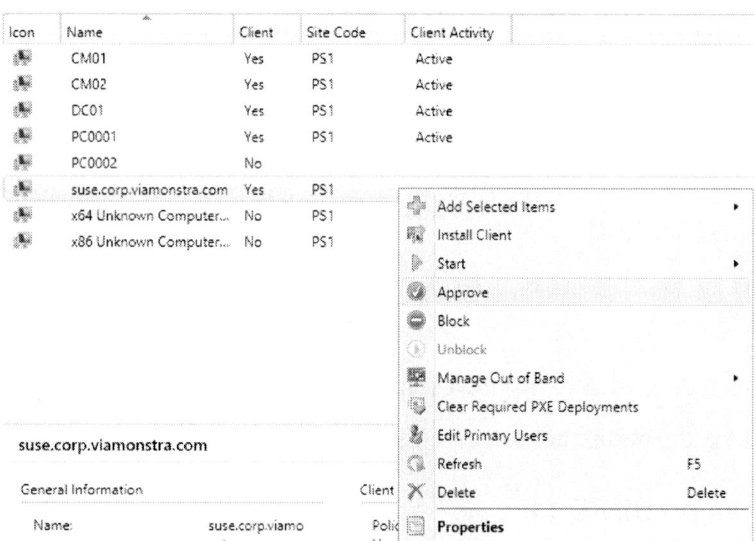

Approving a non-trusted client.

6. Click **Yes** in the **Approve client** dialog box. Notice that Client Activity in the coloumn immediately changes to Active.

7. Log on to the SUSE server, open a terminal session, and navigate to **/opt/microsoft/configmgr/bin**.

8. To restart the ConfigMgr daemon (service), type .**\ccmexec.exe –rs policy** and press **Enter**.

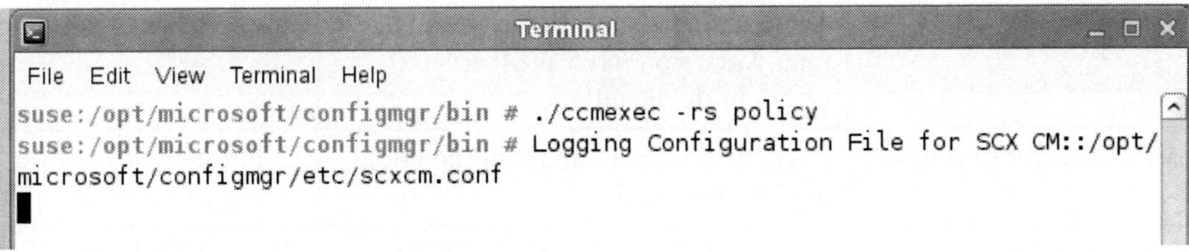

Requesting machine policies on SUSE.

9. While still in the terminal, type .**\ccmexec.exe –rs hinv** to initiate a hardware inventory.

Useful Log Files

The log files in the following table can be used to track client installation and evaluation.

Log File	Description	Location
bgbmgr.log	Records activity about the client Notification Manager component.	Server default
bgbserver.log	Records activity about the Client Notification Manager server like communication with the client and the client notification manager component.	Management point
ccmnotificationagent.log	Records activity about the Client Notification Agent like receiving requests from the client notification manager.	Client default
ccm.log	Records activity about client push attempts and publishing installation properties to Active Directory.	Server default
ccmsetup.log	Records information about downloading the client, installing the prerequisites, and installing the client. This log is the first one you should look at when troubleshooting client installations.	Client %windir%\ccmsetup\log

Log File	Description	Location
Client.msi.log	Records information about installing client.msi. This log file is useful to read when you have WMI-related errors in the installation.	Client %windir%\ccmsetup\log
ClientIDManagerStartup.log	Records information about the client approval process.	Client default
Clientlocation.log	Records information about finding the assigned management point.	Client default
Locationservices.log	Records information about finding local user-facing site system roles like distribution points, management points, and software update points.	Client default
Policyagent.log	Records information about downloading user and machine policies.	Client default
Ccmeval.log	Records information about the evaluation process and the individual rules.	Client default
Ccmsetup.eval.log	Records information about the evaluation process. Check this log file to verify that all needed prerequisites are still installed.	Client %windir%\ccmsetup\log

Chapter 6

Inventory Management and Reporting

Working with inventory has long been one of the strengths in previous ConfigMgr versions and this version is no different. All companies need to know what hardware and software assets are "out there," and guessing is not an option. ViaMonstra has certain requirements when it comes to asset management. For example, management requires that you have the following reporting capabilities:

- Being able to generate a complete list of all computers, with a count for each hardware model, including serial numbers.
- Being able to list all the software installed on a specific computer.
- Being able to tell the specific number of computers that have a specific application installed.
- Being able to collect a custom ViaMonstra registry key.

The data needs to be as up-to-date as possible, while still minimizing network traffic and not causing any performance issues when gathering the data.

Inventory

ConfigMgr basically offers two different inventory processes, one for hardware inventories and one for software. A hardware inventory queries WMI on the client for all information defined in the client agent settings. A software inventory should really be called *file scanning*, as that is what the agent does: scans for files in the locations that you have defined.

The first questions you always have to answer when working with inventory data are *What?* and *Why?*

- What kind of inventory data do you really need?
- Why do you need the inventory data? Is it just because some wise guy in the company requires them or just because you can get them? I have always found that the small word "why" often gets people who have been asking the wrong questions to rethink what they are really asking for. Asking for unnecessary and unrealistic reporting can easily flood the network with data or bring the client computer to its knees due to uncontrolled inventory scanning.

ViaMonstra has already answered these questions, so you know both what you need and why. You need the hardware inventory report to keep track of the computers and the software reports for licensing purposes and to keep track of installed software.

Note: One of the most commonly used types of inventory information is the applications listed in Add/Remove programs. That information is gathered as part of the hardware inventory process.

Configuring Hardware Inventory Data

In Chapter 5, you already configured a daily hardware scan and a weekly software scan. Before you start working with the features, you just need to verify that the settings are correct and that you have inventory data in the database. If you installed ConfigMgr on a Mac OS or UNIX computer, you will learn that the hardware inventory data is not as rich as that from Windows computers. The reason is that neither Mac OS nor UNIX computers have WMI.

Verify Inventory Settings

1. On **CM01**, log on as **VIAMONSTRA\Administrator** and open the **ConfigMgr console**.
2. In the **Administration** workspace, in **Client Settings**, select **Default Client Settings**, and then on the ribbon, click **Properties**.
3. Verify these settings:
    a. Enable Hardware Inventory on clients: **True**
    b. Hardware Inventory, Schedule hardware inventory: **Simple schedule**, **Every 1 day(s)**
    c. Collect MIF Files: **None**
    d. Enable Software Inventory on clients: **True**
    e. Software Inventory, Schedule software inventory: **Simple schedule**, **Every 7 day(s)**
    f. Inventory these file types: ***.EXE**

Real World Note: ConfigMgr creates new tables or modifies existing tables in the site database to accommodate the properties in IDMIF and NOIDMIF files. However, IDMIF and NOIDMIF files are not validated, so they could be used to alter tables that you do not want altered. Valid data could be overwritten by invalid data. Large amounts of data could be loaded, causing delays in all ConfigMgr functions. To mitigate this risk, you should enable IDMIF and NOIDMIF collection only when absolutely necessary. An example of when you want to enable this feature is when you have HP servers and want to use the HP Inventory tools from HP Insight Manager. Those tools will collect additional hardware inventory data and write that information to a NOIDMIF file on the client.

Verify That Inventory Settings Are Working

1. On **CM01**, from the **Start screen**, open the **Configuration Manager** applet; in the **Actions** tab, select **Hardware Inventory Cycle** and click **Run Now**.

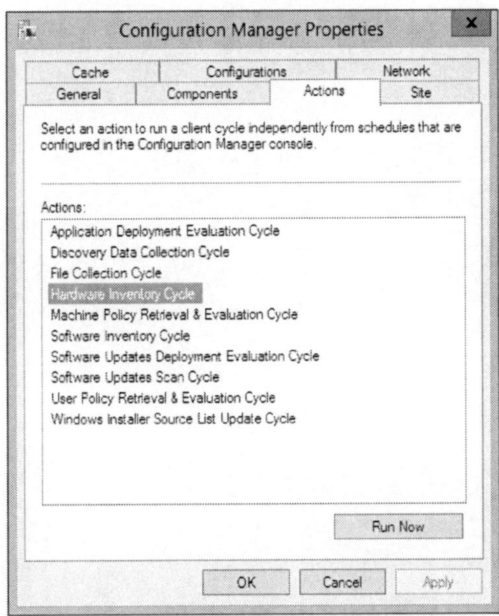

Initiating the hardware inventory action.

2. A message box displays stating that the action was triggered but could take several minutes to complete. Click **OK** and then click **OK** again to close the properties dialog box.
3. Back in the **ConfigMgr console**, select the **Assets and Compliance** workspace and click **Devices**.
4. In the **Search** box, click **Criteria**, select **Name**, type **CM01**, and click **Search**.
5. From the ribbon's **Home** tab, select **Start / Resource Explorer**.
6. Expand the **Hardware** node, and browse through the default set of inventoried items.

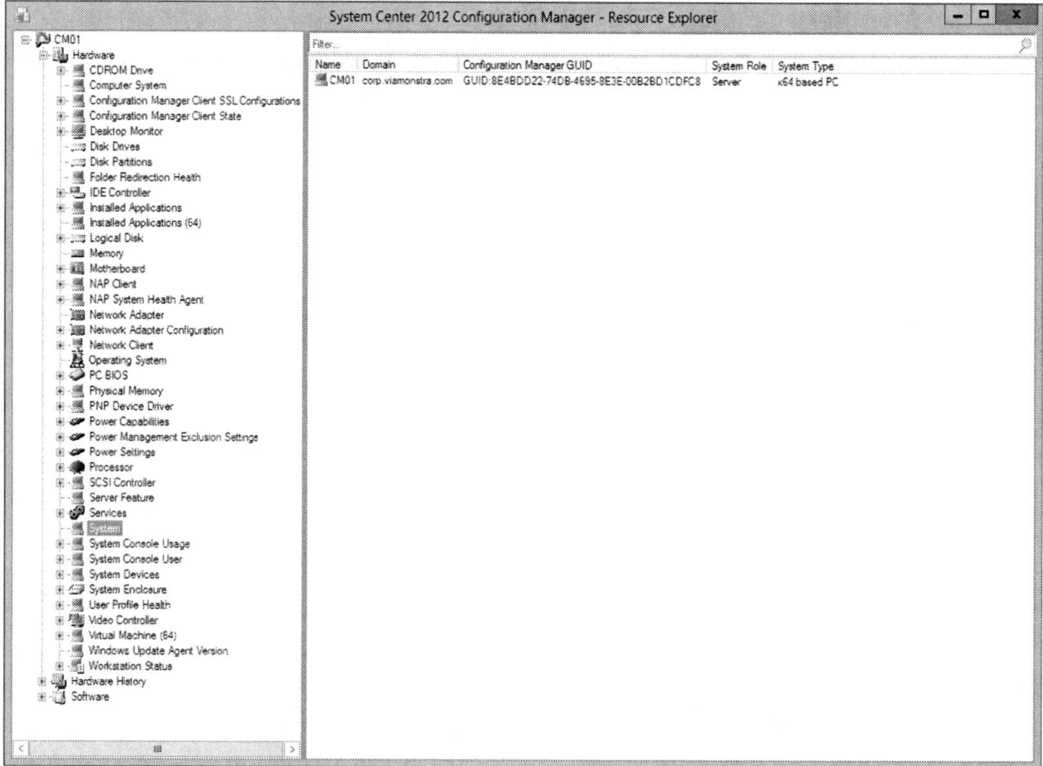

Viewing data in Resource Explorer.

On a UNIX computer you initiate hardware inventory by running .**ccmexec.exe –rs hinv**.

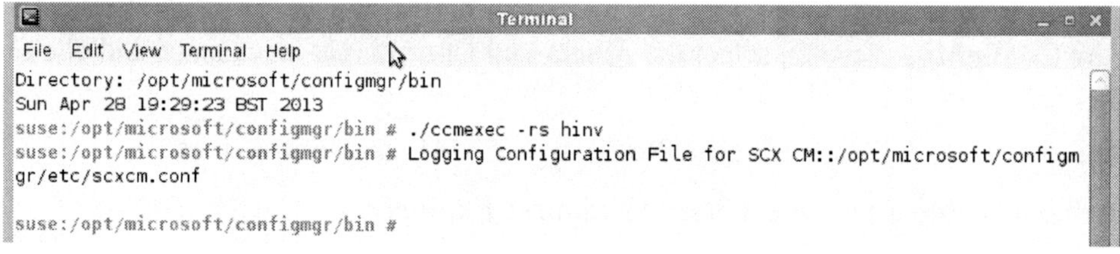

Initiating a hardware inventory in UNIX.

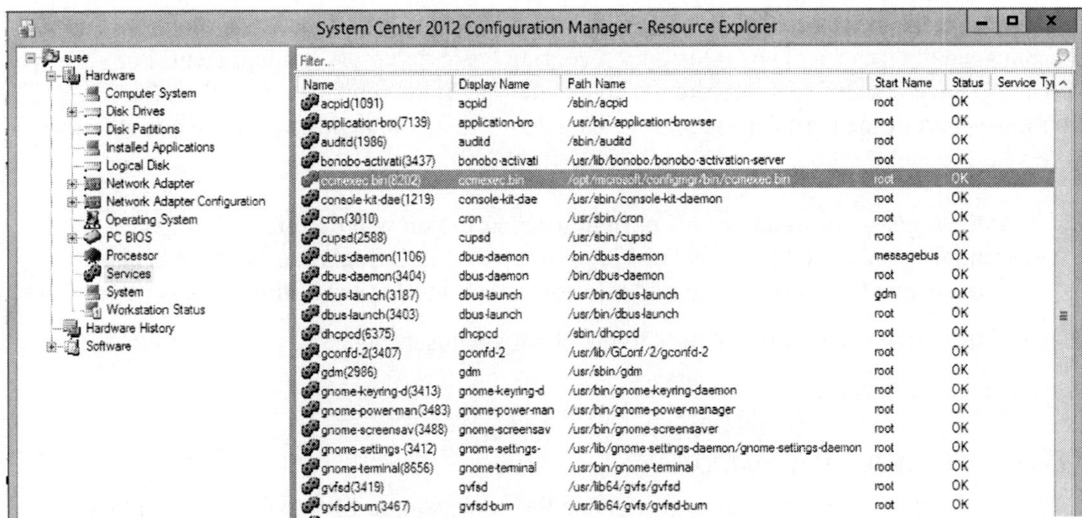

Hardware inventory data from a SUSE server.

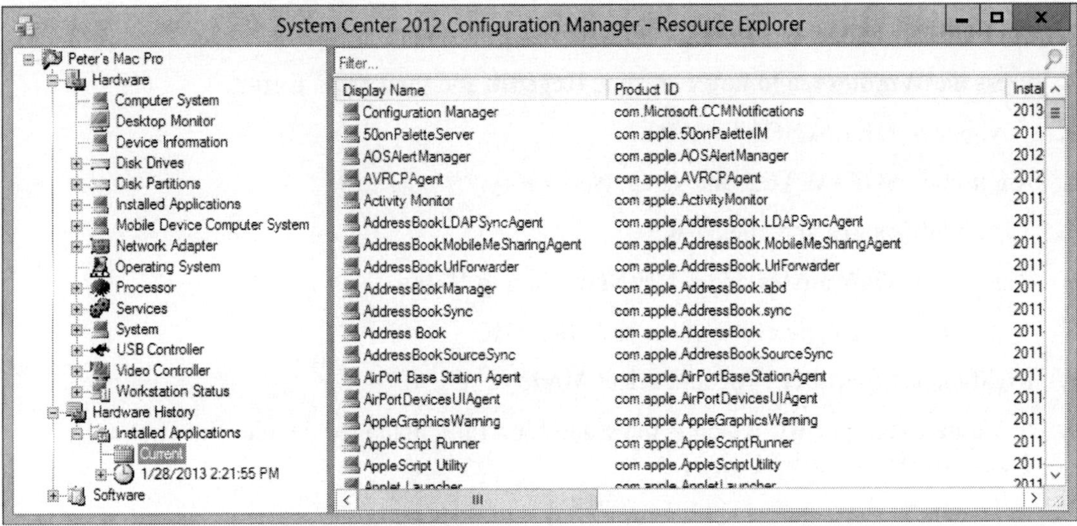

Hardware inventory data from a Mac OS client.

Extending Hardware Inventory

How you extend hardware inventory data depends on what you want gather. If the clients already have the data stored in WMI, all you need to do is add that custom class to the client agent settings. If the data is not yet stored in WMI, then you'll have to add the data to the Configuration.mof file and then add the custom class to the client agent settings. Data added to the Configuration.mof file is automatically added to WMI on the client. You can edit the Configuration.mof file using Notepad. Because there is only one Configuration.mof file per Hierarchy, backing up the file prior to making any changes is highly recommended.

In ViaMonstra, it has been decided to work with two different types of managed devices. Type 01 is fully managed devices and Type 02 is only receiving basic inventory management. For ViaMonstra, I have decided to tattoo the management type in the registry and gather the information as part of the hardware scanning. To achieve this, you need to perform a few things:

1. Add the custom registry information.
2. Add the registry information to Configuration.mof. You will do this with a free community tool called RegKeyToMOF, written by Mark Cochrane. Mark was also gracious enough to allow me to add his tool to the sample files of this book (I tip my hat).
3. Add the newly created WMI class to the client agent settings.
4. Scan and collect the data.

Add Custom Registry Information

In these steps, I assume that you have downloaded the book sample files to C:\Setup on PC0001, which also includes the RegKeyToMOF utility. (Copying them from \\CM01\D$\Setup works great, too. ☺)

1. On **PC0001**, log on as **VIAMONSTRA\Administrator**.
2. Press the **Windows logo key + R**, type **Regedit**, and then press **Enter**.
3. Navigate to **HKLM\SOFTWARE**.
4. Right-click **SOFTWARE** and select **New / Key**.
5. Type **ViaMonstra** and click **OK**.
6. Right-click **ViaMonstra** and select **New / String Value**.
7. Type **ComputerType** as the value and click **OK**.
8. Right-click **ComputerType** and select **Modify**.
9. In **Value data**, type **01**, which is the value for a fully managed device, and click **OK**. Then close the Registry Editor.

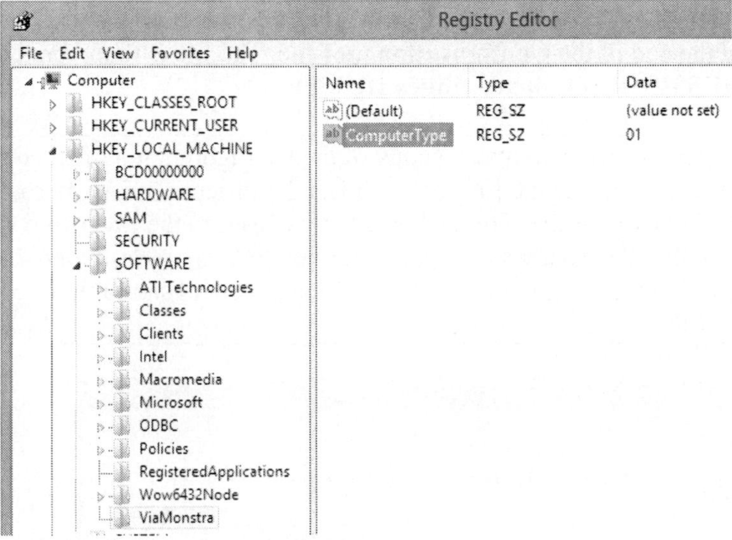
Creating a custom registry key.

10. Run **C:\Setup\RegKey\RegKeyToMofV31.exe**, navigate to **SOFTWARE\ViaMonstra**, and then select **SOFTWARE\ViaMonstra\ComputerType** in the right pane.

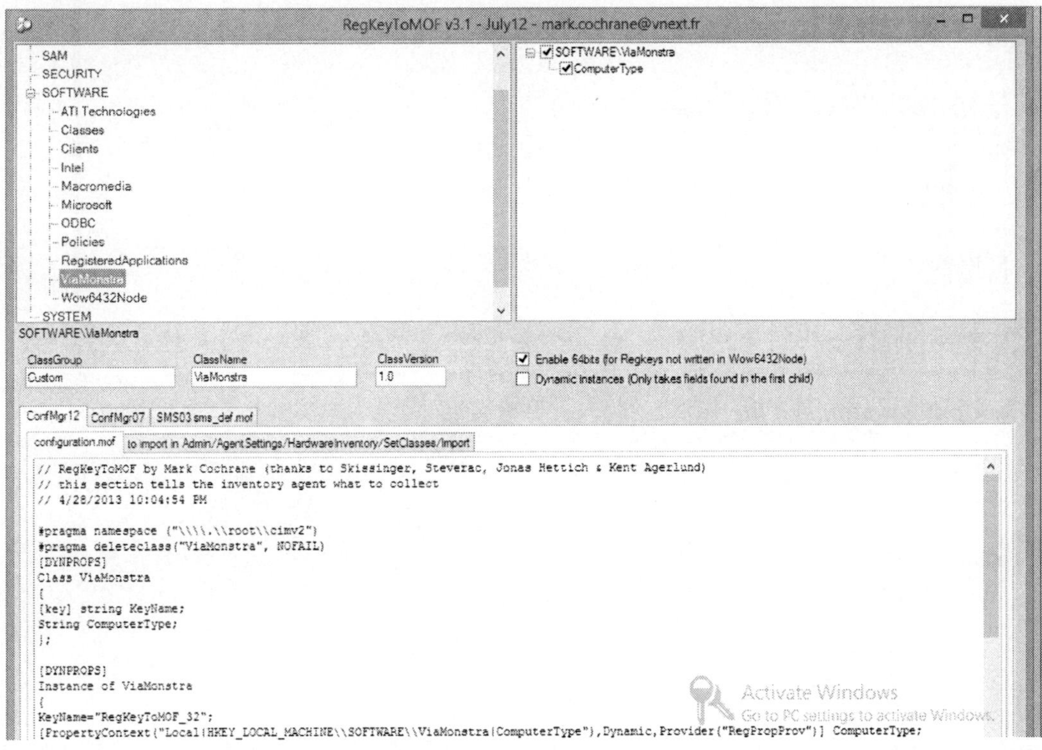
Using RegKeyToMOF.

11. From the lower pane in **RegKeyToMOF**, in the **ConfMgr12** tab, select all the text and paste the information at the end of the **Configuration.mof** file. The file is found on the **CM01** server in **\\CM01\SMS_PS1\inboxes\clifiles.src\hinv**.

> **Real World Note:** It's always a good practice to make a copy of the Configuration.mof file before editing it. ConfigMgr will also make a copy of the file and store it in D:\Program Files\Microsoft Configuration Manager\data\hinvarchive. Furthermore, when adding entries to the file, make sure you add those entries at the end of the file. That way it's easier for you to keep track of any custom changes. The information in the Configuration.mof file is compiled and stored in the database as soon as you save the file.

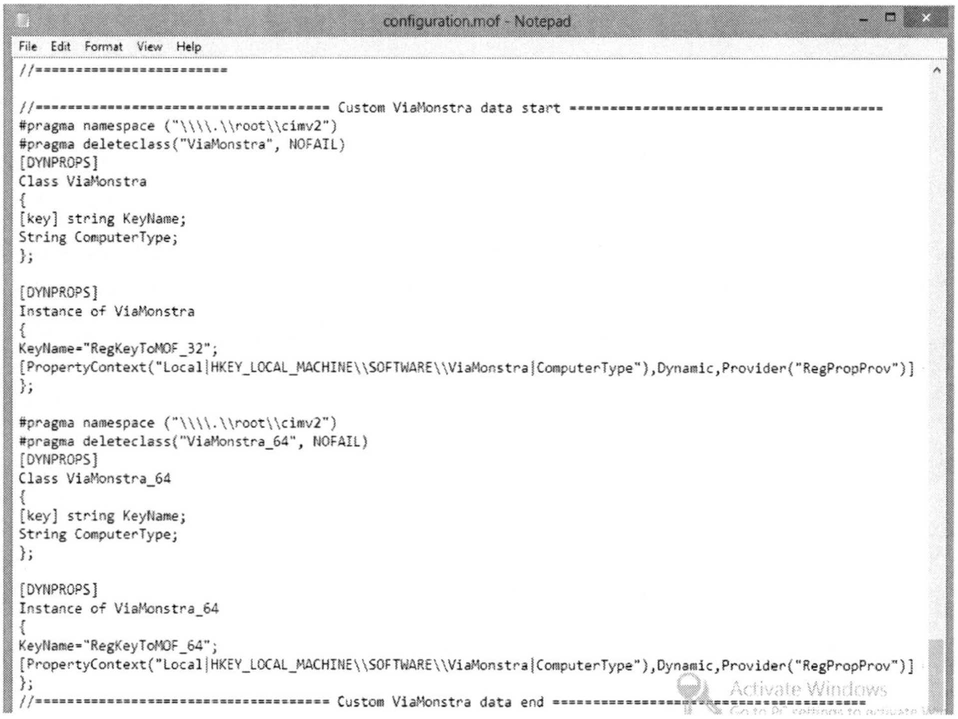

configuration.mof - Notepad

File Edit Format View Help

```
//========================

//==================================== Custom ViaMonstra data start ======================================
#pragma namespace ("\\\\.\\root\\cimv2")
#pragma deleteclass("ViaMonstra", NOFAIL)
[DYNPROPS]
Class ViaMonstra
{
[key] string KeyName;
String ComputerType;
};

[DYNPROPS]
Instance of ViaMonstra
{
KeyName="RegKeyToMOF_32";
[PropertyContext("Local|HKEY_LOCAL_MACHINE\\SOFTWARE\\ViaMonstra|ComputerType"),Dynamic,Provider("RegPropProv")]
};

#pragma namespace ("\\\\.\\root\\cimv2")
#pragma deleteclass("ViaMonstra_64", NOFAIL)
[DYNPROPS]
Class ViaMonstra_64
{
[key] string KeyName;
String ComputerType;
};

[DYNPROPS]
Instance of ViaMonstra_64
{
KeyName="RegKeyToMOF_64";
[PropertyContext("Local|HKEY_LOCAL_MACHINE\\SOFTWARE\\ViaMonstra|ComputerType"),Dynamic,Provider("RegPropProv")]
};
//==================================== Custom ViaMonstra data end ========================================
```

The Configuration.mof file.

12. You can (read *should*) monitor the activity in the **Dataldr.log** file on the server.

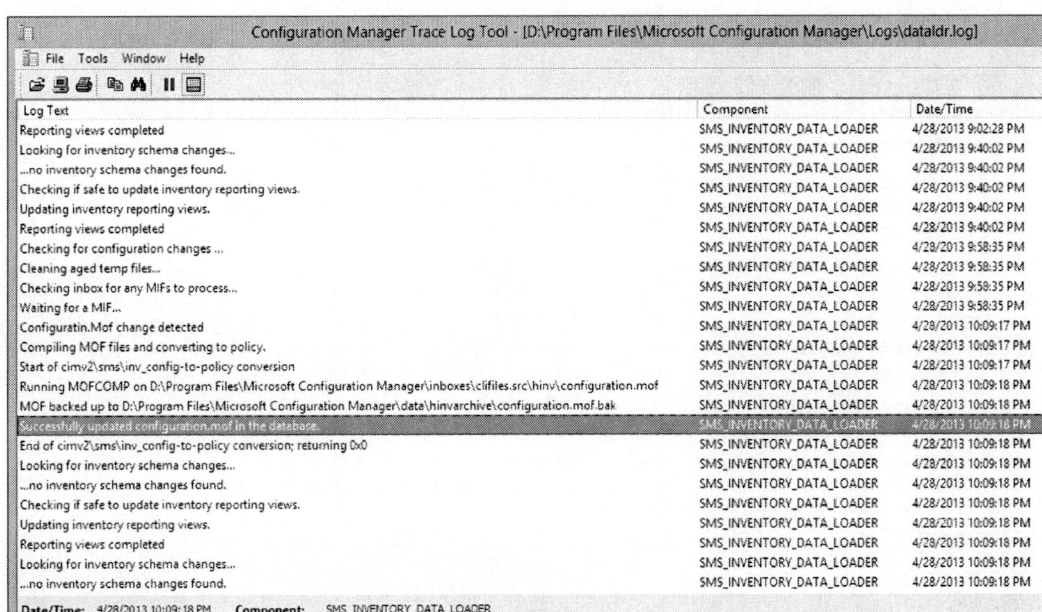

Monitoring the Dataldr.log file on the site server.

13. Clients will read the new settings and add the custom ViaMonstra registry date to WMI after the machine policies have been downloaded and applied. By default, that will happen based on the computer client settings defined in the previous chapter. In order to force a machine policy download, on **PC0001**, open the **Configuration Manager** applet from the **Start screen**; then in the **Action** tab, select **Machine policy retrieval and evaluation cycle** and click **Run Now**.
14. On **CM01**, navigate to the **Administration** workspace, and select **Client settings**.
15. Open the properties for the **Default Client Settings**.
16. Select **Hardware Inventory** and click **Set Classes**.
17. Click **Add / Connect**, and connect to **PC0001**.
18. Select the **ViaMonstra** classes and click **OK**.

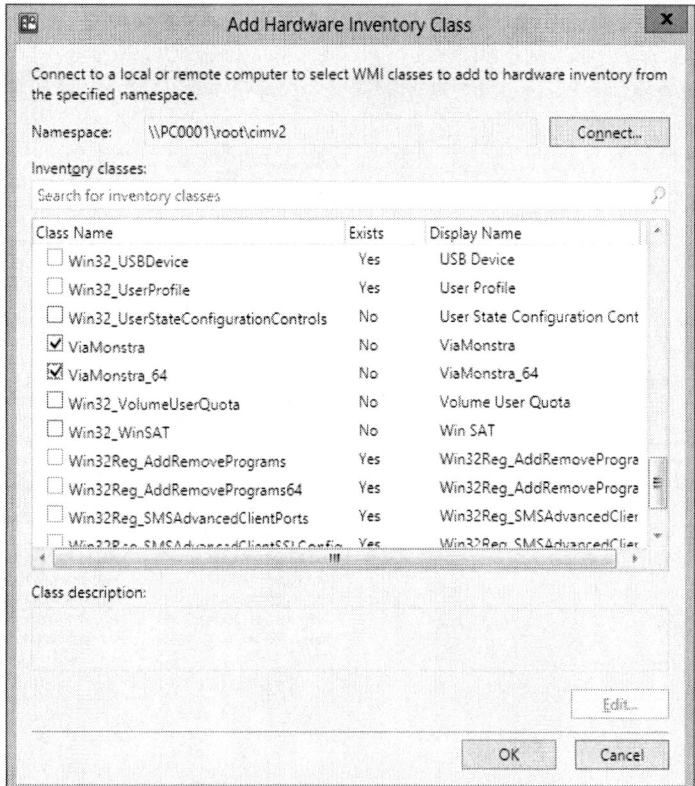

Modifying hardware inventory classes.

19. This enables the ViaMonstra class. Click **OK** twice to close the **Default Settings** dialog box.
20. On **PC0001**, from the **Start screen**, open the **Configuration Manager** applet. From the **Actions** tab, perform a **Machine policy refresh and evaluation cycle** and wait a few seconds.
21. Start a **Hardware Inventory Cycle** action. This will trigger a hardware scan, using all the new information that you have just added to the client agent settings.
22. You can monitor the inventory process by reading **InventoryAgent.log** on the local client.

23. On **CM01**, in the **ConfigMgr console**, open the **Resource Explorer** for **PC0001**. You should be able to find the newly created custom class. If the data is not to be found yet, don't panic; it will appear shortly.

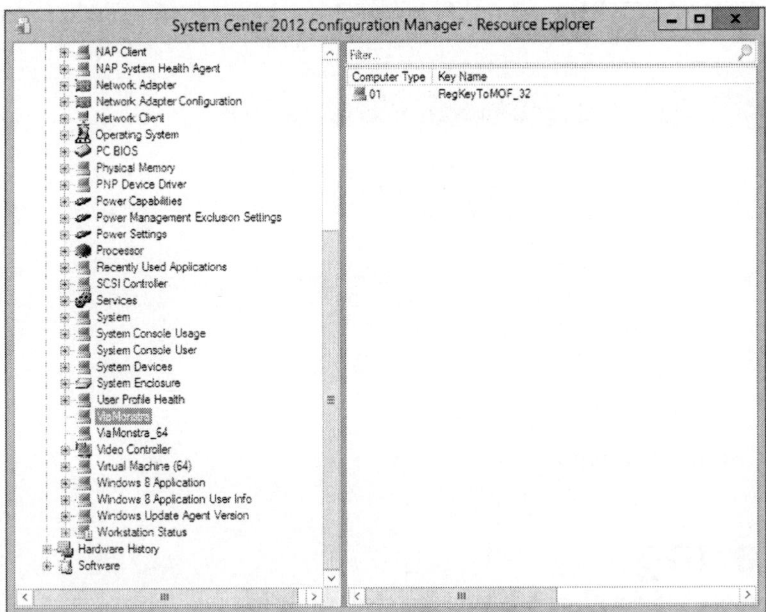

Viewing hardware information using Resource Explorer.

Monitor the Sizes of the Inventory Process Files

One of the important things to know when implementing any inventory solution is the load on the network generated by the client actions. When working with ConfigMgr, at least three different files are generated and uploaded to the management point (hardware, software, and the heartbeat data files). You can monitor the sizes of the files by creating a "secret" file called *archive_reports.sms* and storing that in the inventory temp folder on the client. I always select a group of pilot machines and store the file on those for a few weeks. That way I can easily calculate the average file size for each inventory action.

1. On **PC0001** log on as **VIAMONSTRA\Administrator**.
2. Open **%systemroot%\CCM\Inventory\Temp**.
3. Create a file called **archive_reports.sms** (make sure that you do not create a .txt file).
4. Open the **Configuration Manager** applet from the **Start screen** and perform these actions one at the time:
    a. Initiate a **Discovery Data Collection Cycle**.
    b. Initiate a **Hardware Inventory Cycle**.
    c. Initiate a **Software Inventory Cycle**.

5. Open the **%systemroot%\CCM\Inventory\Temp** folder. You should be able to see three XML files, each containing the data from the three cycles. The files can be deleted any time.
6. Delete the **%systemroot%\CCM\Inventory\Temp\archive_reports.sms** file to revert to the original behavior.

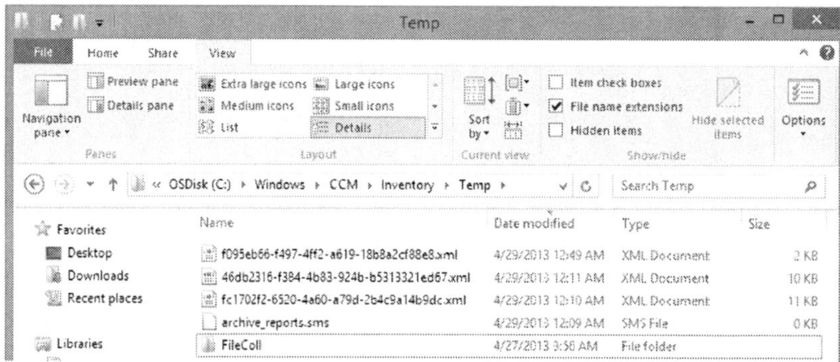

Traffic generated by the inventory actions.

Software Metering

Besides gathering basic inventory information, ViaMonstra also wants to track the usage of a few predefined applications. To do this, you need to create a software metering rule for each of the applications. For the sake of simplicity, I have decided that software metering will be tested using Notepad. That way you do not have to install any other application in your lab environment.

Create a Software Metering Rule

1. On **CM01**, and open the **ConfigMgr console**.
2. In the **Assets and Compliance** workspace, select **Software Metering**.
3. Right-click **Software Metering**, and select **Folder / Create Folder**.
4. Type **Microsoft** and click **OK**.
5. Expand **Software Metering**, select the **Microsoft** folder, and click **Create Software Metering Rule**.
6. In the **Name** box, type **Notepad**.
7. In the **File Name** box, type **notepad.exe**.
8. In **Original File Name**, type **notepad.exe**.
9. The **Version** box should have the * (asterisk) character in it.
10. **Language** should be set to **- Any -**.
11. Click **Next** twice.

12. Click **Close**.

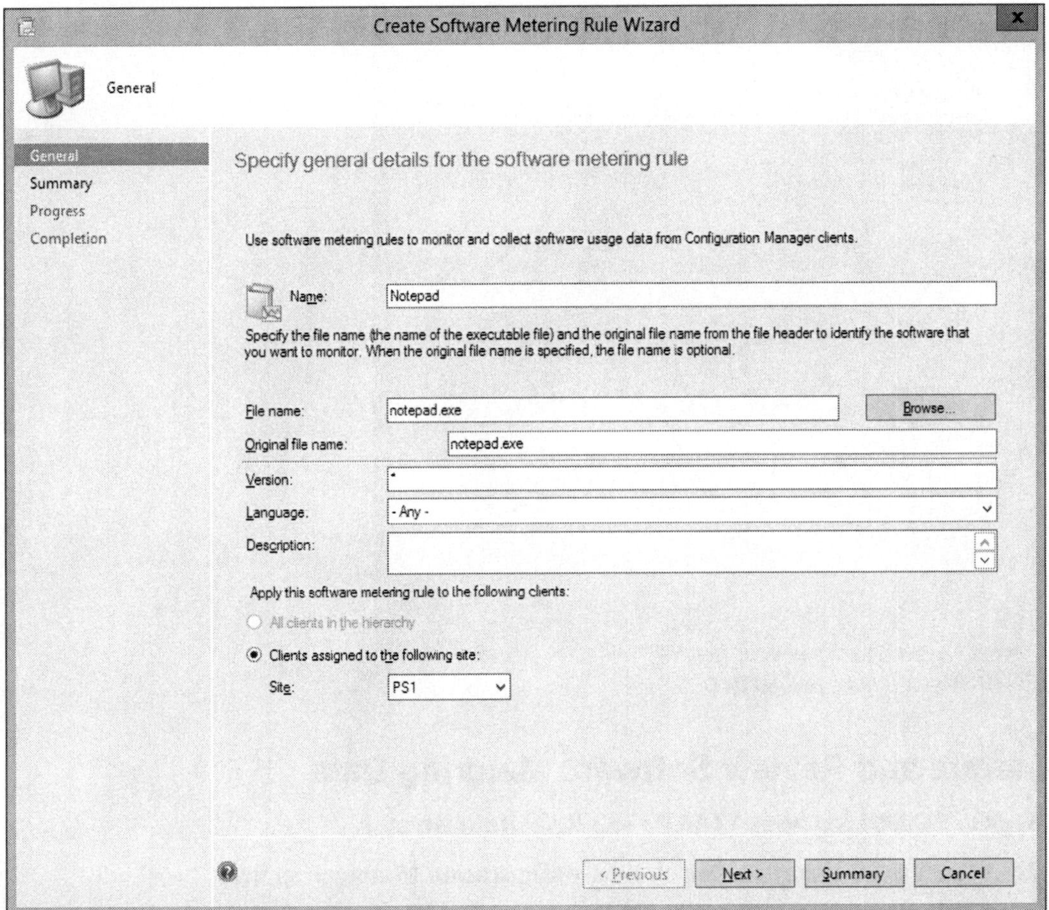

Creating a software metering rule.

Disable Auto Creation of Software Metering Rules

ConfigMgr by default creates disabled software metering rules based on the software.

1. While still in the **Assets and Compliance** workspace, select **Software Metering**.
2. On the ribbon, select **Software Metering Properties**.
3. Clear the **Automatically create disabled metering rules from recent usage inventory** check box and click **OK**.

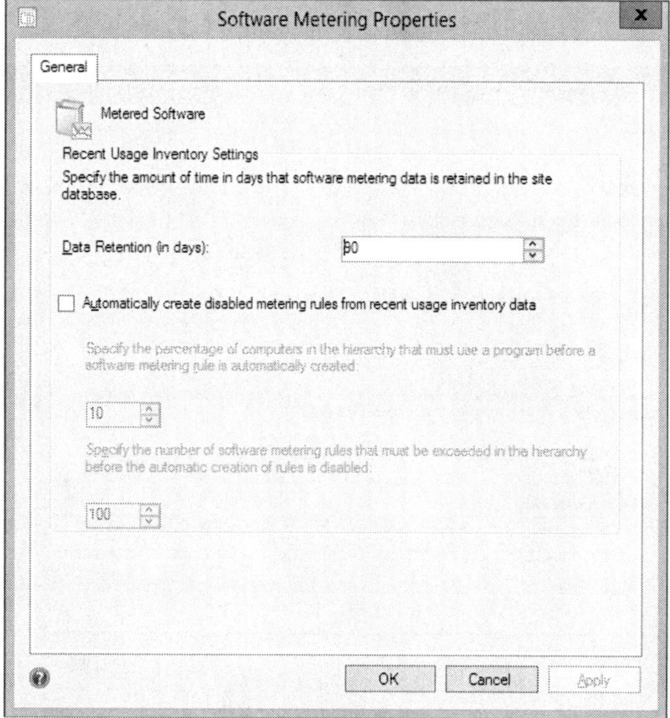

Software metering properties.

Generate and Review Software Metering Data

1. On **PC0001** log on as **VIAMONSTRA\Administrator**.
2. From the **Start screen**, launch the **Configuration Manager** applet.
3. In the **Actions** tab, select **Machine Policy Evaluation and Retrieval Cycle** and click **Run Now**. This action triggers the client to download new policies including the software metering rules.
4. Start **Notepad**.
5. Type **Learning about System Center 2012 Configuration Manager is a blast!**
6. Close **Notepad**.
7. From the **Start screen**, launch the **Configuration Manager** applet.
8. In the **Actions** tab, select **Software Metering Usage Report Cycle** and click **Run Now**. This uploads a report containing all the software metering recorded activity. At the site server, the data is processed by the site maintenance rules. After the processing is done, the usage data will be available in the software metering reports.

The number one reason for working with software metering is to figure out what software you can safely uninstall and where. There is no built-in feature that can assist you; however, you can create custom queries to provide you with the necessary information.

Working with Queries

When working with any database, you always need to create queries. In ConfigMgr, the user creating the query needs access to the administrator console and have at least read permissions to the objects retrieved. Queries often are used for personal ad-hoc purposes, in which a report is created for presenting data to other users in the organization. In ViaMonstra, you start by creating three basic queries using the GUI and one more advanced query using the WMI Query Language (WQL) interface.

Create a Dynamic Query Collection

The first collection you create is a collection that lists all your fully managed clients. You can go through the following steps only if you extended the hardware inventory with the ViaMonstra class as described earlier in this chapter.

1. On **CM01**, open the **ConfigMgr console**.
2. Select the **Assets and Compliance** workspace.
3. Expand **Device Collections**, right-click the **ViaMonstra** folder, and select **Create Device Collection**.
4. Complete the following settings:
    a. Name: **VM All Managed Clients**
    b. Comment: **All ConfigMgr managed client devices**
    c. Limiting collection: Click **Browse** and select **All Systems**.
5. Click **Next**.
6. Click **Add Rule**, **Query Rule**.
7. Name the rule **All Managed Clients** and click **Edit Query Statement**.
8. Select the **Criteria** tab.
9. Click the **yellow icon** and click **Select** to create the criteria.
10. Select **ViaMonstra** as the **Attribute class** and **ComputerType** as the **Attribute**.

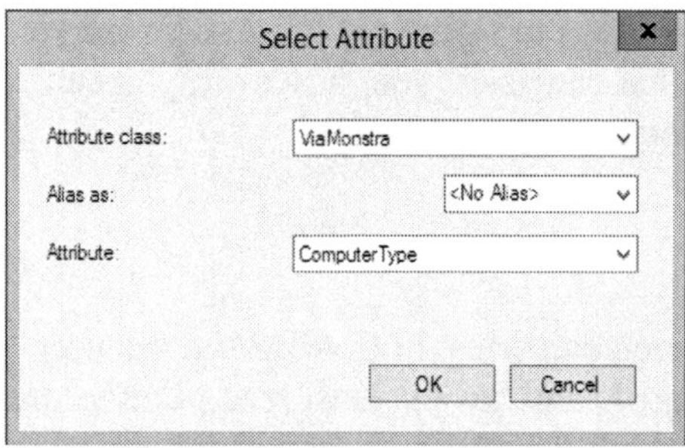

Querying for custom data.

11. Click **OK** to return to the Criterion Properties dialog box.
12. In **Operator**, select **is equal to**, and in **Value**, type **01**.
13. Click **OK** three times and then complete the wizard using the default settings.

Create a Query to List Installed Software

Another commonly used query is one that lists all computers with a specific application installed. The following steps guide you through the creation of a query that lists all SQL 2012 servers installed in the company:

1. Open the **ConfigMgr console**, select the **Monitoring** workspace and select **Queries**.
2. On the ribbon, click **Create Query**.
3. Type **All Servers with SQL installed** as the query name.
4. Click **Edit Query Statement**.
5. In the **General** tab, click **New**.
6. Click **Select** and select the **NETBIOS Name** attribute from the **System Resource** class.
7. Click **OK** twice.
8. Select the **Criteria** tab.
9. Click **New**.
10. Click **Select**.
11. In **Attribute Class**, select **Installed Applications (64)**; and in **Attribute**, select **Display Name**.
12. Click **OK**.
13. Click **Values**.
14. The values include all software products installed. Scroll down to **Microsoft SQL Server 2012 (64-bit)** and click **OK** twice. This returns you to the Criteria tab.
15. Click **OK**, **Next** twice, and then click **Close** to create the query.

16. Select the **All Servers with SQL installed** query, and on the ribbon, click **Run**.

> **Note:** Due to the way data is stored in ConfigMgr, you might get duplicate entries. These duplicates can be removed by selecting the Omit duplicate rows (select distinct) check box in the query statement, a feature you use in the "Create a Query Using Functions()" section later in this chapter.

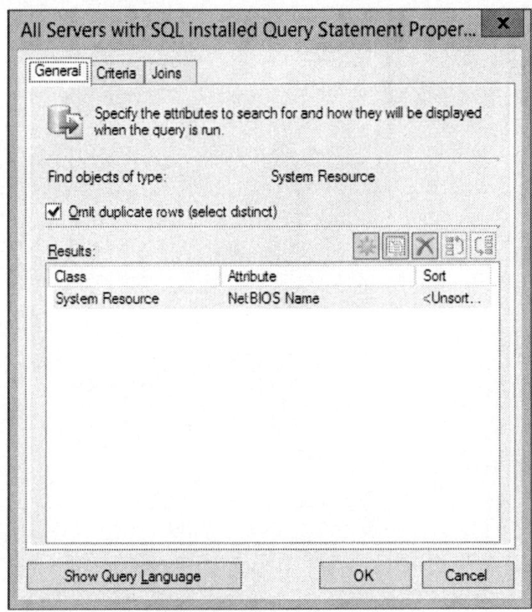

Removing duplicate rows in the query statement.

Create a Subselected Query

A subselected query is one that you use from time to time, such as whenever you need to find objects that do *not* meet a certain criterion, e.g. all servers that do not have SQL Server installed, or all workstations without Office 2013 installed. This query will list the NETBIOS names for all servers without SQL Server 2012 installed.

1. While still in the **Monitoring** workspace, select **Queries**, and then on the ribbon, click **Create Query**.
2. Type **All Servers without SQL installed** as the query name.
3. Click **Edit Query Statement**.
4. In the **General** tab, add this display attribute: **System Resource**, **NETBIOS Name**.
5. Click **OK**.
6. Select the **Criteria** tab.
7. Click **New**, select **SubSelected values** as the criterion type.

8. Click **Select** and select **System Resource, NETBIOS Name**.
9. Click **OK**. This returns you to the **Criterion Properties** dialog box.
10. In **Operator**, select **is not in**.
11. Click **Browse** and select **All Servers with SQL installed**.

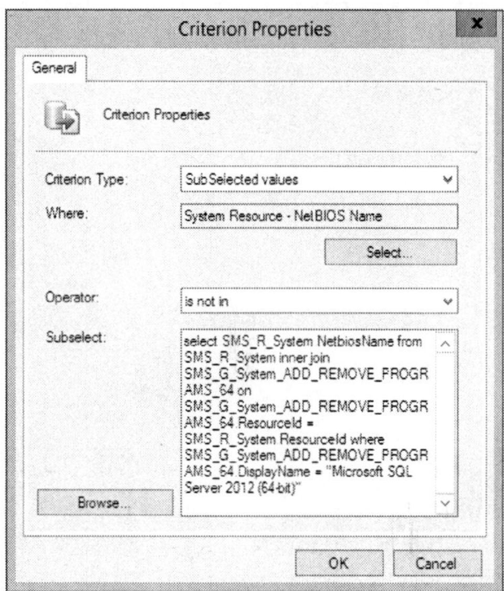

Creating the subselected query.

12. Click **OK**. This returns you to the Criteria tab.
13. Click **New** to build the next criterion.
14. Click **Select**.
15. For **Attribute Class**, select **System Resource**; and for **Attribute**, select **Operating System Name and Version**. Click **OK**.
16. In **Operator**, select **is like**, and in **Value**, type **%Server%**.
17. Click **OK** twice, click **Next** twice, and then click **Close**.
18. Select the query, and on the ribbon, click **Run**.

The Subselected WQL Code

The statement that you created in the wizard is similar to what you see below. If you know you way around WQL, then there is no need to use the GUI to create the queries.

```
select SMS_R_System.NetbiosName from SMS_R_System where
SMS_R_System.NetbiosName not in (select SMS_R_System.NetbiosName
from SMS_R_System inner join SMS_G_System_ADD_REMOVE_PROGRAMS_64
on SMS_G_System_ADD_REMOVE_PROGRAMS_64.ResourceId =
SMS_R_System.ResourceId where
SMS_G_System_ADD_REMOVE_PROGRAMS_64.DisplayName = "Microsoft SQL
Server 2012 (64-bit)") and
SMS_R_System.OperatingSystemNameandVersion like "%Server%"
```

Create a Query Using Functions()

The third query you create for use in ViaMonstra uses one of the famous Date() functions that has existed in SQL since the dawn of time. In this section, you create a query that returns all workstations that haven't had their hardware inventories reported for seven days.

1. While still in the **Monitoring** workspace, select **Queries** on the ribbon, and click **Create Query**.
2. Name the query **Computers with no HW inventory for 7 days** and click **Edit Query Statement**.
3. In the **General** tab, add these display attributes:
   a. System Resource: **NETBIOS Name**
   b. Workstation Status: **Last Hardware Scan (Client Local Time)**
   c. Select the **Omit duplicate rows (select distinct)** check box.
4. Select the **Criteria** tab and click **New** to build the next criterion.
5. Click **Select**.
6. For **Attribute Class**, select **System Resource**; and for **Attribute**, select **Operating System Name and Version**. Click **OK**.
7. In **Operator**, select **is like**, and in **Value**, type **%Workstation%**.
8. Click **OK** and **Show Query Language**, and then type (at the end of the statement):
9. **and (DateDiff(day, SMS_G_System_WORKSTATION_STATUS .LastHardwareScan, GetDate()) > 7)**
10. Save the query and run the query to view the result. If all clients have reported a hardware inventory within seven days, you will see no clients in the result.

Working with Reports

Reporting is a huge part of working with ConfigMgr, which is why you need to have some basic knowledge of SQL Reporting Services. All data that is gathered in the SQL Server database is shown in either a canned report or a custom report that you create. ViaMonstra has a few requirements for reporting, such as being able to automatically mail some reports on a monthly basis, brand the report with company data, add chart objects, and finally create some custom reports.

Changing the Logo on All Canned Reports

When you enable a SQL Reporting Services point, ConfigMgr automatically imports the reports from D:\Program Files\SMS_SRSRP\reports and applies the style and logos to all the reports. You can manually start this process by modifying a registry key as described in the following steps. Before you go through the steps, ensure that you have a custom logo called Report_Header_Right.png. You can find a custom logo for ViaMonstra in the book sample files, in the Branding folder.

1. On **CM01**, open the **D:\Program Files\SMS_SRSRP\Style** folder.
2. Make a backup of the existing **Report_Header_Right.png** file and copy your custom logo to the **Style** folder. Make sure to replace the existing file.
3. Press the **Windows logo key + R**, type **Regedit**, and then press **Enter**.
4. Navigate to **HKLM\SOFTWARE\Microsoft\SMS\SRSRP**.

5. Right-click **SRSInitializeState**, click **Modify**, and change the value to from **1** to **0**.

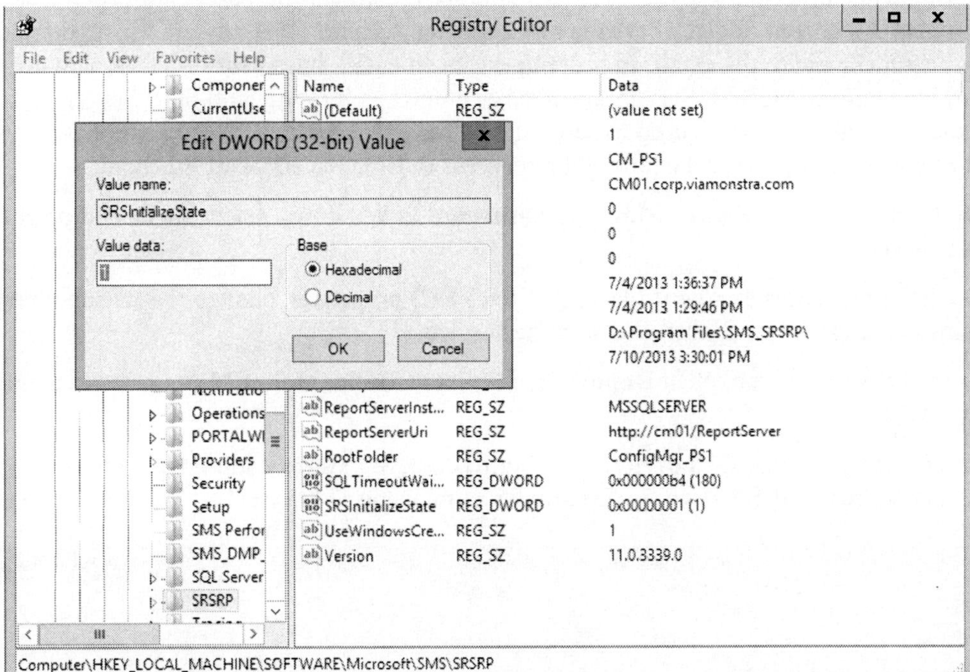

Changing the logo on all reports.

6. Click **OK** and monitor the activity in the **srsrp.log** file on the site server.
7. Wait a few minutes and open any of the canned reports. You should be able to see the new default logo.
8. Open **Internet Explorer** and go to the following URL: **http://CM01/Reports**.

Note: To view the reports on CM01, you should disable IE Enhanced Security Configuration via Server Manager / Local Server.

9. In the **Content** tab, click **ConfigMgr_PS1** to view available reports.
10. Click **Administrative Security** and run the **Administration Activity Log** report.
11. Select **VIAMONSTRA\Administrators**. Notice the logo in the canned report. (Depending on your screen resolution, you may need to scroll to the right in the report to see it.)
12. Close Internet Explorer.

Creating an Email Subscription

When working with subscriptions, you have two options: creating a file-based subscription which stores the report in a shared folder, or creating an email subscription that renders the report and stores it as an attachment to the email. In order to create an email–based subscription, you need to have a working mail server, SQL Server Agent service must be running, and SQL Server Reporting Services must be configured to support emailed subscriptions. ViaMonstra has a Microsoft Exchange 2013 server. Installing the server is outside the scope of this book.

1. On **CM01**, from the **Server Manager** dashboard in Windows, select **Tools** and open the **Service console**.
2. Open the **SQL Server Agent (MSSQLSERVER)** properties, change the startup type to **Automatic (Delayed Start)**, and start the service.
3. From the **Start screen**, open **Reporting Services Configuration Manager**, and connect to **CM01**.
4. In the left pane, click **E-mail Settings**. Configure **CM_SR@viamonstra.com** as the sender address and **EX01.corp.viamonstra.com** as the SMTP server. Then click **Apply**.

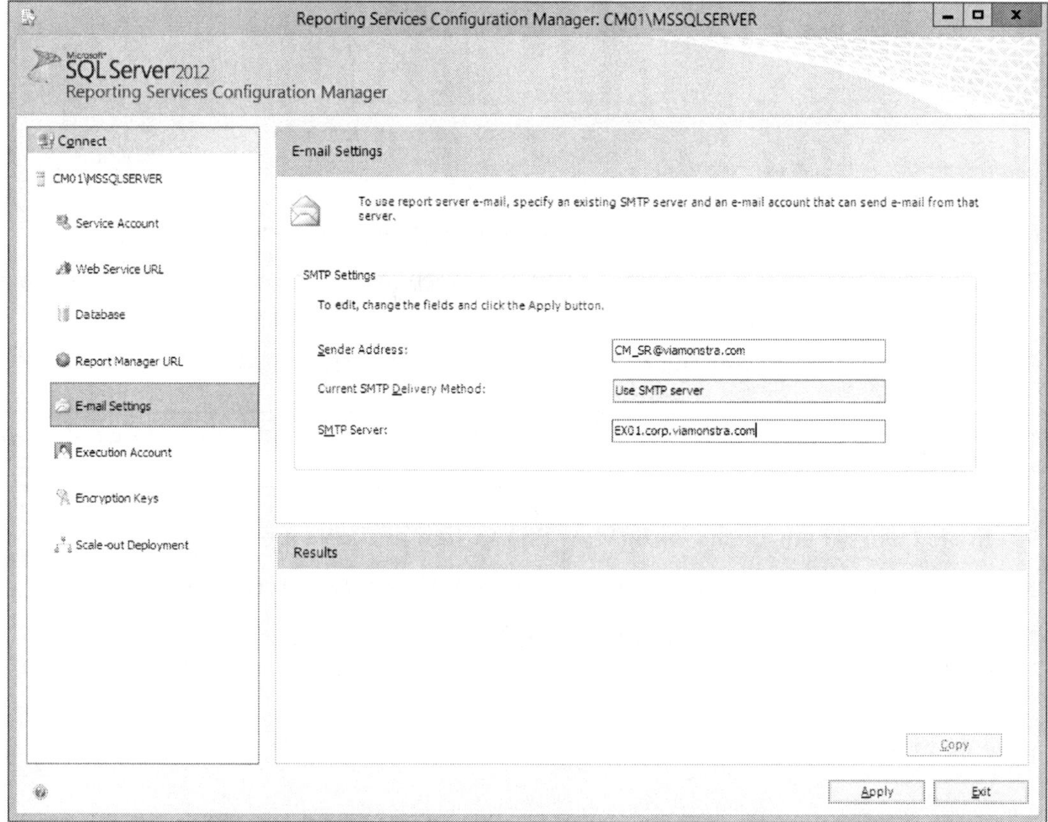

Configuring email support in SQL Server Reporting Services.

5. Click **Exit** to close the reporting configuration tool.
6. Open **Internet Explorer** and connect to **http://CM01/Reports**.
7. Select **ConfigMgr_PS1**, and open the **Client Status** category.
8. Move the mouse over the **Client Status Summary** report until you see a drop-down menu. In the drop-down menu, select **Manage**.
9. In the left pane, click **Subscriptions**.

Note: You also can create subscriptions in the ConfigMgr console.

10. Click **New Subscription**. You can choose between E-mail and Windows File share. Select **E-mail** and configure these settings:
    a. To: **administrator@viamonstra.com**
    b. Render Format: Click the drop-down box, make a note of the different supported formats, and select the **MHTLM** format.
    c. Comment: **Latest client status report**
    d. Click **Select Schedule** and create a weekly new schedule of **every Monday at 6:00**.
    e. Click **OK** to close the Schedule window.
    f. Configure the **Credentials** to **VIAMONSTRA\CM_SR**, and type **Password01** as the password.
    g. Select **All Desktops and Servers** as the collection and **All Configuration Manager Client** versions.
11. Click **OK** to close the New Subscription window.

One of the benefits of using the web interface to create the schedule is the ability to see whether something went wrong during the process. That's not possible from the ConfigMgr console.

Modifying Reports

You can use different tools to create and modify custom reports in SQL Server Reporting Services. Most use either SQL Reporting Builder or Business Intelligence Development Studio (BIDS). In the following sections, you add a custom logo, modify the layout, and add a chart object to an existing report. First you configure ConfigMgr to launch SQL Reporting Builder 3.0 instead of Reporting Builder 2.0.

Configure Configuration Manager 2012 to Launch SQL Reporting Builder 3.0

1. On **CM01**, log on as **VIAMONSTRA\Administrator**; press the **Windows logo key + R**, type **Regedit**, and then press **Enter**.

2. Navigate to **HKLM\SOFTWARE\Wow6432Node\Microsoft\ConfigMgr10 \AdminUI\Reporting**.
3. Edit the **ReportBuilderApplicationManifestName** string from **ReportBuilder_2_0_0_0.application** to **ReportBuilder_3_0_0_0.application** and click **OK**.

Modify an Existing Report

1. On **CM01**, log on as **VIAMONSTRA\Administrator**, and open the **ConfigMgr console** as **Administrator**.
2. Navigate to the **Monitoring** workspace, and select **Reporting / Reports** and then the **Operating System** folder.
3. Select **Count operating system versions**, and on the ribbon, click **Edit**. This launches SQL Reporting Builder 3.0. After you select **Run** (only the first time), it will open the report in edit mode.

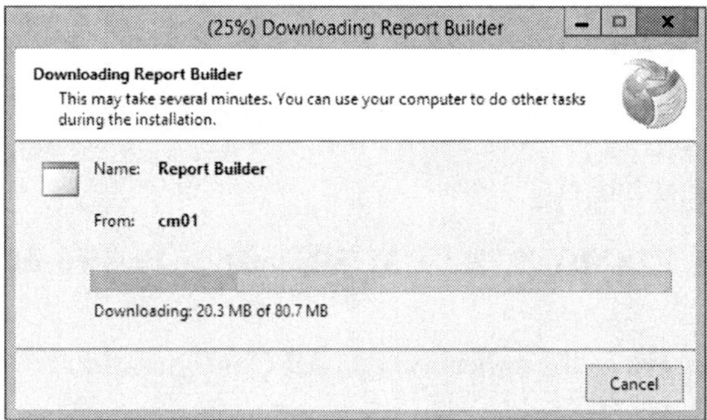

SQL Reporting Builder 3.0 is being installed on the server.

4. Delete the default heading (report title) in the report header, and then the other two expressions in the report body. Expressions are listed as **<<Expr>>**. Right-click each **<<Expr>>** element that has a grey background, and from the menu, select **Delete**.

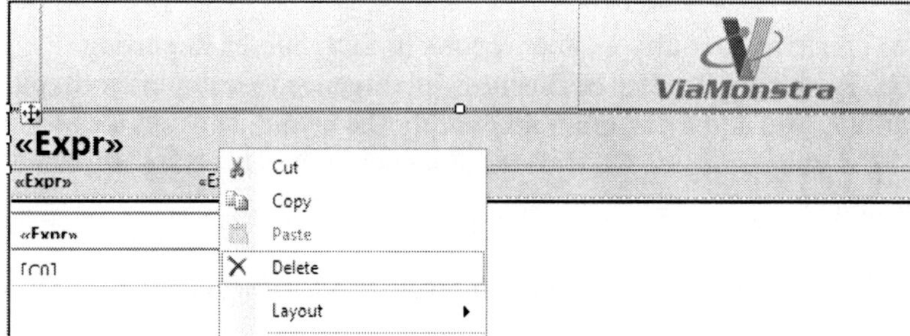

Deleting the default heading (report title) and the other expressions.

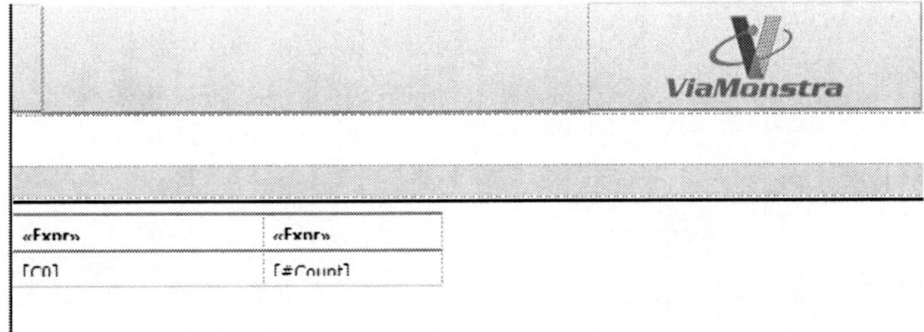

The report after deleting the expressions.

5. On the ribbon, select the **Insert** tab. Click **Text Box** and add a new heading called **Count of Operating Systems in ViaMonstra**. Add the text box to the left in the area below the banner (logo) and resize it to fit the text. Customize the font and text sizes to your liking – but remember other people will have to view the report too. I used Arial size 12, bold, in this example.

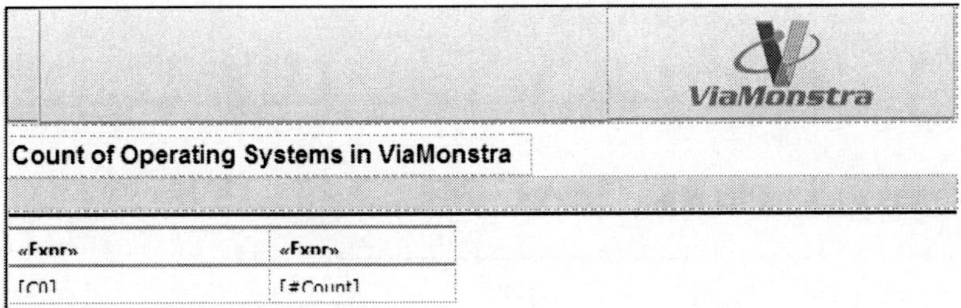

Text box added and resized.

6. From the ribbon's **Insert** tab, select **Chart / Insert Chart**.
7. Insert the chart under the remaining expressions in the report body. You insert the chart by clicking the mouse.
8. Select **Shape** and a **3D pie**.

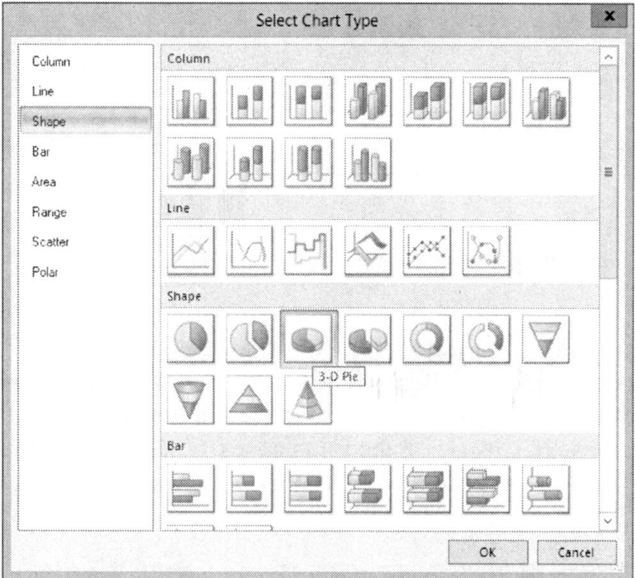

Selecting the 3-D Pie chart.

9. Click **OK**.
10. Resize the chart to be as wide as the report header.

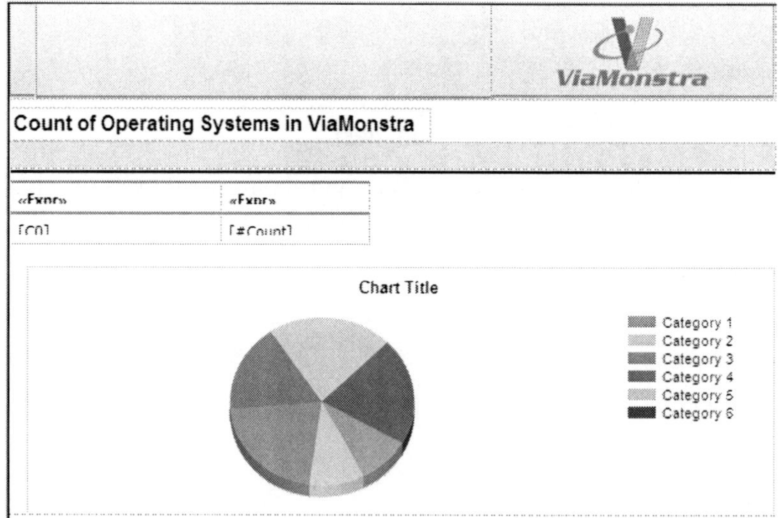

The resized chart.

11. Right-click the chart to display the **Chart Data** window.
12. From the **Report Data** pane, expand **Datasets / DataSet()**.
13. Drag the **C0** field to **Series Groups** in the **Chart Data** area.

14. Drag the **Count** field to the **Values** in the **Chart Data** area.

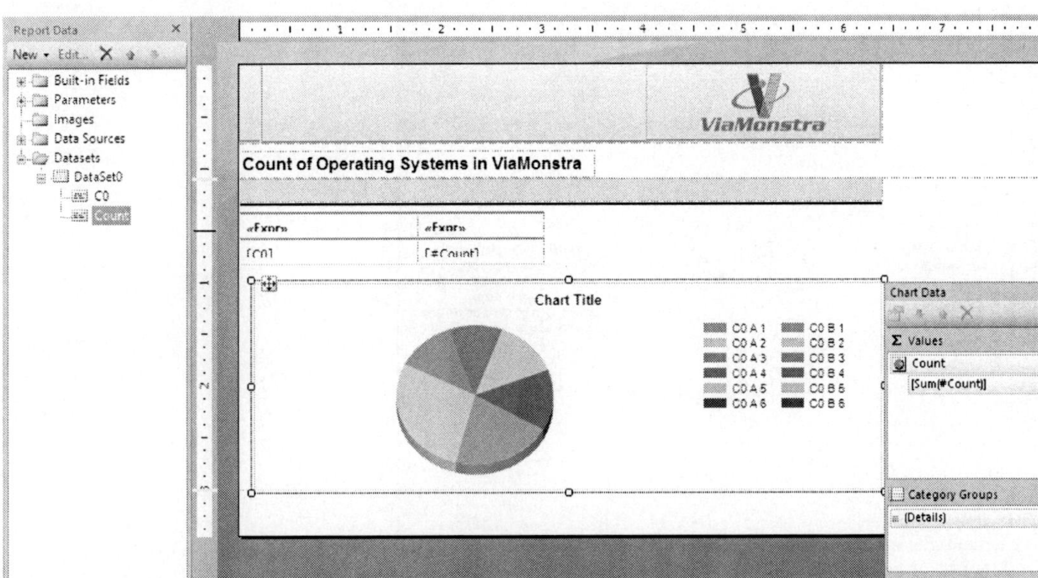

Adding datasets to the chart data.

15. Right-click the chart and select **Show Data Labels**.

16. Right-click the **Chart Title** and select **Delete Title** from the menu.

17. Right-click the lower left footer and select **Insert Textbox.**

18. Right-click the text box and select **Expression**.

19. Type **="Page " &**, then in the **Built-in Fields** node, double-click **PageNumber**; then type **& " of " &**, and in the **Built-in Fields** node, double-click **TotalPages**.

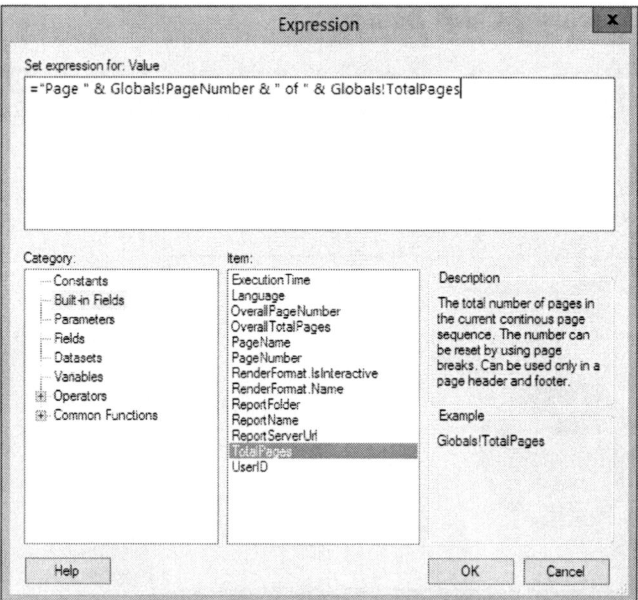

Creating the expression.

20. Click **OK** to close the expression, and then on the ribbon's **Home** tab, click **Run**.

Real World Note: If you find that the user account you're using doesn't have permissions to run the report directly from SQL Report Builder (but you can see the reports fine when using the ConfigMgr console or web browser), make sure the user account is listed as a System User in the Reporting Services Site Settings. To access the Reporting Services Site Settings, start Internet Explorer (iexplore.exe) from an elevated command prompt (run as administrator), navigate to http://cm01/reports, and click Site Settings, which is available only when you run Internet Explorer as administrator.

21. Select the **Reporting Builder** logo in the upper left corner, click **Save As**, name the report **Count operating system in ViaMonstra**, and then close the SQL Report Builder.

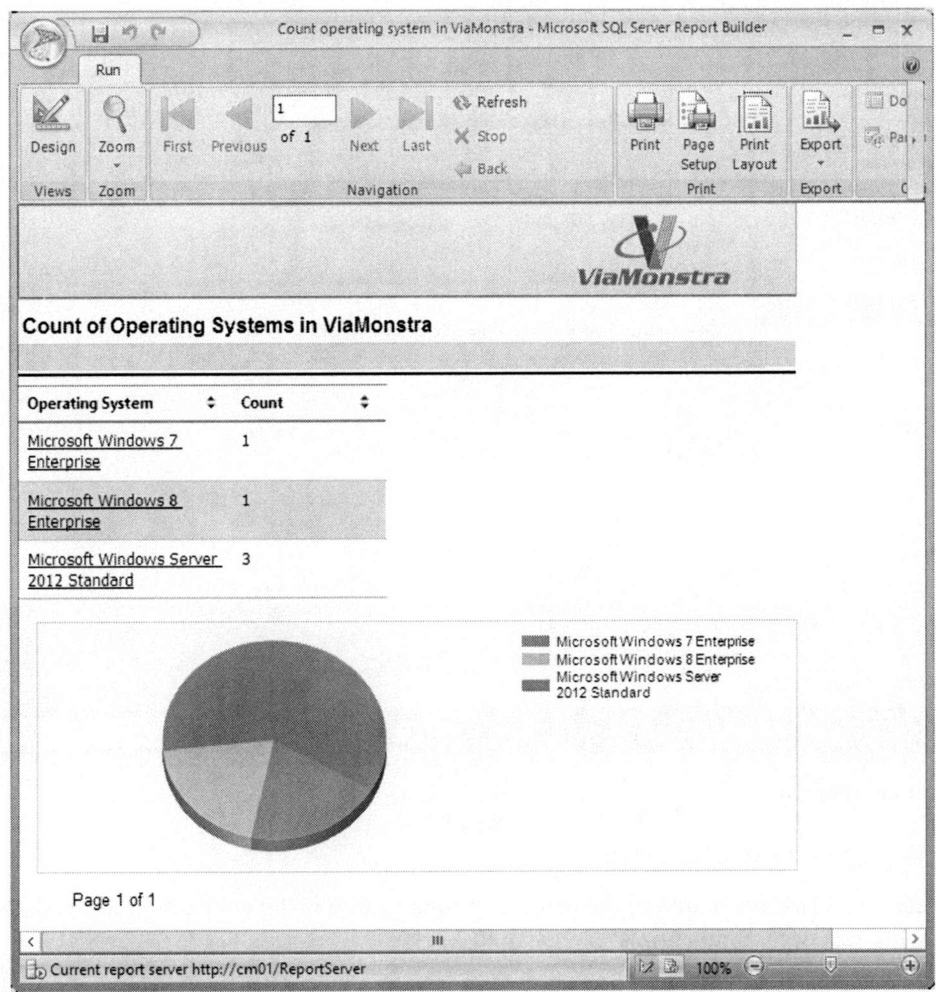

Running the modified report in Report Builder.

Create a Custom Report

You can use SQL Reporting Builder or BIDS (which is really Microsoft Visual Studio 2010 with additional project types that are specific to SQL Server business intelligence) to create custom reports. Usually I prefer BIDS because it gives me a few more choices, like a full development environment. Management wants to see a report with fully managed devices and inventory managed devices. To solve the challenge, you must create a custom report based on the registry information gathered previously in this chapter.

1. From the **Start screen**, open **SQL Server Data Tools** as **Administrator**.
2. On the **Choose Default Environment Settings** page, select **Business Intelligence Settings** and click **Start Visual Studio**.
3. On the **Start Page**, click **New Project**. Then select **Report Server Project Wizard**, name the project **ViaMonstra reports**, and click **OK**.

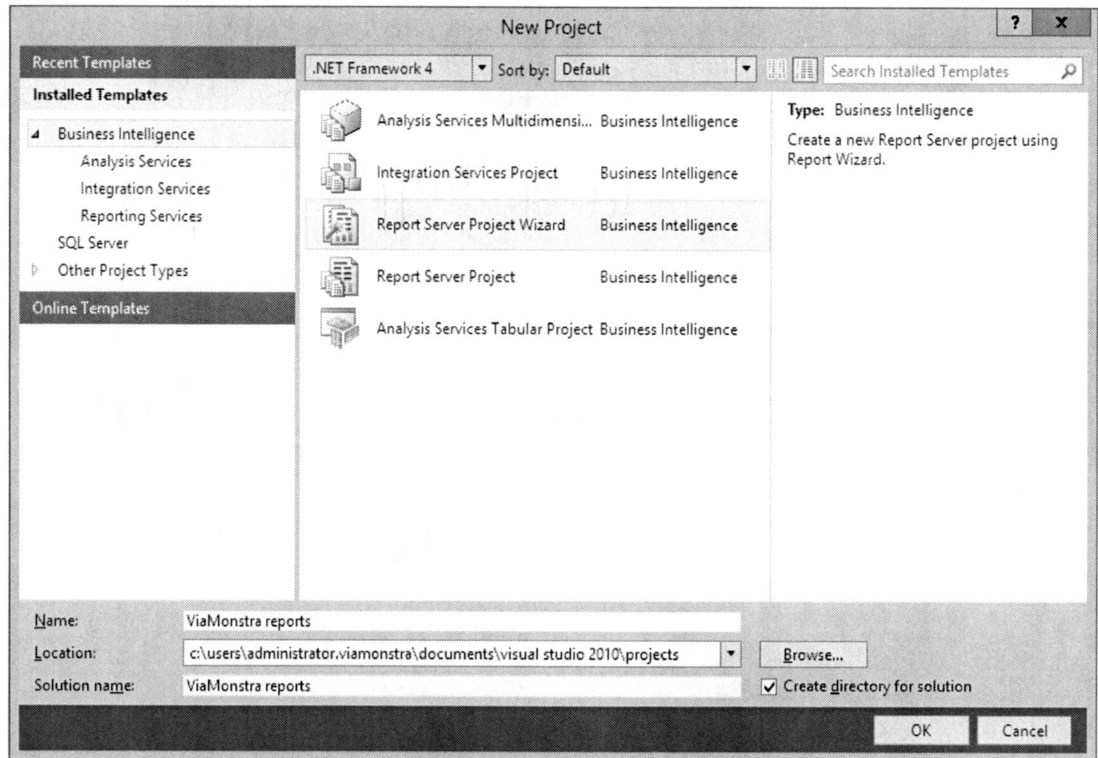

Creating a new project.

4. In the **Report Wizard**, click **Next**.
5. You need to add a data source to the project. A data source is the connection to the data along with the needed credentials.
    a. In **Name**, type **CM2012** and click **Edit**. Use the following settings:
        i. Server name: **CM01**
        ii. Database: Click the drop-down box and select **CM_PS1**.
        iii. Click **OK** to return to the Report Wizard.
    b. Select the **Make this a share data source** check box, and click **Next**.

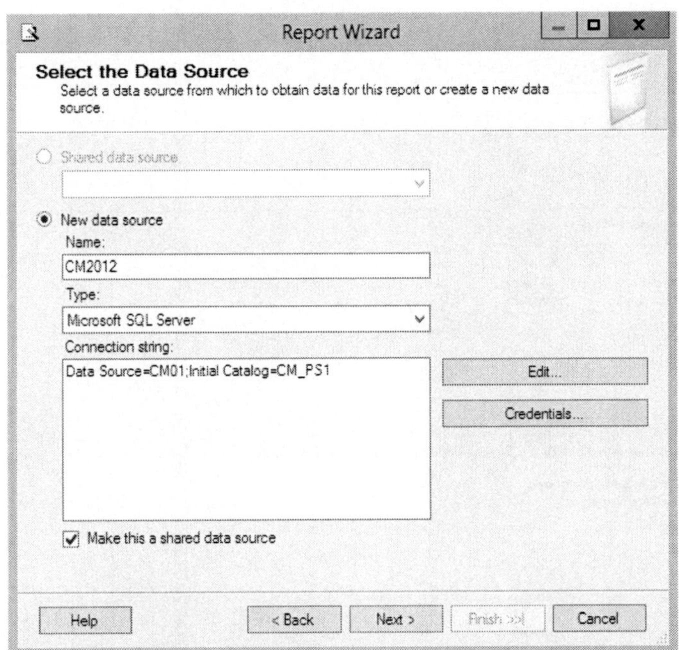

Creating a shared data source.

6. Click **Query Builder** to create the query.
7. In the **Query Designer**, click **Add Table** (the rightmost button on the ribbon) and select **Views**.
8. Select **v_GS_VIAMONSTRA** and **v_R_System** (pressing **Ctrl** to select multiple items), click **Add**, and then click **Close**.
9. From **v_R_System**, drag and drop **ResourceID** on to **ResourceID** in the **v_GS_VIAMONSTRA** view. This creates an Inner Join between the two views.
10. From **v_GS_VIAMONSTRA**, select **ComputerType()**, and from **V_R_System**, select **Netbios_Name()**.
11. On the ribbon, click **Use Group by**.
12. From **v_GS_VIAMONSTRA**, drag another instance of **ComputerType()** to the **Criteria** pane (the second pane from the top that looks like Excel ☺).
13. In **Alias**, type **Total** and then select **Count** in the **Group By** drop-down list.
14. On the ribbon, click **Run** (the exclamation button).

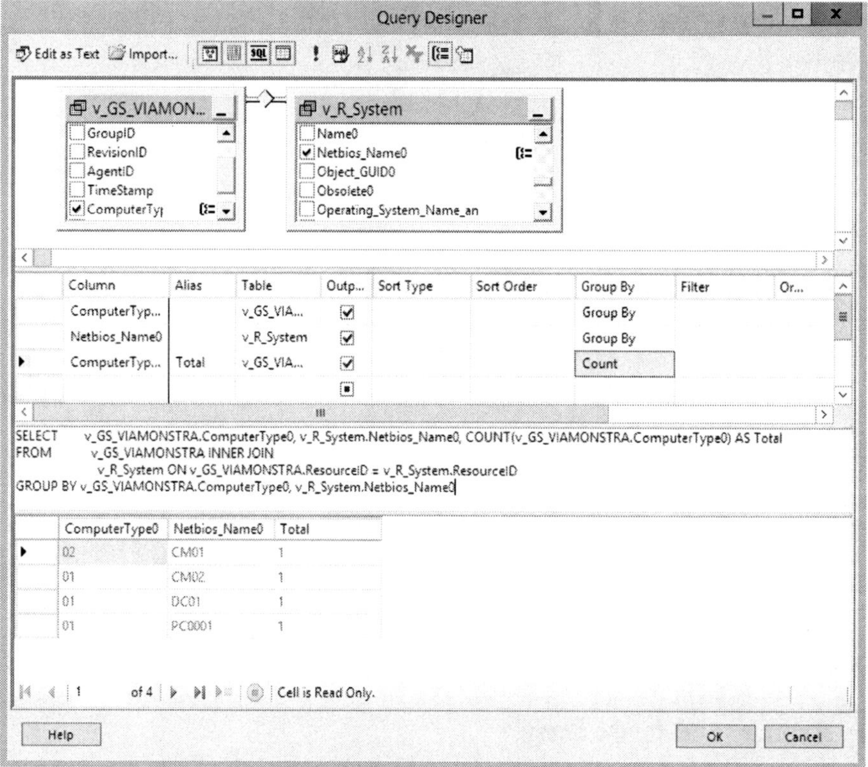

Creating a SQL statement in the Query Designer.

15. Click **OK** and return to the Report Wizard.
16. Click **Next**.
17. On the **Select the Report Type** page, ensure that **Tabular** is selected and click **Next**.

18. On the **Design the Table** page, move **ComputerType()** to **Group**, move **Netbios_Name()** and **Total()** to **Details**, and click **Next**.

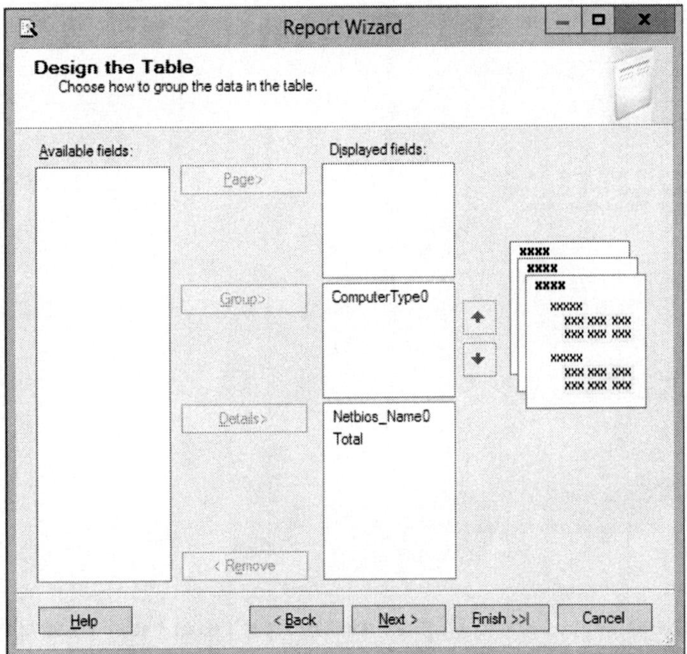

Designing the table.

19. On **Choose the Table Layout** page, use the following settings and click **Next**:
    a. Ensure that **Stepped** is selected.
    b. Select **Include subtotals.**
    c. Select **Enable drilldown.**
20. Select the **Slate** style and click **Next.**
21. On the **Choose the Deployment Location** page, type **ViaMonstra** in the **Deployment folder** text box and click **Next.**

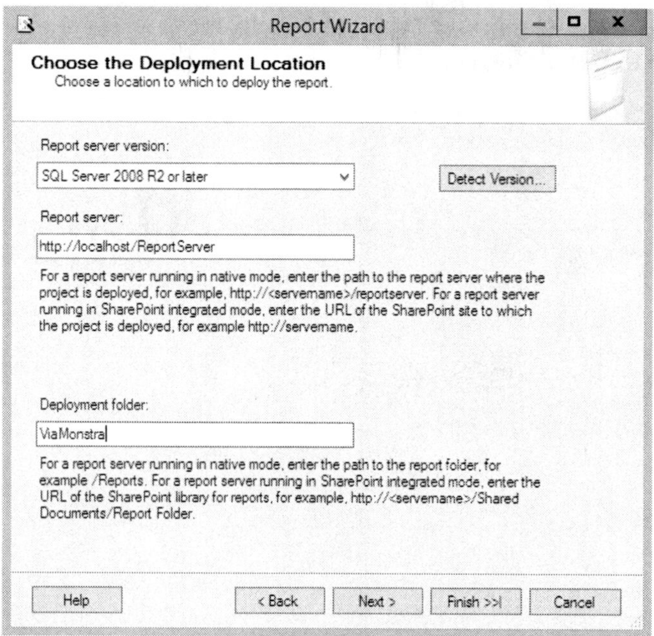

Specifying the report folder.

22. On the **Completing the Wizard** page, for the **Report name**, type **Total Fully Managed and Inventory Managed Clients** and then click **Finish.**
23. Click in the **Total Fully Managed and Inventory Managed Clients.rdl [Design]** pane (the middle pane). Then, from the **Report** menu, select **Add Page Header**.
24. Right-click the **Total Fully Managed and Inventory Managed Clients** title to display the handles.

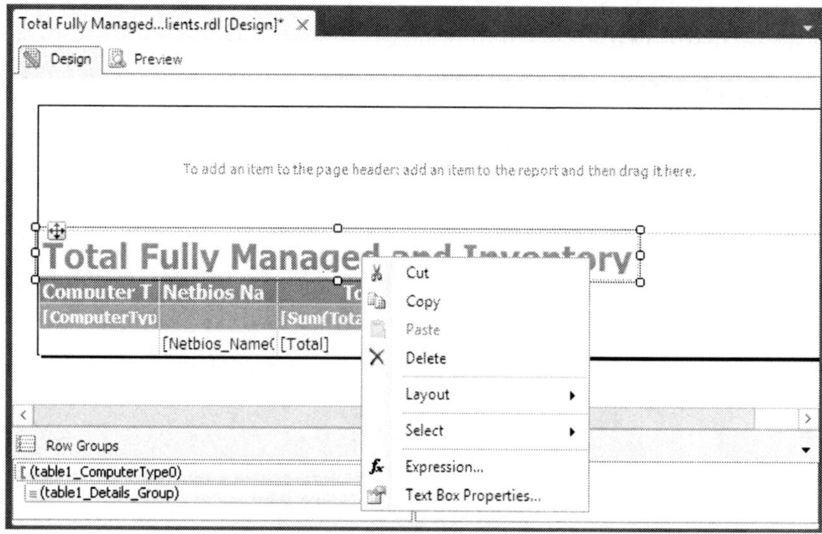

Right-click the title to display the handles.

25. Select the cross, and drag the report title to the page header. Then resize the title box so that you can see the full title within the box.

26. Right-click the page header, and select **Header Properties**. In the **Fill** node, select the **Silver** (grey) fill color, and click **OK**.

27. Right-click the grid below the header, click **Select / table1**, and resize the grid to the same width as the header.

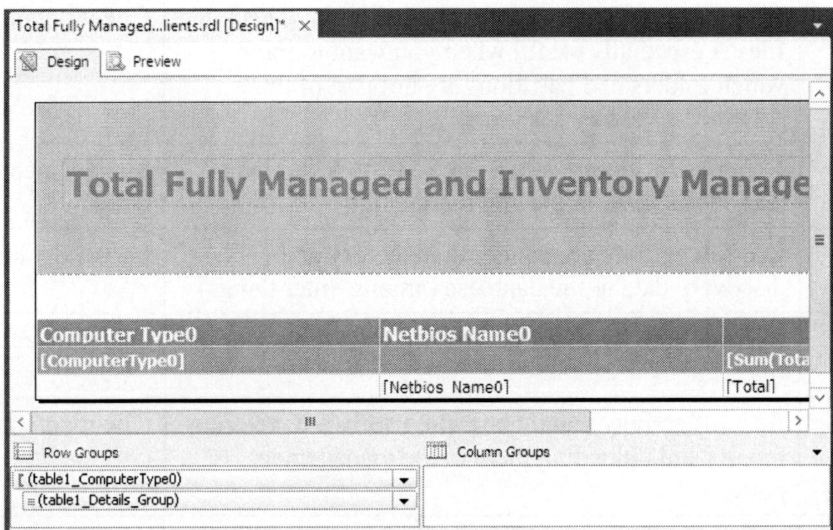

The customized report in the design view.

28. Right-click the **CM2012.rds** shared data source in the **Solution Explorer** and click **Deploy**.

29. Right-click the **Total Fully Managed and Inventory Managed Clients** shared report in the **Solution Explorer** and click **Deploy**.

30. Close **Visual Studio**, save the project, and open **Internet Explorer**. Go to **http://cm01/reports**. Notice the new **ViaMonstra** folder, which contains the newly deployed report.

Home > ViaMonstra > Total Fully Managed and Inventory Managed Clients

1 of 1 100% Find | Next

Total Fully Managed and Inventory Managed Clients

Computer Type0	Netbios Name0	Total
⊟ 01		3
	CM02	1
	DC01	1
	PC0001	1
⊞ 02		1

The custom report.

Useful Log Files

You can use the log files in the following table to track inventory and reporting activity.

Log File	Description	Location
InventoryAgent.log	Records activity about inventory and heartbeat discovery.	Server default
FileSystemfile.log	Records activity about software inventory. This log files is especially useful when you want to track which folders and partitions are not part of the software inventory scanning.	Client default
MP_hinv.log	Converts inventory data from XML to MIF clients and copies them to the site server.	Management point
Dataldr.log	Records activity about adding inventory and discovery data to the database (among other things).	Server default
mtrmgr.log	Records activity about processing software metering rules.	Client default
SWMTRReportGen.log	Records activity about generating software metering reports and uploading them to the management point.	Client default
Srsrp.log	Records activity involving report copies, logos, styles, and applying security.	Server default

Chapter 7

Application Deployment

Like many other companies, ViaMonstra needs to deliver applications to end users. In this chapter, you learn about applications and packages, as well as the deployment process and how to uninstall applications. Working with applications is not just about creating an application and a deployment. You need to have a strategy for how the applications should be made available for the users. Some applications are suitable for device targeting while others are for user targeting. ViaMonstra is very user centric and has a requirement to publish applications to users in a web portal and let them decide when the applications should be installed. Being user centric lowers the burden on your helpdesk due to fewer end-user calls and also assists ViaMonstra in becoming a more agile company.

Content Management Objects

Before going into detail about how you create and deploy applications, I want to take a moment to define processes, describe packages and applications, and ensure the content deployment infrastructure is configured correctly. A distribution point is the site system role where all content—packages, applications, software updates, drivers, and images—are stored and downloaded by the client. Two types of distribution points can be created, *on-premise* or *cloud-based.*

On-Premise Distribution Points

You can install an on-premise distribution point on a server operating system or a client operating system. ViaMonstra has decided to install all distribution points on Windows Server 2012. That provides full support for local PXE services, which is a business requirement. A client OS like Windows 8 does not have support for PXE. Additionally, a client OS cannot service all other content. On-premise distribution points come in two flavors, a *standard distribution point* and a *pull-distribution point.*

The pull-distribution point is a new feature in Service Pack 1 and only differs from a standard distribution point in the way content is distributed. By default the site server controls all content distribution, which can be a very CPU-intensive process when you have many distribution points in a single site. The content distribution process can be throttled and scheduled to mitigate ConfigMgr from flooding the network. A pull-distribution point is not in the same way controlled by the site server, and traffic to the pull distribution point does not honor the bandwidth control or the scheduling. Instead, the site server sends a message to the pull-distribution point informing it that content is available and can be downloaded from one of the pull-distribution point partners. A use case for pull-distribution points is a remote location with three local distribution points. Instead of having the site server process content to all three, you can configure two pull-distribution points and one standard distribution point. That way you will have bandwidth control and scheduling when traffic is distributed to the standard distribution point, and the two pull-distribution points will pull content unthrottled from the standard distribution point.

Creating a New On-Premise Distribution Point

In all remote locations except Liverpool, you will install a local distribution point. The distribution points will be configured to support local clients. This guide assumes that you deployed CM02 per Appendix A and configured your network to allow traffic between the 192.168.1.0/24 and 192.168.2.0/24 subnets.

1. On **CM02** log on as **VIAMONSTRA\Administrator**. From the **Server Manager** dashboard, click **Tools** and open **Computer Management**.
2. Expand **Local Users and Groups** and then **Groups**; right-click the **Administrators** group and select **Add to Group**.
3. Click **Add**, select **Object Types**, **Computers**, and then click **OK**.
4. Type **CM01** and click **OK** twice to add the primary site server computer account to the local Administrators group.
5. On **CM01**, the primary site server, log on as **VIAMONSTRA\Administrator** and verify that you can access **CM02\Admin$**.
6. Using the **ConfigMgr console**, navigate to the **Administration** workspace and select **Site Configuration / Servers and Site System Roles**.
7. On the ribbon's **Home** tab, click **Create Site System Server**.
8. Click **Browse**, type **CM02**, and click **OK**.
9. In **Site code**, select **PS1 - ViaMonstra HQ** and click **Next**.
10. On the **Proxy** page, click **Next**.
11. On the **System Role Selection** page, select **Distribution point** and click **Next**.

12. On the **Distribution point** page, enable **Install and configure IIS if required by Configuration Manager** and click **Next**.

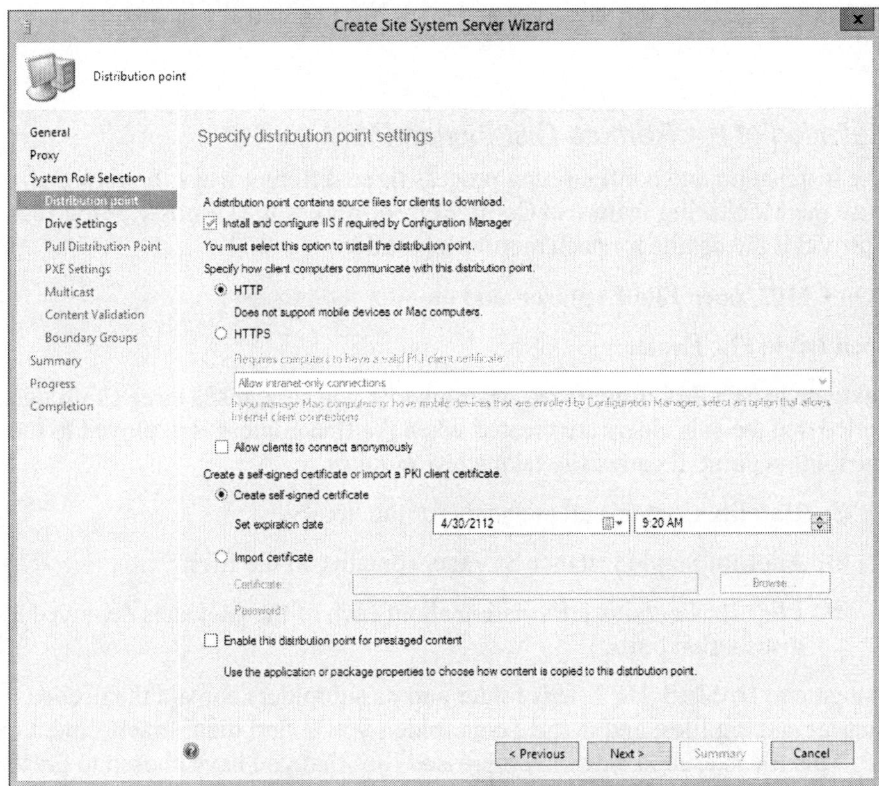

Creating a remote distribution point.

13. On the **Drive Settings** page, configure these settings and click **Next**:
    a. Drive space reserve (MB): **1024**
    b. Primary content library location: **D:**
    c. Secondary content library location: **Automatic**
    d. Primary package share location: **D:**
    e. Secondary package share location: **Automatic**
14. On the **Pull Distribution Point** page, accept the default settings and click **Next**.
15. On the **PXE Settings** page, accept the default settings and click **Next**.
16. On the **Multicast** page, accept the default settings and click **Next**.
17. On the **Content Validation** page, enable **Validate content on a schedule**. Click **Schedule**. Select **Custom interval** and configure a daily schedule starting at 04:00 AM. Click **OK** to close the **Custom Schedule** dialog box and click **Next**.

18. On the **Boundary Groups** page, clear the **Allow fallback source location for content** check box, and click **Next**.
19. On the **Summary** page, read the summary and click **Next** to start the installation.
20. Click **Close**.

Monitor the Installation of the Remote Distribution Point

You can monitor the installation and configuration process three different ways: Review the folders on CM02, use the Monitoring feature in ConfigMgr, or review the ConfigMgr log files. The following list provides the details for each monitoring option:

- Option 1: On **CM02**, open **File Explorer**, and monitor the process:
    a. Open **D:** in File Explorer.
    b. Navigate to **SCCMContentLib**. After a while you should see three subfolders. Notice that the subfolders are created when the first content is deployed to the distribution point. It can easily take a few minutes.
        - **Datalib.** Contains all metadata for the library.
        - **FileLib.** Single Instance Storage, contains all the files.
        - **PkgLib.** Contains information about each of the packages deployed to the distribution point.
    c. Navigate to **D:\SMS_DP$**. This folder and its subfolders contain the needed binaries and log files; and in the Tools folder, you'll find the ExtractContent.exe file. This file is used to extract compressed files that you have chosen to prestage on the remote distribution point.
    d. From the **Server Manager** dashboard, select **Tools** and open **Task Scheduler**. Click **Task Scheduler Library**, **Microsoft**, **Configuration Manager**. Select **Content validation** and the **Actions** tab. Notice the program **D:\sms_dp$\sms\bin\smsdpmon.exe**. This is the scheduled content validation task that you enabled in the wizard. Again, it can take a few minutes before the scheduled task is created.

    In the **Server Manager**, notice that the IIS role is installed.
- Option 2: On **CM01**, open the **ConfigMgr console**, and navigate to the **Monitoring** workspace:
    a. Select **Distribution Status, Distribution Point Configuration Status**.
    b. Select **CM02** and click the **Details** tab. It will take some minutes until all the steps are finalized and configured correctly.

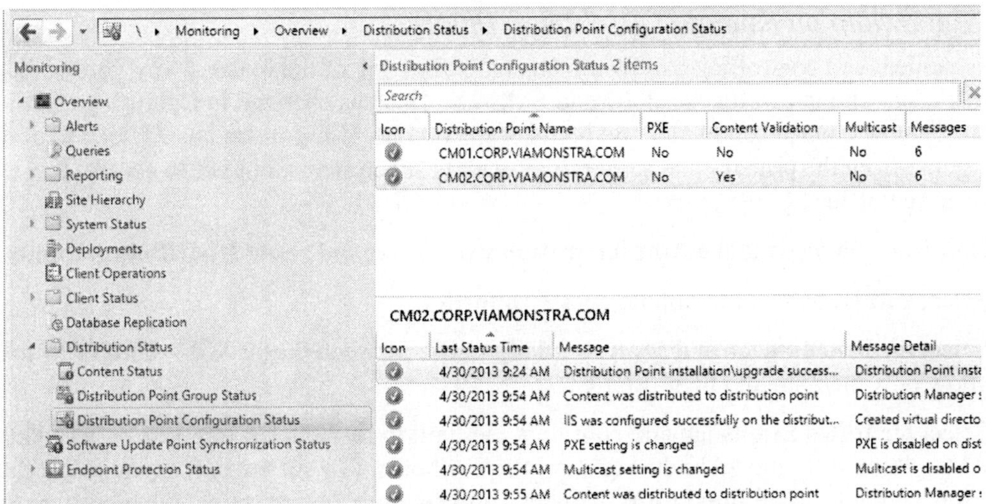

Monitoring the remote distribution point.

> **Real World Note:** You might see a few errors in the Distribution Point Configuration Status. Don't worry, that's very normal. They will disappear when you distribute content. To force the process, navigate to the Software Library workspace, select Application Management, Packages. Open the properties for the Configuration Manager Client Package, select the Content Locations tab and redistribute the package on the new distribution point.

- Option 3: The third way to monitor the process is by reading the **distrmgr.log** file on the site server. Among other things, the log file gives you information about how IIS was installed on the remote server.

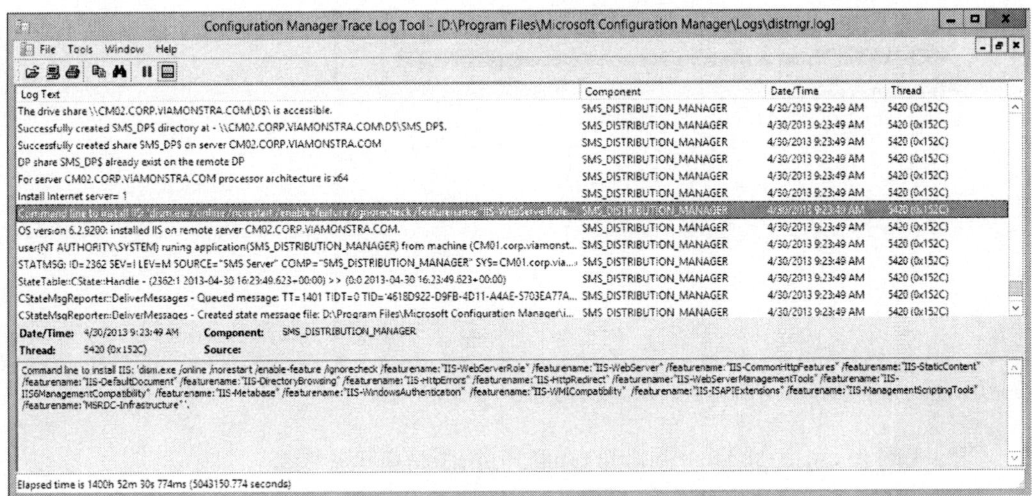

Monitoring the remote distribution point in the distmgr.log file.

Control Bandwidth on Remote Distribution Points

Prestaging content and controlling bandwidth has long been one of the reasons why you would select a secondary site in ConfigMgr 2007 and SMS 2X. This has changed in ConfigMgr 2012 where you can now control bandwidth and hours of operations. ViaMonstra has decided to control all traffic going from the primary site server to all remote site systems, but not to control the upward floating traffic.

1. On CM01, navigate to the **Administration** workspace, and select **Distribution Points**.
2. Select **CM02**, and on the ribbon, click **Properties**.
3. Select the **Schedule** tab and configure daily traffic between **06:00 AM – 08:00 PM** to allow only medium and high priority.
4. Select the **Rates Limits** tab and configure the limit to be **50%** for business hours (06:00 AM – 08:00 PM) and **75%** during non-business hours. (To set the limits, you select the **Limited to specified maximum transfer rates by hour** option, select the blocks on the timeline you want to modify, and then type the percentage number in the **Limit available bandwidth (%)** field.). Then click **OK**.

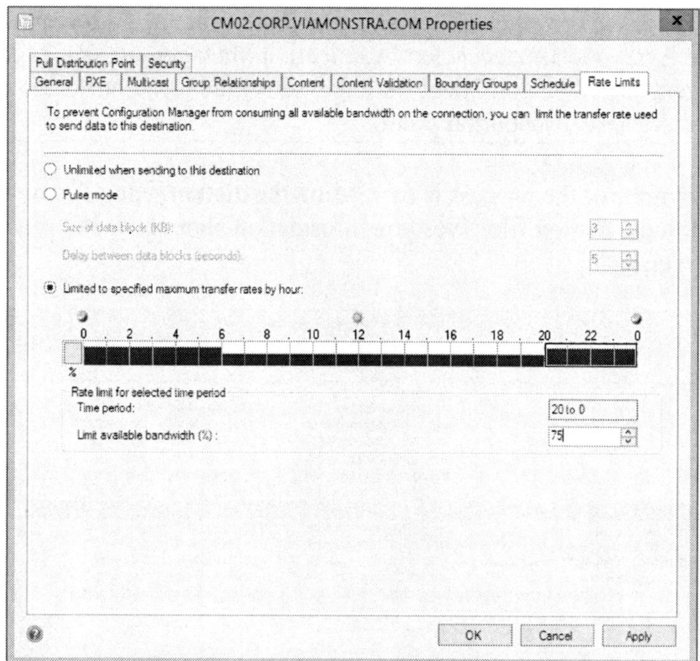

Controlling bandwidth on a remote distribution point.

5. Click **OK** to close the Distribution point Properties dialog box.

Cloud-Based Distribution Point

Any client that is intranet- or Internet-managed can utilize a cloud-based distribution point to download content, though a Windows Azure subscription is required for using cloud-based distribution points. You can use the Client Settings to configure which clients you will allow to fall back to a cloud-based distribution. For ViaMonstra, you will create a POC and test the benefits you can achieve by adding a cloud-based distribution point. The goal for the POC is to determine whether these requirements are fulfilled:

> **Note:** Creating a cloud-based distribution point is an optional configuration and is not needed for the other guides in this book.

- The cloud-based distribution point can be used as a fallback solution.
- Clients fall back to the cloud-based distribution point only when the requested content is not available on the local distribution point or a remote distribution point.
- The solution must not require any modifications to the client communication mode, like requiring a certificate to be installed.
- ViaMonstra must be able to add additional resources when needed, e.g. when opening a new remote office without any local servers.
- ViaMonstra must know the cost of the solution

> **Note:** You need to acquire your own Windows Azure account to use cloud-based distribution points. You can set up a temporary trial account to use for the examples in this book. Note that Microsoft's subscription policy is subject to change, so please make sure you understand the terms of a trial account and any potential costs (http://www.windowsazure.com).

Create a Cloud-Based Distribution Point

A cloud-based distribution point has requirements both internal and external to ConfigMgr. Knowing the high-level steps is good before starting:

1. Create a management certificate and install the certificate on the site server. The certificate only needs to be installed on the site server and will be used to ensure the trust relationship between the site server and Windows Azure.
2. Create a cloud-based distribution point service certificate, and install the certificate on the site server. The certificate is being used to encrypt data and to authenticate the cloud-based distribution point service to the clients. Create a Windows Azure trial account and import the management certificate in Windows Azure.
3. Install a cloud-based distribution point in ConfigMgr.
4. Configure the Client Settings to allow the ConfigMgr client to use the distribution point.
5. Configure a host record in DNS with the IP address of the cloud-based distribution point in order for clients to download content from the distribution point.

> **Note:** Before proceeding with following sections, make sure you have created the required certificates as described in Appendix J.

Create a Windows Azure Trial Account and Import the Certificate

1. Log on to **http://www.windowsazure.com** and create a trial account.
2. Log on to **Windows Azure** with your newly created account.
3. Select **Select Settings.**

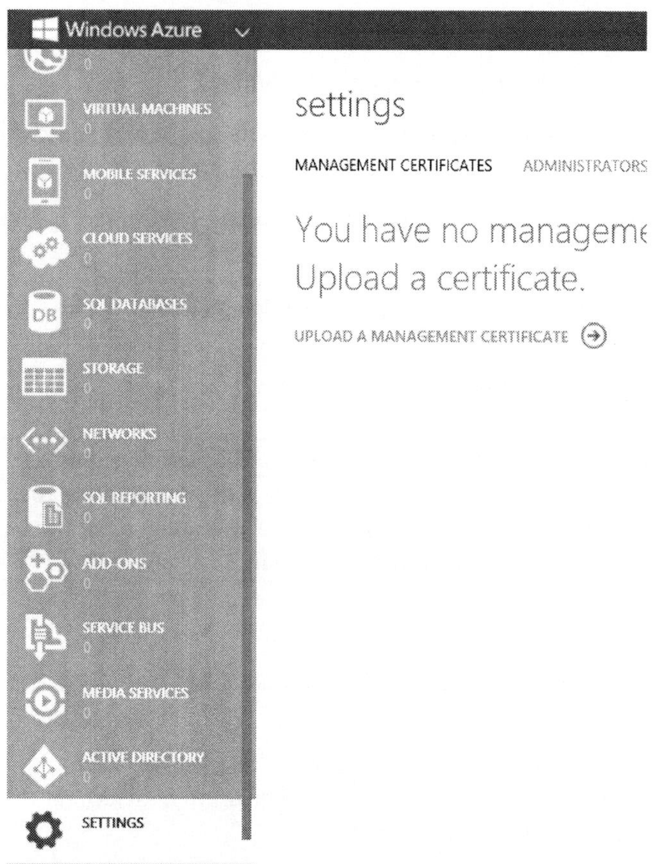

Uploading a management certificate to Windows Azure.

4. Click **Upload a Management Certificate**. Select the **D:\setup\Certificates\clouddp01.cer** certificate.

Create the Cloud-Based Distribution Point

1. Open the **ConfigMgr console**, select **Administration Workspace / Hierarchy Configuration / Cloud.**

2. On the ribbon, click **Create Cloud Distribution Point**.
3. On the **General** page, type the subscription ID from your Azure account. In **Management Certificate**, click **Browse**, select the **D:\Setup\Certificates\clouddp01.pfx** certificate, and click **Next.**
4. On the **Settings** page, select **East US** in **Region,** click **Browse,** and import the **D:\Setup\Certificates\clouddp01SRV.pfx** certificate.Read the Service Certificate warning information, click **OK,** and click **Next**.
5. On the **Alerts** page, keep the recommended storage and transfer alert settings and click **Next**. Configure the expected storage quota and monthly transfer rate, and then finish the wizard.

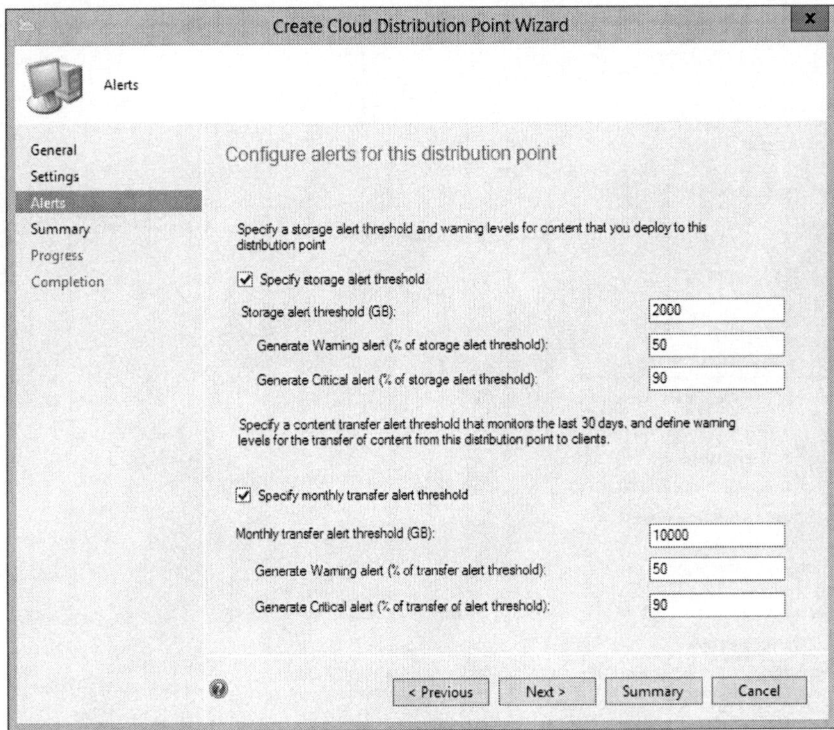

Specifying the estimated monthly usage and storage.

6. Read the **Summary** page and click **Next** to start the configuration.Then, on the **Completion** page, click **Close**.

> **Note:** In the background the CloudDP manager component will connect to Windows Azure and start creating the service. This process can easily take as many as 30–45 minutes. You can monitor the process by reading the clouddpmgr.log file on the site server or by reading the status in the ConfigMgr console. It will change to *Ready* when the process is finished. In this example, we used the same certificate for Windows Azure and the distribution point. It is a best practice to have two different certificates in real-world situations.

Configure DNS

In order for the clients to download content from a cloud-based distribution point, they must be able to resolve clouddp01.corp.viamonstra.com to the cloud-based distribution point IP address. This is done by creating a CNAME record in DNS with the FQDN of the Windows Azure service. Information about the Windows Azure service name can be found in the **Site URL** in Windows Azure.

1. Log on to **Windows Azure**, select **Cloud Services** from the left pane.
2. From the list of cloud services, click the link in front of the service name. This will open the cloud service dashboard. You can find the site URL information on the right-hand side of the dashboard. The site URL name is automatically created when you create the cloud-based distribution point. Copy the **GUID.cloudapp.net**.

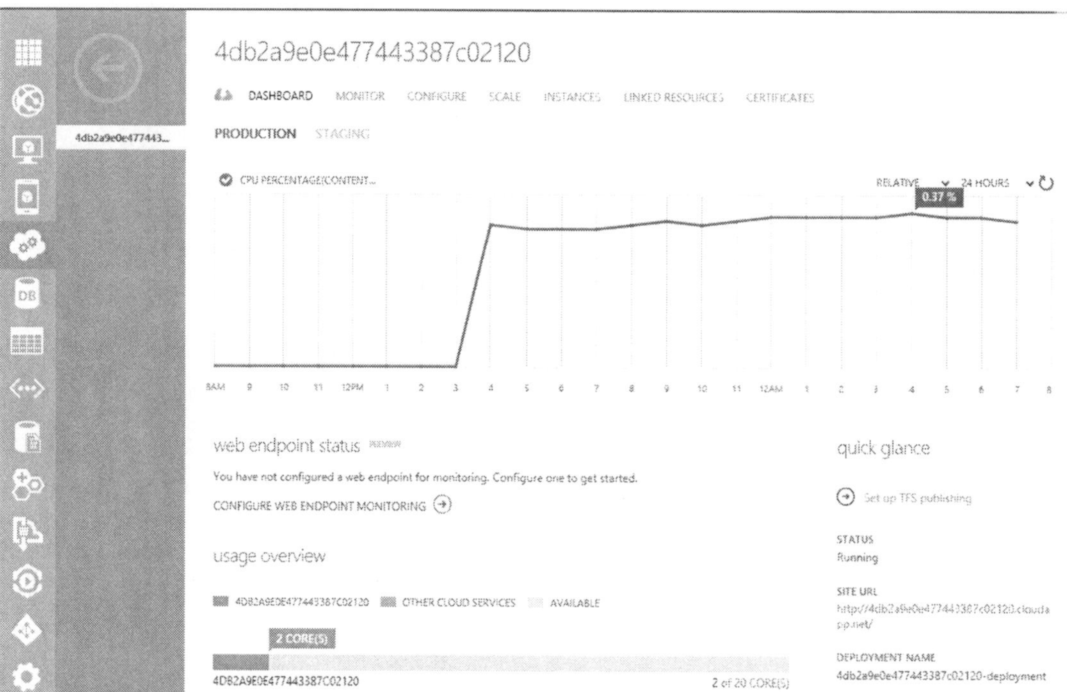

Finding the Windows Azure site URL.

3. On **DC01**, open the **DNS console**.
4. Expand **DC01** and then **Forward Lookup Zones**; right-click **corp.viamonstra.com** and select **New Alias (CNAME).**
5. For **Alias name**, type **clouddp01.**

6. **In Fully qualified domain name (FQDN) for target host** paste the GUID.cloudapp.net information from Windows Azure and click **OK**.

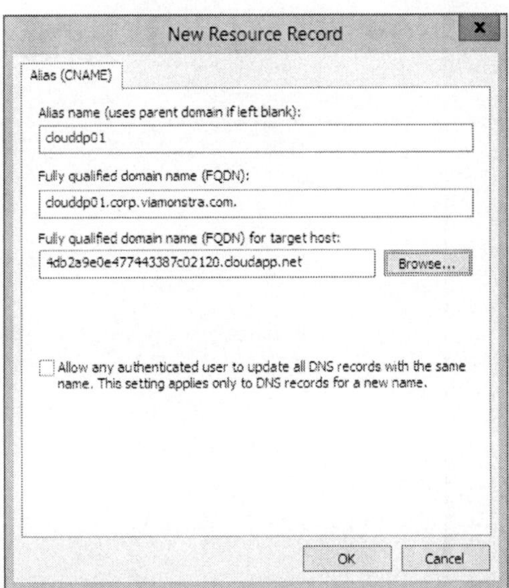

Creating the Windows Azure CNAME record.

Distribution Point Groups

A distribution point group allows you to manage the same content on multiple on-premise and cloud-based distribution points. When you distribute content to a group, all members of that group automatically receive the content. If you add a distribution point to an existing group, that distribution point automatically receives the same content as the rest of the group members. A distribution point can be a member of multiple groups.

1. On **CM01**, log on as **VIAMONSTRA\Administrator** and open the **ConfigMgr console**.
2. Navigate to the **Administration** workspace and select **Distribution Point Groups**.
3. On the ribbon, click **Create Group**.
4. In **Name**, type **All Content**.
5. Select the **Members** tab, click **Add**, select **CM01** and **CM02**, and click **OK**.

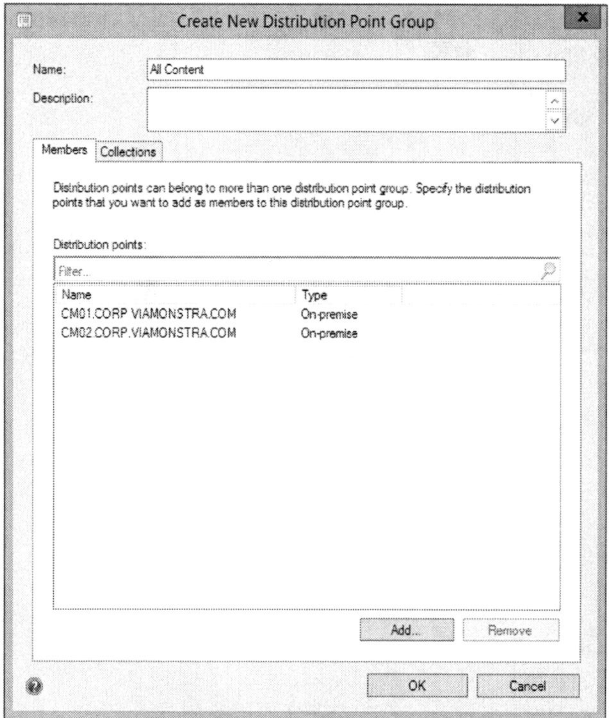

Creating the distribution point group.

6. Click **OK**.

Real World Note: You should always create a distribution point group even if you have a small environment with just a single distribution point. Chances are that you will add a new distribution point in the future. With a distribution point group, it will be easy for you to add the same content to the new distribution point.

Content Boundary Groups

Boundary groups control assignment and content location. In ViaMonstra, the strategy is to allow all clients to fall back to the HQ for content location, but they should always use any local distribution point first. With this strategy, you have to create a unique content lookup boundary group for each remote distribution point.

Create Content Location Boundary Groups

1. On **CM01** , open the **ConfigMgr console**.
2. Navigate to the **Administration** workspace, and select **Hierarchy Configuration**, **Boundary Groups**.
3. On the ribbon, click **Create Boundary Group**; type **CL HQ** as the name; and in the **Boundaries** area, click **Add**.

4. Select the IP range **192.168.1.1 - 192.168.1.254** and click **OK**.
5. Select the **References** tab. In the **Content location** area, click **Add** and select **CM01**.
6. Click **OK**.
7. On the ribbon, click **Create Boundary Group**, type **CL Stockholm** as the name, and click **Add**.
8. Select the IP range **192.168.2.1 - 192.168.2.254** and click **OK**.
9. Select the **References** tab. In **Content location**, click **Add** and select **CM02**.
10. Click **OK**.

Packages

If you are familiar with previous versions of the ConfigMgr, you most likely already have knowledge about packages. Although packages haven't changed in recent versions of ConfigMgr, there are nevertheless still many scenarios where you can benefit from creating a package instead of an application.

When to Use a Package

I often use packages for trivial tasks like running a maintenance script, copying files or other tasks that are machine based. Later in this book, you will learn how to create a package to copy the needed System Center Updates Publisher certificates to all computers. In previous versions of ConfigMgr, it also was very common to create packages to modify registry keys. That is still possible although you might find it easier to solve those challenges using the new Settings Manager feature. Other very useful examples of packages are the packages created using the MDT 2012 task sequence (toolkit, settings, and USMT packages).

Default Packages

By default, ConfigMgr ships with three packages. Two of the packages are found in the Software Library under Application Management / Packages: the Configuration Manager Client package and a User State Migration Tool for Windows 8. The third package is a Configuration Manager Client Upgrade package. That package is not exposed in the Software Library. Navigate to the Monitoring workspace and to Distribution Status / Content Status, and you will be able to see both ConfigMgr client packages. The Configuration Manager Client Upgrade package is used to keep clients up-to-date on the latest version.

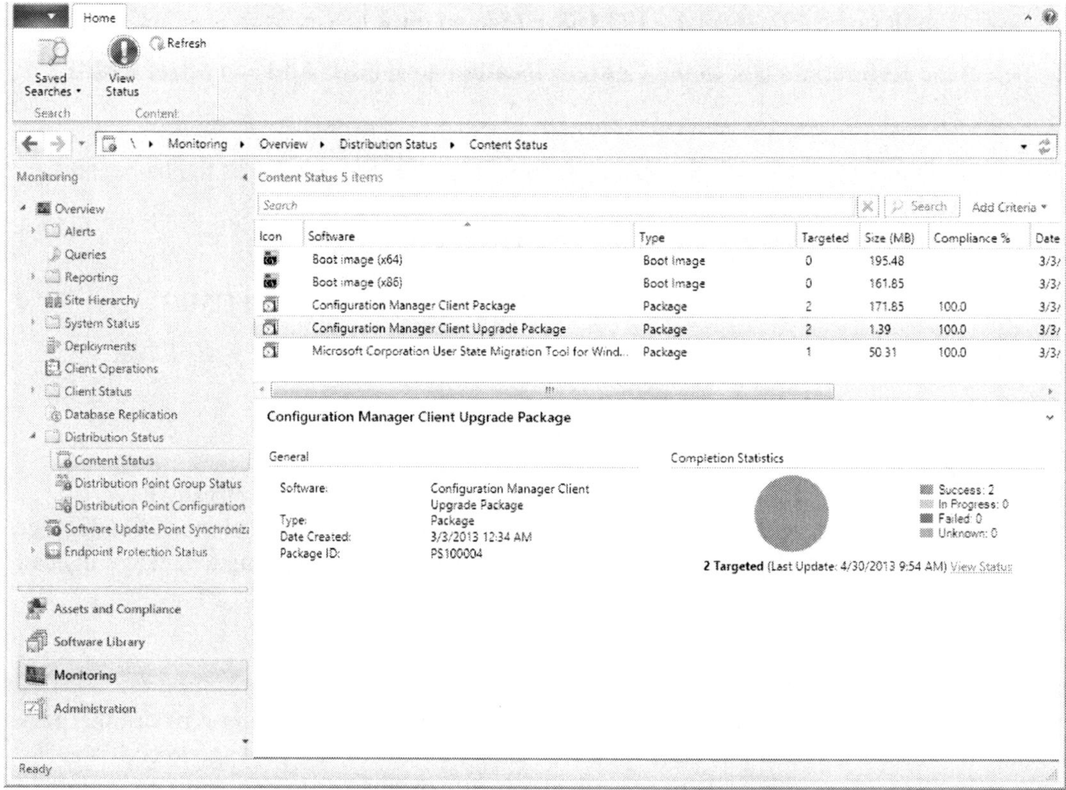

The ConfigMgr client packages.

Automate the ConfigMgr Client Upgrade Process

The built-in client upgrade package will upgrade the ConfigMgr client to the latest service pack. It cannot be used, however, to upgrade the client to the latest available cumulative update.

1. On CM01, open the **ConfigMgr console** and navigate to the **Administration** workspace.
2. Select **Site Configuration / Sites**, and then on the ribbon, click **Hierarchy Settings**.
3. Select the **Automatic Client Upgrade** tab.

4. Select **Upgrade client automatically when new updates are available** and click **OK**.

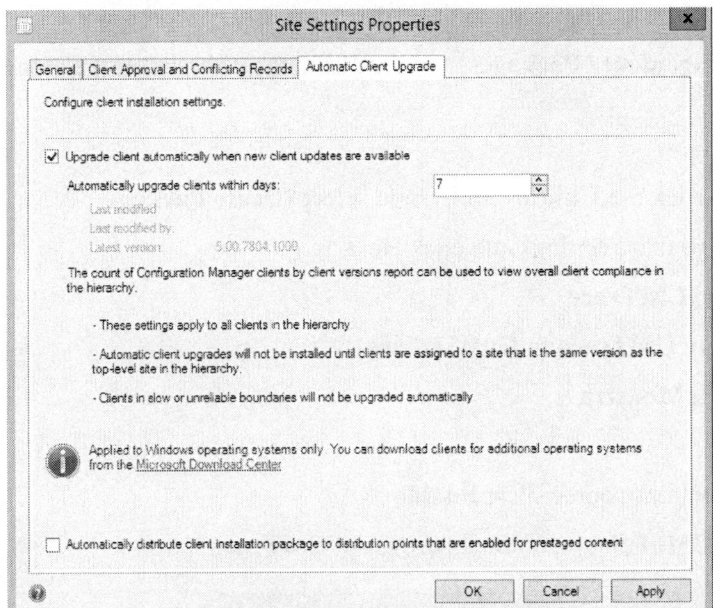

Configuring the automatic client upgrade.

5. Click **OK** to close the **Site Settings Properties** dialog box.

Creating and Deploying Packages

The first package that you create is a PowerShell command that copies CMtrace.exe to %windir%\system32 on all clients. After that, you create a package that configures the business hour setting.

In order to create the packages, you need to place CMtrace.exe and the script in the same folder and use the folder as the source location for the software package. For these steps I assume you have downloaded the book sample files to D:\Setup on CM01.

Create the Package Source

1. On **CM01**, open **File Explorer**, and create the folder **CopyCMTrace** in **D:\Sources\Software**.
2. Copy **CMtrace.exe** from **D:\Setup\CM2012 \SMSSetup\Tools** to **D:\Sources\Software\CopyCMTrace**.
3. Create the folder **BusinessHours** in **D:\Sources\Software**.
4. Copy **Get-CMClientBusinessHours.ps1** and **Set-CMClientBusinessHours.ps1** from **D:\Setup\Scripts** to **D:\Sources\Software\BusinessHours**.

Create the Copy CMTrace Package

1. Open the **ConfigMgr console** and navigate to the **Software Library** workspace.
2. Select **Application Management / Packages**, and then from the ribbon, select **Folder / Create Folder**.
3. Name the folder **Utilities**.
4. Expand **Packages**, right-click the **Utilities** folder, and select **Create Package**.
5. On the **Package** page, type these settings and click **Next**:
    a. Name: **VM_CopyCMTrace**
    b. Description: **Copy CMTrace to C:\Windows**
    c. Manufacturer: **ViaMonstra**
    d. Version: **1.0**
    e. This packages contains source files: **Enable**
    f. Source folder: **\\CM01\Sources$\Software\CopyCMTrace**

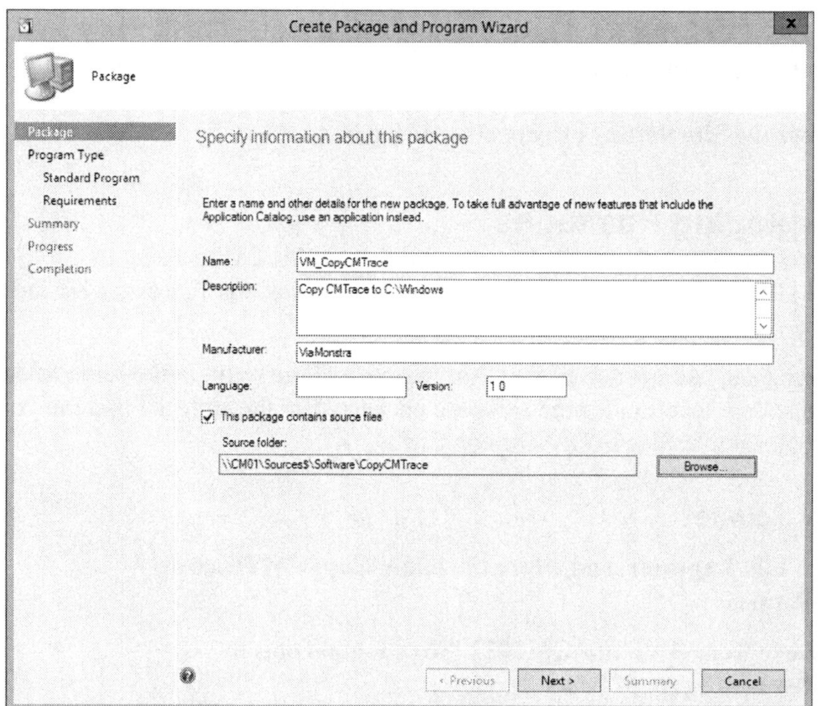

Creating a package.

6. On the **Program Type** page, ensure **Standard program** is selected and click **Next**.

7. On the **Standard Program** page, type these settings and click **Next**:
    a. Name: **CMTrace_Install**
    b. Command line: **powershell.exe -ExecutionPolicy Bypass -Command Copy-Item CMTrace.exe -Destination C:\Windows**
    c. Program can run: **Whether or not a user is logged on**
8. On the **Requirements** page, leave the default settings and click **Next**.
9. On the **Summary** page, read the summary and click **Next** to start the package creation.
10. After the package is created, click **Close** to finish.

Distribute the Package to the Distribution Point Group

1. Select the **VM_CopyCMTrace** package, and on the ribbon's **Home** tab, click **Distribute Content**.
2. On the **General** page, click **Next**.
3. On the **Content Destination** page, click **Add / Distribution Point Group**.
4. Select the **All Content** distribution point group, and click **OK** and **Next**.
5. On the **Summary** page, read the summary and click **Next** to start the content distribution.
6. Close the wizard.

Deploy the Package

Unlike many other applications, this package is deployed as a required package to all computers with a ConfigMgr agent installed. Usually a software deployment requires you to create a custom collection, but this time you use the default **All Desktop and Server Clients** collection.

1. Select the **VM_CopyCMTrace** package, and on the ribbon, click **Deploy**.
2. On the **General** page, click **Browse**, select **All Desktop and Server Clients** collection, and click **Next**. Note that this collection may also contain UNIX and Apple clients. This package will fail on those clients.
3. On the **Content** page, verify that the content is distributed to all on-premise distribution points and click **Next**.
4. On the **Deployment Settings** page, verify that **Purpose** is **Required** and click **Next**.
5. On the **Scheduling** page, click **New** and click **Assign immediately after this event**. Verify that **As soon as possible** is selected for the event, and click **OK** and **Next**.

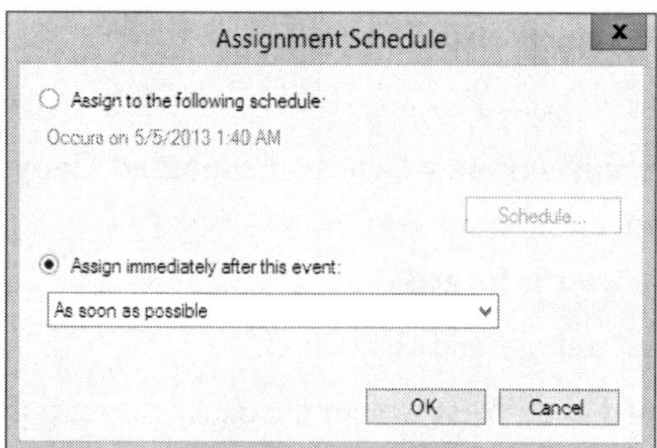

Configuring a deployment to run as soon as possible.

6. On the **User Experience** page, accept the default settings and click **Next**.
7. On the **Distribution Points** page, accept the default settings and click **Next**.
8. On the **Summary** page, read the summary and click **Next** to start the deployment.
9. Close the wizard when the deployment is complete.
10. Navigate to the **Assets and Compliance** workspace and select **Device Collections**.
11. Right-click the **All Desktop and Server Clients** collection, and then select **Client Notification / Download Computer Policy**. Click **OK** in the information dialog box. This action forces all running clients to initiate a machine policy retrieval from the management point. The policy will contain information about the deployment.

Automate Creating Packages Using PowerShell

The section shows an example of how to create a package and a program, and then how to distribute the content to a distribution point group using the built-in cmdlet in Service Pack 1.

1. From the **ConfigMgr console**, launch **PowerShell**.
2. To create the package, type the following command:

```
New-CMPackage -Name "PSH_Copy CMTrace" -Description
"Copy CMtrace to C:\Windows" -Manufacturer "ViaMonstra"
-Version 1.0 -Path "\\cm01\sources$\Software\CopyCMTrace"
```

3. To create the program, type the following command:

```
New-CMProgram -PackageName "PSH_Copy CMTrace"
-StandardProgramName "Copy CMTrace" -RunType Normal
-ProgramRunType WhetherOrNotUserIsLoggedOn -RunMode
RunWithAdministrativeRights -CommandLine "powershell.exe
-ExecutionPolicy bypass -command copy-item CMTrace.exe
-destination C:\Windows"
```

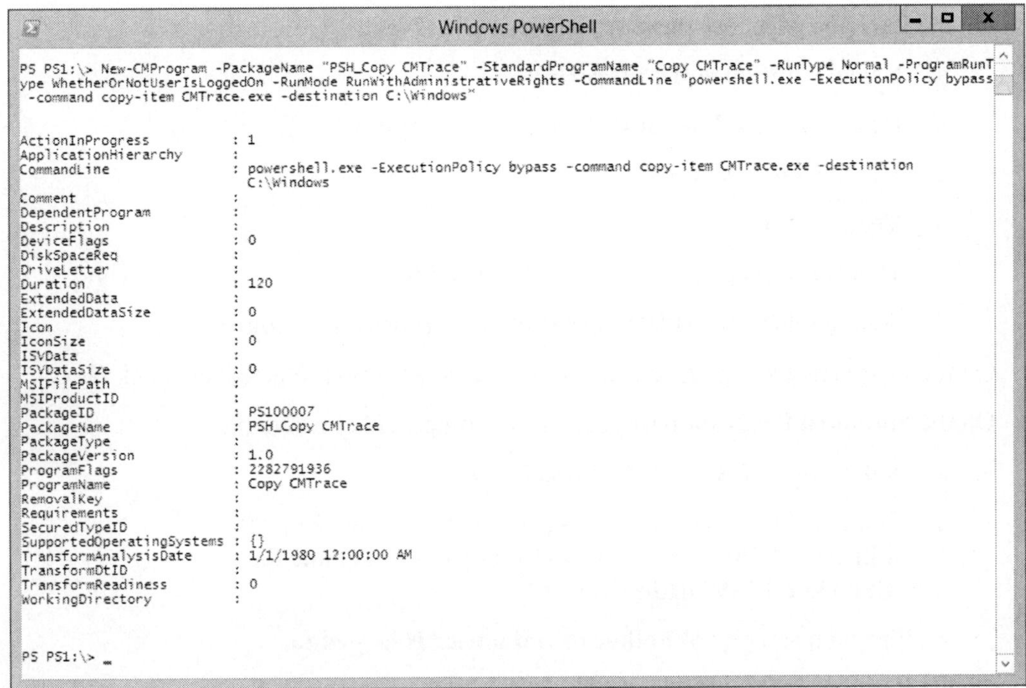

Creating a program using the built-in PowerShell cmdlet.

4. Make a note of the **PackageID**; in this example, it is PS100007.
5. To distribute the content, type the following command:

```
Start-CMContentDistribution -PackageId PS100007
-DistributionPointGroupName "All content"
```

   In this example, PackageId is the unique package identifier.

6. To create the deployment, type the following command:

```
start-CMPackageDeployment -PackageName "PSH_Copy CMTrace"
-StandardProgramName "Copy CMTrace" -CollectionName
"All Desktop and Server Clients" -ScheduleEvent
AsSoonAsPossible -RerunBehavior RerunIfFailedPreviousAttempt
-FastNetworkOption
DownloadContentFromDistributionPointAndRunLocally
-SlowNetworkOption
DownloadContentFromDistributionPointAndLocally
```

Create the Configure Business Hours Package

1. In the **Software Library** workspace, select **Application Management / Packages**.
2. Right-click the **Utilities** folder and select **Create Package**.

3. On the **Package** page, use these settings and click **Next**:
   a. Name: **Configure Business Hours**
   b. Description: **Define local client business hours**
   c. Manufacturer: **ViaMonstra**
   d. Version: **1.0**
   e. This packages contains source files**: Enable**
   f. Source folder: **\\CM01\Sources$\Software\BusinessHours**
4. On the **Program Type** page, ensure **Standard program** is selected and click **Next**.
5. On the **Standard Program** page, use these settings and click **Next**:
   a. Name: **Default Client Business Hours**
   b. Command line: **powershell.exe -ExecutionPolicy Bypass -File .\Set-CMClientBusinessHours.ps1 -StartTime 08 -EndTime 17 -WorkingDays 62**
   c. Program can run: **Whether or not a user is logged on**
6. On the **Requirements** page, leave the default settings and click **Next**.
7. On the **Summary** page, read the summary and click **Next** to start the package creation.
8. After the package is created, click **Close** to finish.

Note: The values used to calculate the weekdays in the PowerShell script are:

1 Sunday, 2 Monday, 4 Tuesday, 8 Wednesday, 16 Thursday, 32 Friday, 64 Saturday

If you want to configure business hours for Friday only, you should specify -WorkingDays 32. If you want to specify Friday and Monday, it is 32 + 2 like this: -WorkingDays 34.

Distribute the Business Hours Package to the Distribution Point Group

The following steps deploy the content to either the cloud-based distribution point or to the All Content distribution point group. Only follow the cloud-based distribution point steps if you have a working cloud-based distribution and a Windows Azure account.

1. Select the **Configure Business Hours** package, and on the ribbon, click **Distribute Content**.
2. On the **General** page, click **Next**.

3. If you have a cloud-based distribution point, do the following:
    a. On the **Content Destination** page, click **Add / Distribution Point**.
    b. Select the **CloudDP01** distribution point, and click **OK** and **Next**.

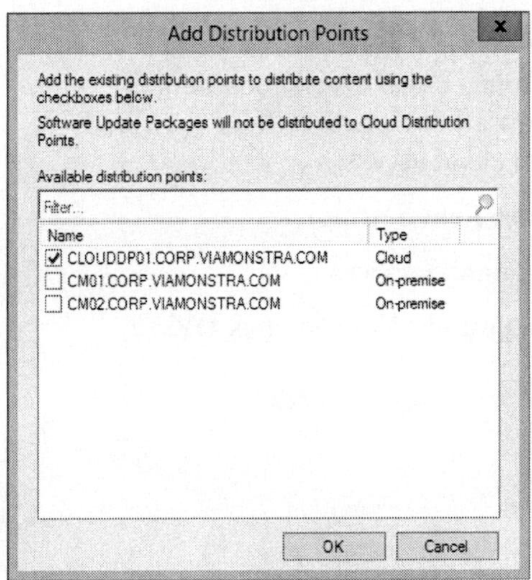

Distributing content to the cloud-based distribution point.

4. If you do not have a cloud-based distribution point, do the following:
    a. On the **Content Destination** page, click **Add / Distribution Point Group**.
    b. Select the **All Content** distribution point group, and click **OK** and **Next**.
5. On the **Summary** page, read the summary and click **Next** to start the content distribution.
6. Close the wizard.

Deploy the Business Hours Package

You deploy this package to all workstations. You can create additional programs with other business hour values and deploy those programs to other collections.

1. Select the **Configure Business Hours** package, and on the ribbon, click **Deploy**.
2. On the **General** page, click **Browse**; then, in the **ViaMonstra** folder, select the **VM All Workstations** collection, and click **Next**.
3. On the **Content** page, verify that the content is distributed to all distribution points and click **Next**.
4. On the **Deployment Settings** page, verify that Purpose is **Required** and click **Next**.
5. On the **Scheduling** page, click **New** and click **Assign immediately after this event**. Verify that **As soon as possible** is selected for the event, and click **OK** and **Next**.
6. On the **User Experience** page, accept the default settings and click **Next**.

7. On the **Distribution Points** page, accept the default settings and click **Next**.
8. On the **Summary** page, read the summary and click **Next** to start the deployment.
9. Close the wizard.

Download Content from a Cloud-Based Distribution Point

You can control which clients can download content from a cloud distribution point by configuring the client settings. In ViaMonstra, you allow all devices to utilize the cloud distribution points. Follow the steps below to configure cloud access:

1. Select the **Administration** workspace and then **Client Settings**.
2. Open the **Default Client Settings**, and select **Cloud Services**.
3. Configure **Allow access to cloud distribution point** to **Yes** and click **OK**.

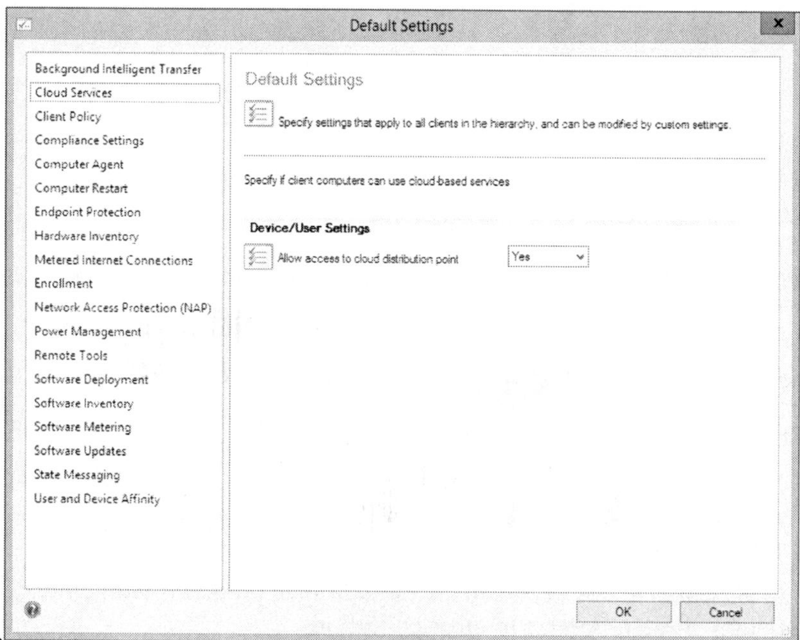

Configure cloud distribution point access.

Verify the New Business Hours on the Client

1. On **PC0001**, log on as **VIAMONSTRA\Administrator** and launch the **Software Center**.
2. Click **Options**, and notice the business hours.
3. Without closing the Software Center, from the **Start screen**, open the **Configuration Manager** applet.
4. In the **Actions** tab, select the **Machine Policy Retrieval & Evaluation Cycle** and click **Run Now**.

5. Close the Configuration Manager applet.
6. Back in the Software Center, select the **Options** tab again and press **F5** to perform a refresh. If the deployment has been executed, you will see the new business hours.

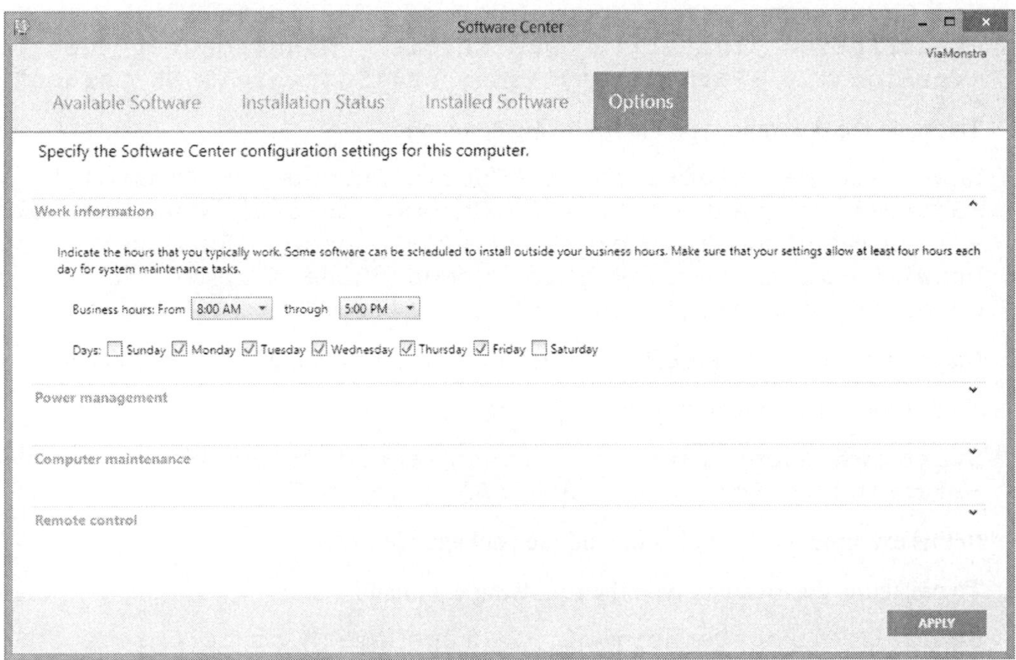

Controlling business hours with PowerShell.

Create Packages for UNIX Clients

There is also support for UNIX clients in the package model. In the following optional example, a standard package and program are deployed to a SUSE 11 X64 server. In these steps, you first create a collection of all SUSE computers and deployments. This guide assumes that you have created the D:\Sources\ Software\SUSE_Chrome folder on CM01, and copied the Google Chrome installation file (google-chrome-stable_current_x86_64.rpm) to the folder.

1. From the **ConfigMgr console**, launch **PowerShell**.
2. To create the collection, type the following command:

```
New-CMDeviceCollection -Name "VM All SUSE Servers"
-LimitingCollectionName "All Systems"
```

3. To create the collection query, type the following command:

```
Add-CMDeviceCollectionQueryMembershipRule -CollectionName
"VM ALL SUSE Servers" -RuleName "All SUSE Systems"
-QueryExpression 'select * from SMS_R_System inner join
SMS_G_System_OPERATING_SYSTEM on
SMS_G_System_OPERATING_SYSTEM.ResourceId =
```

```
SMS_R_System.ResourceId where
SMS_G_System_OPERATING_SYSTEM.Manufacturer like "%SUSE%"'
```

4. To create the package, type the following command:

```
New-CMPackage -Name "Google Chrome SUSE Install"
-Description "Install Google Chrome" -Manufacturer "Google"
-Version 1.0 -Path "\\cm01\sources$\Software\SUSE_Chrome"
```

5. To create the program, type the following command:

```
New-CMProgram -PackageName "Google Chrome SUSE Install"
-StandardProgramName "Google Chrome Install" -RunType Normal
-ProgramRunType WhetherOrNotUserIsLoggedOn -RunMode
RunWithAdministrativeRights -CommandLine " rpm -ivh
google-chrome-stable_current_x86_64.rpm"
```

6. Make a note of the **PackageID** that is returned; in our example, it was PS100009.
7. To distribute the content, type the following command:

```
Start-CMContentDistribution -PackageId PS100009
-DistributionPointGroupName "All content"
```

   In this example, PackageId is the unique package identifier.

8. To create the deployment, type the following command:

```
start-CMPackageDeployment -PackageName "Google Chrome SUSE
Install" -StandardProgramName "Google Chrome Install"
-CollectionName "VM ALL SUSE Servers" -ScheduleEvent
AsSoonAsPossible -RerunBehavior RerunIfFailedPreviousAttempt
-FastNetworkOption
DownloadContentFromDistributionPointAndRunLocally
-SlowNetworkOption
DownloadContentFromDistributionPointAndLocally
```

Monitoring the Deployment

There are several ways you can monitor the deployment.

Use the ConfigMgr Console and the Monitoring Workspace

1. Navigate to the **Monitoring** workspace and select **Deployments**.
2. On the ribbon, click **Run Summarization** and then click **Refresh**.

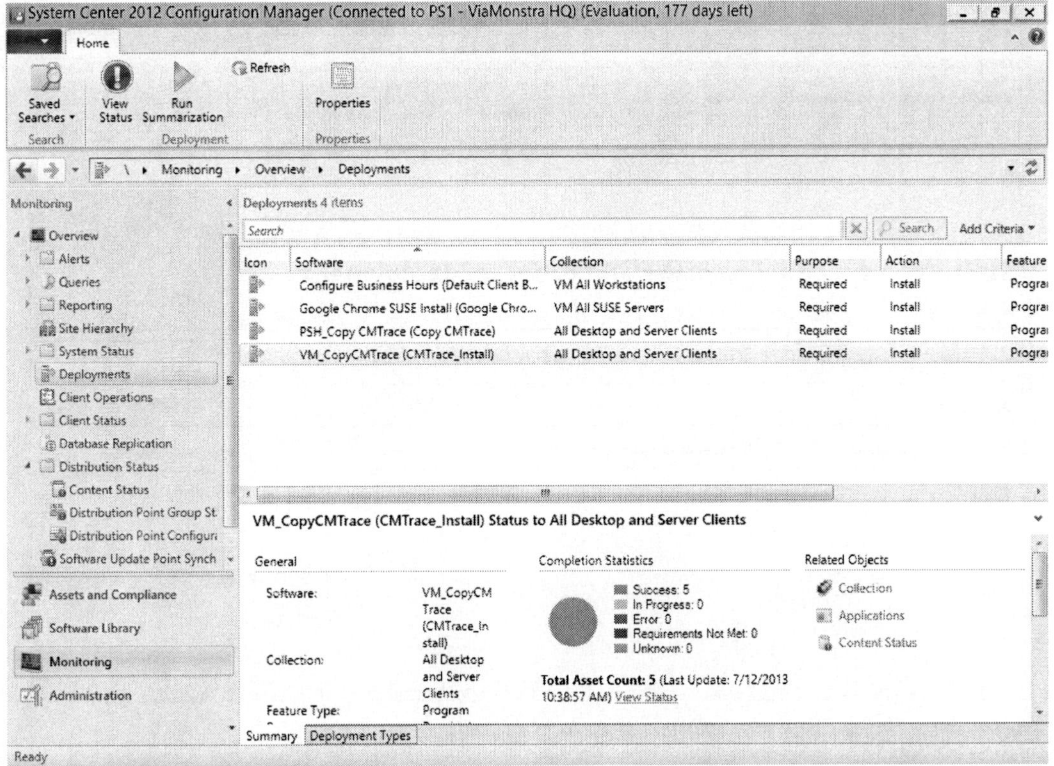

Monitoring the deployment.

Use the Reports

1. Open **Internet Explorer** and go to **http://cm01/reports**.
2. Select the **ConfigMgr_PS1** folder.
3. Select the **Software Distribution - Package and Program Deployment** folder.
4. Run the report **All deployments for a specified package and program**.
5. From the **Package (program)** drop-down list, select **VM_CopyCMTrace (CMTrace_Install)** and click **View Report**.
6. The report lists all deployments for that specific package or program. Click the deployment name to drill into the statistics.

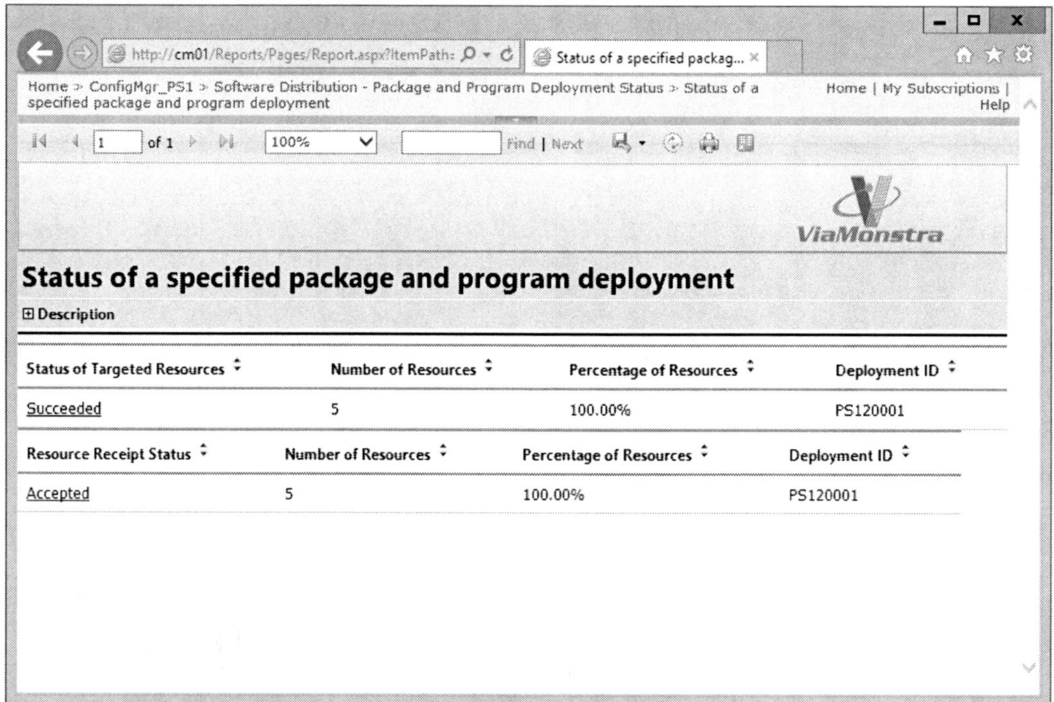

Monitoring the deployment using a standard report.

Applications

I often refer to applications as one of the more "sexy" objects of ConfigMgr. Applications are much more intelligent than packages and allow you as the administrator to gain more control over what happens. Applications are also much more user-centric compared to packages. With the correct requirement rules, you control if and which deployment type is installed to a device. Before creating the applications, you need to understand the basics.

How Applications Are Installed

Applications can be installed automatically without user intervention through the Software Center or from the Application Catalog website point. It's essential that you know when to use the different options. When deploying an application, the deployment can either be required or available (optional):

- A *required* deployment is a deployment that is installed based on either an event or a schedule. The logged on user might have the option to install the application prior to the scheduled deadline.
- An *available*, or optional, deployment requires user interaction and must be started by a logged on user.

Where the Application Will Be Presented	Required Deployment	Available Deployment
User targeted	Software Center	Application Catalog website point and Software Center (once installed)
Device targeted	Software Center	Software Center

The Application

To understand applications, you first need to learn the high-level overview. An application is not a MSI package, nor is it an .exe file. Instead an application represents all possible deployment types for a specific software package. For example, Adobe Reader is one application containing multiple deployment types like App-V, .msi, and .exe. All these different deployment types are all child objects to the same application, but only one of the deployment types will be installed on device. Which one depends on the requirement rules and order of the deployment types.

The following table describes the pages you'll complete when creating your application using the Create Application Wizard.

Application Tab	Description
Application Properties	The first information you have to worry about when creating a new application. The properties should all follow the same naming standard and that way make it easier for the administrators to work with the application in the ConfigMgr console.
Application Catalog	The end-user metadata. The values in the Application Catalog are used by end users when searching for applications or viewing additional information about the application.
References	Information about links between this application and other applications. On this page, you can see whether the application is superseded by another application and whether other applications have dependencies on this application.
Distribution Settings	Information about the distribution settings of the package, such as how the content is distributed to distribution points that are configured for prestaged content only. Here you also find the setting "Distribute the content for this package to preferred distribution points." With this feature enabled, content is automatically distributed to a distribution point when requested by a user or device.

Application Tab	Description
Deployment Type	A list of the associated deployment types and their priorities. Keep in mind that only one of the deployment types is installed on the device. The first deployment type matching all the requirements is installed, and the remaining deployment types are not applied.
Content Locations	A list of the distribution point(s) and distribution point group(s) where the content can be located. You select each distribution point(s) or group(s) and redistribute the package, remove the package from distribution points, and validate the package. The package validation verifies that all the files used by the package are present in the content library and that all HASH values are correct.
Supersedence	Used to create a supersedence relationship between this application and the application you want to supersede.
Security	Security information for the application.

The Deployment Type

Later in this chapter, you configure the deployment types represented by your application. The following table lists and describes the tabs in the Deployment Type properties. The tabs and settings depend on the selected deployment type. ConfigMgr SP1 adds several new deployment types.

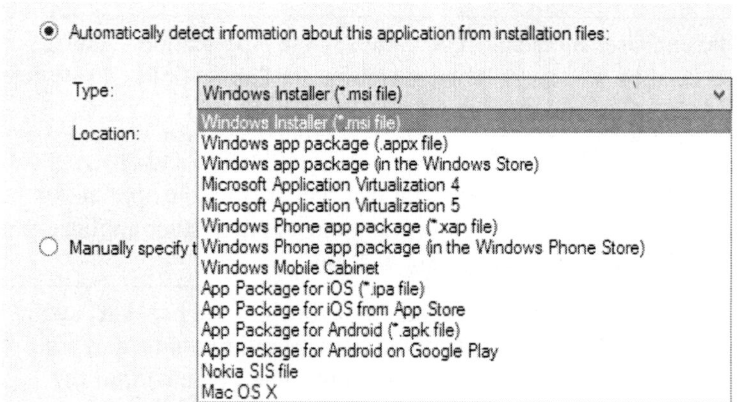

List of the available deployment types in Service Pack 1.

Deployment Type Tab	Description
General	Deployment type properties like name, technology, comments, and language.
Content	Source location and information about Microsoft BranchCache support (which allows clients to share content with other clients on the same subnet). Allowing clients to use a fallback source location for content enables them to use another distribution point as a fallback source for the package in the event that the local distribution point is unavailable. On the Content tab, you also can configure whether the client will be allowed to download the package from a slow connection. A "slow connection" is not based on a real time evaluation, but rather on a setting configured in the boundary group.
Programs	Allows you to specify the install and uninstall program.
Detection Method	Needed for every deployment type. The detection method is used by the client to determine whether that specific deployment type is already present on the device. You can create multiple detection methods like MSI product code, registry, file based, or a custom script.
User Experience	Can be used to configure whether the end user should be able to interact with the installation and whether the installation is intended for a user or device.
Requirements	Also known as *global conditions*. Requirements are evaluated in real-time before the application is downloaded and installed. You can create device, user, and custom requirement rules based on registry values, WMI queries, and much more.
Return Codes	Allows you to specify the return code that the specific deployment type returns in the event of a successful installation, restart required, or failure. I have a dream that one day all software developers start reading the same book and come to a mutual agreement on which return codes to use.
Dependencies	List of other deployment types that this deployment type depends on. One example is that a virtual App-V application depends on the App-V client being installed on the device.
Publishing	Only available for App-V deployment types and defines the icons that are published when "installing" this deployment type. I have "installing" in quotation marks because we are not installing a virtual application like a traditional application.

The Deployment

The settings you can configure on a deployment depend on how and to whom you target the deployment. As mentioned earlier, a deployment can be targeted to a user or device collection, and it can be either available or mandatory (have a deadline for the installation). This table describes the pages you use to configure your deployment.

Deployment Tab	Description
General	Deployment information like software used, collection, and optional comments.
Content	List of the distribution point(s) and distribution point group(s) where the content is available.
Deployment Settings	Information about the deployment action, Install or Uninstall; the purpose of the deployment, Available or Required; and the setting to control whether administrator approval is required in order to install the application. If the deployment has a deadline, you also can configure ConfigMgr to send a wakeup package prior to running the deployment. This setting requires that Wake On LAN has been configured.
Scheduling	Defines the application availability time. If none is specified, the application becomes available as soon as possible. If the deployment is required, you also have the option to configure the installation deadline. When specifying the installation deadline, you have the option to configure whether the time is based on client local time or UTC.
User Experience	Defines how the deployment interacts with the logged on user. If the deployment is required, you have the option to completely hide all notifications, as well as not displaying anything in the Software Center. For available deployments, you can specify the level of notifications shown, but the deployment is always visible in the Software Center. This is also the page where you can choose to ignore maintenance windows for the deployment. By ignoring maintenance windows, you allow the application to be installed outside of any defined maintenance window.
Alerts	Allows you to set alerts for your deployment. The alerts depend on the deployment purpose. For required deployments, you can specify when alerts are created (that is, created in the ConfigMgr console) for failed and missing deployments. If you have OpsMgr 2012 installed, the deployment also can stop the OpsMgr agent. Note that this does not place the OpsMgr 2012 client in real maintenance mode, so you might generate alerts in the OpsMgr console with this feature.

The Collections

For every application, ViaMonstra creates at least two collections. For your Microsoft Office 2013 application, for example, you will have these collections:

- SWU_Office_2013_Pro_X64_Install
- SWU_Office_2013_Pro_X64_Uninstall

The collections are query based and look for members of the corresponding Active Directory user or computer group.

The Application Catalog website point is the site system role that users will connect to when they are "shopping" for software. All user-targeted applications without a deadline will be available in the web catalog.

Create the Active Directory Groups

1. On **DC01**, log on as **VIAMONSTRA\Administrator** and open **Active Directory Users and Computers**.
2. Right-click the **ViaMonstra / Software Groups** OU and select **New / Group**.
3. Create a new security group with these settings:
   a. Group Name: **SW_Office_2013_Install**
   b. Group scope: **Domain local**
   c. Group type: **Security**
4. Create a new group in the same OU with these settings:
   a. Group Name: **SW_Office_2013_Uninstall**
   b. Group scope: **Domain local**
   c. Group type: **Security**
5. Right-click **SW_Office_2013_Install** and click **Properties**.
6. Navigate to the **Members** tab, click **Add**, and add the users **JAP**, **NEP** and **MLG** as members to the group.
7. Click **OK** and close the group properties.
8. Repeat the preceding steps and create the following groups (add the same users to the new Install groups):
   a. **SW_WinRAR_Install**
   b. **SW_WinRAR_Uninstall**
   c. **SW_7-Zip_Install**
   d. **SW_7-Zip Uninstall**

Create the Uninstall Collections

1. On **CM01**, log on as **VIAMONSTRA\Administrator** and open the **ConfigMgr console**.
2. Select the **Assets and Compliance** workspace.
3. Expand **User collections**, right-click the **Software** folder, and select **Create User Collection**.
4. Use these settings:
    a. Name: **SWU_Office_2013_Uninstall**
    b. Comment: **All groups and users in this collection will automatically have Microsoft Office uninstalled.**
    c. Limiting Collection: Click **Browse** and select **All Users and User Groups**.
5. Click **Next**.
6. Enable **Use incremental updates for this collection**.
7. Click **Add Rule / Query Rule**.
8. Name the rule **Office 2013 Uninstall** and click **Edit Query Statement**.
9. Select the **Criteria** tab.
10. Click the **yellow icon** and click **Select** to create the criteria.
11. Select **User Resource** as the **Attribute class** and **Security Group Name** as the **Attribute**.
12. Click **OK** to return to the Criterion Properties dialog box.
13. In **Operator**, select **is equal to**, and in **Value**, type **VIAMONSTRA\SW_Office_2013_Uninstall**.

> **Real World Note:** Normally you also can click Value and select the values from a list. Groups are shown in the list when discovered by the Active Directory User Discovery process; however, empty groups (not containing any user as a member) are not displayed and need to be typed in.

14. Click **OK** three times and return to the Memberships Rules page.
15. Finish the wizard.
16. Repeat the preceding steps and create the following collections (add the related security group via a dynamic collection query):
    a. **SWU_WinRAR_Uninstall**
    b. **SWU_7-Zip_Uninstall**

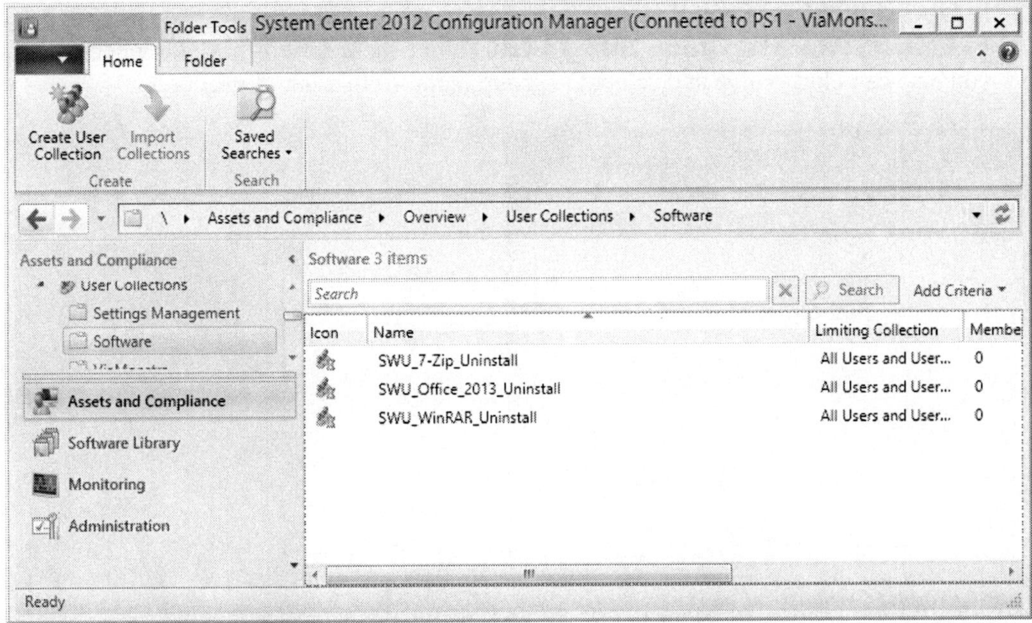

The uninstall collections.

Create the Install Collections

1. Select **User collections**, right-click the **Software** folder, and select **Create User Collection**.
2. Use these settings:
   a. Name: **SWU_Office_2013_Install**
   b. Comment: **All groups and users in this collection will automatically get a version of Microsoft Office installed.**
   c. Limiting Collection: Click **Browse** and select **All Users and User Groups**.
3. Click **Next**.
4. Enable **Use incremental updates for this collection**.
5. Click **Add Rule / Query Rule**.
6. Name the rule **Office 2013 Install**, and click **Edit Query Statement**.
7. Select the **Criteria** tab.
8. Click the **yellow icon** and click **Select** to create the criteria.
9. Select **User Resource** as the **Attribute class** and **Security Group Name** as the **Attribute**.
10. Click **OK** to return to the Criterion Properties dialog box.

11. In **Operator**, select **is equal to**, and in **Value**, type **VIAMONSTRA\SW_Office_2013_Install**. (Since these groups have members, you also can click Value and select the group name from a list of groups.)

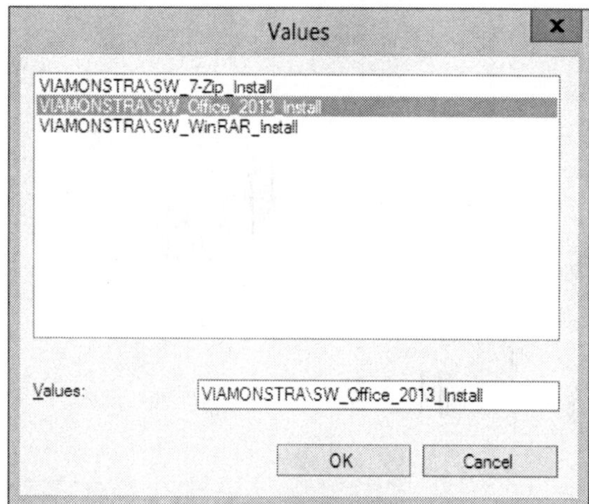

Selecting a value instead of typin; again, only groups with membes are listed.

12. Click **OK** three times and return to the **Memberships Rules** page.
13. Click **Add Rule / Exclude Collections**.
14. Select **Software / SW_ Office_2013_Uninstall**, and click **OK**.
15. Finish the wizard.
16. Repeat the preceding steps and create the following collections (add the related security group via a dynamic collection query, as well as the exclude collections rules):
    a. **SWU_WinRAR_Install**
    b. **SWU_7-Zip_Install**

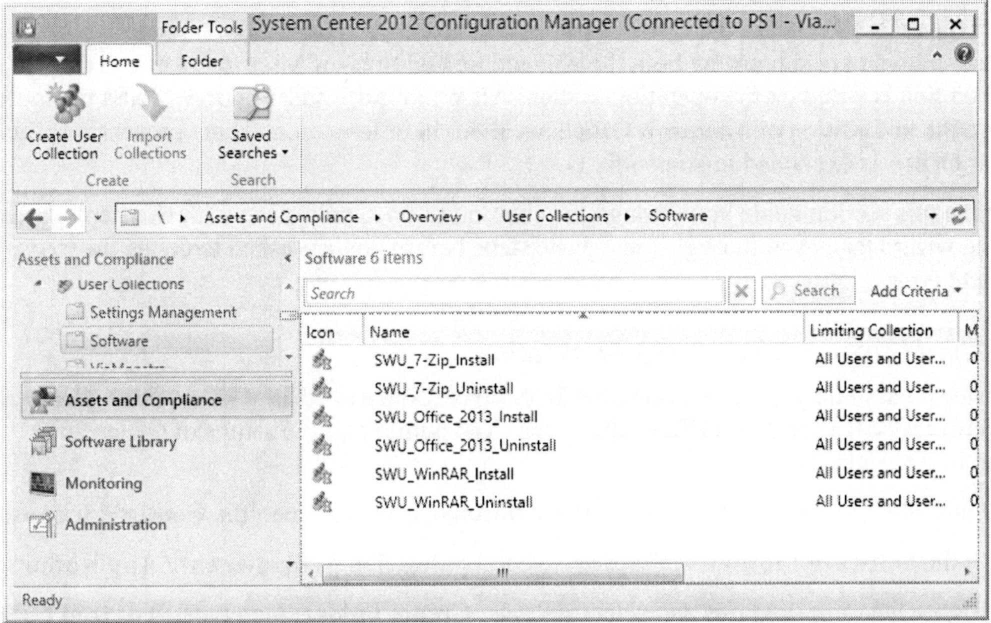

The install collections added.

Automate Creating Dynamic Queries to User Collections Using PowerShell

This optional example shows you how to automate the process of creating a dynamic query on a user collection. Again this is just a sample command, and this action is not needed for the other guides in this book. (You already created the queries in the previous guide.)

1. From the **ConfigMgr console**, select the drop-down list next to the **Home** menu and click **Connect via Windows PowerShell.**
2. Create a user collection by typing the following command:

```
New-CMUserCollection -Name "SWU Office 2013 Install"
-Comment "All users in this collection will get Microsoft
Office 2013 installed" -LimitingCollectionName "All Users
and User Groups"
```

> **Real World Note:** When creating collections for Active Directory groups, you can use the user resources as shown in the preceding example. This approach lists each individual user in the collection. You also can use the user group resource, which lists only the Active Directory group name. Both approaches work as methods to deploy software, but for ViaMonstra, I prefer the user resource method, as it allows us to use the Exclude collection rule in the Uninstall collection to remove users from the Install collection.

Working with Applications

In ViaMonstra, you are supporting both the x32 and x64 editions of Microsoft Office. The installed edition is based on the operating system. All Windows 7 and Windows 8 x64 computers must have the x64 edition of Microsoft Office installed. In order to control the process, configure Microsoft Office as explained in Appendix D.

The steps in this section guide you through the creation of one application with two deployment types. The wizard takes you through some basic steps before you are asked to create the first deployment type.

Create the Microsoft Office 2013 Application

In these steps, I assume you have created the **D:\Sources\Software\MS_Office_2013_Pro_X86** and **D:\Sources\Software\MS_Office_2013_Pro_X64** administrative setups of Office 2013 described in Appendix D.

1. On **CM01**, log on as **VIAMONSTRA\Administrator** and open the **ConfigMgr console**.
2. In the **Software Library** workspace, select **Application Management / Applications**.
3. Right-click **Applications** and select **Folder / Create Folder**; then type **Required User** as the folder name.
4. Expand **Applications**, select the **Required User** folder, and on the ribbon, click **Create Application**.
5. On the **General** page, select **Manually specify the application information** and click **Next**.
6. On the (second) **General** page, specify these application properties and click **Next**:
    a. Name: **Microsoft Office 2013**
    b. Administrator comments: **All Microsoft Office 2013 editions**
    c. Manufacturer: **Microsoft**
    d. Software Version: **2013**
    e. Optional reference: **POmsOff2013** (This is a custom attribute that you can use for whatever purpose. In ViaMonstra, I have decided to type the internal PO number for the software.)
    f. Administrative Categories: Click **Select**, and then click **Create**; type **Core Office application** and click **OK**.
    g. Enable **Allow this application to be installed from the Install Application task sequence action without being deployed**.

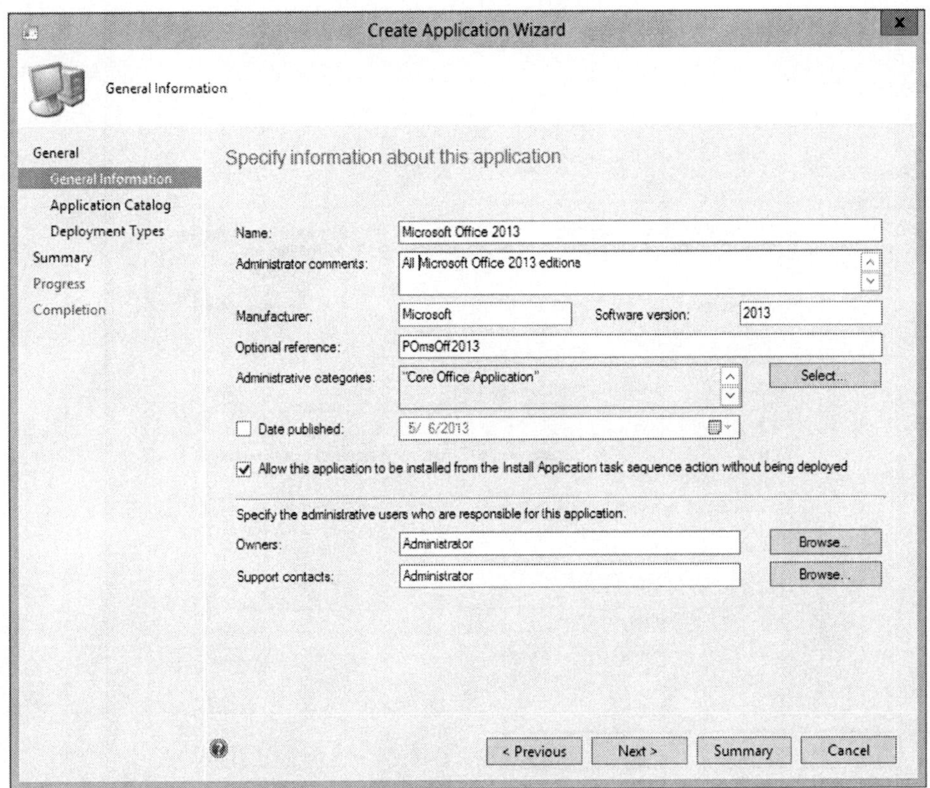

Specifying the application properties.

7. On the **Application Catalog** page, fill out these metadata and click **Next**:
    a. User categories: Click **Edit**, and then click **Create**; type **Office Applications** and click **OK** twice.
    b. User documentation: **http://office.microsoft.com/en-us** (This is a link to the official Microsoft Office site.)
    c. Link text: **Please view the Microsoft Office tutorials before calling service desk.**
    d. Localized description: **Microsoft Office 2013 is our standard Office platform with tools like Word, Excel, OneNote, and PowerPoint.**
    e. Keywords: **Office, Word, Excel, OneNote, PowerPoint**
    f. Icon: Click **Browse** and search for the Office icon file. (In my example, I used the utility from **Iconarchive**—see the Real World Note later in this section—to find all Office-related icons and store them in D:\Sources\Software\Icons.)

Real World Note: Because of a known issue in ConfigMgr 2012 SP1, you might not be seeing all files when browsing for an icon. As a workaround, you can simply type *.* as the file name and all files will be visible in the browse dialog box.

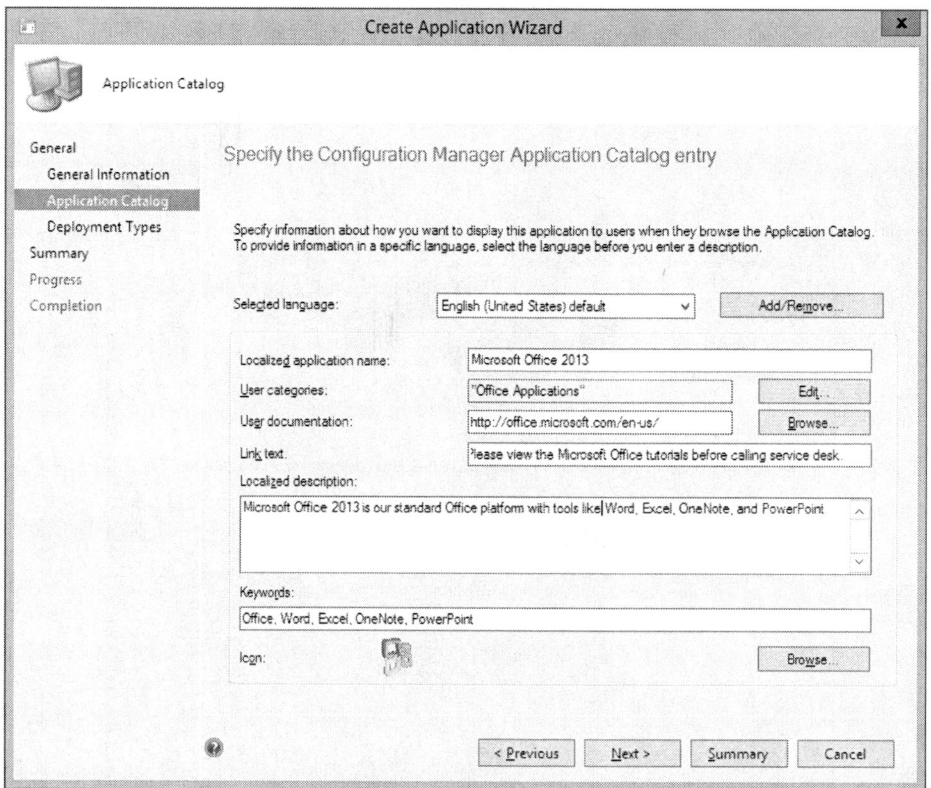

Specifying the application end-user metadata.

Real World Note: Filling out the metadata is a very important step for user-centric deployments. Users can use all the information when searching for applications. One metadata item is specifying the icon. In ViaMonstra, I use http://iconarchive.com, a web site with more than 300,000 downloadable icons, and Icon Extractor, which is an application from http://www.nirsoft.net/utils/iconsext.html.

Create the x64 Deployment Type

1. Still in the **Create Application Wizard**, on the **Deployment Types** page, click **Add** to begin creating the Office 2013 x64 deployment type.
2. On the **General** page, in **Type**, select **Script Installer** and then click **Next**.
3. On the **General Information** page, use this setting and click **Next**:

    Name: **Microsoft Office 2013 x64 MSI**

4. On the **Content** page, specify these settings and click **Next**:

    a. Content location: **\\CM01\Sources$\Software\MS_Office_2013_Pro_X64**

    b. Installation program: **setup.exe**

    c. Uninstall program: **setup.exe /uninstall ProPlus /config .\ProPlus.WW\config.xml**

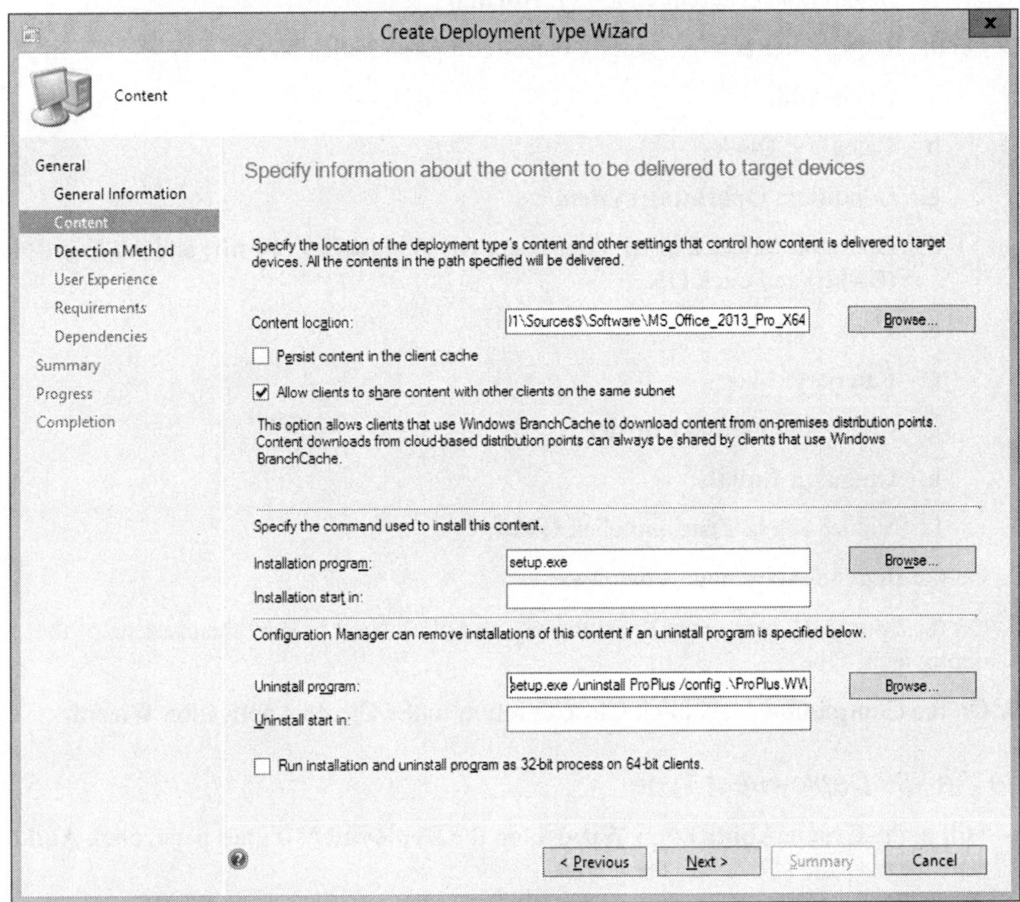

Specifying the install and uninstall commands.

5. On the **Detection Method** page, specify these settings and click **Next**:

    a. Click **Add Clause**, and select **Windows Installer** as the **Setting Type**.

    b. Click **Browse**, navigate to the **D:\Sources\Software\MS_Office_2013_Pro_X64 \proplus.ww** folder, select **proplusww.msi**, and click **Open**.

    c. Click **OK** to close the Detection Rule page.

6. On the **User Experience** page, specify these settings and click **Next**. (The settings for this deployment type are for a user-targeted installation in which the end user is able to follow the installation progress on the monitor.)
    a. Installation behavior: **Install for system**
    b. Logon requirement: **Only when a user is logged on**
    c. Installation program visibility: **Normal**
7. On the **Requirements** page, specify these settings and click **Next**:
    a. Click **Add**.
    b. Category: **Device**
    c. Condition: **Operating system**
    d. Operator: Select **One of**; then select **All Windows 7 (64-bit)** and **All Windows 8 (64-bit)** and click **OK**.
    e. Click **Add**.
    f. Category: **User**
    g. Condition: **Primary device**
    h. Operator: **Equals**
    i. Value: Select **True** and click **OK**.
8. On the **Dependencies** page, click **Next**.
9. On the **Summary** page, read the summary and click **Next** to start the creation of the deployment type.
10. On the **Completion** page, click **Close** to return to the Create Application Wizard.

Create the x86 Deployment Type

1. Still in the **Create Application Wizard**, on the **Deployment Types** page, click **Add** to start creating the x86 deployment type.
2. On the **General** page, in **Type**, select **Script Installer** and then click **Next**.
3. On the **General Information** page, use this setting and click **Next**:

    Name: **Microsoft Office 2013 x86 MSI**
4. On the **Content** page, specify these settings and click **Next**:
    a. Content location: **\\CM01\Sources$\Software\MS_Office_2013_Pro_X86**
    b. Installation program: **setup.exe**
    c. Uninstall program: **setup.exe /uninstall ProPlus /config .\ProPlus.WW\config.xml**

5. On the **Detection Method** page, specify these settings and click **Next**:
    a. Click **Add Clause**, and select **Windows Installer** as the **Setting Type**.
    b. Click **Browse**, navigate to the **D:\Sources\Software\MS_Office_2013_Pro_X86 \proplus.ww** folder, select **proplusww.msi**, and click **Open**.
    c. Click **OK** to close the Detection Rule page.
6. On the **User Experience** page, specify these settings and click **Next**:
    a. Installation behavior: **Install for system**
    b. Logon requirement: **Only when a user is logged on**
    c. Installation program visibility: **Normal**
7. On the **Requirements** page, specify these settings and click **Next**:
    a. Click **Add**.
    b. Category: **Device**
    c. Condition: **Operating System**
    d. Operator: Select **One of**; then select **All Windows 7 (32-bit)** and **All Windows 8 (32-bit)**, and click **OK**.
    e. Click **Add**.
    f. Category: **User**
    g. Condition: **Primary device**
    h. Operator: **Equals**
    i. Value: Select **True** and click **OK**.
8. On the **Dependencies** page, click **Next**.
9. On the **Summary** page, read the summary and click **Next** to start the creation of the deployment type.
10. On the **Completion** page, click **Close** to return to the Create Application Wizard.
11. On the **Deployment Types** page, note your two deployment types and click **Next**.
12. On the **Summary** page, read the summary and click **Next** to start creating the application.
13. On the **Completion** page, click **Close** to return to the ConfigMgr console.

Distribute the MS Office 2013 Application

1. Select the **Microsoft Office 2013** application, and on the ribbon, click **Distribute Content**.
2. On the **General** page, click **Next**.

3. On the **Content** page, click **Next**.
4. On the **General Destination** page, click **Add / Distribution Point Group**. Select **All Content**, click **OK**, and then click **Next**.
5. On the **Summary** page, read the summary and click **Next** to start distributing the content.
6. On the **Completion** page, click **Close** to return to the ConfigMgr console.

Create the WinRAR Application

Usually you should go a long way to ensure that applications can be installed silently without any user interaction. But you will most likely run into scenarios in which you can't (or won't) spend the time needed to repackage the application. The steps below take you through the creation of a WinRAR application. You configure only the most basic application properties and allow the user to interact with the installation. If you have the time, I encourage you to fill out the application metadata just like you did for Microsoft Office 2013.

In these steps, I assume you have downloaded the x86 version of WinRAR 4.20 to D:\Sources\Software\WinRAR on CM01 and added the users mentioned in the corresponding Active Directory security groups.

1. On **CM01**, log on as **VIAMONSTRA\Administrator** and open the **ConfigMgr console**.
2. In the **Software Library** workspace, select **Application Management / Applications**.
3. Right-click **Applications** and select **Folder / Create Folder**. Type **Optional User** as the folder name.
4. Select the **Optional User** folder, and on the ribbon, click **Create Application**.
5. On the **General** page, configure this setting and click **Next**:

   Type: Select **Manually specify the application information**.
6. On the **General Information** page, specify these application properties and click **Next**:
   a. Name: **WinRAR**
   b. Administrator comments: **Our only company supported ZIP application**
   c. Manufacturer: **Rarlab**
   d. Software Version: **4.20**
   e. Optional reference: **POWR**
   f. Administrative Categories: Click **Select**, and the click **Create**; type **Utility** and click **OK**.
7. On the **Application Catalog** page, specify these properties and click **Next**:
   a. User categories: Click **Edit**, click **Create**, type **Utilities**, and click **OK** twice.
   b. User documentation: **http://www.rarlab.com/rarnew.htm**
   c. Link text: **Please read here for the latest information in this version.**

   d. Localized description: **Company Zip application**

   e. Keywords: **Zip**, **WinRAR**, **Compress**, **RAR**

   f. Icon: Click **Browse** and navigate to the **WINRAR icon** file.

8. Click **Add** to start creating the deployment type.
9. On the **General** page, in **Type**, select **Script Installer** and then click **Next**.
10. On the **General Information** page, use this setting and click **Next**:

    Name: **Rarlab WinRAR 4.20 x86 EXE**

11. On the **Content** page, specify these settings and click **Next**:

    a. Content location: **\\CM01\Sources$\Software\WinRAR**

    b. Installation program: **wrar420.exe -s**

    c. Uninstall program: **Uninstall.exe /s**

    d. Uninstall start in: **C:\Program Files (x86)\WinRAR**

12. On the **Detection Method** page, click **Add Clause** and specify these settings; then click **OK** and **Next**.

    a. Setting Type: **File System**

    b. Type: **File**

    c. Path: **C:\Program Files (x86)\WinRAR**

    d. File or folder name: **WinRAR.EXE**

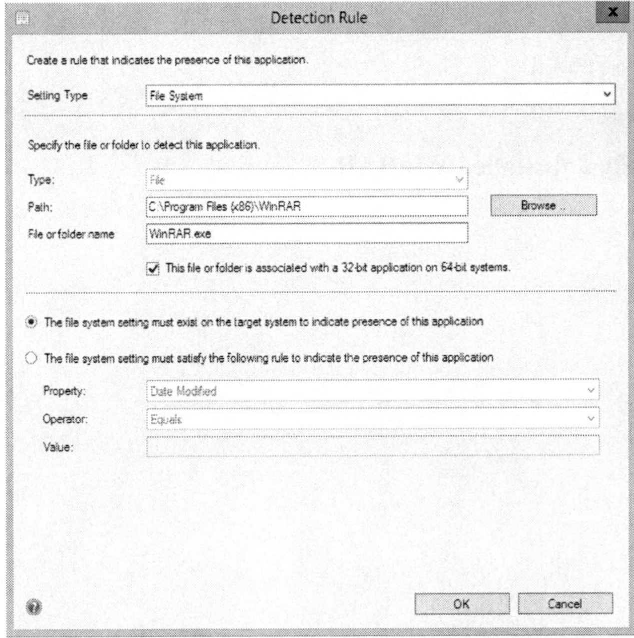

Specifying a detection method.

13. On the **User Experience** page, specify these settings and click **Next**:
    a. Installation behavior: **Install for system**
    b. Logon requirement: **Only when a user is logged on**
    c. Installation program visibility: **Normal**
14. On the **Requirements** page, specify these settings and click **Next**:
    a. Click **Add**.
    b. Category: **Device**
    c. Condition: **Operating System**
    d. Operator: Select **One of**; then select **All Windows 7 (64-bit)**, **All Windows 7 (32-bit), Windows 8 (32-bit)**, **All Windows 8 (64-bit)**, and click **OK**.
15. On the **Dependencies** page, click **Next**.
16. On the **Summary** page, read the summary and click **Next** to start the creation of the deployment type.
17. On the **Completion** page, click **Close** to return to the Create Application Wizard.
18. Select the new **Deployment Type** and click **Edit**.
19. Select the **Return Codes** tab, and notice that there is no return code for a successful uninstall.
20. Click **Add**, configure these settings, and click **OK**:
    a. Return Code Value: **1**
    b. Code Type: **Success (no reboot)**
    c. Name: **Uninstall Success**
    d. Description: **Successfully uninstalled WinRAR**

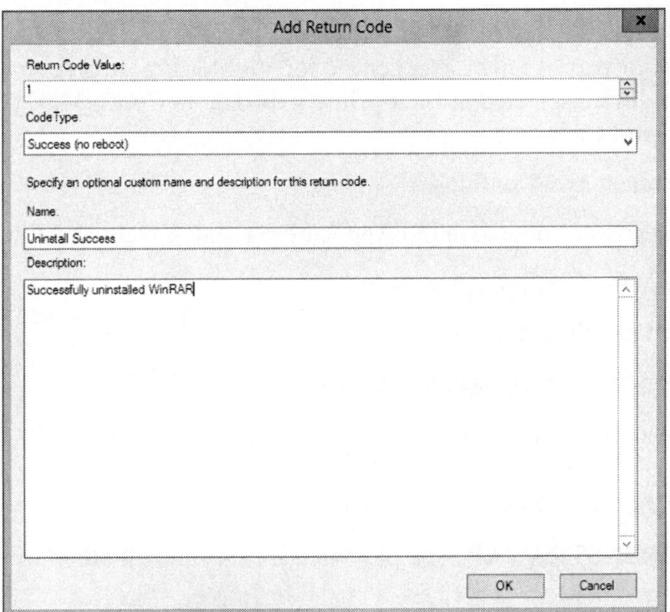

Creating a custom return code.

21. On the **Deployment Types** page, click **Next.**
22. On the **Summary** page, read the summary and click **Next** to start the creation of the application.
23. On the **Completion** page, click **Close** to return to the ConfigMgr console.

Automate Creating Applications Using PowerShell

This example shows you how to automate the process of creating an application and a deployment type using the built-in cmdlet.

1. From the **ConfigMgr console**, launch **PowerShell.**
2. To create the application, type the following command:

```
New-CMApplication -Name "7-zip PoSH" -Manufacturer
"7-Zip.org" -SoftwareVersion "9.20"
```

3. To create a MSI deployment type for the application, type the following command::

```
Add-CMDeploymentType -ApplicationName "7-zip PoSH"
-MsiInstaller -AutoIdentifyFromIntallationFile
-InstallationFileLocation "\\CM01\Sources$\Software\7-Zip
\Windows\7z920-x64.msi" -ForceForUnknownPublisher $True
```

User Device Affinity (UDA)

User Device Affinity or UDA is a major part of going user centric for ViaMonstra. It is company policy that all users have at least one device selected as their primary device. In ConfigMgr, you can specify the primary device in several ways:

1. Automate the process in the client agent settings.
2. Let the end user specify their primary device in the Application Catalog website point.
3. Manually specify the device in the ConfigMgr console.
4. Define the primary user when installing the operating system.
5. Import a CSV file with information about users and devices.
6. Write a custom script to define the relationship.

Specify the Primary Device in the Application Catalog

1. On **PC0001**, log on as **VIAMONSTRA\JAP**. The password for this and all other users is **Password01**.
2. Start **Internet Explorer** and open **http://cm01/CMApplicationCatalog**.
3. Select the **My Devices** tab and enable **I regularly use this computer to do my work.** This option configures the device as the primary device for JAP.

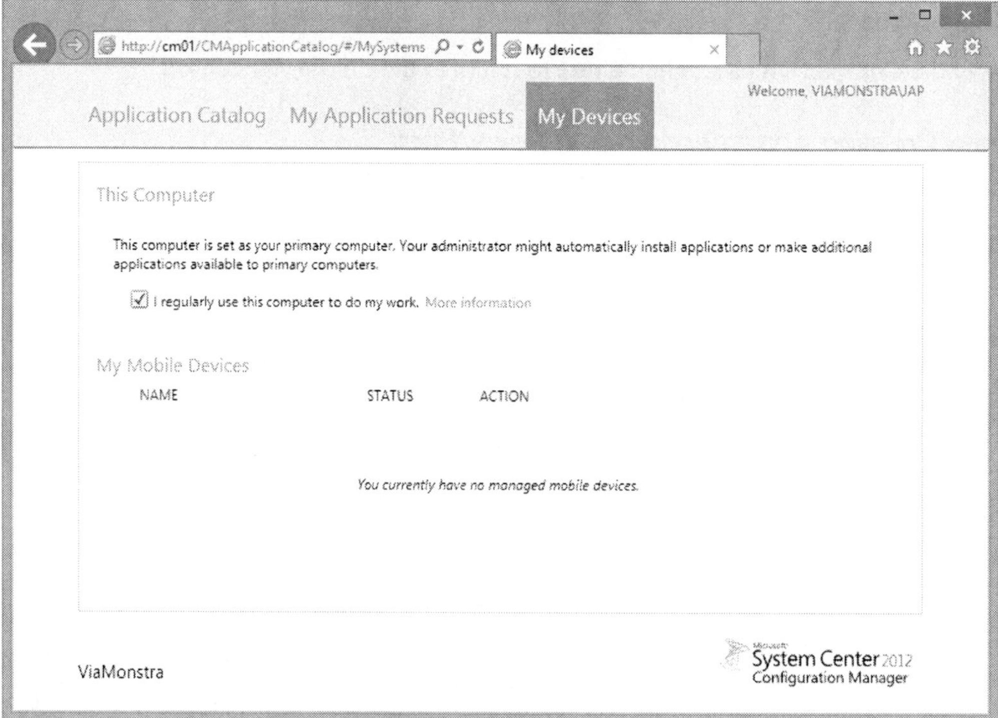

Specifying the primary user in the Application Catalog.

4. On **CM01**, in the **ConfigMgr console**, navigate to the **Assets and Compliance** workspace.
5. In **Devices**, right-click **PC0001** and select **Edit Primary Users**. You should now be able to see the JAP.

   In the Affinity Type, notice that two users are listed. One is Usage Agent Defined (by the client agent settings) and the other one is Catalog Defined.

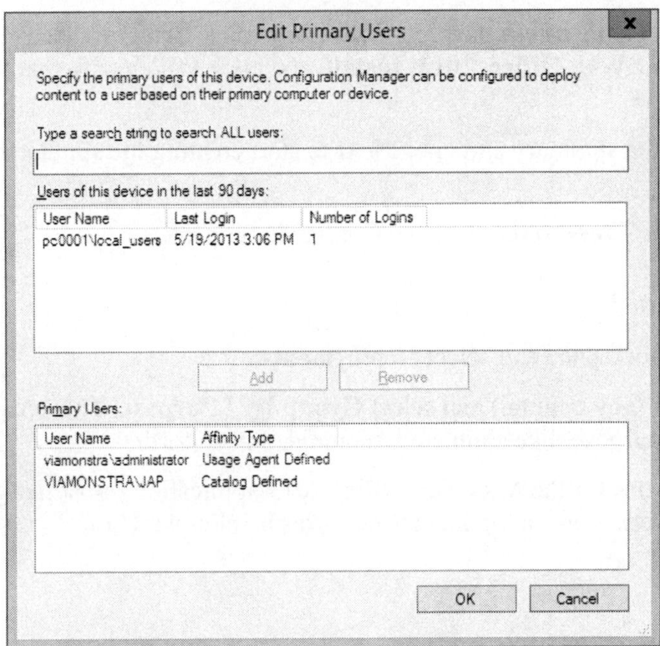

Viewing the primary user for PC0001.

Deployment

A deployment is the process of offering the user or device an application (and sometimes requiring it). Before deploying any application, it's always a very good idea to follow these simple rules:

1. Never deploy any application before you have tested the command line.
2. Never deploy any application to All Systems or All Users except in lab environments.
3. When in doubt, always create a simulated deployment first.

Simulated Deployments

A simulated deployment is almost like a real deployment except that the application is never installed on any device. The purpose of the simulated deployment is to test the requirement rules, dependencies, and detection methods. The simulated deployment will also give you information about how many of each deployment type will be installed.

Create the Simulated Deployment of Microsoft Office 2013

1. On **CM01**, log on as **VIAMONSTRA\Administrator** and open the **ConfigMgr console**.
2. Navigate to **Software Library / Application Management / Applications / Required User**.
3. Select the **Microsoft Office 2013** application, and then from the ribbon, select **Deployment / Simulate Deployment**.
4. On the **Simulate Application Deployment** page, in **Collection**, click **Browse**; then select **User Collections / Software / SWU_Office_2013_Install**, and click **OK**. Verify that the Action is **Install** and click **Next**.
5. On the **Summary** page, read the summary and click **Next** to start creating the simulated deployment.
6. On the **Completion** page, click **Close** to return to the ConfigMgr console.

Monitor the Simulated Deployment

1. Navigate to the **Monitoring** workspace and select **Deployments**.
2. Right-click the column header (any column) and select **Group By / Purpose**. This creates a group for each deployment purpose, like simulated, required, and so forth.
3. Notice the **Completion Statistics** for the Microsoft Office 2013 application (most likely the statistics are not updated yet). You can update the statistics by clicking **Run Summarization** on the ribbon.

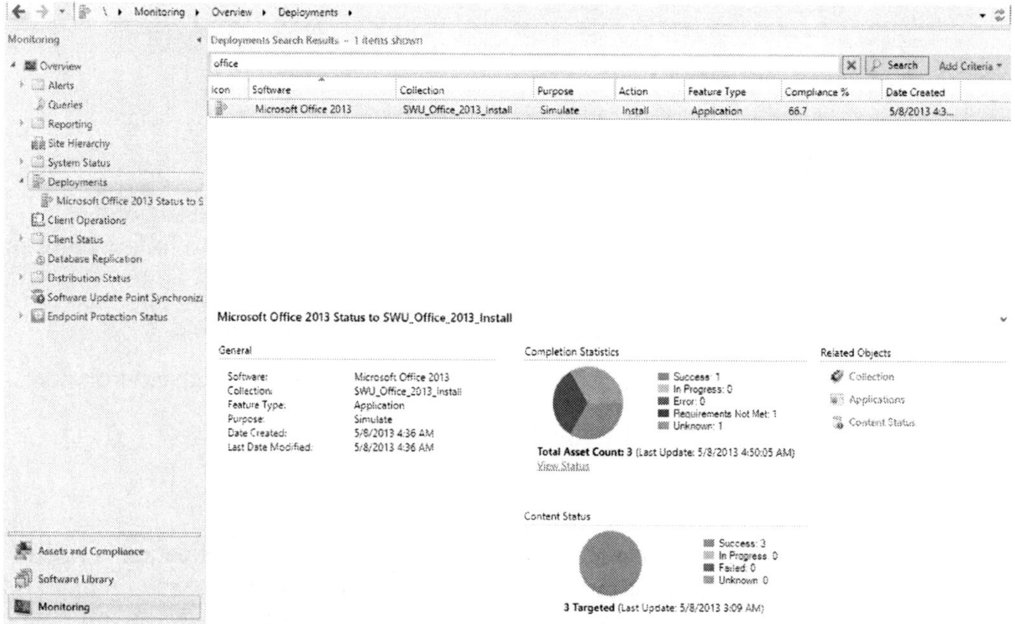

Viewing the simulated deployment status.

4. On the **Summary** tab, click **View Status**. In this view, you get a list of user simulated deployment statuses: succeeded, in progress, error, and requirements not met. You also get a list of users for whom a status is unknown. Users listed in the Unknown tab are users who have not uploaded any states messages about the deployment.
5. Select the deployment again and click the **Deployment Types** tab. In this view, you get a nice chart illustrating the progress of the simulated deployment.

Note: You cannot convert a simulated deployment to a real deployment using the built-in features. However, Greg Ramsey (Enterprise Client Management MVP) posted a PowerShell solution that converts the simulated deployment into a required deployment: http://gregramsey.net/2013/04/17/how-to-promote-an-application-simulation-to-a-required-deployment-in-configmgr-2012-sp1/.

Deploy a Required Application

1. Select the **Software Library** workspace, and then select **Application Management / Applications / Required User**.
2. Select the **Microsoft Office 2013** application. Click the **Deployments** tab, right-click the simulated deployment, click **Delete**, and then click **Yes** in the dialog box. The reason for doing this is that ConfigMgr does not allow you to deploy the same application to the same collection twice.
3. From the ribbon, click **Deployment / Deploy**.
4. On the **General** page, in **Collection**, click **Browse**; then select **User Collections / Software / SWU _Office_2013_Install**, and click **OK**. Click **Next**.
5. On the **Content** page, verify that the content is distributed and click **Next**.
6. On the **Deployment Settings** page, configure these settings and click **Next**:
   a. Action: **Install**
   b. Purpose: **Required**
   c. Enable **Pre-deploy software to the user's primary device**.
7. On the **Schedule Settings** page, configure this setting and click **Next**:

   Installation Deadline: **Current time + 3 days**
8. On the **User Experience** page, configure this setting and click **Next**:

   User Notifications: **Display in Software Center and show all notifications**
9. On the **Alerts Settings** page, configure these settings and click **Next**:
   a. Threshold for successful deployment: Configure a value of **90%** success after **4days** from now. (This setting should trigger a console alert if Microsoft Office is not installed on at least 90% of the primary devices within four days.)
   b. Threshold for failed deployment: Configure a failed value of **5%**.

10. On the **Summary** page, read the summary and click **Next** to start creating the deployment.
11. On the **Completion** page, click **Close** to return to the ConfigMgr console.

Install the Required Application

1. On **PC0001**, log on as **VIAMONSTRA\JAP**.
2. From the **Start screen**, open **Software Center**.

   The application will become available after the next user policy update cycle.
3. Select the **Microsoft Office 2013** application and click **Install**.

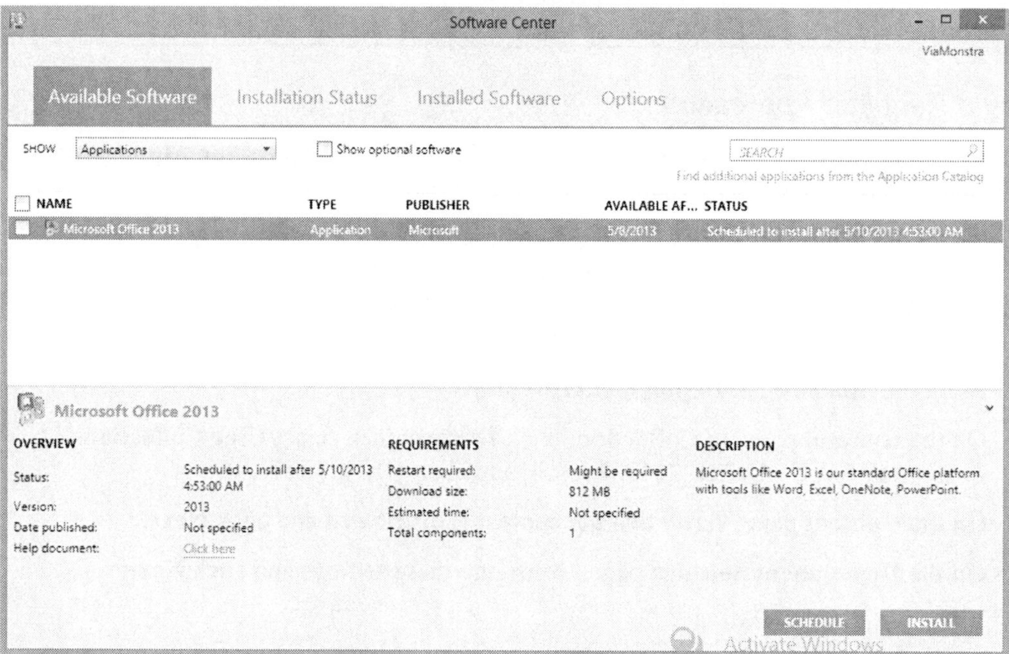

Software available to install.

Deploy an Optional User Application

1. On **CM01**, log on as **VIAMONSTRA\Administrator** and open the **ConfigMgr console**.
2. Select the **Software Library** workspace, and then select **Application Management / Applications / Optional User**.
3. Select the **WinRAR** application.
4. From the ribbon, click **Deployment / Deploy**.
5. On the **General** page, in **Collection**, click **Browse**; then select **User Collections / Software / SWU_WinRAR_Install**, and click **OK** and then **Next**.

6. On the **Content** page, click **Add / Distribution Point Group**. Select **All Content**, and click **OK** and then **Next**.
7. On **Deployment Settings** page, configure these settings and click **Next**:
    a. Action: **Install**
    b. Purpose: **Available**
    c. Enable **Require administrator approval if users request this application.**
8. On the **Schedule Settings** page, click **Next**.
9. On the **User Experience** page, configure this setting and click **Next**:

    User Notifications: **Display in Software Center and show all notifications**
10. On the **Alerts Settings** page, configure this setting and click **Next**:

    Threshold for failed deployment: Configure a failed value of **5%**.
11. On the **Summary** page, read the summary and click **Next** to start creating the deployment.
12. On the **Completion** page, click **Close** to return to the ConfigMgr console.

Install the Optional Application

1. On **PC0001**, log on as **VIAMONSTRA\JAP**.
2. Open **Internet Explorer** and go to **http://cm01/CMApplicationCatalog**.

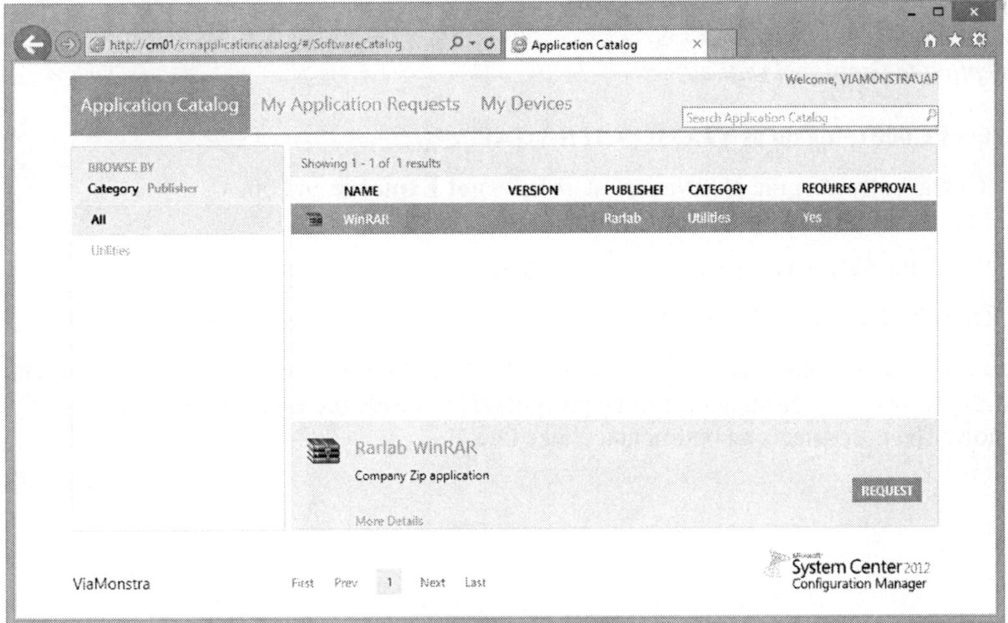

Requesting approval.

3. Select the **WinRAR** application and click **Request**.
4. In the text box, type a message to the administrator like **I really need WinRAR to do my work** and click **Submit**.

   The approval request is written to the ConfigMgr console.
5. On **CM01**, open the **ConfigMgr console**, and navigate to **Software Library / Application Management / Approval Requests**.
6. Select the request from **VIAMONSTRA\JAP**, and on the ribbon, click **Approve**.
7. Type a comment and click **OK**.

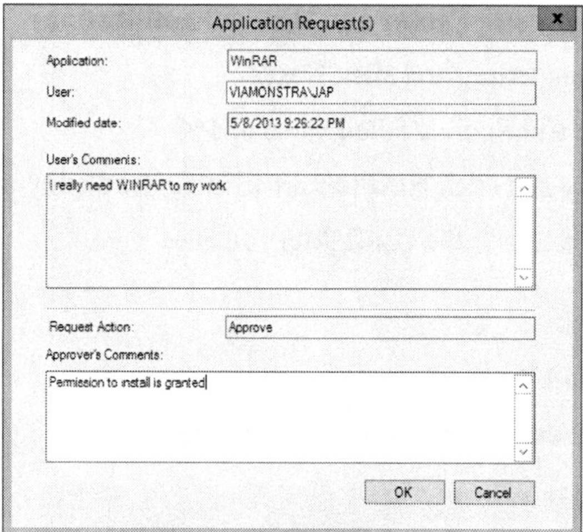

Accepting the approval request.

8. On **PC0001**, log on as **VIAMONSTRA\JAP**.
9. To manually start the installation, start **Internet Explorer** and open **http://cm01/CMApplicationCatalog**.
10. Select the **WinRAR** application and click **Install**.
11. Click **Yes** and start the installation.

You also can wait until the user policy has been refreshed. After that, the user is presented with installation options. The installation can be postponed to outside the user's business hours or started now. The user selects an option and clicks OK.

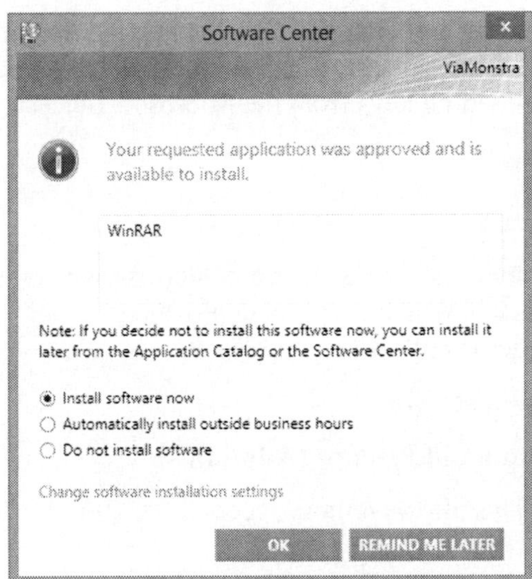

Installation options presented after the application request is approved.

Creating Modern-Style Applications

Creating and deploying modern-style applications for Windows 8 is not that difficult a task. As a matter of fact, it is much less complex than working with traditional Windows applications. In ViaMonstra, you have an in-house modern-style application that you must install on all Windows 8 devices.

Modern-style applications can be deployed in two ways:

- **Deeplinking**. A deployment type in which the application is not installed, but instead the end-user is taken to a specific application in the Windows Store or a company portal.
- **Sideloading**. A deployment type typically used when deploying custom-made in-house applications that are not available in the Windows Store.

Requirements for Modern-Style Applications

There are certain requirements that must be fulfilled before deploying modern-style applications:

- You need an Appx package or link to an existing application in the Windows Store.
- The application must be signed, and the Windows 8 device must trust the signer of the code-signing certificate.
- To install the application, the user must have a valid Microsoft account to access the Windows Store.
- For deeplinking, the application must be installed on a reference device.
- For sideloading, you must configure the registry on the client to allow side-loaded application installations.

- Depending on the Windows version and domain membership, a side-loading key might be required. For Windows 8 Enterprise domain-joined devices, side-loading is not required. For other devices, you must obtain valid side-loading keys from the Microsoft License Service Center.

Creating a Deeplink

In ViaMonstra, you need to make sure that all users have easy access to the modern-style version of Microsoft Lync. To do that, use the following steps to create a deeplink deployment for all users. You must have a valid Microsoft account in order to follow the steps.

1. On **PC0001**, log on as **VIAMONSTRA\Administrator**.
2. Press **[Windows logo key] + X** and click **Command Prompt (Admin).**
3. Type **winrm quickconfig** and press **Enter**. (This allows remote access to PC0001.) When prompted, type **y** and press **Enter**.
4. Open the **Windows Store** and search for **Microsoft Lync**. When you find it, sign in with a valid Microsoft account and install the application.
5. On **CM01**, log on as **VIAMONSTRA\Administrator** and open the **ConfigMgr console**.
6. In the **Software Library**, navigate to **Application Management / Applications / Optional User**.
7. On the ribbon, click **Create Application**.
8. On the **General** page, select these settings and click **Next**:
    a. Type: **Windows app package (in the Windows Store)**
    b. Location: Click **Browse**, and in **Computer name**, type **PC0001** and click **Connect**.
    c. From the list of installed applications, select **Microsoft.LyncMX** and click **OK**.

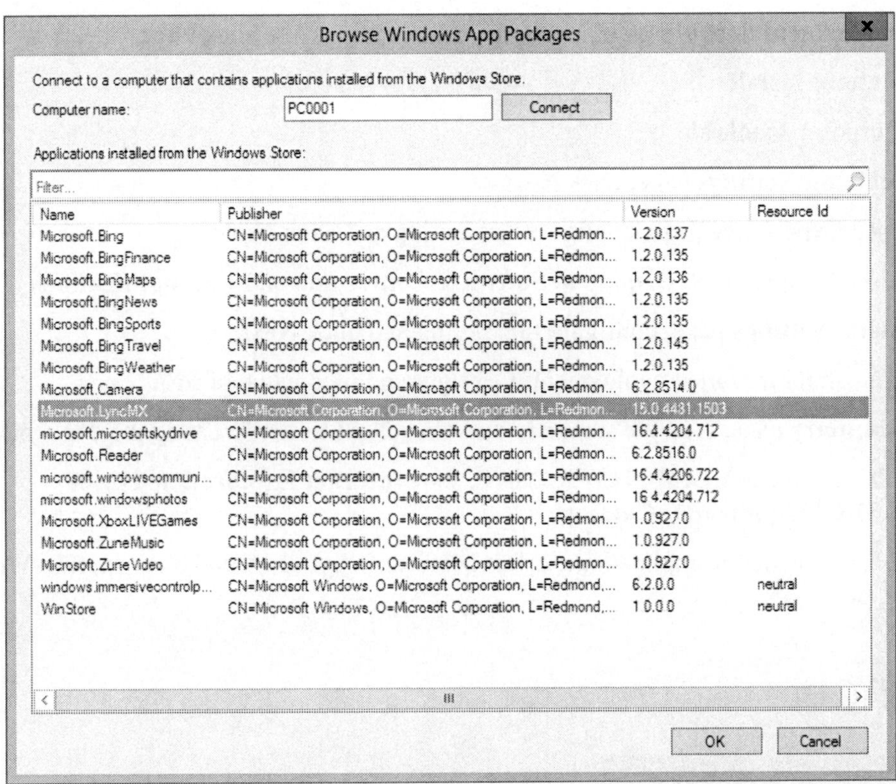

Selecting an installed application from a reference device.

9. On the **Import Information** page, notice all the detailed information about the application and click **Next**.

10. On the **General Information** page, in **Administrative categories**, click **Select** and create a new category called **Communication**. Click **OK** and finish the wizard.

Deploy a Deeplink Application

1. On **CM01**, open the **ConfigMgr console**.
2. Select the **Software Library** workspace, and then select **Application Management / Applications / Optional User**.
3. Select the **Microsoft.LyncMX** application.
4. From the ribbon, click **Deployment / Deploy**.
5. On the **General** page, in **Collection**, click **Browse**; then select the **All Users** collection, click **OK**, and then click **Next**.
6. On the **Content** page, click **Add / Distribution Point Group**. Select **All Content**, click **OK**, and then click **Next**.

7. On the **Deployment Settings** page, configure these settings and click **Next**:

   a. Action: **Install**

   b. Purpose: **Available**

8. On the **Schedule Settings** page, click **Next**.

9. On the **User Experience** page, configure this setting and click **Next**:

   User Notifications: **Display in Software Center and show all notifications**

10. On the **Alerts Settings** page, configure this setting and click **Next**:

    Threshold for failed deployment: Configure a failed value of **5%**.

11. On the **Summary** page, read the summary and click **Next** to start creating the deployment.

12. On **PC0001**, log on as **VIAMONSTRA\JAP**, start **Internet Explorer**, and open **http://cm01/CMApplicationCatalog**.

13. From the list of available applications, select **Microsoft.LyncMX** and click **Install**. When prompted, click **Yes**.

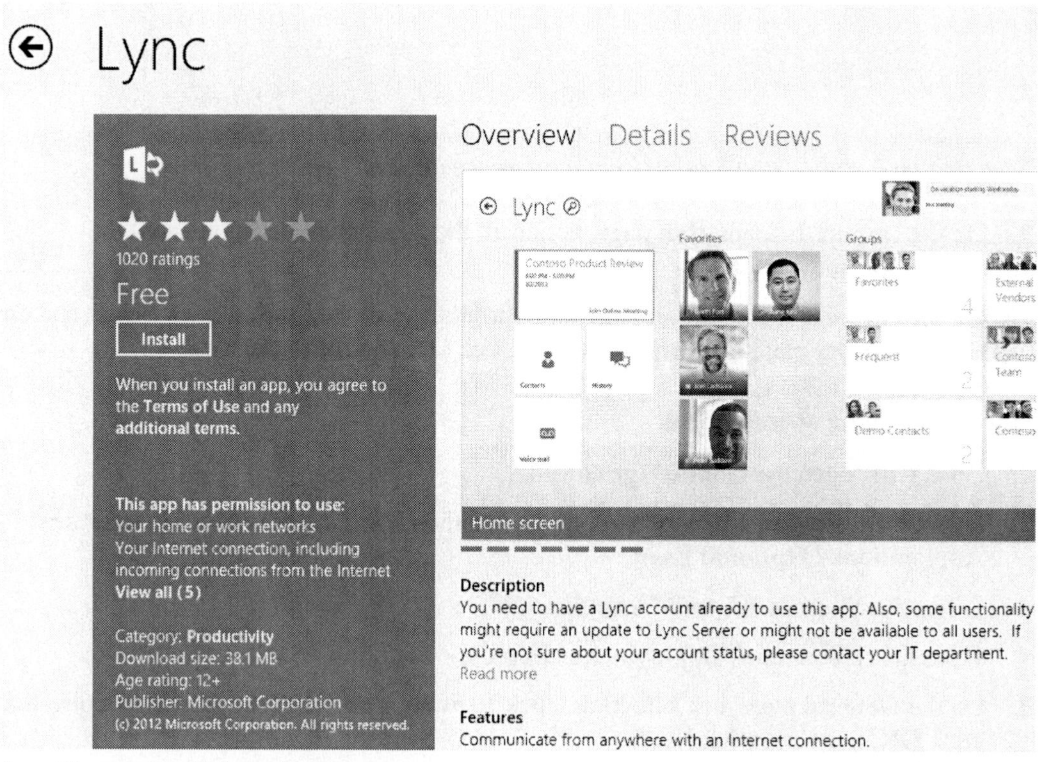

Installing a deeplink application.

14. From the **Windows Store**, click **Install**. When prompted, sign in with a Microsoft account.

Working with Sideloading Applications

ViaMonstra has developed a very important in-house application that must be available to users on all Windows 8 Enterprise devices. Before deploying the application, you first need to create a group policy that enables sideloading and install the certificate on all devices. In these steps, I assume you have downloaded the book sample files which contain the ViaMonstra modern-style application and copied it to D:\Sources\Software\ViaMonstra_ModernStyle on CM01.

1. Create the group policy:
   a. On **DC01**, log on as **VIAMONSTRA\Administrator**, and open the **Group Policy Management console**.
   b. Expand **Forest: corp.viamonstra.com**.
   c. Expand **Domains**.
   d. Right-click the **corp.viamonstra.com** domain and select **Create a GPO in this domain, and Link it here**.
   e. Create a new Group Policy object called **Allow sideloading application** and click **OK**.
   f. Right-click **Allow sideloading application GPO** and select **Edit**.
   g. Expand **Computer Configuration / Policies / Administrative Templates / Windows Components**, and select **App Package Deployment**.
   h. Double-click **Allow All trusted apps to install**, select **Enabled**, and click **OK**.
   i. Close the **Group Policy Management console**.
2. Install the certificate in the Trusted Root store. (Chapter 8 explains how you can use a ConfigMgr package to deploy certificates. In this example, you deploy it manually on PC0001.)
   a. On **PC0001**, log on as **VIAMONSTRA\Administrator**.
   b. From the **Start screen**, open a command prompt as **administrator**, type **MMC**, and press **Enter**.
   c. Press **Ctrl + M** and click **Add** to open the **Add/Remove** snap-in. Select **Certificates** and click **Add**.
   d. Select **Computer account** and click **Next**.
   e. Select **Local computer**, and then click **Finish** and **OK.**
   f. Expand the **Trusted Root Certification Authority** store and click **All Tasks, Import**.
   g. On the **Welcome to the Certificate Import** page, click **Next**.

h. On the **File to Import** page, type **\\CM01\Sources$\Software\ViaMonstra_Modernstyle\ViaMonstra LOB II_1.0.0.0_AnyCPU.cer** and click **Next**.

i. On the **Certificate Store** page, ensure **Trusted Root Certification Authorities** is selected and finish the import.

Create the Application in ConfigMgr

1. In the **Software Library**, navigate to **Application Management\Applications\Optional User**.
2. On the ribbon, click **Create Application**.
3. In the **General** page, select these settings and click **Next**:
   a. Type: **Windows app package (appx file)**
   b. Location: Type **\\cm01\sources$\Software\ViaMonstra_ModernStyle\ViaMonstra LOB II_1.0.0.0_AnyCPU.appx**.
4. On the **Import Information** page, read the imported information and click **Next**.
5. On the **General Information** page, click **Select** and create a **ViaMonstra LOB** category. Click **OK** twice and finish the wizard.

Deploy the Sideloading Application

1. On **CM01**, log on as **VIAMONSTRA\Administrator** and open the **ConfigMgr console**.
2. Select the **Software Library** workspace, and then select **Application Management**, **Applications**, **Optional User**.
3. Select the **ViaMonstra LOB II** application.
4. From the ribbon, click **Deployment / Deploy**.
5. On the **General** page, in **Collection**, click **Browse**; then select the **All Users** collection, click **OK**, and then click **Next**.
6. On the **Content** page, click **Add**, **Distribution Point Group**. Select **All Content**, click **OK**, and then click **Next**.
7. On **Deployment Settings** page, configure these settings and click **Next**:
   a. Action: **Install**
   b. Purpose: **Available**
8. On the **Schedule Settings** page, click **Next**.
9. On the **User Experience** page, configure this setting and click **Next**:

   User Notifications: **Display in Software Center and show all notifications**

10. On the **Alerts Settings** page, configure this setting and click **Next**:

    Threshold for failed deployment: Configure a failed value of **5%**.

11. On the **Summary** page, read the summary and click **Next** to start creating the deployment.
12. On **PC0001**, log on as **VIAMONSTRA\JAP**, start **Internet Explorer**, and open **http://cm01/cmapplication catalog.**
13. Select the **ViaMonstra LOB II** application and click **Install.**

Sideloading modern-style applications.

Creating Mac OS X Applications

In order to install applications on a Mac OS X, the application must first be repackaged on a Mac OS computer with the CMApppUtil tool. ViaMonstra has a few Apple computers, so it has been decided to assist the users with application support. To repackage 7-Zip for Mac, follow these steps:

1. On a **Mac OS X** computer with the CMApppUtil tool installed.
2. Open a terminal, navigate to the **Tools** folder, and type the following command:

   ```
   sudo ./CMAppUtil -c ./7zX_1_71.dmg -o ./
   ```

3. Copy the **7zX.app.cmmac** file to **\\CM01\Sources$\Software\7-Zip\Mac**.

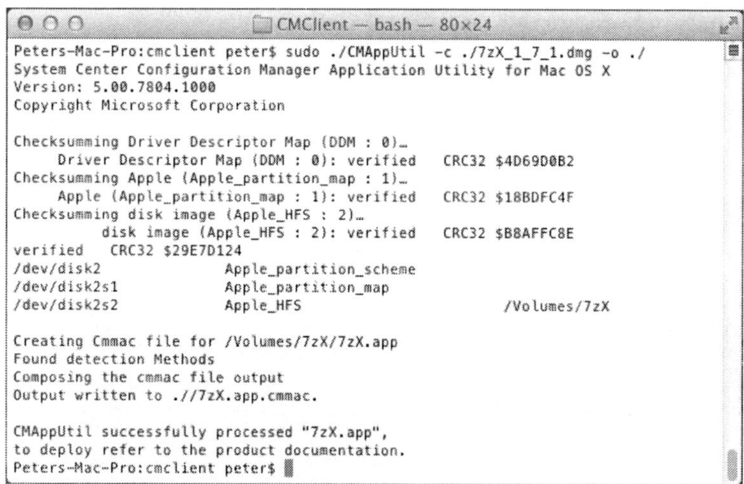

Creating applications on a Mac OS.

Creating the 7-Zip Application for Windows and Mac OS X

The following steps take you through the creation of a 7-Zip application with a MSI deployment type and a Mac OS deployment type. You configure only the most basic application properties. If you have the time, however, I encourage you to fill out the application metadata just like you did for Microsoft Office 2013.

In these steps, I assume you have downloaded 7-Zip 9.20 x64 for Windows to D:\Sources\Software\7-Zip\Windows and 7-Zip for Mac to D:\Sources\Software\7-Zip\Mac on CM01.

1. On **CM01**, log on as **VIAMONSTRA\Administrator** and open the **ConfigMgr console**.
2. In the **Software Library** workspace, select **Application Management / Applications**.
3. Select the **Optional User** folder, and on the ribbon, click **Create Application**.
4. On the **General** page, configure these settings and click **Next**:
   a. Type: **Windows Installer (*.msi file)**
   b. Location: **\\CM01\Sources$\Software\7-Zip\Windows\7z920-x64.MSI**
   c. Click **Yes** when asked about importing this file.
5. On the **Import Information** page, read the information about the imported application and deployment and click **Next**.
6. On the **General Information** page, specify these application properties and click **Next**:
   a. Name: **7-Zip**
   b. Administrator comments: **Our only company supported Zip application**

c. Manufacturer: **7-zip.org**
d. Software version: **9.20**
e. Optional reference: **PO7Z**
f. Administrative Categories: Click **Select**, select **Utility**, and click **OK.**

7. On the **Summary** page, click **Next**, and then click **Close**.
8. Select the **Deployment Types** tab and open the properties for the newly create deployment type.
9. In **Name**, change the name to **7-ZIP 9.20 X64 MSI**.
10. Select the **Requirements** tab and click **Add.**
11. In **Category**, select **Device**; in **Condition**, select **Operating System**; and in the list of operating systems, select **All Windows 7 (64-bit), All Windows 8 (64-bit)**, and **All Windows Server 2012 (64-bit)** and click **OK** twice.
12. To create the Mac OS deployment type, select the **7-Zip** application, and then on the ribbon, click **Create Deployment Type**.
13. On the **General** page, in **Type**, select **Mac OS X, Location**; then type **CM01\Sources$\Software\7-ZIP\Mac\7zX.app.cmmac** and click **Next**.

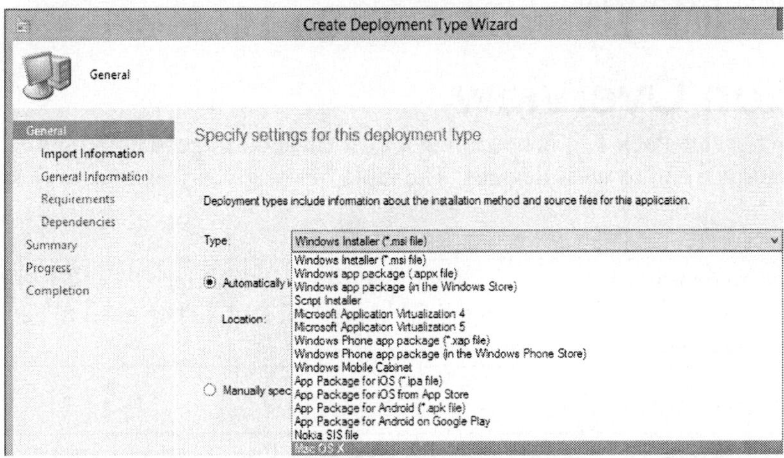

Creating the Mac OS deployment type.

14. On the **Import Information** page, read the information and click **Next**.
15. On the **General Information** page, keep the default settings and click **Next**.

16. On the **Requirements** page, click **Add**, select all the **Mac OS X** operating systems, and click **OK**.

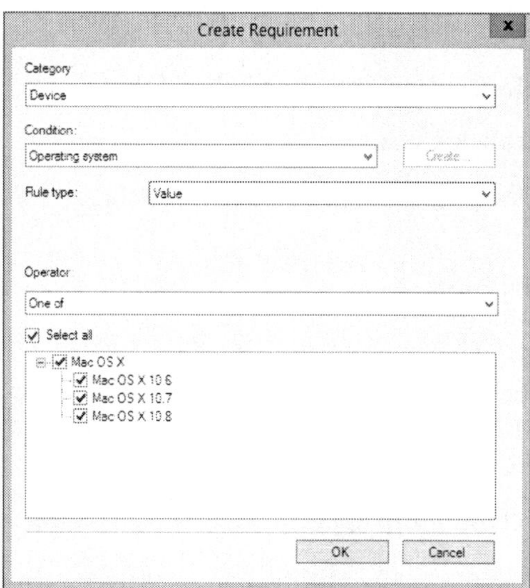

Ensuing the Mac application can be installed only on supported Mac OS X systems.

17. Finish the Deployment Type Wizard.

The Application Overview

With all the new changes in Service Pack 1, it is becoming a little difficult to get a complete overview of what can be deployed and to what devices. The table below gives you an overview of the available choices.

Note: As you learned earlier, to deploy Mac OS X applications using ConfigMgr 2012 SP1, they must first be repackaged on a Mac OS computer with the CMApppUtil tool. (They need to be converted into the Microsoft specified .cmmac format.)

	Windows 8 and Windows RT	**Windows Phone 8**	**Apple iOS**	**Android**	**Mac OS X**	**UNIX**
Deeplink	Yes	Yes	Yes	Yes	No	No
In-house application	*appx	*xap	*.ipa	*.apk	*.MPKG *.PKG *.APP *.DMG	Only through the package model

Uninstall and Superseded Applications

As a natural part of any application life cycle is the decommissioning phase where the application is either superseded with a new version or uninstalled. You can supersede any application with another application as long as both applications are created as applications in the ConfigMgr console.

1. On **CM01**, in the **ConfigMgr console**, select the **7-Zip** application, and then on the ribbon, click **Properties**.
2. Click the **Supersedence** tab.
3. Click **Add**, configure these settings, and click **OK**:
    a. Superseded Application: Click **Browse**, select **Optional User / WinRAR**, and then click **OK**.
    b. New Deployment Type: **7-ZIP 9.20 X64 MSI**
    c. Uninstall: Enable **Uninstall**.

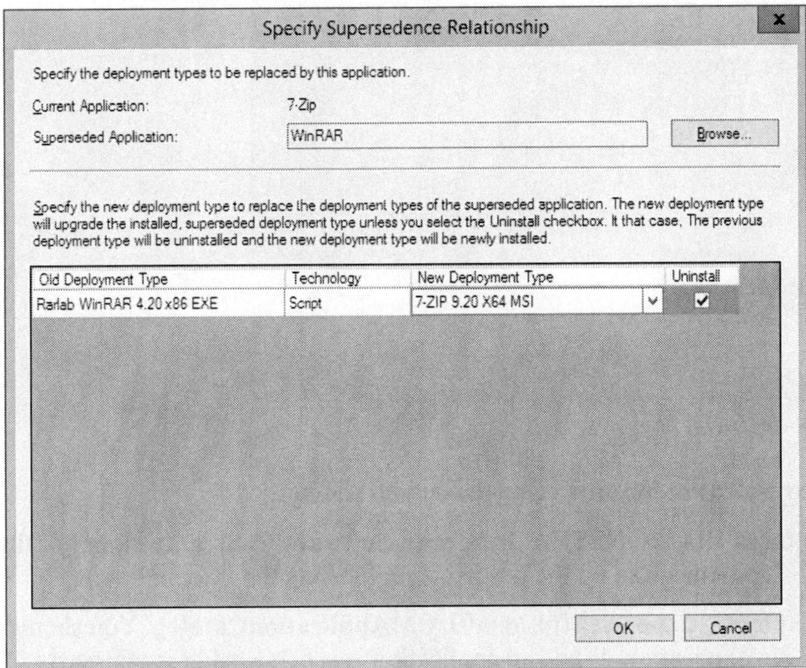

Configuring a supersedence relationship.

4. Click **OK** twice.
5. Select the **7-Zip** application, and from the ribbon's **Home** tab, click **Deployment / Deploy**.
6. On the **General** page, click **Browse** and select **Software / SWU_7-Zip_Install** as the collection; then click **OK** and **Next**.

7. On the **Content** page, click **Add / Distribution Point Group**, and select the **All Content** distribution point group; click **OK** and **Next**.
8. On the **Deployment Settings** page, configure these settings and click **Next**:
    a. Action: **Install**
    b. Purpose: **Available**
    c. Automatically upgrade any superseded versions of this application: **Enabled**

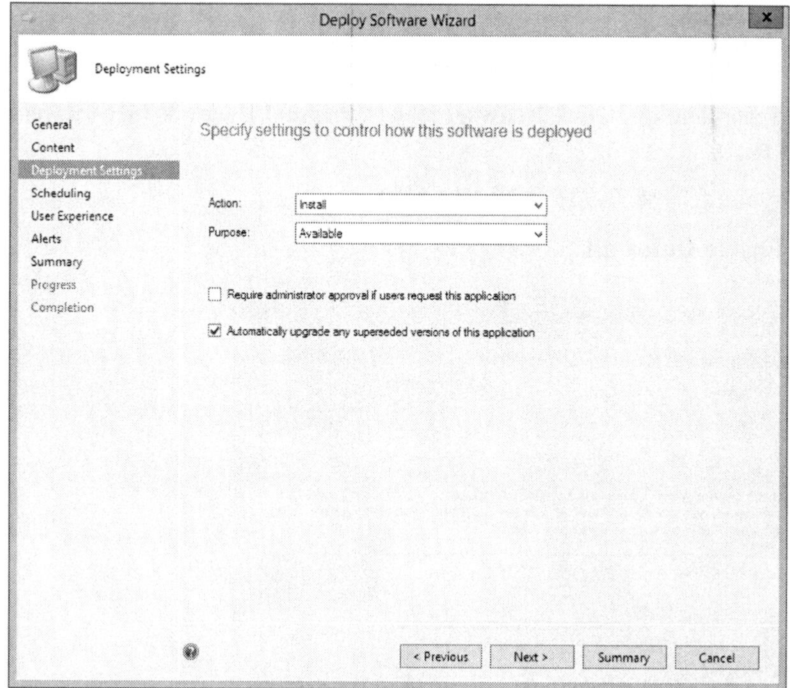

Creating an optional deployment.

9. Finish the **Deploy Software Wizard** using the default settings.
10. On **PC0001**, log on as **VIAMONSTRA\JAP**, open **Software Center**, and monitor the upgrade process. (You can speed up the process by refreshing the User policy.)
11. Start **Internet Explorer**, and open **http://cm01/CMApplicationCatalog**. You should be able to see the 7-Zip application. When an application is superseded, it is removed automatically as an option from the Application Catalog.

Uninstall 7-Zip

1. On **CM01**, log on as **VIAMONSTRA\Administrator** and open the **ConfigMgr console**.
2. Navigate to the **Software Library** workspace, and select the **7-Zip** application.

3. From the ribbon's **Home** tab, click **Deployment / Deploy**; select the **Software / SWU_7-Zip_Uninstall** collection; click **OK** twice; and then click **Next**.
4. On the **Deployment Settings** page, configure the **Action** to **Uninstall,** enable **Pre-deploy software to the users's primary device**, and click **Next**.

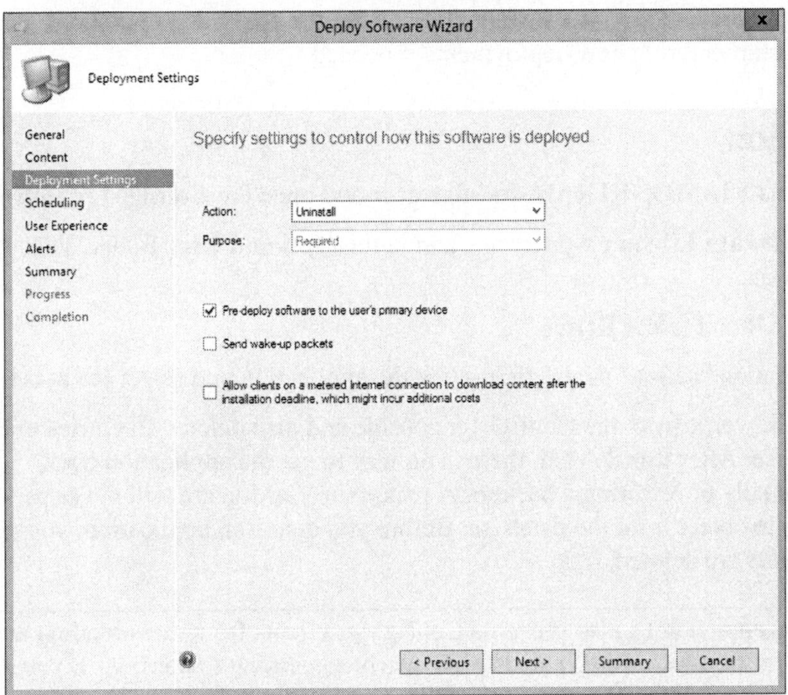

Creating an uninstall deployment.

5. On the **Schedule** page, click **Next**.
6. On the **User Experience** page, select **Software Uninstall**.
7. Finish the **Deploy Software Wizard** using the default settings.
8. On **DC01**, open **Active Directory Users and Computers**.
9. Navigate to the **ViaMonstra / Software Groups** OU. Right-click the **SW_7-Zip_Uninstall** group, select **Properties**, and click the **Members** tab.
10. Click **Add** and add **JAP** as a group member. By adding JAP to the uninstall group, you automatically add her to the corresponding SW_7-Zip_Uninstall collection. Members of that collection are automatically excluded from the SW_7-Zip_Install collection.

Note: If you target an install and an uninstall deployment to the same collection, the install deployment always takes precedence over that uninstall deployment. This is the main reason for always creating an Exclude collection rule in the SW Install collection.

Remove Applications from the ConfigMgr Console

After applications have been uninstalled and are no long supported in ViaMonstra, the policy is to first retire the application and then delete it completely from the ConfigMgr console after 3 months. After an application is retired, no new deployments are available. The application is not automatically uninstalled from any device as a consequence of retiring it in the console. The retirement action is simply to prevent any new installations. After the application is retired, you can always reinstate it and start creating new deployments if needed.

Retire an Application

1. On **CM01**, log on as **VIAMONSTRA\Administrator** and open the **ConfigMgr console**.
2. Navigate to the **Software Library** workspace, and in the **Optional User** folder, select the **WinRAR** application.
3. Right-click **WinRAR** and select **Retire**.

   To make the application "active" again, right-click the application and select **Reinstate**.

Deleting the application removes it from the ConfigMgr console and also deletes all entries of the application from the database. After it is deleted, there is no way to get the application back, except by recreating it manually or restoring a backup. A restore in ViaMonstra will never be started just to restore a single object from the database. Before you delete an application, you need to ensure that all deployments are deleted.

Real World Note: Retiring applications also prevents ConfigMgr clients from downloading and evaluating policies related to the application. This is particularly something to consider if you have many versions of the same application. Retire the older version instead of leaving it active in the ConfigMgr console.

Export an Application

1. On **CM01**, log on as **VIAMONSTRA\Administrator** and open the **ConfigMgr console**.
2. Navigate to the **Software Library** workspace, and in the **Optional User** folder, select the **WinRAR** application.
3. Right-click **WinRAR** and select **Export**.

4. On the **General** page, in **File**, click **Browse**; then navigate to **D:\Setup\Exported Software\WinRAR** (the folder must be manually created), type in **WinRAR**, and click **Next**.

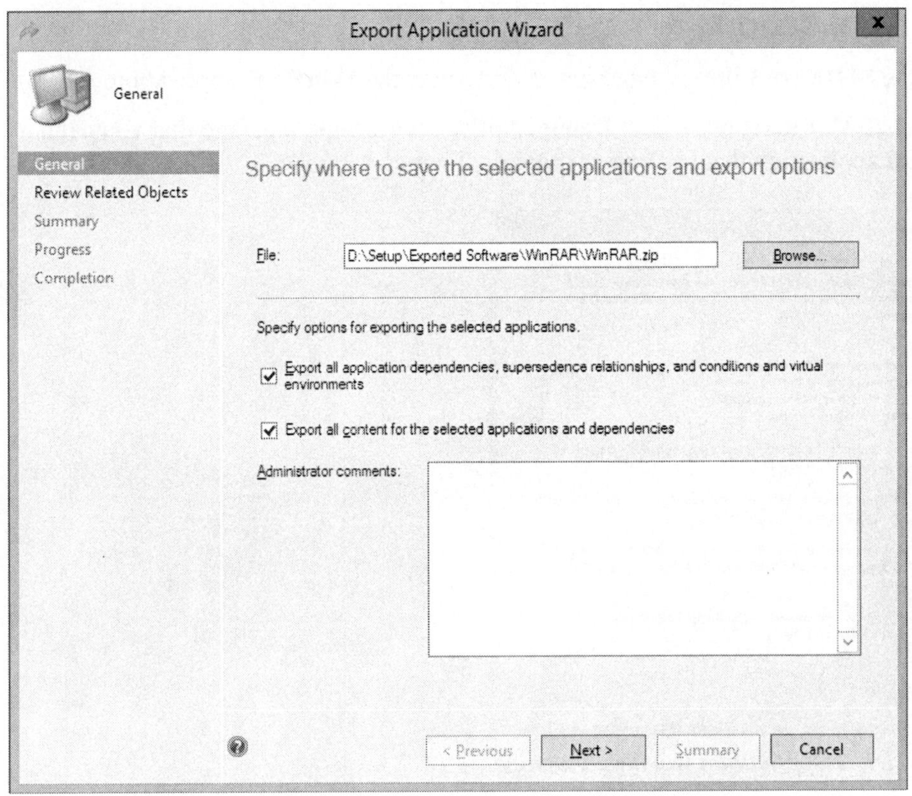

Exporting the WinRAR application.

5. On the **Review Related Objects** page, notice that WinRAR is listed along with the categories and click **Next**.
6. On the **Summary** page, read the summary and click **Next** to start exporting the application.
7. On the **Completion** page, click **Close** to return to the ConfigMgr console.

Retire an Application

1. Go to the **Software Library** workspace, and select the **WinRAR** application.
2. Right-click **WinRAR** and select **Retire**. Notice the status changed from Active to Retired. This does not uninstall the application, but rather prevents administrators from creating new deployments.

Note: To enable a retired appliation, simply select the application and click Reinstate. This allows you to create new deployments.

Delete an Application

1. Go to the **Software Library** workspace, and select the **WinRAR** application.
2. Right-click **WinRAR** and select **Delete**. Notice the warning message that you cannot delete an application that has one or more deployments.

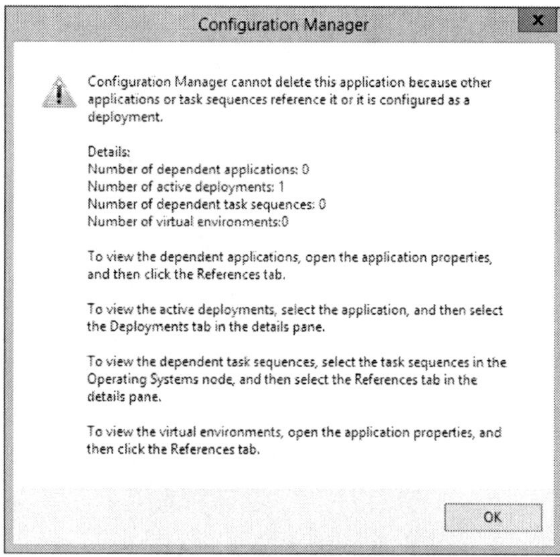

The cannot delete application warning message.

3. Click **OK** in the warning message and select the **Deployments** tab.
4. Right-click the **SWU_WinRAR_Install** deployment and click **Delete**.
5. Click **OK** in the Delete warning dialog box.
6. Right-click the **WinRAR** application and select **Delete**. Notice the warning about permanently deleting the application from ConfigMgr. Click **Yes** to delete the application.

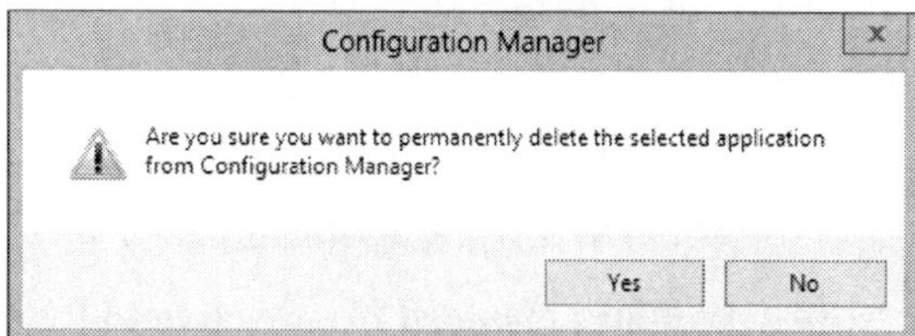

The delete the application warning message.

Import an Application

1. On **CM01**, open the **ConfigMgr console**.
2. Navigate to the **Software Library** workspace, right-click the **User Optional** folder, and select **Import Application**.
3. On the **General** page, in the **File** text box, click **Browse**: then navigate to **\\CM01\D$\Setup\Exported Software\WinRAR**, select the **WinRAR.zip** file, click **Open**, and click **Next**.
4. On the **File Content** page, accept the default settings and click **Next**.
5. On the **Summary** page, read the summary and click **Next** to start the import.
6. On the **Completion** page, click **Close** to return to the ConfigMgr console.

Useful Log Files

This table includes log files you can use to track activity related to your applications and packages.

Log File	Description	Location
execmgr.log	Records information about classical packages and task sequences	Client default
AppIntentEval.log	Records information about the current and intended state of applications, their applicability.	Client default
AppDiscovery.log	Records information about install and uninstall attempts and detection method evaluations.	Client default
ConfigMgrSoftwareCatalog.log	Records the information of the Application Catalog, which includes its use of Silverlight	Client default
SoftwareCenterSystemTasks.log	Records the activities for Software Center prerequisite component validation. This log files is mainly used if Software center is causing problems.	Client default
SoftwareCatalogUpdateEndpoint.log	Records the activities for managing the address for the Web Application Catalog shown in Software Center.	Client default
CAS.log	Records the activities for managing the client cache.	Client default

Log File	**Description**	**Location**
SCClient_<domain>@<username>_1.log	Records the activity in Software Center for the specified user on the client computer	Client default
SCNotify_<domain>@<username>_1.log	Records the activity for notifying users about software for the specified user	Client default
UserAffinity.log	Records details about user device affinity.	Client default
LocationServices.log	Records information about which distribution point used for downloading packages,	Client default
DataTransferService.log	Records all BITS communication for policy and package access.	Client default
ContentTransferManager.log	Records information about BITS and SMB in regards to downloading and accessing packages	Client default
SMSdpmon.log	Records information about the health monitoring scheduled task that is configured on a distribution point	Distribution point .\SMS_DP$\SMS\Logs
smsdpprov.log	Records information about injecting packages into the content library	Distribution point .\SMS_DP$\SMS\Logs

Chapter 8

Software Update Deployment

Keeping Windows and third-party software up-to-date with the latest security updates is a discipline that requires planning and testing. When you plan for software updates, it's very important that you take these factors into consideration:

- It must be easy to approve and deploy new updates.
- No updates must be installed without proper testing.
- All devices must be part of the update plan.
- There must be a plan for the least acceptable compliance level.

Key Elements in Any Software Update Solution

It is important to understand that software update or patch management is much more than deploying some updates to a certain number of client computers. The key to a real software update solution is to look at all the aspects of the process, such as:

- Do you have the required vulnerability intelligence needed to make the correct decisions?
- Do you have a process for detecting all vulnerabilities?
- Do you have a tool or process that enables you to create the correct update packages?
- Do you have a tool that can deploy the updates?

For ViaMonstra, I have defined a real software update management solution like this:

Understanding the Update Components

Server Components

The software update solution consists of two components, an active software update point with WSUS installed and the ConfigMgr client. An active software update point is configured on the top level site hosted on a server with Internet access. Some of the software update's synchronization settings are configured at the CAS and are not available at child sites. All primary sites in the ConfigMgr hierarchy must have an active software update point unlike secondary sites that do not require a software update point.

A High-Level Overview of the Software Update Process

1. The WSUS server synchronizes software update metadata from Windows Update. No binaries will be downloaded as part of this process.
2. The active software update point synchronizes metadata from the WSUS server.
3. The ConfigMgr client performs scanning using metadata from the WSUS server. Compliance state messages are uploaded to the ConfigMgr server through the management point.
4. From the ConfigMgr server, updates are approved and content distributed to distribution point(s).
5. The ConfigMgr client receives the deployment policies, starts downloading required updates from the distribution point to the cache, and installs the updates according to the deadline.

Server Requirements for the Software Update Point

- WSUS 3.0 SP2 or above locally installed
- WSUS administrator console installed on the site server if WSUS is installed remotely

Client Requirements

- Clients must be running Windows Update Agent 3.0 or above.
- The Automatic Updates service must be running.
- There are no group policies pointing to other WSUS server. Configure the client to turn off any automatic updates.

> **Real World Note:** If you have a proxy server, ensure that the software update point can access these sites:
>
> http://windowsupdate.microsoft.com
> http://*.windowsupdate.microsoft.com
> https://*.windowsupdate.microsoft.com
> http://*.update.microsoft.com
> https://*.update.microsoft.com
> http://*.windowsupdate.com
> http://download.windowsupdate.com
> http://download.microsoft.com
> http://*.download.windowsupdate.com
> http://test.stats.update.microsoft.com
> http://ntservicepack.microsoft.com

WSUS Group Policies

The ConfigMgr client receives information about the active software update point as part of the machine policy. The information is merged into local policies as a local WUAU policy. If domain policies for Windows Update are defined, they override the ConfigMgr policies and can cause the clients not to scan correctly.

> **Real World Note:** It's highly recommended to configure a WSUS group policy where the setting "Enable Automatic Updates" is disabled. That way, if for any reason you disable the software update client agent setting, clients will fall back to the group policy and the agent will be disabled. A disabled agent is so much better than having thousands of clients automatically downloading and installing updates using the default Windows settings. The only drawback to this solution is that the Widows Update agent is not upgraded to the latest version. Upgrading the Windows Update agent is a process controlled by WSUS, and it happens only if Configure Automatic Updates is enabled. Unfortunately, there is no longer a stand-alone agent that can be deployed through ConfigMgr. Another way to be safe is by adding the software update point as the WSUS server in a group policy.

Software Update Point Components

When working with a software update point, you have three components that are very interesting to monitor and know about.

WSUS Control Manager

The WSUS Control Manager is responsible for checking the health of the WSUS server. The check is performed once an hour, and you can monitor it by reading the WSUSctrl.log file on the WSUS server.

WSUS Configuration Manager

The WSUS Configuration Manager component initially configures the WSUS settings. You can change these settings any time from the Software Update Point Component properties in ConfigMgr. Most WSUS settings should be configured in the ConfigMgr console. If settings are changed from the WSUS console, they might overwritten by the settings found in ConfigMgr. When I write "might," it is because not all settings can be controlled from the ConfigMgr console.

WSUS Synchronization Manager

The WSUS Synchronization Manager handles the synchronization process between Microsoft Windows Update and the WSUS server and between the WSUS server and the ConfigMgr server. When synchronization is initiated at the top-level site, the software updates metadata is synchronized from Microsoft Update. After a complete synchronization, the WSUS Synchronization Manager synchronizes the software updates metadata from the WSUS database to ConfigMgr. After that process is complete, software updates metadata will be replicated to any child sites.

Planning for Software Updates

Approving and installing updates can be a very easy process when you have some basic understanding of the software update components.

Software Update Collections

Like with any other feature, it is important that your software update solution has a collection design that allows you to ease the administrative work while keeping complete control of the feature. When designing a collection, it's important that you know exactly how you want to control the deployments.

Create Software Update Management Collections

This section guides you through creating the needed software update collections. With those collections, you can create a software update solution where you can minimize the number of deployments and yet still be able control different deployment times.

- **Pilot 1.** A collection used for a simple test to see whether the updates can install and restart the computers without breaking anything.
- **Pilot 2.** A test collection that runs after pilot 1 is accepted. In pilot 2, ViaMonstra will have a subset of computers from different departments. All users are informed about their membership to this group.
- **WRK Production.** The workstation production collection. After pilot 1 and pilot 2 are accepted, members not part of the Excluded collection have the updates installed.
- **WRK Excluded.** The workstation collection for members that for any reason must be excluded in any software update deployment.

- **SRV Automatic.** The collection containing servers where updates are automatically installed and servers restarted in a maintenance window. The collection will only have Include Collection rules, one rule for each of the SRV MW collections.
- **SRV MW.** There will be multiple SRV MW collections, one for each unique maintenance window. ViaMonstra will have four collections, where the first is named SRV MW1. The maintenance windows are used to control when software updates are installed and the servers restarted. For each collection, you create a unique maintenance window.
- **SRV Manual.** The collection containing servers where updates must be manually installed and the server manually restarted.

Create the Active Directory Groups

1. On **DC01**, log on as **VIAMONSTRA\Administrator** and open **Active Directory Users and Computers**.
2. You must create the domain local security groups in the **Software Groups** OU; otherwise, they will not be discovered by the Security Group discovery process.
3. In the **Software Groups** OU, create the domain local security groups in the following table and add the listed computer accounts as members.

Active Directory Security Group	Add These Computers to the Active Directory Group
SUM_Pilot1	PC0001
SUM_Pilot2	
SUM_WRK_Excluded	
SUM_MW1	DC01
SUM_MW2	CM02 EX01 (only if you have set up an Exchange Server)
SUM_MW3	CM03
SUM_SRV_Manual	CM01

Create the Pilot 1 and Pilot 2 Collections

In this guide and the following two, you create the necessary software update collections.

> **Note:** Before you create the following collections, I will warn you that, at the end of this part, there is a PowerShell script that creates all the collections and collection queries, all fully automated. If you can't wait for automation, skip directly to the "Automate Adding Queries to Device Collections Using PowerShell" section a few pages later in this book.

1. On **CM01**, log on as **VIAMONSTRA\Administrator** and open the **ConfigMgr console**.
2. In the **Assets and Compliance** workspace, select **Device Collections** and the **Software Updates** folder.
3. On the ribbon, click **Create Device Collection**.
4. On the **General** page, define these settings and click **Next**:
    a. Name: **SUM Pilot 1**
    b. Comment: **All computers that are part of the first update pilot deployment**
    c. Limiting Collection: Click **Browse**, select the **ViaMonstra** folder, and select **VM All Workstations**.
5. On the **Membership Rules** page, define these settings:
    a. Enable **Use incremental updates for this collection.**
    b. Click **Add Rule / Query Rule.**
    c. Name the rule **SUM Pilot 1** and click **Edit Query Statement.**
    d. Select the **Criteria** tab.
    e. Click the **yellow icon** to build the criteria, and then click **Select.**
    f. Select **System Resource** as the **Attribute class.**
    g. Select **System Group Name** as the **Attribute.**
    h. Click **OK** to return to the Criterion Properties dialog box.

i. Click **Operator** and select **is equal to**; in **Value**, type **VIAMONSTRA\SUM_Pilot1**. (You also can click Value and select the group name from a list of groups.)

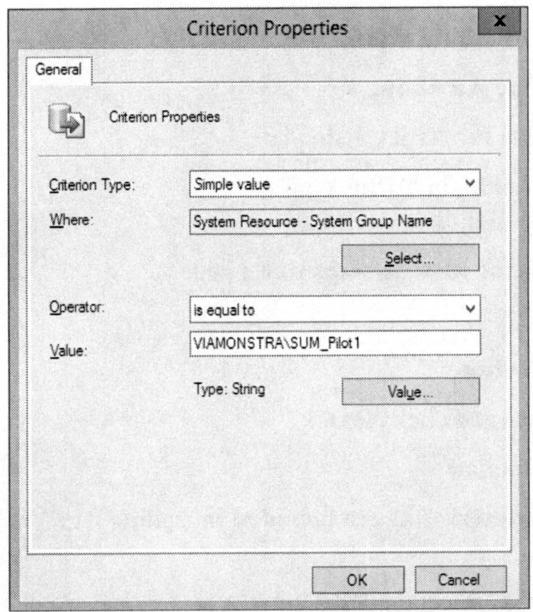

Creating a device collection based on AD group membership.

j. Click **OK three times** to return to the Memberships Rules page.

6. Click **Next** twice, and then click **Close**.
7. Repeat the preceding steps to create the **SUM Pilot 2** collection. Change the collection comment to: **All computers that are part of the second update pilot deployment**.

Create the Workstation Collections

1. While still in the **Software Updates** folder, click **Create Device Collection** on the ribbon.
2. On the **General** page, define these settings and click **Next**:
    a. Name: **SUM Excluded**
    b. Comment: **All workstation computers that are excluded from software updates**
    c. Limiting Collection: Click **Browse**, select the **Root** folder, and select **All Systems**.
3. On the **Membership Rules** page, define these settings and then click **OK**:
    a. Enable **Use incremental updates for this collection**.
    b. Click **Add Rule / Query Rule**.

c. Name the rule **SUM Excluded** and click **Edit Query Statement**.
d. Select the **Criteria** tab.
e. Click the **yellow icon** to build the criteria, and then click **Select**.
f. Select **System Resource** as the **Attribute class**.
g. Select **System Group Name** as the **Attribute**.
h. Click **OK** to return to the Criterion Properties dialog box.
i. Click **Operator** and select **is equal to**; in **Value**, type **VIAMONSTRA\SUM_WRK_Excluded**.
j. Click **OK** three times to return to the Memberships Rules page.

4. Click **Next** twice, and click **Close**.
5. On the ribbon, click **Create Device Collection**.
6. On the **General** page, define these settings and click **Next**:
   a. Name: **SUM Workstation Production**
   b. Comment: **All workstation computers that are included in update management**
   c. Limiting Collection: Click **Browse**, select the **ViaMonstra** folder, and select **VM All Workstations**.
7. On the **Membership Rules** page, define these settings and :
   a. Enable **Use incremental updates for this collection**.
   b. Click **Add Rule / Query Rule**.
   c. Name the rule **SUM Workstation Production** and click **Edit Query Statement**.
   d. Select the **Criteria** tab.
   e. Click the **yellow icon** to build the criteria, and then click **Select**.
   f. Select **System Resource** as the **Attribute class**.
   g. Select **Operating System Name and Version** as the **Attribute**.
   h. Click **OK** to return to the Criterion Properties dialog box.
   i. Click **Operator** and select **is like**; in **Value**, type **%Workstation%**.
   j. Click **OK** three times to return to the Memberships Rules page.
8. Click **Add Rule / Exclude Collections**.
9. Click the **Software Updates** folder, select **SUM Excluded**, and click **OK**.
10. Finish the wizard using the default settings.

Create the Server Collections

1. On the ribbon, click **Create Device Collection**.
2. On the **General** page, define these settings and click **Next**:
   a. Name: **SUM Server MW1**
   b. Comment: **All Servers in Maintenance group 1**
   c. Limiting Collection: Click **Browse**, select the **ViaMonstra** folder, and select **VM All Servers**.
3. On the **Membership Rules** page, define these settings:
   a. Enable **Use incremental updates for this collection**.
   b. Click **Add Rule / Query Rule**.
   c. Name the rule **SUM MW1** and click **Edit Query Statement**.
   d. Select the **Criteria** tab.
   e. Click the **yellow icon** to build the criteria, and then click **Select**.
   f. Select **System Resource** as the **Attribute class**.
   g. Select **System Group Name** as the **Attribute**.
   h. Click **OK** to return to the Criterion Properties dialog box.
   i. Click **Operator** and select **is equal to**; in **Value**, type **VIAMONSTRA\SUM_MW1**. (You also can click Value and select the group name from a list of groups.)
   j. Click **OK** three times to return to the Memberships Rules page.
4. Click **Next** twice, and then click **Close**.
5. Repeat the steps to create the two additional collections for **SUM Server MW2** and **SUM Server MW3**.
6. On the ribbon, click **Create Device Collection**.
7. On the **General** page, define these settings and click **Next**:
   a. Name: **SUM Server Automatic**
   b. Comment: **All servers where updates can be installed according to maintenance windows**
   c. Limiting Collection: Click **Browse**, select the **ViaMonstra** folder, and select **VM All Servers**.

8. On the **Membership Rules** page, define these settings:
   a. Enable **Use incremental updates for this collection**.
   b. Click **Add Rule / Include Collections**; then navigate to the **Software Updates** folder, select the three **SUM Server MW** collections, and click **OK**.

Creating include rules for servers.

9. Finish the wizard using the default settings.
10. On the ribbon, click **Create Device Collection**.
11. On the **General** page, define these settings and click **Next**:
    a. Name: **SUM Server Manual**
    b. Comment: **All servers where updates must be manually installed**
    c. Limiting Collection: Click B**rowse**, select the **ViaMonstra** folder, and select **VM All Servers**.
12. On the **Membership Rules** page, define these settings:
    a. Enable **Use incremental updates for this collection**.
    b. Click **Add Rule / Query Rule**.
    c. Name the rule **SUM Server Manual** and click **Edit Query Statement**.
    d. Select the **Criteria** tab.

e. Click the **yellow icon** to build the criteria, and then click **Select**.
f. Select **System Resource** as the **Attribute class**.
g. Select **System Group Name** as the **Attribute**.
h. Click **OK** to return to the Criterion Properties dialog box.
i. Click **Operator** and select **is equal to**, in **Value**, type **VIAMONSTRA\SUM_SRV_Manual**. (You also can click Value and select the group name from a list of groups.)
j. Click **OK** three times to return to the Memberships Rules page.

13. Click **Next** twice, and then click **Close**.
14. On the ribbon, click **Create Device Collection**.
15. On the **General** page, define these settings and click **Next**:
    a. Name: **SUM Server Non-Managed**
    b. Comment: **All Non-managed SUM Servers**
    c. Limiting Collection: Click **Browse**, select the **ViaMonstra** folder, and select **VM All Servers**.
16. On the **Membership Rules** page, define these settings:
    a. Enable **Use incremental updates for this collection**.
    b. Click **Add Rule / Query Rule**.
    c. Name the rule **All SRV** and click **Edit Query Statement**.
    d. Select the **Criteria** tab.
    e. Click the **yellow icon** to build the criteria, and then click **Select**.
    f. Select **System Resource** as the **Attribute class**.
    g. Select **Operating System Name and Version** as the **Attribute**.
    h. Click **OK** to return to the Criterion Properties dialog box.
    i. Click **Operator** and select **is like**; in **Value**, type **%Server%**.
    j. Click **OK** three times to return to the Memberships Rules page.
    k. Click **Add Rule / Exclude Collections**; then navigate to the **Software Updates** folder, select the three **SUM Server MW** collections, and click **OK**.
17. Finish the wizard using the defaults. You should now have all the needed collections to support the software update feature in ConfigMgr.

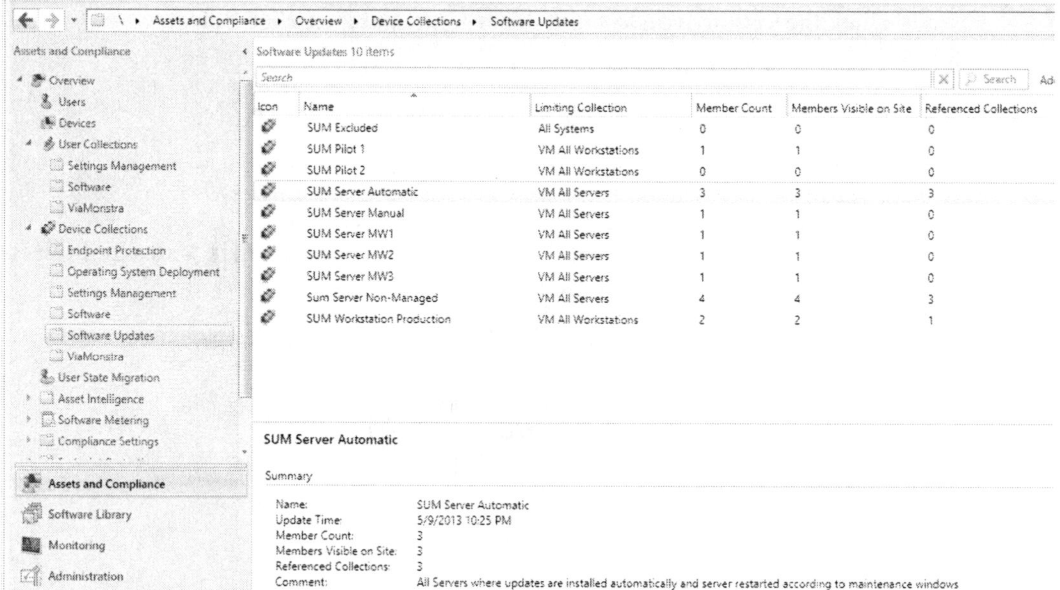

The needed software updates collections.

Automate Adding Queries to Device Collections Using PowerShell

This example can be used to create the previously described complete software update collection structure, including the dynamic query rules. I use the custom cmdlet because the built-in one does not allow you to work with folders. In this example, I assume you have downloaded and extracted the sample files to D:\Setup on CM01.

> **Note:** If you already created all the collections using the manual instructions, please don't run the commands in the following guide.

1. Open **PowerShell** as **Administrator**.
2. Type the following command:

   ```
   cd D:\Setup\Scripts
   ```

3. Type the following command and press **Enter** when prompted:

   ```
   Set-ExecutionPolicy 1 -Force
   ```

> **Real World Note:** Using a number when setting the PowerShell execution policy is just a shortcut command. The full command is Set-ExecutionPolicy -ExecutionPolicy RemoteSigned -Force. The numbers mean the following: 0 is Unrestricted, 1 is RemoteSigned, 2 is AllSigned, 3 is Restricted and 4 is Bypass.

4. Type the following command:

   ```
   . .\CM12_Function_Library_SP1.ps1
   ```

5. Create the entire software update structure by typing the following commands. (They also are available in the Create-SoftwareUpdateCollections.ps1 file in the book sample files if you don't like typing.)

```
Add-CMCollection -SiteCode PS1 -SiteServer CM01 -Name "SUM
Pilot 1" -LimitToCollectionID PS10000B -Folder "Software
Updates" -Type Device -CustomDay 7 -Incremental -Comment
"Software Update pilot 1 members"

Set-CMCollectionQueryRule -SiteCode PS1 -SiteServer CM01
-Query 'select * from SMS_R_System where
SMS_R_System.SystemGroupName = "VIAMONSTRA\\SUM_Pilot1"'
-QueryName "SUM Pilot 1" -QueryType Device -CollectionName
"SUM Pilot 1"

Add-CMCollection -SiteCode PS1 -SiteServer CM01 -Name "SUM
Pilot 2" -LimitToCollectionID PS10000B -Folder "Software
Updates" -Type Device -CustomDay 7 -Incremental -Comment
"Software Update pilot 2 members"

Set-CMCollectionQueryRule -SiteCode PS1 -SiteServer CM01
-Query 'select * from SMS_R_System where
SMS_R_System.SystemGroupName = "VIAMONSTRA\\SUM_Pilot2"'
-QueryName "SUM Pilot 2" -QueryType Device -CollectionName
"SUM Pilot 2"

Add-CMCollection -SiteCode PS1 -SiteServer CM01 -Name "SUM
Excluded" -LimitToCollectionID PS10000A -Folder "Software
Updates" -Type Device -CustomDay 7 -Incremental -Comment
"All Servers and Workstations that should never receive any
updates"

Add-CMCollection -SiteCode PS1 -SiteServer CM01 -Name "SUM
Workstation Production" -LimitToCollectionID PS10000B
-Folder "Software Updates" -Type Device -CustomDay 7
-Incremental -Comment "All workstations"

Set-CMCollectionQueryRule -SiteCode PS1 -SiteServer CM01
-Query 'select * from SMS_R_System where
SMS_R_System.OperatingSystemNameandVersion like
"%workstation%"' -QueryName "All WRK" -QueryType Device
-CollectionName "SUM Workstation Production"

Set-CMCollectionExcludeRule -SiteCode PS1 -SiteServer CM01
-CollectionName "SUM Workstation Production"
-ExcludeCollectionName "SUM Excluded"

Add-CMCollection -SiteCode PS1 -SiteServer CM01 -Name "SUM
Server Manual" -LimitToCollectionID PS10000A -Folder
"Software Updates" -Type Device -CustomDay 7 -Incremental
```

```
-Comment "All servers where updates must be manually
installed"

Set-CMCollectionQueryRule -SiteCode PS1 -SiteServer CM01
-Query 'select * from SMS_R_System where
SMS_R_System.SystemGroupName = "VIAMONSTRA\\SUM_SRV_Manual"'
-QueryName "SUM Server Manual" -QueryType Device -
CollectionName "SUM Server Manual"

Add-CMCollection -SiteCode PS1 -SiteServer CM01 -Name "SUM
Server MW1" -LimitToCollectionID PS10000A -Folder "Software
Updates" -Type Device -CustomDay 7 -Incremental -Comment
"All Servers in Maintenance Window 1"

Set-CMCollectionQueryRule -SiteCode PS1  -SiteServer CM01
-Query 'select * from SMS_R_System where
SMS_R_System.SystemGroupName = "VIAMONSTRA\\SUM_MW1"'
-QueryName "SUM Server MW1" -QueryType Device -
CollectionName "SUM Server MW1"

Add-CMCollection -SiteCode PS1 -SiteServer CM01 -Name "SUM
Server MW2" -LimitToCollectionID PS10000A -Folder "Software
Updates" -Type Device -CustomDay 7 -Incremental -Comment
"All Servers in Maintenance Window 2"

Set-CMCollectionQueryRule -SiteCode PS1 -SiteServer CM01
-Query 'select * from SMS_R_System where
SMS_R_System.SystemGroupName = "VIAMONSTRA\\SUM_MW2"'
-QueryName "SUM Server MW2" -QueryType Device -
CollectionName "SUM Server MW2"

Add-CMCollection -SiteCode PS1 -SiteServer CM01 -Name "SUM
Server MW3" -LimitToCollectionID PS10000A -Folder "Software
Updates" -Type Device -CustomDay 7 -Incremental -Comment
"All Servers in Maintenance Window 3"

Set-CMCollectionQueryRule -SiteCode PS1 -SiteServer CM01
-Query 'select * from SMS_R_System where
SMS_R_System.SystemGroupName = "VIAMONSTRA\\SUM_MW3"'
-QueryName "SUM Server MW3" -QueryType Device -
CollectionName "SUM Server MW3"

Add-CMCollection -SiteCode PS1 -SiteServer CM01 -Name "SUM
Server Automatic" -LimitToCollectionID PS10000A -Folder
"Software Updates" -Type Device -CustomDay 7 -Incremental
-Comment "All Servers where updates are installed
automatically and server restarted according to maintenance
windows"
```

```
Set-CMCollectionIncludeRule -SiteCode PS1 -SiteServer CM01
-CollectionName "SUM Server Automatic"
-IncludeCollectionName "SUM Server MW1"

Set-CMCollectionIncludeRule -SiteCode PS1 -SiteServer CM01
-CollectionName "SUM Server Automatic"
-IncludeCollectionName "SUM Server MW2"

Set-CMCollectionIncludeRule -SiteCode PS1 -SiteServer CM01
-CollectionName "SUM Server Automatic"
-IncludeCollectionName "SUM Server MW3"

Add-CMCollection -SiteCode PS1 -SiteServer CM01 -Name "SUM
Server Non-Managed" -LimitToCollectionID PS10000A -Folder
"Software Updates" -Type Device -CustomDay 7 -Incremental
-Comment "All Non-managed SUM Servers"

Set-CMCollectionQueryRule -SiteCode PS1 -SiteServer CM01
-Query 'select * from SMS_R_System where
SMS_R_System.OperatingSystemNameandVersion like "%Server%"'
-QueryName "All SRV" -QueryType Device -CollectionName "SUM
Server Non-Managed"

Set-CMCollectionExcludeRule -SiteCode PS1 -SiteServer CM01
-CollectionName "SUM Server Non-Managed"
-ExcludeCollectionName "SUM Server MW1"

Set-CMCollectionExcludeRule -SiteCode PS1 -SiteServer CM01
-CollectionName "SUM Server Non-Managed"
-ExcludeCollectionName "SUM Server MW2"

Set-CMCollectionExcludeRule -SiteCode PS1 -SiteServer CM01
-CollectionName "SUM Server Non-Managed"
-ExcludeCollectionName "SUM Server MW3"
```

Automate Creating Include Rules Using the Built-in PowerShell Cmdlet

In this optional example, you create an Include rule for the SUM SRV MW1 collection in the SUM Server Automatic collection using the native cmdlet in ConfigMgr 2012 SP1. (This is just a sample, and these steps are not required for any of the other guides in this book.)

1. Launch **PowerShell** from the **ConfigMgr console**.
2. Type the following command:

```
Add-CMDeviceCollectionIncludeMembershipRule -CollectionName
"SUM Server Automatic" -IncludeCollectionName "SUM Server
MW1"
```

Maintenance Windows

Maintenance windows define when software can be installed on any given computer. Maintenance window also control when a computer reboot can occur. Maintenance windows should be defined based on Active Directory group membership. When a deployment occurs, it is evaluated against each maintenance window on the client. A device will apply maintenance windows from all the collections of which it is a member. Maintenance windows are cumulative which requires some planning. In ViaMonstra, you will create maintenance windows only in the Software Updates collection hierarchy.

Maintenance Window	Active Directory group
Sunday 01:00 – 04:00	SUM_MW1
Monday 01:00 – 04:00	SUM_MW2
Saturday 10:00 – 01:00	SUM_MW3

Create Maintenance Windows

1. On **CM01**, log on as **VIAMONSTRA\Administrator** and open the **ConfigMgr console**.
2. Navigate to the **Assets and Compliance** workspace and select the **Software Update** folder.
3. Select the **SUM Server MW1** collection, and on the ribbon, click **Properties**.
4. Select the **Maintenance Windows** tab, click the **yellow icon**, and create a new maintenance window with these settings:
    a. Name: **MW1 - Sunday 01:00 - 04:00**
    b. Start: **1:00 AM**
    c. End: **4:00 AM**
    d. Recurrence pattern: **Weekly, Sunday**

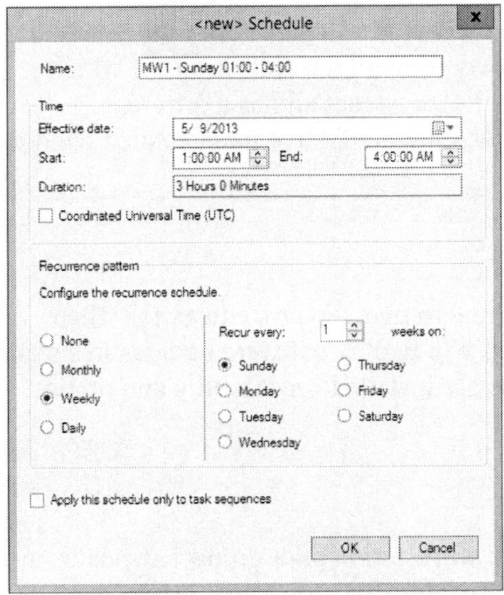

Creating a maintenance window.

5. Click **OK** twice and close the collection properties.
6. Select **SUM Server MW2** and open the collection properties.
7. Select the **Maintenance Windows** tab, click the **yellow icon**, and create a new maintenance window with these settings:
    a. Name: **MW2 - Monday 01:00 - 04:00**
    b. Start: **1:00 AM**
    c. End: **4:00 AM**
    d. Recurrence pattern: **Weekly, Monday**
8. Click **OK** twice and close the collection properties.
9. Select **SUM Server MW3** and open the collection properties.
10. Select the **Maintenance Windows** tab, click the **yellow icon**, and create a new maintenance window with these settings:
    a. Name: **MW3 - Saturday 10:00 - 01:00**
    b. Start: **10:00 PM**
    c. End: **1:00 AM**
    d. Recurrence pattern: **Weekly, Saturday**
11. Click **OK** twice and close the collection properties.

> **Real World Note:** You should only configure maintenance windows on a very limited number of collections. A computer will inherit maintenance windows from all the collections of which it is a member. If the computer is a member of ten different collections that all has a different maintenance window, you end up with a computer for which the effective maintenance window might be 20 hours a day.

Software Updates Procedures

Now when we have the collection design in place, it's time to plan the procedures for when software updates must be deployed. At ViaMonstra, you will deploy software updates in several stages with enough time to validate whether the updates are installed successfully and do not break any business applications or services.

Workstation Software Updates Procedures

1. Approved updates are deployed to computers in workstation pilot group 1. Updates in this group are installed with a deadline as soon as possible.
2. Approved updates are deployed to computers in workstation pilot group 2. Updates in this group have a two-day deadline.
3. After updates are successfully installed in pilot group 2, they can be deployed to all workstations in production. Updates in this group have a one-week deadline. This gives users one week to download and install the updates according to their own business schedules before the updates are applied.

Deployment Group	Updates Released Day x from Release	Deadline Day x from Release
Pilot group 1	Day 2	One day
Pilot group 2	Day 4	Two days
Workstation production	Day 7	Seven days

No computers will be automatically restarted during the update process.

VPN and Remote Locations

All VPN and other remote clients must download and install updates marked as extremely critical and critical, like other workstations in production.

Server Software Update Procedures

1. Approved updates are deployed to computers in workstation pilot group 1. Updates in this group will be installed no later than two days from release.

2. Approved updates are deployed to computers in Server Manual with a purpose of available and no deadline.
3. Approved updates are deployed to computers in Server Automatic with a deadline not ignoring maintenance windows.

Deployment Group	Updates Released Day x from Release	Deadline Day x from Release
Pilot group 1	Day 2	One day
Server Manual	Day 7	No deadline
Server Automatic	Day 7	According to defined maintenance windows

The Software Update Compliance Plan

The Official Microsoft Severity Rating System issues a bulletin for any product vulnerability that could, in Microsoft's judgment, result in multiple systems being affected, no matter how unlikely or limited the impact. The following list describes the different severity ratings:

- **Critical.** A vulnerability whose exploitation could allow the propagation of an Internet worm without user action.
- **Important.** A vulnerability whose exploitation could result in the compromise of the confidentiality, integrity, or availability of users' data, or of the integrity or availability of processing resources.
- **Moderate.** Exploitability is mitigated to a significant degree by factors such as default configuration, auditing, or difficulty of exploitation.
- **Low.** A vulnerability whose exploitation is extremely difficult, or whose impact is minimal.

Note: Ensure that you are familiar with the Microsoft security bulletins and that you subscribe to the monthly newsletter. For more information, visit http://www.microsoft.com/technet/security/bulletin/rating.mspx.

ViaMonstra Severity Rating System

At ViaMonstra, the severity rating system is based loosely upon the Official Microsoft Severity Rating System. As a rule of thumb, Microsoft Critical and Important ratings both become Critical in ViaMonstra's ratings. Similarly, ViaMonstra treats both Microsoft Moderate and Low as Moderate. ViaMonstra also has introduced an "Extremely Critical" rating, which corresponds to what is often referred to as "Zero-Day Exploit."

Microsoft Rating	ViaMonstra Rating
N/A	Extremely Critical ("Zero-Day Exploit")
Critical	Critical
Important	
Moderate	Moderate
Low	

Planning for Compliance

A very important part of planning for software updates is planning for the acceptable compliance level. Without a defined SLA, you never know when management is satisfied and when you have to start working harder to track down the non-compliant devices. Any compliance plan should contain the various severities and multiple achievable success criteria.

Workstation Compliance Success Criteria

ViaMonstra Severity	Success Criterion Week 1	Success Criterion Week 2	Success Criterion Week 3
Extremely critical	100%	100%	100%
Critical	50%	80%	95%
Moderate	50%	75%	90%

Server Compliance Success Criteria

ViaMonstra Severity	Success Criterion Week 1	Success Criterion Week 3	Success Criterion Week 5
Extremely critical	100%	100%	100%
Critical	50%	80%	100%
Moderate	50%	75%	100%

Software Update Components

Update Packages

A software update package is like any other package in ConfigMgr except that it only contains the software update binary files. Deployment packages and deployments are only related in the sense that the update must be present in one available software update package. ViaMonstra has decided to create two update packages per year. The update packages are stored in the same source location as all the other packages using this folder structure:

Software Updates. Top-level share

Software Updates\2013-1. Contains the approved updates for the first half of the year

Software Updates\2013-2. Contains the approved updates for the second half of the year

Software Update Templates

Software update deployments can be controlled by the use of templates. In ViaMonstra, you will have one template for each unique deployment scenario. Unlike previous versions of ConfigMgr, this version allows you to create a new template only when you create a deployment. These are the templates you will create:

- **Pilot 1.** All computers that participate in the first test deployment. This template will require that updates are installed and applied automatically. This deployment will offer full interaction with the end user.
- **Pilot 2.** All computers that participate in the second deployment. All deployments to this collection will be a 100-percent match to the production collection.
- **Workstation Production.** All workstations that are not part of the WRK Excluded collection.
- **Server Automatic.** All servers where an installation and restart will be performed automatically.
- **Server Manual.** All servers where an installation and restart will be performed manually.

Update Groups

An update group is a group of selected software updates that can be deployed to clients and used to track compliance. You can create update groups automatically using the Automatic Update Rule feature or by manually selecting the updates. Within a single update group, you can have zero or multiple deployments. In ViaMonstra, you will create a monthly update group containing all the deployments for that month.

Manually Create Update Groups

Although update groups can be created automatically, there are several scenarios in which you want to manually create an update group. For instance, you might want to create an update group with all required updates and use that update as the foundation for a software update compliance report. Manually creating update groups makes perfectly sense when the update group is created for an ad-hoc task.

1. On **CM01**, log on as **VIAMONSTRA\Administrator** and open the **ConfigMgr console**.
2. Select the **Software Library** workspace, and click **Software Updates / All Software Updates**.

3. Place the cursor in the **Search** column, and on the ribbon, click **Add Criteria**. Select the following criteria and click **Add**. Notice the extra lines with the criteria.
    a. **Expired**
    b. **Superseded**
    c. **Required**
4. Next to **AND Required**, click the link **is less than or equal to**; then select **is greater than or equal to** and type **1**.
5. Change the value in **AND Superseded** from **Yes** to **No**.
6. Change the value in **AND Expired** from **Yes** to **No**.
7. Click **Search**, and you should get a list with all required updates.

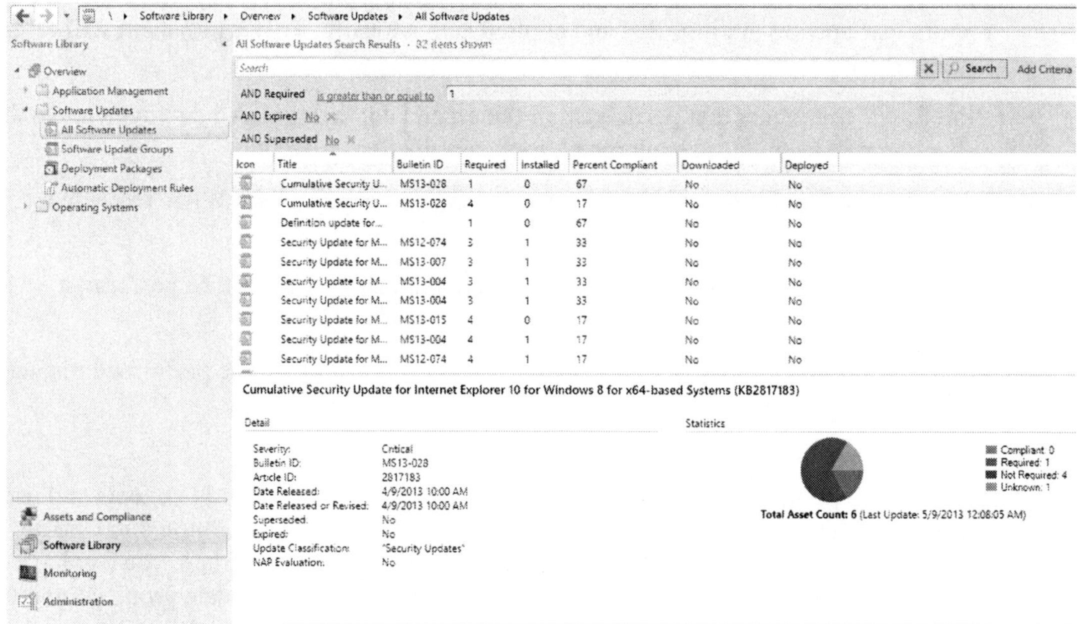

Searching for all required updates.

8. On the ribbon, click **Save Current Search** and save the search as **All Required Updates**.
9. On the ribbon, click **Saved Searches** and select **Manage Searches for Current Node**.

10. Select **All Required Updates** and click **OK**.

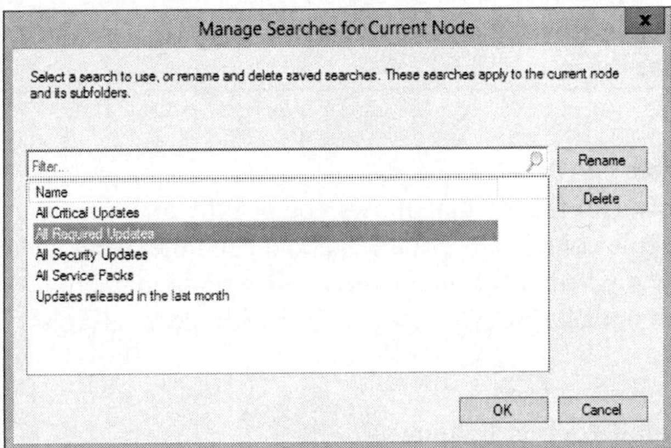

Working with saved searches.

11. Press **Ctrl + A** to select all updates; then right-click and select **Create Software Update Group**.
12. In **Name**, type **All Required Updates** and click **Create**.
13. Select **Software Update Groups** and notice the group. The compliance data are not updated. To update the data, click **Run Summarization** on the ribbon. Select the **All Required updates** update groups and click **Refresh**.

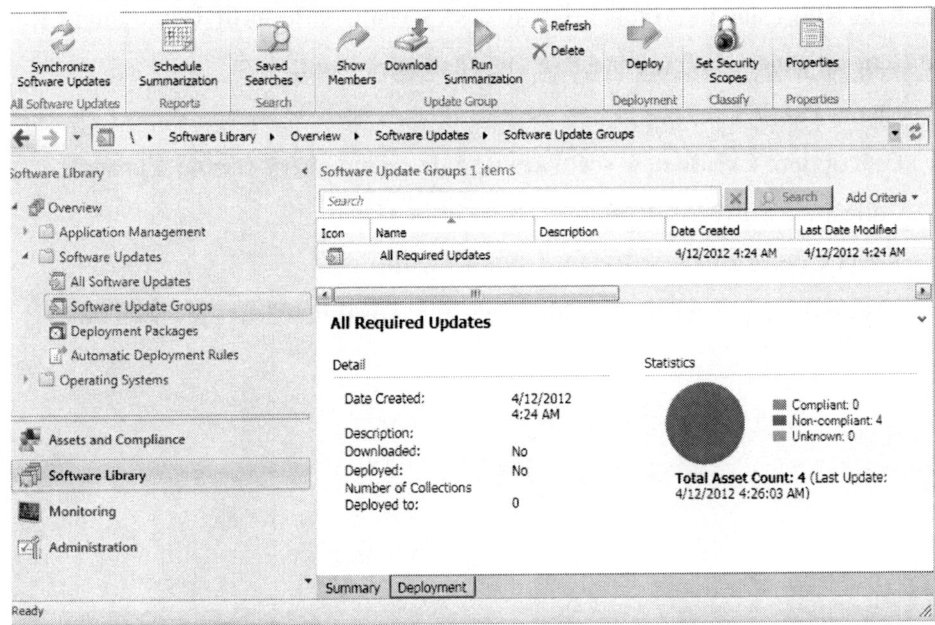

The software update group.

> **Real World Note:** Having a single software update group with too many updates is not a recommended strategy and can be the root cause of all sorts of issues related to software update deployment. You can use the Date Released or Revised criteria to narrow searches. Use the option to specify "is between" when specifying the dates.

Automatic Deployment Rules

Automatic Deployment Rules is a very powerful feature that allows you to fully automate the software update deployment process. The rule contains information about run time, what updates to download, where to store the updates, and whether the deployment will be automatically enabled. In ViaMonstra, you will create an update group for each month with these settings:

- All security and critical updates
- All Windows updates except Windows Server Itanium
- Place all updates in a new update group
- Create the first deployment to the SUM Pilot 1 collection
- Ensure that the deployment is disabled

Create the Patch Tuesday Automatic Deployment Rule

1. On **CM01**, log on as **VIAMONSTRA\Administrator** and open the **ConfigMgr console**.
2. Select the **Software Library** workspace, click **Software Updates / Automatic Deployment Rules**, and then on the ribbon, click **Create Automatic Deployment Rule**.
3. On the **General** page, configure these settings and click **Next**:
    a. Name: **Patch Tuesday**
    b. Description: **Create new software update group every second Tuesday**
    c. Collection: **Software Updates / SUM Pilot 1**
    d. Select **Create a new Software Update Group**
    e. Enable the deployment after this rule is run: **Disable** (Clear the check box.)

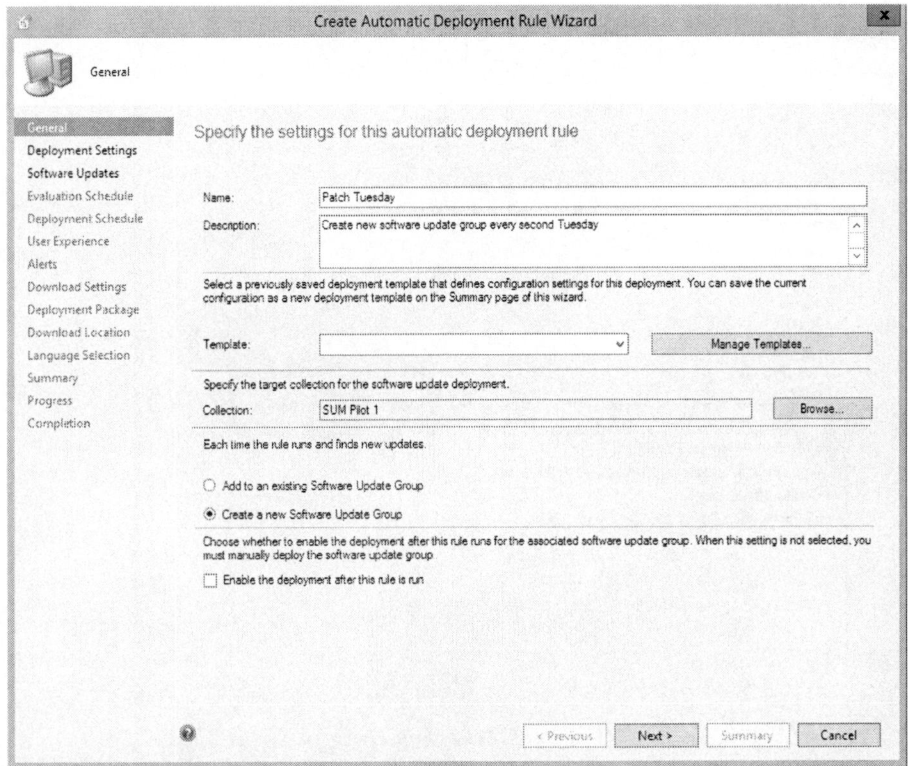

Creating the Patch Tuesday automatic deployment rule.

4. On the **Deployment Settings** page, in **Detail level**, select **Only success and error messages** and then click **Next**.
5. On the **Software Updates** page, configure these settings and click **Next**:
   a. Date Released or Revised: **Last 1 month**
   b. Product: **Office 2013**, **Windows 7**, **Windows 8, Windows Server 2012**
   c. Title: Type **-Itanium** and click **Add -Embedded**.
   d. Update classification: **Critical Updates**, **Security Updates**

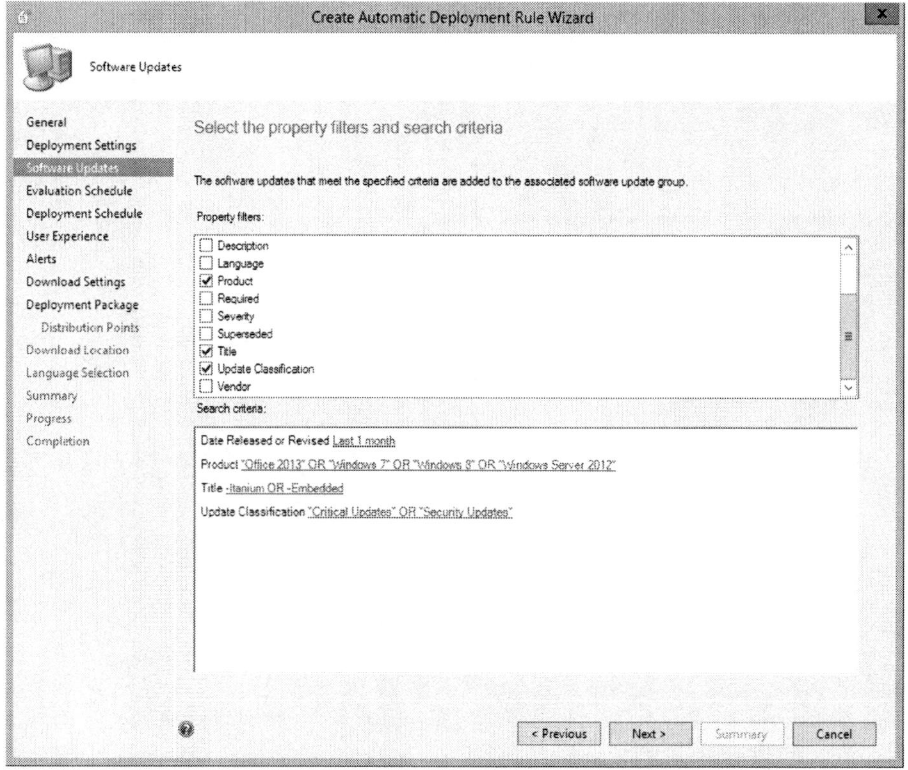

Defining the software updates in the automatic deployment rule.

6. On the **Evaluation Schedule** page, configure this setting and click **Next**:

   Select **Run the rule on a schedule**, click **Customize**, and configure the rule to run **Second Tuesday** every month at **10:00 PM**.

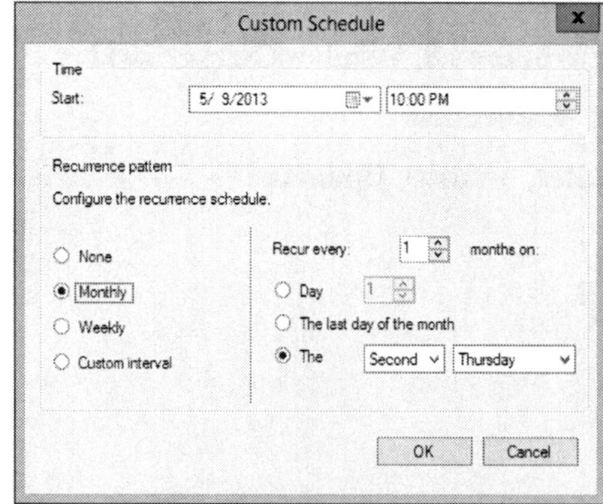

Configuring the automatic deployment rule schedule.

7. Click **OK** to close the Custom Schedule dialog box.

8. On the **Deployment Schedule** page, configure these settings and click **Next**:
    a. Time based on: **Client local time**
    b. Software available time: **As Soon As Possible**
    c. Installation deadline: **As Soon As Possible**
9. On the **User Experience** page, configure these settings and click **Next**;
    a. User visual experience: **Display in Software Center and show all notifications**
    b. Device restart behavior: Enable **Suppress the system restart on the following devices** for **Servers** and **Workstations.**

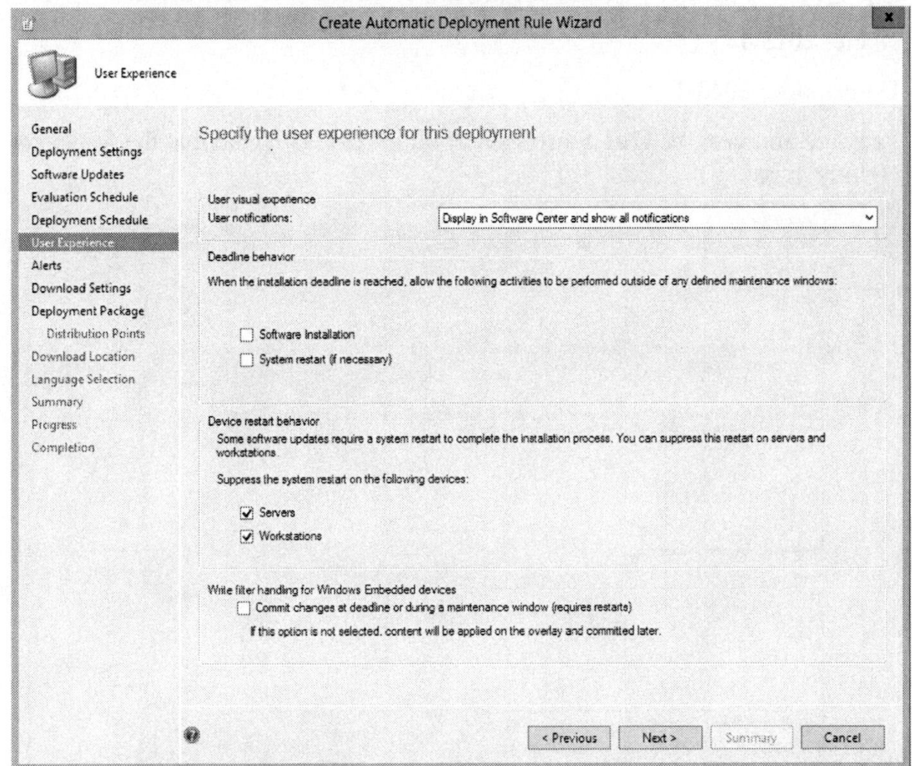

Configuring the user experience.

10. On the **Alerts** page, configure these settings and click **Next**:
    a. Generate an alert when the following conditions are met: **Enable**
    b. Client compliance is below the following percent: **95**
    c. Offset from the deadline: **21 Days**

11. On the **Download Settings** page, configure these settings and click **Next**:

    a. Deployment options for client within a slow or unreliable network boundary: Enable **Download software update from distribution point and install.**

    b. When software updates are not available on any preferred distribution points. Client can download and install software updates from a fallback source location for content: Enable **Download and install software updates from the fallback content source location.**

    c. Enable **If software update are not available on preferred distribution point or remote distribution point, download content from Microsoft Updates.**

12. On the **Deployment Package** page, configure these settings and click **Next**:

    a. Name: **2013-1**

    b. Description: **2013-1**

    c. Package Sources: **\\CM01\Sources$\Updates\2013-1** (Note that the folder must already exist.)

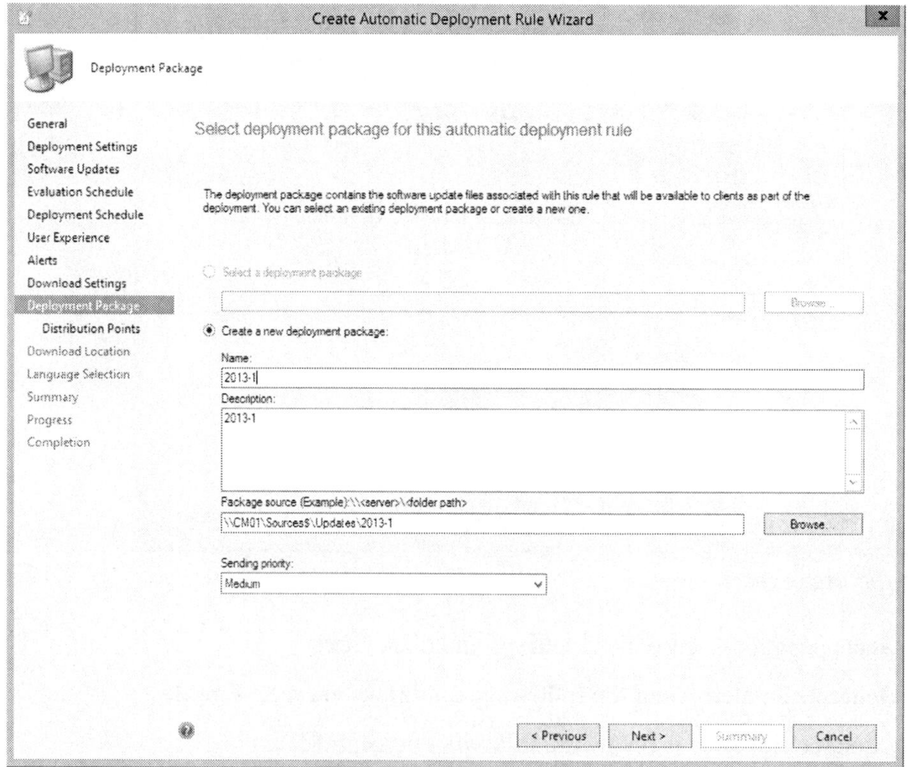

Creating the deployment package.

13. On the **Distribution Points** page, configure this setting and click **Next**:

    Click **Add / Distribution Point Group**; then select the **All Content** distribution point group and click **OK**.

14. On the **Download Location** page, configure this setting and click **Next**:

    Download software update from the Internet: **Enabled**.

15. On the **Language Selection** page, configure this setting and click **Next**:

    Ensure **English** is the only selected language.

16. On the **Summary** page, configure this setting and click **Next**:

    Click **Save As Template**. Type **Pilot 1** in the template **Name** field and click **Save**.

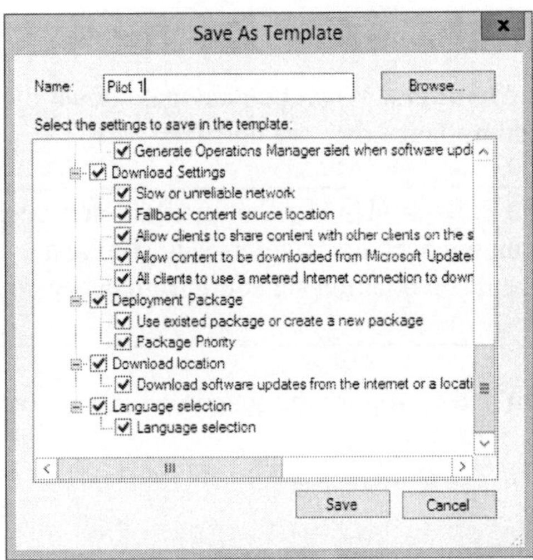

Creating the deployment template.

17. Click **Next,** read the **Completion** page, and click **Close**.

Force the Automatic Deployment Rule to Run

1. Select the **Patch Tuesday** automatic deployment rule, and on the ribbon, click **Run Now**.
2. In the dialog box, click **OK**. The process can easily take a few minutes depending on the number of updates being downloaded. You use CMTrace to monitor the activity along with the number of selected updates in the ruleengine.log. After a few minutes, you will see in the new computer update group being created in the log file.
3. Navigate to **Software Update Groups** and verify that you have a **Patch Tuesday date+time** update group. If you don't see the group yet, press **F5** or click **Refresh**. Right-click the update group, select **Properties**, and rename the update group to **Year + Number of Month + Name of Month**, e.g. **2013 04 April**.

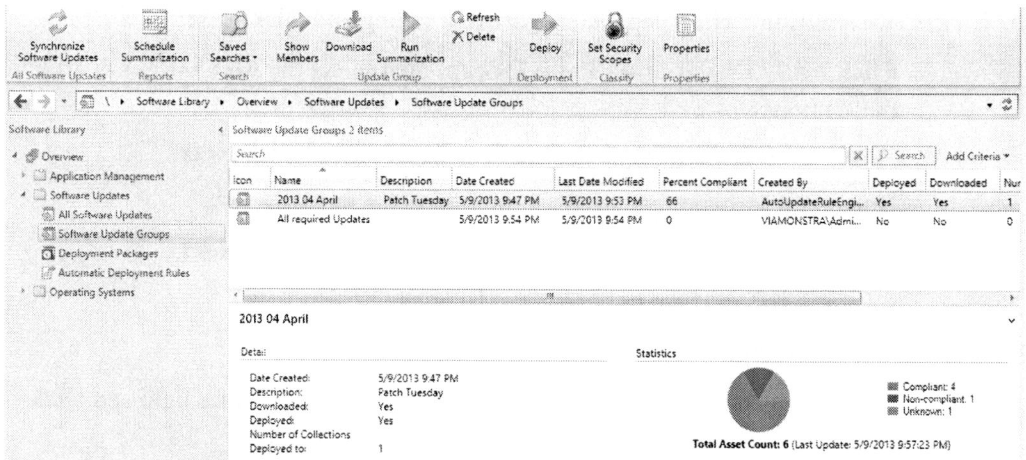

Renaming the automatically created update group.

4. Right-click the update group and select **Show Members**. When you navigate down the different updates in the group, notice that the compliance data are updated.

Real World Note: Compliance data are updated by the Software Update Summarization process. By default, the process runs every hour, which causes an unnecessary load on SQL. Being a medium-sized company, ViaMonstra decided to change the evaluation schedule from every hour to once per day.

5. On the ribbon, click **Schedule Summarization** and configure the schedule to recur every **1 Days**.

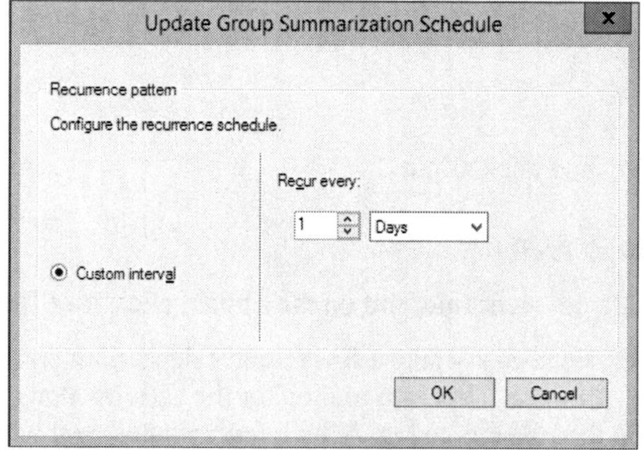

Changing the Update Group Summarization Schedule.

Deployments

The deployment is a child object to an update group. Like any other deployment, it contains information about the installation purpose (required or available), time and day of the deployment, user experience, and so forth. The automatic deployment rule creates only the first deployment target at the pilot collection. The remaining deployments must be created manually. It's absolutely not a time-consuming process when you have the deployment templates created. The following guides take you through the creation of the first deployment in each of the environments. As part of the deployment process, we also create the deployment template.

Enable the Pilot Deployment

1. Navigate to the new **Software Update Group**, select the **Deployment** tab, right-click the automatically created deployment, and click **Properties**.
2. Rename the deployment *Year + Number of Month + Name of Month* Pilot 1, e.g. **2013 04 April Pilot 1**, and click **OK**.

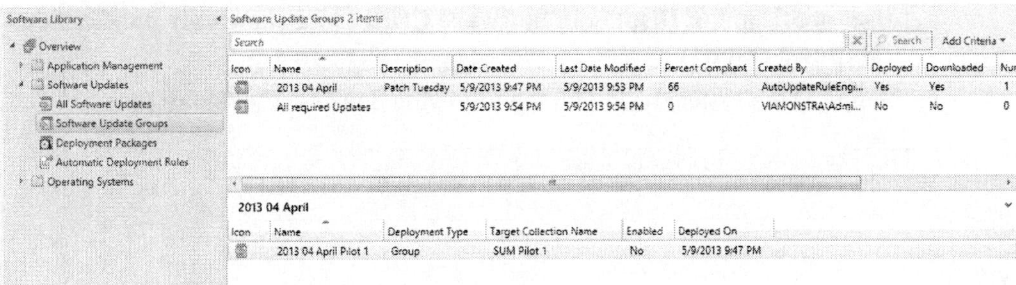

Renaming the automatically created deployment.

3. Right-click the deployment and click **Enable**. This enables the first deployment with an "as soon as possible" deadline. The client downloads the machine policy and starts installing.

> **Real World Note:** If you are working with clients in a VDI environment, consider changing the **Disable deadline randomization** setting to False in the Computer Agent section of the client device settings. This enables a two-hour offset that ensures you don't get 4,000 VDI clients hammering the software update process at the exact same time.

Create the Workstation Production Deployment

You create the workstation production deployment with these settings:

- Limited user experience where only the restart notification is displayed.
- Suppress restart.

Complete the following steps:

1. Navigate to the new **Software Update Group**, and on the ribbon, click **Deploy**.

2. On the **General** page, configure these settings and click **Next**:
    a. Name: WRK *Year + Number of Month + Name of Month* Production, e.g. **WRK 2013 04 April Production**
    b. Description: **April** updates for **all non-excluded** workstations
    c. Collection: **ViaMonstra / SUM Workstation Production**
3. On the **Deployment Settings** page, configure these settings and click **Next**:
    a. Type of deployment: **Required**
    b. Detail level: **All messages**
4. On the **Deployment Scheduling** page, configure these settings and click **Next**:
    a. Software available time: **As soon as possible**
    b. Installation deadline: **7 days from today**
5. On the **User Experience** page, configure these settings and click **Next**;
    a. User notifications: **Display in Software Center and show only notifications for computer restarts**
    b. Suppress the system restart on the following devices: **Workstations**

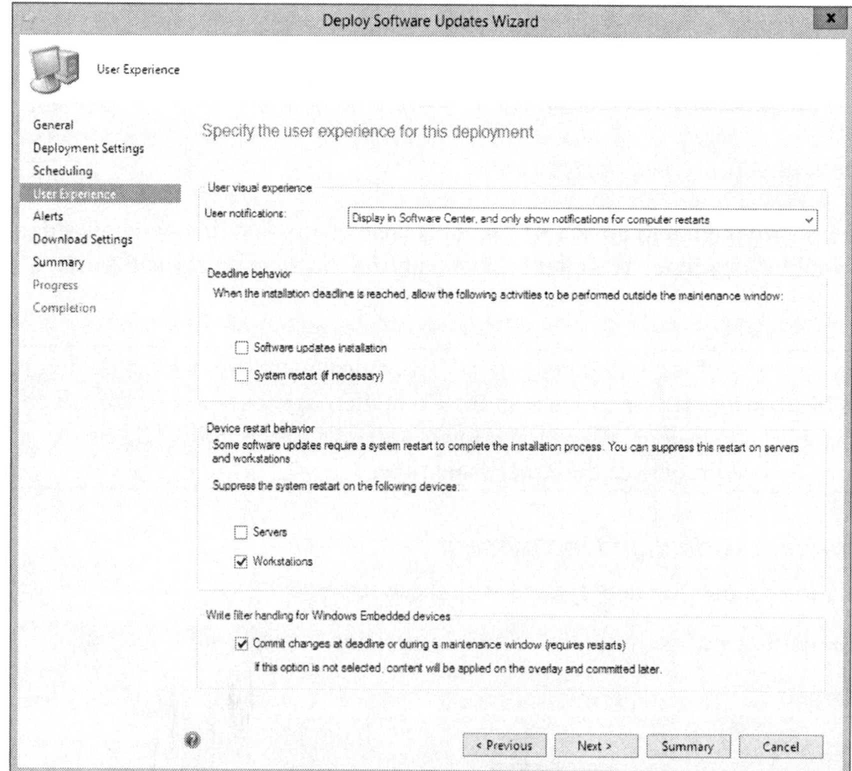

Configuring the user experience for workstations.

6. On the **Alerts** page, configure these settings and click **Next**;
    a. Generate an alert when the following conditions are met: **Enable**
    b. Client compliance is below the following percent: **95**
    c. Offset from the deadline: **21 Days**
7. On the **Download Settings** page, configure these settings and click **Next**:
    a. Deployment options for client within a slow or unreliable network boundary: Enable **Download software update from distribution point and install**.
    b. When software updates are not available on any preferred distribution points. Client can download and install software updates from a fallback source location for content: Enable **Download and install software updates from the fallback content source location**.
    c. Enable **If software update are not available on preferred distribution point or remote distribution point, download content from Microsoft Updates**.
8. On the **Summary** page, click **Save As Template**, type **Workstation Production** as the name, and click **Save**.
9. Click **Next** and then **Close**.

Create the Automatic Server Deployment

You create the Server Automatic deployment with these settings:

- Full user experience where all notifications are displayed.
- Install as soon as possible and restart. The installation deadline will be controlled by the maintenance window.

Complete the following steps:

1. Navigate to the new **Software Update Group**, and on the ribbon, click **Deploy**.
2. On the **General** page, configure these settings and click **Next**:
    a. Name: SRV *Year + Number of Month + Name of Month* Automatic, e.g. **SRV 2012 04 April Automatic**
    b. Description: **All servers that can be updated automatically**
    c. Collection: **SUM Server Automatic**
3. On the **Deployment Settings** page, configure these settings and click **Next**:
    a. Type of deployment: **Required**
    b. Detail level: **All messages**

4. On the **Deployment Settings** page, configure these settings and click **Next**:
   a. Software available time: **As soon as possible**
   b. Installation deadline: **As soon as possible**
5. On the **User Experience** page, configure this setting and click **Next**:

   User notifications: **Display in Software Center and show all notifications**
6. On the **Alerts** page, configure these settings and click **Next**:
   a. Generate an alert when the following conditions are met: **Enable**
   b. Client compliance is below the following percent: **95**
   c. Offset from the deadline: **21 Days**
7. On the **Download Settings** page, configure these settings and click **Next**:
   a. Deployment options for client within a slow or unreliable network boundary: Enable **Download software update from distribution point and install.**
   b. When software updates are not available on any preferred distribution points. Client can download and install software updates from a fallback source location for content: Enable **Download and install software updates from the fallback content source location.**
   c. Enable **If software update are not available on preferred distribution point or remote distribution point, download content from Microsoft Updates.**
8. On the **Summary** page, click **Save As Template**, type **Server Automatic** as the name, and click **Save.**
9. Click **Next** and then **Close.**

Create the Manual Server Deployment

You create the Server Manual deployment with these settings:

- Full user experience where all notifications are displayed.
- Updates are only made available but never installed automatically.

Complete the following steps:

1. Navigate to the new **Software Update Group**, and on the ribbon, click **Deploy.**
2. On the **General** page, configure these settings and click **Next**:
   a. Name: SRV *Year + Number of Month + Name of Month* Manual, e.g. **SRV 2013 04 April Manual**
   b. Description: **All servers that must be updated manually**
   c. Collection: **SUM Server Manual**

3. On the **Deployment Settings** page, configure these settings and click **Next**:
    a. Type of deployment: **Available**
    b. Detail level: **All messages**
4. On the **Deployment Settings** page, configure this setting and click **Next**:

    Software available time: **As soon as possible**
5. On the **User Experience** page, configure this setting and click **Next**:

    User notifications: **Display in Software Center and show all notifications**
6. On the **Alerts** page, click **Next**.
7. On the **Download Settings** page, configure these settings and click **Next**:
    a. Deployment options for client within a slow or unreliable network boundary: Enable **Download software update from distribution point and install**.
    b. When software updates are not available on any preferred distribution points. Client can download and install software updates from a fallback source location for content: Enable **Download and install software updates from the fallback content source location**.
    c. Enable **If software update are not available on preferred distribution point or remote distribution point, download content from Microsoft Updates**.
8. On the **Summary** page, click **Save As Template**, type **Server Manual** as the name, and click **Save**.
9. Click **Next** and then **Close**.

Automate Creating Deployments Using PowerShell

This is an example on how to create a software update deployment using the built-in cmdlet in Service Pack 1:

1. From the **ConfigMgr console**, launch **PowerShell**.
2. To create the deployment, type the following command:

```
Start-CMSoftwareUpdateDeployment -CollectionName "SUM Pilot
2" -DeploymentType Required -SendWakeUpPacket $true
-VerbosityLevel OnlyErrorMessages -TimeBasedOn LocalTime
-UserNotification DisplayAll -SoftwareInstallation $True
-AllowRestart $False -RestartServer $False
-RestartWorkstation $True -GenerateSuccessAlert $False
-PercentSuccess 95 -TimeValue 21 -TimeUnit Days
-DisableOperationsManagerAlert $True
-GenerateOperationsManagerAlert $False -ProtectedType
RemoteDistributionPoint -UnprotectedType NoInstall
-UseBranchCache $False -DownloadFromMicrosoftUpdate $false
```

```
-AllowUseMeteredNetwork $false -SoftwareUpdateGroupName
"2013 04 April" -DeploymentName "2013 04 April Pilot 2"
-DeploymentAvailableDay(Get-date) -DeploymentExpireTime
(Get-Date)
```

How and When Updates Are Downloaded to the Client

Clients only download required software updates, regardless of the number of updates in the software update package. If a deployment purpose is required, then updates start downloading when the client reads the machine policy. Updates remain in cache and are applied according to the deadline in the deployment. If a deployment purpose is available, then updates are downloaded when the client initiates the installation.

Monitor the Deployments

1. On **PC0001**, from the **Start screen**, open the **Configuration Manager** applet.
2. On the **Actions** tab, select **Software Updates Deployment Evaluation Cycle** and click **Run Now**. It might take a few minutes for the client to perform the evaluation cycle.

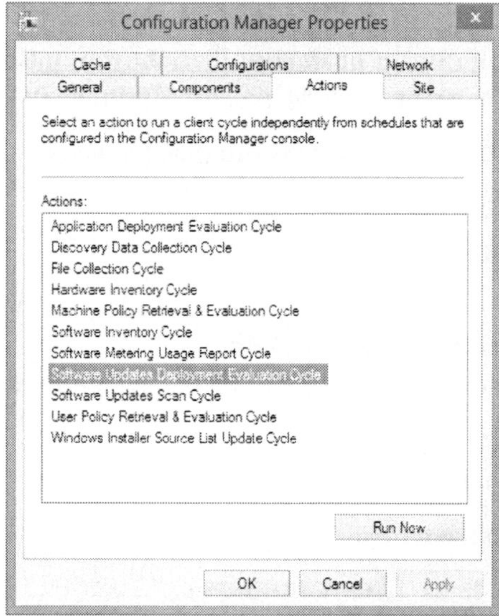

Initiating the software update evaluation cycle.

3. From the **Start screen**, open the **Software Center**.

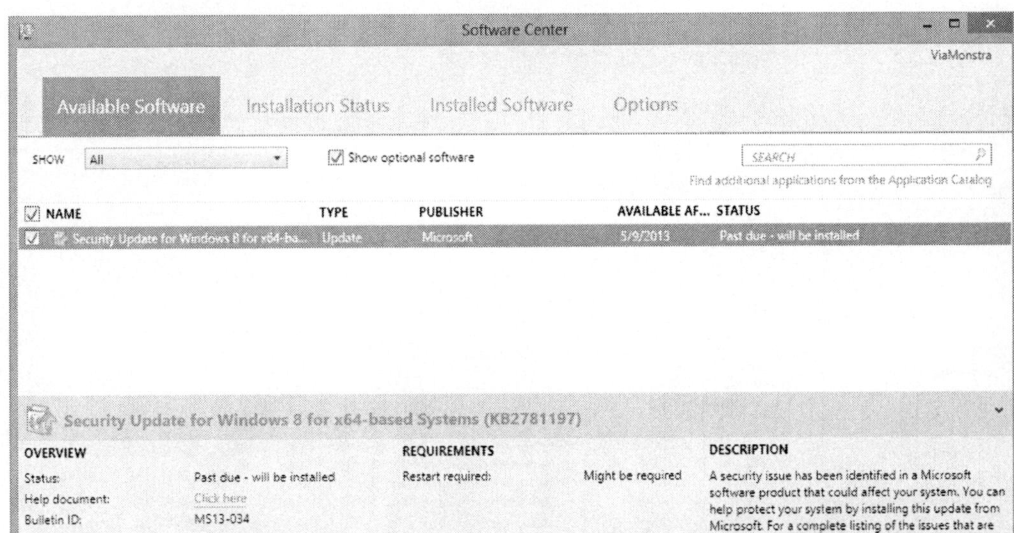

Monitoring the deployment from the Software Center.

4. Select the updates to install, click **INSTALL SELECTED**, and click **OK**.
5. Click **Restart** after all the updates are installed.
6. On **CM01**, open the **ConfigMgr console**.
7. Navigate to the **Monitoring** workspace, and select **Deployments**.
8. Type **2013 04 April** in the search field. You should see the four deployments.
9. Select the deployment target for the **SUM Pilot 1 Deployment** collection and click **View Status** in the dashboard.
10. Depending on your maintenance windows, you should be able to see the deployment states as either **Compliant** or **In Progress**. If the status is **Unknown**, click **Run Summarization and Refresh**.

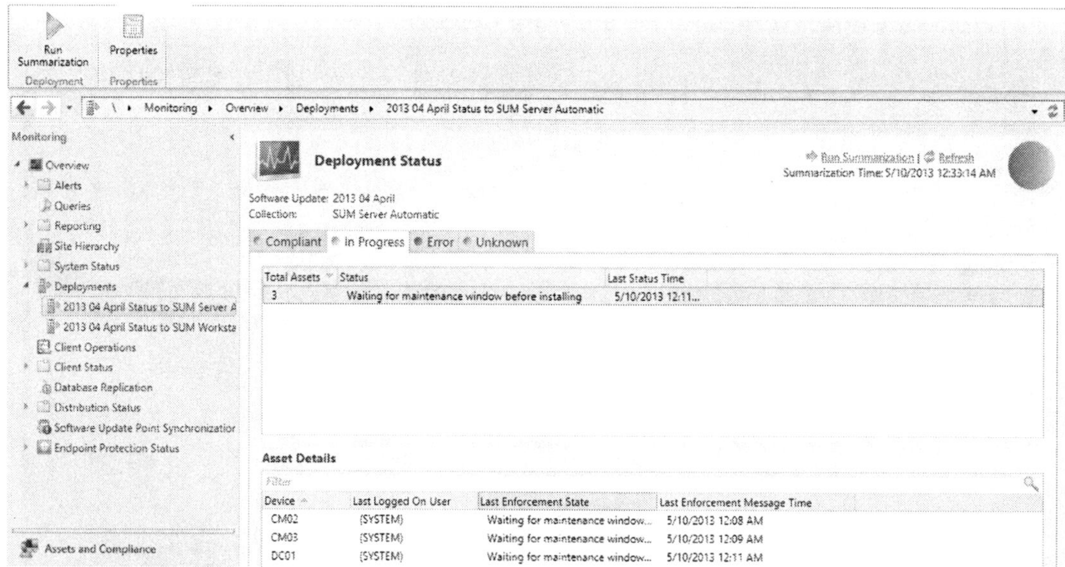

Monitoring the server automatic deployment.

11. In the **In Progress** tab, select **DC01** and click **More Details.**

Detailed deployment summary

12. Select the **Software Updates** tab and see the number of updates that will be installed during the next maintenance window.

13. Close the **Asset Message** window.

Monitor the Deployments Using Reports

1. Open **Internet Explorer** and go to **http://CM01/Reports/Pages/Folder.aspx**.
2. Navigate to **ConfigMgr_PS1 / Software Updates - C Deployment States**, and run the report **States 1 - Enforcement states for a deployment**.
3. In **Deployment**, select the **SRV 2013 04 Automatic** deployment and click **View Report**.

House Cleaning and Deleting Expired Updates

As time goes by, updates will be superseded or expired by Microsoft. Expired updates are not requested by any client. In ConfigMgr 2012 SP1 a built-in process will automatically perform a cleanup and remove expired updates from deployments and delete the binaries from both distribution points and the source location. ConfigMgr has a non-configurable maintenance task that automatically removes expired updates from distribution points and from the package source. The process, however, does not remove updates that are still part of a deployment. For that reason, you should incorporate a process to remove expired updates from active deployments.

Find and Remove Expired Updates from Deployments

1. On **CM01**, open the **ConfigMgr console**.
2. Select the **Software Library** workspace, and click **Software Updates / All Software Updates**.
3. Place the cursor in the **Search** column, and on the ribbon, click **Add Criteria**.
4. Select **Expired** from the list of criteria. Notice the extra line with the criteria.
5. Click **Search**. You should get a list with all expired updates.
6. On the ribbon, click **Save Current Search** and save the search as **All Expired updates**.
7. On the ribbon, click **Saved Searches** and select **Manage Searches for Current Node**.
8. Select **All Expired Updates** and click **OK**.

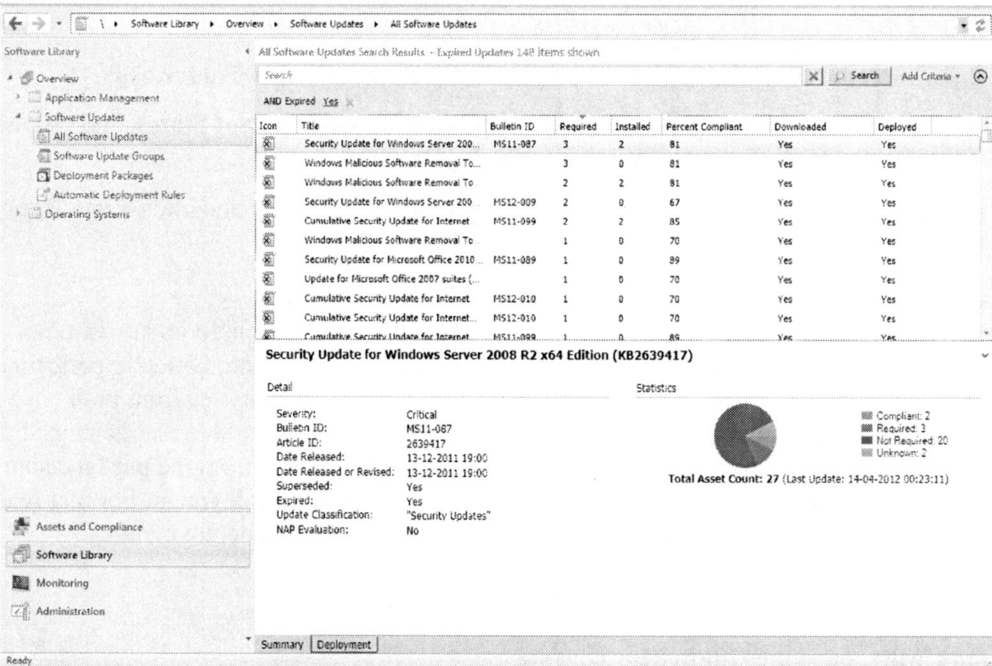

Finding all expired updates.

9. Press **Ctrl + A** to select all the updates, and then on the ribbon's **Home** tab, click **Edit Membership**.

Removing updates from deployments. This sample screenshot displays a few additional software update groups.

10. Remove the updates by unchecking each of the update groups. Note that the illustration above is not taken from the ViaMonstra installation.
11. Click **OK** to return to the **ConfigMgr console**.

Deploy Custom Software Updates

Any software update policy should contain more than just a focus on Windows updates. Out of the box, there is no real good way to deploy third-party updates with ConfigMgr. What most organizations do is integrate either Microsoft System Center Updates Publisher (SCUP) or a third-party solution like Secunia CSI or Solarwinds Patch Manager.

System Center Updates Publisher (SCUP)

SCUP 2011 is a free updates publishing and authoring application. You can benefit from this application by downloading free catalogs from vendors like Adobe, HP, and Dell, or by subscribing to some of the catalogs that are not free, like the SCUPdates and PatchMyPC catalogs. Furthermore, you can author your own updates and publish those to WSUS. The benefit of using SCUP vs. application deployment in ConfigMgr is the detection methods. As with any Microsoft update, your updates will be installed only if the computer requires the update. SCUP provide ViaMonstra with update creation and update deployment, which are two out of the four elements in the Software Update Management solution.

You can download SCUP 2011 from http://tinyurl.com/7llvmvy.

SCUP Requirements

- Supported Operating Systems
- Windows Vista, Windows 7, Windows 8, Windows Server 2008, Windows Server 2008 R2, Windows Server 2012
- Update WSUS-KB2530390-x64.exe if running on Windows Server 2008 or Windows Server 2008 R2
- Windows Server Update Services (WSUS) 3.0 SP2 or above
- .NET Framework 4.0
- Trusted Signing Certificate

Install and Configure SCUP 2011

1. On **CM01**, log on as **VIAMONSTRA\Administrator**.
2. Download **SCUP 2011** from **http://tinyurl.com/7jfd8kk** and save the file in **D:\Setup\SCUP 2011**.
3. Open a **command prompt** with administrative privileges, navigate to **D:\Setup\SCUP 2011**, and run **SystemCenterUpdatesPublisher.msi**.
4. Click **Next** to start the installation.

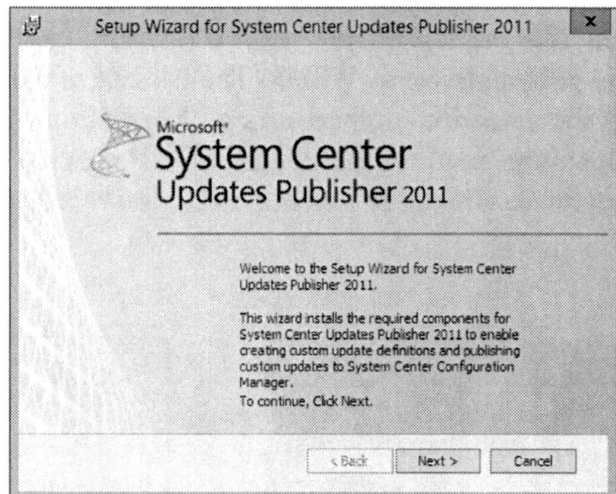

Installing SCUP 2011.

5. Click **Next**. (Do **not** install the Microsoft Windows Server Update Services 3.0 SP2 hotfix, as it's already included on WSUS 4.0.)
6. Accept the license terms and click **Next**.
7. Modify the installation location to **D:\Program Files (x86)\System Center Updates Publisher 2011**, and finish the wizard using the default settings.

Configure SCUP

You'll need to configure SCUP before you can use the application to publish updates. The configuration integrates SCUP with WSUS, creates the needed WSUS certificate, and integrates with ConfigMgr.

1. On **CM01**, from the **Start screen**, right-click **System Center Custom Publisher** and select **Run as administrator**.

2. Click the top menu, above the ribbon, to the left of the **Home** tab, select **Options**.

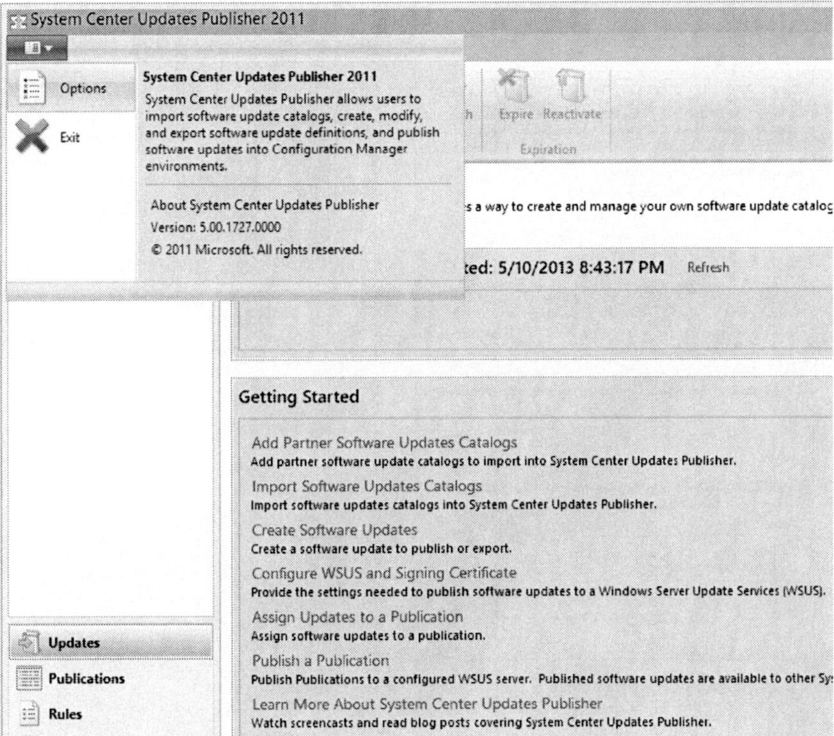

Configuring the SCUP options.

3. Select **Enable publishing to an update server** and click **Test Connection**.

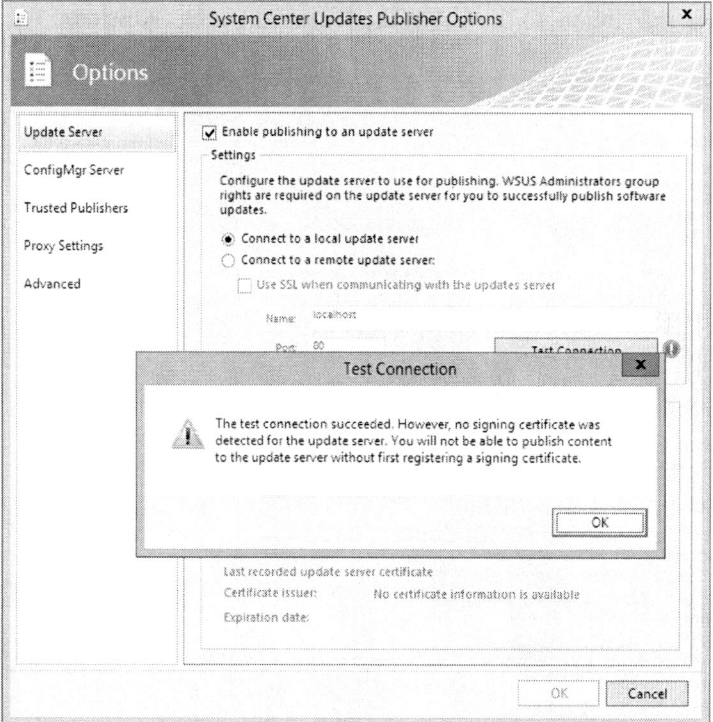

Configuring SCUP as a publishing server.

4. Read the Information about the signing certificate and click **OK**.
5. In **Signing Certificate**, click **Create** and then **OK**.

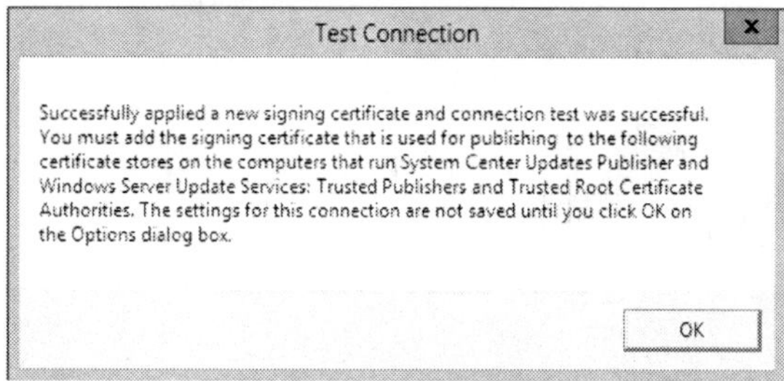

Creating the signing certificate.

6. In the left pane, select **ConfigMgr Server**.
7. Enable **Configuration Manager integration**.
8. Click **Test Connection** and click **OK**.
9. In **Requested client count threshold**, type **5**. This value specifies how many clients in ConfigMgr must request the update before SCUP downloads the binaries and changes the update status from automatic to full. Only updates that are deployed with full content can be installed on a client.

10. In **Package source size threshold (MB)**, type **20**. This value specifies that maximum file size of the update. You can still deploy updates beyond the size, but SCUP will not automatically convert the update into a full content update.
11. Click **OK** to save the changes.

Configuring ConfigMgr integration.

Prepare the Certificate

The certificate must be deployed the local Trusted Root Certification Authorities and Trusted Publisher certificate stores. There are several ways to do that. I often prefer creating a package in ConfigMgr because I don't always have access to Active Directory and the Group Policy Management Console (GPMC). The certificate must be installed on the ConfigMgr server and all clients.

1. On **CM01**, log on as **VIAMONSTRA\Administrator**.
2. Press **Windows logo key + X** and click **Command Prompt (Admin).**
3. At the command prompt, type **MMC** and press **Enter**.
4. Press **Ctrl + M** and click **Add** to open the **Add/Remove** snap-in. Select **Certificates** and click **Add**.
5. Select **Computer account** and click **Next**.

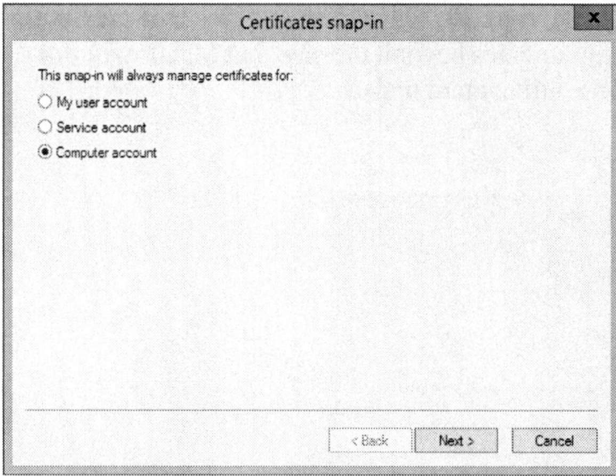

Opening the computer certificate store.

6. Select **Local Computer**, and then click **Finish** and **OK**.
7. Select **Certificates / WSUS / Certificates**.
8. Right-click the **WSUS Publisher Self-signed** certificate, and then select **All Tasks**, **Export**.

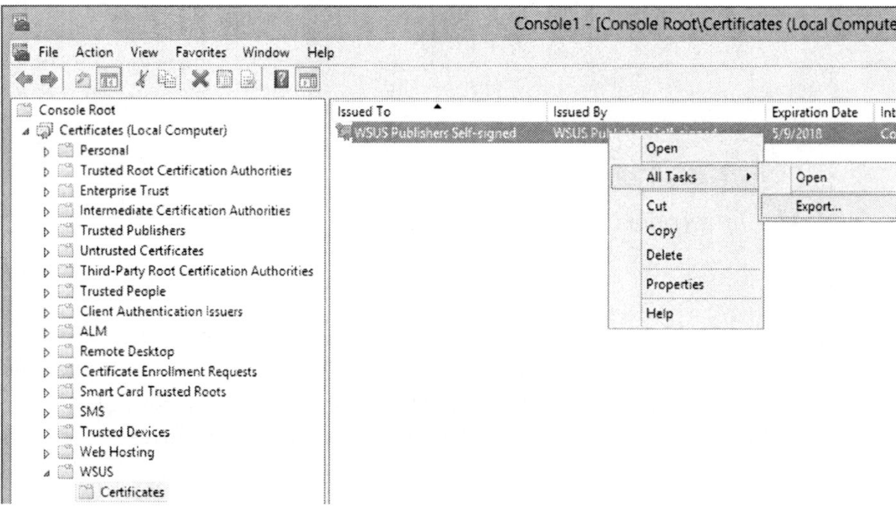

Exporting the WSUS self-signed certificate.

9. In the **Certificate Export Wizard**, click **Next**.
10. On the **Export Private Key** page, make sure **No, do not export the private key** is selected and click **Next**.
11. On the **Export File Format** page, accept the default settings and click **Next**.

12. Save the certificate as **scup2011.cer** in **D:\Sources\Software\SCUP Certificate**. Note that you need to create the folder first.
13. Click **Next**, **Finish**, and **OK** to close the wizard.

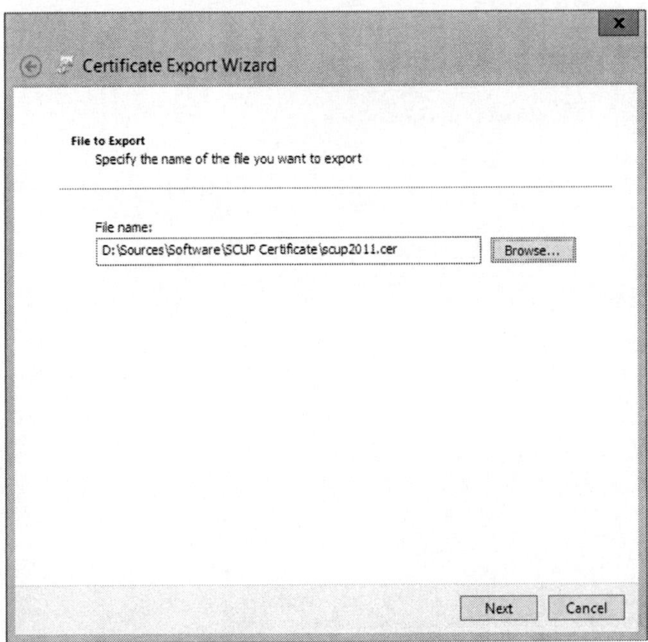

Exporting the certificate.

Create a Package and Deployment

The next step in the process is to deploy the certificate to all client computers. The installation is a simple command line and as such a good candidate for a package and not an application. You can install the certificate in the local certificate store by running the certutil.exe command. Certutil is found in C:\Windows\System32 on the Windows 7 and Windows 8 clients.

1. Open the **ConfigMgr console** and navigate to the **Software Library** workspace.
2. Select **Application Management / Packages / Utilities**, and then on the ribbon, click **Create Package**.
3. On the **Package** page, type these settings and click **Next**:
   a. Name: **SCUP 2011 Certificate**
   b. Description: **Install the WSUS publishing certificate into trusted publisher and trusted root certificate stores**
   c. Manufacturer: **ViaMonstra**
   d. Version: **1.0**
   e. This packages contains source files: **Enable**

f. Source folder: **\\CM01\Sources$\Software\SCUP Certificate**

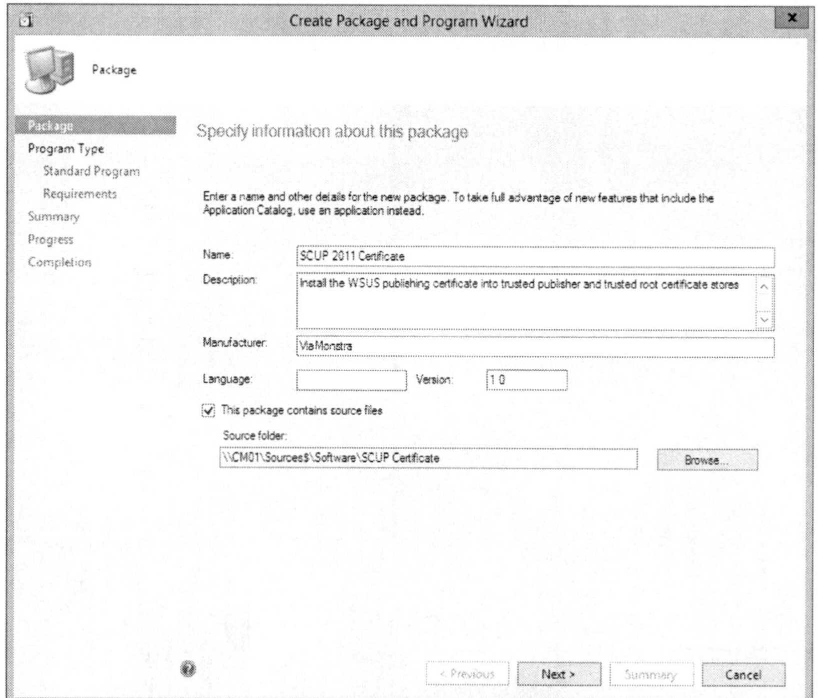

Creating the WSUS certificate package.

4. On the **Program Type** page, select **Standard program** settings and click **Next.**
5. On the **Standard Program** page, configure these settings and click **Next**:
    a. Name: **Import WSUS certificate into Root**
    b. Command line: **certutil.exe -addstore Root scup2011.cer**
    c. Program can run: **Whether or not a user is logged on**
6. On the **Requirements** page, click **Next.**
7. On the **Summary** page, read the summary, click **Next** to start creating the package, and then click **Close.**
8. Select the **SCUP 2011 Certificate** package, and on the ribbon, click **Create Program.**
9. On the **Program Type** page, select **Standard program** settings and click **Next.**
10. On the **Standard Program** page, configure these settings and click **Next**:
    a. Name: **Import WSUS certificate into Trusted**
    b. Command line: **certutil.exe -addstore TrustedPublisher scup2011.cer**
    c. Program can run: **Whether or not a user is logged on**

11. On the **Requirements** page, configure these settings and click **Next**:
    a. Run another program first: **Enable**
    b. Package: Click **Browse**, select **Utilities / ViaMonstra SCUP 2011 Certificate 1.0**, and click **OK**.
    c. Program: **Import WSUS certificate into Root**
12. On the **Summary** page, read the summary, click **Next** to start creating the package and **Close**.
13. Click **Finish**.
14. Select the **SCUP 2011 Certificate** package, and on the ribbon, click **Distribute Content**.
15. On the **General** page, click **Next**.
16. On the **Content Destination** page, select **Add / Distribution Point Group**.
17. Select the **All Content** distribution point group, click **OK**, and then click **Next**.
18. On the **Summary** page, read the summary and click **Next** to start the distribution.
19. Click **Close**.
20. Select the **SCUP 2011 Certificate** package, and on the ribbon, click **Deploy**.
21. On the **General** page, configure these settings and click **Next**:
    a. Software: Click **Browse** and select **Import WSUS certificate into Trusted**.
    b. Collection: Click **Browse** and select the **All Desktop and Server Clients** collection.
22. On the **Content** page, verify that the content is distributed to all distribution points and click **Next**.
23. On the **Deployment Settings** page, verify that purpose is **Required** and click **Next**.
24. On the **Scheduling** page, click **New** and then click **Assign immediately after this event**. Verify that **As soon as possible** is selected as the event, click **OK** and **Next**.
25. On the **User Experience** page, click **Software installation** to allow the program to run outside a maintenance window (the second check box on the page) and then click **Next**.
26. On the **Distribution Points** page, accept the default setting and click **Next**.
27. On the **Summary** page, read the summary and click **Next** to start the deployment.
28. Click **Close**.

Import Custom Updates

The easiest way to get started with SCUP is by importing existing update catalogs. The free catalogs aren't that rich and often require additional testing. For those organizations that have Adobe Reader and Adobe Flash installed, I recommend starting with the Adobe catalog.

1. From the **Start screen**, open **System Center Updates Publisher**.
2. Navigate to the **Catalogs** workspace, and on the ribbon, click **Add Catalogs**.
3. Select all the **Adobe Systems** catalogs and click **Add**.

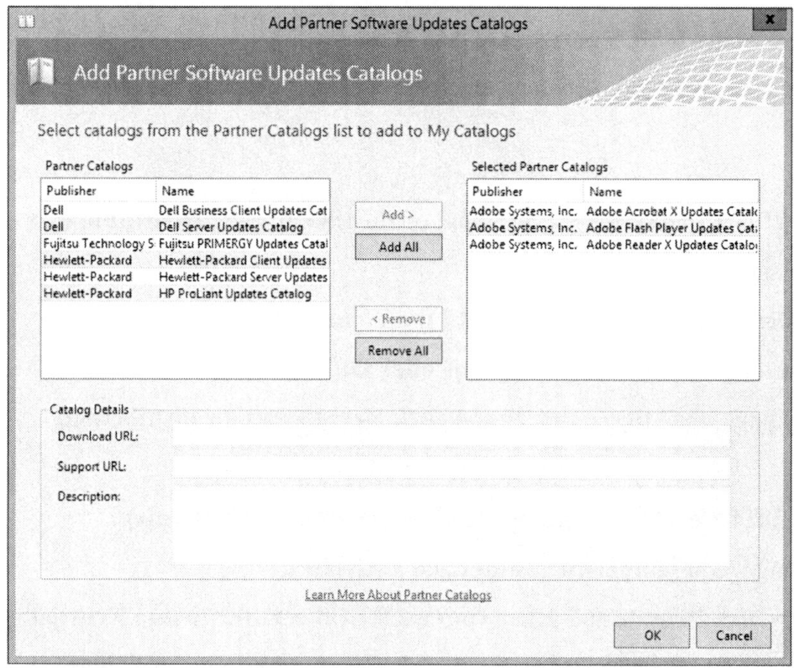

Adding the Adobe updates.

4. Click **OK** and navigate to the **Updates** workspace.
5. On the ribbon, click **Import**, select all catalogs, and click **Next** twice.
6. When prompted, select **Always accept content from "Adobe Systems, Incorporated"**, and click **Accept**. Click **Close** to finish the import.

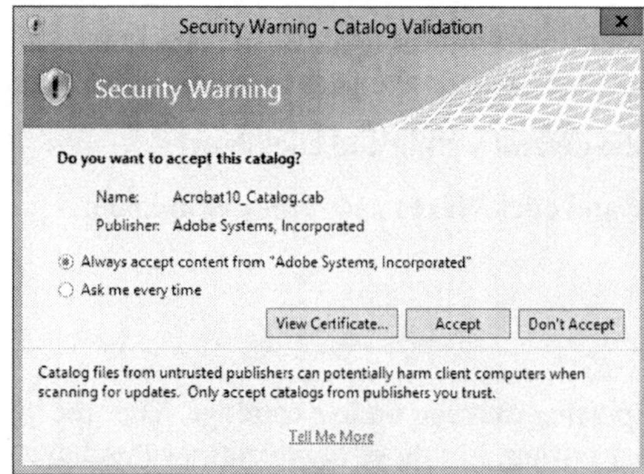

Accepting content from Adobe.

Import Configuration Manager 2012 SP1 Cumulative Update 2

You can install ConfigMgr 2012 cumulative updates as traditional ConfigMgr packages or through SCUP using the SCUP cab file. Follow these steps to use the ConfigMgr 2012 SP1 CU2 cab file:

> **Note:** This guide assumes that you have installed CU2 per the instructions in Appendix I. Don't worry if you haven't, however, as it's an optional guide. You can simply skip this guide and continue with the next one.

1. From the **Start screen**, open **System Center Updates Publisher**.
2. Navigate to the **Catalogs** workspace, and on the ribbon, click **Add**.
3. Specify these settings and click **OK**:
    a. Catalog Path: **\\cm01\SMS_PS1\hotfix\KB2854009\SCUP\2854009.cab**
    b. Publisher: **Microsoft**
    c. Name: **ConfigMgr2012SP1CU2**
    d. Description: **ConfigMgr 2012 SP1 CU2 update**
    e. Support URL: **http://support.microsoft.com/kb/2854009**
4. Navigate to the **Updates** workspace.
5. On the ribbon, click **Import**, select the **ConfigMgr2012SP1CU2** catalog, and click **Next** twice.
6. When promted, accept the certificate and finish the import.

Publish Updates

Before you can start deploying custom updates through ConfigMgr 2012, you first have to publish them from SCUP into WSUS. When publishing updates, you have three options for each update. You can publish them as *metadata*, *full content*, or *automatic*.

- **Metadata.** When published as metadata, updates can be used only to track compliance. Metadata is not enough to install the update.
- **Full content.** Full content tells SCUP to download all the binaries needed for the update and publish them along with metadata to WSUS.
- **Automatic.** This option chooses either metadata or full content depending on the ConfigMgr integration that you have configured. SCUP 2011 performs a WMI query against ConfigMgr 2012 for all updates marked as automatic. If the update is required by more than the a specific number of hosts and the update binary size is less than the valued specified, then updates are published with full content; otherwise, updates are published with metadata only.

Publications

A publication is a list of updates that you have selected to work with. Usually you create a publication list and add the updates you to want to publish. By doing that, it is easier to find and manage the published updates. ViaMonstra has decided to create a new publication list every month using the same naming standard as that used for update groups.

Real World Note: Make sure the certificates have been deployed to **CM01** before publishing custom updates.

Publish Custom Updates

1. From the **Start screen**, open **System Center Updates Publisher**.
2. Navigate to **Adobe Systems, Inc / Adobe Flash Player**. Select the latest **Flash Player** versions (both the 32-bit and x64-bit plugins), and then on the ribbon, click **Assign**.
3. Select **Full Content** as the publication type. Select **Assign software updates to a new publication**, name the new publication **2013 04 April**, and click **OK**.

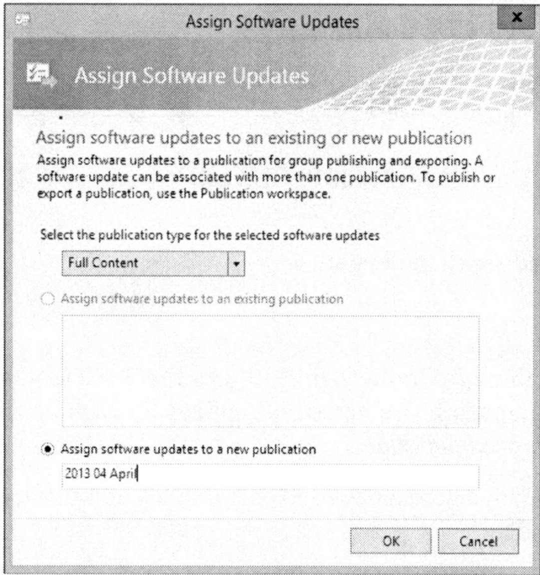

Creating the publication.

4. Navigate to **Adobe Systems, Inc / Adobe Reader**. Select the latest Reader version, and then on the ribbon, click **Assign** and assign the update with **Full Content** to the **2012 06 April** publication.
5. Navigate to the **Publications** workspace and select **2013 06 April**. You should see all updates in the publication. On the ribbon, click **Publish**.
6. On the **Publish Options** page, click **Next**.

7. On the **Summary** page, read the summary and click **Next** to start publishing the updates.
8. On the **Confirmation** page, click **Close**.
9. Select the **Updates** workspace and navigate to **Microsoft – Local Publish / System Center 2012 Configuration Manager**.
10. Select the two client upgrades, and on the ribbon, click **Assign**.
11. Select **Full Content** as the publication type. Select **Assign software updates to a new publication**, name the new publication **ConfigMgr 2012 SP1 CU2**, and click **OK**.
12. From the **Publications** workspace, select **ConfigMgr 2012 SP1 CU2** and click **Publish**.
13. On the **Publish Options** page, click **Next**.
14. On the **Summary** page, read the summary and click **Next** to start publishing the updates.
15. When prompted to accept the certificate, select **Always accept content from "Microsoft Corporation"** and click **Accept**.
16. On the **Confirmation** page, click **Close**.
17. Open the **ConfigMgr console** and navigate to the **Software Library** workspace.
18. Select **Software Updates / All Software Updates**, and then on the ribbon, click **Synchronize Software Updates**. Click **Yes** in the dialog box and start the synchronization process. The first synchronization process synchronizes information about new products from WSUS.
19. Once the synchronization process is finished, select the **Administration** workspace and navigate to **Site Configuration / Sites**.
20. Right-click **PS1 – ViaMonstra HQ** and select **Configure Site Components / Software Update Point**.
21. From the **Products** tab, select **Adobe Systems, Inc**, and **Microsoft – Local Publisher**.

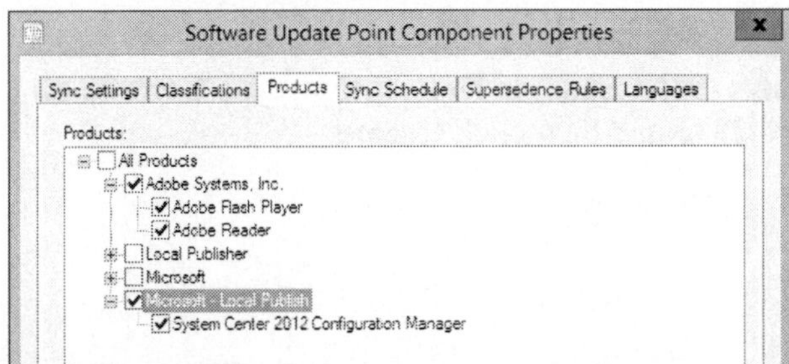

Including the new products in the synchronization process.

22. Select the **Classifications** tab, check **Update Rollup**, and click **OK**. This is needed to synchronize the ConfigMgr cumulative updates.

23. Navigate to the **Software Library** workspace and initiate another Software Update synchronization process.

24. Even though the in-console monitoring has improved a lot, it's still valuable to use the log files as they give you much more detailed real-time information. Open **D:\Program Files\Microsoft Configuration Manager\Logs\wsyncmgr.log** and monitor the process.

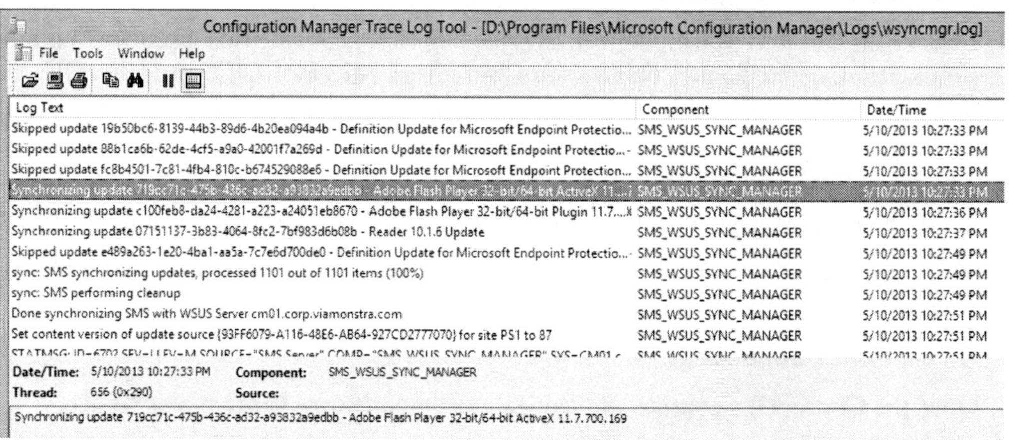

Monitoring the wsyncmgr.log file.

25. Open the **ConfigMgr console**, navigate to the **Software Library** workspace, and select **All Software Updates**.

26. Place the cursor in **Search**, and on the ribbon, click **Add Criteria**.

27. From the list of criteria, select **Vendor**.

28. Notice that **Adobe Systems, Inc** is selected in the Search Criteria (not really magic, the list is sorted alphabetically). Click **Search**.

29. Select all the **Adobe Systems** updates, and on the ribbon, click **Create Software Update Group**.

30. Type **2013 04 April Custom Updates** as the name; in **Description**, type **Contain all custom updates published in April 2013** and then click **Create**.

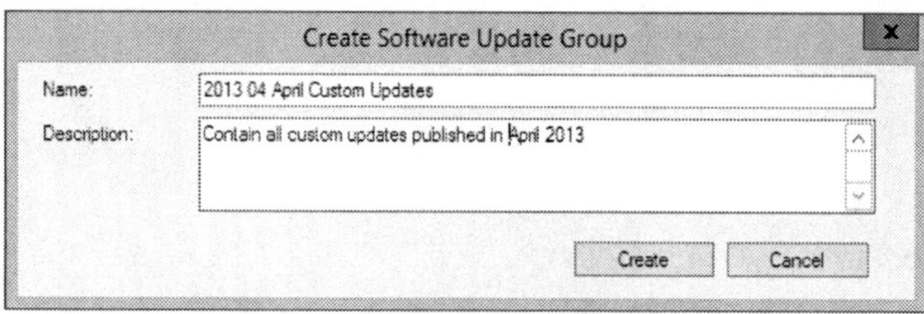

Creating a custom software update group.

31. Place the cursor in **Search**, and on the ribbon, click **Add Criteria**.

32. From the list of criteria, select **Vendor**.

33. Notice that **Adobe Systems, Inc** is selected in the **Search Criteria** (not really magic, as the list is sorted alphabetically). Click **Search**.
34. Select all the **Adobe Systems** updates, and on the ribbon, click **Create Software Update Group**.
35. Type **2013 04 April Custom Updates** as the name; in **Description**, type **Contain all custom updates published in April 2013** and then click **Create**.
36. From the **Vendor** list select **Microsoft – Local Publish**. You should now see the two System Center 2012 Configuration Manager cumulative updates.
37. Select both updates, and on the ribbon, click **Create Software Update Group** and name it **System Center 2012 SP1 CU2**.

The rest of the deployment process is similar to deploying Windows updates. ConfigMgr client does not treat third-party updates any differently than normal Windows updates. Having said that, in ViaMonstra, I prefer to create separate software update groups for the third-party updates and not mix them with our "normal" Microsoft Patch Tuesday updates.

Real World Note: Always manage the entire live cycle from the SCUP console. That includes expiring and deleting updates. When you expire and update from SCUP, the metadata are automatically synchronized to WSUS and ConfigMgr.

Other Third-Party Software Update Solutions

As mentioned earlier in this chapter, a proper software update solution must provide the administrator with vulnerability intelligence information and be able to detect vulnerabilities without having to define manually what to scan for. SCUP does not offer that, which is why ViaMonstra plans to look at the other available solutions. After scanning the market, ViaMonstra found two products that can be integrated with ConfigMgr. These are CSI from Secunia and Patch Manager from Solarwinds. The features ViaMonstra is looking for are:

- **Integration.** Secunia and Solarwinds both offer a ConfigMgr administrator console plugin.
- **Custom packages.** Secunia and Solarwinds both offer custom packages. There is a minor difference in some of the packages, but they can all be installed silent. Some of the tested packages like Adobe Reader, Adobe Flash, SUN Java, and Apple iTunes also offer support to disable automatic update features and remove icons from the user desktop. These features will save ViaMonstra administrators hours of repackaging time.
- **Custom reports and dashboard.** Secunia and Solarwinds both offer custom reports and dashboards. In this category, Secunia is a little different in that it also provides ViaMonstra with complete vulnerability intelligence information taken from a cloud-based database.

- **Download information.** Secunia CSI can be downloaded from http://tinyurl.com/p2he2jp, and Solarwinds Patch Manager can be downloaded from http://tinyurl.com/or3bhuo.

You can request a POC from both vendors in either your production or a lab environment.

Useful Log Files

You can use the log files in the following table to track activity related to your software updates.

Log File	Description	Location
WCM.log	Records information about the SUP configuration, subscribed categories, classifications, and languages on the SUP server.	Server default
wsyncmgr.log	Records information about the synchronization process.	Server default
wctrl.log	Records information about the configuration, database connectivity, and health of the WSUS server.	Server default
scup.log	Records information about downloading and synchronizing custom updates to WSUS.	%temp% on the computer with the SCUP console installed
patchdownloader.log	Records information about downloading software updates from the update source to the specified source location for the Update package.	Client default on the computer from which the download was initiated
ruleengine.log	Records information about processing the automatic update rules.	Server default
windowsupdate.log	Default Windows Update agent log file. Records activity about scanning and installing updates.	C:\windows
WUAHandler.log	Records information about searching for updates	Client default
UpdatesDeployment.log	Records information about deployment, evaluations, and enforcements on the client.	Client default
UpdatesHandler,log	Records information about compliance scanning, and the download and installation of updates on the client.	Client default

Log File	Description	Location
UpdateStore.log	Records information about the compliance of updates that are scanned as part of the compliance scanning.	Client default
SoftwareDistribution.log	Records information about the software updates that are synchronized from the update source to the WSUS database	WSUS server %program files%\Update Services\Logfiles

Chapter 9

Endpoint Protection

Malware protection has over the years become more and more important. With ConfigMgr 2012, managing malware in a client environment has never been easier. The System Center Endpoint Protection feature is completely integrated with ConfigMgr without the need to install an additional reporting server or new database. Configuring and managing the solution can be divided into three major areas:

- Configuring the site system role and definition update settings
- Configuring the client settings and malware policies
- Configuring alerts and monitor the environment

Your first step before configuring your solution, however, is preparing for it by creating the proper collections. That is where I'll start.

Preparing for Endpoint Protection

Like with any other feature, it is important that your antimalware solution has a collection design that allows you to ease the administrative work while keeping complete control of the feature. When designing collections, it's important that you allow for a pilot group, applying different malware policies and excluding computers from being controlled by Endpoint Protection.

Endpoint Protection Collections

This section guides you through creating the needed Endpoint Protection collections. With those collections, you can create an Endpoint Protection solution in which you can run a pilot and allow for different malware templates.

- **EP Pilot 1.** Contains all computers that participate in the pilot test.
- **EP Workstation Production.** All workstations in production that will have the Endpoint Protection client installed.
- **EP Excluded.** Computers that for any reason must be excluded from installing the Endpoint Protection client.
- **EP Server ConfigMgr.** All System Center 2012 ConfigMgr servers.
- **EP Server Domain Controllers.** All Windows domain controllers.
- **EP All Client.** Will include all EP collections and be used as target collection for the Endpoint Protection definitions deployments.

Create the Endpoint Protection Collections

1. On **CM01**, open the **ConfigMgr console**.
2. In the **Assets and Compliance** workspace, in **Device Collections**, select the **Endpoint Protection** folder.
3. On the ribbon, click **Create Device Collection**.
4. On the **General** page, define these settings and click **Next**:
   a. Name: **EP Pilot 1**
   b. Comment: **All computers that are part of the SCEP pilot**
   c. Limiting Collection: Click **Browse** and select **All Systems**.
5. On the **Membership Rules** page, define this setting and click **Next**:

   Click **Add Rule / Direct Rule**.
6. On the **Welcome** page, click **Next**.
7. On the **Search Resources** page, type **PC0001** in **Value** and click **Next**.
8. On the **Select Resources** page, select **PC0001** and click **Next**.

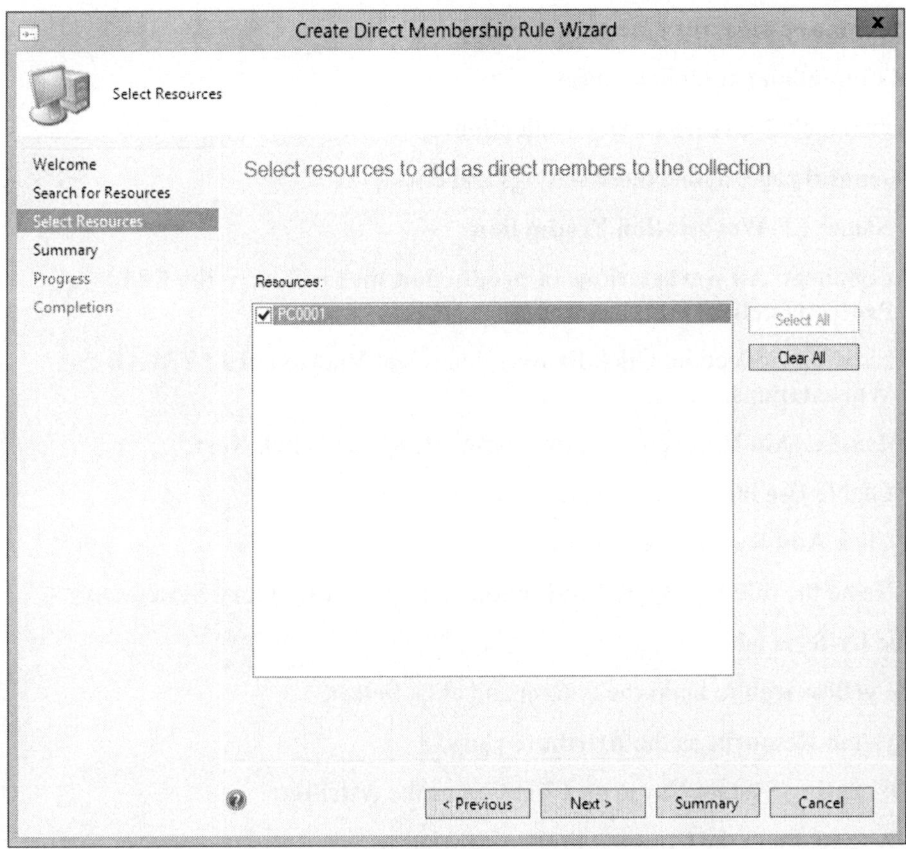

Creating a direct membership rule.

9. On the **Summary** page, read the summary and click **Next**.
10. On the **Completion** page, click **Close**.
11. On the **Membership Rules** page, verify that you have a direct rule and click **Next**.
12. On the **Summary** page, read the summary and click **Next**.
13. On the **Completion** page, click **Close**.

Create the Workstation Collections

1. On the ribbon, click **Create Device Collection**.
2. On the **General** page, define these settings and click **Next**:
    a. Name: **EP Excluded**
    b. Comment: **All computers that are excluded from Endpoint Protection**
    c. Limiting Collection: Click **Browse** and select **All Systems**.
3. On the **Membership Rules** page, click **Next** and **OK** in the warning message.

4. On the **Summary** page, read the summary and click **Next**.
5. On the **Completion** page, click **Close**
6. On the ribbon, click **Create Device Collection**.
7. On the **General** page, define these settings and click **Next**:
    a. Name: **EP Workstation Production**
    b. Comment: **All workstations in production that will have the Endpoint Protection client installed**
    c. Limiting Collection: Click **Browse** and select **ViaMonstra / VM All Workstations**.
8. On the **Membership Rules** page, define these settings and click **Next**:
    a. Enable **Use incremental updates for this collection**.
    b. Click **Add Rule / Query Rule**.
    c. Name the rule **EP WRK Production** and click **Edit Query Statement**.
9. Select the **Criteria** tab.
10. Click the **yellow icon** to build the criteria and click **Select**.
11. Select **System Resource** as the **Attribute class**.
12. Select **Operating System Name and Version** as the **Attribute**.
13. Click **OK** to return to the Criterion Properties window.
14. Click **Operator** and select **is like** in **Value** type **%Workstation%**.
15. Click **OK** three times and return to the **Memberships Rules** page.
16. Click **Add Rule / Exclude Collections**.
17. Click the **Endpoint Protection** folder, select **EP Excluded** and click **OK**.

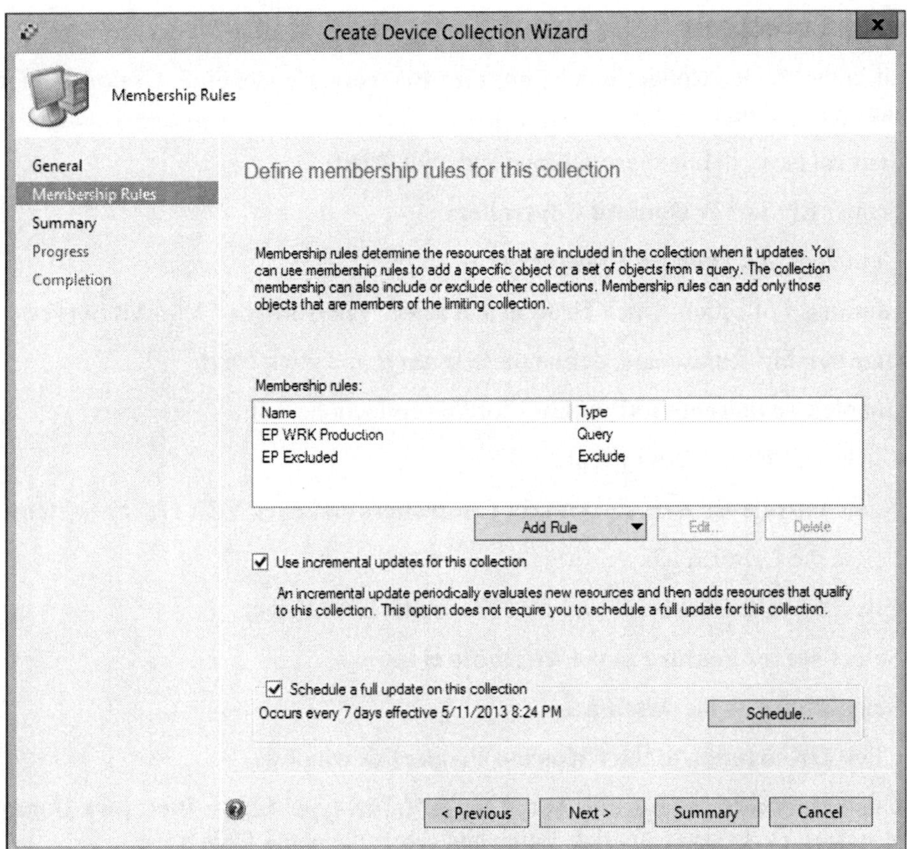

Creating the EP Workstations collection.

18. Finish the Create Device Collection Wizard using the default settings.

Automate Creating Exclude Rules in Collections Using PowerShell

In this optional example, you create an Exclude rule for the EP Excluded collection in the EP Workstation Production collection. (This is just a sample command and is not required for any of the guides in this book.)

1. From the **ConfigMgr console**, launch **PowerShell.**
2. To create the collection **Exclude** rule, type the following command:

```
Set-CMCollectionExcludeRule -SiteCode PS1 -SiteServer CM01
-CollectionName "EP Workstation Production"
-ExcludeCollectionName "EP Excluded"
```

Create the Server Collections

1. While still in the **Device Collections / Endpoint Protection** node, click **Create Device Collection** on the ribbon.
2. On the **General** page, define these settings and click **Next**:
    a. Name: **EP Server Domain Controllers**
    b. Comment: **All Domain Controllers**
    c. Limiting Collection: Click **Browse** and select **ViaMonstra / VM All Servers**.
3. On the **Membership Rules** page, define these settings and click **Next**:
    a. Enable **Use incremental updates** for this collection.
    b. Click **Add Rule / Query Rule**.
    c. Name the rule **EP Server Domain Controllers** and click **Edit Query Statement**.
    d. Select the **Criteria** tab.
    e. Click the **yellow icon** to build the criteria and click **Select**.
    f. Select **Server Feature** as the **Attribute class**.
    g. Select **Name** as the **Attribute**.
    h. Click **OK** to return to the **Criterion Properties** window.
    i. Click **Operator** and select **is equal to**; in **Value**, type **Active Directory Domain Services**. (You also can click Value and select the name from a list.)
    j. Click **OK** three times to return to the Memberships Rules page.
4. Finish the wizard using the default settings.
5. On the ribbon, click **Create Device Collection**.
6. On the **General** page, define these settings and click **Next**:
    a. Name: **EP Server ConfigMgr**
    b. Comment: **All System Center 2012 ConfigMgr servers**
    c. Limiting Collection: Click **Browse** and select **ViaMonstra / VM All Servers**.
7. On the **Membership Rules** page, define these settings and click **Next**:
    a. Enable **Use incremental updates** for this collection.
    b. Click **Add Rule / Query Rule**.
    c. Name the rule **EP Server ConfigMgr** and click **Edit Query Statement**.
    d. Select the **Criteria** tab.
    e. Click the **yellow icon** to build the criteria and click **Select**.

f. Select **Installed Applications (64)** as the **Attribute class**.

g. Select **Display Name** as the **Attribute**.

h. Click **OK** to return to the Criterion Properties dialog box.

i. Click **Operator** and select **is like**; in **Value**, type **Microsoft System Center 2012 Configuration Manager%**. Click **OK** three times to return to the Memberships Rules page.

8. Finish the wizard using the default settings.

Create the EP All Client Collection

1. On the ribbon, click **Create Device Collection**.
2. On the **General** page, define these settings and click **Next**:
   a. Name: **EP All Clients**
   b. Comment: **All clients with SCEP installed**
   c. Limiting Collection: Click **Browse** and select **All Systems**.
3. On the **Membership Rules** page, define these settings and click **Next**:
   a. Click **Add Rule / Include Collections**.
   b. Navigate to the **Endpoint Protection** folder and select all EP collections except **EP Excluded** and click **OK**.

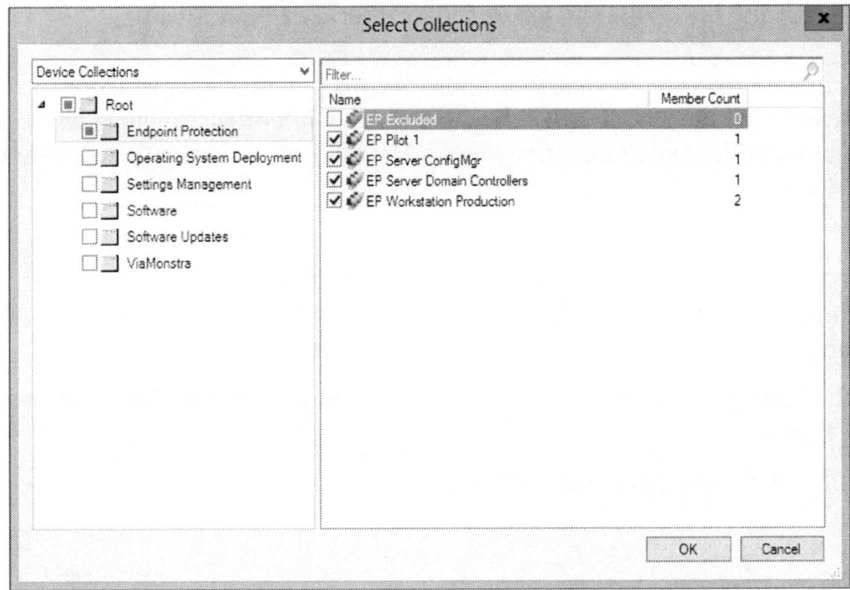

Create the EP All client collection

4. Finish the wizard using the default settings.

Configuring the Site System Role and Definition Update Settings

Install the Endpoint Protection Site System Role

1. On **CM01**, log on as **VIAMONSTRA\Administrator** and open the **ConfigMgr console**.
2. Navigate to the **Administration** workspace and select **Site Configuration / Servers and Site System Roles**.
3. Select **CM01**, and on the ribbon, click **Add Site System Roles**.
4. On the **General** page, click **Next**.
5. On the **Proxy** page, click **Next**.
6. On the **System Role Selection** page, select **Endpoint Protection point**, accept the warning message, and click **Next**.
7. On the **Endpoint Protection** page, read and accept the license terms and then click **Next**.
8. On the **Microsoft Active Protection Service** page, select **Advanced membership** and click **Next**.
9. On the **Summary** page, read the summary and click **Next** to enable the site system role.
10. On the **Completion** page, click **Close**.
11. Open the **EPSetup.log** file on the site server and monitor the EP installation.

Real World Note: A System Center Endpoint Protection client is installed automatically on the site server when you enable the site system role. The client is not a full protected client and is assigned a special malware policy called Reporting Server Default Policy. This policy does not enable real-time protection.

Configure Automatic Deployment of Definitions

One way to keep definition files up to date is by creating an automatic deployment rule using the software update feature:

1. Navigate to the **Software Library** workspace and select **Software Updates / Automatic Deployment Rules**.
2. On the ribbon, click **Create Automatic Deployment Rule**.

3. On the **General** page, configure these settings and click **Next**:
    a. Name: **Endpoint Protection Definitions**
    b. Collection: **Endpoint Protection / EP All clients**
    c. Enable: **Add to an existing Software Update Group**
    d. Enable: **Enable the deployment after this rule is run**

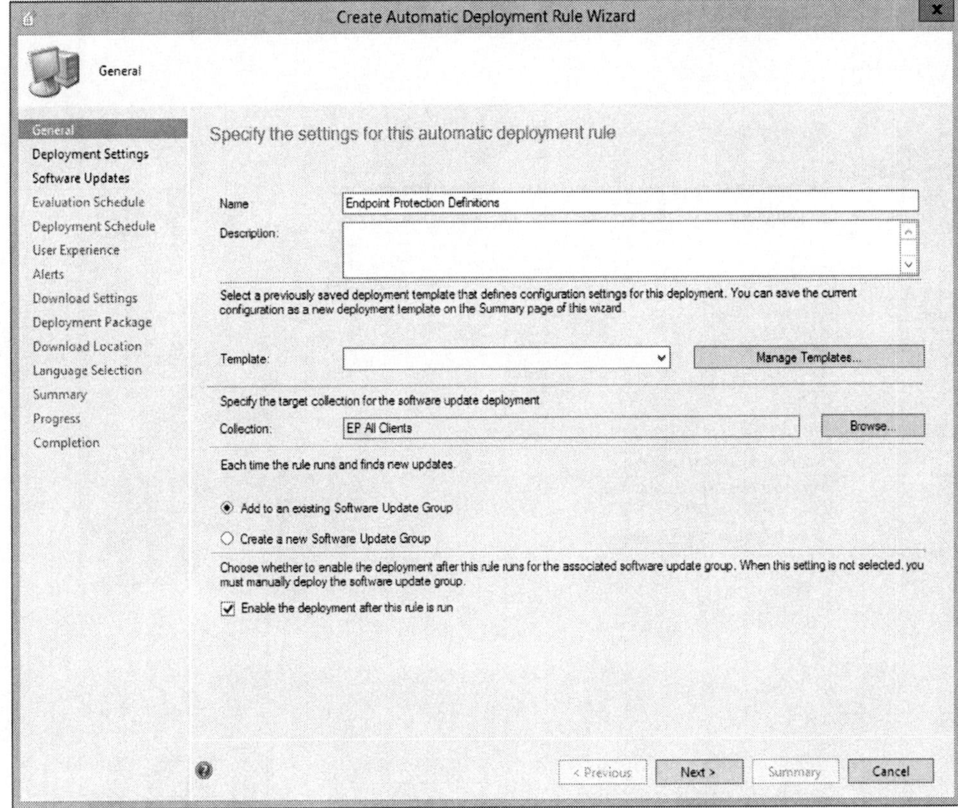

Creating an automatic deployment rule.

4. On the **Deployment Settings** page, select **Only error messages** and click **Next**.

5. On the **Software Updates** page, select these settings and click **Next**:
    a. Date Released or Revised: **Last 6 days**
    b. Product: **Forefront Endpoint Protection 2010**
    c. Superseded: **No**
    d. Update classification: **Definition Updates**

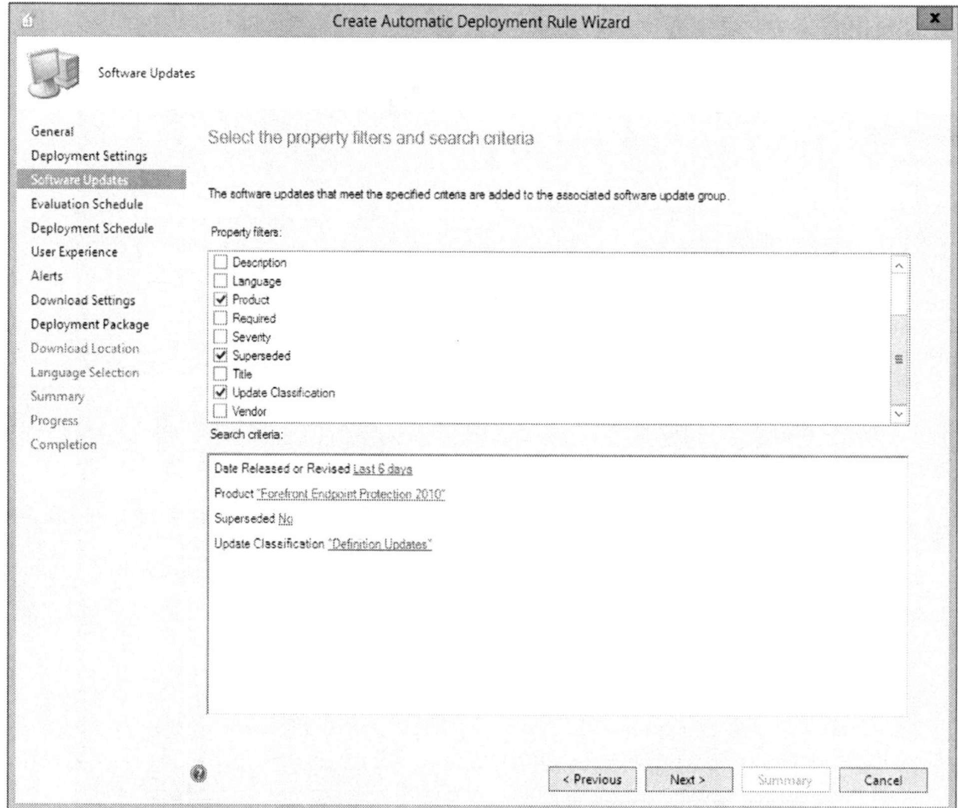

Filtering the definition updates.

6. On the **Evaluation Schedule** page, ensure **Run the rule after any software update point synchronization** is selected and click **Next**.
7. On the **Deployment Schedule** page, configure these settings and click **Next**:
    a. Software available time: **As soon as possible**
    b. Installation deadline: **As soon as possible**

8. On the **User Experience** page, configure these settings and click **Next**:
    a. User notifications: **Hide in Software Center and all notifications**
    b. Deadline behavior: Enable **Software Installation**.
    c. Device Restart Behavior: Enable **Servers and Workstations**.

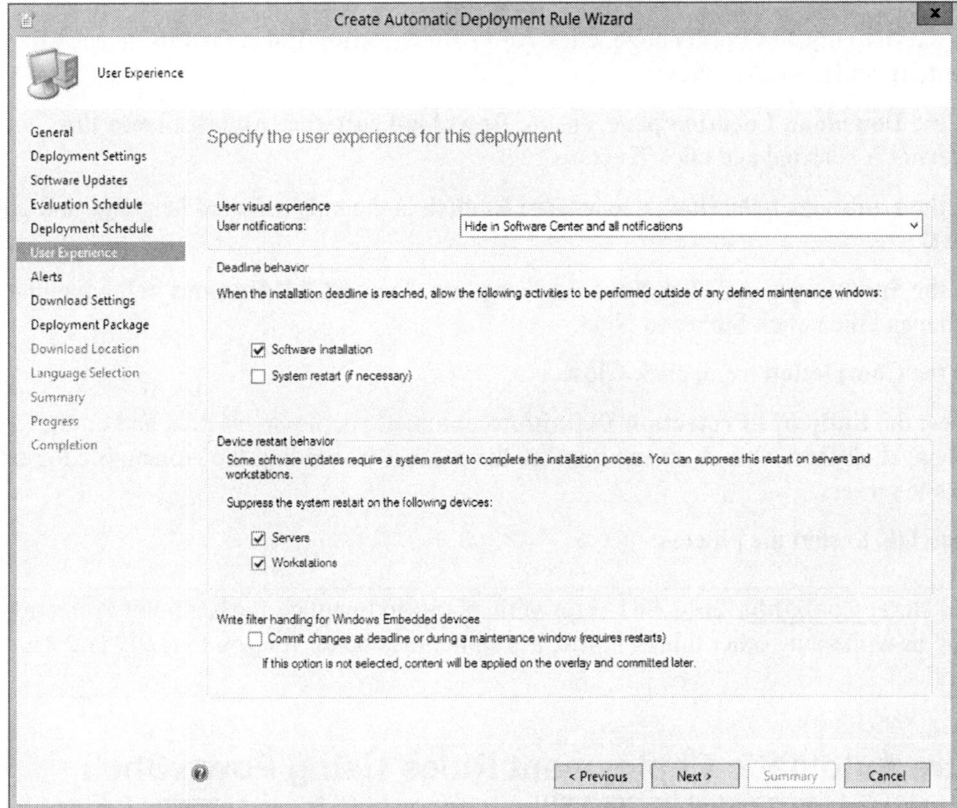

Hiding update activity for the user.

9. On the **Alerts** page, click **Next**.
10. On the **Download Settings** page, configure these settings and click **Next**:
    a. Deployment options for clients within a slow or unreliable network: **Download software updates from distribution point and install**
    b. Deployment options for when updates are not available on any preferred distribution points: **Download software updates from distribution point and install**
    c. Enable **If software updates are not available on preferred distribution point or remote distribution, download content from Microsoft Updates**.

11. On the **Deployment Package** page, create a new deployment package with these settings and click **Next**:

    a. Name: **EP Definition Updates**

    b. Description: **EP Definition Updates**

    c. Package Sources: **\\CM01\Sources$\Updates\Definitions**.

12. On the **Distribution Points** page, click **Add / Distribution Point Group**, select **All Content**, and then click **Next**.

13. On the **Download Location** page, ensure **Download software updates from the Internet** is selected and click **Next**.

14. On the **Language Selection** page, ensure **English** is the only selected language and click **Next**.

15. On the **Summary** page, click **Save As Template**. Type **SCEP Updates** in the template name, and then click **Save** and Next.

16. On the **Completion** page, click **Close**.

17. Select the **Endpoint Protection Definitions** automatic deployment rule, and on the ribbon, click **Run Now**. You can monitor the process by reading the **ruleengine.log** on the site server.

18. Click **OK** to start the process.

> **Real World Note:** ConfigMgr 2012 SP1 ships with a built-in template for Endpoint Protection updates. But, as with many other things in life, it's sometimes better for you to really understand how this works.

Configure Automatic Deployment Rules Using PowerShell

If you have upgraded your ConfigMgr 2012 SP1 installation to CU2 per Appendix I, one of the built-in cmdlet lets you create automatic deployment rules, but a requirement is that you reference an existing package in your script. The following example first creates a software update package that is used in the automatic deployment rule:

> **Note:** The following example requires that you have upgraded your ConfigMgr 2012 SP1 installation to CU2 per the instructions in Appendix I. If you have not done this, you can simply skip this optional sample, as it's not required for the other guides in this book.

1. On **CM01**, from the **ConfigMgr console**, launch **PowerShell**.
2. Using **File Explorer**, create the **D:\Sources\Updates\SCEP** folder.

3. To create the software update package, type the following command:

```
$Arguments = @{Name = "SCEP"; Description = "Software Update
package SCEP def"; PkgSourceFlag = 2; PkgSourcePath =
"\\CM01\Sources$\Updates\SCEP"}
```

4. Type the following command:

```
Set-WmiInstance -Namespace "root\sms\Site_PS1" -Class
SMS_SoftwareUpdatesPackage -Arguments $Arguments
```

```
Administrator: Windows PowerShell
PS D:\Setup\scripts> $Arguments = @{Name = "SCEP"; Description = "Software Update package SCEP def"; PkgSourceFlag = 2; PkgSourcePath = "\\CM01\Sources$\Updates\SCEP"}
PS D:\Setup\scripts> Set-WmiInstance -Namespace "root\sms\Site_PS1" -Class SMS_SoftwareUpdatesPackage -Arguments $Arguments

__GENUS                     : 2
__CLASS                     : SMS_SoftwareUpdatesPackage
__SUPERCLASS                : SMS_PackageBaseclass
__DYNASTY                   : SMS_BaseClass
__RELPATH                   : SMS_SoftwareUpdatesPackage.PackageID="PS100018"
__PROPERTY_COUNT            : 43
__DERIVATION                : {SMS_PackageBaseclass, SMS_BaseClass}
__SERVER                    : CM01
__NAMESPACE                 : root\sms\Site_PS1
__PATH                      : \\CM01\root\sms\Site_PS1:SMS_SoftwareUpdatesPackage.PackageID="PS100018"
ActionInProgress            : 1
AlternateContentProviders   :
Description                 : Software Update package SCEP def
```

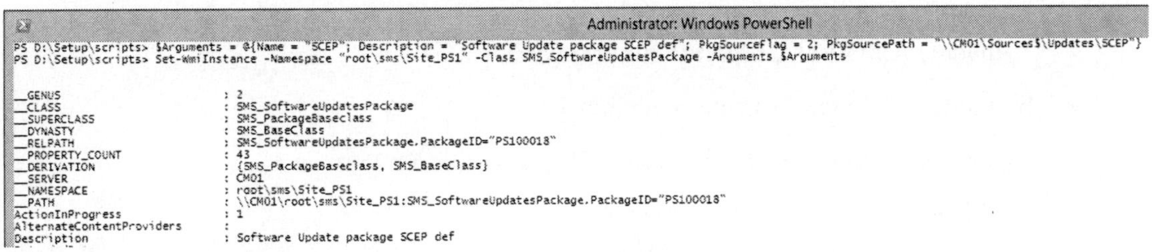

Creating a software update package using PowerShell.

5. Type the following command:

```
New-CMSoftwareUpdateAutoDeploymentRule -CollectionName
"EP All Clients" -AddToExistingSoftwareUpdateGroup $true
-EnabledAfterCreate $True -SendWakeUpPacket $true
-UpdateClassification "Definition Updates"
-DateReleasedOrRevised "Last6day" -Product "Forefront
Endpoint Protection 2010" -Superseded $false -RunType
RunTheRuleAfterAnySoftwareUpdatePointSynchronization
-DeploymentPackageName "SCEP" -Name "SCEP Updates"
-VerboseLevel OnlyErrorMessages -DownloadFromInternet $true
-AvailableImmediately $True -DeadlineImmediately $True
-UseUtc $false -UserNotification HideAll -
AllowUseMeteredNetwork $false -SuccessPercentage 90
-AlertTime 7 -AlertTimeUnit Days -SuppressRestartServer
$false -SuppressRestartWorkstation $false
```

Configuring Client Settings and Malware Policies

You control the SCEP client installation through Client Settings. This allows you to create a custom set of settings and deploy to a group of pilot computers. Endpoint Protection automatically removes existing antimalware client software on the computer prior to installing the new SCEP client. This works for some but not all antimalware clients. The only way for you to make sure that it will work in your environment is to test, test, and test. The following clients will be removed:

- Symantec AntiVirus Corporate Edition version 10
- Symantec Endpoint Protection version 11
- Symantec Endpoint Protection Small Business Edition version 12
- McAfee VirusScan Enterprise version 8
- Trend Micro OfficeScan
- Microsoft Forefront Codename Stirling Beta 2
- Microsoft Forefront Codename Stirling Beta 3
- Microsoft Forefront Client Security v1
- Microsoft Security Essentials v1
- Microsoft Security Essentials 2010
- Microsoft Forefront Endpoint Protection 2010
- Microsoft Security Center Online v1

Note: If any of the preceding clients are not automatically removed, make sure that you remove the password from the client.

After the client is installed, you can control the antimalware policies by editing the default client antimalware policy or creating one or more custom policies. A client can only apply a single policy, and in the event of a conflict, the policy order value determines which one is applied. The one with the lowest value will take precedence over any higher value policies.

Installing and Managing SCEP Clients

Install the Client on the EP Pilot Collection

1. On **CM01**, log on as **VIAMONSTRA\Administrator** and open the **ConfigMgr console**.
2. Navigate to thc **Administration** workspace.

3. Select **Client Settings**, and on the ribbon, click **Create Custom Client Device Settings**.
4. In **Name**, type **Endpoint Protection**.
5. From the list of custom settings, select **Endpoint Protection** and configure these settings:
    a. Manage Endpoint Protection on client computers: **Yes**
    b. Install Endpoint Protection client on client computers: **Yes**
    c. Automatically remove any previously installed antimalware software before Endpoint Protection is installed: **Yes**
    d. Suppress any required computer restarts after the Endpoint Protection client is installed: **Yes**
    e. Disable alternate sources: **Yes**

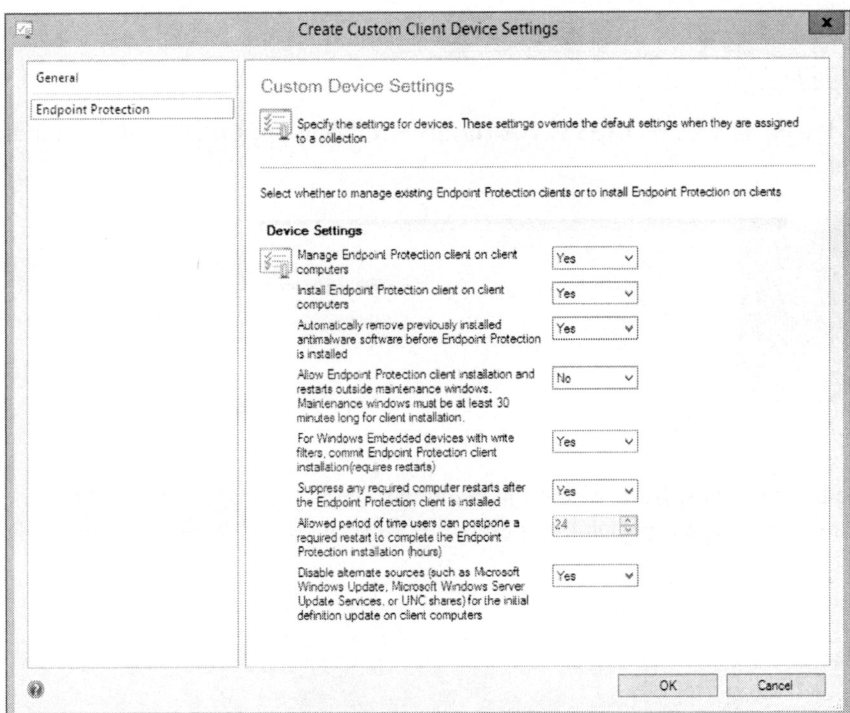

Configuring SCEP client properties.

6. Click **OK** to close the custom settings.
7. From the list of available client settings, select **Endpoint Protection**, and on the ribbon, click **Deploy**.
8. Navigate to the **Endpoint Protection** folder, select **EP Pilot 1** and click **OK**.
9. The installation starts as soon as the machine policy is updated.

10. You can monitor the installation in the **Deployments** section of the **Monitoring** workspace, or from the **EndpointProtectionAgent.log** file on the client.

Real World Note: To install the client manually, use SCEPInstall.exe /s /q /policy "full path to policy".

Verify the SCEP Client

Installing the client will take place as soon as the machine policy has been updated. The client will be installed from a local source using this command line:

C:\Windows\ccmsetup\SCEPInstall.exe" /s /q /NoSigsUpdateAtInitialExp /policy "C:\Windows\CCM\EPAMPolicy.xml"

After the client is installed, it connects to the ConfigMgr infrastructure and starts updating the SCEP engine and definitions.

View the Local SCEP Agent

1. On **PC0001**, log on as **VIAMONSTRA\Administrator** and open the **SCEP** icon in the notification area.

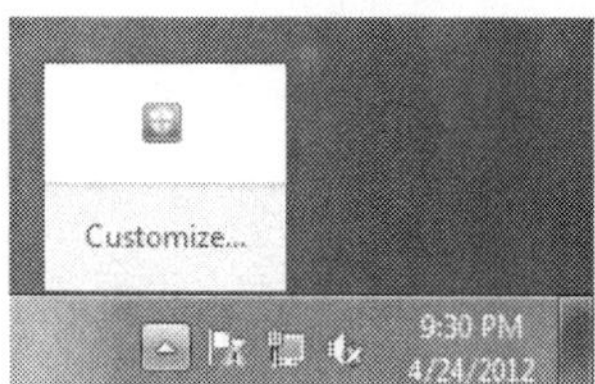

Opening the local SCEP settings.

The interface has four tabs, from which the client can read information about the protection status and, depending on the malware policy, also modify the settings.

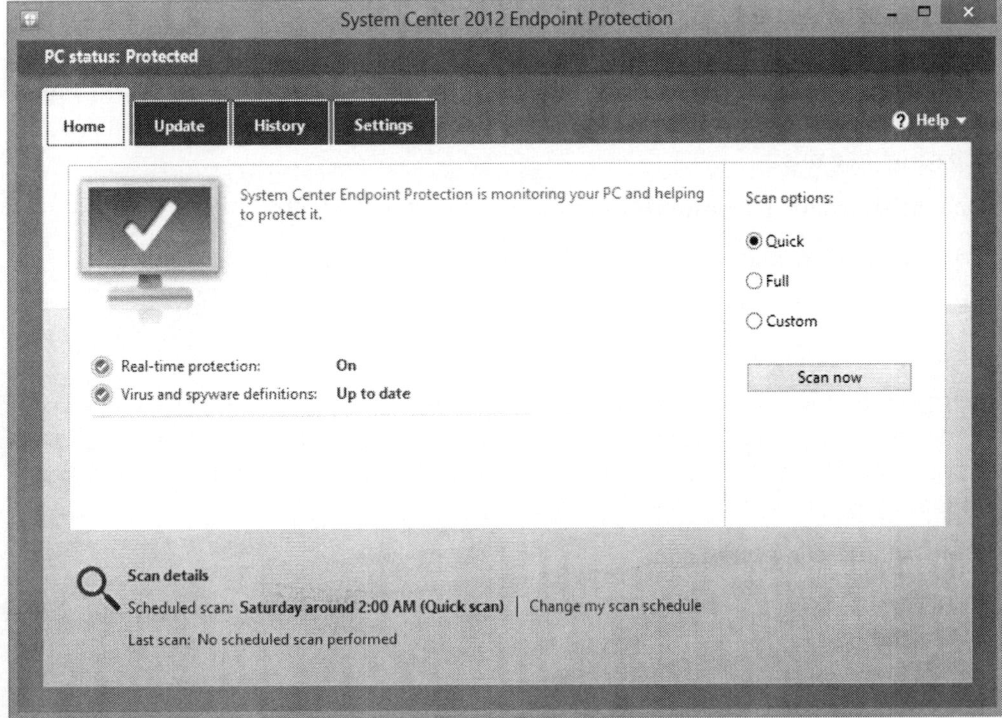

The SCEP client interface.

2. To view additional information, click the drop-down arrow next to **Help** and select **About System Center Endpoint Protection**.

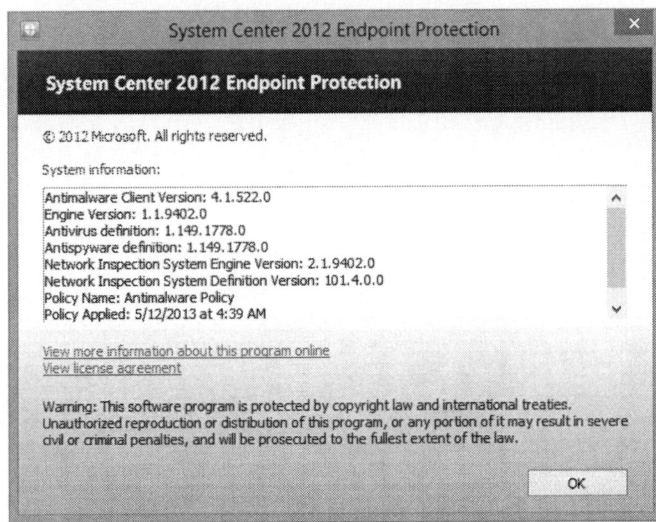

The SCEP system information.

3. Click **OK** to close the system information.

View the Applied Policies

Unlike the ConfigMgr 2012 RTM version, with SP1, information about the applied antimalware policies is no longer available via the client help file. The information, however, is still stored in WMI, which allows you to view information either using a WMI browser or by creating a PowerShell script like this:

1. On **CM01**, from the **ConfigMgr console**, launch **PowerShell**.
2. To view all the applied antimalware policies, type the following command:

   ```
   $EmptyPolicy= @()
   ```

3. Type the following command:

   ```
   $EPPolicy = Get-wmiObject -namespace
   "Root\ccm\Policy\Machine\ActualConfig" -query "Select Name
   from CCM_AntiMalwarePolicyClientConfig" | ForEach-Object
   {$EmptyPolicy+=$_.Name}
   ```

4. Type the following command:

   ```
   $EmptyPolicy | Group-Object | Select-Object -Property Name
   -Unique
   ```

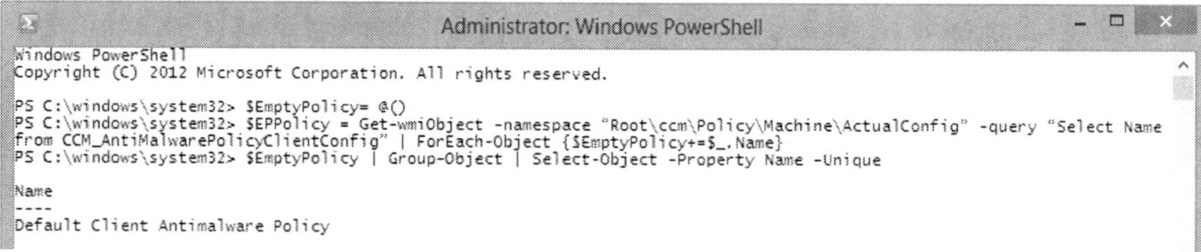

View all applied antimalware policies.

Edit the Default Antimalware Policy

An antimalware policy is used to control how clients are protected against different types of malware. Malware means "malicious software," which is software or a piece of code designed to steal sensitive data or otherwise gain access to your computer. When creating an antimalware policy, you can control things like when to run a scan, excluding files and processes from the scan, enabling real-time protection, and much more. A ConfigMgr SP1 client can read and apply settings from multiple antimalware policies unlike ConfigMgr RTM clients that could only apply a single policy. In ViaMonstra, you define all the global settings in the existing Default Antimalware policy and create custom policies for exceptions like unique exclusion rules for SQL server. In ViaMonstra, the default malware policy must include these settings:

- A daily quick scan
- A weekly full scan, workstations scan every Friday morning at 9:00 and servers based on the server role
- Scan email
- Scan USB devices
- Enable real-time protection
- Configure **updates distributed from Microsoft update** as the second download source
- Exclude the folders being used by the ConfigMgr client agent

Complete these steps:

1. On **CM01**, log on as **VIAMONSTRA\Administrator** and open the **ConfigMgr console**.
2. Navigate to the **Assets and Compliance** workspace, expand **Endpoint Protection**, and then select **Antimalware Policies**.
3. Select the **Default Client Malware Policy**, and on the ribbon, click **Properties**.

4. Click **Scheduled scans** and configure these settings:
    a. Run a schedule scan on client computers: **Yes**
    b. Scan type: **Full Scan**
    c. Scan day: **Friday**
    d. Scan time: **9 AM**
    e. Run a daily quick scan on client computers: **Yes**
    f. Daily quick scan schedule time: 12 PM
    g. Check for the latest definition updates before running a scan: **Yes**
    h. Limit CPU usage during scans to (%): **30**

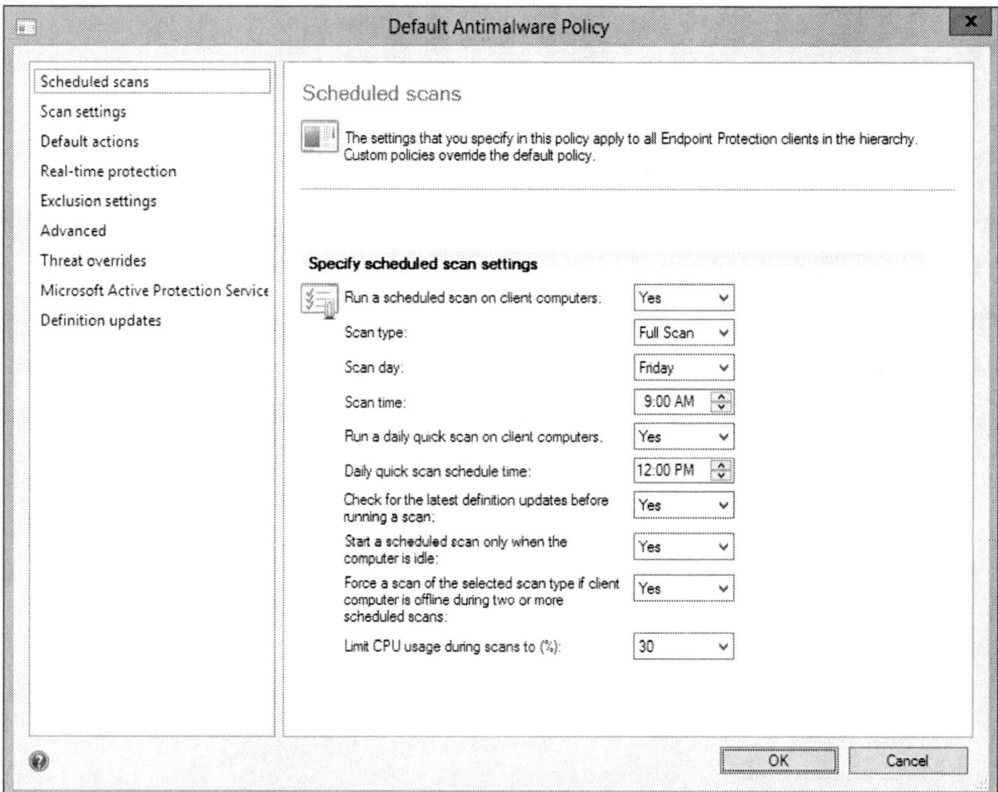

Modifying the default antimalware scheduled scan settings.

5. Click **Scan settings** and configure these settings:
   a. Scan email and email attachments: **Yes**
   b. Scan removable storage devices such as USB drives: **Yes**

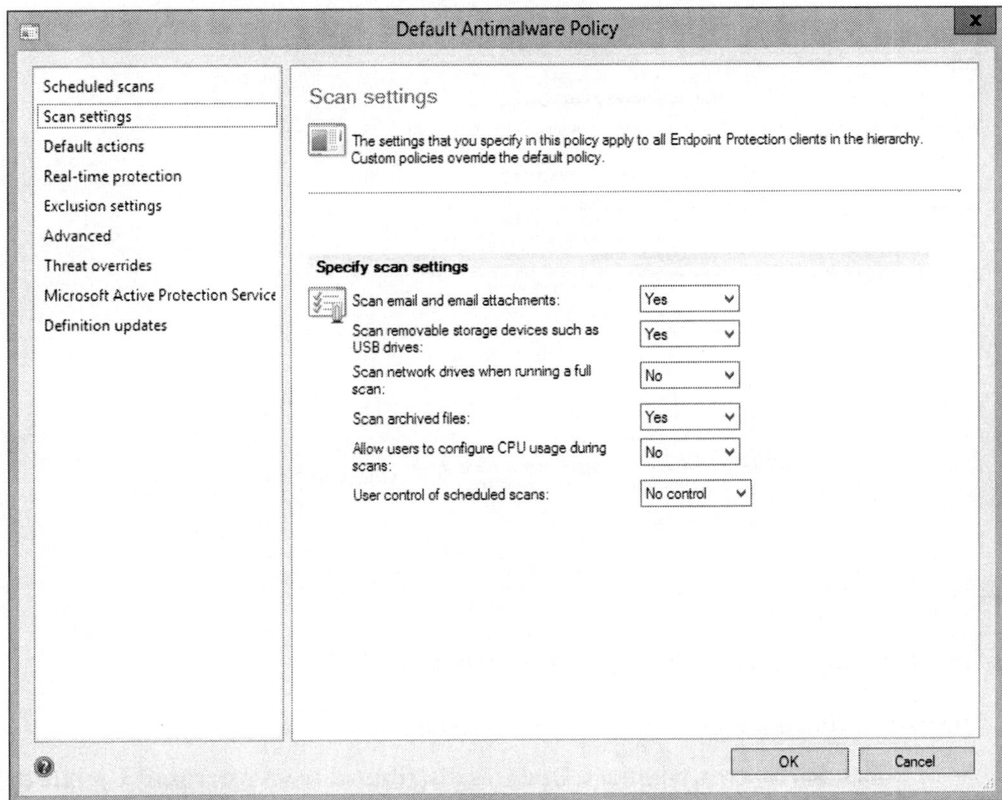

Configuring the default antimalware scan settings.

6. Click **Advanced** and configure this setting:

   Show notifications messages to users on client computer: **Yes**

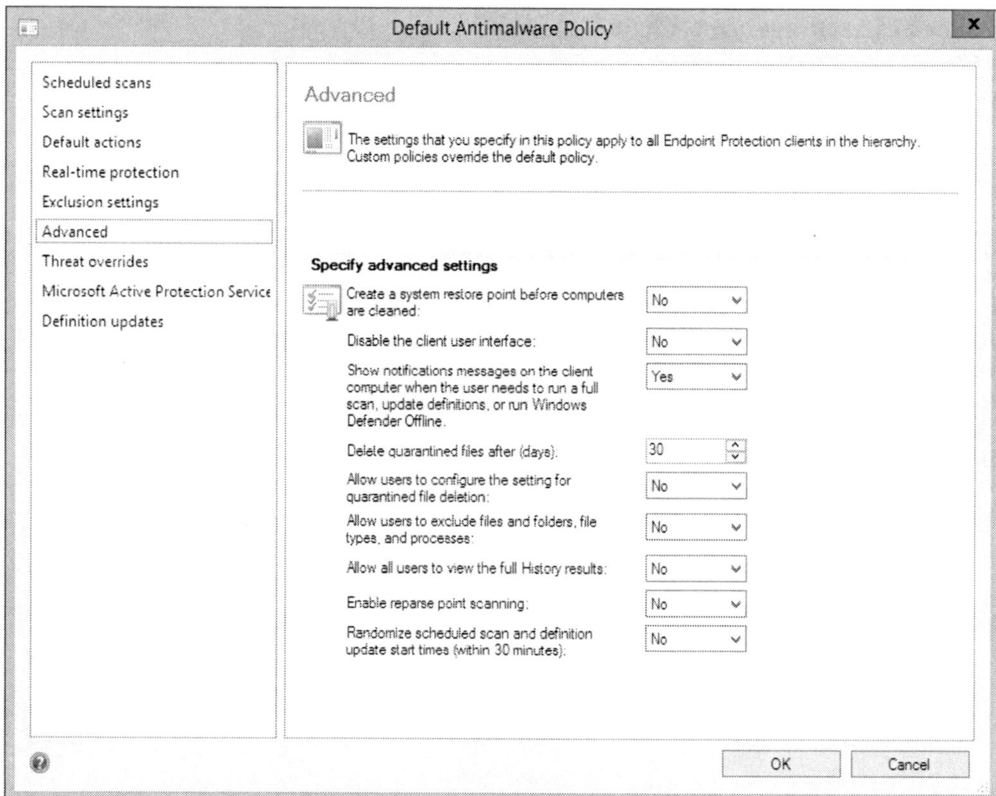

Configuring the default antimalware advanced settings.

7. Click **Definition updates** and configure this setting:

   Click **Set Source**, configure **Updates distributed from Microsoft Update** to be second in the list, and then click **OK**.

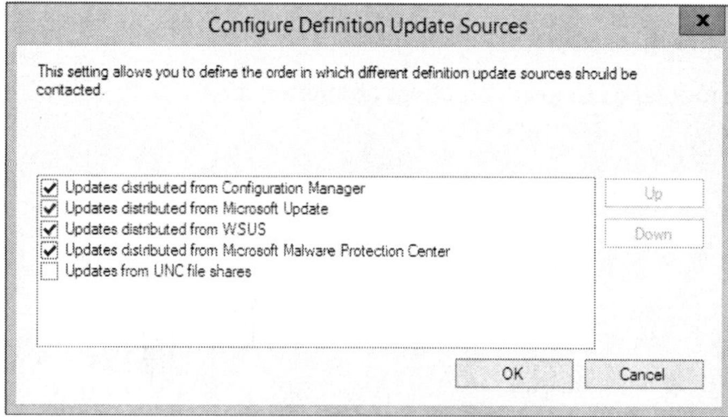

Configuring the definition update sources.

8. Click **OK**.

Create an Antimalware Policy for ConfigMgr 2012 Servers

1. Open **D:\Program Files\Microsoft Configuration Manager\AdminConsole\XmlStorage\EPTemplates** and copy **SCEP12_Default_CfgMgr2012.xml** to the desktop.
2. Rename the file **SCEP12_ViaMonstra_CfgMgr2012.xml**.
3. Open the template using notepad, replace all instances of **%programfiles%\Microsoft Configuration Manager** with **D:\Program Files\Microsoft Configuration Manager**.
4. Save the file and copy it to **D:\Program Files\Microsoft Configuration Manager\AdminConsole\XmlStorage\EPTemplates**.
5. Navigate to the **Assets and Compliance** workspace and select **Endpoint Protection**.
6. Select **Antimalware Policies**, and on the ribbon, click **Import**.
7. Scroll down the list of XML files, select **SCEP12_ViaMonstra_CfgMgr2012.xml** and click **Open**.
8. Select **Real-time protection** and configure this setting:

   Enable real-time protection: **No**

9. Select **Exclusion settings**, and next to **Excluded files and folders**, click **Set**, and scroll down to review the new exclusion settings.

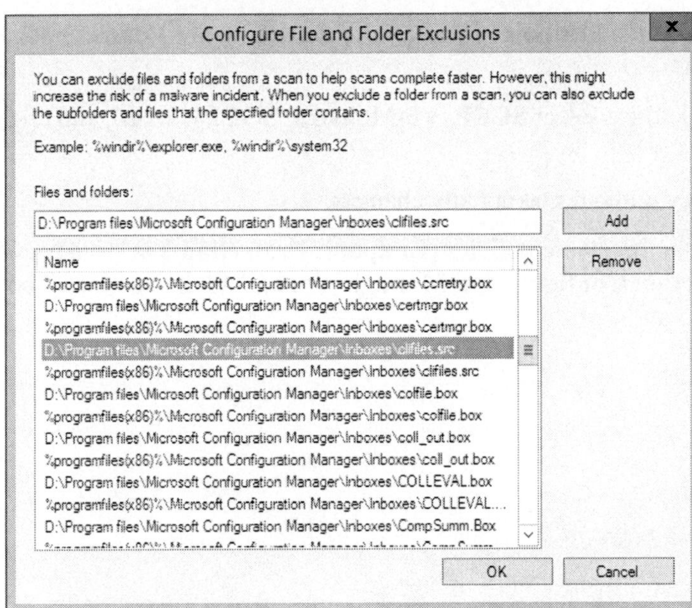

Custom-made exclusions.

10. Click **OK twice**.

11. Open **D:\Program Files\Microsoft Configuration Manager\AdminConsole\XmlStorage\EPTemplates** and copy **FEP_Default_SQL2008.xml** to the desktop.
12. Rename the file **SCEP_ViaMonstra_SQL2012.xml**.
13. Open the template using **Notepad** and replace these instances:
    a. **Name and Description** from **Endpoint Protection SQL 2008** to **Endpoint Protection ViaMonstra SQL 2012**
    b. **%ProgramFiles%\Microsoft SQL Server\MSSQL10.MSSQLSERVER \MSSQL\Binn\SQLServr.exe** with **D:\Program Files\Microsoft SQL Server \MSSQL11.MSSQLSERVER\MSSQL\Binn\SQLServr.exe**
    c. **%ProgramFiles%\Microsoft SQL Server\MSRS10.MSSQLSERVER \Reporting Services\ReportServer\Bin\ReportingServicesService.exe** with **D:\Program Files\Microsoft SQL Server\MSRS11.MSSQLSERVER \Reporting Services\ReportServer\Bin\ReportingServicesService.exe**
    d. **%ProgramFiles%\Microsoft SQL Server\MSAS10.MSSQLSERVER\OLAP \Bin\MSMDSrv.exe** with **D:\Program Files\Microsoft SQL Server \MSAS11.MSSQLSERVER\OLAP\Bin\MSMDSrv.exe**
14. Save the file and copy it to **D:\Program Files\Microsoft Configuration Manager\AdminConsole\XmlStorage\EPTemplates**.
15. In the **ConfigMgr console**, in the **Endpoint Protection / Antimalware Policies** node, click **Import** on the ribbon.
16. Scroll down the list of XML files, select **SCEP_ViaMonstra_SQL2012.xml**, and click **Open**.
17. Click **OK** to close the policy without making any changes.
18. Select both of the two new antimalware policies (**Endpoint Protection ViaMonstra SQL 2012** and **Endpoint Protection Configuration Manager 2012**), and then on the ribbon, click **Merge**.

19. Type **Configuration Manager 2012** as the **New Policy Name**, and configure the **Endpoint Protection Configuration Manager 2012** as the **Base Policy**.

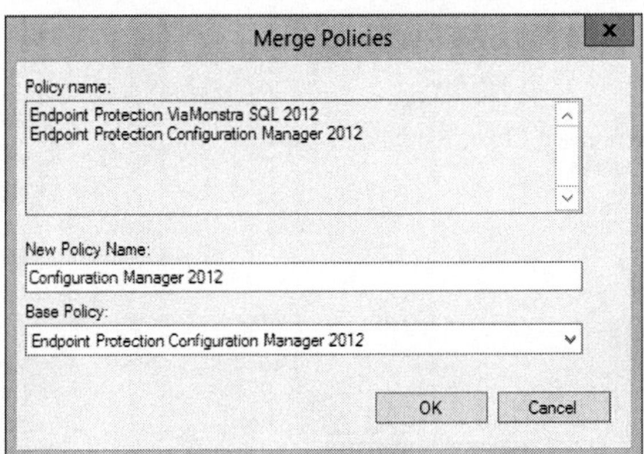

Merging antimalware policies.

20. Click **OK**.

> **Note:** Antimalware policies can be applied in the same manner as Device and User Client settings. You can create all the company-specific settings in the default policy and add exceptions to those rules in custom policies.

Deploy Endpoint Protection

When the pilot phase is over, it's time to deploy the Endpoint Protection client to all other computers in the environment:

1. On **CM01**, log on as **VIAMONSTRA\Administrator** and open the **ConfigMgr console**.
2. Navigate to the **Administration** workspace.
3. Click **Client Settings,** select the **Endpoint Protection**, and on the ribbon, click **Deploy**.
4. Select **Endpoint Protection / EP All Clients** and click **OK**.

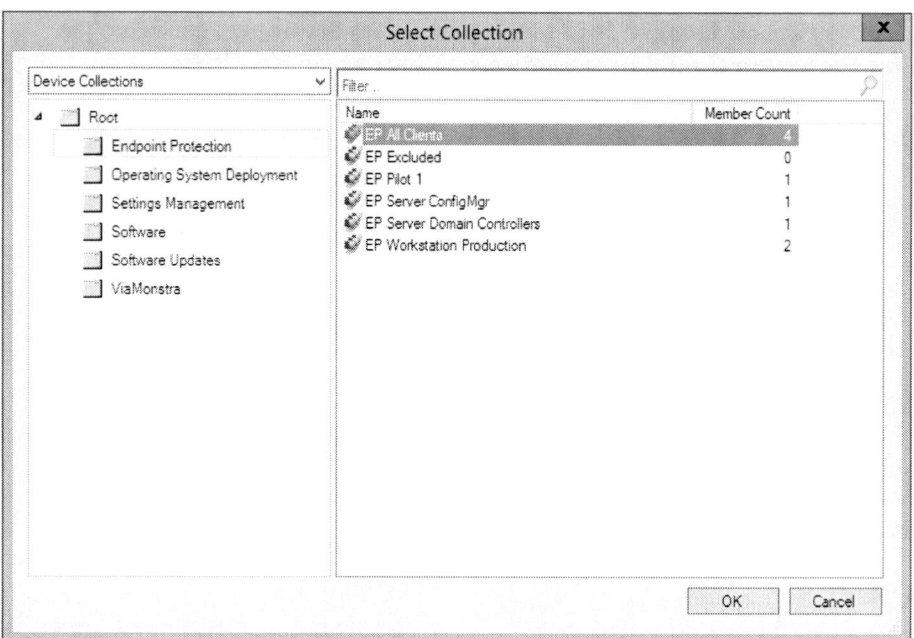

Deploying Endpoint Protection to all EP clients.

Deploy the ConfigMgr 2012 Antimalware Policy

1. Navigate to the **Assets and Compliance** workspace.
2. Navigate to **Endpoint Protection / Antimalware Policies**.
3. Select the **Configuration Manager 2012** policy, and on the ribbon, click **Deploy**.
4. Select the **Endpoint Protection / EP Server ConfigMgr** collection and click **OK**.

Real World Note: One issue you will run into is dealing with false positives. False positives are situations in which a program is flagged as malicious but is not. Classic examples are remote tools like Dameware. You configure which programs should be treated as false positives and not flagged in the Threat Override section of an antimalware policy.

Configuring Alerts and Monitor Malware Activity

Endpoint Protection is at present the only feature in ConfigMgr where you can configure email alert settings. As part of the planning process, you must plan for when you receive alerts and how you will react to those.

Configure Collection Alerts

Alerts are used to control when email notifications are being sent and whether collections are visible on the Endpoint Protection dashboard. It's not uncommon to have different alert settings for different workstations and servers.

1. In the **Assets and Compliance** workspace, select **Device Collections** and the **ViaMonstra** folder.
2. Right-click the **VM All Workstations** collection and select **Properties**.
3. Select the **Alerts** tab, and enable **View this collection** on the **Endpoint Protection** dashboard.
4. Click **Add** and enable all the Endpoint Protection rules. Click **OK** to close the dialog box.
5. Select the different conditions and notice the definitions.

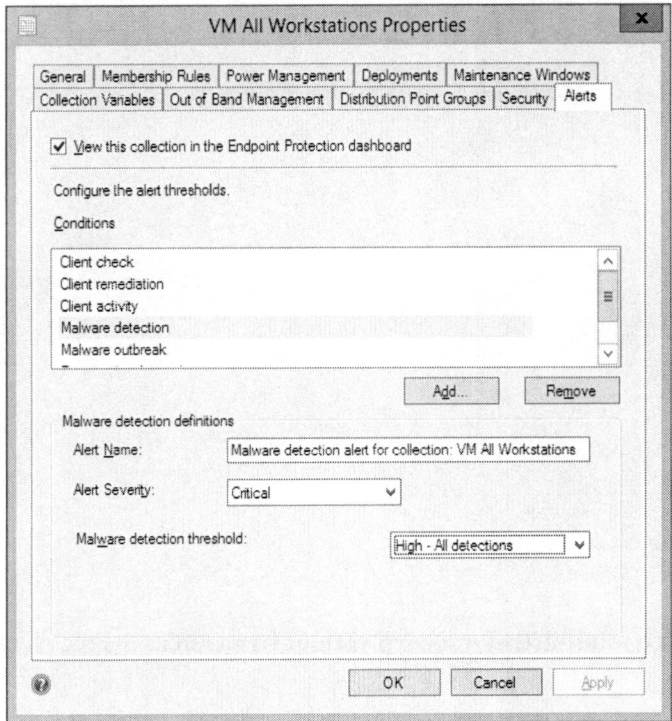

Configuring Endpoint Protection alerts.

6. Click **OK** and close the collection properties.
7. Repeat the steps for the **VM All Servers** collection found in the **ViaMonstra** folder.

Configure Email Settings

To verify that email works, you need to have an SMTP Server available. In this sample, I use the EX01.corp.viamonstra.com mail server.

1. Navigate to the **Administration** workspace, and select **Site Configuration / Sites**.
2. From the ribbon, select **Settings / Configure Site Components / Email Notification**.

3. Select **Enable email notification** and configure these settings:
    a. Enable email notification for Endpoint Protection alerts: **True**
    b. FQDN or IP Address of the SMTP server: **EX01.corp.viamonstra.com**
    c. SMTP Connection Account: **None (anonymous access)**.
    d. Sender address for email alerts: **administrator@corp.viamonstra.com**

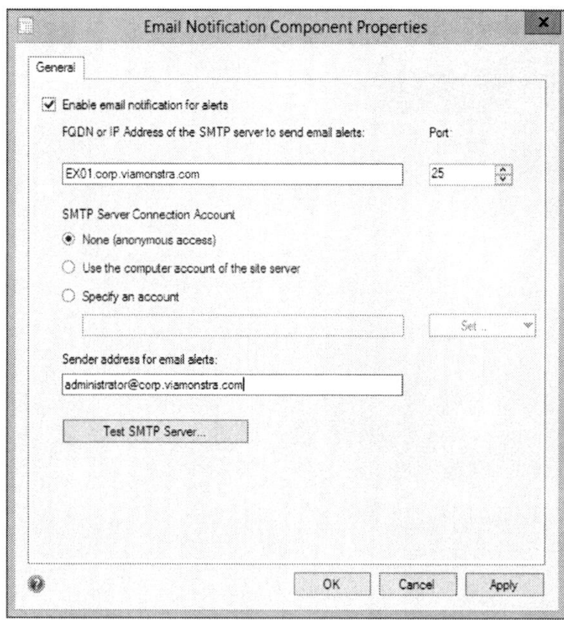

Configuring email notifications

4. Click **Test SMTP Server**, type **administrator@corp.viamonstra.com** as the recipient, and click **Send test email**.
5. Click **Close** and **OK**.

Real World Note: Configuring email notification requires knowledge about the SMTP server and the ports used by the mail server. There is no guarantee the specific settings in the book can be used in your environment.

Configure Email Subscriptions

1. In the **Monitoring** workspace, select **Alerts / Subscriptions**.
2. On the ribbon, click **Create Subscription**; then configure the following settings and click **OK**:
    a. Name: **Server Malware alerts**
    b. Email address: **Serverteam@viamonstra.com**
    c. Email language: **English**
    d. Click in Filter and type **VM All Servers.**
    e. Alert: Enable **All the malware alerts**.

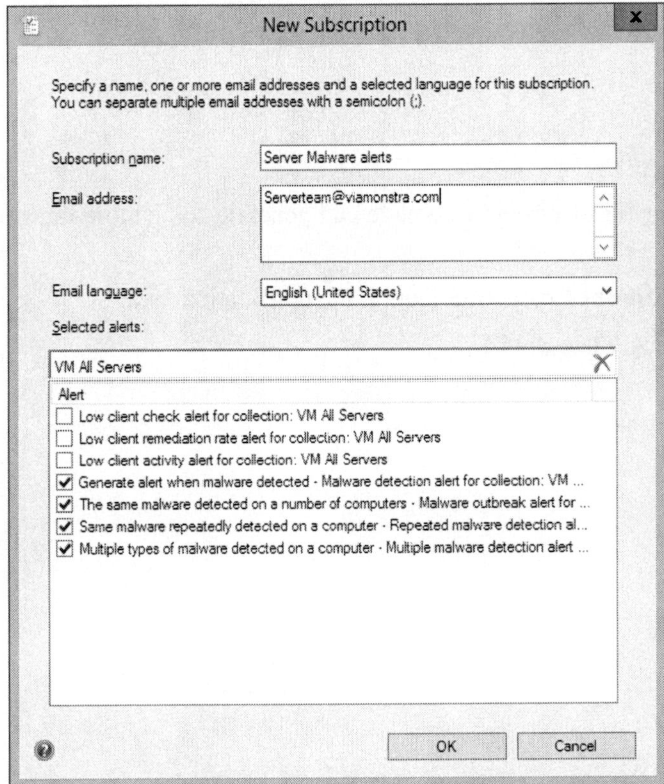

Creating new a malware email subscription.

3. Click **OK**.
4. Repeat the steps and create alerts for the **VM All Workstations** collection. All malware mails must be mailed to **desktopteam@viamonstra.com**.

Monitor Malware Activity

Monitoring malware activity is a daily task that you can perform either from within the ConfigMgr console using the Endpoint Protection dashboard or by reading one the Endpoint Protection reports. To create activity, you can download a safe malware from http://www.eicar.org/85-0-Download.html. The malware is completely harmless and can be used to test the antimalware client.

1. On **PC0001**, log on as **VIAMONSTRA\Administrator** and open **Internet Explorer**.
2. Type **http://www.eicar.org/85-0-Download.html** and download the **eicar_com.zip** file to the desktop. You should receive an Endpoint Protection alert the very second you choose to download the file.

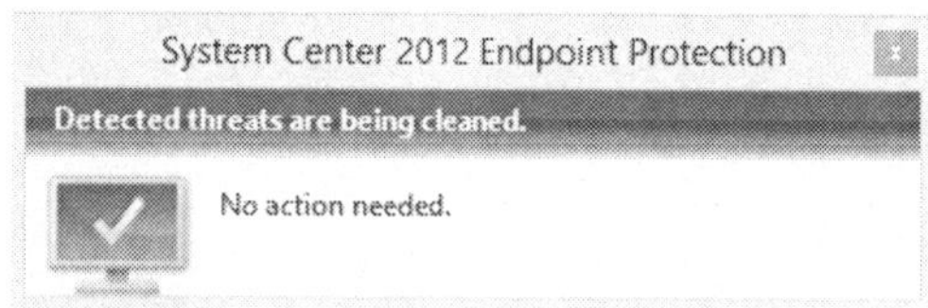

Generating malware activity.

3. It's safe to download the other files from the web page and generate some more malware activity.
4. Open the **System Center Endpoint Protection** icon in the notification area.
5. Select the **History** tab and click **View details**.

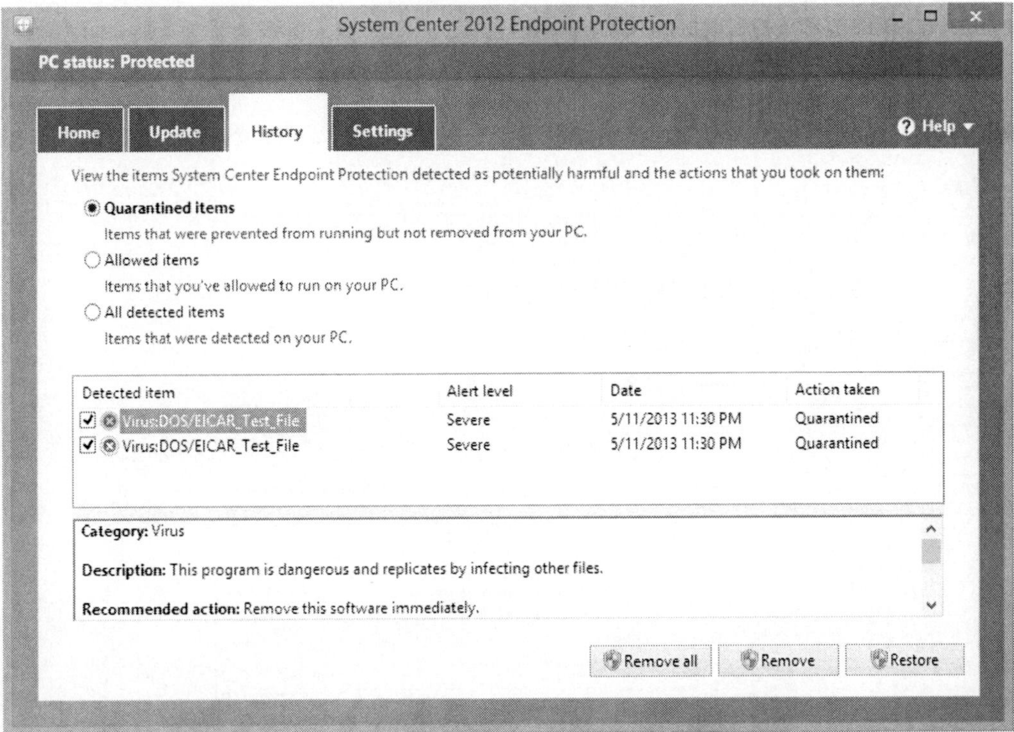

Viewing malware activity on the client.

6. From the detailed view, you can remove or restore any of the quarantined items. By selecting **Allowed items**, you can view the specific files that you have configured as false positives, which allows them to run on your computer even if Endpoint Protection mistakenly considers them to be malware.

View Malware in the ConfigMgr Console

1. In the **Monitoring** workspace, select **System Center 2012 Endpoint Protection**.

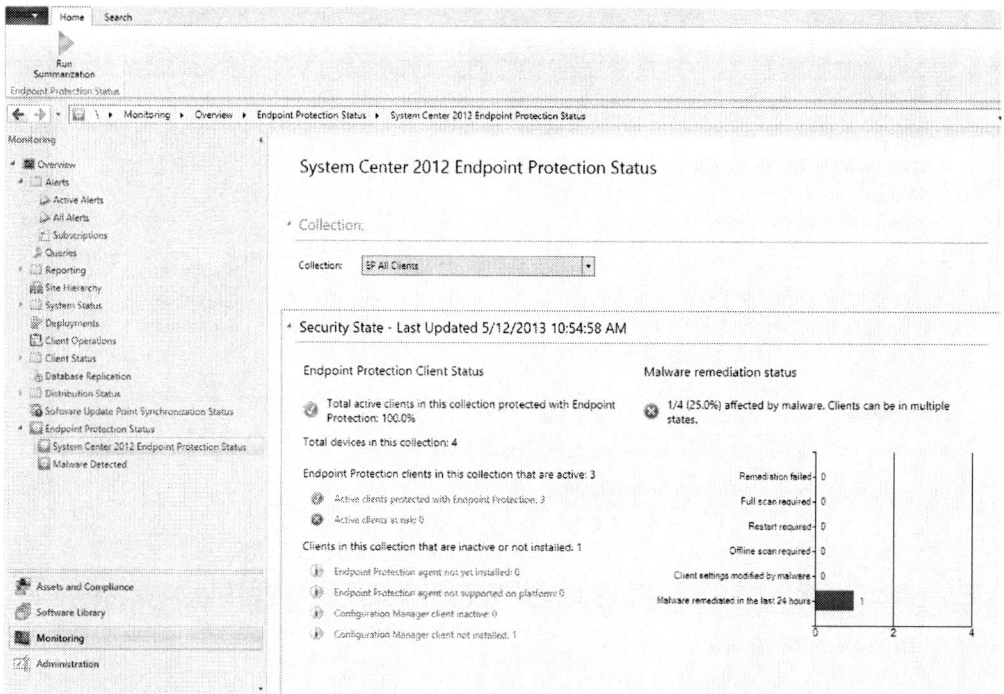

The Endpoint Protection dashboard.

2. Notice the Malware remediation status in the right column. Click the **Malware remediated in the last 24 hours** chart.
3. The click creates a query-based node containing all devices for which malware has been remediated within the last 24 hours.
4. Select the **Malware Detail** tab and notice the information about the malware.

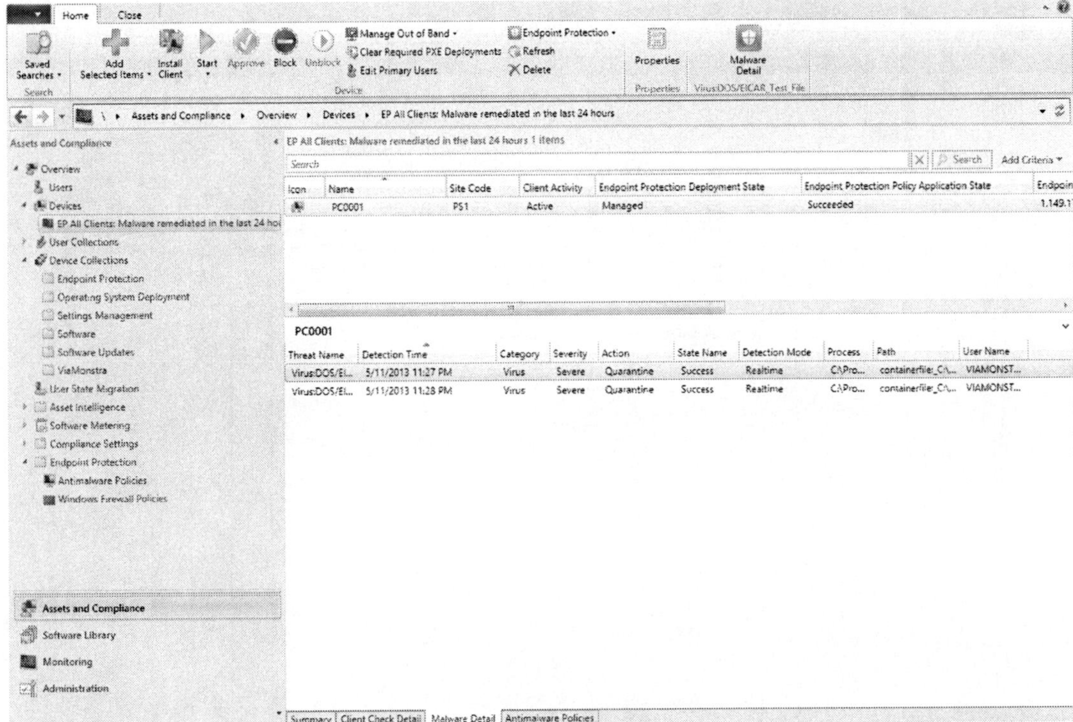

Viewing malware information in the ConfigMgr console.

5. Provided that you have configured the alerts, malware outbreaks and detections also will create critical alerts. Select the **Monitoring** workspace and navigate to **Alerts**.

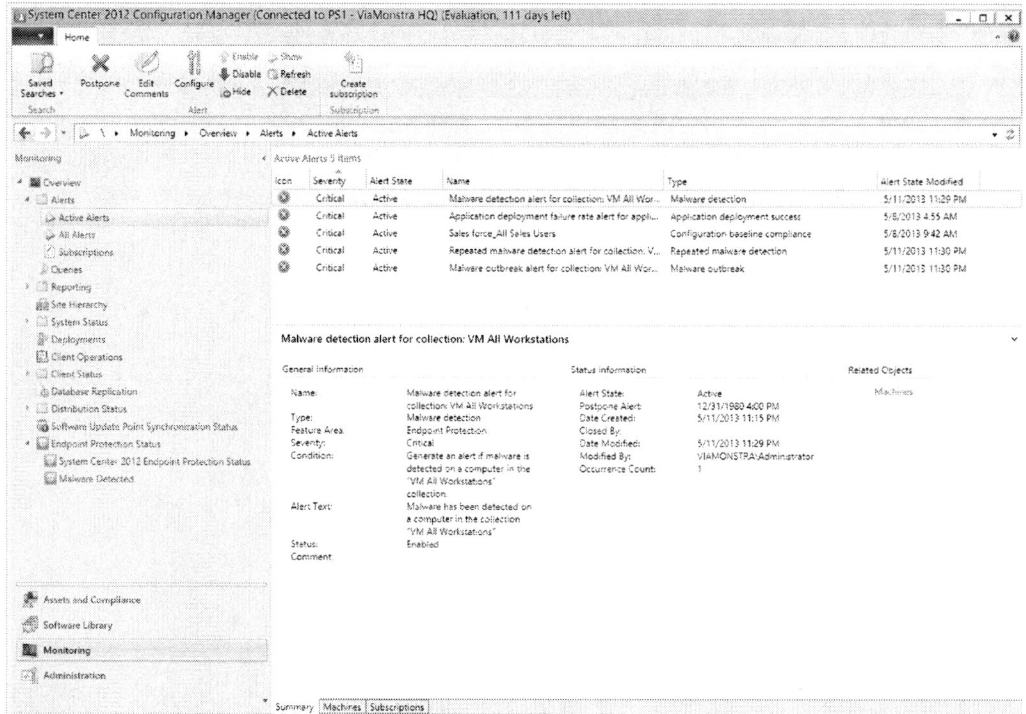

Malware detection alert.

If you configured email support, then alerts also trigger an email message.

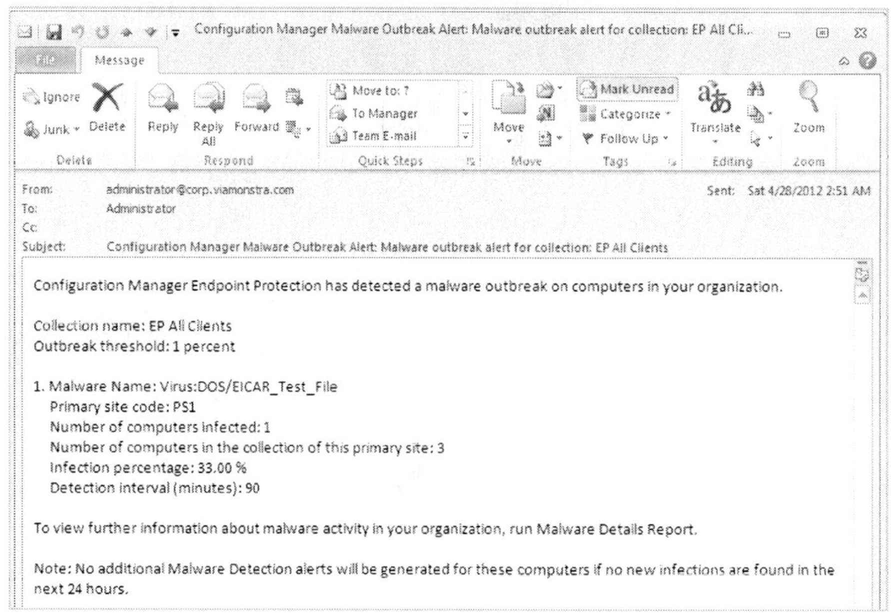

SCEP email notification.

> **Note:** You can use the use the Client Notification feature to initiate Endpoint Protection actions from the ConfigMgr console. Select a collection and click Endpoint Protection on the ribbon. From here you can force a full or quick scan, or initiate a definition download.

View Malware Information Using Reports

1. On CM01, open **Internet Explorer** and open **http://cm01/reports**.
2. Select the **ConfigMgr_PS1** folder and the **Endpoint Protection** subfolder.
3. Select the **Antimalware overall status and history** report; then from the collection list, select **EP All Clients** and click **View Report**. The dashboard report is like a cockpit providing you with the high-level overview. If you want to dig a bit deeper, all you need to do is click one of the chart objects. That action will launch one of the hidden Endpoint Protection reports with detailed information.

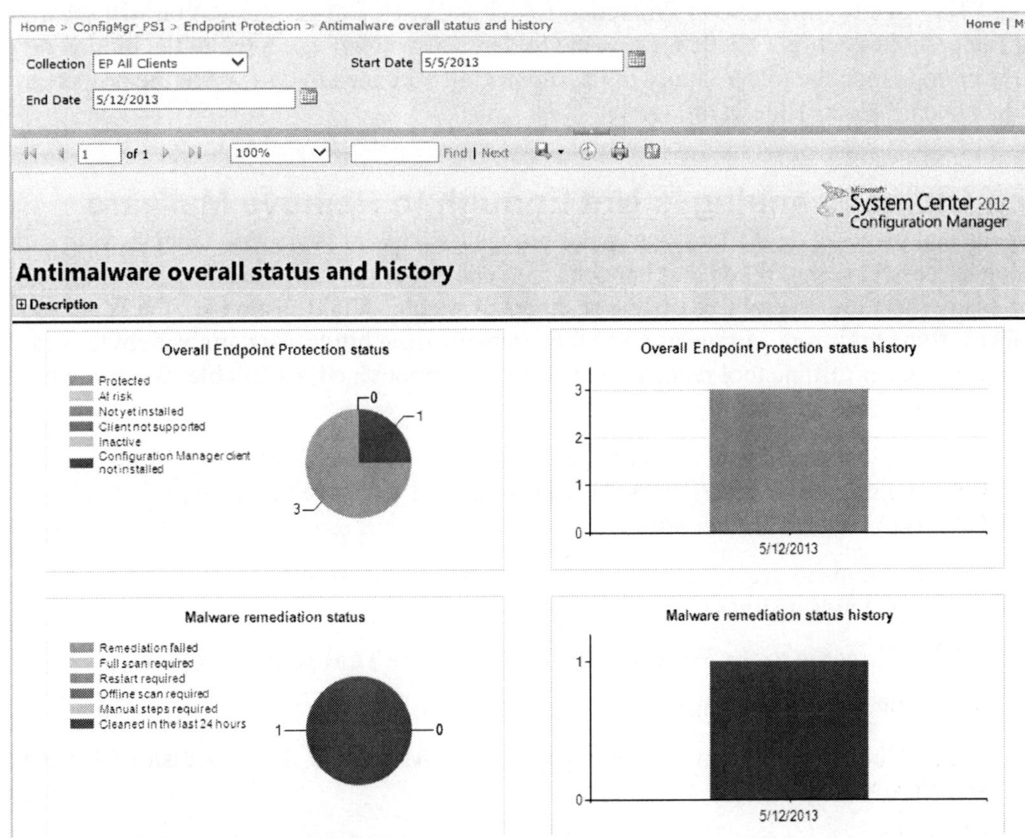

The Endpoint Protection dashboard.

4. Click the **Malware remediation status** chart.

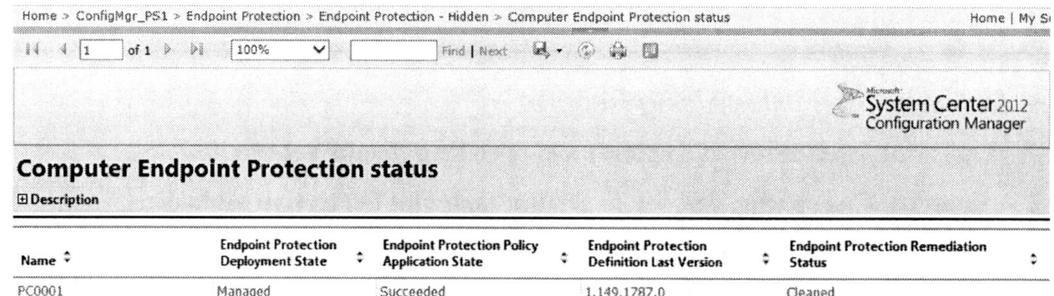

Malware remediation report.

Note: To view the hidden Endpoint Protection reports, open the report manager in Internet Explorer. Navigate to the Endpoint Protection folder and click Details View. You will see a folder called Endpoint Protection - Hidden. Click the folder, and you will see a list of the hidden reports. If you want to unhide the folder or any of the reports, all you need to do is open the properties for the object and deselect "Hide in tile view."

When Online Scanning Is Not Enough to Remove Malware

It happens that malware on the local computer prevents Endpoint Protection from starting and finishing successful scans. When that happens, you can either reinstall the computer or run an offline scan. There are several free offline scanners available. ViaMonstra uses the Windows Defender Offline tool from Microsoft and Malwarebytes from http://www.malwarebytes.org/. The Microsoft Defender Offline tool requires that you have remote media available like an USB stick or CD/DVD, or create an .ISO file.

1. On your Host machine, download the **Windows Defender Offline** tool from **http://go.microsoft.com/fwlink/?LinkID=232461** and save the file to **C:\Setup\Tools\offlinescanner**.
2. Open a command prompt as **administrator** and run **mssstool64.exe** from **C:\Setup\Tools\offlinescanner**.
3. On the **Welcome to the Windows Defender Offline Tool** page, click **Next**.
4. Accept the license agreement.
5. On the **Choose your startup media** page, select **As an ISO file on a disk (Advanced)** and click **Next**.
6. On the **Choose a location for the ISO file** page, select **C:\Setup\Tools\offlinescanner** and click **Next**.

7. On the **ISO file creation complete** page, click **Finish**.

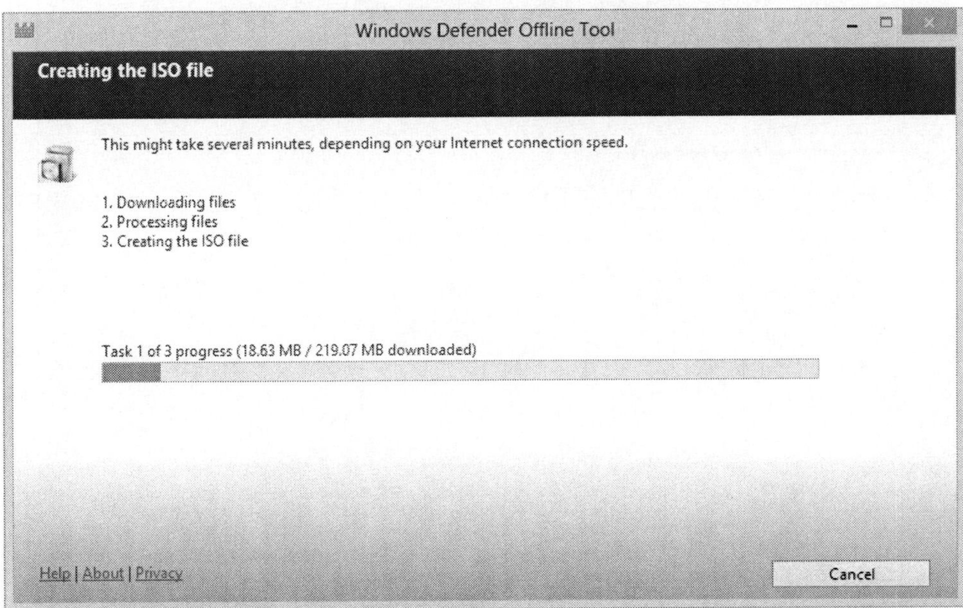

The offline ISO file being created.

8. Mount the **ISO file** on **PC0001** and restart **PC0001**.
9. When prompted, press any key to boot from the ISO file.
10. Windows Defender will automatically start the offline scan. When the scan is finished, restart the computer.

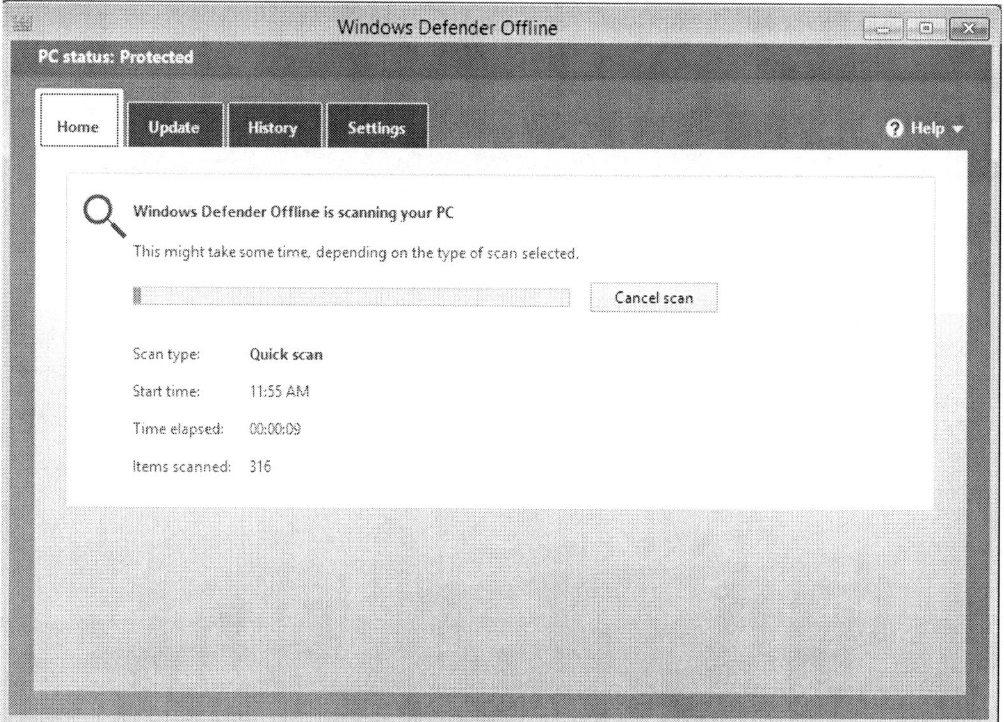

Windows Defender Offline scan.

Note: The %programfiles%\Microsoft Security Client\MpCdmRun.exe utility on the client can be used to perform a variety of client actions, such as gathering log information about the activity, updating signature files, and much more. Run MpCmdRun.exe –h for a list of commands.

Useful Log Files

You can use the log files in the following table to track activity related to your software updates.

Log File	**Description**	**Location**
EPCtrlMgr.log	Records details about the synchronization of malware threat information from the Endpoint Protection role server into the Configuration Manager database.	Site system server hosting the role

Log File	Description	Location
EPMgr.log	Monitors the status of the Endpoint Protection site system role.	Site system server hosting the role
EPSetup.log	Provides information about the installation of the Endpoint Protection site system role.	Site system server hosting the role
EndpointProtectionAgent.log	Records details about the installation of the Endpoint Protection client and the application of antimalware policy to that client.	Client default
MPLog-XX.log	Records Endpoint Protection activity on the client side.	C:\ProgramData\Microsoft\Microsoft Antimalware\Support
MPDetection-XX.log	Records details about each case of malware detected on the system.	C:\ProgramData\Microsoft\Microsoft Antimalware\Support
NisLog.txt	Records details about the Network Inspection System.	C:\ProgramData\Microsoft\Microsoft Antimalware\Network Inspection System\Support

Chapter 10

Operating System Deployment

Operating system (OS) deployment is one of the most commonly used features in ConfigMgr. If you are familiar with ConfigMgr 2007, you will quickly discover that the OS deployment features haven't changed that much. One of the nice new features, however, is the ability to service your operating system images offline from within the ConfigMgr console.

After reading this chapter, you will be able to configure support for OS deployment, deploy your images, and manage your drivers in your environment.

Planning for Operating System Deployment

Before you deploy any operating system, you need to plan what kind deployment scenarios you must support and whether you have the needed infrastructure to support those demands. The infrastructure planning mostly includes creating user accounts, configuring site system roles, and integrating with Microsoft Deployment Toolkit (MDT).

Configuring the Required Infrastructure

Configure the Network Access Account

Before you are able to use the OS deployment features, you need to verify that the Network Access Account (CM_NAA) is working. The Network Access Account is used to establish a connection from WinPE to a distribution point and download the image.

1. In the **Administration** workspace, navigate to **Site Configurations\Security**.
2. Select **Accounts and open the properties for VIAMONSTRA\CM_NAA**.
3. Click **Set** and click **Verify**.
4. In **Password** and **Confirm Password**, type **Password01**.
5. For the **Network share**, type **\\CM01\SMS_PS1** and click **Test connection**.

6. Click **OK** three times.

Verifying the Network Access Account.

Install and Configure WDS

Windows Deployment Services, or WDS, is only one of the different methods that you can use to start the image installation process. Many prefer WDS because an installation can be initiated by simply pressing F12 on keyboard. You can install and configure WDS manually prior to configuring the PXE feature on the distribution point role. If WDS is not installed, ConfigMgr automatically installs it when you enable the PXE role on a distribution point. For ViaMonstra, I like to have control and for that reason have installed WDS, as described in Appendix A.

Configure a PXE-Enabled Distribution Point

1. On CM01, in the **Administration** workspace, select **Distribution Points**.
2. Select **CM01.CORP.VIAMONSTRA.COM**, and on the ribbon, click **Properties**.
3. Select the **PXE** tab.
4. Select the **Enable PXE support for clients** check box, and click **Yes** in dialog box.

5. Configure the following settings:
    a. Allow this distribution point to respond to incoming PXE requests: **Enabled**
    b. Enable unknown computer support: **Enabled**, and click **OK** after reading the warning message about enabling unknown computer support.
    c. Require a password when computers use PXE: **Enabled**, and supply a secret password.
    d. User device affinity: **Allow user device affinity with automatic approval**.

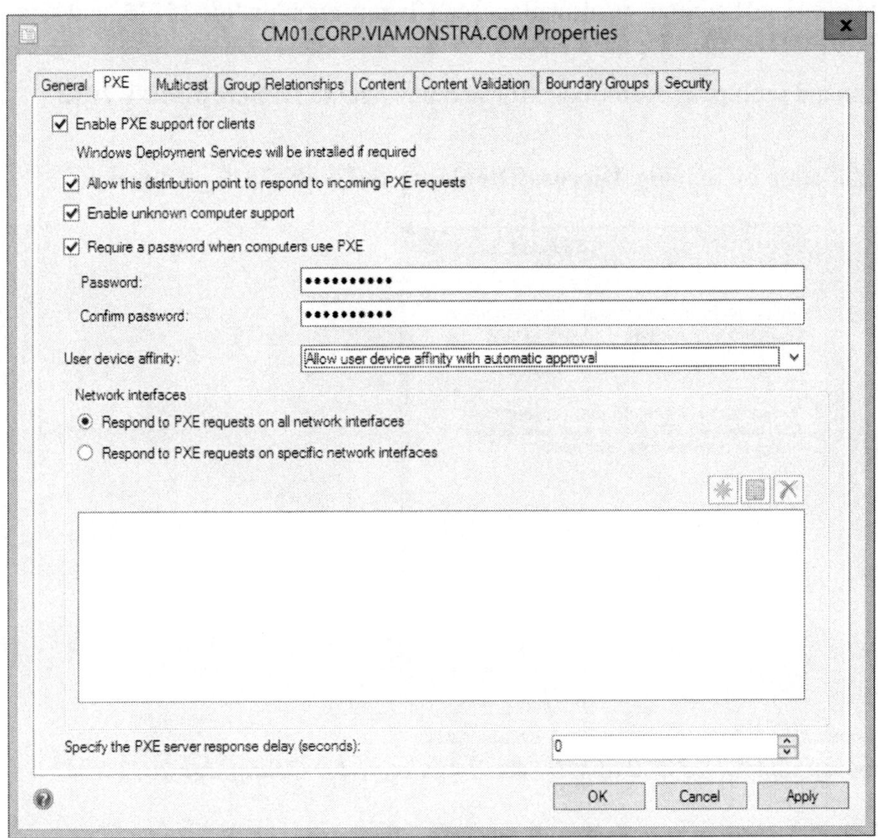

Enabling and configuring PXE support.

6. Click **OK**.

Note: You can monitor the WDS installation command by reading the distmgr.log file on the site server. The log file will tell you the exact command line used, which is very helpful when you are documenting your environment.

Install and Configure MDT 2012 Update 1

Your next step in configuring an OS deployment is to install Microsoft Deployment Toolkit (MDT) 2012 Update 1. MDT is not a requirement for OS deployment in ConfigMgr, but is used frequently to ease the process of building task sequences and because of the massive number of cool scripts that ships with the product. It allows you to create a smooth Zero Touch deployment experience.

1. On **CM01**, log on as **VIAMONSTRA\Administrator**.
2. Download the latest version of **Microsoft Deployment Toolkit 2012 update 1** from **http://www.microsoft.com/en-us/download/confirmation.aspx?id=25175**, and save the file in **D:\Setup\MDT 2012 Update 1**.
3. Open a command prompt as **Administrator** and navigate to **D:\Setup\MDT 2012 Update 1**.
4. Start the installation by running **MicrosoftDeploymentToolkit2012_x64.msi**.

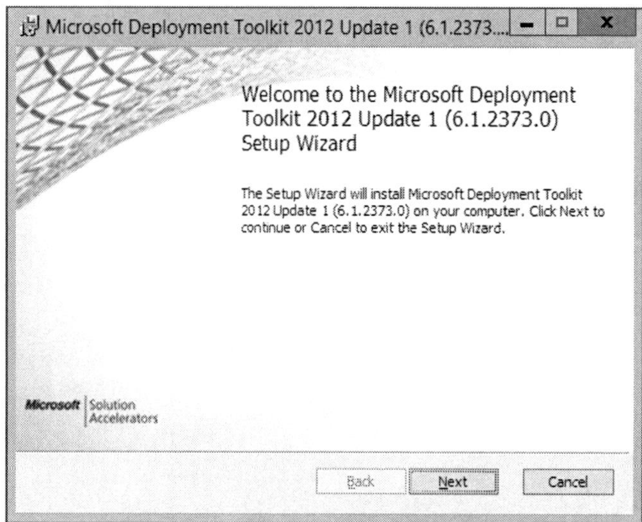

You need to have version 6.1.2373.0 of MDT 2012 Update 1 for ConfigMgr 2012 SP1.

5. Go through the installation and accept all the default settings.
6. From the **Start screen**, launch **Deployment Workbench**.
7. Using the **Deployment Workbench**, right-click **Deployment Shares** and select **New Deployment Share**.
8. On the **Path** page, configure the **Deployment share path** to **D:\MDTProduction** and click **Next.**

9. On the **Share** page, configure the share name to **MDTProduction$** and click **Next**.
10. On the **Descriptive Name** page, type **MDT** and click **Next**.
11. On the **Options** page, keep the defaults and click **Next**.
12. On the **Summary** page, read the summary and click **Next**.
13. On the **Confirmation** page, click **Finish**.

Note: Notice the View Script button on the Confirmation page. You can use it to find the needed PowerShell script used to create the deployment share.

Create the Logs$ Share

With MDT, you are able to create extra logging of your deployment process. To store the log files, you need to create a share where MDT can store the log files.

1. Using **File Explorer**, create the **D:\Logs** folder and share it as **Logs$**.
2. Allow the **Everyone** group **Change** permissions (Sharing Permissions).

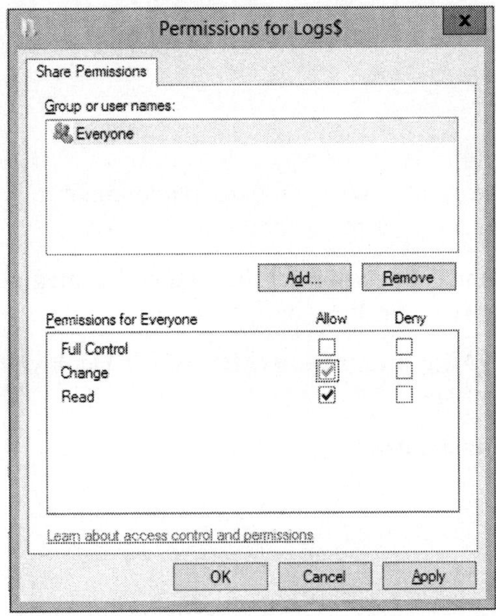

Everyone must have change share permissions.

3. Allow the **CM_NAA** user account **Modify** permissions (NTFS Permissions).

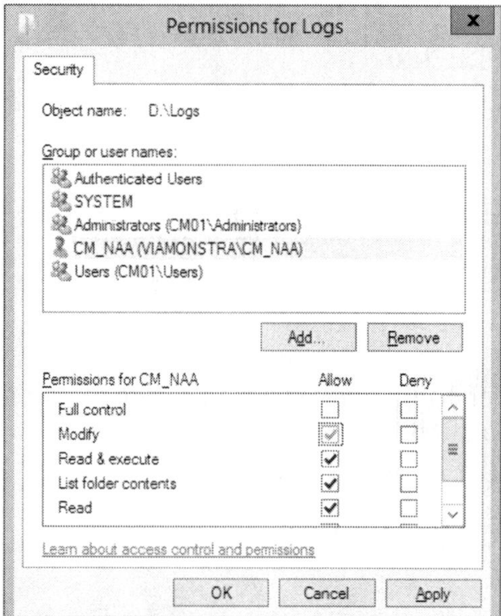

The Network Access Account must have modify permissions.

Configure ConfigMgr 2012 Integration

MDT integrates with the ConfigMgr Console. The integration gives you extra deployment options, like enhanced task sequences and boot images with scripting support.

1. Close the **ConfigMgr console** before continuing. The reason for this is that the integration adds console extensions that are applied when you start the ConfigMgr console.
2. From the **Start screen**, run **Configure ConfigMgr Integration** (Microsoft's Deploymnet Toolkit utility) and configure the following settings:
   a. Site Server Name: **CM01.corp.viamonstra.com**
   b. Site code: **PS1**

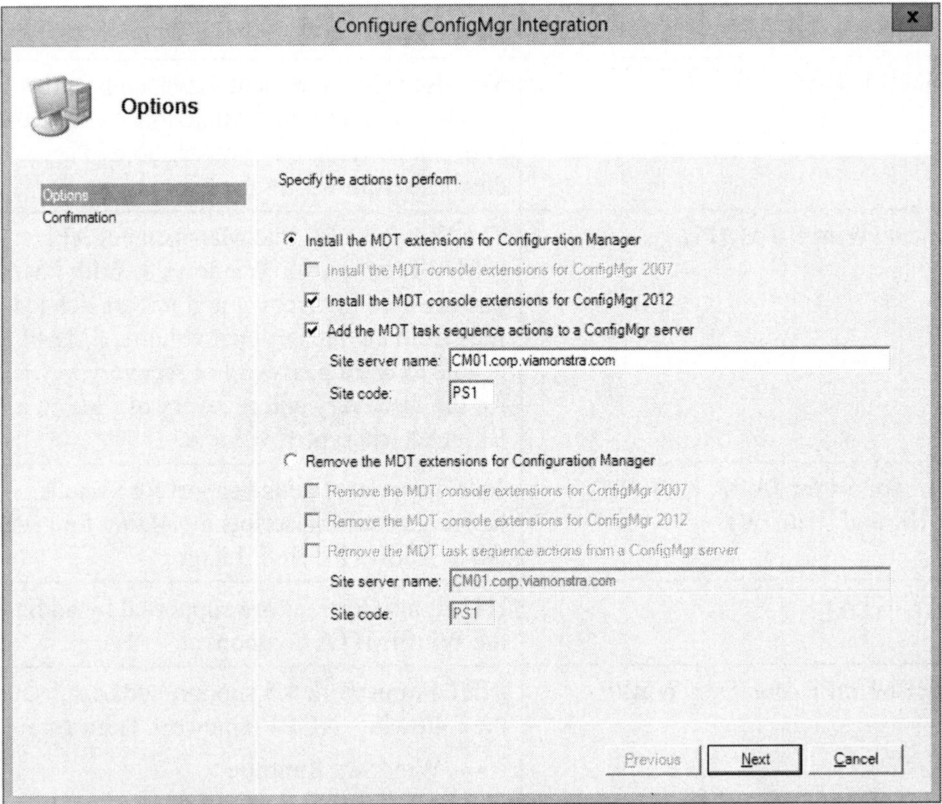

Integrating MDT 2012 with ConfigMgr 2012.

3. Click **Next**, and then click **Finish** to configure the integration.

Boot Images

Boot images are essential to the OS deployment process. The boot image is used to establish contact between the computer and the network. A boot image contains a version of Windows PE, the needed NIC and storage drivers, and any logic that you find needed to start the deployment process (scripts, tools, and so forth).

Before ConfigMgr 2012 SP1, I always created custom boot images due to the lack of component support found in the default boot images. With SP1, support for modifying boot images has been greatly improved. Within the ConfigMgr console, you can add the components in the following table.

Component	Description
Database (WinPE-MDAC)	You use this component toadd support for ODBC, OLE DB, and Microsoft ADO to the boot image. This way you are able to access a database from within the boot image.
File management (WinPE-FMAPI)	The Windows PE File Management API (FMAPI) is new for Windows 8. With FMAPI, you are able to discover and restore deleted files from an unencrypted volume. FMAPI also is able to use a password or recovery key file for the discovery and recovery of files on a Bitlocker-encrypted volume.
Fonts (WinPE support for JA-JP. KO-KR, ZH0CN, ZH-HK and ZH0TW)	This component adds support for various languages/writing scripts by adding font files to the Windows PE Boot Image.
HTML (WinPE-HTA)	HTML applications are supported by adding the WinPE-HTA component.
Microsoft .NET (WinPE-Dot3Svc, WinPE-NetFx4)	.NET Framework 4.5 support adds a subset of the following .NET Framework features: • Windows Runtime • .NET Framework Fusion APIs • Windows Control Library event logging • .NET Framework COM Interoperability • .NET Framework Cryptography Model
Network (WinPE-PPPoE and WinPE-RNDIS)	The WinPE-PPPoE component enables you to use PPPoE to create a VPN tunnel to your office. The WinPE-RNDIS component enables network support for devices that implement the Remote NDIS specification over USB.
Recovery (WinPE-WinReCfg)	The WinPE-WinReCfg component contains the Winrecfg.exe tool, which allows you to configure Windows RE settings on offline operating system images.
Setup (WinPE-LegacySetup, WinPE-Setup, WinPE-Setup-Client and WinPE-Setup-Server)	The Setup components add content of the \Sources folder of the Windows media to the boot image.

Component	Description
Storage (WinPE-EnhancedStorage)	New for Windows 8, this component adds enhanced storage functionality to enable support for encrypted drives and implementations that combine Trusted Computing Group and IEEE 1667.
Windows PowerShell (WinPE-DismCmdlets, WinPE-Powershell3 and WinPE-StorageWMI)	These components add native support for Windows PowerShell.

Customize the Default Images

You can enhance the boot images by following the next steps. In this example, you add Powershell 3.0 support to the boot image.

1. On **CM01**, using the **ConfigMgr console**, select **Operating Systems / Boot Images** in the **Software Library** workspace.
2. Select **Boot image (x64**, and on the ribbon, click **Properties**.
3. Select the **Optional Components** tab and click on the **yellow icon**.
4. Select **Windows Powershell (WinPE-PowerShell3)** and click **OK** in the message box that states that another required component will be added.

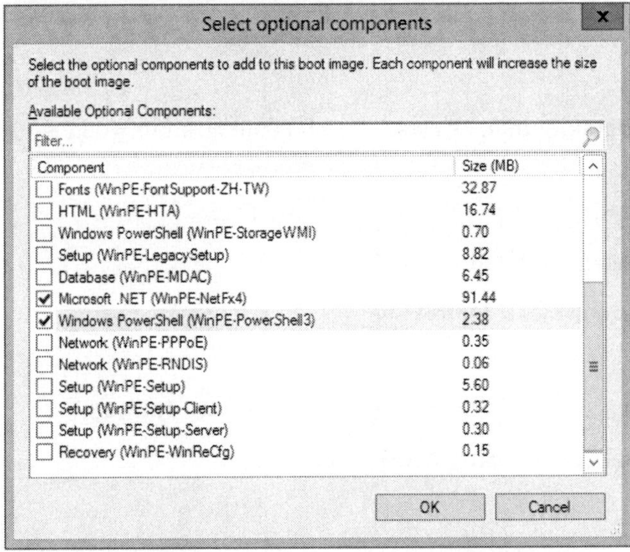

Adding optional components to the boot images.

5. Click **OK**.

6. In the **Customization** tab, change the scratch space to **512 MB** and enable **Enable command support (testing only)**.
7. In the **Data Source** tab, note that the **Deploy this boot image from the PXE-enabled distribution point** option is enabled by default (new in ConfigMgr 2012 SP1).
8. Click **OK** and click **Yes** in the message box that states that the boot images need to be updated.
9. In the **Update Distribution Point Wizard**, click **Next** and close the wizard when the boot image is finished.
10. Under the **Boot Images** node, select both default boot images, and on the ribbon, click **Distribute Content**.
11. On the **General** page, click **Next**.
12. On the **Content Destination** page, click **Add / Distribution Point Group**. Select the **All Content** group, and then click **OK** and **Next**.
13. On the **Summary** page, click **Next**.
14. On the **Completion** page, click **Close**.

Note: Enable command support only in a lab environment, or for testing. The Network Access Account name and password can be discovered during the WinPE phase and can be found in clear text.

Create Custom Boot Images

If you still want to create your own custom boot images using the MDT integration, you can do so by following the next steps:

1. Using **File Explorer**, create these folders:
    - **D:\Sources\OSD\Bootimages\MDTboot\x64**
    - **D:\Sources\OSD\Bootimages\MDTboot\x86**
2. Open the **ConfigMgr console**.
3. In the **Software Library** workspace, select **Operating Systems / Boot Images**.
4. On the ribbon, select **Create Boot Image using MDT**.

5. On the **Package Source** page, specify the package source folder: **\\CM01\Sources$\OSD\Bootimages\mdtboot\x64**. Click **Next**.

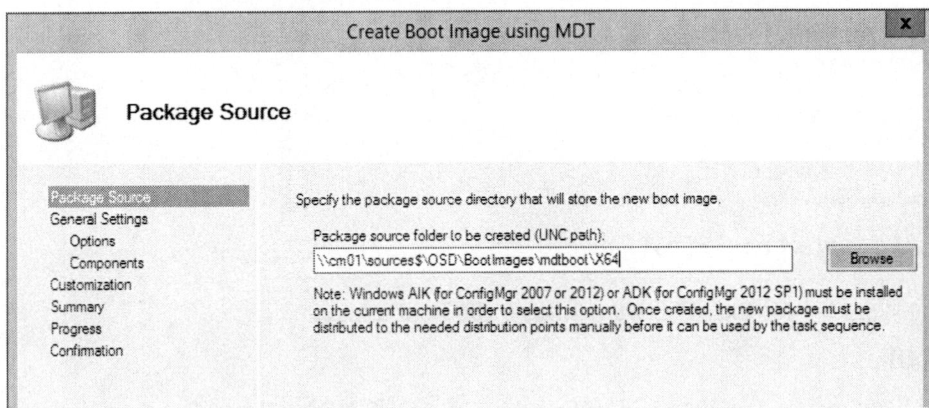

Specifying the package source for the x64 boot image.

6. On the **General Settings** page, configure these settings and click **Next**:
   a. Name: **MDTBoot Image x64**
   b. Version: **1.0**
   c. Comments: **Custom MDT Boot image**
7. On the **Options** page, configure these settings and click **Next**:
   a. Platform: **x64**
   b. Scratch space: **512MB**
8. On the **Components** page, leave the default settings and click **Next**.
9. On the **Customization** page, leave the default settings and click **Next**.
10. On the **Summary** page, read the summary and click **Next**.
11. Repeat steps 4–10 and create a custom **x86** boot image.

Distribute the MDT Boot Images

To be able to use the MDT boot image, you need to deploy it to the distribution points:

1. In the **Software Library** workspace, select **Operating Systems / Boot Images**.
2. Select the **MDTBoot Image x64**.
3. Open the **Properties**.

4. Select the **Data Source** tab, enable **Deploy this boot image from the PXE-enabled distribution point**, and click **OK**.

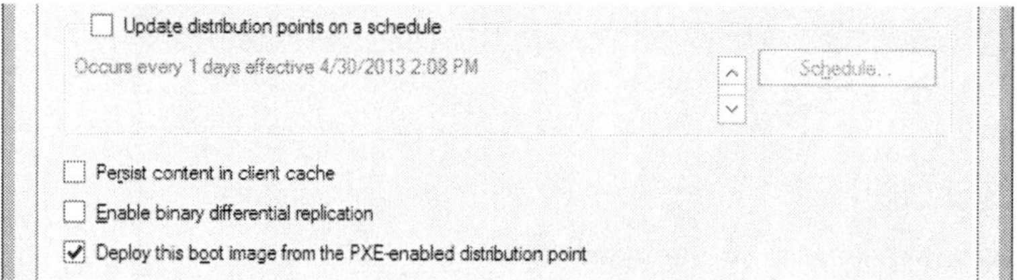

Enabling PXE support on the boot image.

5. Repeat steps 1-4 for the **MDTBoot Image x86** boot image.
6. Click **OK**.
7. Select both custom boot images, and on the ribbon, click **Distribute Content**.
8. On the **General** page, click **Next**.
9. On the **Content Destination** page, click **Add / Distribution Point Group**. Select the **All Content** group, and click **OK** and then **Next**.
10. On the **Summary** page, click **Next**.
11. On the **Completion** page, click **Close**.

Configure State Migration Point

When using OS deployment in your environment, you might want to preserve local data on your workstations and laptops. To be able to preserve the local data, you need to configure the state migration point. You can use the state migration point to store the user state data that are gathered during the OS deployment process by the User State Migration Toolkit. Data stored on the state migration point is encrypted, and to preserve disk space, you can configure how many days the data will stored on the server.

1. In the **Administration** workspace, select **Site Configuration / Servers and Site System Roles**.
2. Select the **\\CM01.corp.viamonstra.com** server, and on the ribbon's **Home** tab, click **Add Site System Roles**.
3. On the **General** page, click **Next**.
4. On the **Proxy** page, click **Next**
5. On the **System Role Selection** page, click **State migration point** and click **Next**.
6. On the **State Migration Point** page, click the **yellow icon**.

7. Configure these settings, and then click **OK**:
    a. Folder details and in Storage : **D:\StateMigration\Storage1**
    b. Maximum clients: **500**
    c. Maximum free space: **20 GB**

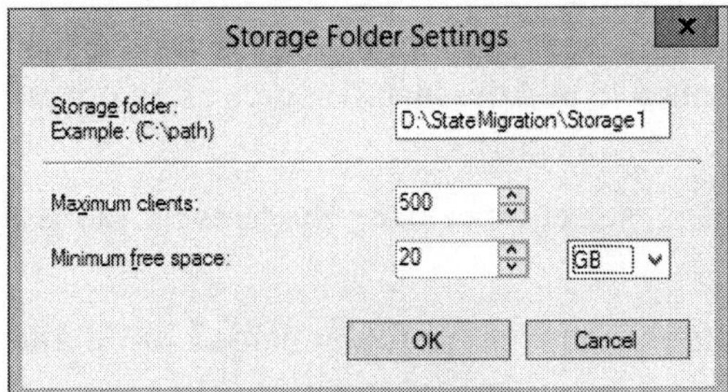

Configuring the storage folder.

8. In the **Deletion policy** section, configure **Delete after** to **7 days**. It is not wise to delete the data immediately, so choose a value that suites your needs. Before refreshing numerous workstations to Windows 8, monitor the disk space to ensure that the user data can be kept for the configured amount of time.

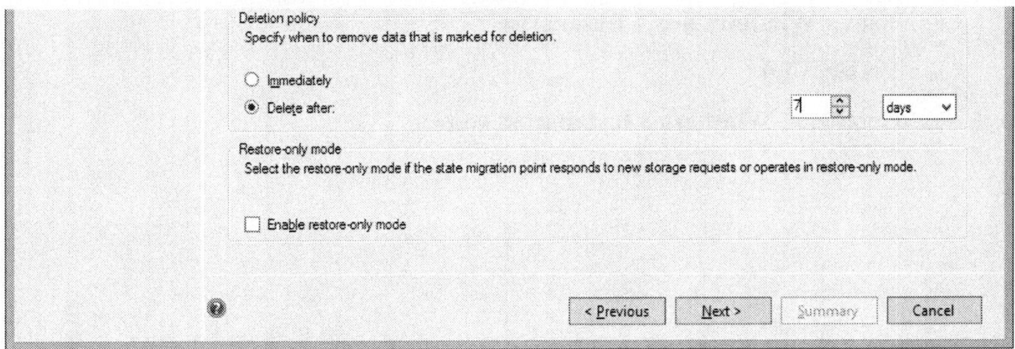

Configuring the storage folder and deletion policy.

9. On the **Configure the Boundary Groups** page, ensure that **CL HQ** is added and click **Next**.
10. On the **Summary** page, read the summary and click **Next**.
11. On the **Completion** page, click **Close**.

Real World Note: If you have a large environment, you can create as many storage folders as your disk size permits. When sizing your state migration point, look at the number of OS deployments that need to be done, how long the user state needs to be stored, and the average size of the user state.

Add an Operating System Install Source

Before you are able to create your custom Windows image, you need to add the source content of the operating system that you want to deploy. ViaMonstra wants to create and deploy a custom and fully patched Windows 8 image, so add the Windows 8 source to Configuration Manager. In order to complete the following steps, you need the Windows 8 source files copied to D:\Sources\OSD\OSSources\Win8X64Ent on CM01.

Because Windows 8 uses WinPE 4.0 and setup.exe is no longer supported, you cannot use the operating system installers anymore. Therefore, you need to add the Install source as an operating system image to ConfigMgr 2012.

1. On **CM01**, in the **Software Library** workspace, select **Operating Systems / Operating System Images**.
2. On the ribbon's **Folder** tab, click **Create Folder**, and create a folder named **Build and Capture**.
3. Expand the **Operating System Images** node, select the **Build and Capture** folder, and on the ribbon's **Home** tab, click **Add Operating System Image**.
4. On the **Data Source** page, type **\\cm01\sources$\OSD\OSSources\Win8X64Ent \sources\install.wim** in **Path**, and then click **Next**
5. On the **General** page, configure these settings and click **Next**:
    a. Name: **Windows 8 x64 Enterprise**
    b. Version: **1.0**
    c. Comment: **Windows 8 installation source**

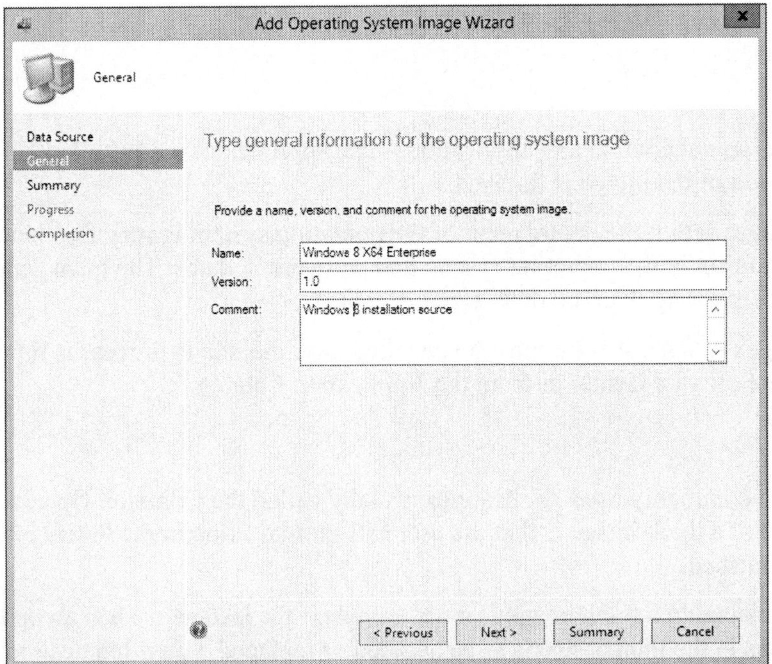

Adding metadata to the operating system installer package.

6. On the **Summary** page, read the summary and click **Next**.
7. On the **Completion** page, click **Close**.
8. Distribute the operating system install package to all distribution points. Select the **Windows 8 x64 Enterprise** operating system image package, and on the ribbon, click **Distribute Content**.
9. On the **General** page, click **Next**.
10. On the **Content Destination** page, click **Add / Distribution Point Group**. Select the **All Content** group, and then click **OK** and **Next**.
11. On the **Summary** page, click **Next**.
12. On the **Completion** page, click **Close**.

Creating a Custom WIM Image

Now you are set to create a custom Windows 8 image. Depending on the SLAs for deployment time, you can choose for different kind of images: thin, thick, and hybrid. There is no absolute right or wrong; but before deciding on a strategy, you need to know the differences between the three image types.

Types of Images

Thin Images

Thin images are images that do not contain any applications. The applications are installed separately after the installation of the image is finished.

A big advantage of thin images is that the deployment of the operating system is very fast, since the image is small and contains only the operating system and software updates. The management of thin images is less time consuming than the other types of images.

A disadvantage of thin images is that software must be installed after the image process is finished either automatically, via the Software Center or from the Application Catalog.

Thick Images

Thick images contain all the commonly used applications, usually called the Common Operating Environment. An advantage of a thick image is that the user can start working immediately after the deployment process is finished.

A big disadvantage is that managing a thick image is more complex; for instance, when an update for an application that resides in the images needs to be updated or replaced, you often need to recreate the image. This can be a time-consuming task. One scenario for which a thick image is a disadvantage is a developer image where the end user (the developer) is reinstalling the operating system once a week and the image deployment time must be kept at a minimum.

Hybrid Images

Hybrid images are the best of both thin and thick images. This type of image allows you to add, for instance, Microsoft Office 2013 to your image. The rest of the applications can be installed during the operating system deployment process or via the Software Center or Application Catalog.

The offline servicing feature within Configuration Manager 2012 allows you also to update the Microsoft Office 2013 application without needing to recreate the operating system image.

Creating the Custom Windows 8 Image

For ViaMonstra, I have decided to go for a hybrid Windows 8 image with Microsoft Office 2013 that is fully patched with the latest approved software updates.

Before you can deploy a custom image, you first need to create the reference image. You can install the reference OS by hand, make changes to it, and capture the reference OS. You also can automate the build and capture of the Windows 8 installation, the customizations, and the installation of Microsoft Office 2013. This way you know that you always have the same golden version of your Windows 8 operating system. To be able to automate the build and capture process, you need to create a build and capture task sequence.

> **Real World Note:** Always use a virtual machine to create a reference image of an operating system. By using a virtual machine, you add only a limited number of drivers during the process.

Create a New Microsoft Office 2013 Application

Before creating the build and capture task sequence, you have to create a new Microsoft Office 2013 application. The application you created in Chapter 7 has two deployment types which are not supported when installing the application through a task sequence. The easiest way to create a new application is simply to copy the existing application created in Chapter 7 and modify it.

1. On **CM01**, using the **ConfigMgr console**, expand **Application Management** in the **Software Library** workplace, then expand **Applications**, and select the **Required User** folder.
2. Right-click the **Microsoft Office 2013** application and select **Copy**.
3. Right-click the new **Microsoft Office 2013-copy** application and select **Properties**
4. In the **General** tab, change the name to **Microsoft Office 2013 OSD**.
5. In the **Deployment Types** tab, delete the **Microsoft Office 2013 x32 MSI** deployment type. Then select the **Microsoft Office 2013 x64 MSI** deployment type and click **Edit**.
6. In the **User Experience** tab, change the **Logon Requirement** to **Whether or not a user is logged on**.
7. On the **Requirements** tab, delete the operating system and primary device requirements and click **OK** twice.
8. Distribute the new application to all distribution points. Select the **Microsoft Office 2013 OSD** application, and from the ribbon, click **Deployment / Distribute Content**.
9. On the **General** page, click **Next**.
10. On the **Content** page, click **Next**.
11. On the **Content Destination** page, click **Add / Distribution Point Group**. Select the **All Content** group, click **OK** and **Next**, and then complete the wizard.

Create the Build and Capture Task Sequence

1. On **CM01**, using **File Explorer**, create the **D:\Sources\OSD\Images\Windows8** folder and grant the **VIAMONSTRA\CM_NAA** account **modify** permissions to it (NTFS Permissions).
2. In the **Software Library**, select **Operating Systems / Task Sequences**.
3. On the ribbon's **Folder** tab, click **Create Folder** and create a folder named **Build and Capture**.
4. Expand the **Task Sequences** node, select the **Build and Capture** folder, and on the ribbon's **Home** tab, click **Create Task Sequence**.

5. On the **Create New Task Sequence** page, select **Build and Capture a reference operating system image** and click **Next**.

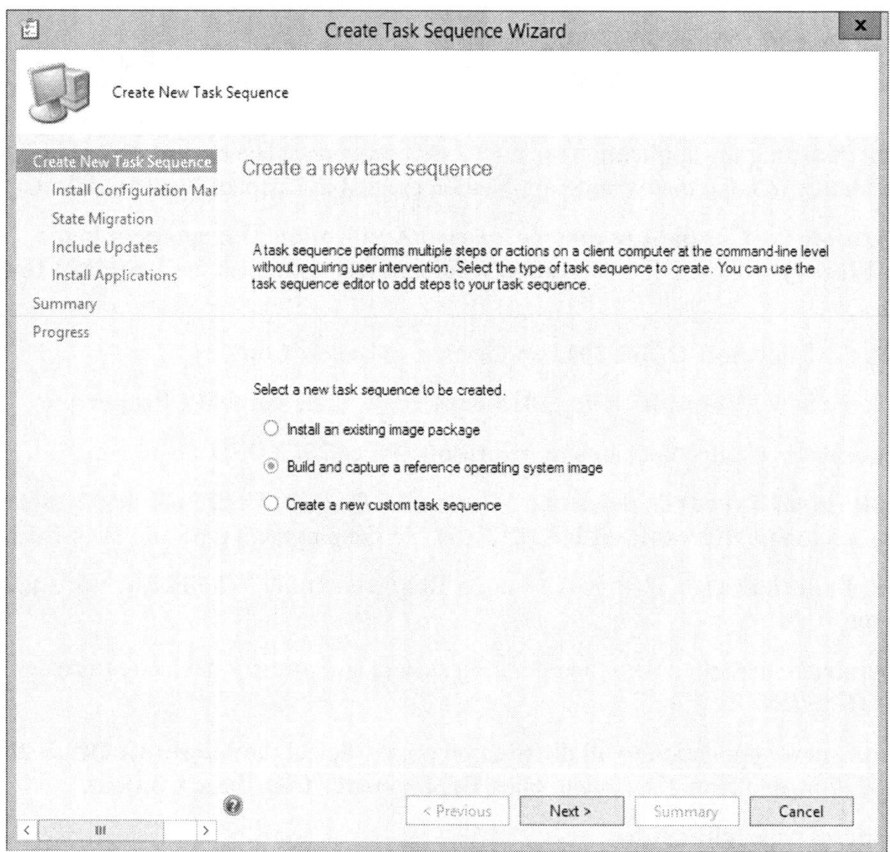

Creating the build and capture task sequence.

6. On the **Task Sequence Information** page, configure these settings and click **Next**:
   a. Name: **Build and Capture Windows 8 Enterprise x64**
   b. Boot image: **Boot image (x64) 6.2.9200.16384 en-US**
7. On the **Install Windows** page, configure these settings and click **Next**:
   a. Image Package: Click **Browse** and select **Build and Capture / Windows 8 x64 Enterprise 1.0 en-US**
   b. Product key: <leave empty>
   c. Always use the same administrator password: **Password01**

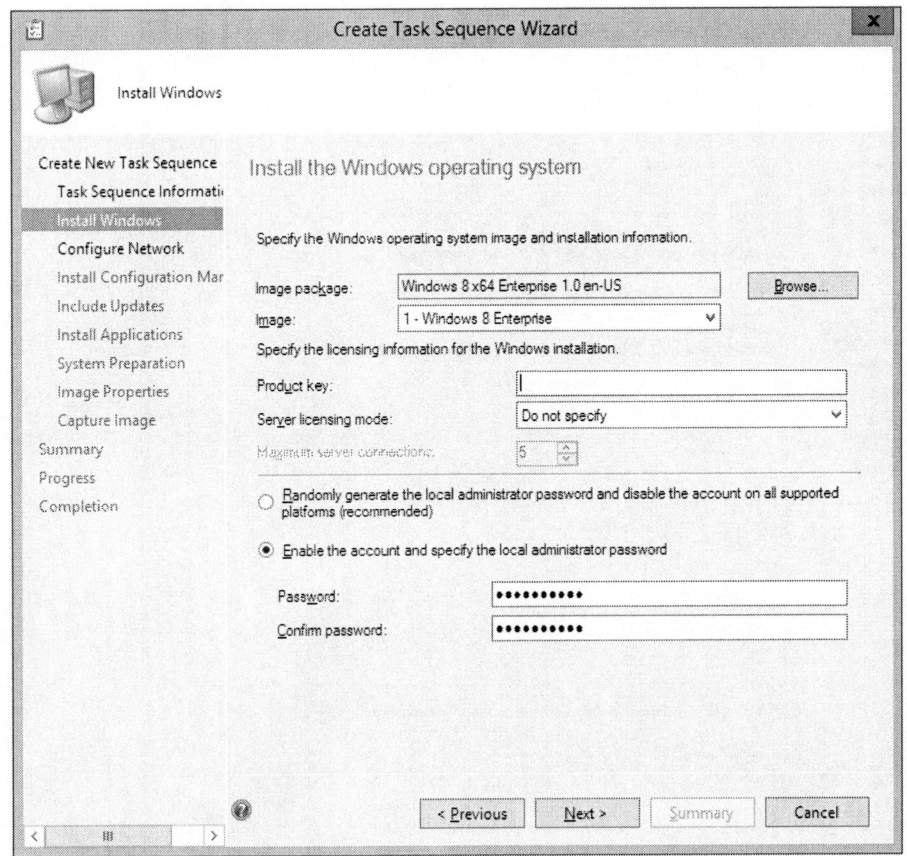

Specifying the OS install files.

8. On the **Configure Network** page, configure this setting and click **Next**:

    Join a Workgroup: **CM2012Install**

9. On the **Install Configuration Manager** page, click **Browse**, select the **Configuration Manager Client Package**, ensure that **SMSMP=CM01.CORP.VIAMONSTRA.COM** is added in **Installation properties**, and click **Next**.
10. On the **Include Updates** page, select **All Software Updates** and click **Next**.
11. On the **Install Applications** page, configure these settings and click **Next**:
    a. Click the **yellow icon** and select the **Required User / Microsoft Office 2013 OSD** application.
    b. Enable **If an application installation fails, continue installing other applications in the list.**

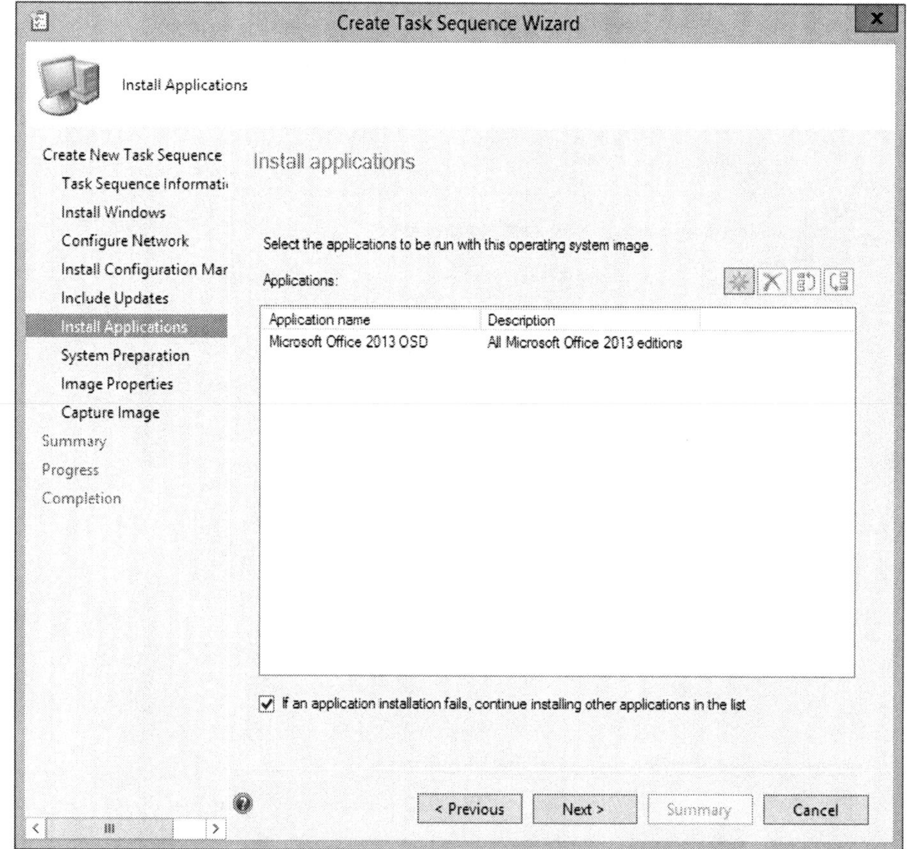

Adding a single application in the task sequence.

12. On the **System Preparation** page, click **Next**.
13. On the **Image Properties** page, configure these settings and click **Next**:
    a. Creator: **ViaMonstra Administrator**
    b. Version: **1.0**
    c. Comments: **Fully patched Windows 8 and Microsoft Office 2013 image created 01/06/2013**.
14. On the **Capture Image** page, configure these settings and click **Next**:
    a. Path: **\\cm01\sources$\OSD\Images\Windows8\Win8_X64_Ent_v1.wim**
    b. Account: **VIAMONSTRA\CM_NAA** (with password **Password01**).
    c. Click **Test connection** (notice the default share), and after a successful test, click **OK**.
15. On the **Summary** page, read the summary and click **Next**.
16. On the **Completion** page, click **Close**.

Deploy the Build and Capture Task Sequence

Now that the build and capture task sequence is created, you need to deploy the task sequence:

1. Navigate to the **Software Library**, and select **Operating Systems / Task Sequences / Build and Capture**.
2. Select the **Build and Capture Windows 8 Enterprise x64** task sequence, and on the ribbon, click **Deploy**.
3. On the **General** page, in **Collection**, click **Browse**; select the **All Unknown Computers** collection and click **Next**. You also can choose to import a known computer to an existing collection and specify that.
4. On the **Deployment Settings** page, configure these settings and click **Next**:
    a. Action: **Install**
    b. Purpose: **Available**
    c. Make available to the following: **Only media and PXE**

    In ConfigMgr 2012 Service Pack 1, you are able to make the task sequence available for the four deployment methods in the following table.

Deployment Method	**Description**
Only ConfigMgr clients	The deployment of the task sequence is available only for clients where the ConfigMgr 2012 client is installed. This method is used often for computer refresh scenarios.
Only ConfigMgr clients, media, and PXE	The deployment of the task sequence is available for clients where the ConfigMgr 2012 client is installed, while booting via PXE or task sequence media. This method is used often for computer refresh, new computer, or replace computer scenarios.
Only media and PXE	The deployment of the task sequence is available only for computers booting via task sequence media or PXE. This method is used often for bare metal deployment or new computer scenarios, or when you want to completely wipe an existing computer.
Only media and PXE (hidden)	The deployment of the task sequence is available only for computers booting via task sequence media or PXE when you know how to access the task sequence via the deployment ID. This method is used often for testing purposes.

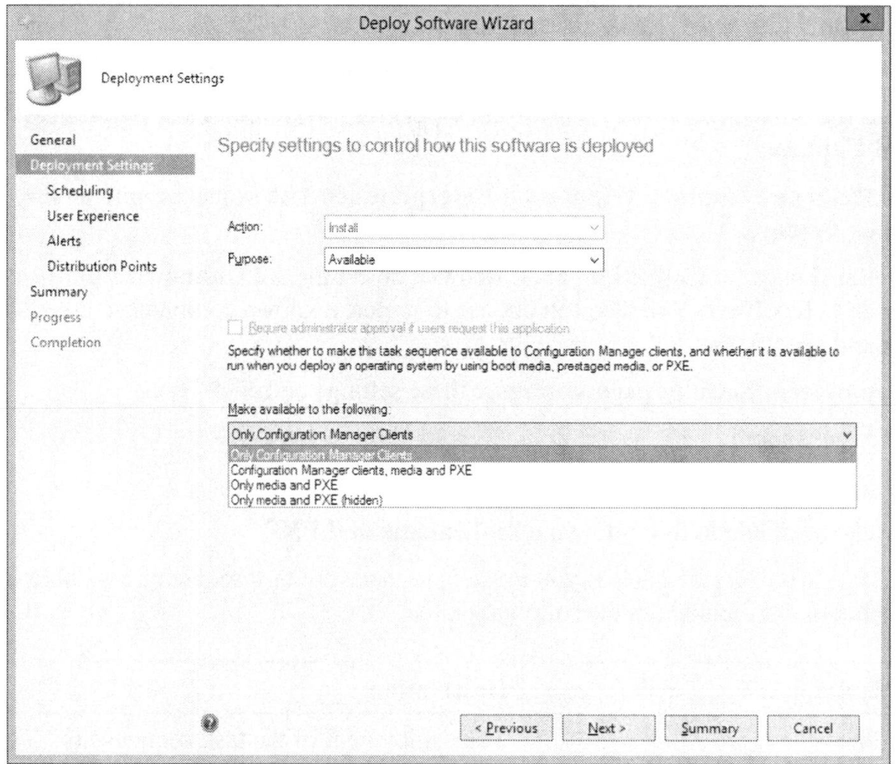

Configuring the deployment as available.

5. On the **Scheduling** page, leave the default and click **Next**.
6. On the **User Experience** page, leave the default and click **Next**.
7. On the **Alerts** page, leave the default and click **Next**.
8. On the **Distribution Points** page, leave the defaults and click **Next**.
9. On the **Summary** page, read the summary and click **Next**.
10. On the **Completion** page, click **Close**.

Note: You can use the built-in task sequence variable SMSTSPreferredAdvertID to specify the task sequence deployment ID you want to run. By adding some logic to a script, you can build some very dynamic deployment solutions.

Deploy Updates to the All Unknown Device Collection

In the next section, you start the deployment of the build and capture task sequence; but, in order for the reference image to install the software updates, you need to deploy them to the All Unknown Computers collection. In the example, you deploy "only" the updates from April. In the real world, you need to deploy all released updates to patch the image fully.

1. On **CM01**, using the **ConfigMgr console**, navigate to the **Software Library** workplace. Expand **Software Updates**, and select **Software Update Groups**.
2. Right-click the **2013 04 April** software update group and select **Deploy**.
3. On the **General** page, configure these settings and click **Next**:
   a. Deployment Name: **WRK 2013 04 April OSD**
   b. Description: **Updates for OSD**
   c. Collection: **All Unknown Computers**
4. On the **Deployment Settings** page, configure these settings and click **Next**:
   a. Type of deployment: **Required**
   b. Detail level: **Only successes and error messages**
5. On the **Scheduling** page, configure these settings and click **Next**:
   a. Time based**: UTC**
   b. Software available time: **As soon as possible**
   c. Installation deadline: **As soon as possible**
6. On the **User Experience** page, accept the default settings and click **Next**.
7. On the **Alerts** page, accept the default settings and click **Next**.
8. On the **Download Settings** page, configure these settings and click **Next**:
   a. Deployment options for client within a slow or unreliable network boundary: Enable **Download software update from distribution point and install**.
   b. When software updates are not available on any preferred distribution points, the client can download and install software updates from a fallback source location for content: Enable **Download and install software updates from the fallback content source location**.
9. On the **Summary** page, click **Save As Template**, type **Workstation OSD** as the name, and click **Save**.
10. Click **Next**, and then click **Close**.

Add a Workgroup PKI Certificate to the Build and Capture Process

If HTTPS is enabled in your environment, you need to add a PKI certificate to the build and capture process. Because the OS you are going to capture is part of a workgroup, the ConfigMgr client won't have a certificate and won't be able to communicate with the primary site. Therefore, you need to configure a certificate that can be used for ConfigMgr clients in the workgroup. The certificate must be installed on the reference computer before installing the ConfigMgr client. For information about creating the certificate, please read Appendix J.

1. Copy the **CM2012 Workgroup Certificate** certificate to **\\cm01\Sources$\OSD\SW\Settings\Win8SettingsBC**.
2. Create an **unattend.xml** with the following content and copy this file to **\\cm01\Sources$\OSD\SW\Settings\Win8SettingsBC**:

```
<?xml version="1.0" encoding="utf-8"?>
<unattend xmlns="urn:schemas-microsoft-com:unattend">
   <settings pass="specialize">
      <component name="Microsoft-Windows-Deployment"
       processorArchitecture="amd64"
       publicKeyToken="31bf3856ad364e35"
       language="neutral"
       versionScope="nonSxS"
       xmlns:wcm="http://schemas.microsoft.com/WMIConfig
          /2002/State"
       xmlns:xsi="http://www.w3.org/2001
          /XMLSchema-instance">
         <RunSynchronous>
            <RunSynchronousCommand wcm:action="add">
               <Description>Import Certificate</Description>
               <Order>1</Order>
               <Path>cmd /c certutil -f -p Password01
                -importpfx
                C:\_SMSTaskSequence\wgpki.pfx</Path>
            </RunSynchronousCommand>
         </RunSynchronous>
      </component>
   </settings>
   <cpi:offlineImage cpi:source="" xmlns:cpi="urn:schemas
    -microsoft-com:cpi" />
</unattend>
```

3. On **CM01**, using the **ConfigMgr console**, navigate to the **Software Library** workplace. Expand **Application Management** and select **Packages**. Click **Create Package**, supply the following information, and click **Next**:
   a. Name: **Settings Package for Windows 8 Build and Capture**
   b. Select: **This Package contains source files**
   c. Source Folder: **\\cm01\Sources$\OSD\SW\Settings\Win8SettingsBC**
4. Select **Do not create a program** and click **Next**.
5. On the **Summary** page, click **Next**.
6. Click **Close** after the creation of the package is complete.
7. Distribute the package to the distribution point group **All Content**.
8. In the **ConfigMgr Console**, navigate to **Operating Systems\Task Sequences**, select **Build and Capture Windows 8 Enterprise x64**, and click **Edit**.

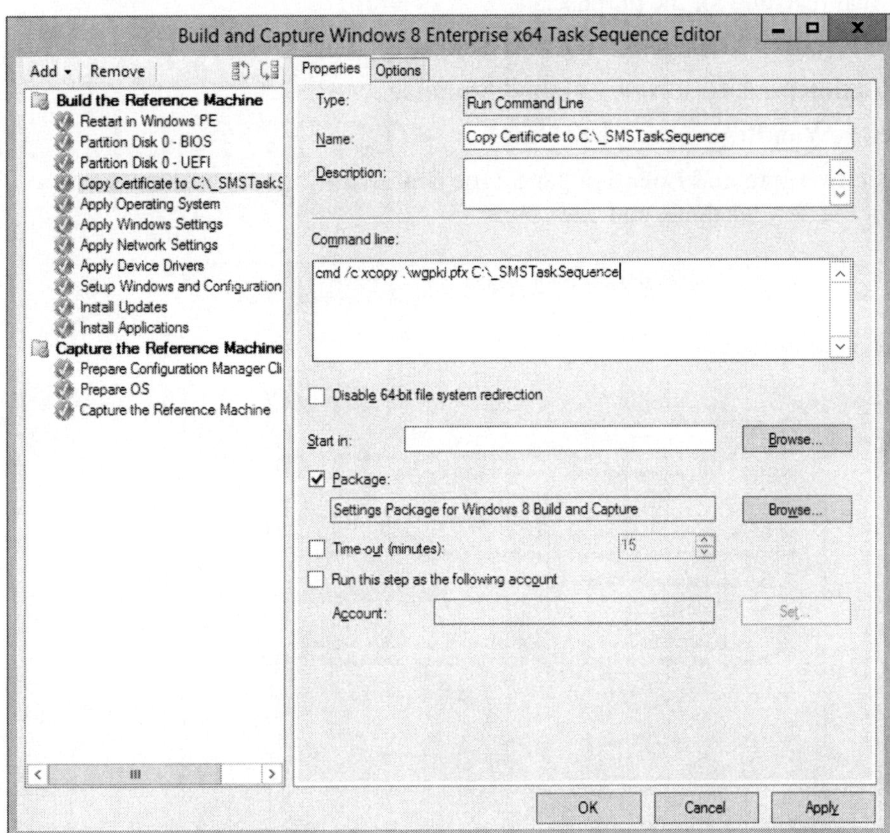

Changing the Build and Capture task sequence.

9. Add a **Command Line** task beneath the Partition tasks via **Add**, **General** and supply the following information:
    a. Name: **Copy Certificate to C:_SMSTaskSequence**
    b. Command line: **cmd /c xcopy .\wgpki.pfx C:_SMSTaskSequence**
    c. Package: **Settings Package for Windows 8 Build and Capture**
10. Select the **Apply Operating System** task and change the following settings:
    a. Select **Use an unattended or Sysprep answer file for a custom installation**.
    b. Package: **Settings Package for Windows 8 Build and Capture**
    c. File name: **unattend.xml**
11. Click **OK** to close the task sequence.

Start the Deployment

The next logical step in the process is to start the deployment. For ViaMonstra, you use Hyper-V to create a new virtual machine for the purpose:

1. Launch the **Hyper-V Manager** on the host computer.
2. From the **Action** pane, click **New / Virtual Machine**.
3. On the **Before You Begin** page, click **Next**.
4. On the **Specify Name and Location** page, type **BuildAndCapture** as the name, specify a location for the new machine, and click **Next**.

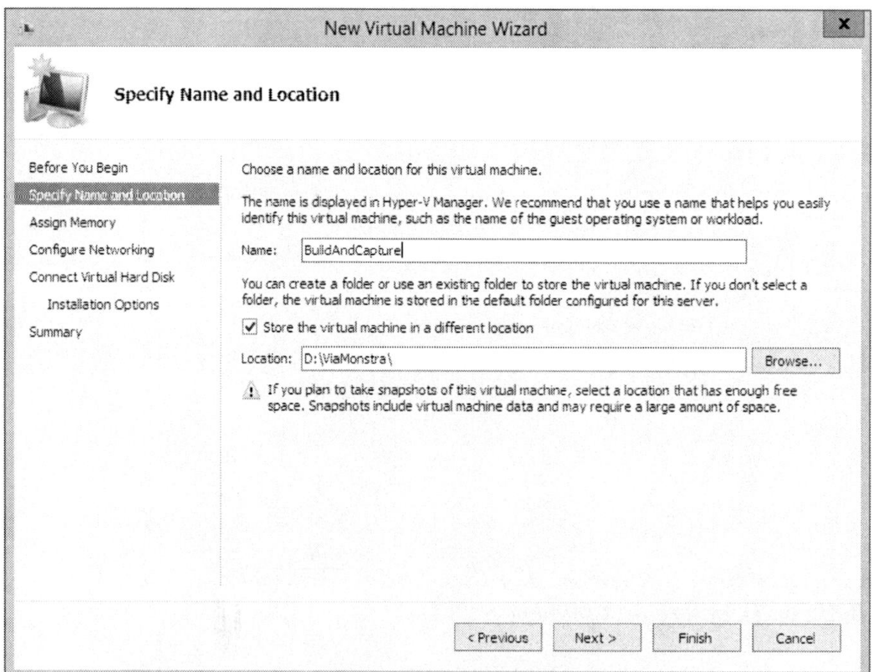

Creating a new virtual machine.

5. On the **Assign Memory** page, assign **1024** MB (or as much as you can) and click **Next.**
6. On the **Configure Networking** page, configure the same network as the site server and click **Next**.
7. On the **Connect Virtual Hard Disk** page, leave the defaults and click **Next**.
8. On the **Installation Options** page, select **Install an operating system from a network-based installation server** and click **Next.**

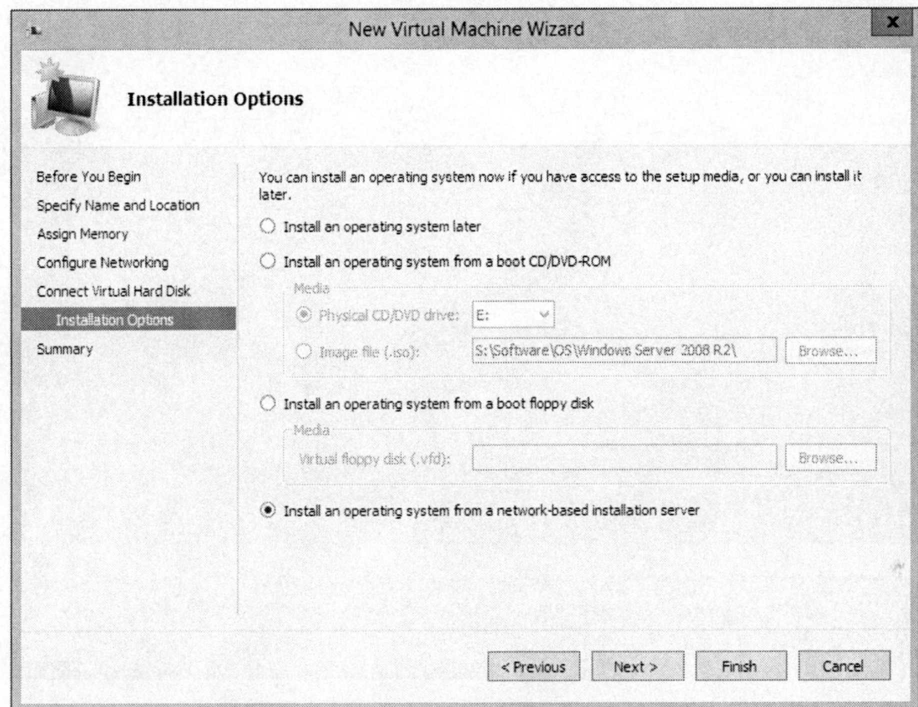

Configuring the virtual machine to boot from PXE.

9. On the **Summary** page, read the summary and click **Finish**.
10. Start the new **BuildAndCapture** machine.

11. When prompted, press **F12** to initiate the PXE process.

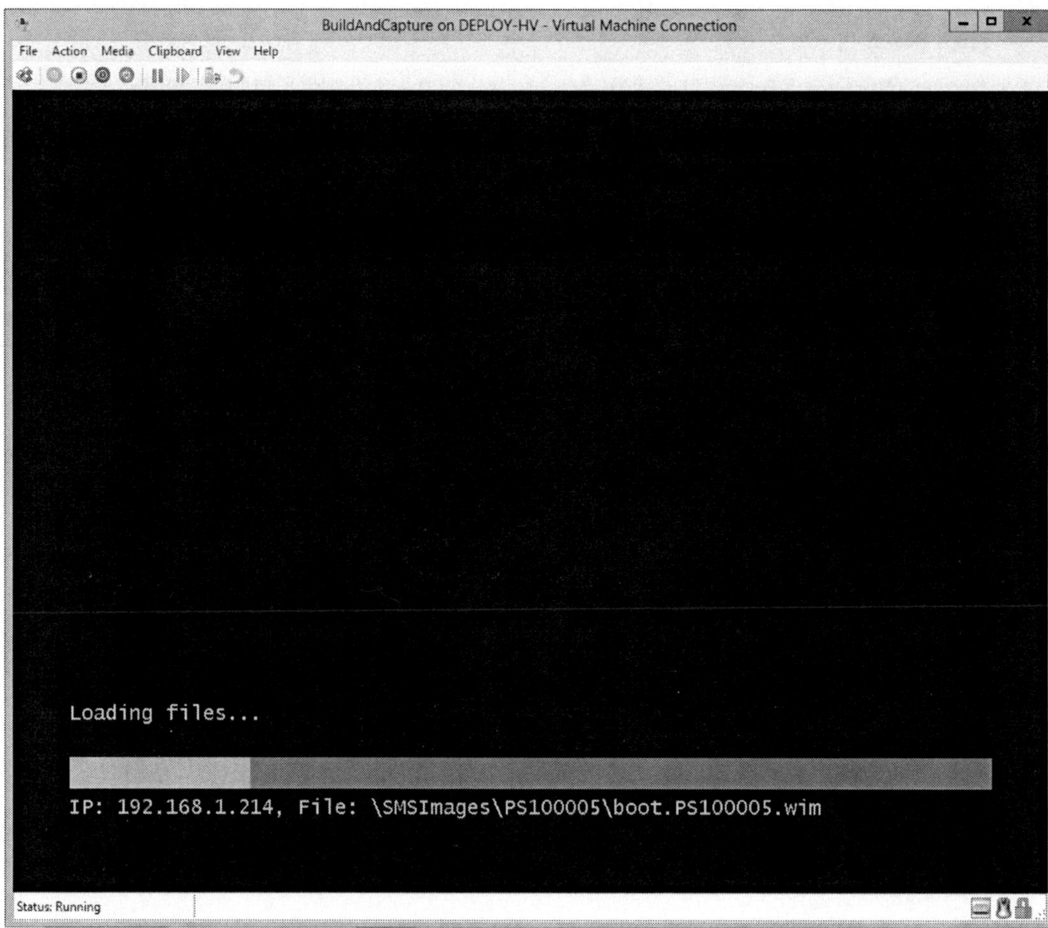

Downloading the boot image using PXE.

12. Type the PXE password and click **Next**.
13. Select the **Build and Capture Windows 8 Enterprise x64** task sequence and click **Next**.

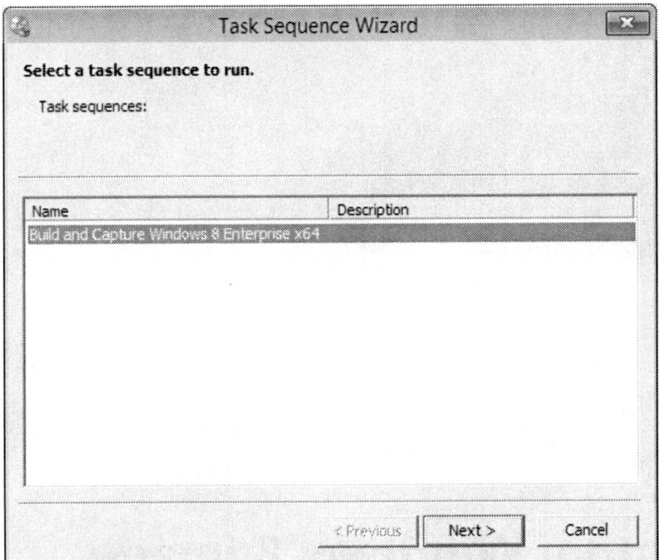

Starting the Build and Capture task sequence

The operating system will be installed and captured to the configured location. After this step is complete, you are able to proceed with the OS image deployment, which is covered in the next section.

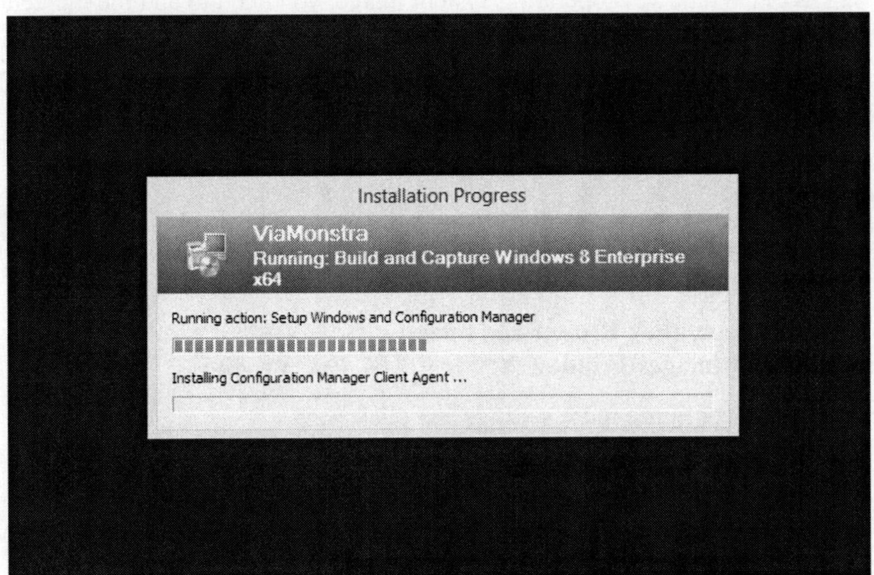

The reference image being deployed and installing the ConfigMgr Client Agent.

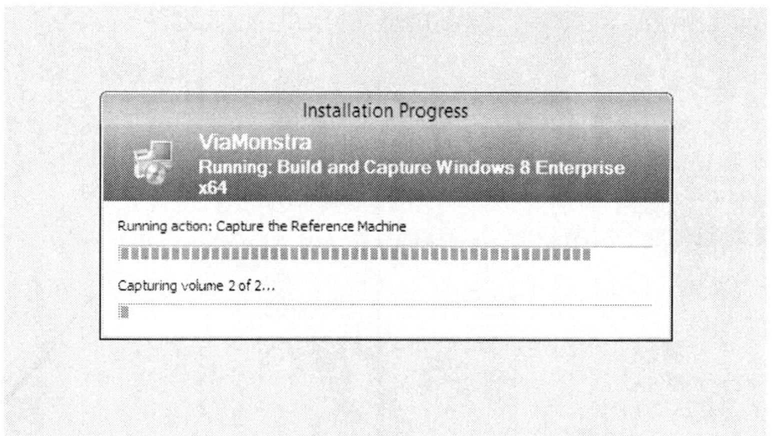

Creating the Windows 8 WIM image.

Deploying the Custom Windows 8 Image

Now that you have a custom Windows 8 image, you can add this operating system image to ConfigMgr and start deploying the image to your workstations.

Adding a Custom Windows 8 Operating System Image

After creating a fresh custom Windows 8 operating system image, you need to add the image to ConfigMgr and distribute it to all of your distribution points:

1. Navigate to the **Software library** workspace, and select **Operating Systems / Operating System Images**.
2. On the ribbon's **Folder** tab, click **Create Folder** and create a folder named **Deploy Production**.
3. Navigate to the **Deploy Production** folder, and on the ribbon's **Home** tab, click **Add Operating System Image**.
4. On the **Data Source** page, click **Browse** and select **\\cm01\sources$\OSD\Images\Windows8\Win8_X64_Ent_v1.wim**.
5. On the **General** page, configure these settings and click **Next**:
    a. Name: **Windows 8 Enterprise x64**
    b. Version: **1.0**
    c. Comments: **Standard ViaMonstra corp image**

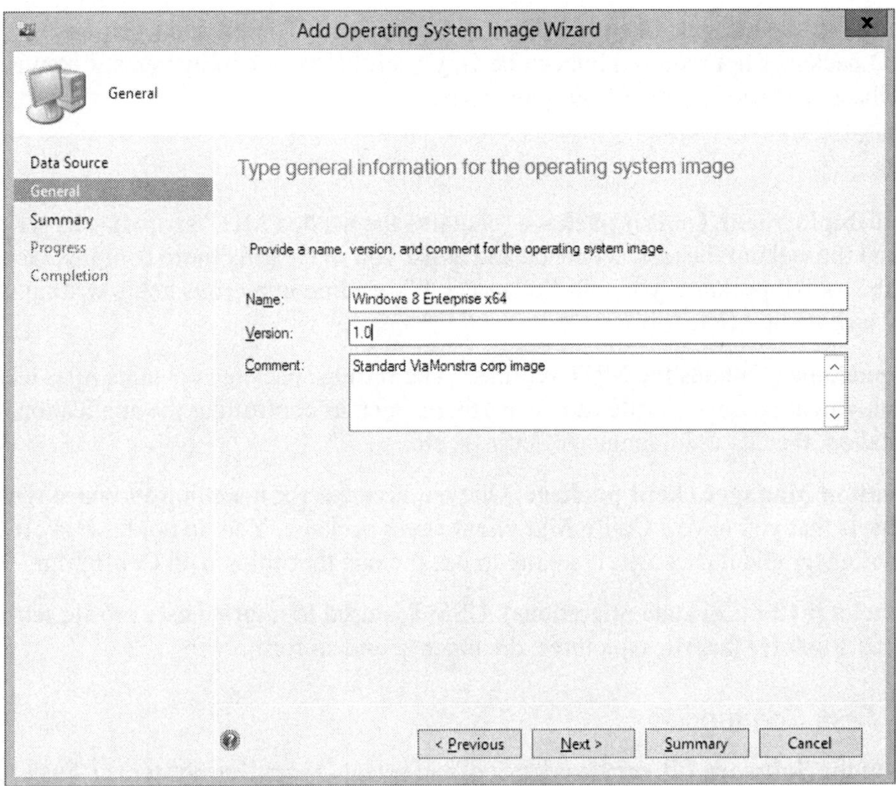

Adding a custom image.

6. In the **Summary** page, read the summary and click **Next**.
7. On the **Completion** page, click **Close**.
8. Select the **Windows 8 Enterprise x64** image, and on the ribbon, click **Distribute Content**.
9. On the **General** page, click **Next**.
10. On the **Content Destination** page, click **Add / Distribution Point Group**. Select the **All Content** group, and click **OK** and then **Next**.
11. On the **Summary** page, click **Next**.
12. On the **Completion** page, click **Close**.

Creating a Deploy Task Sequence

To be able to deploy the custom Windows 8 image, you need to create a task sequence. The task sequence is the engine that takes care of the unattended installation of the Windows 8 image. The task sequence wizard in ConfigMgr assists you in creating a basic bare metal deployment task sequence. However, if you also want to support other deployment scenarios, you will find it easier to work with the MDT 2012 Update 1 task sequences. When creating the first task sequence, you are asked to create several packages, like the Microsoft Deployment Toolkit and a settings package. The OSD packages not required but can be very useful in your deployments. Likewise, you can reuse all these packages in other task sequences.

OSD Packages

- **Microsoft Deployment Toolkit package** (contains the needed MDT scripts). The scripts can be used throughout the task sequence and assist you in creating more complex tasks. Without the toolkit package, you will find yourself spending numerous hours writing what is already written by Microsoft.
- **Settings package** (contains the MDT settings). The settings package contains rules used in the deployment process. A rule can be anything, such as controlling the application being installed, the OU used, language settings, etc.
- **Configuration Manager client package**. One requirement for installing an image with ConfigMgr is that you have a ConfigMgr client agent package. You do not have to create a new ConfigMgr client package; it's okay to use the one that ships with ConfigMgr.
- **USMT package** (for user state migrations). USMT is used to migrate user profile settings like Internet Explorer favorites, pictures, documents, and so forth.

Create a MDT Task Sequence

1. Navigate to the **Software Library** workspace, and select **Operating Systems / Task Sequences**.
2. On the ribbon's **Folder** tab, click **Create Folder** and create a folder named **Deploy Production**.
3. Navigate to the **Deploy Production** folder, and on the ribbon's **Home** tab, click **Create MDT Task Sequence**.
4. On the **Choose Template** page, select **Client Task Sequence** and click **Next**.

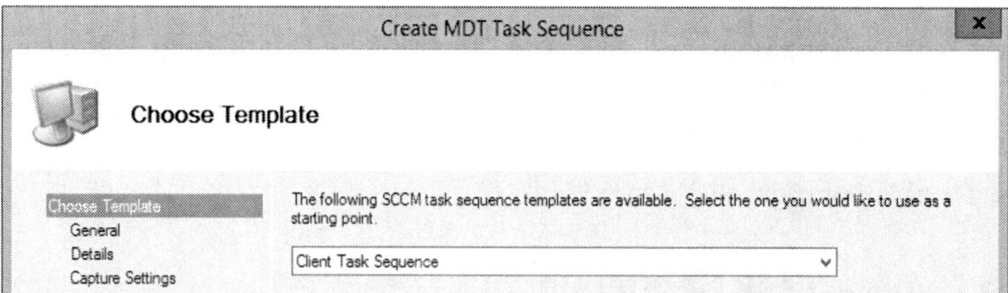

Selecting the client task sequence template.

5. On the **General** page, configure these settings and click **Next**:
    a. Task sequence name: **Windows 8 Enterprise Eng x64**
    b. Task sequence comments: **ViaMonstra Corp image**

6. On the **Details** page, configure these settings and click **Next**:
    a. Join Workgroup or Domain
        i. Join a domain: **corp.viamonstra.com**
        ii. Account: **VIAMONSTRA\CM_JD**
        iii. Password: **Password01**
    b. Windows Settings
        a. User name: **ViaMonstra**
        b. Organization name: **ViaMonstra**
        c. Product key: supply product key or leave blank if you are using a KMS.

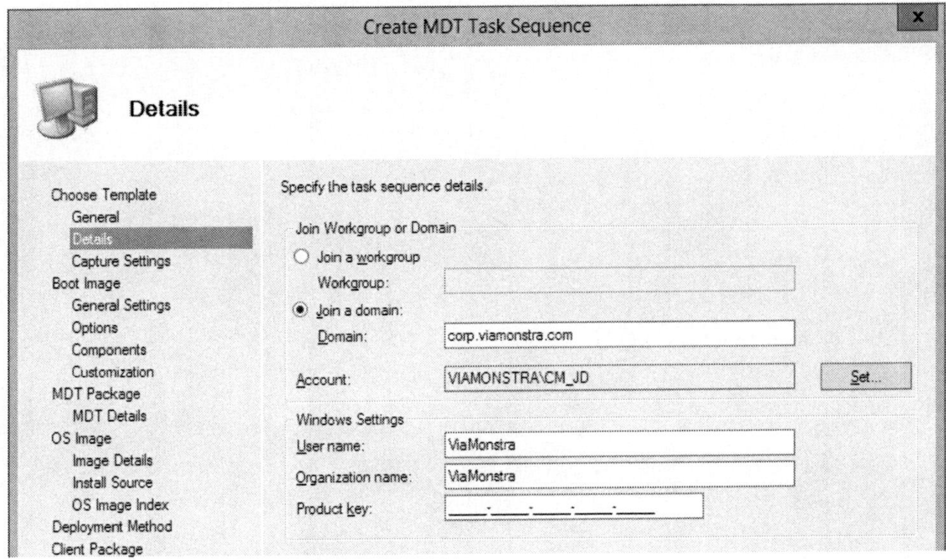

Configuring the domain information.

7. On the **Capture Settings** page, configure this setting and click **Next**:

    This task sequence will never be used to capture an image: **Enabled**

8. On the **Boot Image** page, configure this setting and click **Next**:

    In **Specify an existing boot image package**, click **Browse**, select the **MDT Boot Image x64 1.0 en-US** boot image package, and click **OK**.

9. On the **MDT Package** page configure this setting and click **Next**:

    Select **Create a new Microsoft Deployment Toolkit Files Package**, and in the **Package source folder to be created (UNC path)** text box, type **\\CM01\Sources$\OSD\SW\Toolkit**.

10. On the **MDT Details** page, configure these settings and click **Next**:
    a. Name: **Deployment Toolkit package**
    b. Version: **2012 update 1**
    c. Language: **US**
    d. Manufacturer: **Microsoft**
11. On the **OS Image** page, configure this setting and click **Next**:

    Select **Specify an existing OS image**, click **Browse**, select **Windows 8 Enterprise x64 1.0 en-US** from the **Deploy Production** folder and click **OK**.

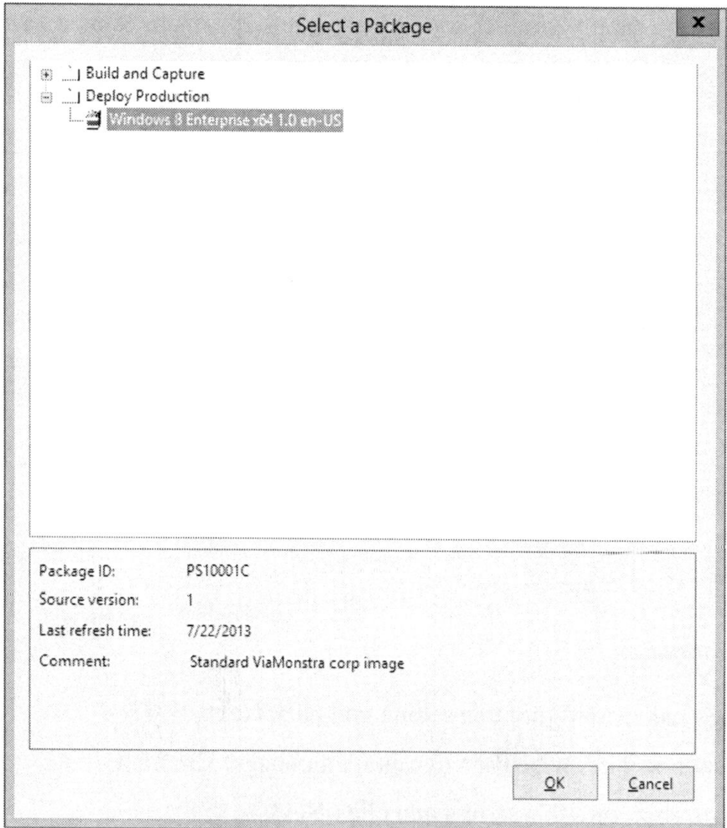

Selecting the operating system image file.

12. On the **OS Image Index** page, select index number **2**.

Note: If you select the incorrect index, the deployment will break. Index 2 contains the Windows 8 operating system image that was previously captured.

13. On the **Deployment Method** page, accept the default settings and click **Next.**

14. On the **Client Package** page, configure this setting and click **Next**:

    Select **Specify a ConfigMgr client package**, click **Browse**, select the **Microsoft Corporation Configuration Manager Client Package**, and click **OK**.

15. On the **USMT Package** page, configure the following setting and click **Next**:

    Select **Specify an existing USMT package,** click **Browse**, select **Microsoft Corporation User State Migration Tool for Windows 8 6.2.9200.16384**, and click **OK**.

16. On the **Settings Package** page, configure this setting and click **Next**:

    Click **Create a new settings package**; in **Package source folder to be created (UNC Path)**, type **\\CM01\Sources$\OSD\SW\Settings\Win8Settings**.

17. On the **Settings Details** page, configure these settings and click **Next**:

    a. Name: **Windows 8 Deploy Settings**

    b. Version: **1.0**

    c. Language: **US**

    d. Manufacturer: **Microsoft**

18. On the **Sysprep Package** page, select **No Sysprep package is required** and click **Next**.

19. On the **Summary** page, read the summary and click **Next** to start creating the task sequence and the packages.

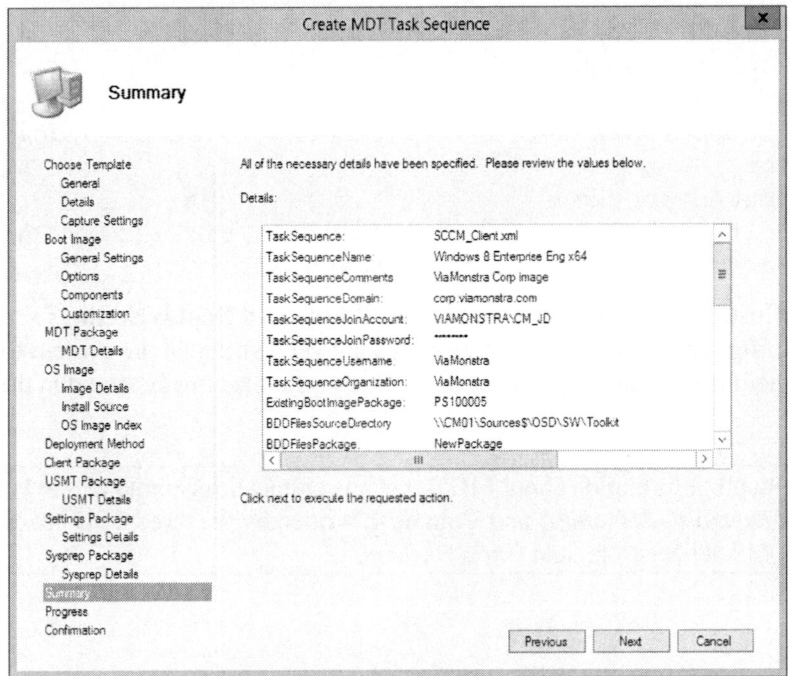

Summary of all settings and packages for the MDT task sequence.

20. On the **Confirmation** page, click **Finish**.
21. Move the new task sequence to the **Deploy Production** folder.

Note: Even if you were in the Deploy Production folder when creating the task sequence, it's created in the root of the Task Sequences node.

Edit the Rules (Settings Package)

After finishing the creation of the MDT task sequence, you need to change some rules in the CustomSettings.ini file within your settings package. The settings package is customizable; you are able to change the Unattend.xml and CustomSettings.ini files. In CustomSettings.ini, you are able to edit the existing rules and add new rules.

1. Use **File Explorer** to open **\\cm01\sources$\OSD\SW\Settings\Win8Settings**, and open **CustomSettings.ini** using **Notepad**.
2. Edit the **CustomSettings.ini** file so it reflects the settings file in the example below. You also can find the CustomSettings.ini file along with the other files and scripts used in this book.

```
[Settings]
Priority=Default
Properties=OSDMigrateConfigFiles,OSDMigrateMode

[Default]
SLShare=\\CM01\logs$
DoCapture=NO
ComputerBackupLocation=NONE
BDEInstallSuppress=YES
MachineObjectOU=ou=workstations,ou=viamonstra,dc=corp,dc=via
monstra,dc=com
OSDMigrateMode=Advanced
OSDMigrateAdditionalCaptureOptions=/ue:*\* /ui:VIAMONSTRA\*
OSDMigrateConfigFiles=Miguser.xml,Migapp.xml
```

3. After editing the **CustomSettings.ini** file, update the **Windows 8 Deploy Settings** package in the **ConfigMgr console**. Even if you have not yet distributed the content for this package, you still need to update it because the first version is already stored in the content library.

Real World Note: For in-depth information about MDT custom settings, I recommend that you acquire *Deployment Fundamentals* – Volume 3 and Volume 4, written by the three OSD "über geeks" Johan Arwidmark, Mikael Nyström, and Chris Nackers.

Distribute the MDT Packages

After editing the CustomSettings.ini file, you need to distribute the newly created packages. You can do this via the packages themselves, but it is easier to distribute the content via the newly created task sequence. This way you are certain that all the content referenced by the task sequence is distributed to the distribution points. The approach also checks whether the related boot image and Windows 8 image are distributed.

1. Navigate to the **Software Library** workspace, and select **Operating Systems / Task Sequences / Deploy Production**. You should see the newly created task sequence **Windows 8 Enterprise x64**. If not, refresh the console view.
2. Select the **Windows 8 Enterprise Eng x64** task sequence, and on the ribbon, click **Distribute Content**.
3. On the **General** page, click **Next**.
4. On the **Content Destination** page, verify that all packages and images referenced by the packages are listed, and then click **Next**.

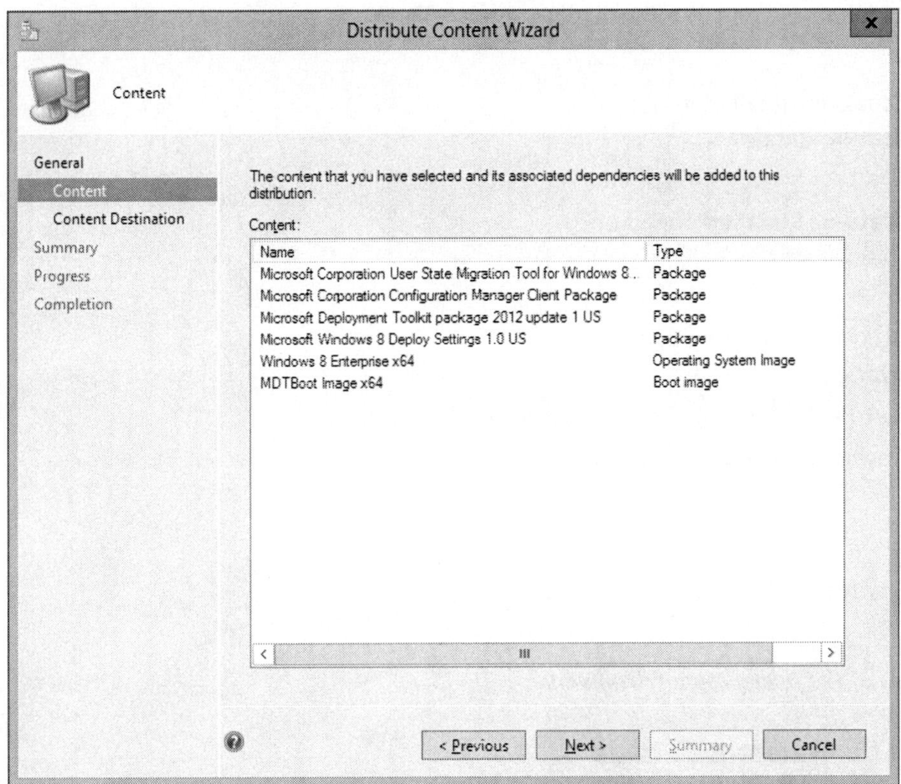

An easy way to ensure that all packages referenced by the task sequence are distributed.

5. On the **Content Destination** page, click **Add / Distribution Point Group**; then select **All Content** and click **OK** and **Next**.

6. On the **Summary** page, read the summary and click **Next**.
7. On the **Completion** page, click **Close**.

Applications in the OS Deployment Process

There are several ways to deploy applications as part of the OS deployment process. Applications can be deployed in five different phases of the process. In which phase you plan to deploy the application, depends on factors like:

- The importance of deployment speed
- The number of applications you want to deploy
- Whether you want to deploy applications before a user is assigned as primary user for a device
- Whether you want to deploy applications before the user is logged on

The operating environment consists of five layers, and each one represents another way or method of installing applications on your Windows 8 operating system.

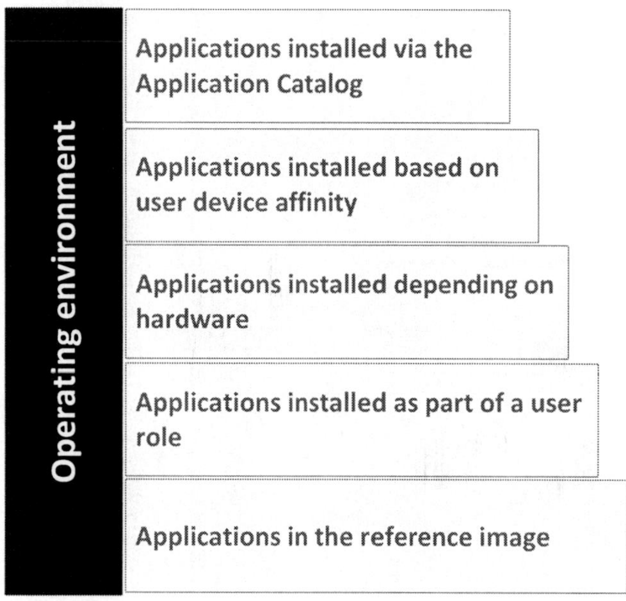

Application layers of the operating environment.

Applications in the Reference Image

The reference image includes Windows 8 and Microsoft Office 2013, with all the approved software updates in place. After the reference image is created, you are able to service the image by incorporating approved software updates offline.

Applications Installed as Part of a User Role

Depending on group membership, user role applications can be installed via a ConfigMgr task sequence when the user next logs on, or via the Software Center or Application Catalog from which the users can install or request software that is available for them.

Applications Installed Depending on Hardware

With a task sequence, you are able to install applications for different hardware types. For instance, you can specify what software in installed depending on the type of hardware.

In the task sequence, you are allowed to add conditions to a task. A condition can be a WMI query which checks what kind of hardware you are using, or a task sequence variable. Depending on the condition, a task will run or not. As an example, you can use the task sequence variable IsLaptop to install certain applications only on laptops.

1. In the **Software Library** workspace, select **Operating Systems / Task Sequences / Deploy Production**.
2. Select the **Windows 8 Enterprise x64** task sequence you created earlier, and on the ribbon, click **Edit**.
3. Go to the **State Restore** phase of the task sequence, select the **Install Application** task, and select **Options.**

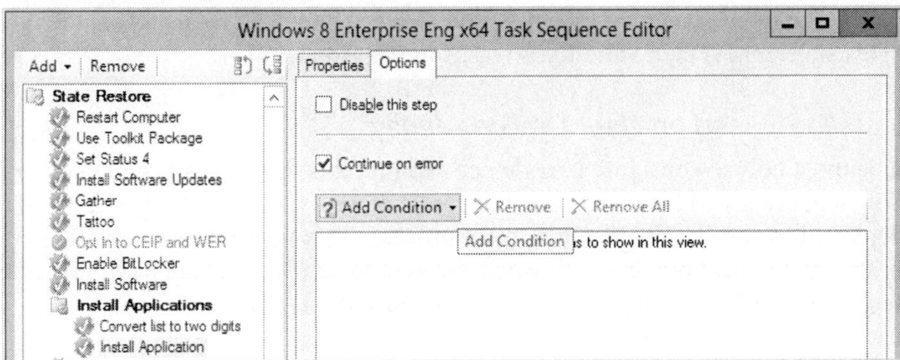

Selecting the Install Application task.

4. Click **Add Condition**, and select **If Statement** with the option **All conditions**.
5. Click **Add Condition**, and select **Task Sequence Variable**.

6. Use the following values:
    a. Variable: **IsLaptop**
    b. Condition: **equals**
    c. Value: **True**

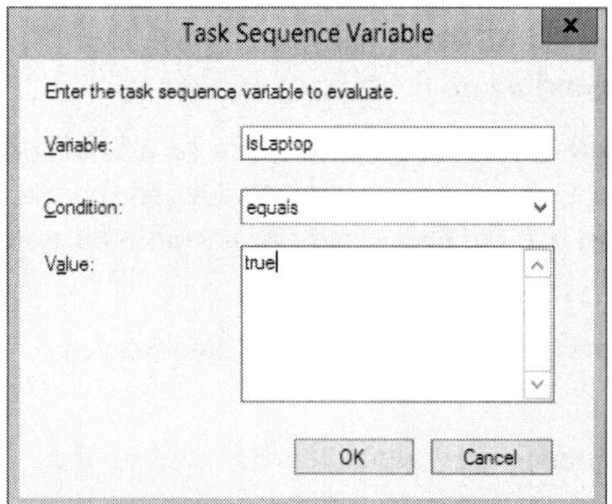

Setting the task sequence variable.

7. Select **OK** twice to submit the values and close the task sequence.

Instead of configuring the IF statement on one task, you also can create a group and set the statement there. This statement is then valid for all tasks in the group.

Applications Installed Based on User Device Affinity

In Chapter 6, you learned how to configure user device affinity; this feature also can be integrated with the OS deployment process. This means that the applications that are normally deployed to the user can be deployed as part of the OS deployment process. This way a user can work immediately after the deployment process is finished. Be sure to configure the deployment of the applications as **required** and that the application is **deployed automatically according to schedule whether or not a user is logged on**.

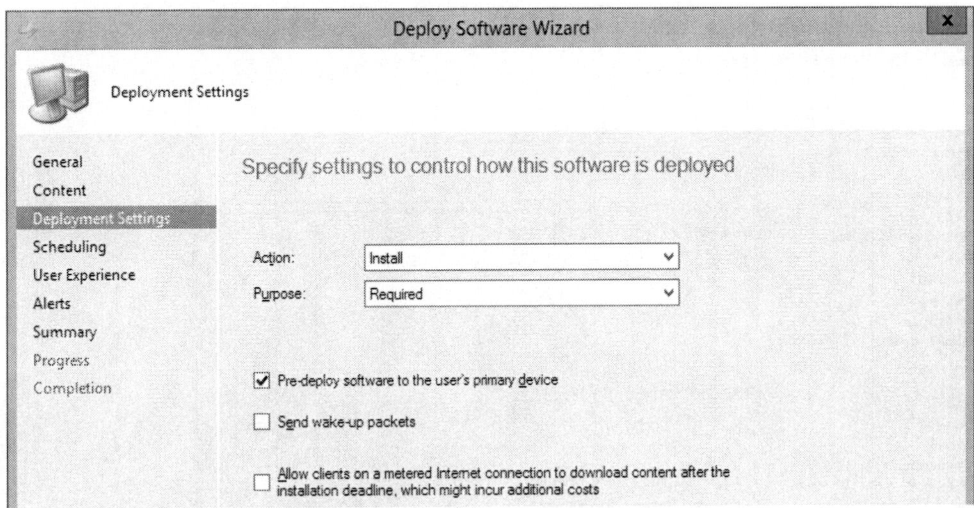

Configuring the application deployment.

Applications Installed via the Application Catalog

In Chapter 6, you learned how to configure applications and deploy those to the Application Catalog. Applications deployed to the Application Catalog are not part of the OS deployment process but still worth mentioning in this model.

Integrating Endpoint Protection

When deploying a new operating system without an Endpoint Protection solution, the machine may be vulnerable to possible viruses or other unwanted software. A safe solution is embedding the Endpoint Protection solution in your OS deployment environment.

To install the Endpoint Protection client while installing Windows 8, you need to do the following:

1. In the **Software Library** workspace, select **Operating Systems / Task Sequences / Deploy Production**.
2. Right-click **Windows 8 Enterprise Eng x64** and select **Edit**.
3. Go to the **Install Applications** group and select **Add / General / Run Command line**.
4. Configure the task with the following settings:
    a. Name: **SCEP Install**
    b. Command line: **SCEPInstall.exe /s /q /policy "ep_defaultpolicy.xml"**
    c. Package: **Configuration Manager Client Package**

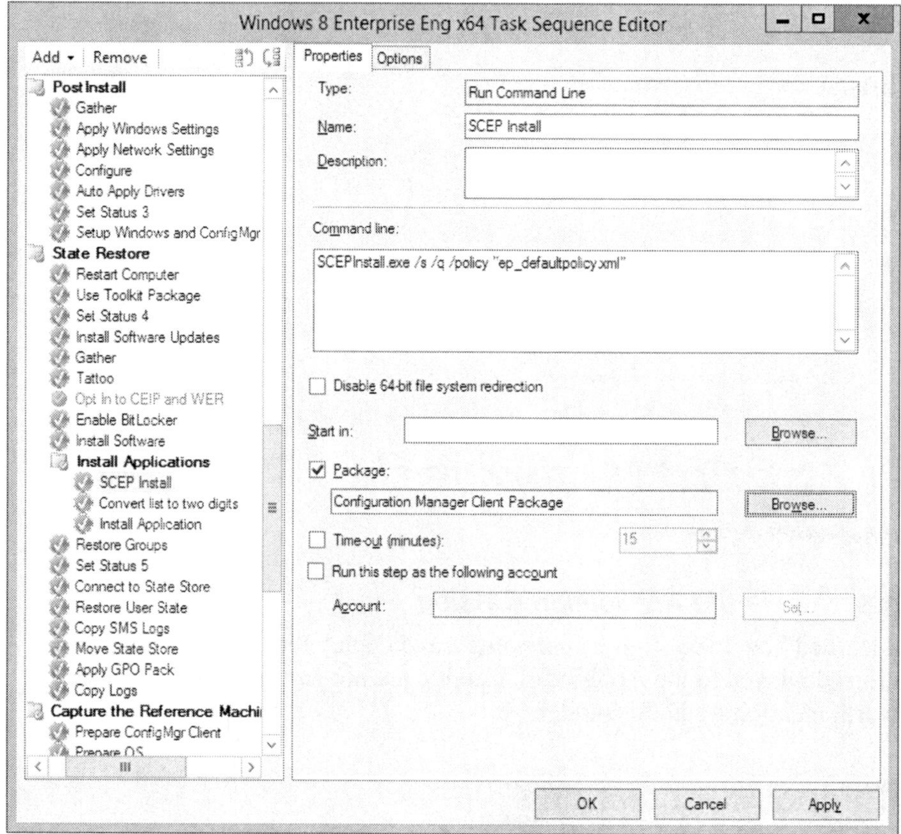

The SCEP install task.

5. Select **OK** to save the settings of the task sequence.

Real World Note: The file ep_defaultpolicy.xml is part of the standard Configuration Manager Client Package. If you want a custom file, you can install the client manually by using SCEPInstall.exe /s /q /policy "full path to policy".

Refreshing Windows 7 to Windows 8

After preparing the ViaMonstra environment for deploying a new custom Windows 8 image, it is time to migrate the Windows 7 workstations to Windows 8. Before you are able to do that, you need to deploy the task sequence to a collection with your old Windows 7 workstations.

Real World Note: Never deploy any OS task sequence to members of the All System collection. Always use one or more specific collections for the Windows 7 migrations.

Create a Custom Collection

1. In the **Asset and Compliance** workspace, select **Device Collection / Operating System Deployment**, and then on the ribbon, click **Create Device Collection.**
2. On the **General** page, enter the following details and click **Next**:
   a. Name: **OSD Refresh Windows 8**
   b. Limiting Collection: Click **Browse** and select **All Systems.**
3. On the **Membership Rules** page, click **Add Rule / Direct Rule.**
4. On the **Welcome** page, click **Next.**
5. On the **Search for Resources** page, in **Value**, type **PC0002** and click **Next.**
6. On the **Select Resources** page, select **PC0002** from the list and click **Next.**
7. On the **Summary** page, read the summary and click **Next.**
8. On the **Completion** page, click **Close** and return to the Membership Rules page.
9. On the **Membership Rules** page, click **Next.**
10. On the **Summary** page, read the summary and click **Next.**
11. On the **Completion** page, click **Close.**

Deploy the Refresh Machine Task Sequence

1. Navigate to the **Software Library** workspace and select **Operating Systems, Task Sequences, Windows 8 Enterprise x64**; then on the ribbon, click **Deploy.**
2. On the **General** page, click **Browse**; then in the **Operating System Deployment** folder, select the just created collection **OSD Refresh Windows 8** collection and click **Next.**
3. On the **Deployment Settings** page, ensure the **Purpose** is **Required** and that the availability for **Only Configuration Manager Clients** is selected. Click **Next** to continue. You also can configure the deployment to be Available; by doing that, you are not forcing the upgrade.
4. On the **Scheduling** page, click **New** in **Assignment Schedule**, click the **Schedule** button, and configure the assignment schedule to one week from now. Click **OK** twice and then **Next.**
5. On the **User Experience** page, configure the following Notification setting and click **Next**:

   Allow users to run the program independently of assignments: **Enable**

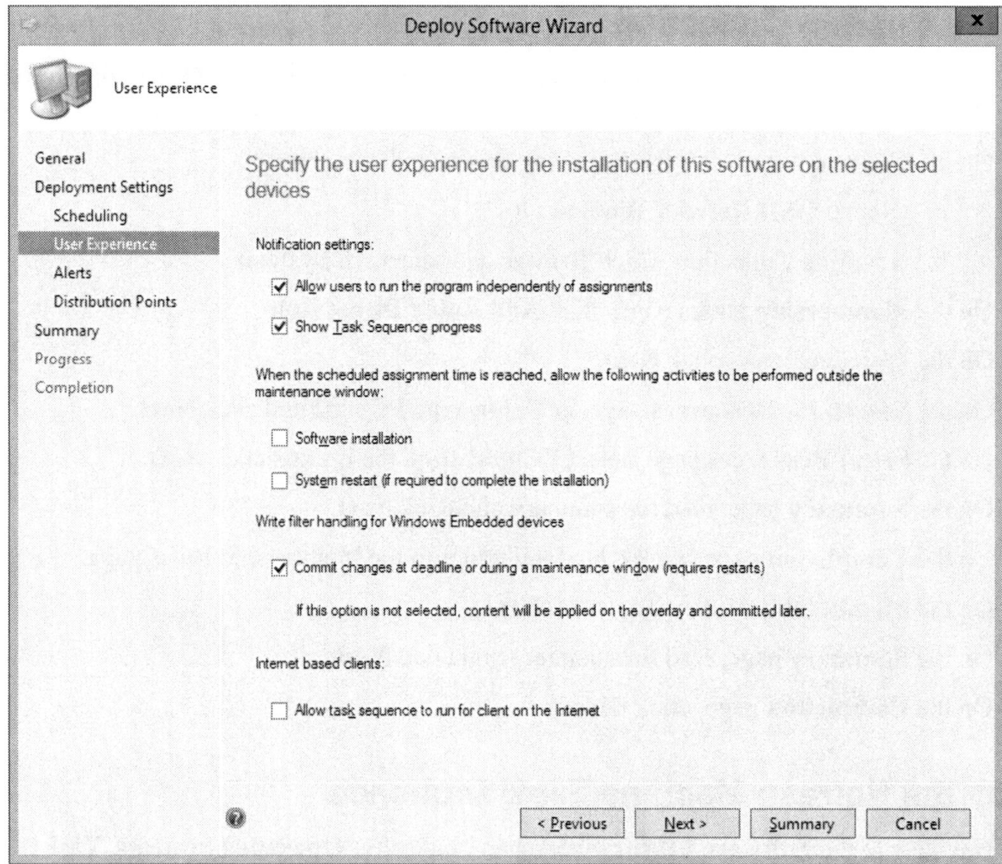

Allowing the end user to run the deployment prior to deadline.

6. On the **Alerts** page, configure these settings and click **Next**:
    a. Create a deployment alert when the threshold is lower than the following: **Enable**
    b. Percent success: **95**
    c. After: **a date 8 days from now**
    d. Create a deployment alert when the threshold is higher than the following: **Enable**
    e. Percent failure: **1**
7. On the **Distribution Points** page, click **Next**.
8. On the **Summary** page, read the summary and click **Next**.
9. On the **Completion** page, click **Close**.

Run the Refresh Task Sequence

1. On **PC0002**, log on as **VIAMONSTRA\JAP** and perform a few changes on the desktop, like changing the wallpaper, create some shortcuts, and so forth.
2. Log off the computer to save the profile.
3. Log back on to **PC0002** as **VIAMONSTRA\JAP**, open the **Control Panel**, and navigate to the **Configuration Manager** icon in the **System and Security** category.
4. In **Configuration Manager Properties**, select the **Actions** tab, select **Machine Policy Retrieval & Evaluation Cycle**, and click **Run Now**.
5. From the **Start menu**, launch **Software Center**.
6. In the **Software Center**, click **Show Operating System**, select **Windows 8 Enterprise Eng x64**, and click **INSTALL**. In the warning message, click **INSTALL OPERATING SYSTEM**.

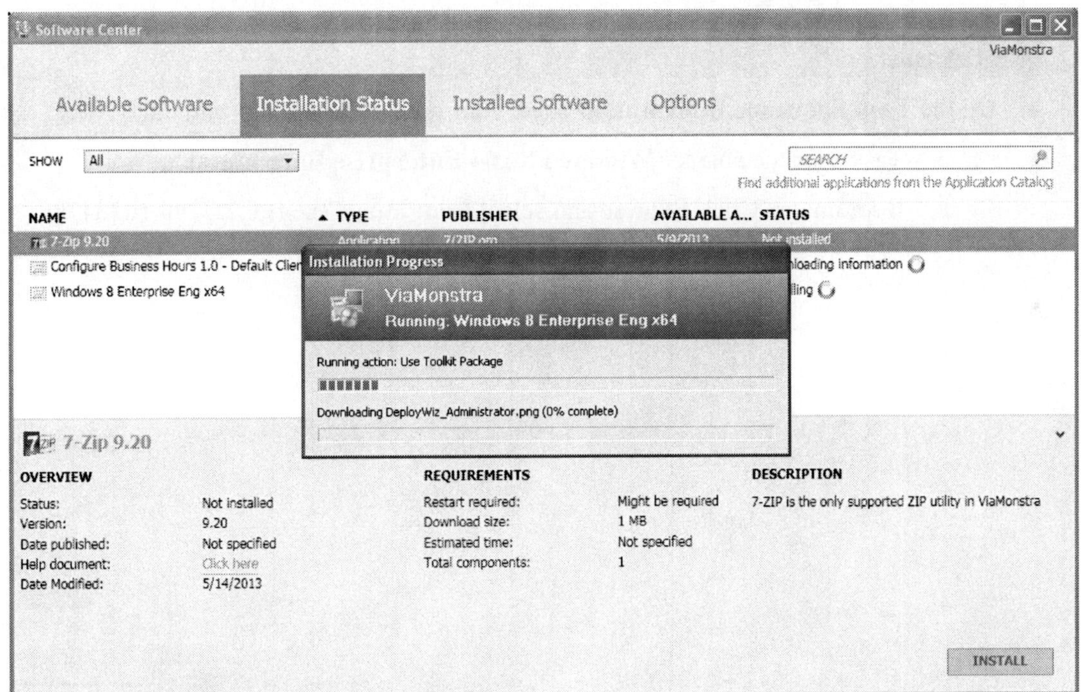

Starting the refresh of Windows 7 to Windows 8.

7. After you select **INSTALL OPERATING SYSTEM**, the task sequence starts and prepares the installation of Windows 8.

After the deployment is finished, notice that the documents on the desktop were preserved during the update to Windows 8. The User State Migration Toolkit and the earlier configured state migration point took care of this.

Bare Metal Deployment

When a new workstation comes out of the box, you want to be sure that it receives the corporate Windows 8 image without too much administrative effort. ConfigMgr supports bare metal deployment by enabling you to add a resource record for a new machine manually or by using the Unknown Computer support. You can use the existing MDT task sequence to perform a bare metal deployment or create a new task sequence. For the fun of it, create a new ConfigMgr task sequence so that you can compare the MDT task sequence with a native ConfigMgr task sequence. You will not use this task sequence in the other guides.

Create a Configuration Manager Deploy Task Sequence

1. In the **Software Library** workspace, select **Operating Systems / Task Sequences / Deploy Production**.
2. On the ribbon's **Home** tab, click **Create Task Sequence**.
3. On the **Create New Task Sequence** page, select **Install an existing image package** and click **Next**.
4. On the **Task Sequence Information** page, configure these settings and click **Next**:
    a. Task sequence name: **Windows 8 x64 Enterprise Bare Metal**
    b. Boot image: Click **Browse** and select **Boot image (x64) 6.2.9200.16384 en**.

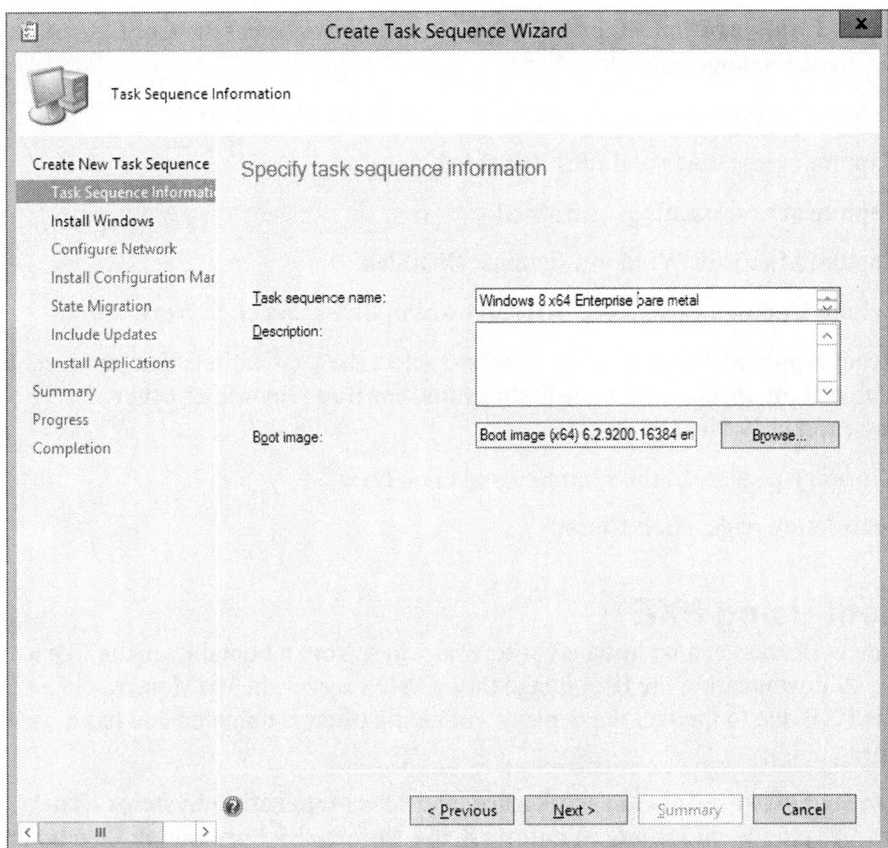

Creating the bare metal task sequence.

5. On the **Install Windows** page, configure these settings and click **Next**:
   a. Image package: Click **Browse** and select the **Deploy Production / Windows 8 x64 Enterprise** image.
   b. Deselect **Configure task sequence for use with Bitlocker**.
   c. Select **Enable the account and specify the local administrator password**, and assign **Password01** as the password.
6. On the **Configure Network** page, configure these settings and click **Next**:
   a. Join a domain: **corp.viamonstra.com**
   b. Domain OU: **LDAP://OU=Workstations,OU=ViaMonstra,DC=corp, DC=viamonstra,DC=com**
   c. Account: **VIAMONSTRA\CM_JD** with **Password01** as password. Click **Verify** and then **Test connection**.

7. On the **Install Configuration Manager** page, click **Browse**, select the **Configuration Manager Client Package**, and click **Next**.
8. On the **State Migration** page, configure these settings and click **Next**:
   a. Capture user settings and files: **Disabled**
   b. Capture network settings: **Disabled**
   c. Capture Microsoft Windows settings: **Disabled**
9. On the **Include Updates** page, select **All software updates** and click **Next**.
10. On the **Install Application** page, click **New** and select the applications that you want to install. Enable **If an application installation fails, continue installing other applications** and click **Next**.
11. On the **Summary** page, read the summary and click **Next**.
12. On the **Completion** page, click **Close**.

Deploy a Client Using PXE

The image deployment process can be initiated in several ways, from a bootable media like a DVD, CD, USB or by downloading the boot image thru a WDS server. In ViaMonstra our preferred method is PXE due to the fact the deployment media often is outdated and has a tendency to disappear.

1. Navigate to the **Software Library** workspace, and select **Operating Systems / Task Sequences / Deploy Production / Windows 8 x64 Enterprise bare metal**; then on the ribbon, click **Deploy**.
2. On the **General** page, configure this setting and click **Next**:

   Collection: Click **Browse**, select the **All Unknown computers** collection, and click **OK**.
3. On the **Deployment Settings** page, configure these settings and click **Next**:
   a. Purpose: **Available**
   b. Make available to the following: **Only media and PXE**.

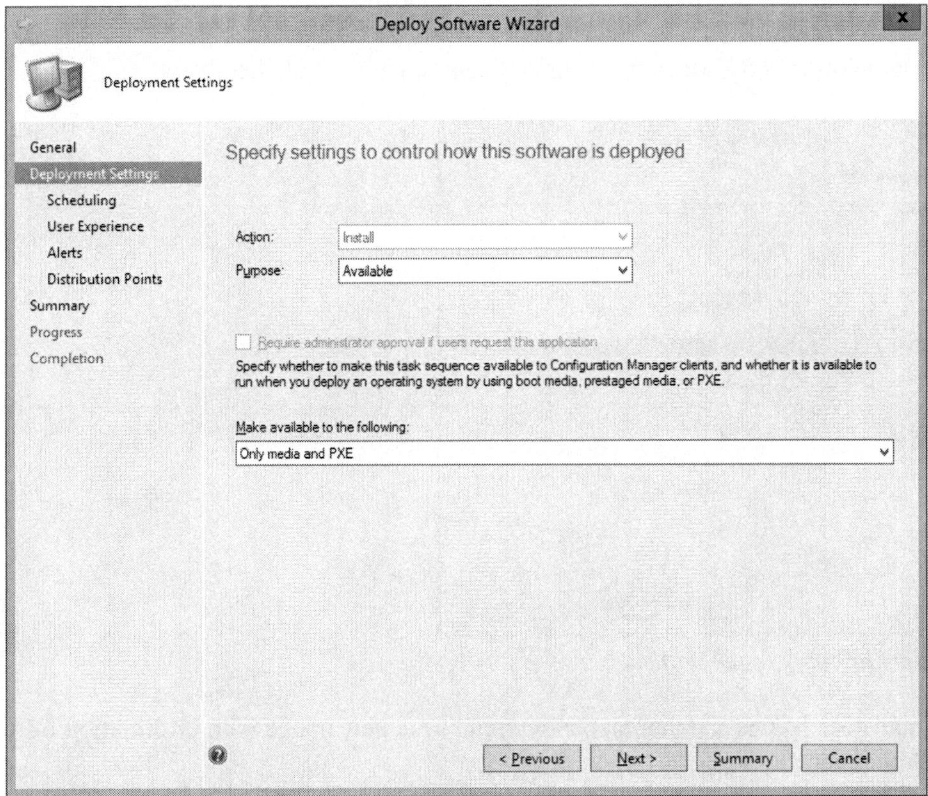

Creating an available deployment task sequence.

4. On the **Scheduling** page, keep the default settings and click **Next**.
5. On the **User Experience** page, keep the default settings and click **Next**.
6. On the **Alerts** page, configure the threshold for a failed deployment failure to **1%** and click **Next**.
7. On the **Distribution Points** page, keep the default settings and click **Next**.
8. On the **Summary** page, read the summary and click **Next**.
9. On the **Completion** page, click **Close**.

Deploy the Bare Metal Client

Before you can start deploying the client, you need to create a new virtual machine named PC0003. (Use the same configuration as when you created the virtual machine for the reference image earlier in this chapter.)

1. Create a new virtual machine named **PC0003** and start it.
2. Start the PXE deployment process by pressing **F12** during the **PC0003** virtual machine startup.

3. In the **Welcome to the Task Sequence** wizard, type **Password01** and click **Next**.
4. Select the **Windows 8 Enterprise Eng x64** task sequence and click **Next**.

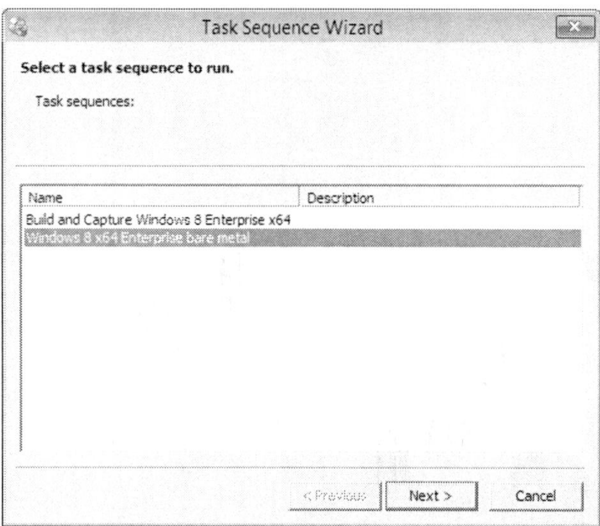

Selecting the bare metal task sequence.

The installation begins and automatically applies the new image with information from the task sequence.

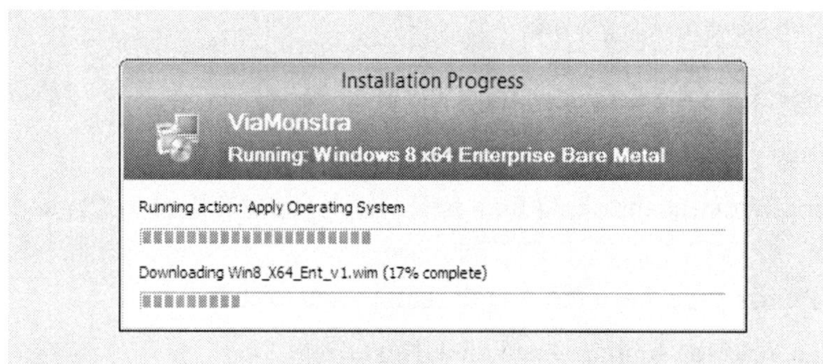

Downloading the custom WIM file.

Import Computer Information

Another way of deploying bare metal computers is to import information about the new computers into ConfigMgr. You can do this with the following procedure:

1. In the **Assets and Compliance** workspace, Expand **Device Collections** and select the **Operating System Deployment** folder.
2. On the ribbon, click **Create Device Collection**.

3. On the **General** page, configure these settings and click **Next**:
    a. Name: **OSD Bare Metal**
    b. Comment: **Computers added to this collection will be able to start a bare metal deployment**
    c. Limiting Collection: **All Systems**
4. Finish the wizard using the default settings. (Accept the warning about having no members in the collection.)
5. In the **Assets and Compliance** workspace, select **Devices**.
6. On the ribbon, click **Import Computer Information**.
7. On the **Select Source** page, select **Import single computer** and click **Next**.
8. On the **Single Computer** page, configure these settings and click **Next**:
    a. Computer name: **PC0004**
    b. MAC Address: 00:00:00:00:00:00 (Type the actual MAC Address. You can see the MAC Address when performing a PXE boot.)

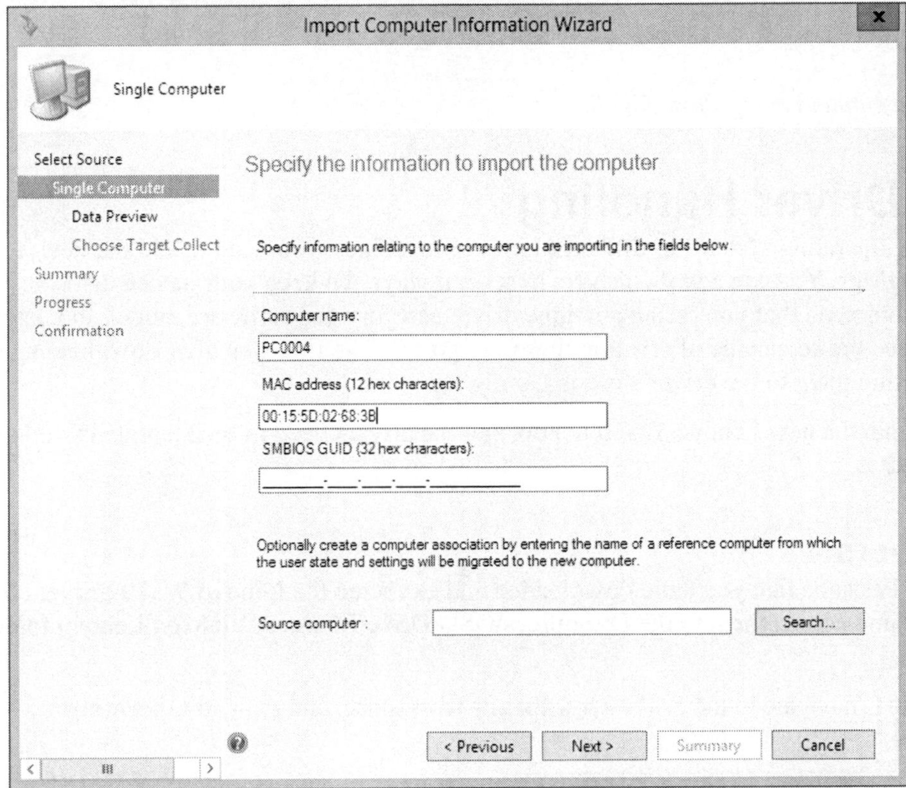

Importing a computer.

9. On the **Data Preview** page, confirm the information and click **Next**.
10. On the **Choose Target Collection** page, configure this setting and click **Next**:
11. Add computers to the following collection: Click **Browse** and in the **Operating System Deployment** folder, select the **OSD Bare Metal** collection.
12. On the **Summary** page, read the summary and click **Next**.
13. On the **Completion** page, click **Close**.

Automate Importing Computers Using PowerShell

In this example, you import a new computer object into the OSD Bare Metal collection:

1. Launch **PowerShell** from the **ConfigMgr console**.
2. Type the following command:

```
Import-CMComputerInformation -ComputerName PC0005
-MacAddress "00:15:5D:02:68:00" -CollectionName "OSD Bare
metal"
```

Importing computers using PowerShell.

Device Driver Handling

When deploying operating systems to different kinds of machines, you need to add the device drivers to ConfigMgr. You can add the drivers in several ways. To keep your device drivers structured, I recommend that you create a unique driver category per hardware model. In a later stage, you will see the advantage of creating these categories. The first step after downloading the drivers is importing them to the driver store in ConfigMgr.

ViaMonstra acquired a new Lenovo W510 laptop, and the drivers need to be integrated within the deployment process.

Import Drivers

In this example I assume that you have downloaded and extracted the Lenovo W510 drirvers for Windows 8 x64 and copied them to the D:\Sources\OSD\DriverSources\Win8x64\Lenovo folder on CM01.

1. On **CM01**, navigate to the **Software Library** workspace, and expand **Operating Systems**.
2. Right-click **Drivers** and click **Folder / Create Folder**.
3. Name the folder **Windows 8 x64**.

4. Right-click the root of the **Drivers** node and select **Import Driver**.
5. On the **Locate Driver** page, configure this setting and click **Next**:

   In **Source folder**, type **\\cm01\sources$\OSD\DriverSources\Win8x64\Lenovo**.

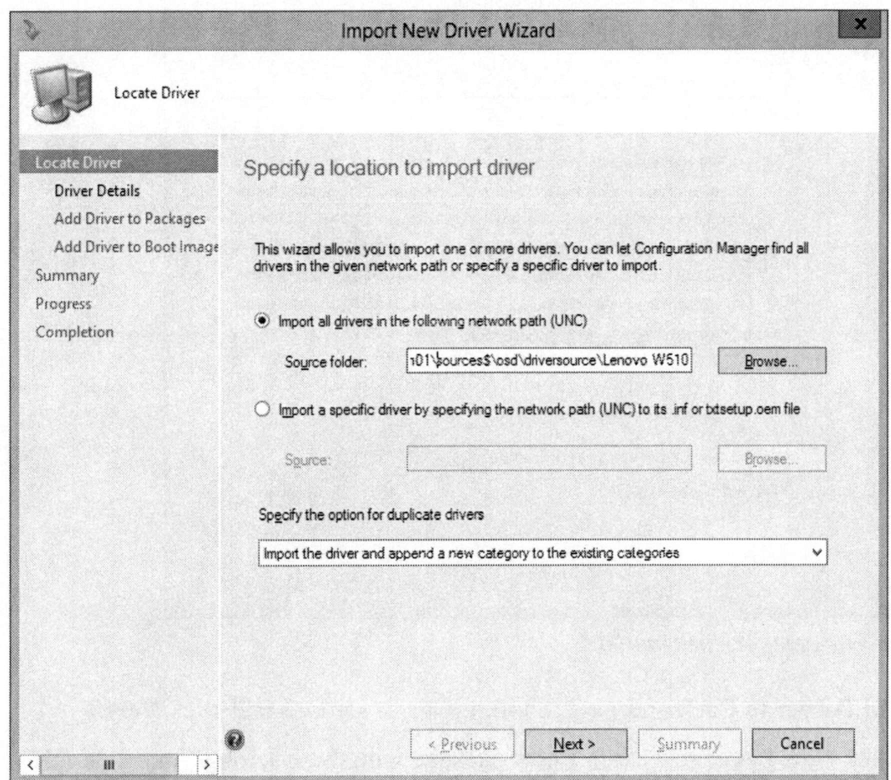

Specifying the source driver source location.

6. On the **Driver details** page, configure this setting and click **Next**:

   Click **Categories**, click **Create**, and create a category called **Windows 8 x64 Lenovo W510**; then click **OK** twice.

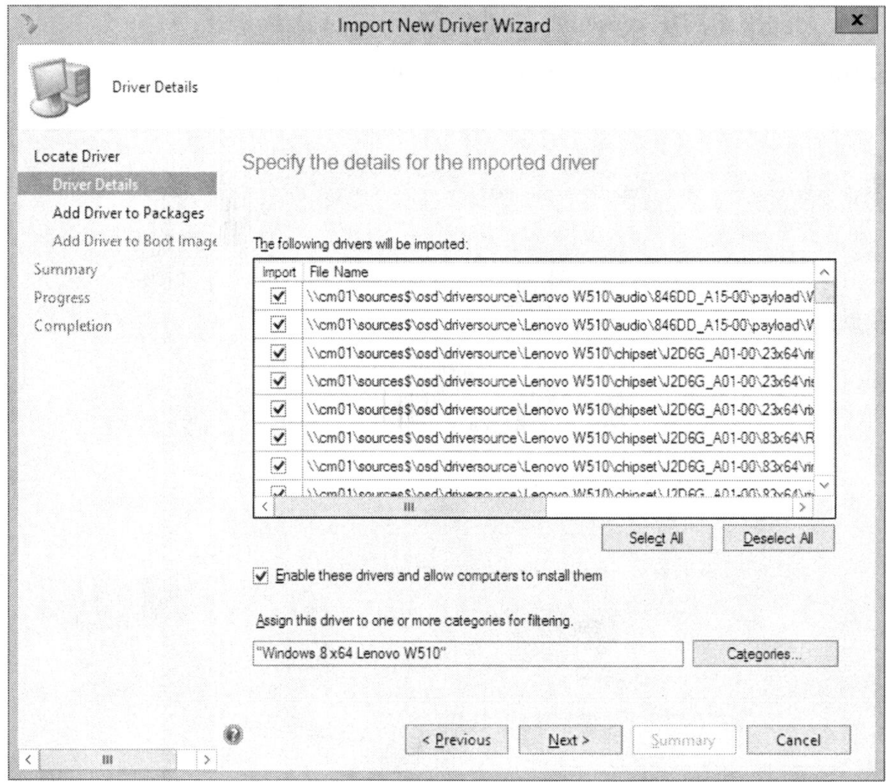

Assigning a unique category per model.

7. On the **Add Driver to Packages** page, configure these settings and click **Next**:

    Click **New Package**. Create a new package with these settings and click **OK**.

    i. Name: **Windows 8 x64 Lenovo W510**

    ii. Path: **\\cm01\sources$\OSD\DriverPackages\Win8x64\Lenovo\W510**

8. On the **Add Driver to Boot Images** page, leave the defaults and click **Next**.
9. On the **Summary** page, read the summary and click **Next**.
10. On the **Completion** page, click **Close**.
11. After the drivers are imported, you will find them in the **Drivers** root and not the folder you created. Select all the drivers with the category **Windows 8 x64 Lenovo W510**; on the ribbon, click **Move**; and then move them to the **Windows 8 x64** folder.

Deploy the Driver Package

You now need to deploy the new driver package to the distribution points within your environment:

1. Select **Drivers Packages**. You should see the newly created **Windows 8 Lenovo x64 W510** driver package.
2. Select the driver package, and on the ribbon, click **Distribute Content**.
3. Distribute the package to the **All Content** distribution point group.

Modify the Task Sequence to Include Driver Packages

When deploying device drivers as part of the operating system deployment process, you are able to do that in several different ways. The standard MDT task sequence, like the one you created earlier, comes with an Auto Apply Drivers task. This task lets the PnP process within WinPE determine which drivers from the driver store must be installed. This method works but also can determine the wrong driver for a specific device, even if you configure the task to use the created category.

A better way of implementing drivers in your deployment process is to use the Apply Driver Package task in the task sequence. You need to configure the task to run only when the specific hardware needs that driver package. You can do this by adding a WMI query to the task.

The following steps show you how to configure the task:

1. In the **Software Library**, select **Operating Systems / Task Sequences / Deploy Production**.
2. Right-click **Windows 8 Enterprise Eng x64** and select **Edit**.
3. Navigate to the **Post Install** group. Right-click **Auto Apply drivers** and select **Delete**.
4. Click **Yes** to delete the step.
5. From the menu, select **Add / Drivers / Apply Driver Package**.
6. In **Name**, type **Apply Driver Package Lenovo W510**.
7. For **Driver Package**, click **Browse** and select the **Windows 8 x64 Lenovo W510** driver package.

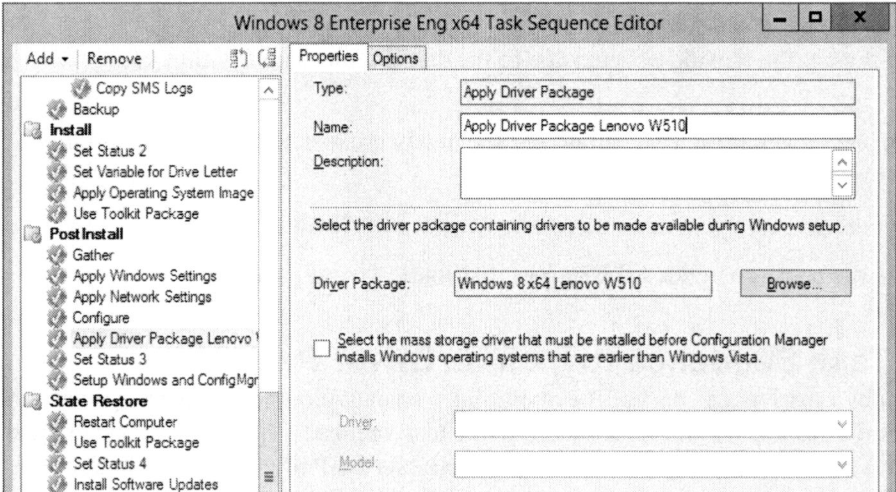

Applying a driver package.

8. Select the **Options** tab, click **Add Condition** and select **Query WMI**.
9. In **WQL Query**, type the following:

   SELECT * FROM Win32_ComputerSystem WHERE Model LIKE "4319%"

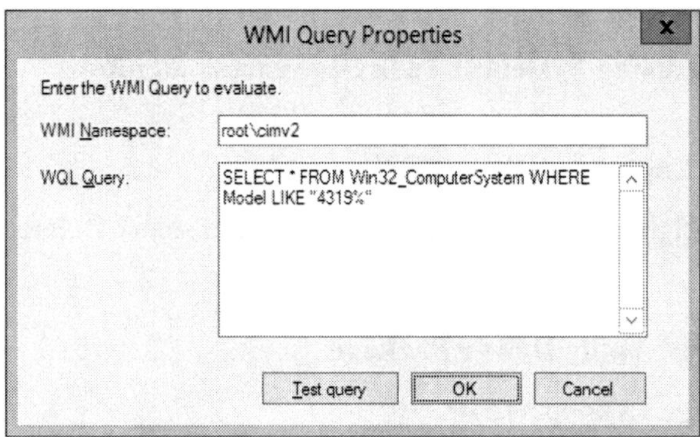

Configuring the task sequence with the WMI query.

10. Click **OK** to close and save the task sequence.

Note: You can get the model number in many ways. One is opening a command prompt and typing **wmic computersystem get model** on the target computer.

Maintaining a WIM Image

After creating a custom WIM image, you definitely need to have a strategy for how often you want to update the reference image. ConfigMgr allows you deploy software updates to the WIM image directly from the console. To keep your deployment process quick and the golden image safe from security breaches, you should service your WIM image offline at least four times a year with security updates. Waiting longer extends the deployment process because the approved software updates will have to be installed during this process.

1. In the **Software Library** workspace, select **Operating Systems / Operating System Images**.
2. In **Deploy Production**, select **Windows 8 Enterprise x64**, and on the ribbon, click **Schedule Updates.**
3. On the **Choose Updates** page, select the updates you want to inject into the image and click **Next**.

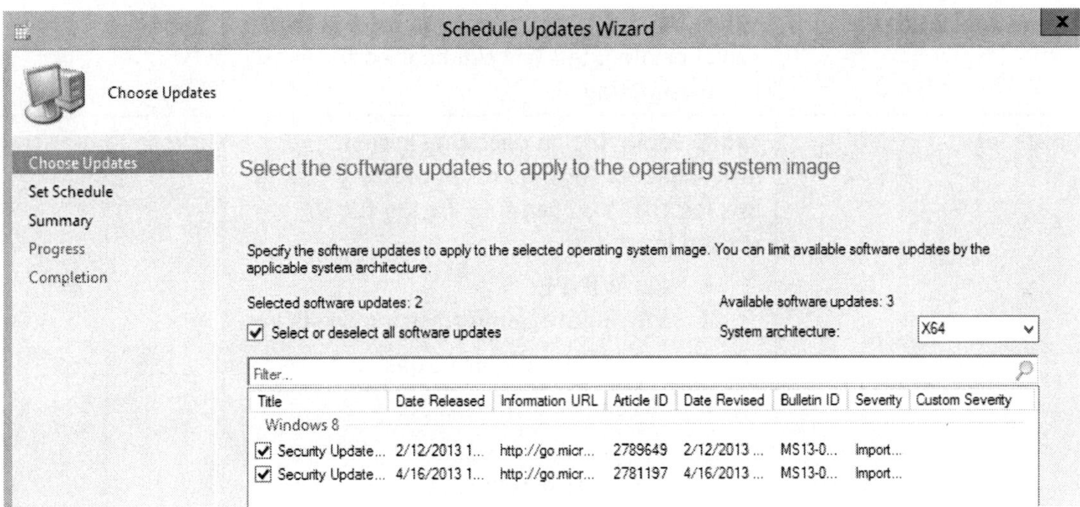

Selecting the updates that need to be injected.

4. On the **Set Schedule** page, configure a schedule or select **As soon as possible** and click **Next.**
5. In the **Update Operating System Image** window, select the updates and click **Next.**
6. On the **Summary** page, read the summary and click **Next.**
7. On the **Completion** page, click **Close.**

Note: To monitor the updates to be installed and those that are installed, open the image properties and check the Servicing tab for those that are to be installed and the Installed Updates tab for those that already are installed in the image.

Useful Log Files

You can use the log files in the following table to track the OS deployment activity.

Log File	Description	Location
OSDImageproperties.log	This log file records activity about maintaining the boot images.	Server
OfflineServicingMgr.log	When you service your WIM images offline, this log file tells you everything about the offline servicing process and helps you to troubleshoot the process.	Server
Smspxe.log	This log file provides information about the PXE role on the Configuration Manager distribution point.	Server
Drivercatalog.log	When importing or updating drivers in the driver catalog, this file can be used for troubleshooting.	Server
Smsts.log	While deploying an operating system, the task sequence logs the result of every task in this log file. You can find the log file in several locations: • On WINPE: x:\windows\temp\smstslog\smsts.log • <CCM Install Dir>\Logs • %Temp%\SMSTSLOG • <largest fixed partition> _SMSTaskSequence • %Windir%\System32\Ccm\Logs • %Windir%\SysWOW64\Ccm\Logs • <largest fixed partition> \SMSTSLOG	Client
setupact.log	This Windows Installation log file is useful for troubleshooting installation failures.	Client C:\Windows\panther

Chapter 11

Compliance Settings

The ConfigMgr 2012 compliance settings feature is an updated version of ConfigMgr 2007's Desired Configuration Management. The compliance settings feature allows you to run a check on your clients against a set of rules. Those rules are called configuration items (CIs) that are grouped together in a configuration baseline. You can easily create your own CIs and baselines, or you can download preconfigured configuration packs from http://tinyurl.com/c7rlc34.

There is a wealth of different configuration packs ranging from Microsoft best practice for securing your environment to regulations configuration packs from organizations like SOX.

Configuration Items

A CI is a rule containing one or more checks that are evaluated by the client. A CI contains a setting type and a set of compliance rules. In the setting type, you define what setting you want to check and the compliance rules determine what happens if the client reports noncompliance. For some of the settings, you are able to remediate the settings automatically. You can create different CIs for your mobile devices: "normal" Windows devices and Mac OS devices.

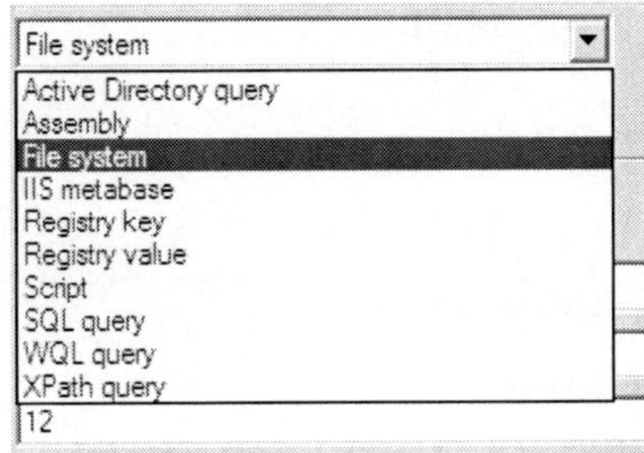

A list of the available setting types in a Windows CI.

Note: Auto-remediate only works for these setting types: Script, Registry and WMI.

Baselines

A baseline is a collection of CIs that you deploy to a user or device collection. The baseline can be deployed as "monitor only," or you can enable remediation. If you enable remediation, then all CIs configured for automatic remediation automatically remediate the compliance setting from noncompliant to compliant.

Creating CIs and Baselines

In ViaMonstra, you won't allow servers to run the automatic ConfigMgr client remediation, but you still want the client to upload client health information. To achieve that, you can either use the command line notifyonly=true when installing the client, or modify this registry value HKLM\Software\Microsoft\CCM\Ccmeval\NotifyOnly from False to True.

Create a Device CI

1. On **CM01**, in the **Assets and Compliance** workspace of the **ConfigMgr console**, select **Compliance Settings / Configuration Items**.
2. Right-click **Configuration Items**, and select **Folder / Create Folder**.
3. Type **Server Compliance** as the folder name and click **OK**.
4. Expand **Configuration Items**, select the **Server Compliance** folder, and on the ribbon, click **Create Configuration Item**.
5. On the **General** page, configure these settings and click **Next**:
    a. Name: **Disable automatic client remediation**
    b. Categories: Click **Categories**, select **Server**, and click **OK**.
6. On the **Supported Platforms** page, click **Next**.
7. On the **Settings** page, click **New** and configure these values:
    a. Name: **Disable automatic client remediation**
    b. Setting type: **Registry value**
    c. Data type: **String**
    d. Hive: Click **Browse** and complete the following settings:
        i. Computer name: Type **DC01** and click **Connect**.
        ii. Select **DC01**, navigate to **HKEY_LOCAL_MACHINE / SOFTWARE / Microsoft / CCM / CcmEval**, and select the **NotifyOnly** key.
        iii. Select **The registry value must exist on the client device.**
        iv. Select **The registry value must satisfy the following rule if present** and set it for **Equals TRUE**.
        v. Click **OK**.

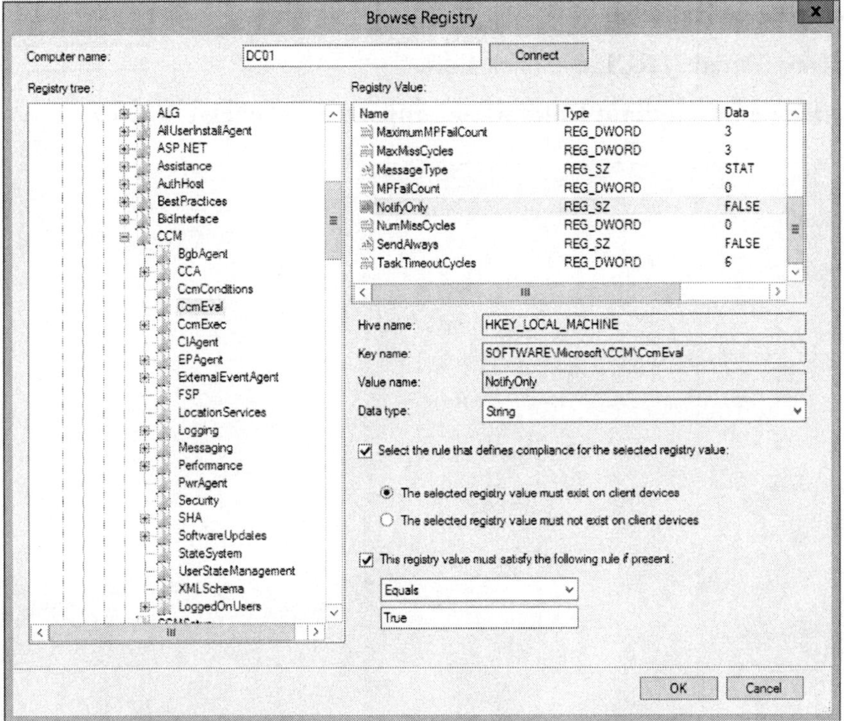

Selecting the registry key.

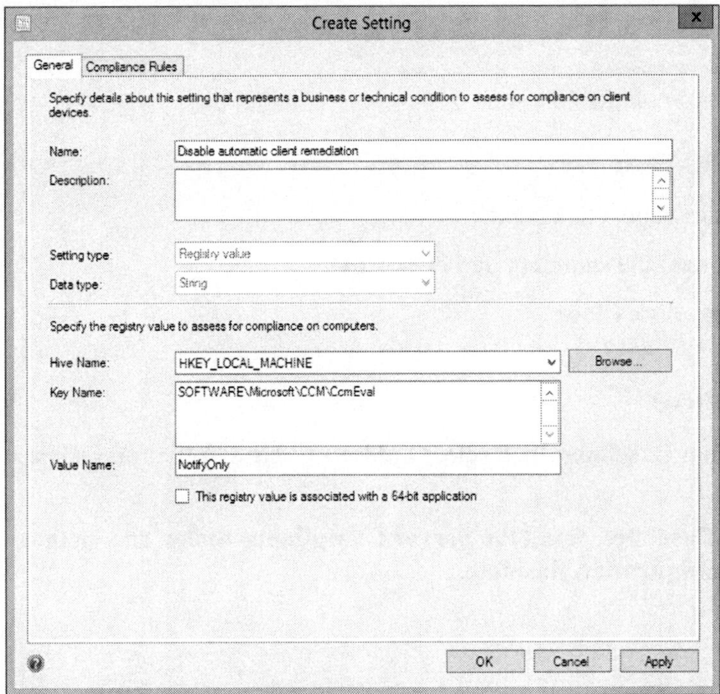

The final registry settings.

8. Select the **Compliance Rules** tab.
9. Select **NotifyOnly Equals TRUE** and click **Edit**.
10. Enable **Remediate noncompliant Rules when supported** and click **OK** twice.

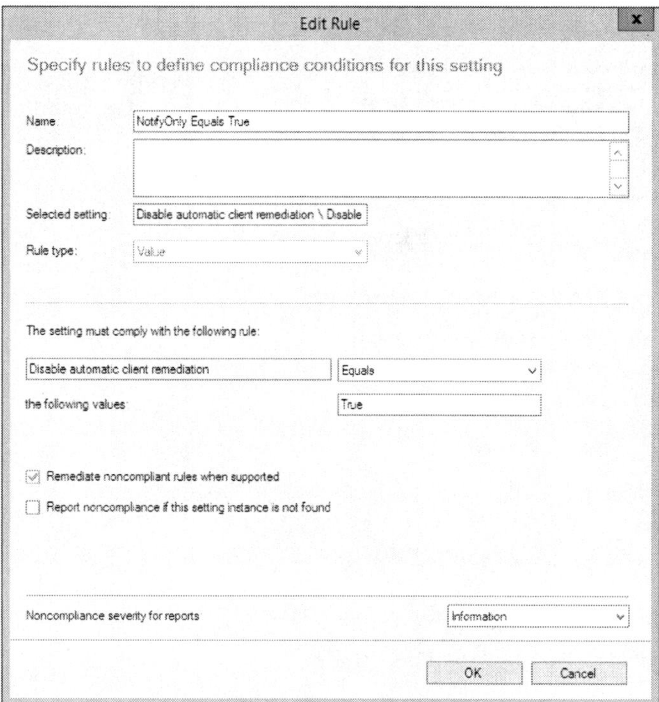

Enabling automatic remediation on the CI.

11. On the **Settings** page, click **Next**.
12. On the **Compliance Rules** page, click **Next**.
13. On the **Summary** page, read the summary and click **Next**.
14. On the **Completion** page, click **Close**.

Create a Device Baseline

1. Right-click **Configuration Baselines**; then select **Folder / Create Folder** and name it **Server Compliance**.
2. Expand **Configuration Baselines**, select the **Server Compliance** folder, and on the ribbon, click **Create Configuration Baseline**.

3. Configure a baseline with these settings and click **OK**:
    a. Name: **Server Compliance**
    b. Configuration data: Click **Add / Configuration Items**. Select **Disable automatic client remediation**, and then click **Add** and **OK**.
    c. Click **Categories**, select **Server**, and click **OK** twice.

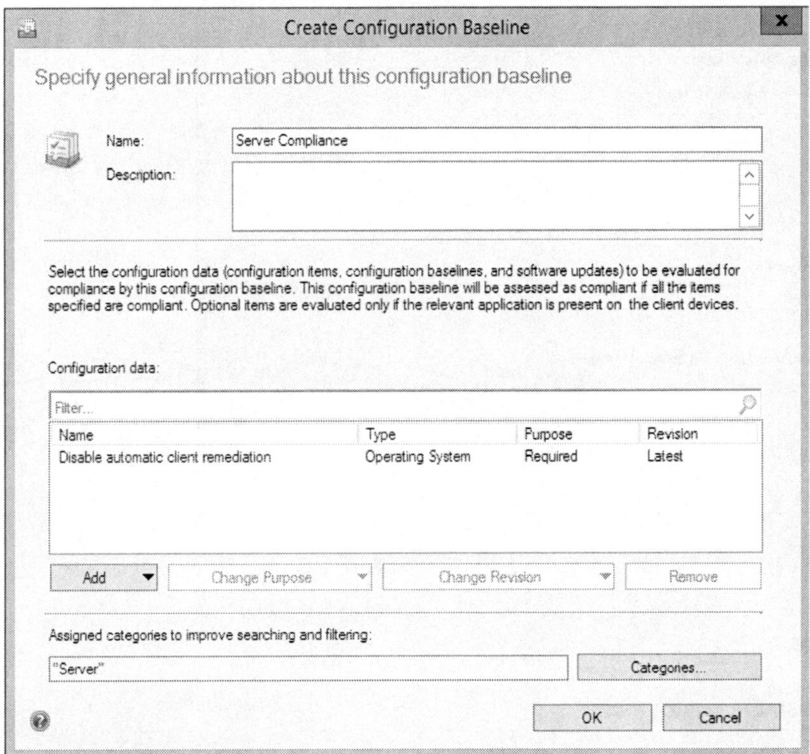

Creating the baseline.

Deploy the Baseline

1. Back in the **ConfigMgr console**, select the newly create **Server Compliance** baseline, and on the ribbon, click **Deploy**.
2. Configure these settings and click **OK**:
    a. Remediate noncompliant rules when supported: **Enabled**
    b. Allow remediation outside the maintenance window: **Enabled**
    c. Generate an alert: **Enabled** and configured for **90%**
3. Click **Browse** and from **Device Collections**, select the **ViaMonstra / VM All Servers** collection.

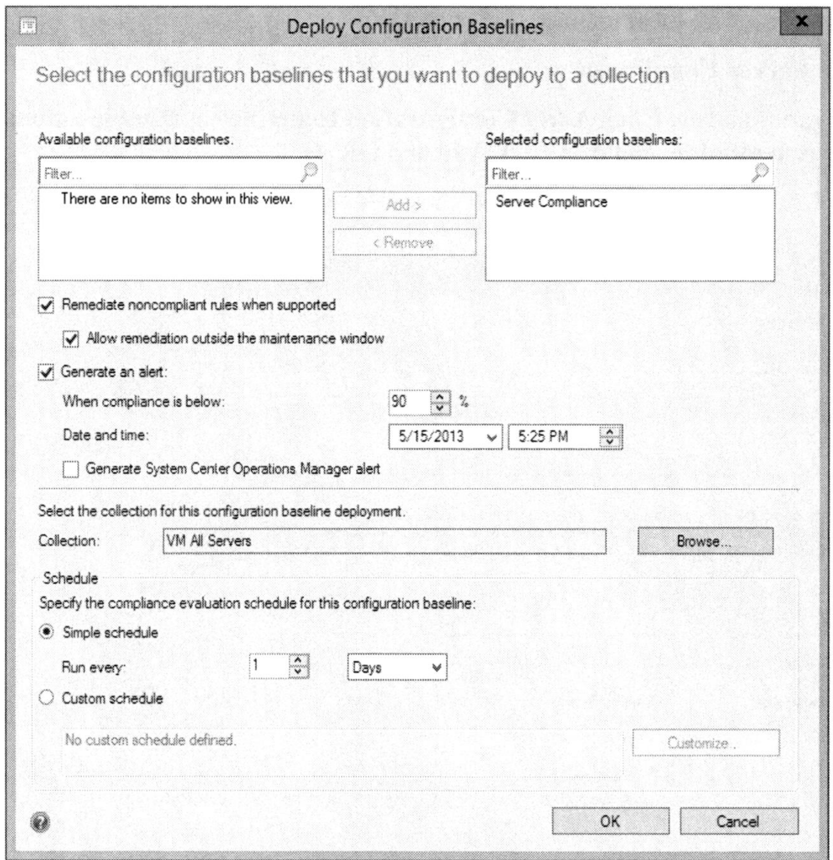

Deploying a baseline.

4. Click **OK** to finish the deployment.

Create a User CI

1. In the **Assets and Compliance** workspace, select **Compliance Settings / Configuration Items**.
2. Right-click **Configuration Items**, and select **Folder / Create Folder**.
3. Type **Desktop Compliance** as the folder name and click **OK**.
4. Select the **Desktop Compliance** folder, and on the ribbon, click **Create Configuration Item**.
5. On the **General** page, configure these settings and click **Next**:
    a. Name: **IE Proxy Enabled**
    b. Categories: Click **Browse**, select **Client**, and click **OK**.

6. On the **Supported Platforms** page, leave all operating systems selected and click **Next**.
7. On the **Settings** page, click **New** and configure these settings:
    a. Name: **IE Proxy Enabled**
    b. Setting type: **Registry value**
    c. Data type: **String**
    d. Click **Browse** and complete the following settings:
        i. Navigate to **My Computer / HKEY_CURRENT_USER / Software / Microsoft / Windows / CurrentVersion / Internet Settings** and select the **ProxyEnable** key.
        ii. Select **This registry value must satisfy the following rule if present** and set it for **Equals 0**.
        iii. Click **OK**.

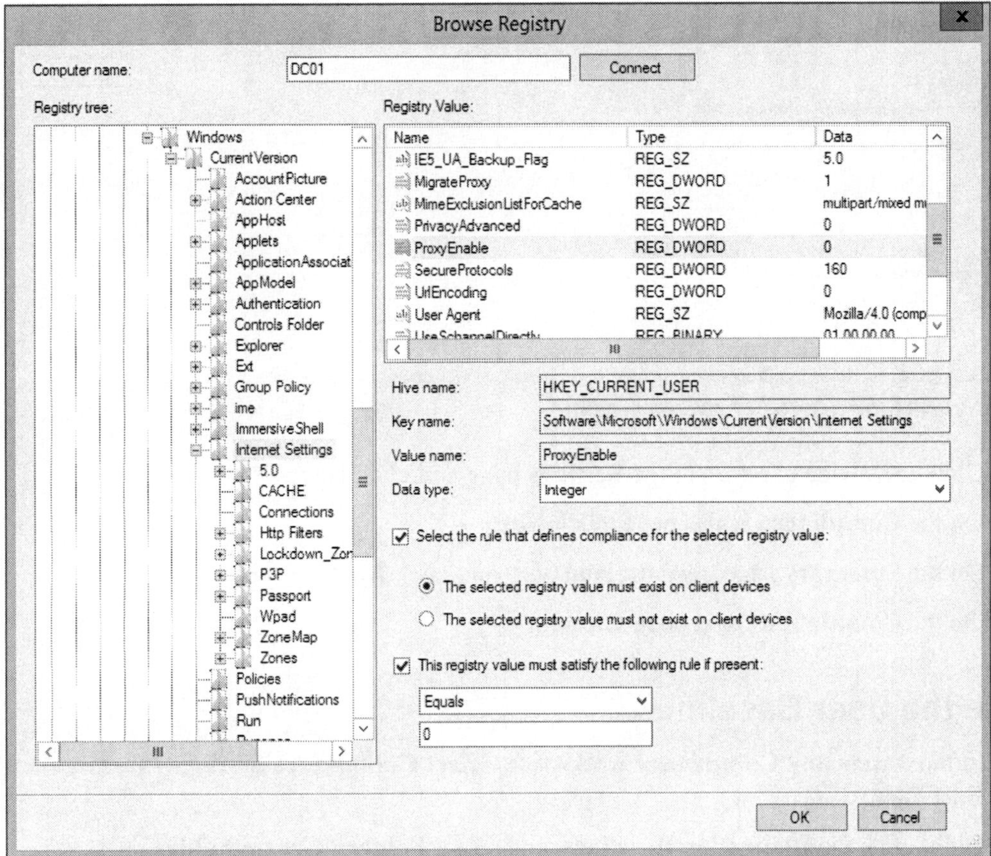

Using a reference machine to create the CI.

8. Select the **Compliance Rules** tab.

9. Select **ProxyEnable Equals 0**, click **Edit**, and configure this setting:

   Remediate noncompliant rules when support: **Enabled**

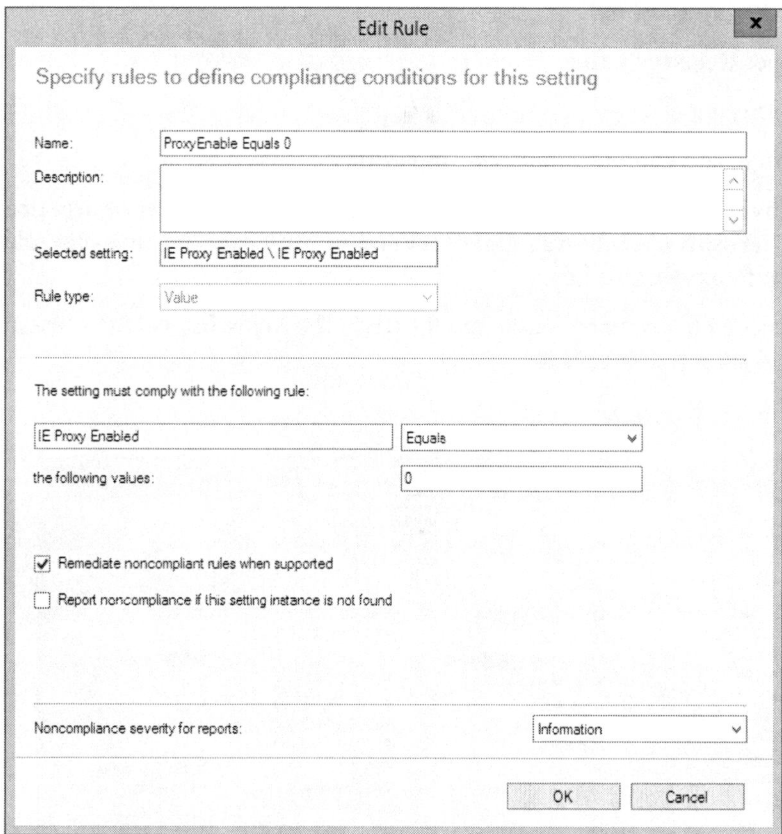

Configuring the user CI to auto-remediate.

10. Click **OK** twice to return to the **Settings** page and click **Next**.
11. On the **Compliance Rules** page, click **Next**.
12. On the **Summary** page, read the summary and click **Next**.
13. On the **Completion** page, click **Close**.

Create the User Baseline

1. In the **Assets and Compliance** workspace, select **Compliance Settings / Configuration Baselines**.
2. Right-click **Configuration Baselines**, and select **Folder / Create Folder**.
3. Type **Desktop Compliance** as the folder name and click **OK**.

4. Select the **Desktop Compliance** folder, and on the ribbon, click **Create Configuration Baseline**.
5. In the **Name** box, type **Desktop Compliance**.
6. Click the **Add** button and select **Configuration Items.**
7. Select the **IE Proxy Enabled** CI, click **Add**, and click **OK**.
8. Click **Add / Software Updates**.
9. In the **Add Software Updates** dialog box, navigate to **Critical Updates / Microsoft / Windows 8**, and select **282241 Update for Windows 8 x64-based Systems (KB282241)**.

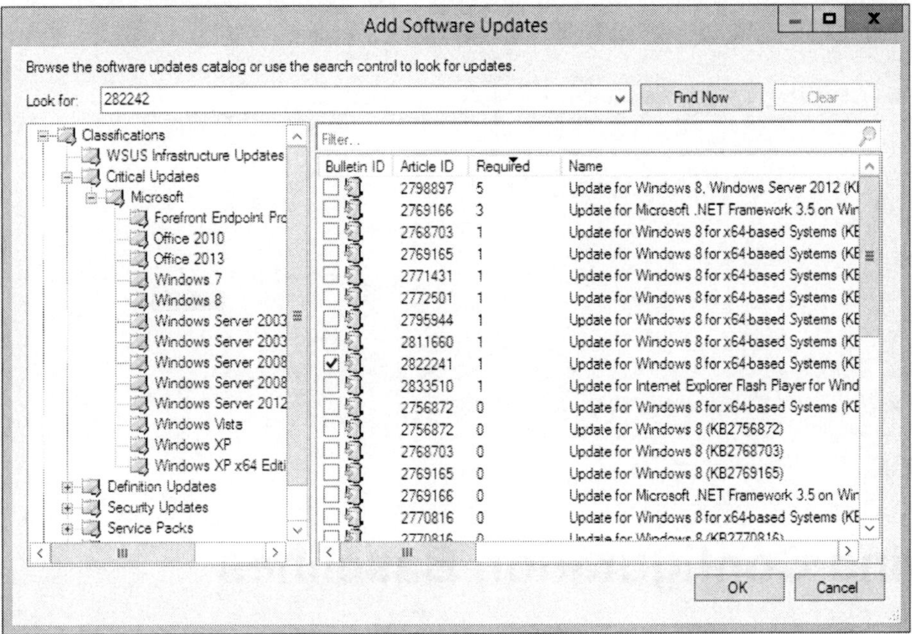

Adding a required update to the baseline.

10. Click **Categories**, select **Client**, and click **OK**.

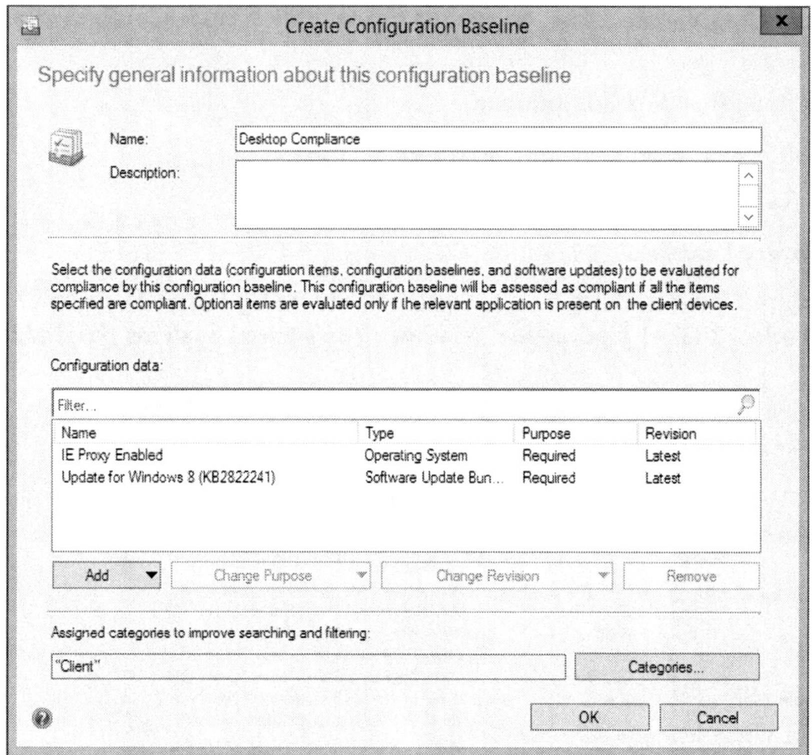

A baseline with a mix of user and computer settings.

11. Click **OK**.

Deploying Configuration Baselines

Deploy the Baseline to Computers

1. In the **Assets and Compliance** workspace, select **Compliance Settings / Configuration Baselines / Desktop Compliance**.
2. Select **Desktop Compliance**, and on the ribbon, click **Deploy**.
3. Configure these settings and click **OK**:
    a. Generate an alert: **Enabled**
    b. When compliance is below: **90 percent**
    c. Collections: From **Device Collections**, select **ViaMonstra / VM All Workstations** and click **OK**.
4. Click **OK**.

Deploy the Baseline to Users

1. In the **Assets and Compliance** workspace, select **Compliance Settings / Configuration Baselines / Desktop Compliance**.
2. Select **Desktop Compliance**, and on the ribbon, click **Deploy**.
3. Configure these settings and click **OK**:
    a. Generate an alert: **Enabled**
    b. When compliance is below: **90 percent**
    c. Collections: From **User Collections**, select **All Users** and click **OK**.
4. Click **OK**.

Generate a Noncompliant Scenario

1. On **PC0001**, log on as **VIAMONSTRA\Administrator**.
2. Open **Internet Explorer**, and from the **Tools** menu, open the **Internet Options**.
3. Select the **Connections** tab and click **LAN settings**.
4. Enable **Use a proxy server for your LAN** and click **OK**.

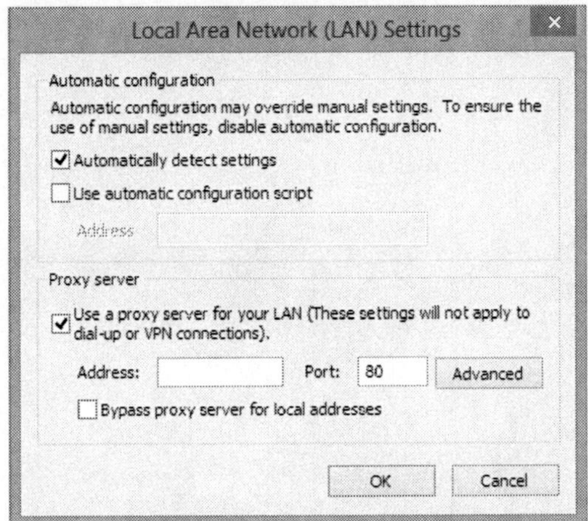

Configuring IE to use a non-valid proxy server.

5. Click **OK** to close the Internet Options.

Verify Baselines

1. On **PC0001** log on as **VIAMONSTRA\Administrator**.
2. From the **Start screen**, open the **Configuration Manager** applet.
3. Select the **Actions** tab, highlight **Machine Policy Retrieval & Evaluation Cycle**, and click **Run Now**.
4. Click **OK** in the message and select the **Configurations** tab.

   If the machine policy has been applied correctly, you will be able to see the Client Policy. Notice that the Compliance state is Unknown, that's because the baseline has not yet been evaluated.
5. Select **Desktop Compliance** and click **Evaluate**.

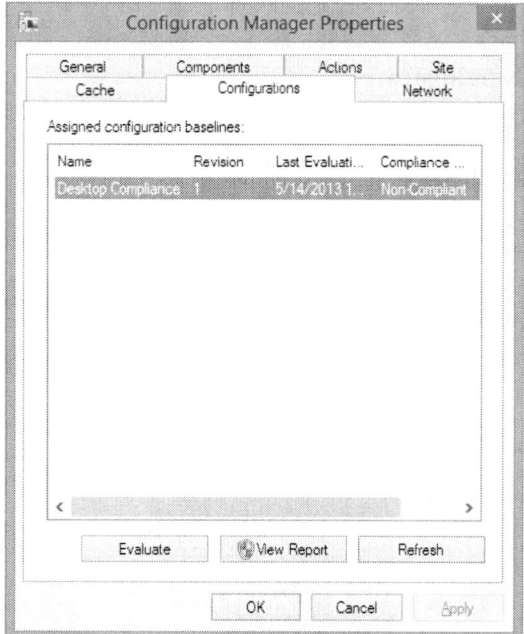

Manually running a compliance evaluation.

6. Click the **View Report** button.
7. From **Summary**, click the **IE Proxy Enabled** link, which takes you to the rule.

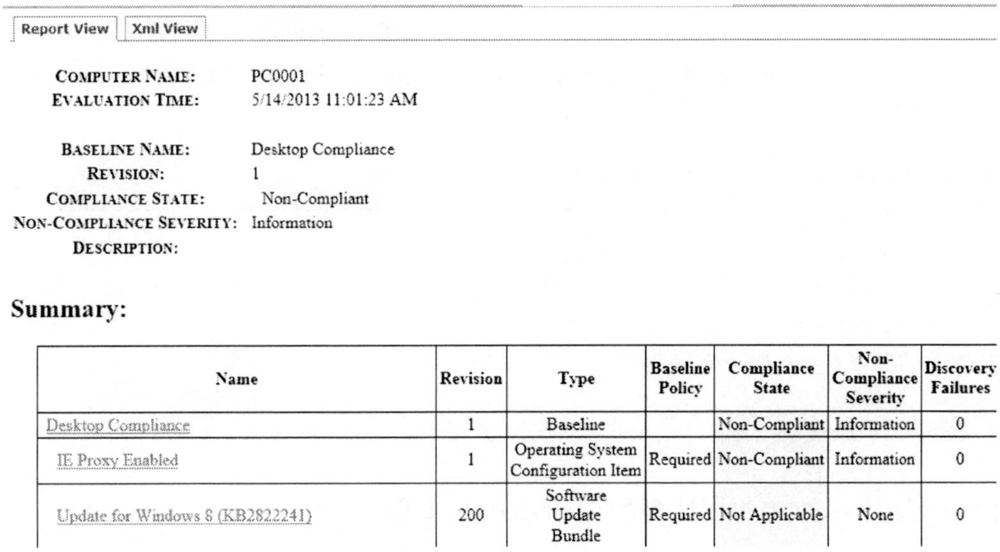

Report View | Xml View

COMPUTER NAME: PC0001
EVALUATION TIME: 5/14/2013 11:01:23 AM

BASELINE NAME: Desktop Compliance
REVISION: 1
COMPLIANCE STATE: Non-Compliant
NON-COMPLIANCE SEVERITY: Information
DESCRIPTION:

Summary:

Name	Revision	Type	Baseline Policy	Compliance State	Non-Compliance Severity	Discovery Failures
Desktop Compliance	1	Baseline		Non-Compliant	Information	0
IE Proxy Enabled	1	Operating System Configuration Item	Required	Non-Compliant	Information	0
Update for Windows 8 (KB2822241)	200	Software Update Bundle	Required	Not Applicable	None	0

The compliance report. Notice that the rule is listed as Non-Compliant.

8. Close the report.

Verify Baselines Using Reporting

1. On **CM01**, log on as **VIAMONSTRA\Administrator** and open the **ConfigMgr console**.
2. In the **Monitoring** workspace, select **Deployments**.
3. In **Search**, type **Desktop Compliance** and press **Enter**. You most likely do not have any compliance information yet.
4. Select both **Desktop Compliance** deployments; then on the ribbon, click **Run Summarization**, and click **OK** in the information dialog.
5. Select **Reporting / Reports**.
6. In the search box, type **summary compliance**.
7. From the list of reports, select **Summary compliance by Configuration baseline**, and then on the ribbon, click **Run**.
8. Click the **Desktop Compliance** baseline link to open the sub report. Notice that the report lists both CIs and a unique compliance level for each CI.

9. Scroll the report to the right until you can see the **Non-Compliant** column.
10. In the **IE Proxy Enabled** row, click the **Non-Compliant** link (4). This opens another sub-report showing all the users that are noncompliant

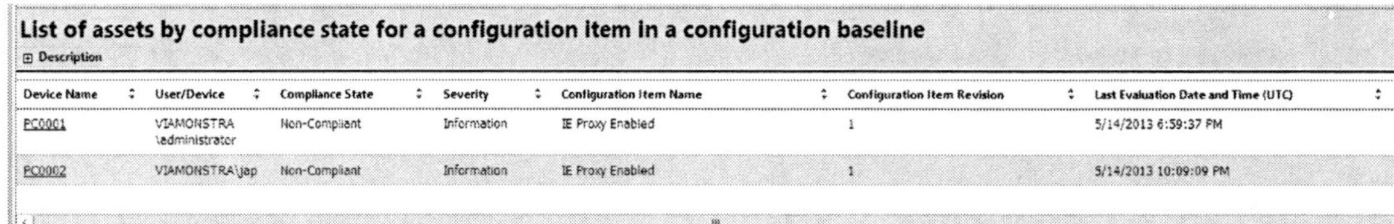

List of assets by compliance state for a configuration item in a configuration baseline
Description
Device Name
User/Device
Compliance State
Severity
Configuration Item Name
Configuration Item Revision
Last Evaluation Date and Time (UTC)
PC0001
VIAMONSTRA \administrator
Non-Compliant
Information
IE Proxy Enabled
1
5/14/2013 6:59:37 PM
PC0002
VIAMONSTRA\jap
Non-Compliant
Information
IE Proxy Enabled
1
5/14/2013 10:09:09 PM

Showing a list of noncompliant users.

11. Close the reports.

Create a Collection with Noncompliant Objects

1. In the **Assets and Compliance** workspace, select **Compliance Settings / Configuration Baselines / Desktop Compliance**.
2. Select **Desktop Compliance** and click **Deployments**.
3. Select the **All Users** deployment, and from the ribbon, click **Create New Collection / Non-compliant**.

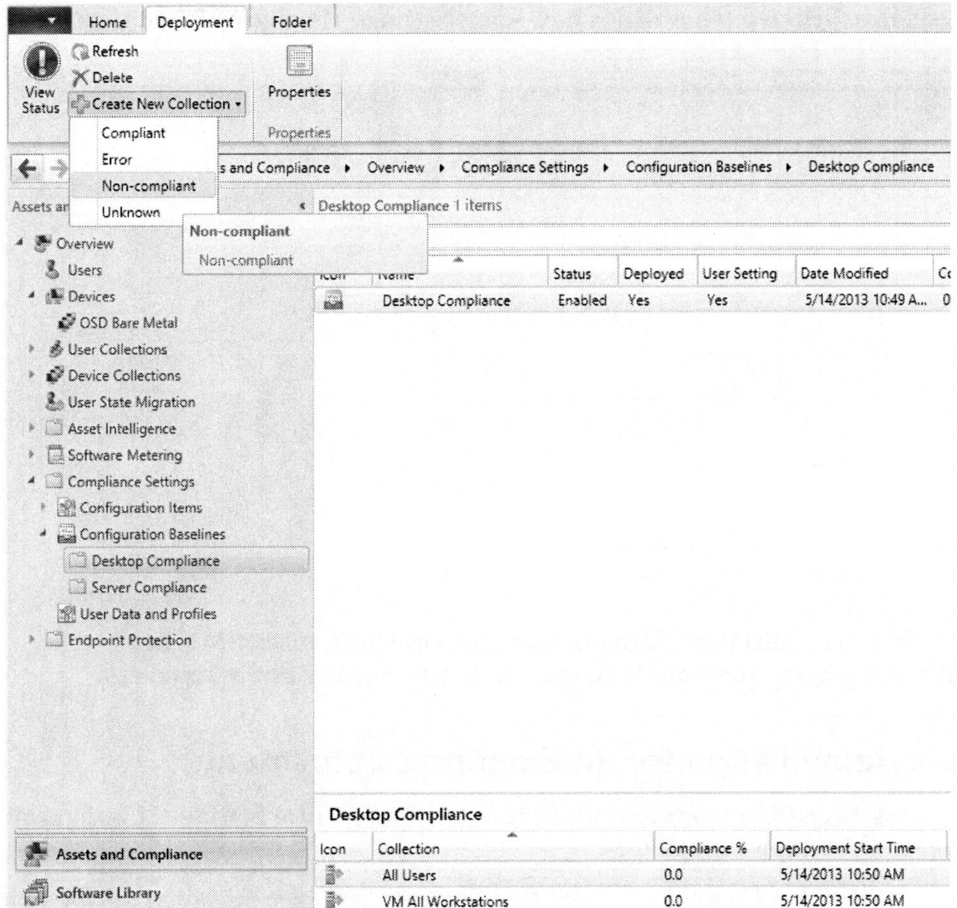

Creating a dynamic collection containing noncompliant users.

4. On the **General** page, configure this setting and click **Next**:

   Name: Add a **SM** prefix to the default name. That way you have a unique prefix for the compliance settings collections.

5. On the **Membership Rules** page, configure this setting and click **Next**:

   Use incremental updates for this collection: **Enabled**

6. On the **Summary** page, read the summary and click **Next**.
7. On the **Completion** page, click **Close**.
8. Select **User Collections**, right-click the new **SM Client Policy_All Users_Noncompliant** collection and select **Move**.

9. In the **Move Selected Items** dialog box, select **Settings Management** and click **OK**.

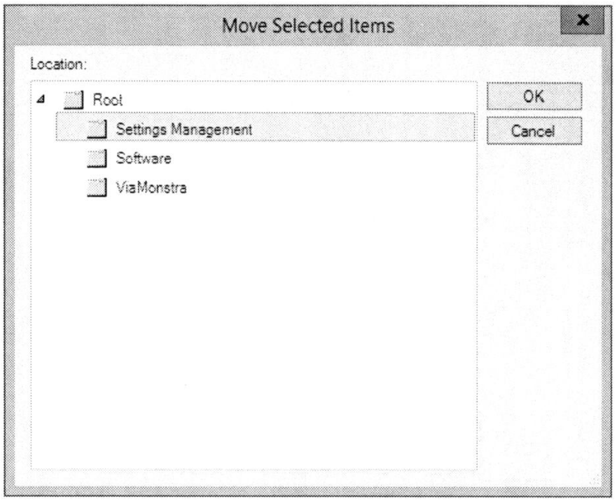

Moving a collection.

10. From the **User Collection / Settings Management** folder, select **SM Client Policy_All_Users_Noncompliant**; then on the ribbon, click **Show Members**.

Configure Remediation for an Existing Deployment

1. In the **Assets and Compliance** workspace, select **Compliance Settings / Configuration Baselines / Desktop Compliance**.
2. Select the **Desktop Compliance**, click **Deployments**, and open the properties for the **All Users** deployment.
3. Configure these settings and click **OK**:
    a. Remediate noncompliant rules when supported: **Enabled**
    b. Allow remediation outside of the maintenance window: **Enabled**

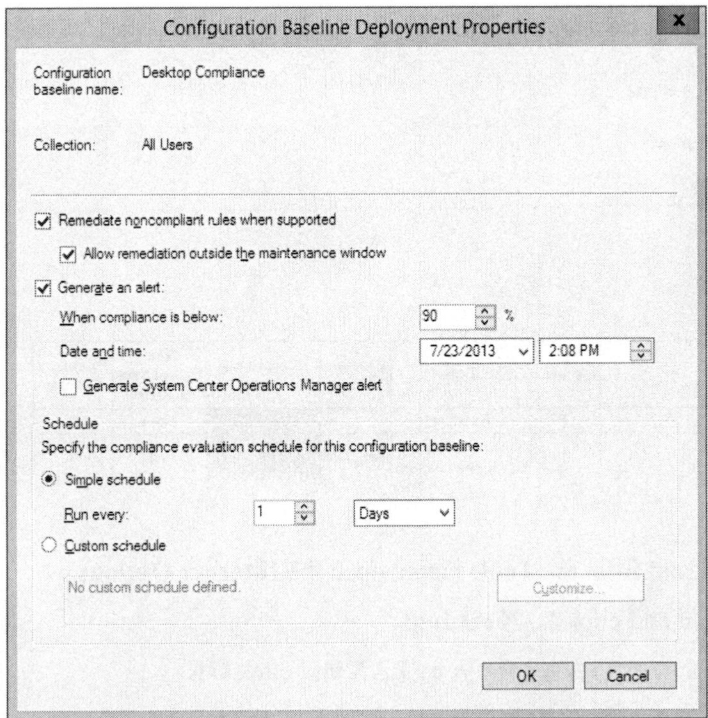

Enabling remediation on an existing deployment.

Remediate a Noncompliant User

1. On **PC0001**, log on as **VIAMONSTRA\Administrator**.
2. Perform a **Machine policy refresh** and a **User policy refresh** from the **Configuration Manager** client agent on the **Start screen**.
3. Select the **Configuration** tab and click **Evaluate**. The Compliance State should change from **Non-Compliant** to **Compliant**.
4. Click **View Report** and notice that the user is now compliant. The computer has been compliant all along.

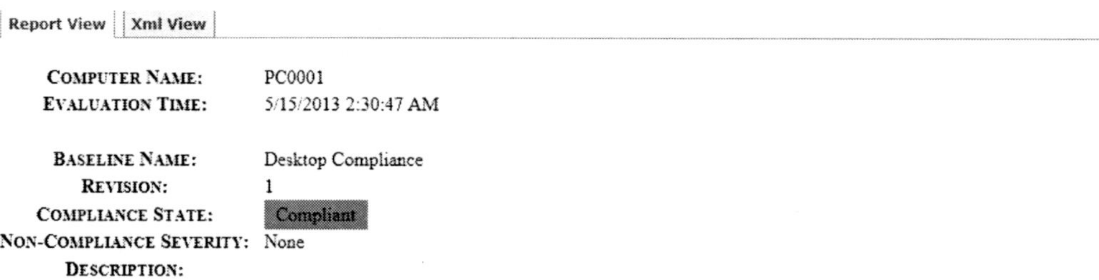

Report View | Xml View

COMPUTER NAME: PC0001
EVALUATION TIME: 5/15/2013 2:30:47 AM

BASELINE NAME: Desktop Compliance
REVISION: 1
COMPLIANCE STATE: Compliant
NON-COMPLIANCE SEVERITY: None
DESCRIPTION:

Summary:

Name	Revision	Type	Baseline Policy	Compliance State	Non-Compliance Severity	Discovery Failures
Desktop Compliance	1	Baseline		Compliant	None	0
IE Proxy Enabled	1	Operating System Configuration Item	Required	Compliant	None	0

The user is now compliant.

5. Open **Internet Explorer**, and from the **Tools** menu, open the **Internet Options**.
6. Select the **Connections** tab and click **LAN settings**.
7. Notice the setting in **Use a proxy server for your LAN** and click **OK**.

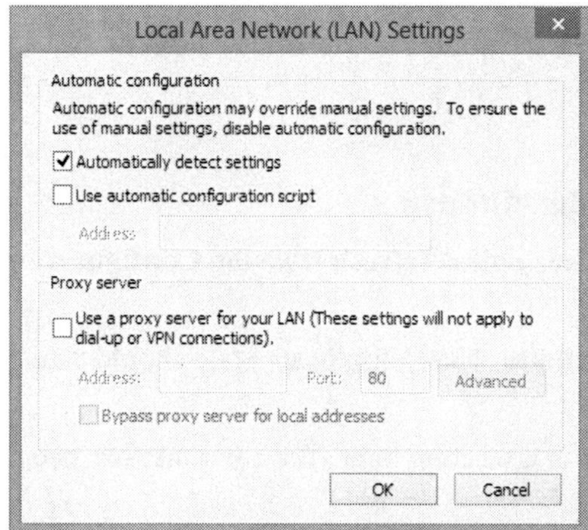

IE proxy settings after remediation.

8. Click **OK** to close the Internet Options.

User Data and Profiles

User data and profiles is a feature that has been around in Microsoft environments for a very long time, but only through Active Directory and Group Policy objects. The feature allows administrators to manage and report on user profile settings, like folder redirections, offline files, and roaming profiles. The benefits of controlling user data and profiles in ConfigMgr, rather than

Active Directory, are mainly flexibility and the fact that you can configure the feature in a reporting only mode. Settings are created and deployed in the same manner as any other deployment.

In Viamonstra, it's important that users in the Sales department store all documents on a file server, but also be able individually to make files available as offline copies. To achieve this goal ViaMonstra will implement the new SP1 user data and profiles feature.

For the steps below, I assume you have created a security group in Active Directory called *Sales* and a user device collection with all group members called *SM Sales* in the Settings Management folder.

1. On **CM01**, log on as **VIAMONSTRA\Administrator**, open **File Explorer**, and create this folder:

   E:\Userdata

2. Share **Userdata** with the following settings:

   a. Share name: **Userdata$**

   b. Share permissions: **Everyone** have **Full Control**

   c. Security: **Administrators, SYSTEM, CREATOR OWNER** all have **Full Control**

   d. Security: **Authenticated Users** have **Read & Execute, List Folder Contents, Read**

3. In the **ConfigMgr console**, in the **Administration** workspace, select **Client Settings.**

4. Open the **Workstation** properties, select **Compliance Settings**, configure **Enable User Data and Profiles** to **Yes**, and click **OK**.

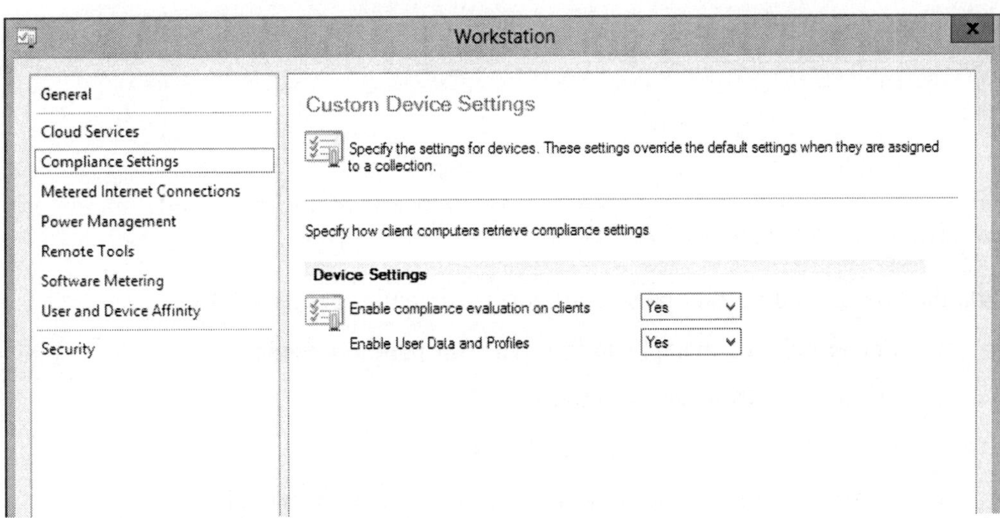

Enabling user data and profiles.

5. In the **Assets and Compliance** workspace, select **Compliance Settings / User Data and Profiles**.
6. On the ribbon, click **Create User Data and Profiles Configuration Item**.
7. On the **General** page, configure these settings and click **OK**:
    a. Name: **Sales dept Folder settings**
    b. Description: **Sales department offline and folder redirection settings**
    c. Folder redirection: **Enabled**
    d. Offline files: **Enabled**

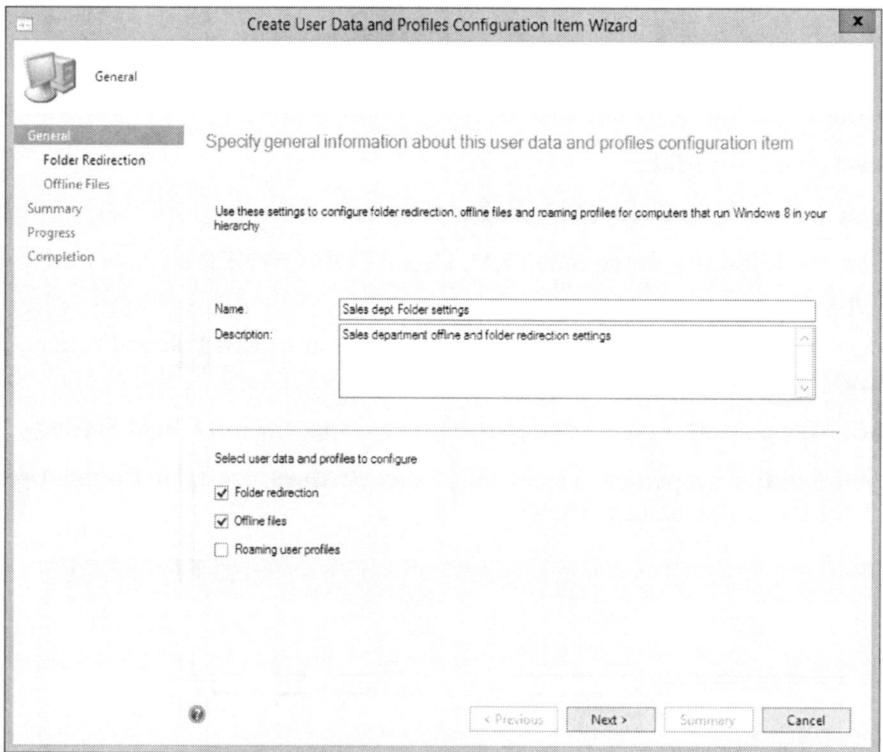

Controlling user profile and folder settings.

8. On the **Folder Redirection** page, configure these settings and click **OK**:
    a. Folder redirection applicability: **Only on primary device**
    b. Documents: **Redirect to remote**
    c. Redirect to the specified folder: **\\CM01\Userdata$**
    d. Configure threshold for error and warning events: **Enabled**
9. On the **Offline Files** page, enable **Offline files** and click **Next**.

10. On the **Summary** page, read the summary and click **Next**.
11. On the **Completion** page, click **Close**.

Deploy the User Data and Profile settings

1. In the **Assets and Compliance** workspace, select **Compliance Settings / User Data and Profiles**.
2. On the ribbon, select **Sales dept Folder settings** and click **Deploy**.
3. Configure these settings and click **OK**:
    a. Collection: **Settings Management / SM Sales**
    b. Remediate noncompliant rules when supported: **Enabled**
    c. Generate an alert: **Enabled**
    d. When compliance is below: **90 percent**
4. Click **OK**.
5. On **PC0001**, log on as **VIAMONSTRA\JAP** and open **File Explorer**.
6. Open the properties for the **Documents** folder and notice the folder redirection.

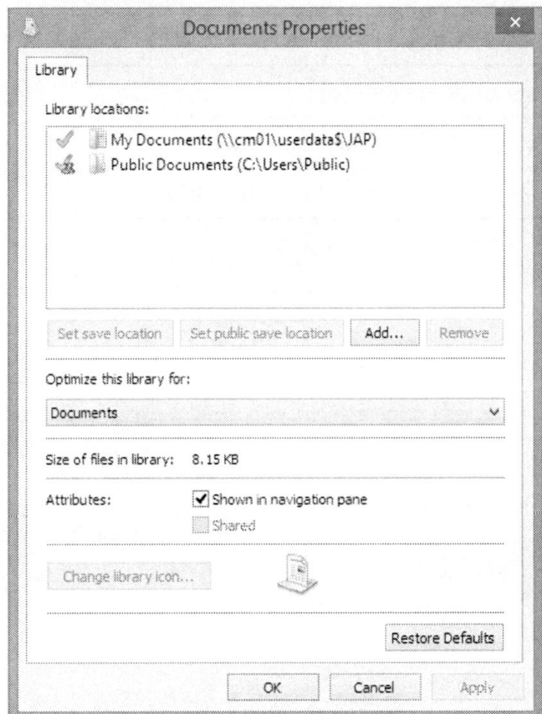

Documents folder redirected.

7. Create a folder and a file in the **Documents** folder.
8. Right-click the newly created file, open its properties, and notice the **Offline** tab.

Note: It's not uncommon that you can configure conflicting settings in ConfigMgr and Active Directory. Most of the time an Active Directory setting will override a ConfigMgr setting. However, with user data and profiles, a ConfigMgr setting will win a conflict.

Useful Log Files

The log files in the following table contain useful compliance settings activity information.

Log File	Description
Statemessage.log	Contains the state messages send by CI ID and baseline ID
Ciagent.log	Conatins details about the CIs in the baselines
Cistatestore.log	Contains details about the CI versions cached
PolicyAgent.log	Requests policies by using the Data Transfer service (to look for new Inventory classes to report)
PolicyAgentProvider.log	Records policy changes
PolicyEvaluator.log	Records new policy settings
Dcmagent.log	Contains details about dcmagent jobs
Dcmreporting.log	Contains details about the baselines evaluated
CcmUsrCse.log	Contains details about user data and profile settings.

Chapter 12

Planning for Backup and Recovery

As with any application, you need to plan for backup and also test the restore process at least once. Unlike previous versions, ConfigMgr 2012 relies on SQL Server only when restoring the site. This gives you the opportunity to select whether you want to run backups internally from the ConfigMgr console, or you want to configure backup only from SQL Server. For ViaMonstra, I have decided to configure backup from within the ConfigMgr console.

The Backup

To create a complete backup of your ConfigMgr site, you can configure the Backup ConfigMgr Site Server maintenance task. The site maintenance task automatically includes a backup of:

- The ConfigMgr SQL database
- The needed folders on the primary site server
- The needed registry keys on the primary site server.

Note: One of the more common misunderstandings about ConfigMgr 2012 is that administrators believe that the only supported backup method is the built-in backup maintenance task. The fact is that a normal SQL backup also is a supported and often better solution. During a native SQL backup job, data is compressed and no ConfigMgr services are stopped in the process. The benefit of using the ConfigMgr site maintenance task is that you are not required to have any knowledge of SQL.

Configure Backup

In ViaMonstra, you need a daily backup of ConfigMgr. Configuring the backup should be one of the first things you do, which is why you did it in Chapter 4. The following steps verify the backup configuration you did in Chapter 4:

1. Navigate to the **Administration** workspace, and select **Site Configuration / Sites**.
2. Select the site, and from the ribbon, click **Settings / Site Maintenance**.
3. Select the **Backup Site Server** task and click **Edit**. Verify that the task is enabled.
4. Verify that the **Backup Destination** is configured.

5. Verify that **Enable alerts** for backup task failures is enabled and click **OK** twice.

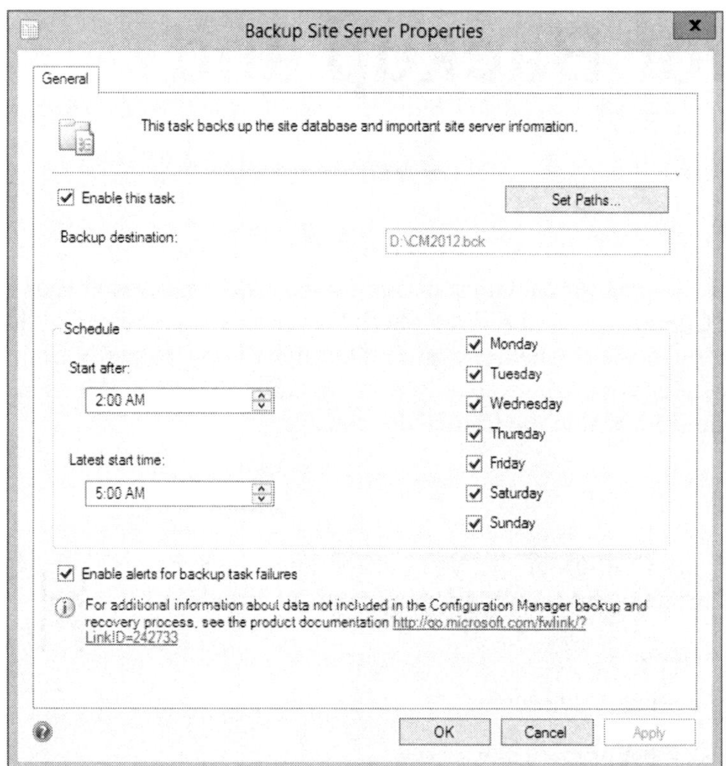

Configuring a daily backup.

What Happens When a Backup Runs

When ConfigMgr starts a backup, the SMS_SITE_BACKUP service starts and performs a backup based on the information that is stored in the backup control file, located in:

D:\Program files\Microsoft Configuration Manager\Inboxes\smsbkup.box\smsbkup.ctl

The backup process automatically creates a folder and stores the backup files in that folder. ConfigMgr automatically overwrites the backup files each time it performs a backup.

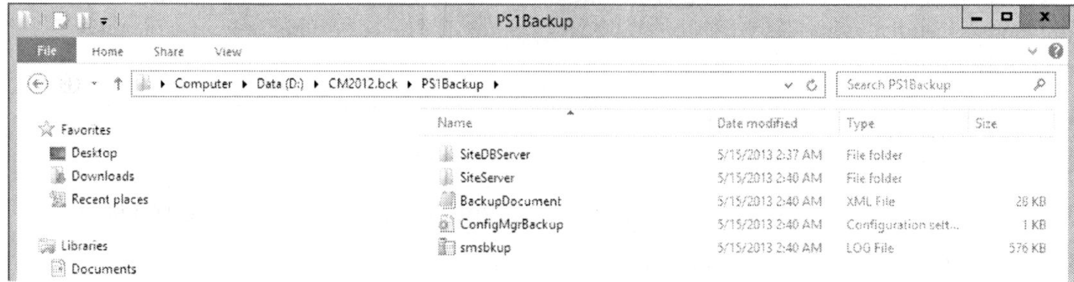

The files and folders created by the backup process.

Real World Note: It's highly recommended to store the backup files on another server or archive the Backup Snapshot to another server. You can automate the process by writing the needed commands and saving them to a file called AfterBackup.bat in:

D:\Program files\Microsoft Configuration Manager\inboxes\smsbkup.box

ConfigMgr automatically processes whichever command it finds in that specific file.

Manually Start Backup

If necessary, you can start the backup process manually:

1. On **CM01**, log on as **VIAMONSTRA\Administrator**.
2. Open a command prompt as **Administrator**.
3. Type **Net Start SMS_Site_Backup** and press **Enter** to start the backup process.

Back Up the Secondary Site and Remote Site Systems

There are no backup options for a secondary site, but with Service Pack 1, you still have a recovery option. The restore process reinstalls the secondary site using the configuration from the original installation. After the "restore," ConfigMgr locates the old content library on the secondary server and uses that to build the new content library. Restoring the content library is the main concern because otherwise you have to restore all the content to the server manually. If the restore process is unable to detect the content library, a plan B is to prestage content on remote distribution points and thus save a lot of network bandwidth and replication time, as explained in Appendix E. To restore a secondary site server, complete the following steps.

Note: These steps assume that you have installed a secondary site per the instructions in Appendix F.

1. On CM01, log on as **VIAMONSTRA\Administrator**.
2. From the **Administration** workspace, navigate to **Site Configuration / Sites** and select **S01 - secondary Site, Liverpool**.
3. On the ribbon, click **Recover Secondary Site** and click **OK** in the warning message.

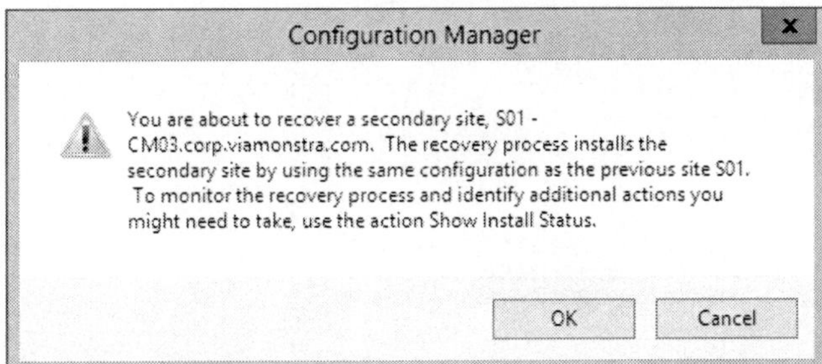

Performing a secondary site recovery.

4. To monitor the process, click **Show Install Status** on the ribbon or use the log.

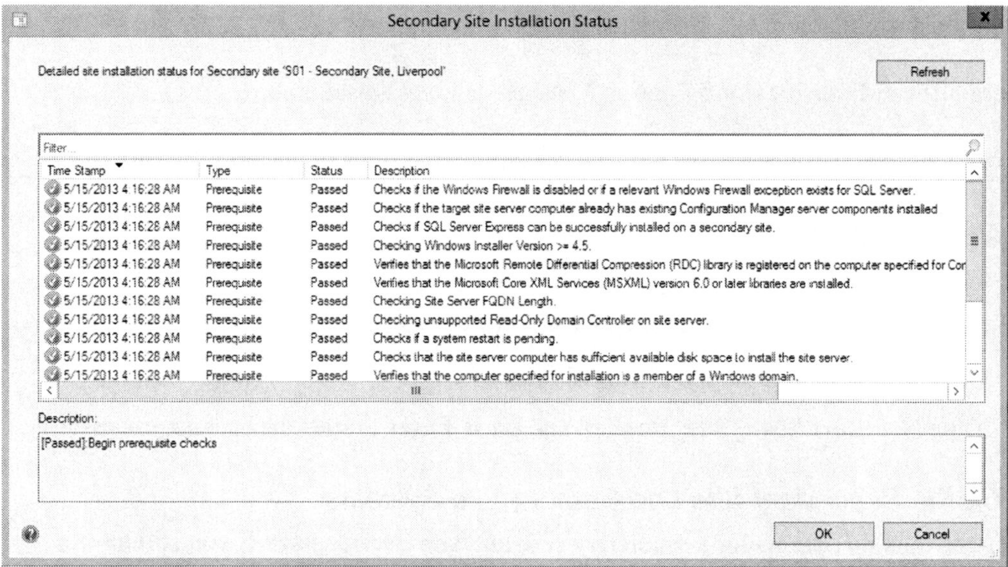

Monitoring the secondary site restore process.

5. On the secondary site server, the restore process starts by running this command: **/script D:\SMS_BOOTSTRAP.ini /nouserinput**. A quick look in the **SMS_BOOTSTRAP.ini** file reveals that it is an upgrade process.

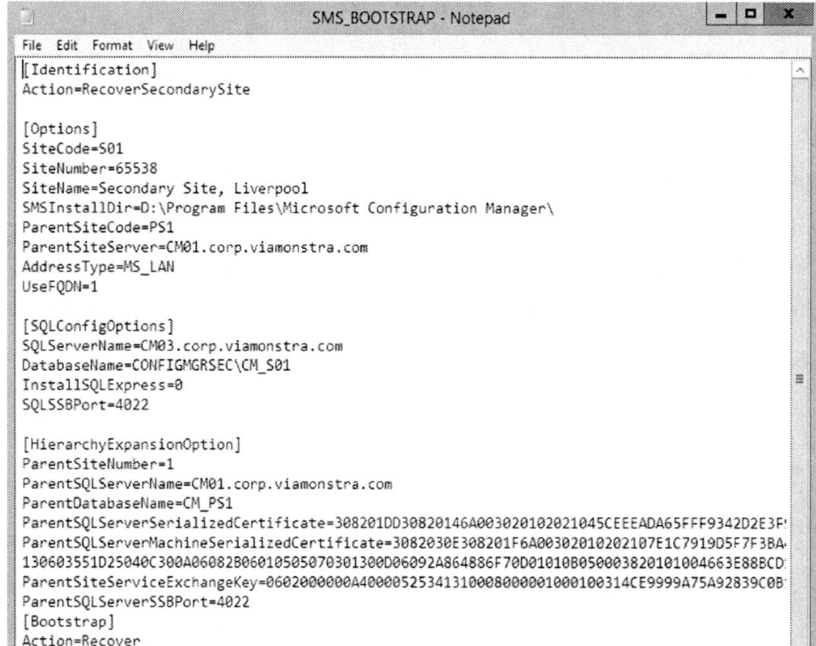

The SMS_BOOTSTRAP.ini file.

What Is Not Included in the Backup

ViaMonstra uses several non-core ConfigMgr services to support its ConfigMgr environment. Those services along with some additional ones are not part of the site maintenance backup process and must be included in the overall backup plans:

- Microsoft Deployment Toolkit (MDT)
- Site system roles
- The content library
- SQL Server Reporting Services and custom reports
- WSUS database
- System Center Updates Publisher (SCUP)

Note: You can create a maintenance job in SQL to back up the non-ConfigMgr databases. The only exception is the SCUP database, which by default is stored in the installer's user profile.

What Happens When a Site or Site System Fails

ConfigMgr is a system made up of a site server and multiple site system roles. Some of the site system roles provide fault tolerance by allowing multiple instances of the same role. Other roles, including the site server, do not offer multiple instances of the same role.

The Site Server Is Down

If the site server is down, you will not be able to perform any site administration. Remote site system roles and clients will still work to some extent. However, in most cases, deployments will not run, and clients will be limited to working with cached information and inventory. You can create SQL replicas on the management points to minimize the consequences of a failed site server. A SQL replica installed on the management point continues to service ConfigMgr clients as though nothing has happened. Of course, you cannot create any new deployments until the site server is restored.

Fault tolerance options: **None**

SQL Server Database

If the SQL Server is down, life's not good. You will not be able to perform any site administration, and clients will be able to work only with cached information. Although you can install SQL in a cluster, I usually recommend spending the money on better hardware, including more and faster disks, and ensuring that you have tested a full recovery in production.

Move the Site Database

You need to run a site reset on order to move the site database to another SQL Server. Prior to running the site reset you need to copy the database to the new SQL server.

Fault tolerance options: **Install SQL Server in a cluster**.

SMS Provider

If the SMS provider is down, no administrators will be able to connect to the database and perform any administration of the site. You can install multiple instances of the SMS provider for fault tolerance. In that event, the console will automatically perform a failover after five unsuccessful attempts. For performance reasons, it's recommended that you install the SMS provider on the database, the primary site server, and lastly on any other server. You can add another provider by running a site reset and selecting **Modify SMS provider information**.

Fault tolerance options: **Install multiple providers**.

Management Point

The management point is the primary contact between the client and the site server. If the management point fails, clients will not be able to upload or download any inventory data or new policies. Unlike previous versions, ConfigMgr 2012 enables clients to download a list of management points automatically. In the event that one is not responding, the client automatically selects another management point from the list.

Fault tolerance options: **Install 10 management points**.

Distribution Point

The distribution point is needed anytime a client requires access to a package. After a distribution point is selected for a package, the client retries that distribution point for 8 hours and then performs a different source location request. If the package is not available at the primary distribution point, the client uses a remote distribution point (if one is configured). You can configure the distribution point as a fallback source in the properties for the site system role, as we did previously for the distribution point in the datacenter.

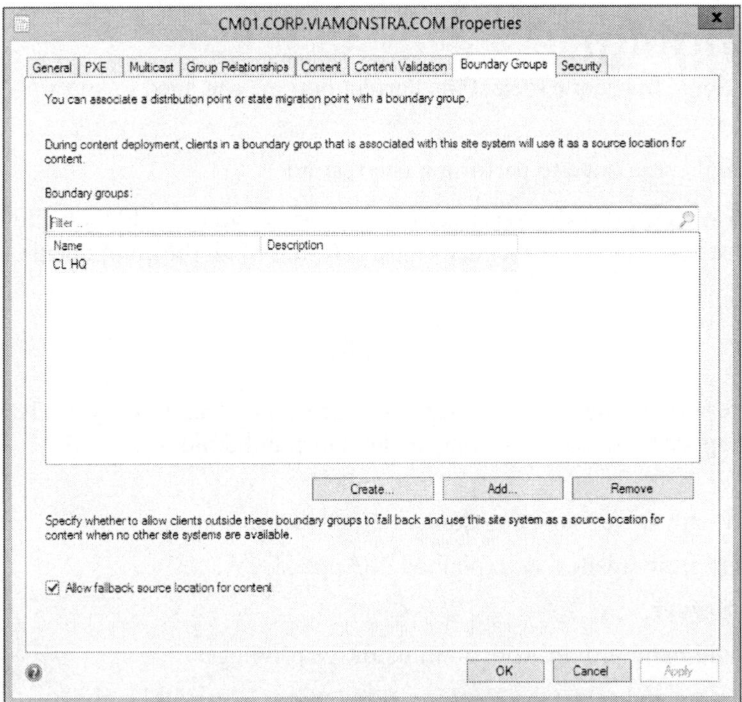

Distribution point configured as a fallback source.

If the package is not available at either the default distribution point or the fallback distribution point, the client can fall back to a cloud-based distribution point.

Fault tolerance options: **Install multiple distribution points** and/or a cloud distribution point.

Software Update Point

The software update is initiated by the client when it performs an online scan of software updates. If the first software update point is not responding, the client tries again four times every 30 minutes. After that, the client selects another software update point and configures that as its preferred software update point. Note that the client does not fall back to the old software update point. If no software update points are available, the client cannot scan for any new software updates and will not upload any new compliance data.

Fault tolerance options: **Either install multiple Software Update Points** or **Install a Windows NLB with multiple WSUS servers**.

Recovering ConfigMgr

ConfigMgr offers a few recover options. In order to select the correct option, you need to know what you want to restore:

- If data is lost or the server fails, you have to perform a site restore.
- If you experience problems with ConfigMgr services or components, you should try a site reset. A site reset does not restore any data, but performs a reinstall of all the components, including services.

Perform a Site Restore

In order to recover a ConfigMgr site server, you need a server with same name and disk layout. It doesn't have to be the same operating system version as long as the name and domain membership are the same.

1. Install the operating system with same name and domain membership.
2. Install all needed ConfigMgr prerequisites, as explained in Appendix A.
3. Install and configure **SQL Server**.
4. On the site server, open a command prompt with administrative privileges.
5. Start the ConfigMgr installation and select the **Recover Site** option. You will be given several recovery options; select **Recover this site server using an existing backup**.
6. On the **Before You Begin** page, click **Next**.
7. On the **Getting Started** page, select **Recover a site** and click **Next**.

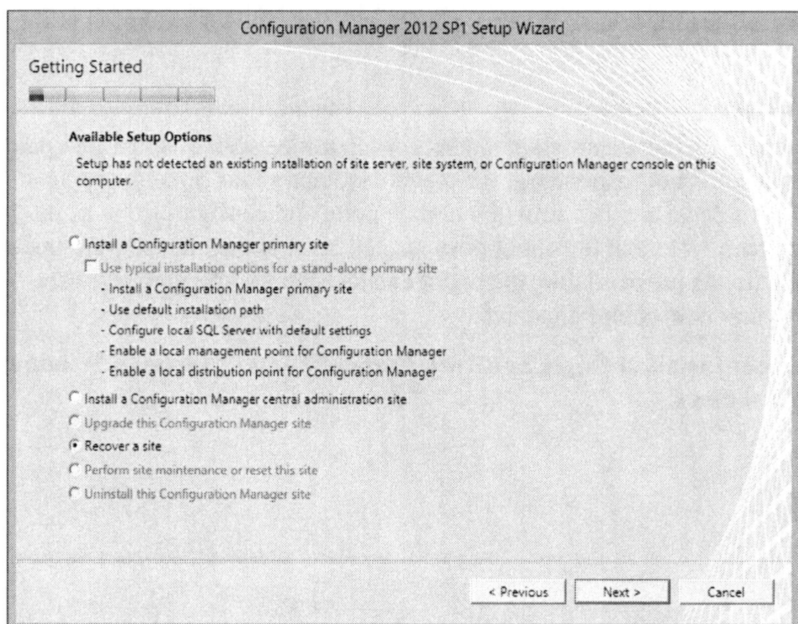

Starting the recovery process.

8. On the **Site Server and Database Recovery Options** page, configure these settings and click **Next**:
    a. Recover this site server using an existing backup: Click **Browse** and navigate to **D:\CM2012.BCK\PS1Backup**.
    b. Recover the site database using the backup set at the following location: Click **Browse** and navigate to **D:\CM2012.BCK\PS1Backup**.

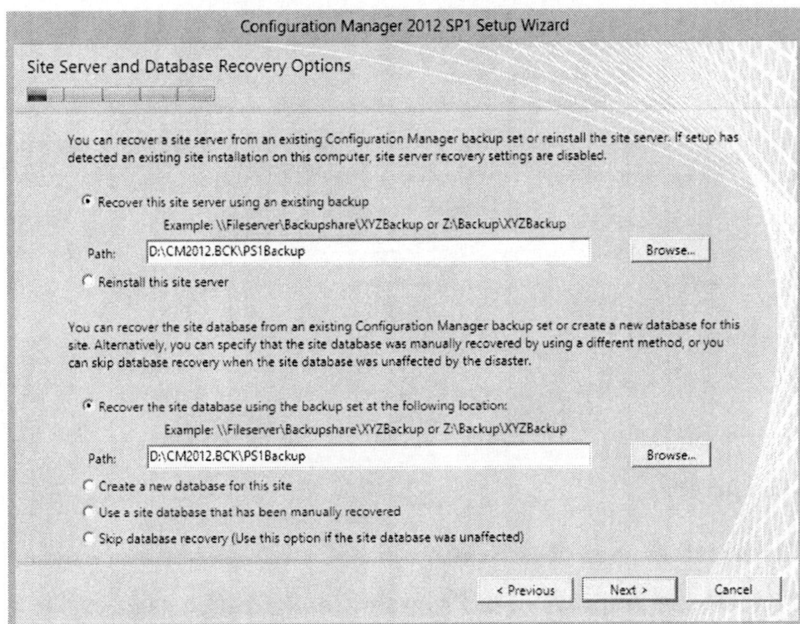

Selecting the backup files.

9. On the **Site Recovery Information** page, click **Next**. This page is only used if you are storing a CAS or a primary child site.
10. On the **Product Key** page, select **Install this product as an evaluation** and click **Next**.
11. On the **Microsoft Software License Terms** page, accept the license terms and click **Next**.
12. On the **Prerequisites License** page, accept all license terms and click **Next**.
13. On the **Updated Prerequisite** page, select **Use previously downloaded updates from the following location**; then type **D:\Setup\CM2012DL** and click **Next**.

14. On the **Site and Installation** page, modify the installation folder to **D:\Program Files\Microsoft Configuration Manager**, and click **Next**.

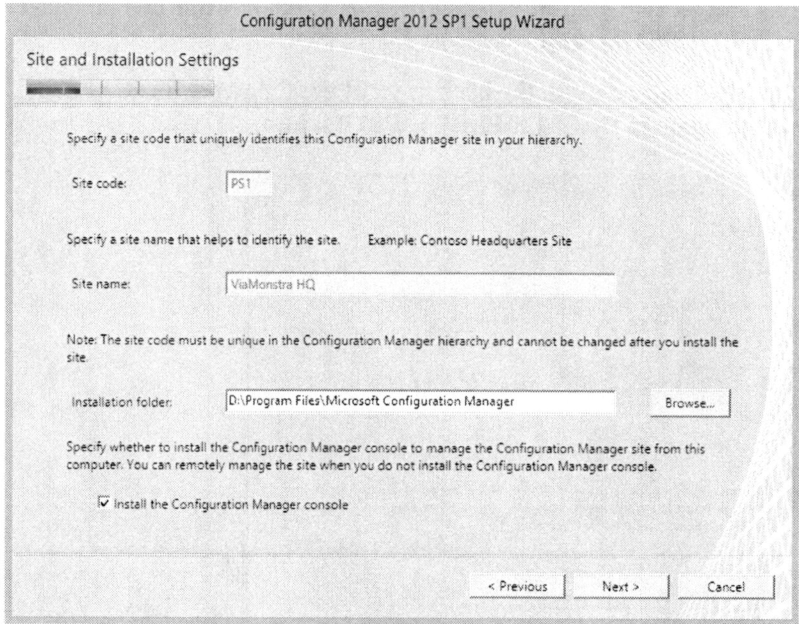

Specifying the installation folder.

15. On the **Database Information** page, click **Next**.
16. On the **Customer Experience Improvement Program Configuration** page, enable **Join the Customer Experience Improvement Program,** and click **Next**.
17. On the **Settings Summary** page, review the summary and click **Next**.
18. On the **Prerequisites** page, click **Begin Install.**
19. On the **Install** page, click **Next**.

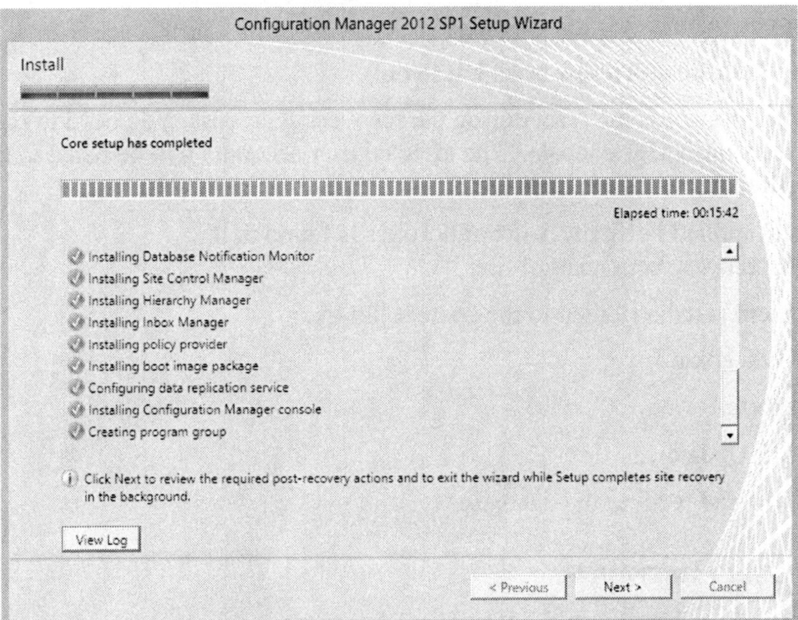

The restore is finished.

20. On the **Finished** page, make a note of all the post recovery tasks and click **Close**.

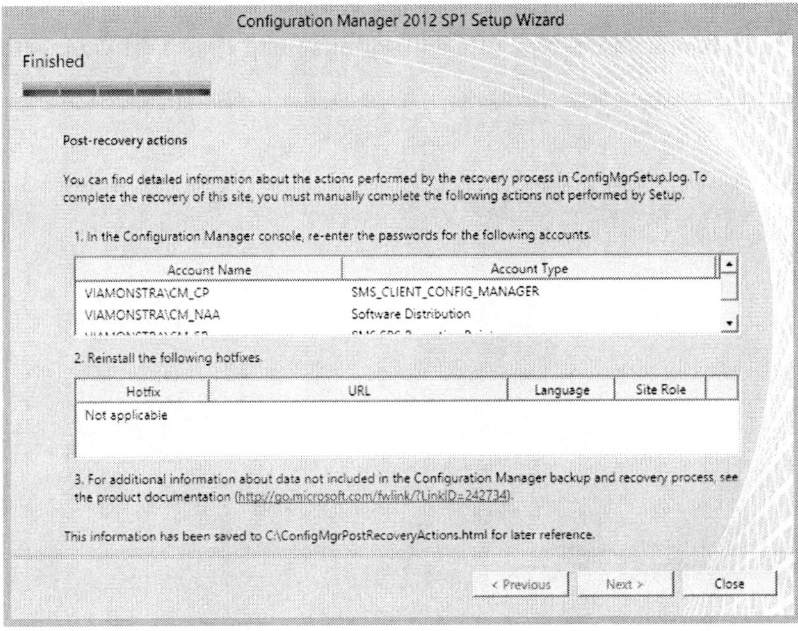

Information about post-recovery tasks.

Post-Recovery Tasks

After the site is recovered, there are still a few tasks left to do:

1. All ConfigMgr user passwords are reset during the recovering process. You need to reset the passwords in the ConfigMgr console. The effected user accounts will be listed in the C:\ConfigMgrPostRecoveryActions.html file.
2. Reinstall previously applied hotfixes. A list of hotfixes is found in the C:\ConfigMgrPostRecoveryActions.html file.
3. Ensure that all content is redistributed to the content library.
4. Restore the WSUS database.
5. Restore custom reports.
6. Reinstall MDT 2012 Update 1.
7. Reinstall SCUP 2011 and recover the database.

Reset the ConfigMgr User Passwords

1. In the **Administration** workspace, select **Security / Accounts**.
2. Select the **VIAMONSTRA\CM_CP** account, and on the ribbon, click **Properties**.
3. Click **Set**.
4. Type the password twice.
5. Click **Verify**, and in **Network share**, type **\\PC0001\admin$** and click **Test Connection**.

Verifying the account.

6. Click **OK** three times to close the account properties.
7. Repeat the steps for the remaining accounts. If you want to verify the new password, create a connection to **\\DC01\SYSVOL**.

Perform a Site Reset

A site reset reinstalls site components, reset permissions, and restore registry keys.

1. From the **Start screen**, launch **Configuration Manager Setup**.
2. On the **Before You Begin** page, click **Next**.
3. On the **Available Setup Options** page, click **Perform site maintenance or reset this Site** and click **Next**.
4. On the **Site Maintenance** page, select **Reset site with no configuration changes** and click **Next**.

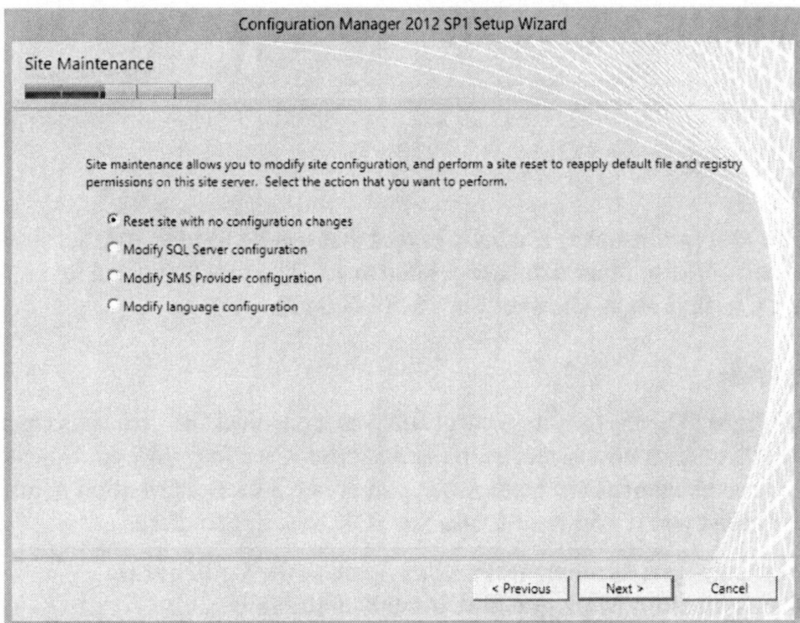

Starting the site reset process.

5. Click **Yes** in the message box.
6. On the **Configuration** page, click **Close**.

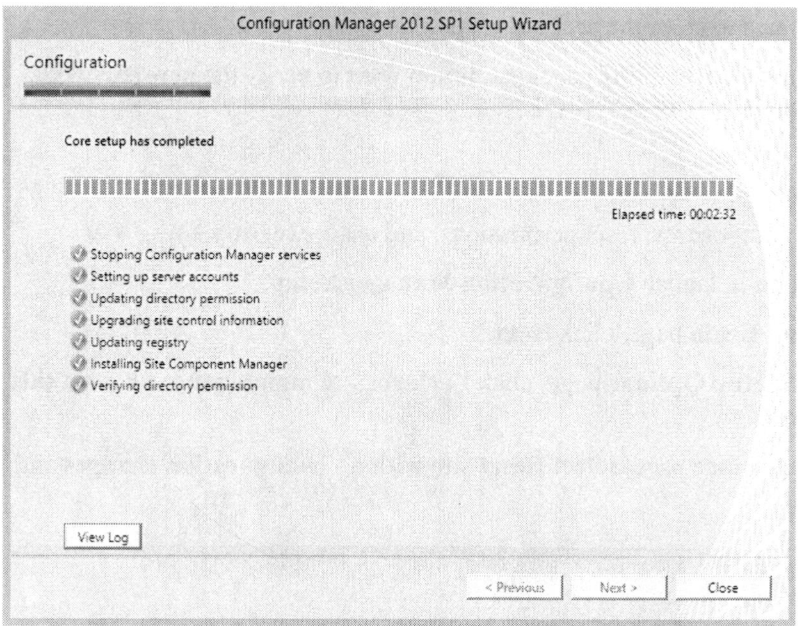

The site reset finished successfully.

The Preinst.exe Tool

The Hierarchy Maintenance tool (preinst.exe) is a built-in tool that can be used to stop services, dump the site control file, and perform other database-related tasks. The tool is located in D:\Program files\Microsoft Configuration Manager\bin\x64\00000409.

Dump the Site Control File

In previous versions of ConfigMgr/SMS, the site control file was a physical file. This has changed in ConfigMgr 2012, as the site control now is stored in the database. Creating a site control can be useful when you want to see what changes are made when you create a new distribution point. Having this knowledge can assist you if you want to use the SDK to script solutions.

1. Open a command prompt as **Administrator** and navigate to the **D:\Program files\Microsoft Configuration Manager\bin\X64\00000409** folder.
2. Run **preinst.exe /dump PS1**. This creates the sitectrl_PS1.cto in the root of the drive.
3. Rename the **sitectrl_PS1.cto** file **sitectrl_PS1.old**.
4. Perform the installation of the new distribution point.
5. Run **sitectrl_PS1.cto** again.
6. Compare the two files to see what you need to include in your script.

Other Preinst.exe Command Lines

- **/stopsite** signals ConfigMgr to stop the site component manager service. After the service is restarted, the site component manager performs a site reset.
- **/delsite S01** deletes child site information from the database. This is useful if a secondary site server was not successfully removed.
- **/deljob PS1** deletes all jobs targeted to site PS1.
- **/keyforparent** creates the public key PS2.CT4 in the root of the drive from which the command is run. You must copy the file manually to the hman.box inbox on the primary site server.
- **/keyforchild** creates the public key PS1.CT6 in the root of the drive from which the command is run. You must copy the file manually to the hman.box inbox on the secondary site server.

Note: Preinst.exe has several other command lines. Just run preinst.exe without any command to get a list of available commands.

Chapter 13

A Tribute to the Communities

I have never before in my career as an IT consultant experienced a richer and more dedicated community than the System Center Configuration Manager community. It seems like most ConfigMgr administrators play an active role in the community, contributing custom reports, scripts, deep technical blog posts, videos, and freeware utilities that assist us all in our daily work. In this chapter, I'll document the forums and blogs that I use.

Forums

MyITforum

The mother of all System Management forums in the universe. Especially in the beginning of my SMS voyage, I learned a lot from those guys. At MyITforum, you'll find most of the documents that you need, ranging from blog posts to videos to wikis. I'm a huge admire of the work done by Rod Trent and Ron Crumbaker. You guys have helped more people than you can ever imagine.

http://myitforum.com

Microsoft TechNet

Microsoft TechNet has come a very long way in recent years. I do not know what they feed the technical writers at Microsoft, but they seem to work around the clock, constantly updating the technical articles. Besides the TechNet articles, you also will find the TechNet forums. The forums are monitored by Microsoft, but it is most often community members who are answering everyday questions. From the answers, you will often learn a lot, pick up best practices from industry experts, and generally gain access to a wealth of knowledge.

http://technet.microsoft.com/en-us/ms376608.aspx

http://social.technet.microsoft.com/Forums/en-US/category/systemcenter2012configurationmanager

System Center Central

System Center Central is more than just a ConfigMgr community. Here you will also find lots of information about all the other System Center products in the family. Besides a very active forum, you will also find interviews, documentation, and very useful articles on how to work with the different System Center products.

http://www.systemcentercentral.com

Windows-Noob

This site was founded in 2006 by Niall Brady (ConfigMgr MVP), who wanted to make step-by-step guides available to the public, that use screenshots to describe the process from start to finish for everything ConfigMgr-related, particularly OSD. The site has plenty of step-by-step guides for System Center 2012 Configuration Manager and has a lively and very active forum full of loyal followers.

http://www.windows-noob.com

Blogs

It's been a while since I dropped my daily newspaper subscription. Instead, I spend the first 10–20 minutes every morning with coffee and a quick look at my RSS feeds.

Official Blogs from Microsoft

- Official ConfigMgr Team Blog: http://blogs.technet.com/b/configmgrteam
- System Center on Technet Edge: http://technet.microsoft.com/en-us/edge/system-center.aspx
- The Configuration Manager Support Team Blog: http://blogs.technet.com/b/configurationmgr
- Michael Niehaus: http://blogs.technet.com/b/mniehaus/
- RSS feed for recent KB articles for ConfigMgr 2007 and ConfigMgr 2012: http://support.microsoft.com/common/rss.aspx?rssid=12769&in=en-us

Blogs from the Community

- Kent Agerlund: http://blog.coretech.dk/author/kea
- Johan Arwidmark: http://www.deploymentresearch.com
- Greg Ramsey: http://gregramsey.wordpress.com
- Kaido Järvemets: http://cm12sdk.net/ and http://blog.coretech.dk/author/kaj
- Matthew Hudson: http://sms-hints-tricks.blogspot.com
- Peter Daalmans: http://www. configmgrblog.com
- Jason Sandys: http://blog.configmgrftw.com
- Chris Nackers: http://www.chrisnackers.com
- Maik Koster: http://myitforum.com/cs2/blogs/maikkoster/rss.aspx
- Garth Jones: http://smsug.ca

- Jakob G. Svendsen: blog.coretech.dk/jgs
- Jörgen Nilsson: http://ccmexec.com
- Raphael Perez: http://wmug.co.uk/blogs/dotraphael
- Rob Marshall: http://wmug.co.uk/blogs/r0b/default.aspx
- Niall C. Brady: http://www.niallbrady.com
- Cliff Hobbs: http://www.faqshop.com/wp/author/cliff
- Ronni Pedersen: http://www.ronnipedersen.com
- Torsten Meringer: http://www.mssccmfaq.de
- Jean-Sébastien Duchêne: http://www.systemcentertouch.fr
- Mikael Nystrom: http://deploymentbunny.com
- John Marcum: http://myitforum.com/cs2/blogs/jmarcum/archive/2012/03/01/160763.aspx
- John Nelson aka Number 2: http://myitforum.com/cs2/blogs/jnelson/archive/2011/09/20/159499.aspx
- Sherry Kissinger: http://myitforum.com/cs2/blogs/skissinger/default.aspx
- James Bannon: http://www.jamesbannanit.com/
- Nicolai Henriksen: http://www.sccm.biz/
- Brian Mason: http://mnscug.org/

Community Tools

There are many free community tools that can be very beneficial to use in your ConfigMgr 2012-related projects. The tools in the following section are the ones that I always use. Besides these, you can find a wealth of other tools that are worth taking a closer look at. You can find them via web searches and others in the communities who post to forums or blogs, including those mentioned previously in this chapter.

The Right Click Tools

The famous right click tools are a console extension that allows you to trigger actions on the clients directly from the ConfigMgr console. There are several different right click tools available.

http://tinyurl.com/5zl9cy

The following link will take you to a blog post that explains how you can create your own custom tools:

http://tinyurl.com/7bhffyk

Client Center

The tool is designed for IT Professionals to troubleshoot SMS/SCCM client-related issues. The SCCM Client Center provides a quick and easy overview of client settings, including running services and SCCM settings in a good user-friendly interface. The tool is developed by fellow MVP Roger Zander.

http://sourceforge.net/projects/smsclictr

WMI and PowerShell Explorer

This is a powerful WMI tool that allows you to connect to and work with WMI locally and remotely. With the tool you can browse WMI namespaces, classes, methods, properties and class instances. Besides being a WMI browser the tool is also PowerShell Explorer from where you can easily navigate in the Powershell modules, access online helpfile and and download hundreds of PowerShell examples.

http://blog.coretech.dk/kaj/coretech-wmi-and-powershell-browser/

Automatic Email Application Approval

By default, application approvals must be done from within the ConfigMgr console. If you have Service Manager 2012, you can use that to implement an approval process.

The solution consists of a website and a web service. None of them have to be installed on the same server. Also there is no requirement to install any the components on the site server.

http://blog.coretech.dk/download/CAA-0.9.0.zip

GUI to Modify Third-Party License Information

ConfigMgr 2007 and 2012 allow you to import license information from a CSV file. The data are shown in the License 15A – General License Reconciliation Report. The problem for many is that it's often a bit too difficult to create the CSV file in the correct format. Highly inspired by the CM2007 AILW utility, Coretech created a new tool that's compliant with both ConfigMgr 2007 and ConfigMgr 2012.

http://blog.coretech.dk/download/CTAILW.zip

Auto Install Warning

One question that is seen again and again in the news forums is "How can I configure a custom message prior to running an application?" This utility—Auto Install Warning—is installed on each client in the hierarchy. The utility allows you to write custom text and add a company logo that will be shown before the actual deployment begins.

http://blog.coretech.dk/jgs/coretech-auto-install-warning-1-0-3-freeware-update/

OSD Frontends

In this book, you have learned how to start OS deployments using the unknown computers collection or by importing a computer object into the ConfigMgr console. As you dig deeper into the OSD feature, you quickly discover a need for automating the process one step further. That automation is often done by adding an OSD frontend from which the end user can initiate the deployment process by selecting a few options like location, keyboard layout, additional applications, operating system, and so forth. The following are several good options:

- windows-noob.com FrontEnd HTA: http://tinyurl.com/bo9gcb3
- Johan Arwidmark's Pretty Good Frontend: http://prettygoodfrontend.codeplex.com
- Maik Koster's MDT Web FrontEnd: http://tinyurl.com/7dqv2sb

Distribution Point Utlization Monitor

This tool gives you information about how much traffic is downloaded from each distribution point and by whom. The tool comes with some standard reports that provide you with all the details.

http://blog.coretech.dk/kea/coretech-distribution-point-utilization-monitor/

RegKeyToMOF

RegKeyToMOF is used to create custom hardware inventory classes based on registry information entries and format them correctly for the Configuration.mof file.

http://myitforum.com/cs2/files/folders/152945/download.aspx

Package Source Changer

As you start migrating from ConfigMgr 2007 to ConfigMgr 2012, one of the requirements is that the package source used for packages must be a UNC and accessible from ConfigMgr 2012. I have seen many site installations in which the package source is either a local source on the site server or a UNC pointing to the site server. In either case, you must somehow update the package source before starting the migration. The Package Source Changer can be used to change the package source in ConfigMgr 2007 before you migrate the packages, or after the packages are migrated to ConfigMgr 2012.

http://blog.coretech.dk/jgs/coretech-package-source-changer/

User Groups

No matter where you are located, you will most likely be able to find a System Center user group in your area. User groups are community driven and are a great opportunity for you to share your thoughts, ideas, and daily challenges. The easiest way to find a local user group is to "Bing" "System Center User Group".

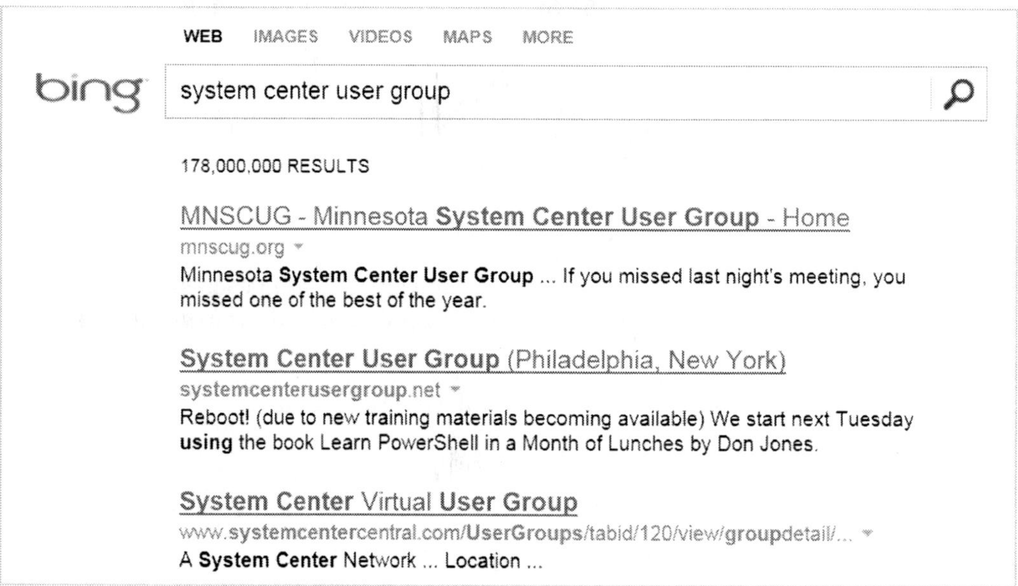

178,000,000 results for "System Center User Group."

Appendix A

Using the Hydration Kit to Build the POC Environment

Here are the detailed steps for installing and configuring the hydration kit provided in the book sample files. This kit, along with some post-configuration tasks described in this appendix, allows you to build the same virtual environment, using either Hyper-V or VMware, that is used for this book.

Note: The password for the accounts created by the hydration kit is Password01 (including the Administrator account).

To follow the guides in this appendix, you need to download the book sample files that are available on http://www.deploymentfundamentals.com.

Real World Note: As you learned in Chapter 2, you use virtual machines for the proof-of-concept environment, and if you have a powerful host, you can run them all on the same machine (for lab and test purposes). If you assign the minimum amount of memory, you can complete all steps on a host with 16 GB of RAM, even though 32 GB of RAM is preferred.

If you are thinking about using the same setup in a production environment, you probably want to separate the virtual machines onto multiple hosts. And you do remember that you should run at least one domain controller on a physical machine, right?

The Base Servers

Using the hydration kit and some post configurations, you build the following list of servers. The server setups for the New York site are fully automated. The servers in the Liverpool and Stockholm sites are deployed only with the base operating system since you need to verify things such as network connectivity between the sites before doing the final configuration.

New York Site Servers (192.168.1.0/24)

- DC01, Domain Controller, DNS, and DHCP
- CM01, Member Server (Primary Site Server)

Stockholm Site Server (192.168.2.0/24)

CM02, Member Server (Remote Location Distribution Point)

Liverpool Site Server (192.168.3.0/24)

CM03, Member Server (Secondary Site Server)

Real World Note: If you only want a smaller lab and test environment to learn about ConfigMgr 2012 SP1, you can start out by deploying only the New York site servers and clients.

The Base Clients

In addition to the servers, you also use a few clients throughout the book guides. Using the hydration kit, you build the following list of clients. The hydration kit clients are assigned to the New York site. I decided not to have any ready-made clients in the Liverpool or Stockholm sites, so you will need to deploy new clients to these sites if you choose to use them.

PC0001 is used in most chapters as the main ConfigMgr 2012 client. The Windows 7 client (PC0002) is needed only if you want to do the Windows 7 to Windows 8 migration guide in Chapter 10.

New York Site Clients (192.168.1.0/24)

- PC0001, Windows 8 Enterprise x64
- PC0002, Windows 7 Enterprise SP1 x64

Setting Up the Hydration Environment

Hydration is the concept of using MDT 2012 Update 1 Lite Touch offline media to do fully automated builds of entire lab, proof-of-concept, or production environments.

How Does the Hydration Work?

The hydration kit that you download is just a folder structure and some scripts. The scripts help you create the offline media, and the folder structure is there for you to add your own software and licenses when applicable. You also can use trial versions for the lab software, as well. The overview steps are the following:

1. Install MDT 2012 Update 1 and ADK.
2. Extract the hydration kit from the book sample files (download from http://www.deploymentfundamentals.com).
3. Create an MDT 2012 Update 1 deployment share using one of the sample scripts.
4. Populate the folder structure with setup media (either full versions or trial).

5. Build the offline media (big ISO) by updating the offline media item in the MDT 2012 Update 1 deployment share.
6. Create a few virtual machines, boot them on the offline media (ISO), select what servers or clients they should become, and a few hours later you have the base setup.

Prepare the Downloads Folder

In the following steps, you need to have access to the book sample files and the other software listed in the following guide. The steps are performed on the machine (client or server) that you use to manage Hyper-V or VMware, which if you are using Hyper-V, also can be the Hyper-V host.

1. On the machine (client or server) that you use to manage Hyper-V or VMware, create the **C:\Downloads** folder.
2. Download the following software:
    - The book sample files (http://www.deploymentfundamentals.com)
    - MDT 2012 Update 1
    - ADK (after downloading the 1 MB setup from Microsoft, run the adksetup.exe to download all the other components of ADK.

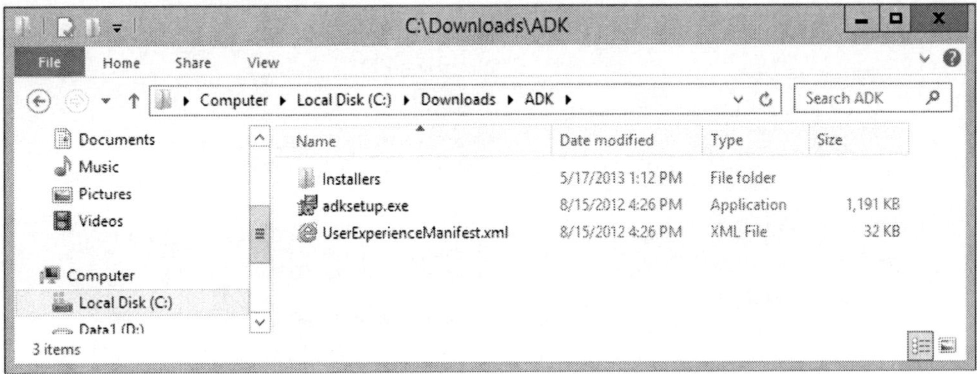

The ADK folder, after running adksetup.exe and downloading the about 2.5 GB of installers (and the UserExperienceManifest.xml file).

    - Windows Server 2012 Standard (trial or full version)
    - Windows 7 Enterprise SP1 x64 (trial or full version)
    - Windows 8 Enterprise x64 (trial or full version)
    - BGInfo

> **Note:** The hydration kit is built for volume license media. If using retail media, like some of the MSDN or TechNet licenses, the automatic install will stop and prompt you for the operating system product keys.

Prepare the Hydration Environment

The machine (client or server) that you use to manage Hyper-V or VMware needs to have PowerShell installed, and I assume that you have downloaded the book sample files.

Note: MDT 2012 Update 1 requires local administrator rights/permissions. You need to have at least 45 GB of free disk space on C:\ for the hydration kit and at least 200 GB of free space for the volume hosting your virtual machines. Also make sure to run all commands from an elevated PowerShell command prompt.

Create the Hydration Deployment Share

1. On the Windows machine that you use to manage Hyper-V or VMware, install **ADK** (**adksetup.exe**) selecting only the following components:
   a. **Deployment Tools**
   b. **Windows Preinstallation Environment (Windows PE)**

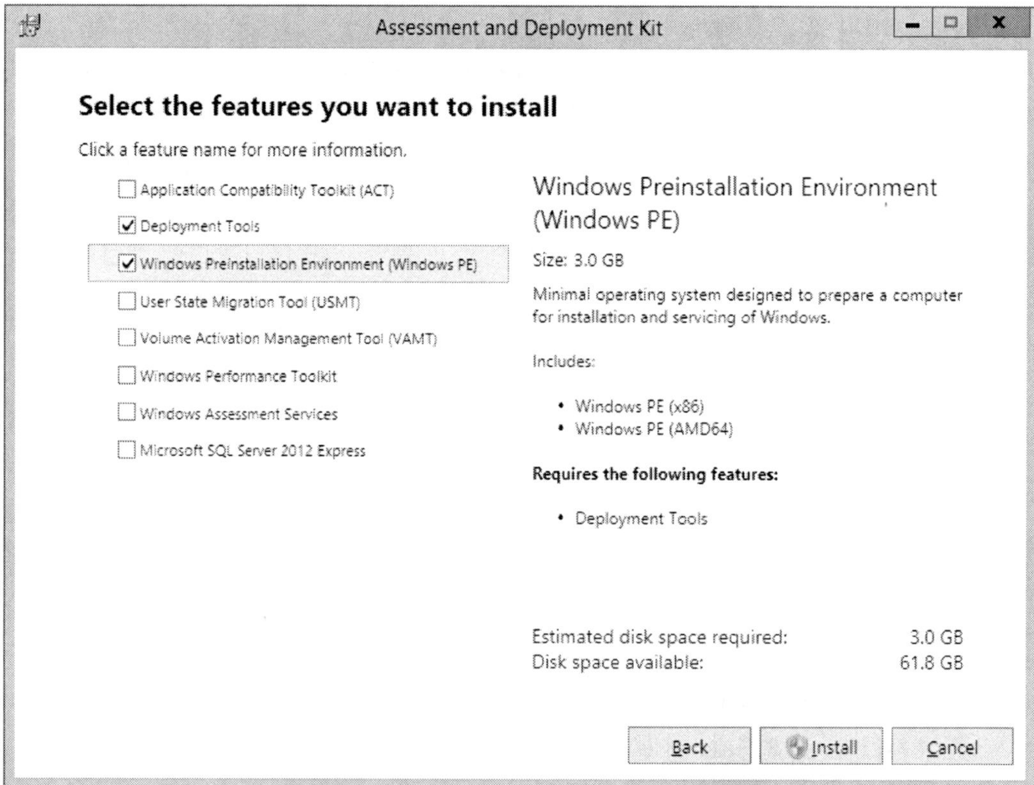

The ADK setup.

2. Install **MDT 2012 Update 1** (**MicrosoftDeploymentToolkit2012_x64.msi**) with the default settings.

3. Extract the book sample files to **C:\Downloads** and copy the **HydrationCM2012SP1MTF** folder to **C:**.
4. You should now have the following folder containing a few subfolders and PowerShell scripts:

   C:\HydrationCM2012SP1MTF\Source

5. In an elevated (run as **Administrator**) **PowerShell** command prompt, configure **Execution Policy** in PowerShell by typing the following command:

```
Set-ExecutionPolicy Unrestricted -Force
```

6. In the **PowerShell** command prompt, navigate to the hydration folder by typing the following command:

```
Set-Location C:\HydrationCM2012SP1MTF\Source
```

7. While still in the **PowerShell** command prompt, with location (working directory) set to **C:\HydrationCM2012SP1MTF\Source**, create the hydration deployment share by typing the following command:

```
.\CreateHydrationDeploymentShare.ps1
```

Populate the Hydration Deployment Share with the Setup Files

1. Copy the **BGInfo** file (**bginfo.exe**) to the following folder:

   C:\HydrationCM2012SP1MTF\DS\Applications\Install - BGInfo\Source

2. Copy the **Windows Server 2012** installation files (the content of the ISO, not the actual ISO) to the following folder:

   C:\HydrationCM2012SP1MTF\DS\Operating Systems\WS2012

3. Copy the **Windows 8 Enterprise x64** installation files (the content of the ISO, not the actual ISO) to the following folder:

   C:\HydrationCM2012SP1MTF\DS\Operating Systems\W8X64

4. Copy the **Windows 7 Enterprise SP1 x64** installation files (again, the content of the ISO, not the actual ISO) to the following folder:

   C:\HydrationCM2012SP1MTF\DS\Operating Systems\W7X64SP1

Create the Hydration ISO (MDT 2012 Update Offline Media Item)

1. Using **Deployment Workbench** (available on the **Start screen**), expand **Deployment Shares**, and expand **Hydration CM2012 SP1 MTF**.
2. Review the various nodes. The **Applications**, **Operating Systems** and **Task Sequences** nodes should all have some content in them.

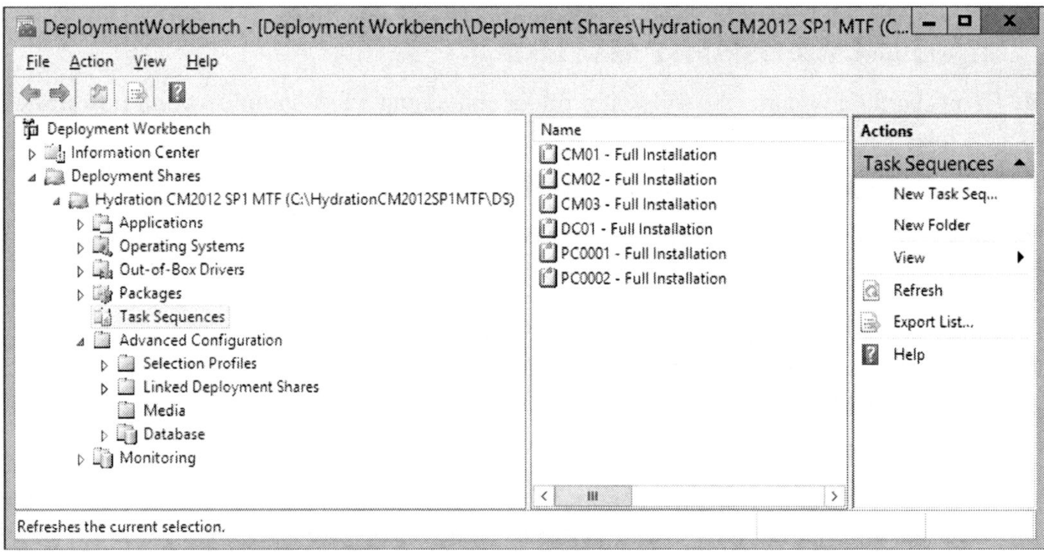

The Hydration CM2012 SP1 MTF deployment share, listing all task sequences.

3. Expand the **Advanced Configuration** node, and then select the **Media** node.
4. In the right pane, right-click the **MEDIA001** item, and select **Update Media Content**.

Note: The media update will take a while to run, a perfect time for a coffee break. ☺

After the media update, you will have a big ISO (HydrationCM2012SP1MTF.iso) in the C:\ HydrationCM2012SP1MTF\ISO folder. The HydrationCM2012SP1MTF.iso will be about 10 GB in size.

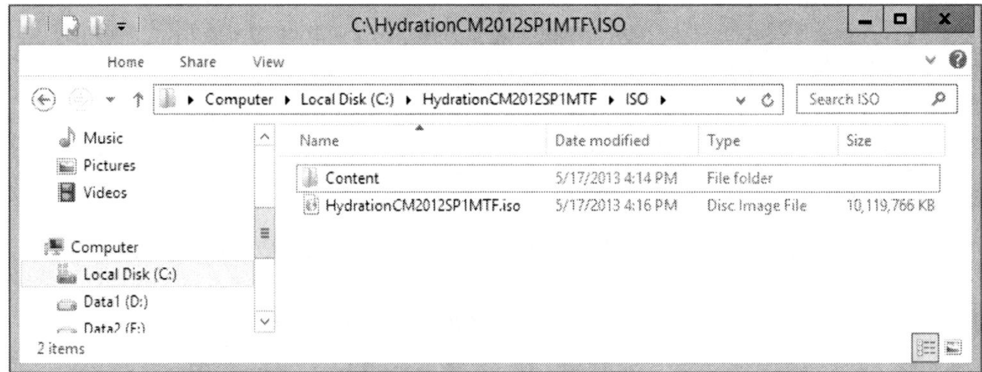

The HydrationCM2012SP1MTF.iso media item.

Real World Note: Everything you do in the Deployment Workbench (and more) can be done via PowerShell. This means that the media item also can be updated via PowerShell. I have added a sample script that will run the update media content action in the hydration kit. Check out the UpdateHydrationMediaItem.ps1 script in the C:\HydrationCM2012SP1MTF\Source\Extra folder. If you are using Hyper-V on Windows Server 2012 to build your virtual machines, please also check out the CreateVirtualMachines.ps1 script in the same folder.

The Virtual Machines for the New York Site

The following steps assume that you have a dedicated network for the New York site. In my environment, I'm using 192.168.1.0/24 with a default gateway of 192.168.1.254.

Deploy DC01

This is the primary domain controller used in the environment, and it also is running DNS and DHCP.

1. Using **Hyper-V Manager** or **VMware Sphere**, create a virtual machine with the following settings:
    a. Name: **DC01**
    b. Memory: **1 GB** (minimum; 2 GB is recommended)
    c. Hard drive: **60 GB** (dynamic disk)
    d. Network: The virtual network for the New York site
    e. Image file (ISO): **C:\HydrationCM2012SP1MTF\ISO\HydrationCM2012SP1MTF.iso**
2. Start the **DC01** virtual machine. After booting from **HydrationCM2012SP1MTF.iso**, and after WinPE has loaded, select the **DC01** task sequence.

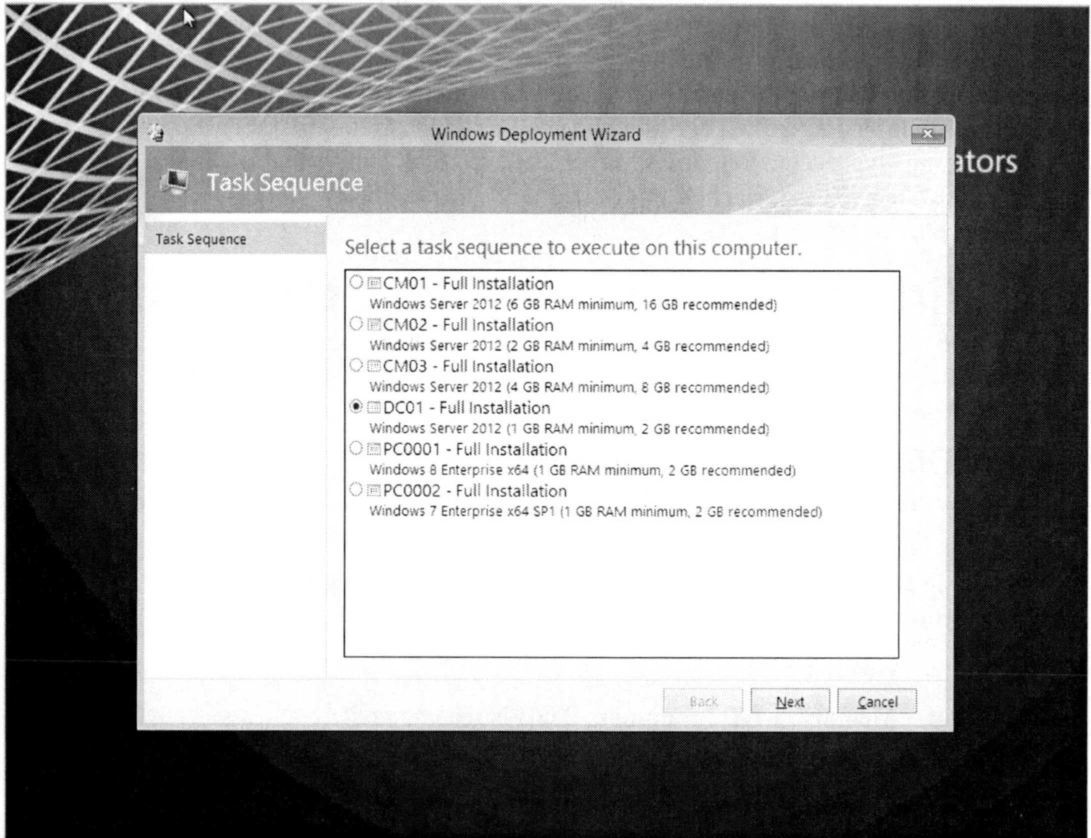

Starting the DC01 virtual machine on the HydrationCM2012SP1MTF.iso.

3. Wait until the setup is complete and you see the **Hydration completed** message in the final summary. Leave DC01 running while installing the other servers and clients.

Deploy CM01

CM01 is the ConfigMgr 2012 primary site server. Before continuing, make sure DC01 is still running (CM01 joins the domain during setup). In addition to the core Windows Server 2012 operating system setup, the CM01 task sequence also installs ConfigMgr 2012 SP1 prerequisites like IIS, .BITS and Remote Differential Compression, WDS, and .NET Framework.

1. Using **Hyper-V Manager** or **VMware Sphere**, create a virtual machine with the following settings:
    a. Name: **CM01**
    b. Memory: **6 GB** (minimum; 16 GB is recommended)
    c. Hard drive #1: **72 GB** (dynamic disk)
    d. Hard drive #2: **650 GB** (dynamic disk)

> **Note:** If using Hyper-V, connect both hard drives to IDE Controller 0 (Location 0 and 1). If using a Hyper-V SCSI disk for hard drive #2, you need to add additional logic to the hydration kit to set the SCSI disk online and rearrange the assigned drive letters.

   e. Network: The virtual network used for the New York site
   f. Image file (ISO): **C:\HydrationCM2012SP1MTF\ISO\HydrationCM2012SP1MTF.iso**

2. Start the **CM01** virtual machine. After booting from **HydrationCM2012SP1MTF.iso**, and after WinPE has loaded, select the **CM01** task sequence.
3. Wait until the setup is complete and you see the **Hydration completed** message in the final summary.

> **Real World Note:** For production use or large scale tests, each volume used for the primary site server should be a separate local disk array or a separate volume from the SAN. For lab and test purposes, using two disks for all volumes is fine.

Deploy PC0001

This is a client running Windows 8 Enterprise x64 in the corp.viamonstra.com domain.

1. Using **Hyper-V Manager** or **VMware Sphere**, create a virtual machine with the following settings:
   a. Name: **PC0001**
   b. Memory: **1 GB** (minimum; 2 GB is recommended)
   c. Hard drive: **60 GB** (dynamic disk)
   d. Network: The virtual network dedicated for the New York site
   e. Image file (ISO): **C:\HydrationCM2012SP1MTF\ISO\HydrationCM2012SP1MTF.iso**
2. Start the **PC0001** virtual machine. After booting from **HydrationCM2012SP1MTF.iso**, and after WinPE has loaded, select the **PC0001** task sequence.
3. Wait until the setup is complete and you see the **Hydration completed** message in the final summary.

Deploy PC0002

This is a client running Windows 7 Enterprise SP1 x64 in the corp.viamonstra.com domain.

1. Using **Hyper-V Manager** or **VMware Sphere**, create a virtual machine with the following settings:
   a. Name: **PC0002**
   b. Memory: **1 GB** (minimum; 2 GB is recommended)

   c. Hard drive: **60 GB** (dynamic disk)
   d. Network: The virtual network used for the New York site.
   e. Image file (ISO): **C:\HydrationCM2012SP1MTF\ISO \HydrationCM2012SP1MTF.iso**

2. Start the **PC0002** virtual machine. After booting from **HydrationCM2012SP1MTF.iso**, and after WinPE has loaded, select the **PC0002** task sequence.
3. Wait until the setup is complete and you see the **Hydration completed** message in the final summary.

The Virtual Machine for the Stockholm Site

The virtual machine for the Stockholm site is needed only if you want to learn how ConfigMgr works with a remote distribution point.

The guides in this section assume that you have a dedicated network for the Stockholm site. In my environment, I'm using 192.168.2.0/24 with a default gateway of 192.168.2.1. You also need to have routing enabled between the networks.

Real World Note: If the virtual network used for your virtual machines does not have internet access, you can use a separate Windows Server 2012 virtual machine, with Routing and Remote Access enabled, as a gateway. For more details on using a virtual router, see this article by Johan Arwidmark: http://tinyurl.com/usingvirtualrouter.

Deploy CM02

This is the ConfigMgr 2012 remote distribution point in the Stockholm site.

1. Using **Hyper-V Manager** or **VMware Sphere**, create a virtual machine with the following settings:
   a. Name: **CM02**
   b. Hard drive: **300 GB** (dynamic disk)
   c. Memory: **2 GB** (minimum; 4 GB is recommended)
   d. Network: The virtual network dedicated for the Stockholm site
   e. Image file (ISO): **C:\HydrationCM2012SP1MTF\ISO \HydrationCM2012SP1MTF.iso**
2. Start the **CM02** virtual machine. After booting from **HydrationCM2012SP1MTF.iso**, and after WinPE has loaded, select the **CM02** task sequence.
3. Wait until the setup is complete and you see the **Hydration completed** message in the final summary. Then continue to the next section ("Configure CM02").

Configure CM02

After the hydration is complete, you need to join it to the domain:

1. On **CM02**, log on as **Administrator** using the password **Password01**.
2. Join **CM02** to the **corp.viamonstra.com** domain and reboot.
3. On **DC01**, move the **CM02** computer account to the **ViaMonstra / Servers** OU.

The Virtual Machine for the Liverpool Site

The virtual machines for the Liverpool site are needed only if you want to learn how ConfigMgr works with a secondary site.

The guides in this section assume that you have a dedicated network for the Liverpool site. In my environment, I'm using 192.168.3.0/24 with a default gateway of 192.168.3.1. You also need to have routing enabled between the networks.

Deploy CM03

This is the ConfigMgr 2012 secondary site server in the Liverpool site.

1. Using **Hyper-V Manager** or **VMware Sphere**, create a virtual machine with the following settings:
   a. Name: **CM03**
   b. Memory: **4 GB** (minimum; 8 GB is recommended)
   c. Hard drive: **300 GB** (dynamic disk)
   d. Network: The virtual network dedicated for the Liverpool site
   e. Image file (ISO): **C:\HydrationCM2012SP1MTF\ISO\HydrationCM2012SP1MTF.iso**
2. Start the **CM03** virtual machine. After booting from **HydrationCM2012SP1MTF.iso**, and after WinPE has loaded, select the **CM03** task sequence.
3. Wait until the setup is complete and you see the **Hydration completed** message in the final summary. Then continue to the next section ("Configure CM03").

Configure CM03

After the hydration is complete, you need to join it to the domain:

1. On **CM03**, log on as **Administrator** using the password **Password01**.
2. Join **CM03** to the **corp.viamonstra.com** domain and reboot.
3. On **DC01**, move the **CM03** computer account to the **ViaMonstra / Servers** OU.

Appendix B

PowerShell Scripts

In this book, you will find several PowerShell examples based on the default ConfigMgr 2012 SP1 cmdlets and a custom cmdlet. The custom cmdlet is a library of useful ConfigMgr-related functions used to create objects like folders, collections, packages, applications, and to install things such as the site system prerequisites. The cmdlet is developed exclusively for the purpose of this book. The cmdlet used in the book is CM12_Function_Library_SP1.ps1.

Getting Started with the Built-in Cmdlets

To access the built-in cmdlets, you need to launch the PowerShell ConfigMgr module. You can do this by launching PowerShell from the ConfigMgr console, which also launches the module. To do this, follow these steps:

1. Open the **ConfigMgr console**, and from the top left menu, click **Connect via Windows PowerShell**.

Launching PowerShell with the built-in ConfigMgr module.

2. From a **PowerShell** command prompt, type **A** (to always trust the publisher) and press **Enter**.
3. Type the following command to list all the ConfigMgr cmdlets:

```
Get-Command -Module ConfigurationManager
```

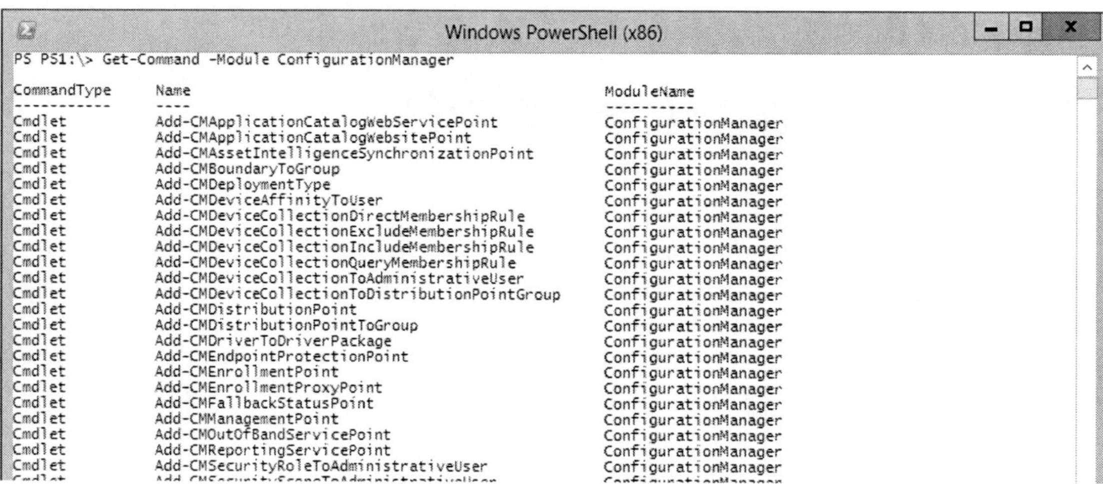

Listing all built-in ConfigMgr cmdlets.

You also can launch the ConfigMgr module manually from an existing PowerShell (x86) session using the following steps:

1. From **PowerShell (x86)**, type the following command:

   ```
   Import-Module -Name D:\Program Files\Microsoft Configuration Manager\AdminConsole\bin\ConfigurationManager.psd1
   ```

2. Change the connection context to **PS1** by typing the following command:

   ```
   Set-Location PS1:\
   ```

3. To verify that the **Powershell ConfigMgr module** is loaded, type the following command:

   ```
   Get-PSdrive -PSProvider cmsite
   ```

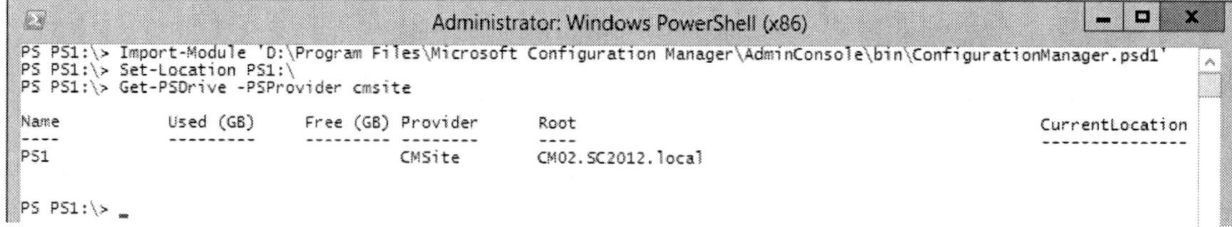

Importing the ConfigMgr module from an existing PowerShell session.

Getting Started with the Custom Powershell Module

1. Copy the **CM12_Function_Library_SP1.ps1 module** to **D:\Setup\Scripts**.
2. From the taskbar, right-click **PowerShell** and select **Run as Administrator**.

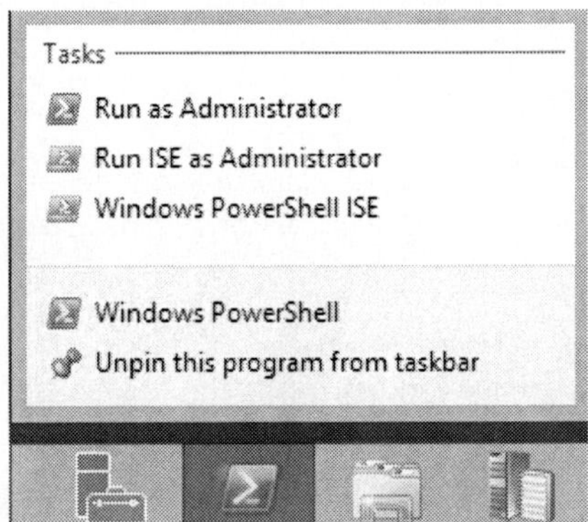

Starting PowerShell as administrator.

3. Type the following command:

```
cd d:\setup\scripts
```

4. Type the following command and press **Enter** when prompted:

```
Set-ExecutionPolicy 1
```

5. To load the library, type the following command. (Notice the space between the two dots.)

```
. .\CM12_Function_Library_SP1.ps1
```

6. To get a list of functions, type the following command:

```
Get-Help .\CM12_Function_Library_SP1.ps1
```

```
Administrator: Windows PowerShell
Windows PowerShell
Copyright (C) 2012 Microsoft Corporation. All rights reserved.

PS C:\windows\system32> d:
PS D:\> cd .\Setup
PS D:\Setup> cd .\scripts
PS D:\Setup\scripts> . .\CM12_Function_Library.ps1
PS D:\Setup\scripts> Get-Help .\CM12_Function_Library.ps1

NAME
    D:\Setup\scripts\CM12_Function_Library.ps1

SYNOPSIS
    This CM12 Function Library contains many functions


SYNTAX
    D:\Setup\scripts\CM12_Function_Library.ps1 [<CommonParameters>]


DESCRIPTION


RELATED LINKS
    Http://depsharee.blogspot.com
    Http://blog.Coretech.dk

REMARKS
    To see the examples, type: "get-help D:\Setup\scripts\CM12_Function_Library.ps1 -examples".
    For more information, type: "get-help D:\Setup\scripts\CM12_Function_Library.ps1 -detailed".
    For technical information, type: "get-help D:\Setup\scripts\CM12_Function_Library.ps1 -full".
    For online help, type: "get-help D:\Setup\scripts\CM12_Function_Library.ps1 -online"
```

Getting help.

7. To get a list of examples, type the following command:

   `.\Get-Help CM12_Function_Library_SP1.ps1 -Examples`

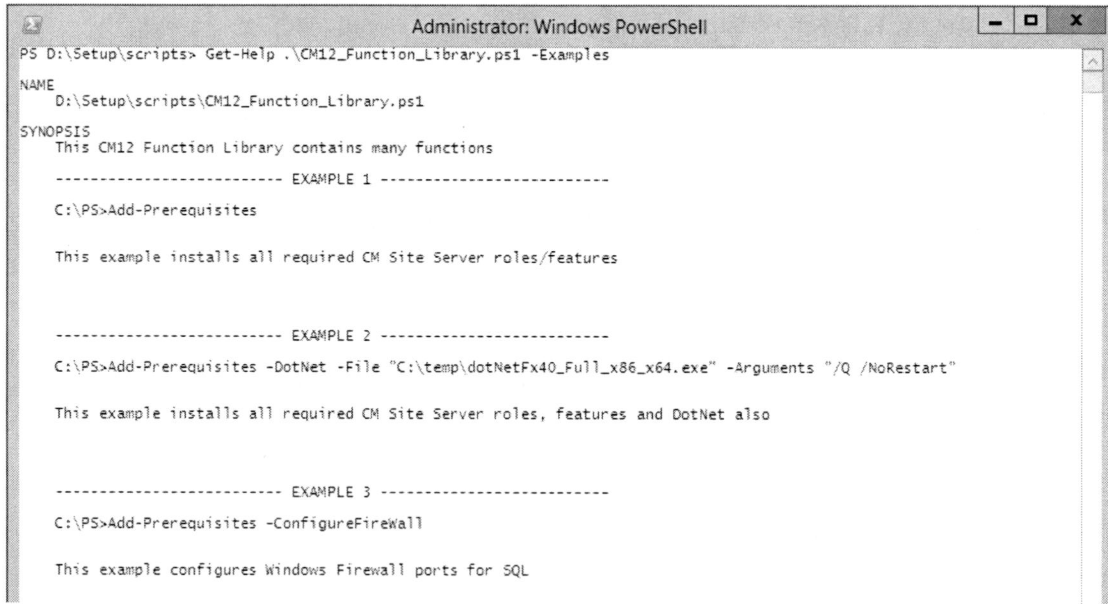

```
Administrator: Windows PowerShell
PS D:\Setup\scripts> Get-Help .\CM12_Function_Library.ps1 -Examples

NAME
    D:\Setup\scripts\CM12_Function_Library.ps1

SYNOPSIS
    This CM12 Function Library contains many functions

    -------------------------- EXAMPLE 1 --------------------------

    C:\PS>Add-Prerequisites

    This example installs all required CM Site Server roles/features



    -------------------------- EXAMPLE 2 --------------------------

    C:\PS>Add-Prerequisites -DotNet -File "C:\temp\dotNetFx40_Full_x86_x64.exe" -Arguments "/Q /NoRestart"

    This example installs all required CM Site Server roles, features and DotNet also



    -------------------------- EXAMPLE 3 --------------------------

    C:\PS>Add-Prerequisites -ConfigureFireWall

    This example configures Windows Firewall ports for SQL
```

Showing the different PowerShell examples.

Appendix C

Changes Made to Active Directory

Here is a list of the Active Directory objects that are created in the various guides throughout the book.

Object Type	Name
OU	Security Groups
OU	Software Groups
OU	Workstations
OU	Servers
OU	Service Accounts
OU	Users
User	CM_CP
User	CM_SR
User	CM_SQ
User	CM_EX
User	CM_NAA
User	CM_JD
User	SrvAdmin
User	WrkAdmin
User	JAP (domain user), full name Julie Petersen
User	SAN (domain user), full name Suzanne Angelhart
User	MAC (domain user), full name Mark Carragher
User	MLG (domain user), full name Michael L Gerrad
User	NEP (domain user), full name Nanna E Petersen
User	SMA (domain user), full name Sofie M Andersen

Object Type	Name
User	WKO (domain user), full name Wally Konig
User	BOP (domain user), full name Bob Paisly
Group	ConfigMgr_Servers
Group	LocalCorpAdmins
Group	Mac Users
Group	Sales
Group	Server Admins
Group	Workstation Admins
Group	SW_Office_2013_Install
Group	SW_Office_2013_Uninstall
Group	SW_WinRAR_Install
Group	SW_WinRAR_Uninstall
Group	SW_7-Zip_Install
Group	SW_7-Zip_Uninstall
Group	SUM_Pilot_1
Group	SUM_Pilot_2
Group	SUM_WRK_Excluded
Group	SUM_MW1
Group	SUM_MW2
Group	SUM_MW3
Group	SUM_SRV_Manual

Appendix D

Creating the Office 2013 Application

As with previous versions of Microsoft Office, you don't install Office 2013 using a single MSI file. Instead the install is invoked by running Setup.exe, which combines a language-neutral core package with one or more language-specific packages. In ViaMonstra, the business language is English, and you do not support any language packages. You do support installing Office 2013 to existing computers while showing the installation progress bar and also supporting a silent installation used in the image process. For ViaMonstra, you use the volume license version of Office 2013 because it offers additional installation options, like administrative setup.

Office setup goes through the following list of phases. As the administrator, you can influence the installation by adding a custom XML file, configuring an MSP file, and adding updates to the Update folder. Some of the settings that you can specify in the XML file also can be added to the MSP file. In the event of a conflict, settings from the XML file take precedence.

1. Runs Setup
2. Checks prerequisites
3. Reads XML data
4. Builds the feature tree
5. Creates a local installation source on the user's computer
6. Installs Office
7. Applies the customization file
8. Applies software updates

Prepare Office 2013 for Deployment

For these steps, you need to have a volume license version of Office 2013. The retail editions do not support administrative installs.

1. The first step in the process is to create the installation point. Create a folder and copy the entire content to the folder. In my example, I copied the content from the x64 edition of Office 2013 Professional Plus to **D:\Sources\Software\MS_Office_2013_Pro_X64** on **CM01**. If you want to add additional language support or Office versions, just copy the content to the same folder. When prompted to overwrite existing files, select **No**. (The files that would be overwritten are the common language-neutral files.)

2. On **CM01**, start the **OCT** (Office Customization Tool) by pressing the **Windows logo key + R**, typing **setup.exe /admin**, and then pressing **Enter**.
3. Select the Office version you want to customize and click **OK**. (This example uses Office 2013 Professional Plus x64 for the customization.)

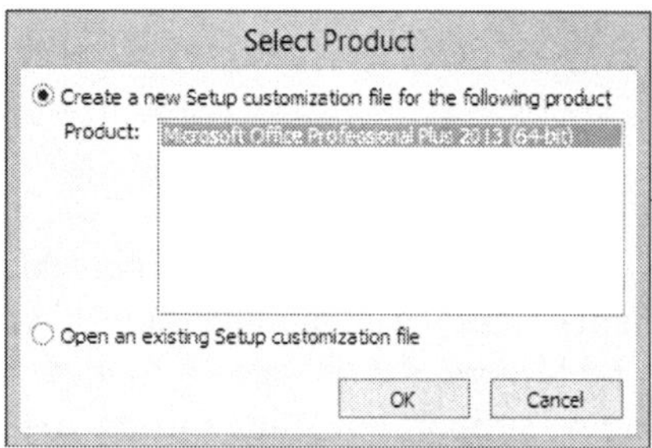

Selecting the Office 2013 version.

4. Select **Install location and organization name** and configure the following setting:

   Organization name: **ViaMonstra**

5. Select **Licensing and User Interface** and complete the following:
   a. Select **Use KMS client key**.
   b. Select **I accept the terms in the license agreement**.
   c. For **Display level**, select:
      i. **Basic** (shows the user a welcome screen, progress bar, and error messages but does not require any user input)
      ii. **Suppress modal**
      iii. **No cancel** (prevents the user from cancelling the installation)

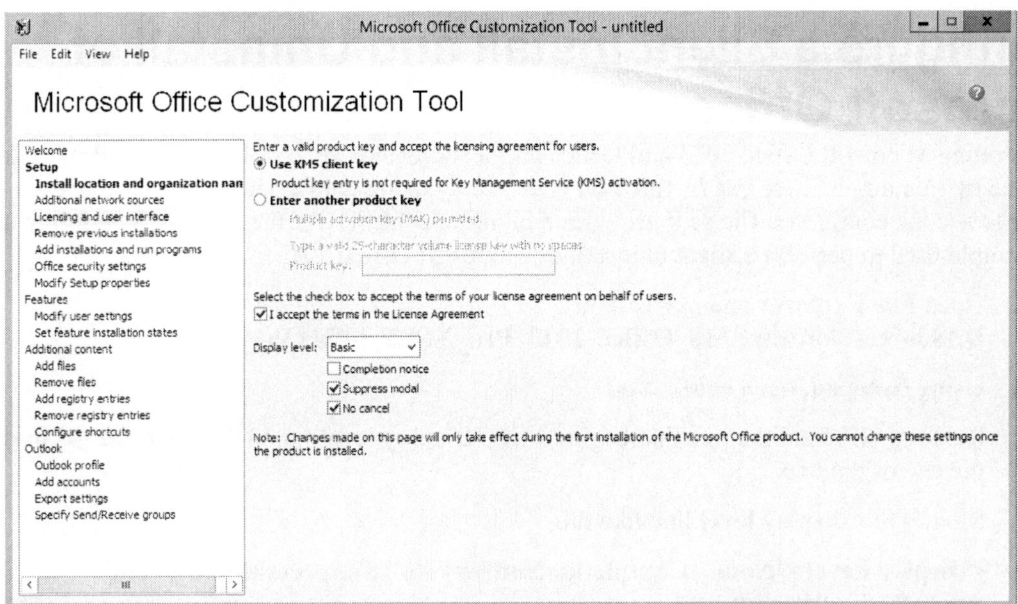

Customizing the Office GUI.

6. Select **Modify Setup properties** and complete the following:

   Click **Add** and type **SETUP_REBOOT** for the property name and **Never** as a value. (This allows ConfigMgr to control the reboot.)

7. Select **File / Save** and save the file as **1_VM.MSP** in the **D:\Sources\Software \MS_Office_2013_Pro_X64\updates** folder. All patches in the Updates folder are applied automatically (in alphabetic order) during installation. You can place the file in another folder if you are using setup.exe /adminfile.

Add Service Pack Files and Updates

As of this writing (June 2013), there is no service pack for Microsoft Office 2013. However, I am certain that one will be released eventually. When that happens, follow these steps to inject the updates into the installation:

1. On **CM01**, download **Microsoft Office 2013 Service Pack 1** to a folder.

2. Open a command prompt as **Administrator** and navigate to the folder containing the downloaded service pack file.

3. Type **<servicepack-filename.exe>/extract:D:\Setup\Office2013SP1** and press **Enter**. This command extracts all the files to **D:\Setup\Office2013SP1**.

4. Copy all the files from **D:\Setup\Office2013SP1** to **D:\Sources\Software\MS_Office_2013_Pro_X64\Updates**. All the files added to the Updates folder are applied automatically as the last step in the Office installation.

Configure a Silent Install and Uninstall of Microsoft Office

Uninstalling Microsoft Office 2013 and Office applications like Microsoft Visio and Project can be done by running msiexec.exe /x {product code} or by using config.xml. For ViaMonstra, I prefer to use the config.xml file as it provides a bit more control over the process. The following is an example used to perform a silent uninstall of Microsoft Office 2013:

1. Open **File Explorer** and navigate to **D:\Sources\Software\MS_Office_2013_Pro_X64\ProPlus.WW**.
2. Using **Notepad**, open **config.xml**.
3. Remove **<!--** from the line that begins with **<Display level=**, and then remove **-->** from the end of the line.
4. Modify the **Display level** line like this:

   <Display Level="None" CompletionNotice="No" SuppressModal="Yes" AcceptEula="Yes" />
5. Remove **<!--** from the line that begins with **<Logging Type**, and then remove **-->** from the end of the line.
6. Remove **<!--** from the line that begins with **<Setting Id**, and then remove **-->** from the end of the line.
7. Modify the **Setting Id** line like this:

   <Setting Id="SETUP_REBOOT" Value="Never" />

```
config.xml - Notepad
File Edit Format View Help
<Configuration Product="ProPlus">

         <Display Level="None" CompletionNotice="No" SuppressModal="Yes" AcceptEula="Yes" />

        <Logging Type="standard" Path="%temp%" Template="Microsoft Office Professional Plus Setup(*).txt" />

        <!-- <USERNAME Value="Customer" /> -->

        <!-- <COMPANYNAME Value="MyCompany" /> -->

        <!-- <INSTALLLOCATION Value="%programfiles%\Microsoft Office" /> -->

        <!-- <LIS CACHEACTION="CacheOnly" /> -->

        <!-- <LIS SOURCELIST="\\server1\share\Office;\\server2\share\Office" /> -->

        <!-- <DistributionPoint Location="\\server\share\Office" /> -->

        <!-- <OptionState Id="OptionID" State="absent" Children="force" /> -->

        <Setting Id="SETUP_REBOOT" Value="Never" />

        <!-- <Command Path="%windir%\system32\msiexec.exe" Args="/i \\server\share\my.msi" QuietArg="/q" ChainPosition="after" Execute="install" /> -->

</Configuration>
```

Configuring config.xml to perform a silent uninstall.

8. Save the file. Note that you also can use this file to perform a silent installation of Microsoft Office.

Configure Another Silent Install and Uninstall of Microsoft Office

Repeat the previous steps in this appendix to also create an administrative install and uninstall of the x86 version of Office 2013. Store the Office 2013 x86 installation files in **D:\Sources\Software\MS_Office_2013_Pro_X86** on **CM01**.

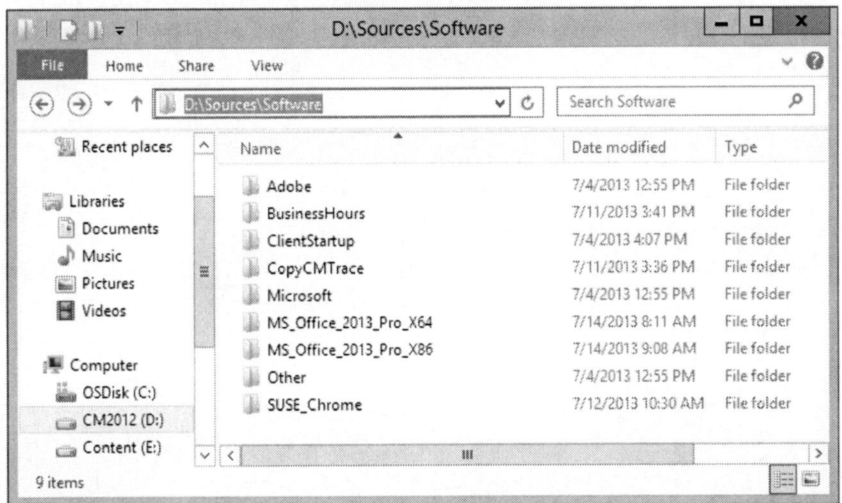

The D:\Sources\Software folder after adding administrative setups of both x86 and x64 versions of Office 2013.

Appendix E

Prestaging Content on Remote Distribution Points

Prestaging content has long been a feature only available for content that was distributed between site servers. This has changed in ConfigMgr 2012, with which you can now prestage all content. ConfigMgr will create a file with the prestaged content from an existing distribution. For that reason, the content must exist on at least one distribution point before you can create the prestaged content file. In this appendix, the boot images are used as examples.

1. In the **ConfigMgr console**, navigate to the **Software Library** workspace, and select **Operating Systems / Boot Images**.
2. Select the two custom **boot images**, and on the ribbon, click **Create Prestage Content File**.
3. On the **General** page, click **Browse**, save the file **D:\Setup\boot.pkgx**, and click **Next**.
4. On the **Content** page, click **Next**.
5. On the **Content Locations** page, configure this setting and click **Next**:

   Click **Add**, select **CM01.CORP.VIAMONSTRA.COM**, and click **OK**.

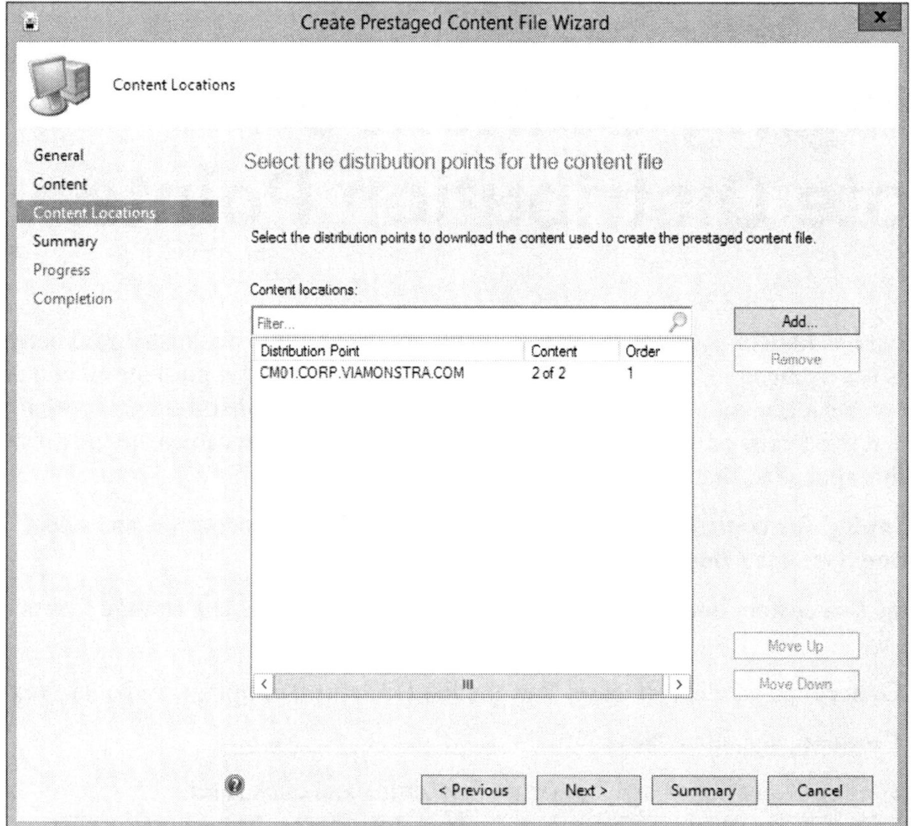

Selecting the source distribution point.

6. On the **Summary** page, read the summary and click **Next**.
7. On the **Completion** page, click **Close**.
8. Copy the **boot.pkgx** file to a remote device for transporting purposes.
9. Log on to the remote distribution point and copy the **boot.pkgx** from the remote device to **D:\SMS_DP$\SMS\Tools**.
10. Open a command prompt as **Administrator** and navigate to **D:\SMS_DP$\SMS\Tools**.
11. Type **ExtractContent.exe /P:D:\SMS_DP$\SMS\Tools\boot.pkgx** and press **Enter**. Notice that you get an error if the content is already present on the remote distribution point. In that case, use the command line /F to force the files to become prestaged.

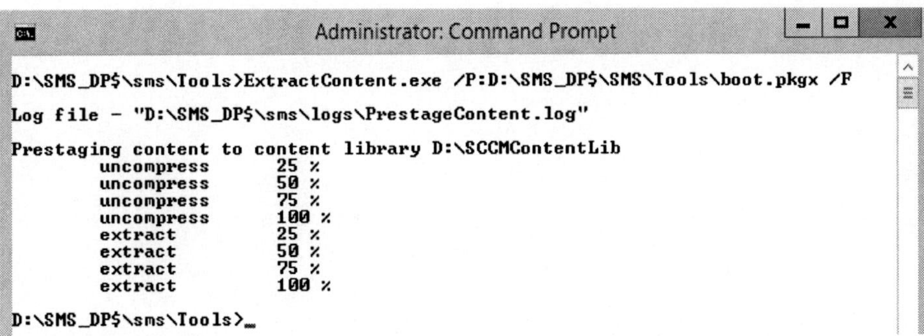

```
D:\SMS_DP$\sms\Tools>ExtractContent.exe /P:D:\SMS_DP$\SMS\Tools\boot.pkgx /F

Log file - "D:\SMS_DP$\sms\logs\PrestageContent.log"

Prestaging content to content library D:\SCCMContentLib
        uncompress      25 %
        uncompress      50 %
        uncompress      75 %
        uncompress      100 %
        extract         25 %
        extract         50 %
        extract         75 %
        extract         100 %

D:\SMS_DP$\sms\Tools>_
```

Prestaging packages.

12. Use **CMTrace.exe** to open **D:\SMS_DP$\sms\logs\PrestageContent.log**. From this log file, you are able to monitor the process.
13. On **CM01**, open the **ConfigMgr console** and navigate to the **Software Library** workspace.
14. Select **Operating Systems / Boot Images**, and distribute the content of both boot images to the remote distribution point. ConfigMgr will not redistribute the content because the remote distribution point has uploaded a state message with information about the content being prestaged.

Appendix F

Creating a Secondary Site

Due to the many infrastructure changes in ConfigMgr 2012, many companies are never required to install a secondary site server. However, if you do have a remote location with several thousand users, it is a good idea to consider a secondary site. Other valid reasons for configuring secondary sites are to offload some of the content processing from the site server, or when you have more than 250 distribution points in a single primary site. For each new secondary site, there is support for adding up to 250 distribution points. The steps in this appendix take you through the installation and configuration of a secondary site server.

Prerequisites for Installing the Secondary Site Server

Before installing the secondary site server, you need to ensure that these prerequisites are met:

1. Ensure that the user account installing the secondary site is a member of the local administrator group on the secondary site server.
2. Ensure that the secondary site server computer account has permissions to the System Management container in Active Directory.
3. Configure SQL Firewall ports.
4. Install Remote Differential Compression (RDC).
5. Install BITS.
6. For site-specific system role requirements, install all the prerequisites listed in Appendix A.
7. Run the prerequisites checker from the ConfigMgr 2012 SP1 installation media. (The order in which you perform the first six prerequisites is not important; however, this one must be done last.)

Note: If you have applied ConfigMgr 2012 SP1 CU2, you can't install secondary sites using the Copy installation source files over the network from the parent site server Installation Source Files option. This issue has been corrected in the following hotfix:

> "FIX: Errors when you try to install or recover a secondary site in System Center 2012 Configuration Manager": http://support.microsoft.com/kb/2867422

Run the Prerequisites Checker

It's a very good idea to run the prerequisite check before starting the secondary site installation. If you start the installation and the prerequisites are not met, you end up spending hours troubleshooting the failure and determining why it occurred.

1. Before you proceed with the rest of these steps, ensure that **CM03** is member of the **ConfigMgr_Servers** group in Active Directory and that the **ConfigMgr_Servers** group is a member of the local **Administrator** group on **CM03**.
2. On **CM01**, open the command prompt as **Administrator**.
3. Navigate to the **ConfigMgr 2012 SP1 installation media**.
4. Run this command from SMSSETUP\BIN\X64:

   prereqchk.exe /SEC cm03.corp.viamonstra.com /INSTALLSQLEXPRESS /Ssbport 4022 /Sqlport 1433

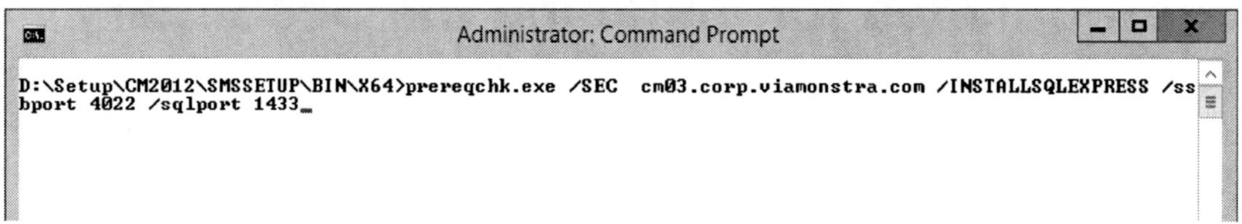

Running the prerequisites check on a secondary site server.

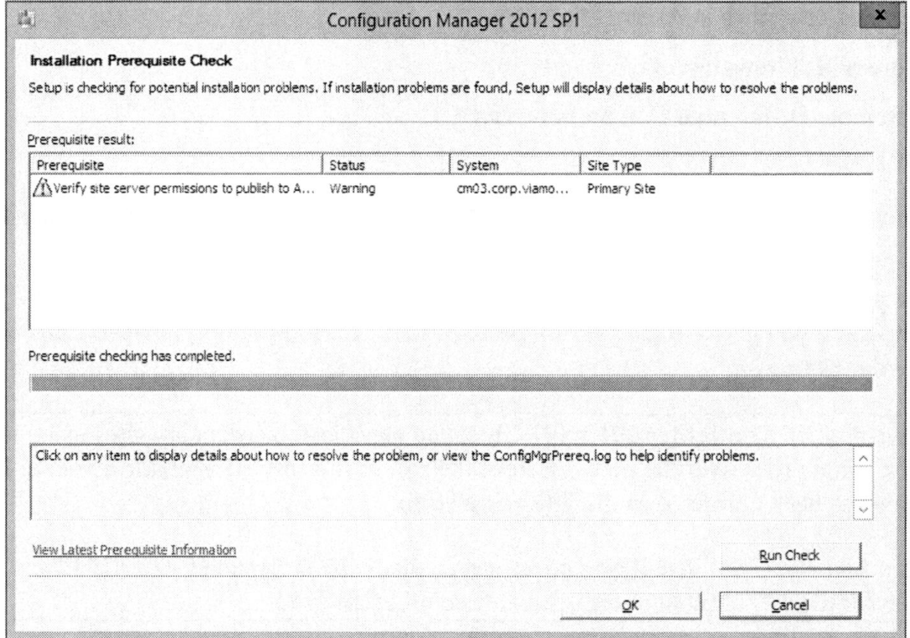

The warning about publishing data is a known issue and can safely be ignored.

5. Click **OK** to close the prerequisites checker.

Install the Secondary Site Server

Note: If you have upgraded CM01 to ConfigMgr 2012 SP1 CU2, install the http://support.microsoft.com/kb/2867422 hotfix before continuing.

1. On **CM01**, open the **ConfigMgr console**.
2. Navigate to the **Administration** workspace and select **Site Configuration / Sites**.
3. On the ribbon, click **Create Secondary Site**.
4. On the **Before You Begin** page, click **Next**.
5. On the **General** page, configure these settings and click **Next**:
    a. Site Code: **S01**
    b. Site Server Name: **CM03.corp.viamonstra.com**
    c. Site Name: **Secondary site, Liverpool**
    d. Installation folder: **D:\Program files\Microsoft Configuration Manager**

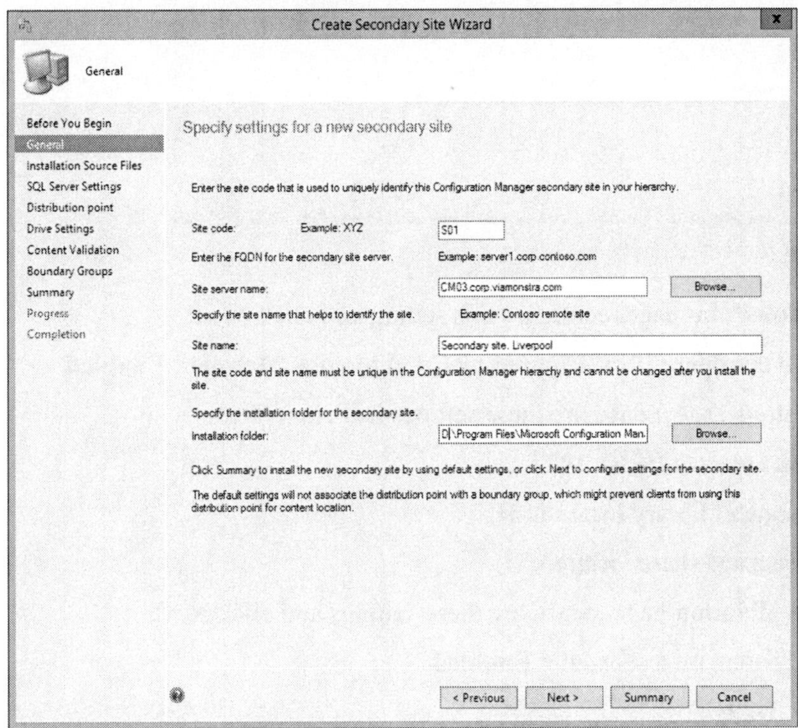

Configuring the site server information.

6. On the **Installation Source Files** page, select **Copy installation source files over the network from the parent site server** and click **Next.**
7. On the **SQL Server Settings** page, keep the default settings and click **Next**. The default settings will install SQL Server Express 2012 RTM.

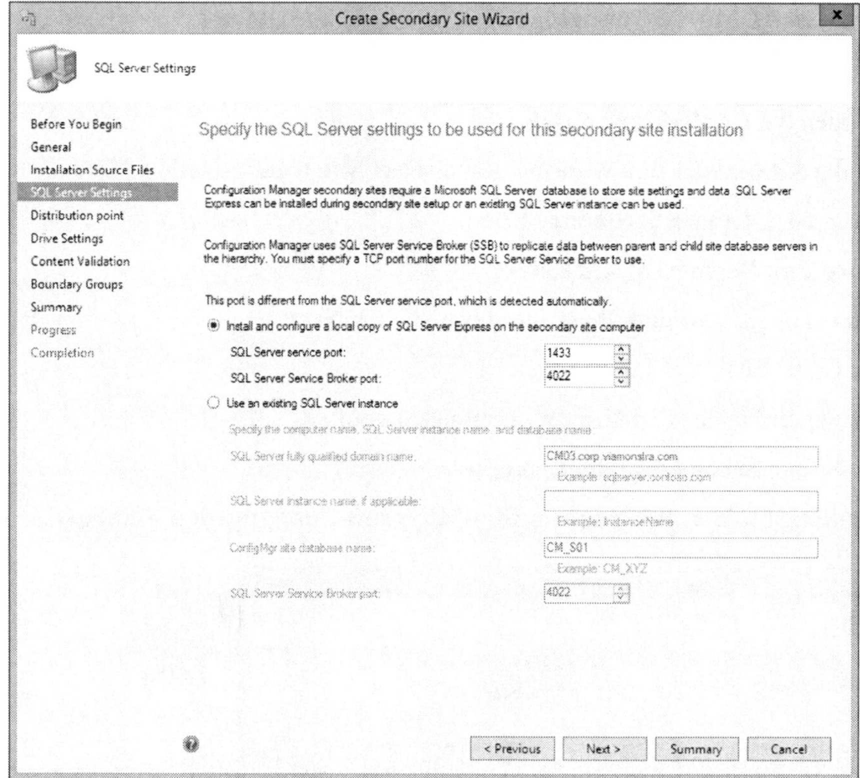

Specifying the local SQL Server.

8. On the **Distribution Point** page, configure this setting and click **Next**:

   Install and configure IIS if required by Configuration Manager: **Enabled**

9. On the **Drive Settings** page, configure these settings and click **Next**.
   a. Drive space reserve (MB): **1024**
   b. Primary content library location: **D**
   c. Primary package share location: **D**
10. On the **Content Validation** page, configure these settings and click **Next**:
    a. Validate content on a schedule: **Enabled**
    b. Schedule: **Daily**
11. On the **Boundary Groups** page, leave the default settings and click **Next**.

12. On the **Summary** page, read the summary and click **Next**.

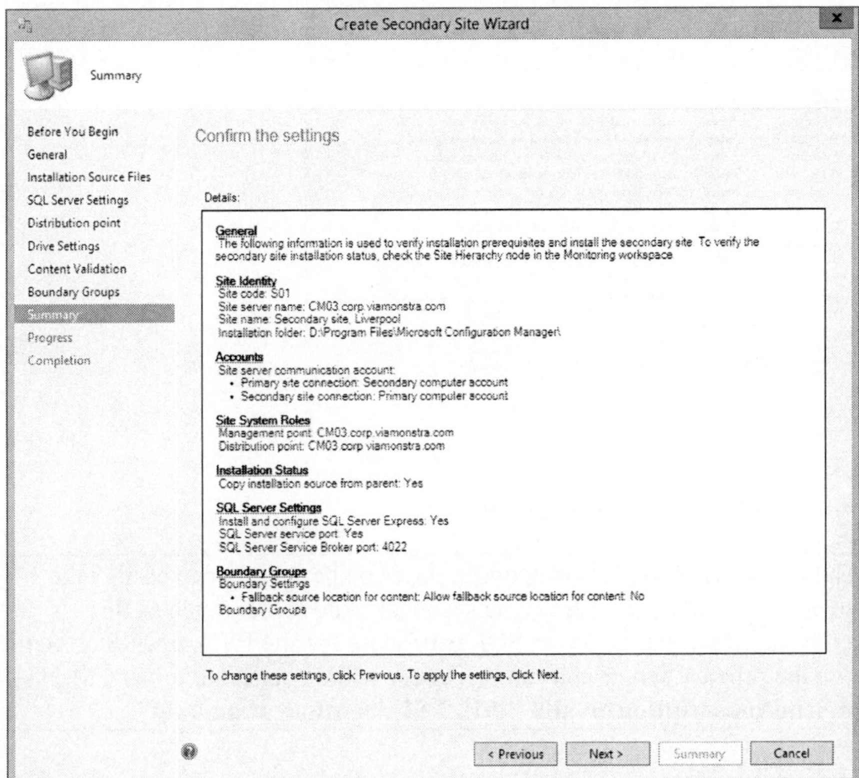

Secondary site server installation summary.

13. On the **Completion** page, click **Close**.

14. You can monitor the installation status by clicking **Show Install Status** on the ribbon.

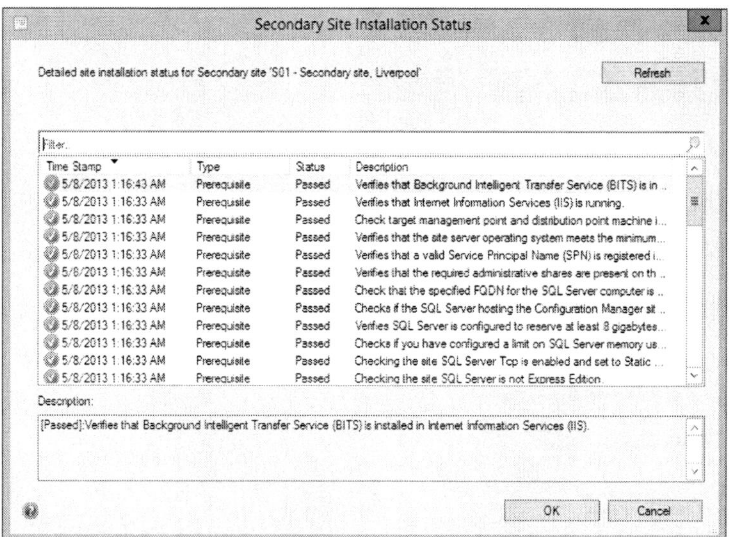

Monitoring the installation status in near realtime.

> **Real World Note:** The initial synchronization between the two site servers can easily take 10–15 minutes. If you see errors in the hman.log file on the secondary site server (such as this CheckParentSQLServerCertificate: Failed to get SQL certificate for site PS1), open SQL Server Management Studio on the primary server and run this query while connected to the CM_PS1 database: **Exec spDrsSendSubscriptionInvalid 'S01','PS1','configuration data'**.

Post-Installation SQL Server Express Updates

The ConfigMgr installation wizard installs only SQL Server Express version 11. 0.2100.60, which is SQL Server Express 2012 RTM. After the secondary site server installation is done, you should upgrade to SQL Server Express 2012 SP1. You can download SQL Express 2012 SP1 from http://www.microsoft.com/en-us/download/details.aspx?id=35579.

1. On **CM03**, log on as **VIAMONSTRA\Administrator**.
2. From the **Server Manager**, select the **Tools** menu and open **Services**.
3. Stop these three services:
   a. **SMS Agent host (the Management Point service)**
   b. **SMS Executive**
   c. **SMS Site Component Manager**

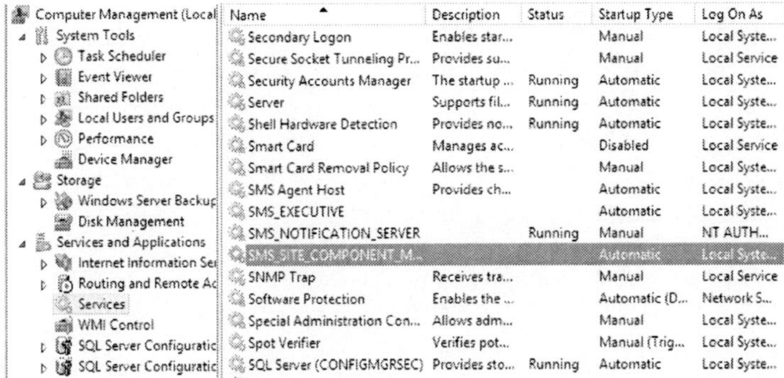

Stopping the main ConfigMgr services.

4. Open a command prompt as **administrator**, and navigate to the folder containing the **SQL 2012 SP1** update.
5. Run the following command:

```
SQLEXPR_x64_ENU.exe /Action=Patch
/IAcceptSQLServerLicenseTerms /AllInstances /Quiet
```

6. After the upgrade is finished, restart the three ConfigMgr services and the SQL Server (**CONFIGMGRSEC**) service.

   The new SQL Server Express version will be 11.0.3000.0

Verify the Secondary Site Installation

For me, the easiest way to verify that the installation has started is by looking at the log files. After the installation is done, I monitor the status of the secondary site in the ConfigMgr console:

1. In the **Administration** workspace, select **Site Configuration / Sites**.

   Here you see the status of the secondary site server. After a successful installation (and refresh of the console), the State will be listed as Active.

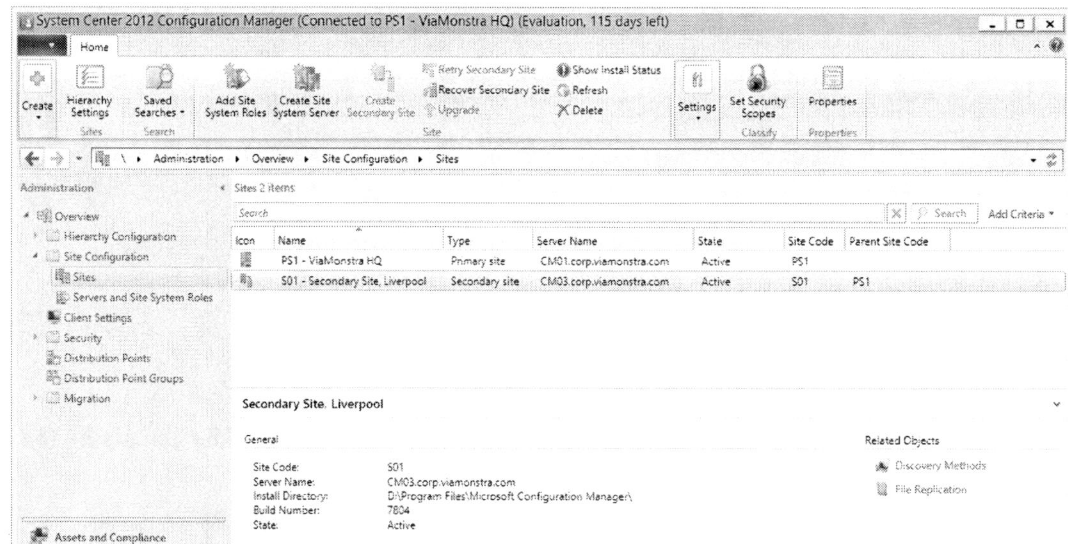

Active secondary site.

2. Open the **Monitoring** workspace and select **Site Hierarchy**. Here you see a Hierarchy diagram and the overall status of the sites.

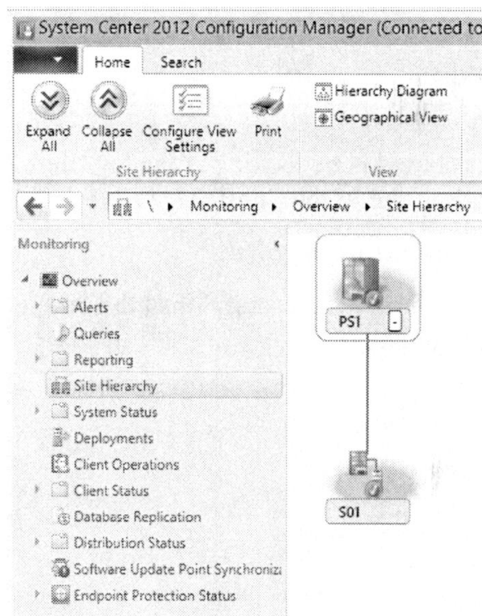

Viewing the hierarchy status.

3. On the ribbon, click **Configure View Settings** and select the **Site Location** tab.
4. Configure these settings and click **OK**:
    a. For site **PS1**, type **New York, United States** in **Location**.
    b. For site **S01**, type **Liverpool, United Kingdom** in **Location**.

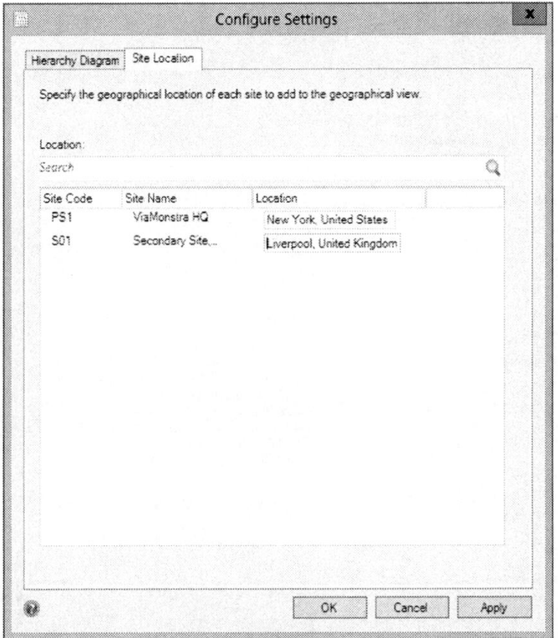

Configuring Bing Map location settings.

5. Back in the site hierarchy settings, click **Geographical View** on the ribbon .

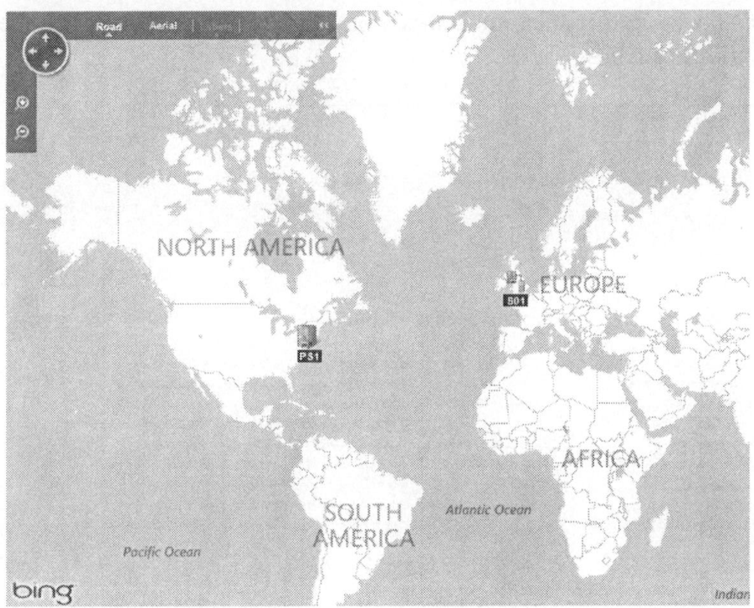

The Bing Map showing the two locations.

6. In the **Monitoring** workspace, select **Database replication**.

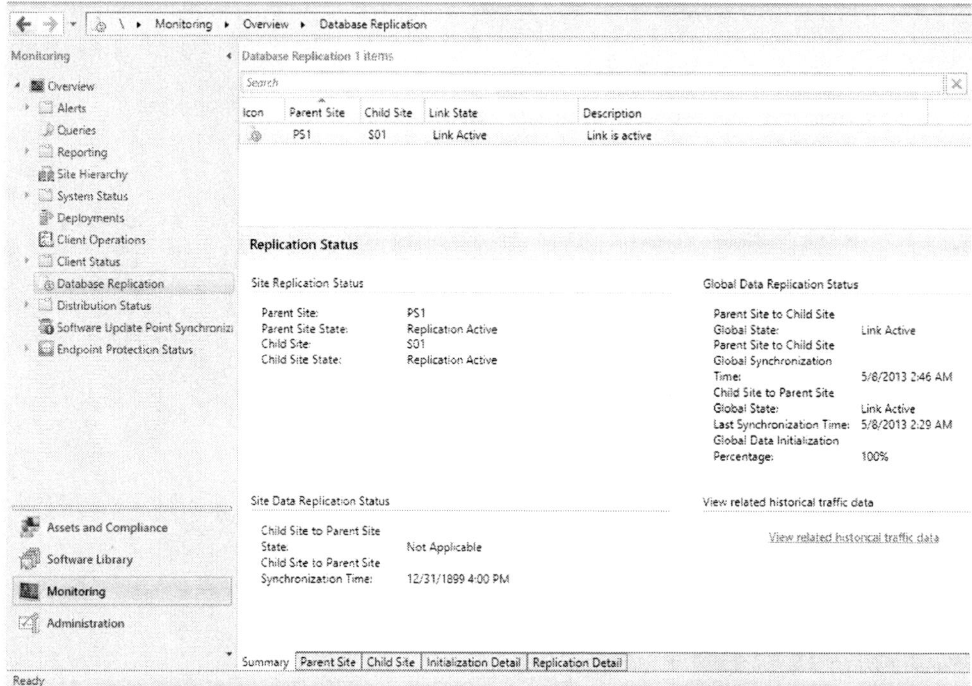

Monitoring database replication.

7. The Summary tab lists the overall replication status. For detailed information, click the **Parent Site** or the **Child Site** tab.

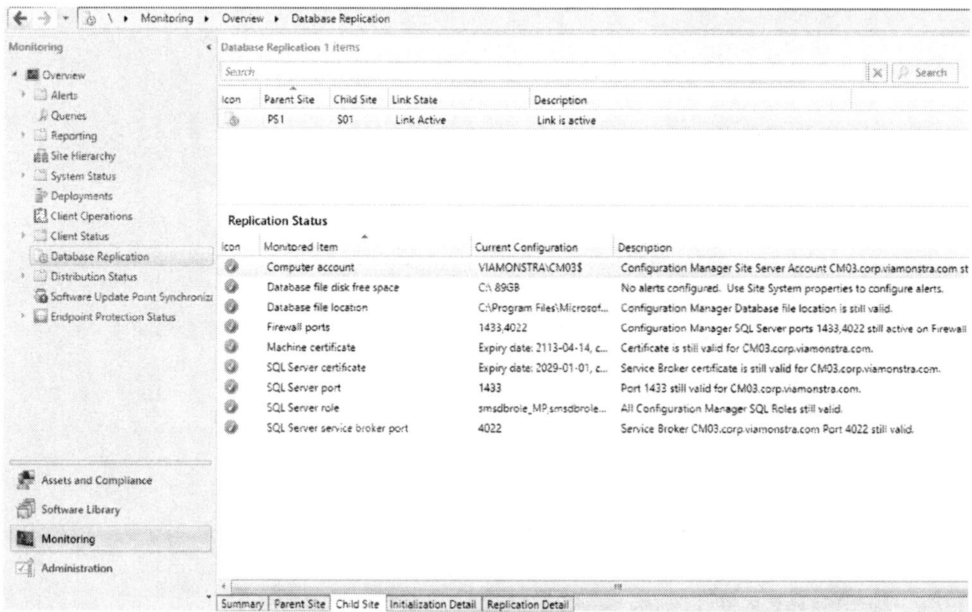

Detailed information about the parent site replication status.

Post-Secondary Site Tasks

After the secondary site is installed, it's time to configure the site which includes the following tasks:

- Configuring boundaries and boundary groups to service local clients only
- Creating a new distribution point group or adding the distribution point to an existing distribution point group
- Installing and configuring additional site system roles

Configure the Secondary Site to Service Local Clients Only

1. In the **Administration** workspace, navigate to **Hierarchy Configuration / Boundaries**.
2. Select the IP address range boundary that is used in Liverpool (**192-168.3.1 - 192.168.3.254**), and from the ribbon, select **Add Selected Items / Add Selected Items to New Boundary Groups**.
3. On the **General** page, configure these settings and then click the **References** tab:
    a. Name: **CL Liverpool**
    b. Description: **Content location boundary group for Liverpool**
4. On the **Reference** tab, configure this setting and click **OK**:

    Click **Add**, and from the list of distribution points, select **\\CM03.corp.viamonstra.com**.

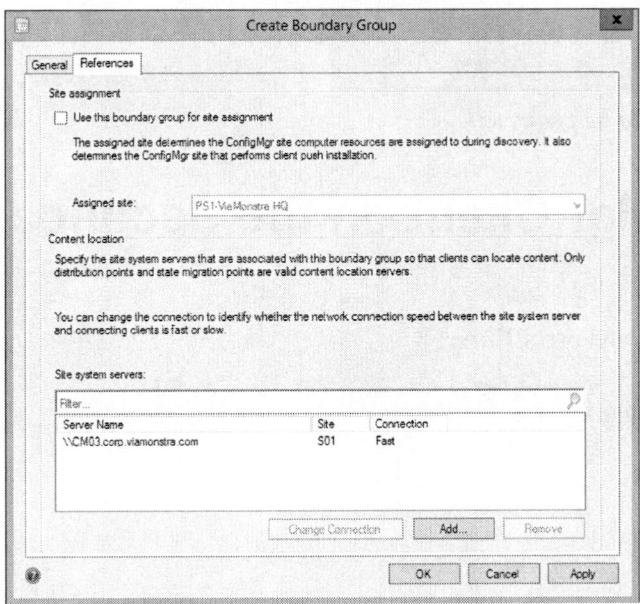

Creating the secondary site boundary group.

5. Still in the **Administration** workspace, navigate to **Site Configuration / Servers / Site System Roles**.
6. Select the **\\CM03.corp.viamonstra.com** server and open the **Distribution Point** properties.
7. Select the **Group Relationship** tab, click **Add**, select **All Content**, and click **OK**.
8. Select the **Boundary Groups** tab, remove the checkmark in **Allow fallback source location for content** and click **OK**.

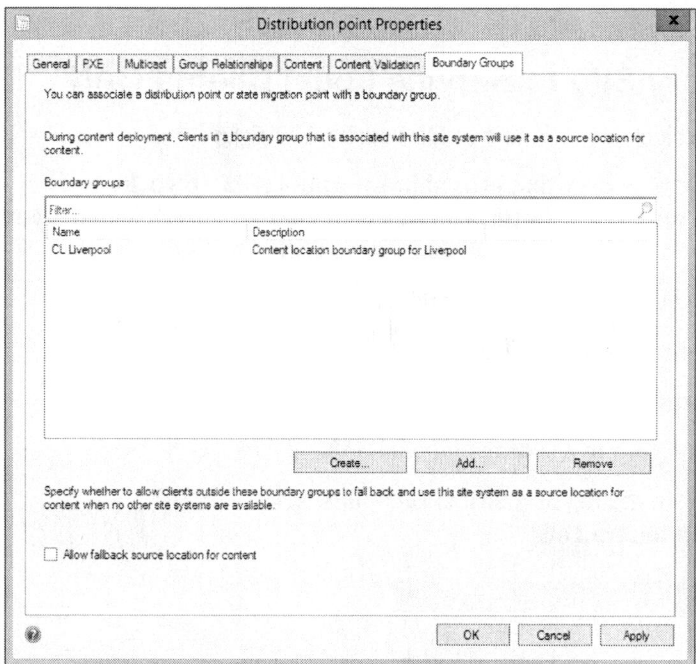

Configuring the distribution point to be protected.

Install the ConfigMgr Client on the Secondary Site Server

1. Open **Run**, type the following, and press **Enter**:

```
\\CM01\SMS_PS1\Client\ccmsetup.exe SMSsitecode=PS1
/MP:CM03.CORP.VIAMONSTRA.COM
```

2. Open the **Configuration Manager** Properties on the **Start screen**. Notice the site and management point information

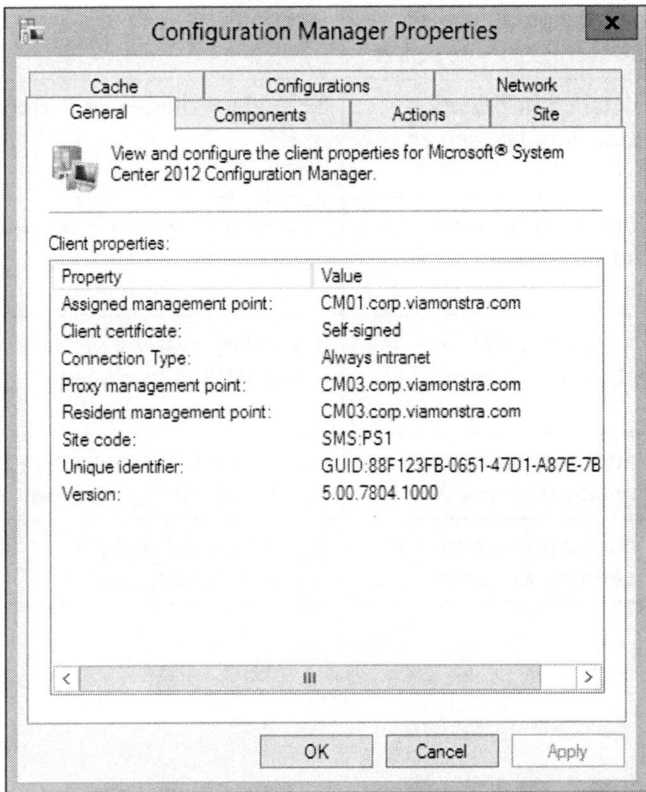

A ConfigMgr client in a secondary site.

Real World Note: Don't panic when you check the assigned site code after the client is installed. The ConfigMgr client will always be assigned to a primary site, never to a secondary site. To control that the client is using the local distribution point and management point, check these log files on the client: clientlocation.log, locationservices.log, contenttransfermanager.log, and cas.log.

Useful Log Files

You can use the log files in the following table to track activity related to the secondary site installation process.

Log File	Description	Location
Hman.log	Gives you information about running the prerequisites check on the secondary site server	Parent site server default log location

Log File	Description	Location
ConfigMgrPrereq.log	Gives you detailed information about running the prerequisites check on the secondary site server	Parent site server default log location
ConfigMgrSetup.log	Gives you detailed information about the secondary site server installation	Secondary site server in the root of C:\
SiteComp.log	Gives you information about installing the site system components.	Secondary site server default log location
Sender.log	Gives you information about sending content data between the sites	Secondary site and primary site server default log location
Despool.log	Gives you information about receiving content from another site	Secondary site and primary site server default log location
Rcmctrl.log	Gives you information about the SQL replication between the sites	Secondary site and primary site server default log location

Appendix G

Migrating from ConfigMgr 2007

With previous versions of ConfigMgr you were able to do an in-place upgrade of the old version. That is not possible with ConfigMgr 2012. In order to preserve existing ConfigMgr 2007 objects, you need to use the built-in ConfigMgr 2012 migration tool. With this tool, you can migrate several primary ConfigMgr 2007 sites into a single ConfigMgr 2012 site.

In this appendix, you learn how to migrate a ConfigMgr 2007 hierarchy consisting of a primary site server, a secondary site server, and a remote distribution point. Note that none of these machines are part of the hydration kit.

Computers Used in This Appendix

ConfigMgr 2007 servers:

- Primary site server: cm01.sc2012.local
- Secondary site server: cm01ss01.sc2012.local
- Remote distribution point: cm01dp

ConfigMgr 2012 server:

Primary site server: cm02.sc2012.local

Planning for Migration

When migrating from ConfigMgr 2007 to ConfigMgr 2012, you need to be sure to plan the migration correctly. First of all, you need to prepare your environment so that you can migrate the objects to the new ConfigMgr 2012 environment:

1. Service Pack 2 for ConfigMgr 2007 needs to be installed on all site servers. It doesn't matter if R2 or R3 is installed.
2. There is no support for users and devices in one collection. Create separate collections for users and devices.
3. Collections with more than one query rule are not supported.
4. A site code is a unique entity. Use a new site code in your ConfigMgr 2012 environment.
5. Upgrade your branch distribution points to Windows 7.

6. Be sure that your package source is always a UNC path. Local paths will not work when migrating the objects to a new ConfigMgr 2012 server.
7. Plan which objects you need to migrate and what is easier to recreate.
8. Investigate the need for migrating custom reports.
9. If you integrated MDT in ConfigMgr 2007, plan how to migrate the custom steps in your task sequences.
10. If you have custom boot images in ConfigMgr 2007, those will have to be recreated.

Note: With Service Pack 1, it also is possible to migrate from one ConfigMgr 2012 Service Pack 1 site to another ConfigMgr 2012 Service Pack 1 site. The process is the same as when migrating from ConfigMgr 2007.

Preparing the Configuration Manager 2007 Environment

To be able to use the migrated packages, you must be sure that all packages are using an UNC path to point to the package source. In this example, CM01 is the name of the ConfigMgr 2007 primary site server. The site server has been used to store the package source files locally in D:\Sources\Software. The location has also been shared as \\CM01\SCCM_Sources$.

Check Package Source Locations from ConfigMgr 2007

1. Log on to the ConfigMgr 2007 server (**CM01**).
2. Open the **ConfigMgr console** and navigate to **Computer Management\Software Distribution\Packages**. Open the **package properties** for **Adobe Reader 9.3** (for instance) and select the **Data Source** tab. You can right-click the package and select Properties to open the package properties. Notice the source directory.

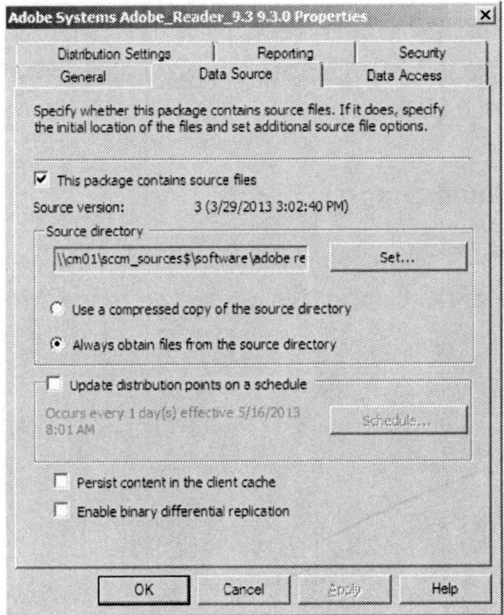

Package with an UNC source path.

3. Click **OK** to close the properties.
4. Open the **package properties** for **Adobe Reader 7.0** and select the **Data Source** tab. Notice the source directory.

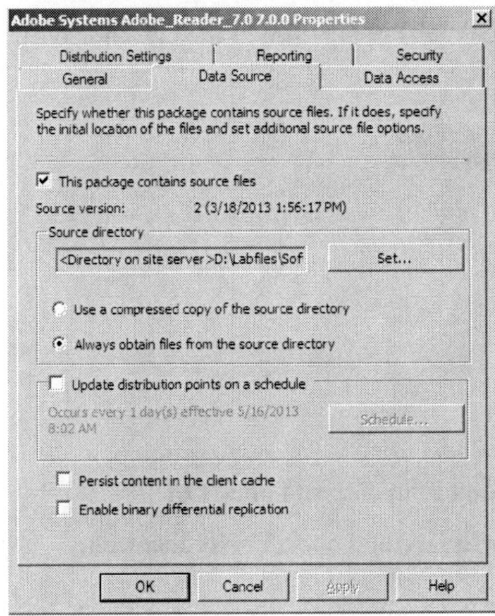

Package with a local source path.

5. Click **OK** to close the properties.

Install and Configure the Package Source Change Utility

One of the community tools mentioned earlier in this book is the Package Source Changer that can be downloaded from http://blog.coretech.dk/jgs/coretech-package-source-changer/. The tool is also part of the book sample files.

1. Run **PackageSourceChanger.exe** with as **administrator**.
2. Accept the license terms and click **Configuration**.
3. In **Configuration**, you need to type the name of the ConfigMgr site server; type **CM01** and click **Save**.

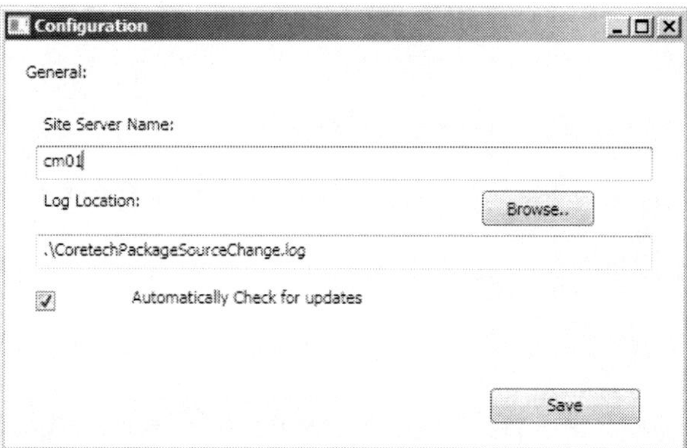

Configuring the utility to connect to the CM2007 server.

4. Click **List** to get a list of all package source locations being used in the current ConfigMgr 2007 site server.

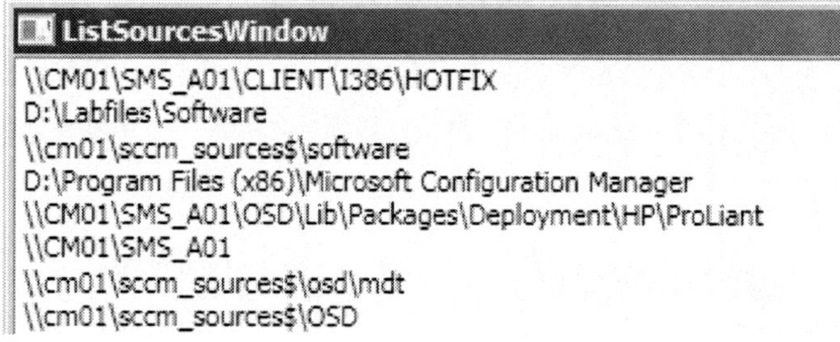

All package source locations.

5. From the list, select the source location you want to update and click **OK**.
6. In **Replace**, type **\\CM02\SCCM_Sources\Software** and click **Verify location**.
7. Select **Copy content from Old to new source**.
8. Click **Select Packages**. Select the applications that you want to move from the list and click **Save**.

Selecting the packages for which you want to change the package source.

9. Click **Start** to start the package source update process.

Package sources are changed and the source is copied to the new CM01 server.

10. Repeat the step again for every different package source, for instance **D:\Sources**.
11. Back in the ConfigMgr console, open the **Adobe Reader 7.0** package properties and select the **Data source** tab.

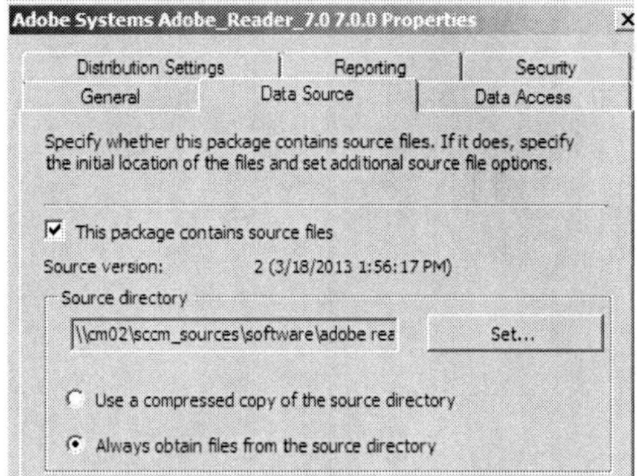

Checking the source of the package.

12. Verify that the source is correct and click **OK**.

Real World Note: Please plan carefully when you update the package source on a site. The distribution manager will refresh the package on all distribution points when the package source is updated. If you have a large site and you have to continue supporting the ConfigMgr 2007 site for a long period, then perform the package source change in ConfigMgr 2012 after you have done the package migration. That way, you are not affecting the existing production environment. You can check the distmgr.log file on the ConfigMgr 2007 server to monitor the package update process.

Remove Boundaries

1. Open the **ConfigMgr console**.
2. Navigate to **Site Database\Site Management\Site Settings\Boundaries**, and delete all boundaries.

Note: You are not forced to remove the boundaries in ConfigMgr 2007, but by removing the boundaries, you clean up the System Management container in Active Directory. ConfigMgr 2012 and ConfigMgr 2007 do not have overlapping boundaries as long as you do not create any site assignment boundary groups in ConfigMgr 2012.

Migrating from CM2007

Configure the Data Source Hierarchy

1. Log on to the ConfigMgr 2012 primary site server (in this appendix **CM02)** and open the **ConfigMgr console**.
2. Select the **Administration** workspace.
3. Navigate to **Overview / Migration / Active Source Hierarchy**.
4. On the ribbon, click **Specify Source Hierarchy**.
5. In **Top-Level Configuration Manager 2007** site server, type **cm01. sc2012.local**.
6. In **Source site access accounts**, click **Set, New Account**, **Browse**; type **sc2012\administrator**. Click **Check names** and click **OK**.
7. Type the account password twice and click **Verify**.
8. Type the name of the ConfigMgr 2007 server and the database name and click **Test connection**. Click **OK** after testing the connection,

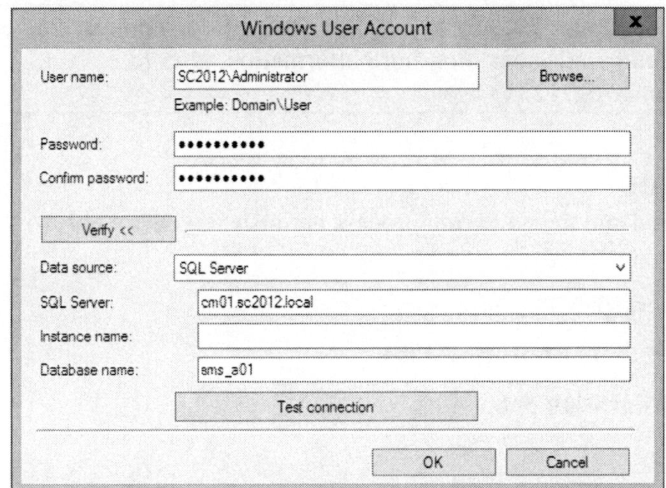

Specifying the account used to connect to ConfigMgr 2007.

9. Back at **Specify Source Hierarchy**, select **Enable distribution point sharing for the source site server** and click **OK** twice. This starts the gathering process and collects metadata from the CM2007 hierarchy.
10. The gathering process can take a few minutes. Open **migmctrl.log** and monitor the process.
11. Click **Close** when the gathering process is finished.

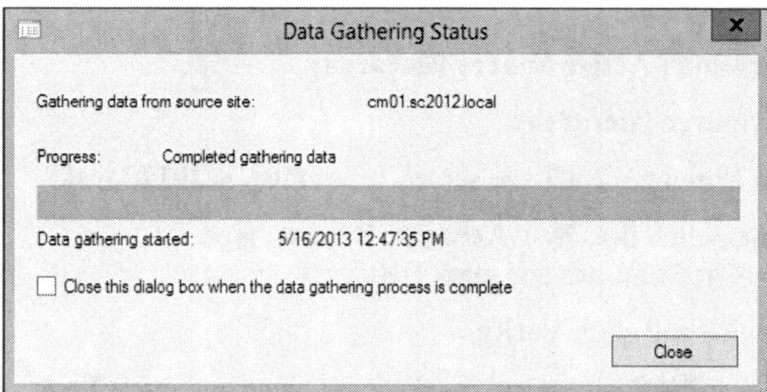

The data gathering process reading information from your CM 2007 environment.

> **Note:** You do not have to use the administrator account to perform a migration. You can create a custom migration account with required permissions. For more information, refer to http://technet.microsoft.com/en-us/library/gg712313.aspx.

Migrate Software Packages

After the source hierarchy is configured and the gathering process is finished, you are able to migrate ConfigMgr objects like packages:

1. Select the **Administration** workspace.
2. Navigate to **Overview / Migration / Migration Jobs**.
3. On the ribbon, click **Create Migration Job**.
4. In **Name**, type **Packages**.

5. In **Job type**, select **Object migration** and click **Next**.

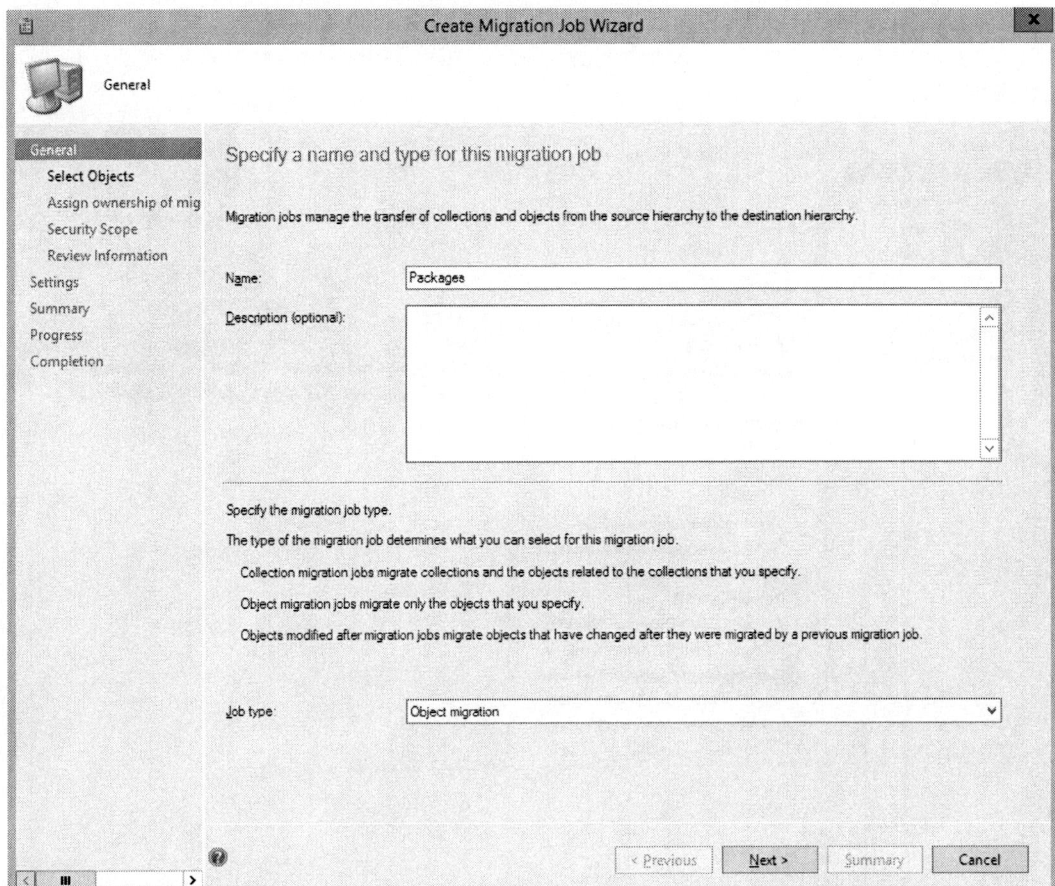

Creating an object migration job.

6. Select **Software Distribution**, select the packages you want to migrate, and click **Next**.

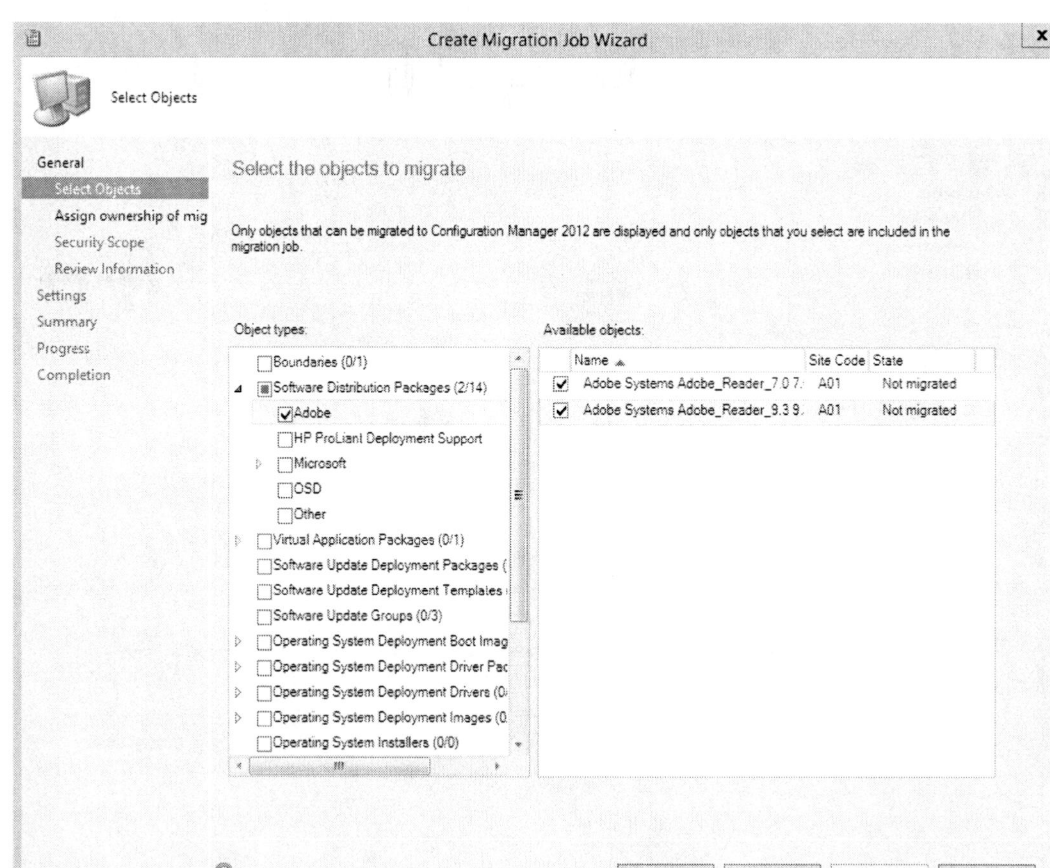

Selecting the packages you want to migrate.

7. On the **Assign ownership of migrated objects** page, click **Next**.
8. Select the **Default** security scope and click **Next**.

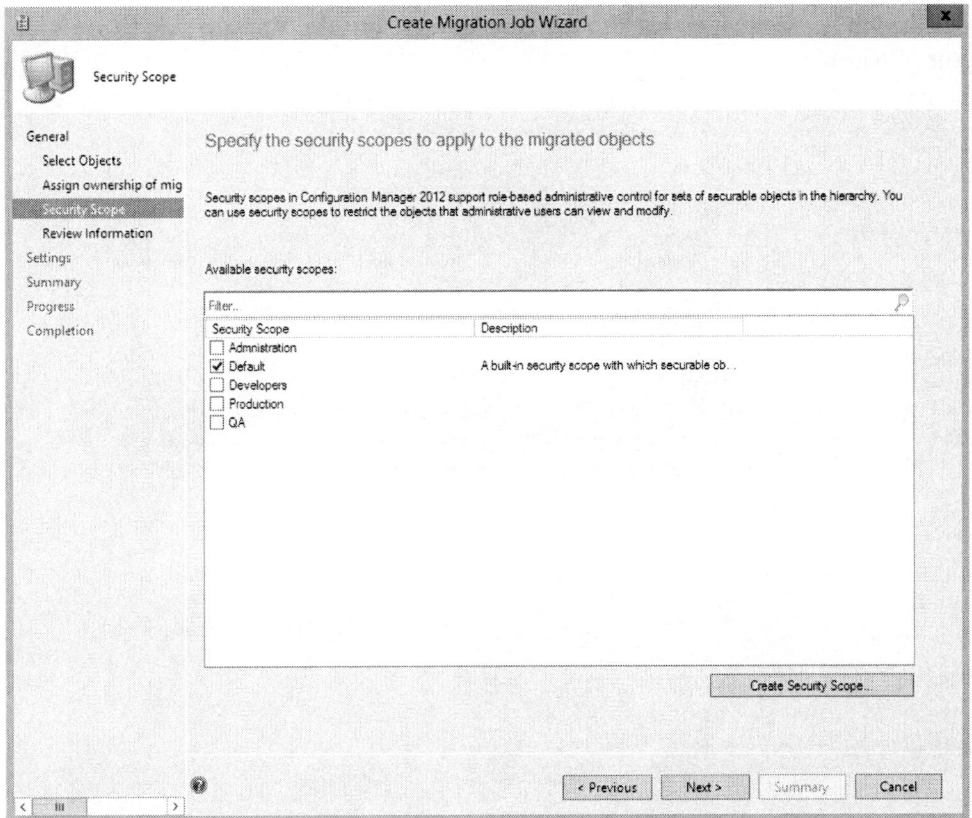

Selecting the security scope.

9. Review the migration information and click **Next**.
10. Click **Schedule the migration job**, assign a schedule for the job to begin, and click **Next**.
11. Click **Next** and **Close**.

12. After the job has started, go back to the **ConfigMgr console**. You are able to see a job status of **Running**.

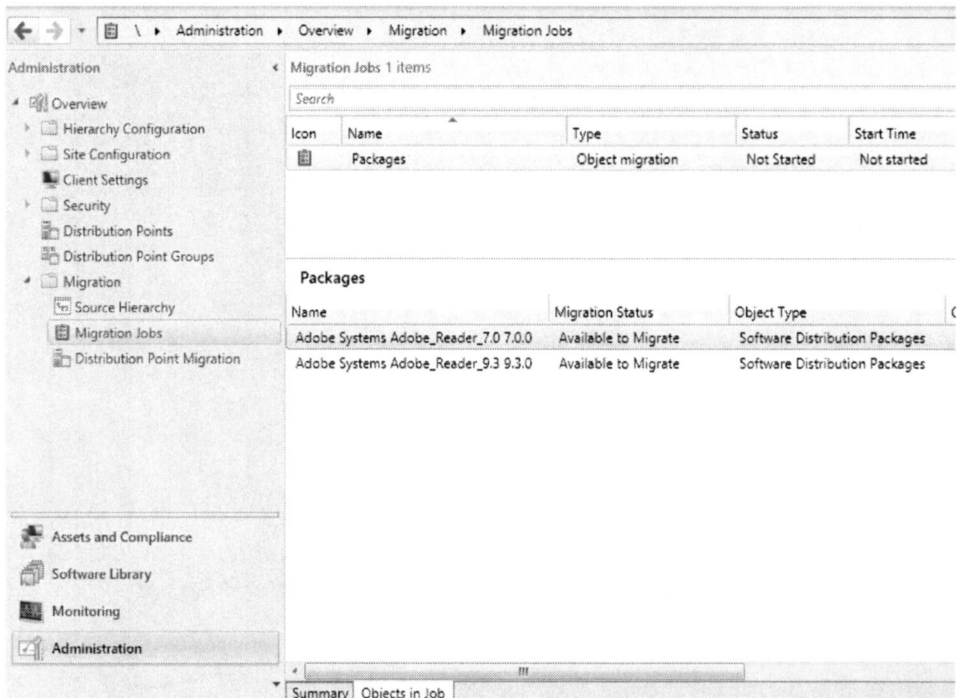

Monitoring the migration of the objects.

13. After the job is complete, refresh the view in Migration Jobs and the status should display **Migrated**.

The Package Conversion Manager

The Package Conversion Manager is a utility from Microsoft that can assist you in converting traditional packages into the application model. The utility integrates into the ConfigMgr console and adds extra options to the Software Library workspace.

Install the Package Conversion Manager

1. Close the **ConfigMgr console**.
2. Download the **Package Conversion Manager** from **http://www.microsoft.com/en-us/download/details.aspx?id=34605**.
3. Run **PCMSP1Setup-ENU.exe** with administrative privileges from your download location.
4. Click **Next**, **Accept the License terms**, and click **Install**.
5. Restart the **ConfigMgr console**.

Convert Packages

In the following example, you convert the MSI versions of Adobe Reader X, Adobe Reader 9.30 and Adobe Reader 7.0. Not all packages can be converted automatically, but the wizard provides you with readiness information for each package that has been analyzed. Note that in this example one readiness state is automatic and two are manual.

1. Select the **Software Library** workspace and navigate to **Packages / Adobe**. Right-click the columns above the packages and select **Readiness**.
2. Select the **Adobe** packages, and on the ribbon, click **Analyze Package**.

   After analyzing the packages, ConfigMgr 2012 lists the readiness state for each package.

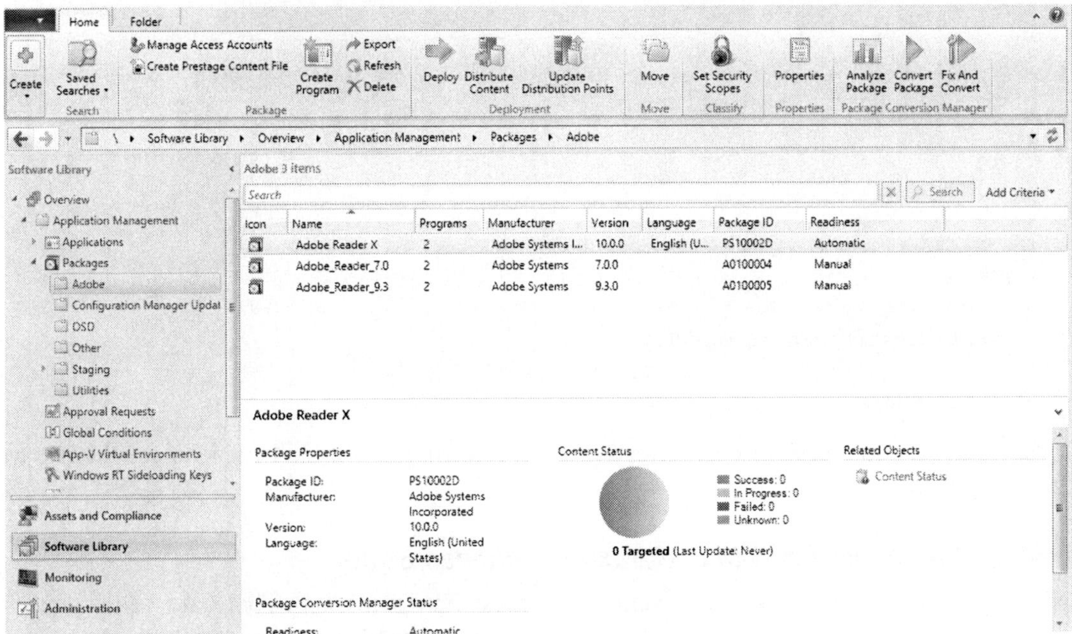

See the readiness state of the packages.

3. Select the **Adobe Reader** X package, right-click the packages, and select **Convert Package**.
4. Click **OK**.

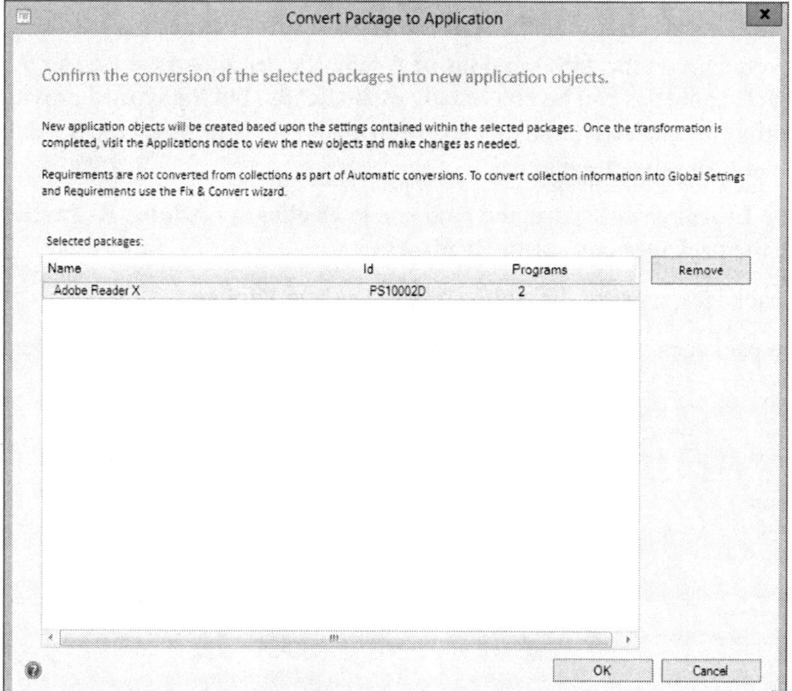

The package conversion completed.

5. Click **Close**.
6. Navigate to **Applications**. After a console refresh, you should be able to see the two new applications.

Analyze the Packages with a Manual Readiness State

There can be several reasons why a package readiness state is manual. That state means your package can be converted but you have to do some manual work first. For assistance with the process, select the package and click Fix and Convert on the ribbon.

The command line is an issue with older ConfigMgr 2007 packages that are imported using the package import feature is the command line.

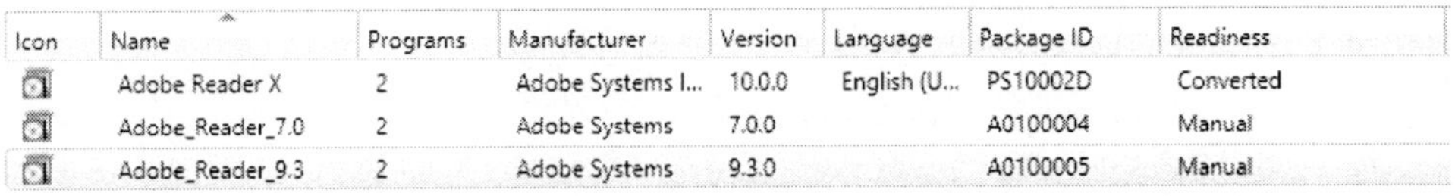

Icon	Name	Programs	Manufacturer	Version	Language	Package ID	Readiness
	Adobe Reader X	2	Adobe Systems I...	10.0.0	English (U...	PS10002D	Converted
	Adobe_Reader_7.0	2	Adobe Systems	7.0.0		A0100004	Manual
	Adobe_Reader_9.3	2	Adobe Systems	9.3.0		A0100005	Manual

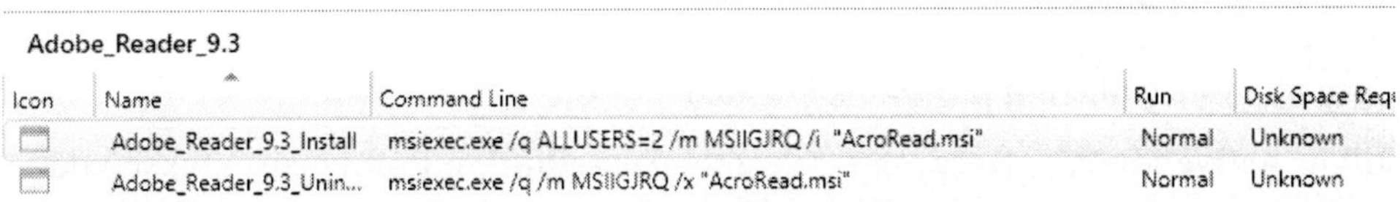

Adobe_Reader_9.3

Icon	Name	Command Line	Run	Disk Space Req
	Adobe_Reader_9.3_Install	msiexec.exe /q ALLUSERS=2 /m MSIIGJRQ /i "AcroRead.msi"	Normal	Unknown
	Adobe_Reader_9.3_Unin...	msiexec.exe /q /m MSIIGJRQ /x "AcroRead.msi"	Normal	Unknown

Standard program command line from an imported package in ConfigMgr 2007.

To fix that issue, open the program command lines and remove the parameter /M MSIIGJRQ and run the package analyzer again. The readiness state will be changed from Manual to Automatic. This approach only fixes issues with packages using the /M command line. You will likely run into other issues that must be fixed in different ways.

Note: The Package Conversion Manager is a neat little tool, but it's not the correct solution for migrating all packages. Sometimes it is just easier to create the application manually and not use an existing package.

Distribution Point Sharing

Distribution point sharing is a feature used while the migration is in progress and you have a mix of ConfigMgr 2007 and ConfigMgr 2012 clients. It allows the ConfigMgr 2012 clients to make use of a ConfigMgr 2007 distribution point. It's not a feature you implement for long, only long enough to ensure that all clients have been successfully migrated to ConfigMgr 2012. After that's done, you upgrade the distribution point or the secondary site server to a ConfigMgr 2012 distribution point.

1. You already enabled distribution point sharing when you created the source connection to the ConfigMgr 2007 hierarchy. If you didn't enable distribution point sharing, then select the **Administration** workspace.
2. Navigate to **Overview / Migration / Active Source Hierarchy**.
3. Select the existing **Source Hierarchy** connection, and on the ribbon, click **Configure**.
4. Select **Enable distribution point sharing for this source site** and click **OK**.

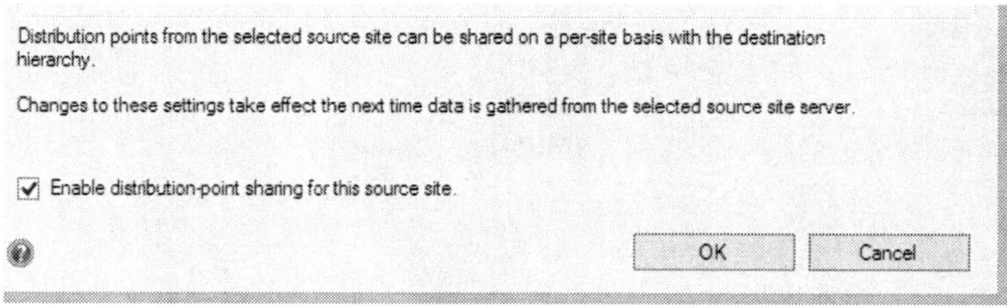

Sharing the distribution points.

5. Click **Close** after the gathering process is finished.
6. While still in **Active Source Hierarchy**, select the **Distribution Points** tab. You should be able to see a list of the available DPs.

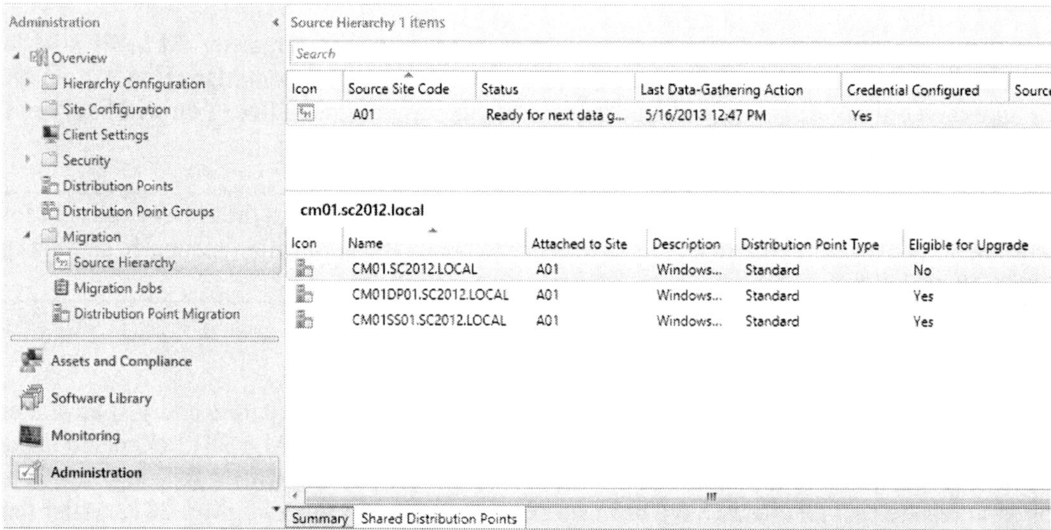

The shared distribution points are listed.

Upgrade the Distribution Point

1. Select the **Administration** workspace.
2. Navigate to **Overview / Migration / Active Source Hierarchy**.
3. Select the **Shared Distribution Point** tab, select the distribution point you want to upgrade, and on the ribbon, click **Upgrade**.
4. On the **General** page, in **Site Code**, select the primary site and click **Next**. This instructs the ConfigMgr 2007 site server to uninstall the remote distribution point and then install and assign it to the ConfigMgr 2012 primary site. During the process all existing packages are preserved on the distribution point and, after a successful upgrade, injected into the ConfigMgr 2012 content library.

5. On the **Distribution Point** page, select **Install and configure IIS if required by Configuration Manager** and click **Next**.
6. On the **Drive Settings** page, configure the **Primary content library** and **Primary package share location** to match the remote distribution point and click **Next**.
7. On the **PXE Settings** page, click **Next**.
8. On the **Content Validation** page, enable a daily schedule and click **Next**.
9. On the **Boundary Groups** page, note the existing boundary groups. Those are automatically migrated when you enabled distribution point sharing. Uncheck the **Allow fallback source location for content** option and click **Next**.
10. On the **Content Conversion** page, note the number of packages that will be converted and click **Next**.

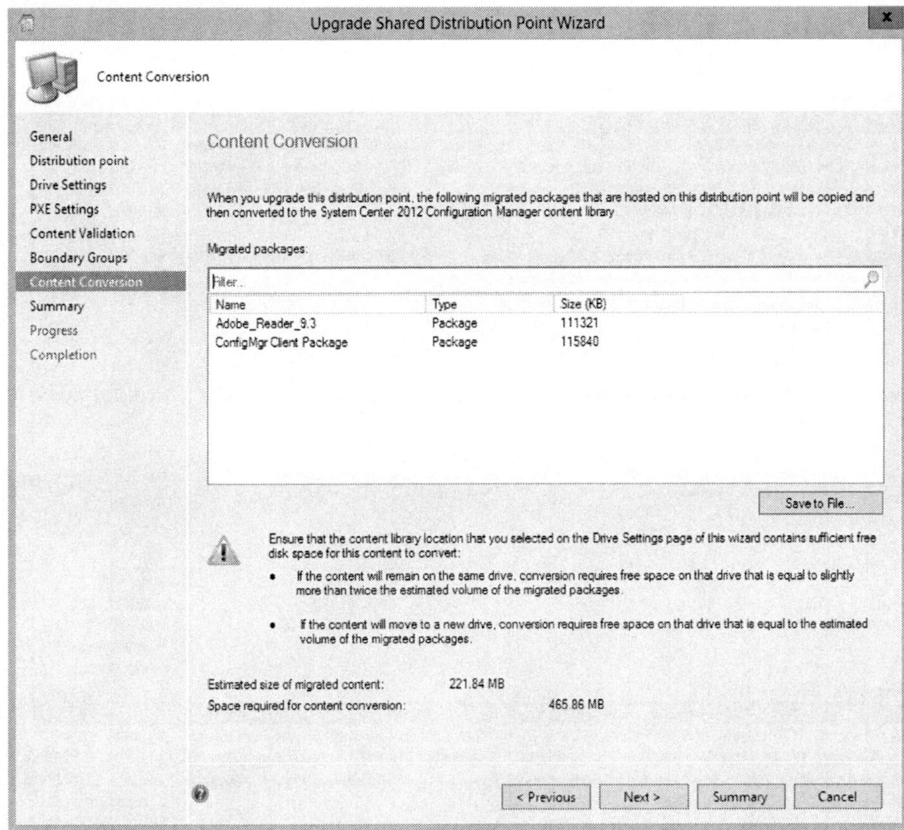

List of content that will be converted.

11. Click **Next** and **Close** to start the upgrade process.

Upgrade Secondary Site Servers

Upgrading the secondary site server is almost the same process as upgrading an existing distribution point. The only difference is that once the upgrade wizard is finished, it instructs the secondary site server to perform an uninstall of the entire site. This process happens in two phases and takes longer than performing a normal distribution point upgrade.

The first phase is the uninstall process, and the second phase happens after the next Data Gathering process. The Data Gathering process automatically runs several times per day and also can be initiated manually by selecting the active source hierarchy and clicking Gather Data Now on the ribbon.

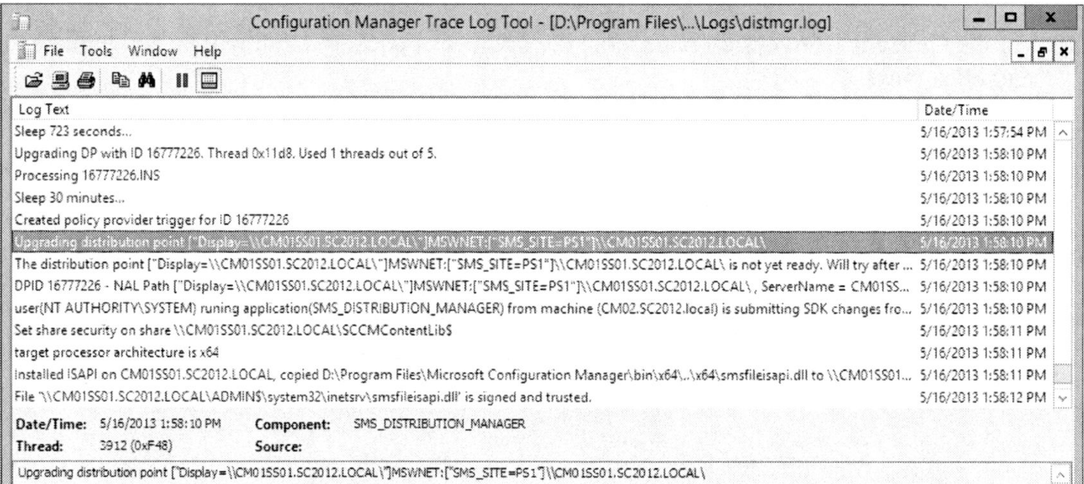

Monitor the secondary site uninstall process in C:\ConfigMgrSetup.log on the secondary site server.

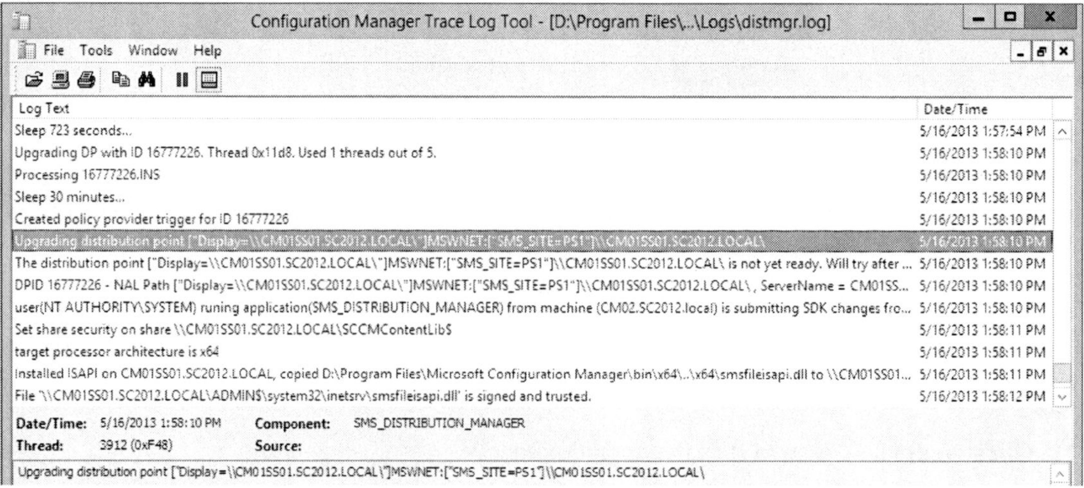

Monitor the distribution point installation in the distmgr.log file on the primary site server after running a Data Gathering process.

Migrate Collection

Collections can be migrated as single objects or along with the content that is associated with the collection, such as advertisements, packages, and task sequences. To migrate collections, follow these steps:

1. Select the **Administration** workspace.
2. Navigate to **Overview / Migration / Migration Jobs**.
3. On the ribbon, click **Create Migration Job**.
4. In **Name**, type **Collections**.
5. In **Job type**, select **Collection migration** and click **Next**.

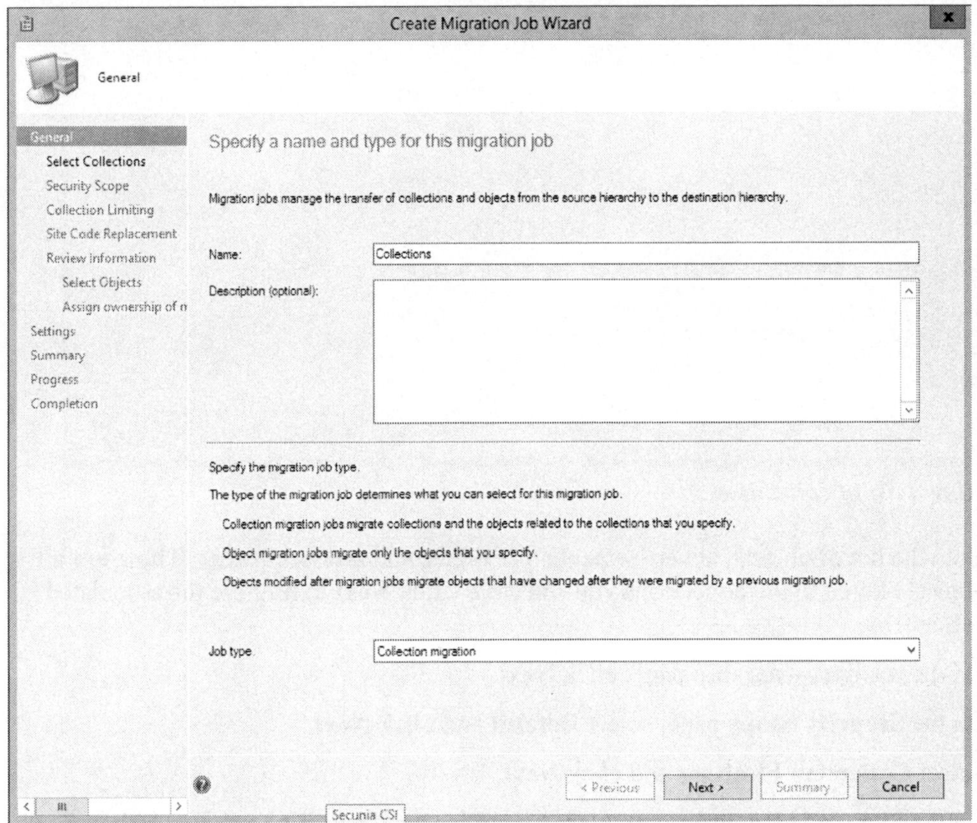

Configuring the migration job type.

6. Select the collections you want to migrate and click **Next**.

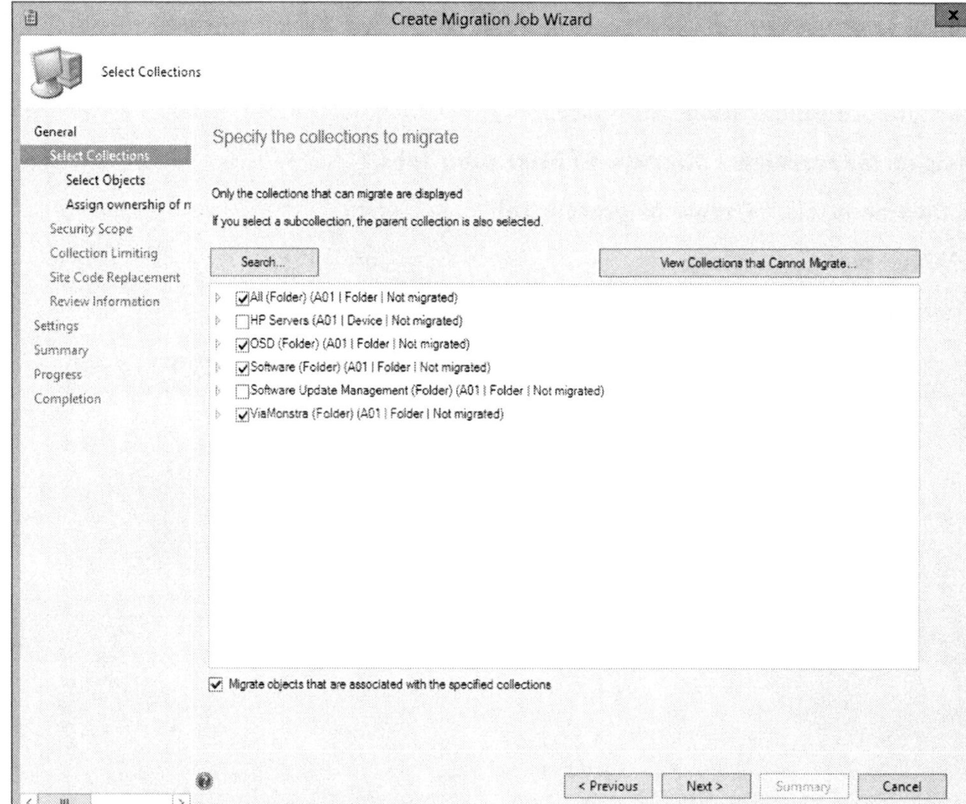

Selecting a list of collections.

7. Note the list of objects, advertisements, packages, and task sequences. Those are all objects related to the collections you selected. Click **Next** to migrate the associated collections.
8. On the **Assign ownership** page, click **Next**.
9. On the **Security Scope** page, select **Default** and click **Next**.
10. Select **Collection Limiting** and click **Next**.
11. On the **Site Code Replacement** page, a list of collections will be shown if those collections contained a hardcoded site code in ConfigMgr 2007. Since ConfigMgr 2012 has another site code, you are able to select that new site code from the drop-down box.

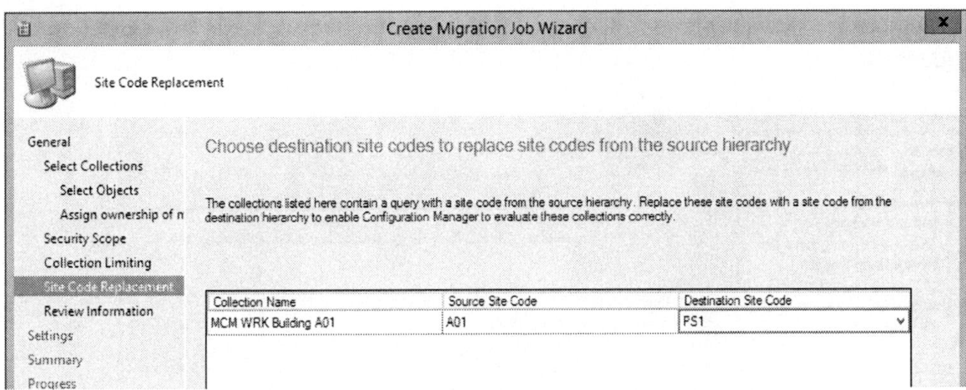

Replacing a hardcoded site code in a collection query.

12. Click **Next** to run the migration job now.
13. Click **Next** and **Close**.
14. Monitor the **migmctrl.log** file; it will contain information about the migration process.

Migrate Task Sequences

Task sequences can be challenging to migrate if they contain MDT steps like Use Toolkit Package or Gather. A good tip for migrating your task sequences is to follow the steps below in ConfigMgr 2007:

1. In **ConfigMgr 2007**, create a new empty task sequence.
2. Open the new empty task sequence.
3. Open the task sequence you want to migrate and copy any custom steps to the clipboard.

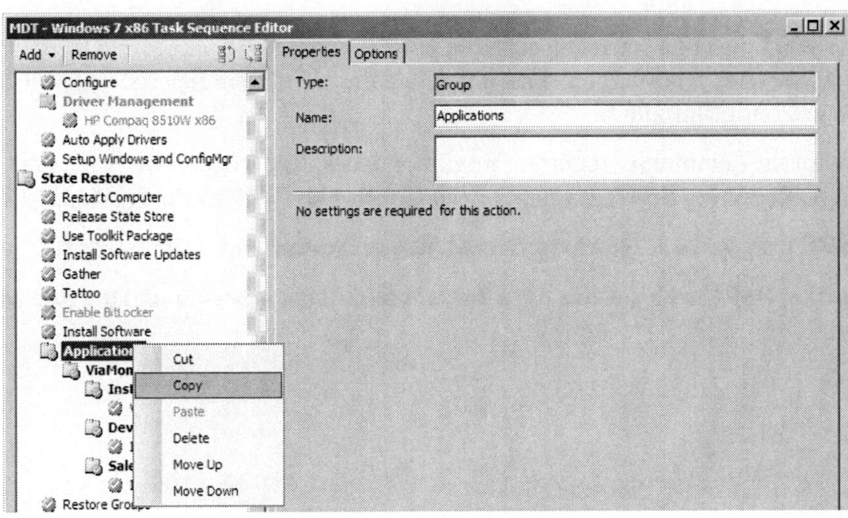

Copying custom steps from an existing task sequence.

4. Navigate to the new empty task sequence and paste the custom steps from existing task sequence.

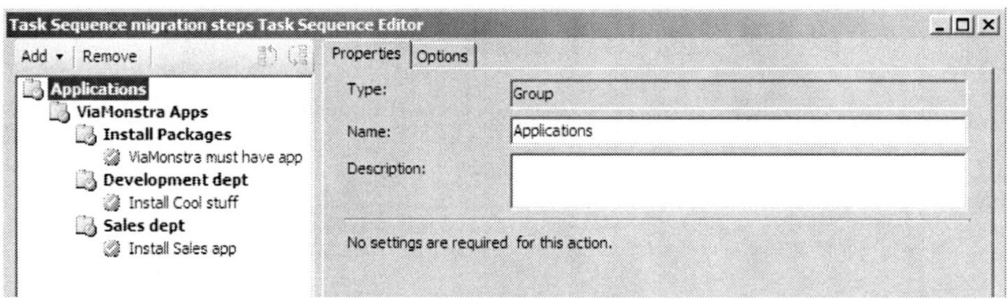

A new task sequence with all the custom steps ready for migration.

5. Migrate the new task sequence to Configmgr 2012 and copy the custom steps to a new ConfigMgr task sequence.

Migrate Software Updates

This book is written based on best practices and how I operate in real life. To be honest, you are better off not migrating your software updates. Instead, create new objects in ConfigMgr 2012, such as new templates, automatic deployment rules, and software update packages.

Migrate Reports

There is no supported upgrade path from classic ConfigMgr 2007 reports to ConfigMgr 2012 SQL Reporting Services reports. However, that is not the same as saying it cannot be done. To migrate classic reports from ConfigMgr 2007, follow these steps.

1. In **ConfigMgr 2007**, install **ConfigMgr 2007 R2** or **R3** along with **SQL Reporting Services**.
2. In **ConfigMgr 2007**, install a reporting services point and convert the required reports to SQL Reporting Services reports. This does not delete the old classic reports, and you can still run those in ConfigMgr 2007.
3. Download one of the community reporting migration tools, like ReportSync.v1.0, and convert the SQL Reporting Services reports from ConfigMgr 2007 to ConfigMgr 2012.
4. In **Source SSRS web service**, type **http://cmo1/ReportServer** and the password.
5. In the **Destination SSRS web service**, type **http://cmo2/ReportServer** and the password.

6. From the **Tools** menu, select **Map Datasources**; then in **Destination**, select **/ConfigMgr_PS1** and click **Set**.

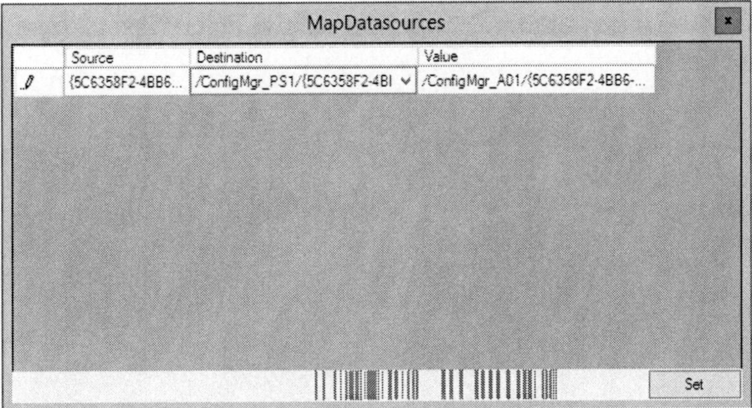

Modifying the report datasource.

7. Back in the **ReportSync** window, click **Load** in both web service columns; then select the reports you want to migrate and the destination folder.
8. Click **Sync** to begin the migration process, and click **OK** when done.

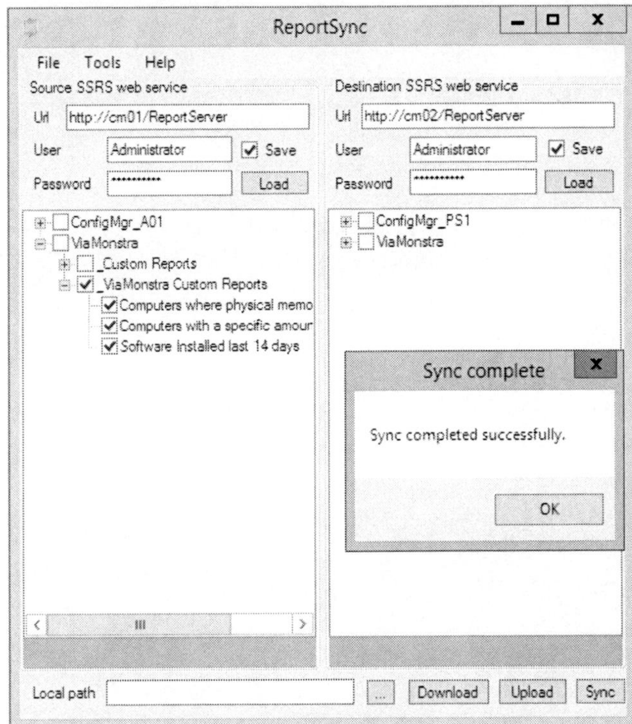

Using a community tool to migrate reports.

Monitor the Migration Process

1. Open the **Monitor** workspace and select **Reporting**, **Reports**.
2. In **Search**, type **Migration** and press **Enter**. You should see five reports in the Migration folder.

Appendix H

Naming Standards

Throughout this book, I have created several different objects like collections, packages, applications, deployment types, update groups, and so forth. The tables in this appendix list the naming standards that I have typically followed.

Naming Conventions for Collections and Folders

Object	**Naming Convention**
Collection	Collection prefix + Description SUM Workstation Production

Naming Conventions for Software

Object	**Naming Convention**
Package	Manufacturer Application Version Optional Language Optional **Microsoft Visio 2013**
Program	Application Action Architecture **Visio Install x86**
Deployment	Application Action **Visio Install**
Application	Manufacturer Application Version **Microsoft Office 2013**
Deployment type	Application Version Architecture Language **Office 2013 x86**

Naming Conventions for Software Updates

Object	**Naming Convention**
Update Group	Year Month value Month name **2012 06 June**

Object	Naming Convention
Templates	(WRK/SRV) Description **WRK Production**
Deployments	(WRK/SRV) Year Month number Month name Target Vendor (Optional Type) **WRK 2013 06 June Pilot 1**
Deployment Packages	Year First/Second half Vendor (Optional Type) **2013-1**
Automatic Deployment Rules	Description **Patch Tuesday**

Naming Conventions for Operating System

Object	Naming Convention
Driver categories	OS Architecture Make Model **Windows 8 x64 Lenovo W510**
Driver packages	OS Architecture Make Model **Windows 8 Lenovo x64 W510**
Task Sequences	Descriptive name OS Architecture **Build and Capture Windows 8 Enterprise x64**
Boot images	Descriptive name Architecture **MDTBoot Image x64**
Images	Descriptive name OS Architecture Version **Win8_x64_Ent_v1**

Appendix I

Upgrading to Service Pack 1

Upgrading ConfigMgr 2012 RTM to Service Pack 1 is not a difficult task, but still a task that requires planning, testing, and a fallback plan. As a general rule of thumb, all ConfigMgr upgrades use a top-down approach. In order, you upgrade the Central Administration Site, primary sites, any remote administration consoles, secondary sites, and finally all the clients.

Planning and Testing

The planning process is where you make sure your operating system, database, and hardware are still supported, and that you have all the necessary prerequisites, like required hotfixes, the Windows ADK, and so forth. The following list includes the steps that ViaMonstra walks through before upgrading.

Note: It's a very good idea to resolve any issues or problems that you have in the existing environment before starting the upgrade process. Navigate to the Monitoring workspace, select System Status, and walk through Site Status and Component Status. Any critical status must be investigated before proceeding with the upgrade.

1. Download and install the WSUS hotfix to add support for Windows 8 and Server 2012 from **http://support.microsoft.com/kb/2734608**.
2. Back up the SQL database and restore a copy of the database on an instance that is not hosting the production database. Perform a destructive test upgrade of the database to Service Pack 1. The test upgrade *must* be performed on the database copy.
3. Uninstall **Windows Automated Installation Kit** (WAIK).
4. Download **Windows Assessment and Deployment Kit** (Windows ADK).
5. Download the ConfigMgr SP1 prerrquisite files.
6. Run the **SP1 prerequisite checker** tool and verify that all required prerequisites are installed and configured correctly.
7. Plan for a restart of all site servers.

Needless to say that you should never install or upgrade directly in your production environment until you have performed a successful upgrade in a test environment.

Upgrade WSUS

In this process, I assume you have downloaded the X64 version of update 2734608 from http://support.microsoft.com/kb/2734608 and placed the update in D:\Setup\SP1\WSUS.

1. Open **File Explorer** and navigate to **D:\Setup\SP1\WSUS**.
2. Right-click **WSUS-KB2734608-x64.exe** and select **Run as administrator**.

Test Upgrade the Database

Ever since the SMS days, Microsoft has recommended that you perform a test upgrade of the database prior to performing a real upgrade. The test upgrade must be performed on a SQL instance that is not hosting the production database. In ViaMonstra, you installed a new SQL 2008 R2 CU6 instance called CM12TestUpgrade on server CM01. You will attach the database backup generated by the Site Maintenance task earlier in this book. The backup is stored in D:\CM2012.BCK\PS1Backup\SiteDBServer on server CM01. It's important that this copy of the database is not the only copy. The backup files can't be used once you have performed the test upgrade process. For that reason, you will end up with a non-valid backup. I assume that you have downloaded a valid copy of System Center 2012 Configuration Manager SP1 and placed the files in D:\Setup\CM2012SP1.

1. Download the **SQL Server Native Client 11.0** from **http://go.microsoft.com/fwlink/?LinkID=239648&clcid=0x409** and save the copy in **D:\Setup\SP1\SQLClient**.
2. Open a command prompt with administrative privileges.
3. Navigate to **D:\Setup\SP1\SQLClient** and run **sqlncli.msi**. Install the tool using the default settings.
4. On server **CM01**, start **SQL Server Management Studio** and connect to **CM01\CM12testUpgrade**.
5. Click **New Query**, type the following text, and click **Execute**. A copy of the script can also be found in the AttachSQL.txt file with the companion content for this book.

```
USE [master]

GO

CREATE DATABASE [CM_PS1] ON

( FILENAME =
N'D:\CM2012.BCK\PS1Backup\SiteDBServer\CM_PS1.mdf' ),

( FILENAME =
N'D:\CM2012.BCK\PS1Backup\SiteDBServer\CM_PS1_log.LDF' ),

( FILENAME =
N'D:\CM2012.BCK\PS1Backup\SiteDBServer\CM_PS1_2.mdf' ),

( FILENAME =
N'D:\CM2012.BCK\PS1Backup\SiteDBServer\CM_PS1_3.mdf' ),
```

```
( FILENAME =
N'D:\CM2012.BCK\PS1Backup\SiteDBServer\CM_PS1_4.mdf' ),
( FILENAME =
N'D:\CM2012.BCK\PS1Backup\SiteDBServer\CM_PS1_5.mdf' ),
( FILENAME =
N'D:\CM2012.BCK\PS1Backup\SiteDBServer\CM_PS1_6.mdf' ),
( FILENAME =
N'D:\CM2012.BCK\PS1Backup\SiteDBServer\CM_PS1_7.mdf' ),
( FILENAME =
N'D:\CM2012.BCK\PS1Backup\SiteDBServer\CM_PS1_8.mdf' ),
FOR ATTACH
GO
```

6. Open a command prompt with administrative privileges.
7. Navigate to **D:\Setup\CM2012SP1\SMSSETUP\BIN\X64** and type **Setup.exe /testdbupgrade CM01\CM12TestUpgrade**.

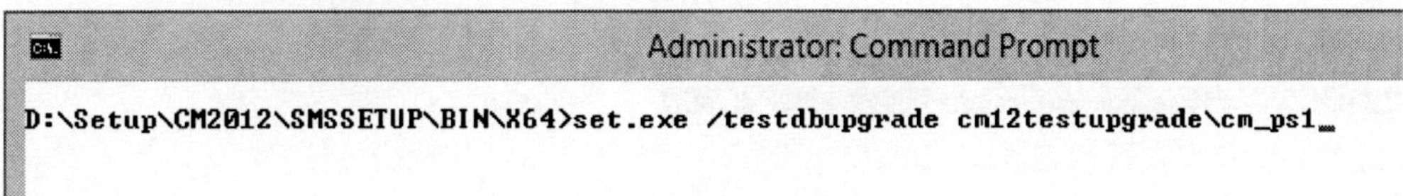

Performing the database test upgrade.

8. Click **Begin TestDBUpgrade** and accept the database size warning message.

Configuration Manager 2012 SP1
Installation Prerequisite Check
Setup is checking for potential installation problems. If installation problems are found, Setup will display details about how to resolve the problems.
Prerequisite result:
Prerequisite | Status | System | Site Type
All required prerequisite tests have complete... | Success
Prerequisite checking has completed.
Click on any item to display details about how to resolve the problem, or view the ConfigMgrPrereq.log to help identify problems.
View Latest Prerequisite Information
Run Check
Begin TestDBUpgrade
Cancel

Starting the test upgrade process.

9. ConfigMgr will display a final warning message before starting the process. Click **Yes** and accept the warning.

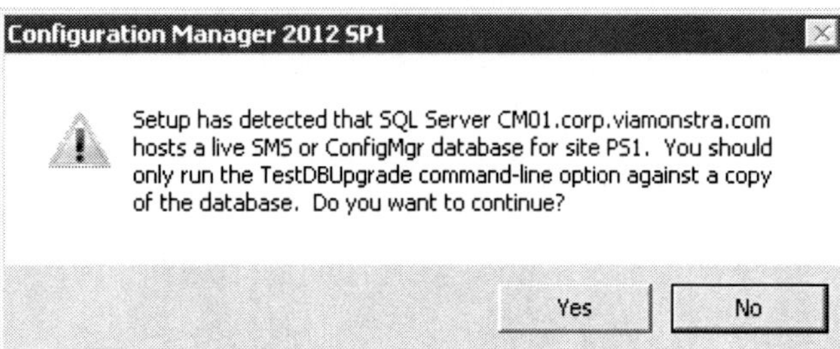

Database warning message.

After a successful upgrade you will see a line in ConfigMgrSetup.log saying "Configuration Manager Setup has successfully upgraded the database."

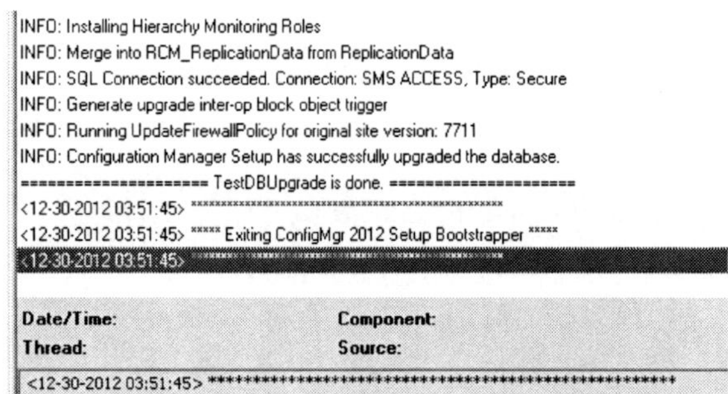

Successful test upgrade of the database.

Note: The process will write to the very same log files as the real upgrade process. I recommend monitoring the test upgrade process reading C:\ConfigMgrPrereq.log and ConfigMgrSetup.log.

Uninstall WAIK and Install Windows ADK

Windows Assessment and Deployment Kit is a replacement for WAIK and a required component if you plan to deploy operating systems with ConfigMgr. Windows ADK is not a single tool but a kit containing multiple utilities like Microsoft USMT, Windows PE etc. Only 3 of the tools are required by ConfigMgr those are USMT, Windows PE and the Deployment Tools. I assume you have downloaded Windows ADK from http://www.microsoft.com/en-us/download /details.aspx?id=30652 and stored adksetup.exe in D:\Setup\SP1\ADK.

1. On **CM01**, open **Programs and features** in the **Control Panel**. Select **Windows Automated Installation Kit** and click **Uninstall**.
2. When prompted to verify the uninstall, click **Yes**.
3. Open a command prompt as **administrator** and run **D:\Setup\SP1\ADK\adksetup.exe**.
4. On the **Specify location** page, accept the defaults and click **Next**.

5. On the **Join the CEIP program** page, click **Yes** and proceed.
6. On the **License Agreement** page, accept the license terms and click **Next**.
7. On the **Select the features you want to install** page, select **Deployment Tools, Windows PE**, and **USMT**, and then click **Install**.

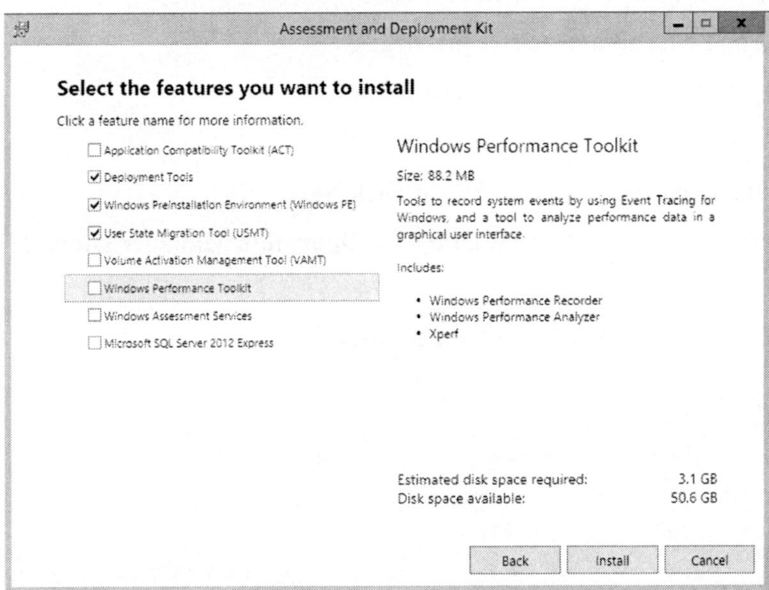

Select the required ADK features.

8. Click **Close** when the installation is finished.

Download the ConfigMgr SP1 Prerequisites Files and Run the Prerequisite Checker

Downloading the SP1 prerequisites files and running the prerequisites checker prior to the actual upgrade is considered a very good idea. Too often have I witnessed an upgrade attempt fail due to missing requirements or database issues. This can easily lead to several IT pros wasting precious time and not being able to perform a successful upgrade in their assigned maintenance window.

1. Open a command prompt with administrative privileges.
2. Navigate to **D:\Setup\CM2012SP1\SMSSETUP\BIN\X64**, type **SetupDL.exe D:\Setup\SP1\CM12SPDL**, and press **Enter**.
3. Once all 56 files have been downloaded, type **prereqchk.exe /LOCAL**. Notice that you will get error messages about an existing ConfigMgr installation and a dedicated SQL instance. You can safely ignore those errors as you are not going to perform a new installation but upgrade the existing installation.
4. Click **Cancel** and close the command prompt.
5. Restart the server. A restart is not required but is a very good idea.

Upgrade Primary Site with Service Pack 1

Upgrading to Service Pack 1 is almost identical to performing the initial installation except that you have an existing environment that you need to ensure will have as little downtime as possible. In this guide, I assume you have downloaded ConfigMgr 2012 SP1 to D:\Setup\CM2012SP1.

1. On **CM01**, log on as **VIAMONSTRA\Administrator**.
2. Open a command prompt with administrative privileges.
3. Navigate to **D:\Setup\CM2012SP1** and type **splash.hta**.
4. Click **Install**.
5. On the **Before You Begin** page, read the notes and click **Next**.
6. On the **Getting Started** page, select **Upgrade this Configuration Manager site** and click **Next**.

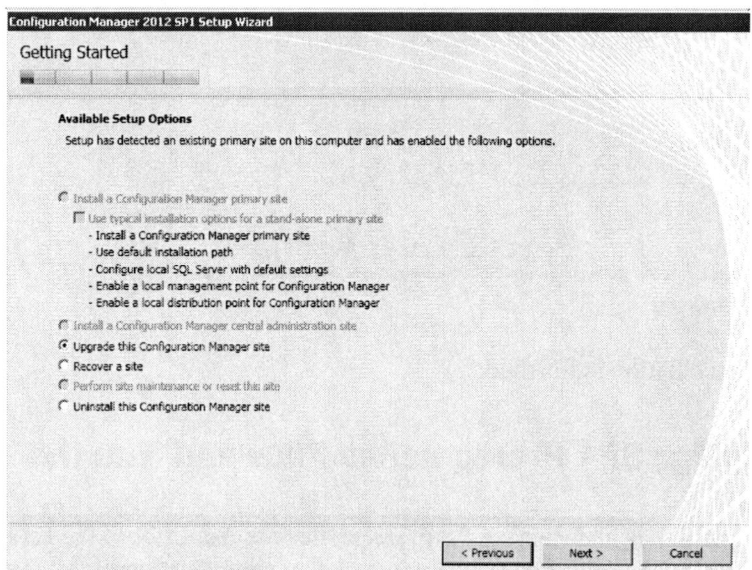

Upgrading a primary site server.

7. On the **Product Key** page, enter your 25-character product key, or select **Install this product as an evaluation** if you don't have the key at the present time, and click **Next**.
8. On the **Microsoft Software License Terms** page, click **I accept these license terms**, and then click **Next**.
9. On the **Prerequisite Licenses** page, accept the prerequisite license terms and click **Next**.
10. On the **Prerequisite Download** page, click **Use previously downloaded files**; use the **Browse** button to select the **D:\Setup\SP1\CM12SPDL** folder, and click **Next**.
11. On the **Server Language Selection** page, ensure that **English** is the only selected language and click **Next**.

12. On the **Client Language Selection** page, select the client languages you wish to support in your environment and click **Next**.
13. On the **Settings Summary** page, review the summary and click **Next**.
14. On the **Prerequisite Checker** page, click **Begin Install** to start the upgrade. Notice that you do not have any SQL errors like you had when running the prerequisites tool.
15. The upgrade process can easily take 20–40 minutes. Once the upgrade is finished, click **Close**.

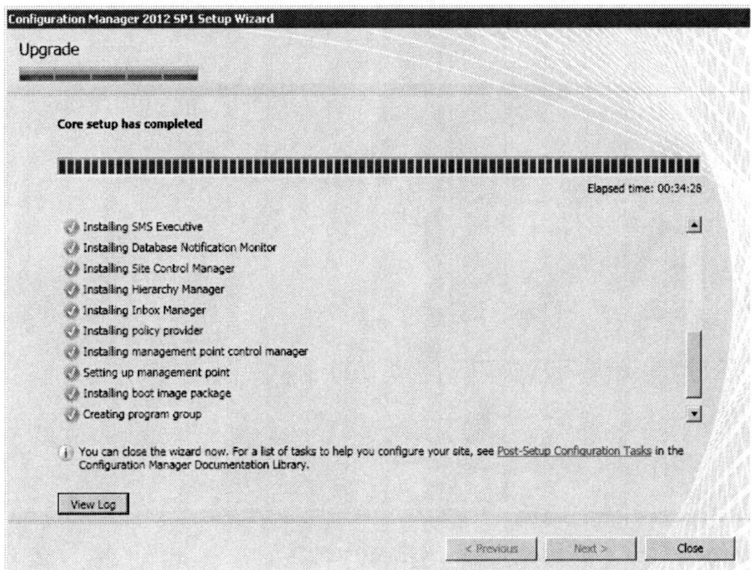

ConfigMgr successfully upgraded with SP1.

16. Check **C:\ConfigMgrSetup.log** and monitor the installation.

> **Note:** ConfigMgr performs a site reset after the upgrade. During a site reset, all components and site systems are reinstalled and default permissions are re-applied. This process and the upgrade process can be closely monitored by reading the sitecomp.log, C:\ConfigMgrPrereq.log, and ConfigMgrSetup.log files.

Upgrade Secondary Site with Service Pack 1

Upgrading the secondary site can be performed from within the ConfigMgr console or by running setup on the site server. In ViaMonstra we have decided to perform the installation within the ConfigMgr console. It's good practice to run the prerequisites checker prior to upgrading as described earlier in this appendix. You also need to ensure that the SQL server on the secondary site is not configured to use dynamic ports.

1. On **CM03**, start the **SQL Server Configuration Manager** from the **Start screen**.
2. Select **SQL Server Network Configuration, Protocols for CONFIGMGRSEC**.

3. Right-click **TCP/IP** and click **Properties**.
4. Select the **IP Addresses** tab and scroll down to **IPALL**. Delete the entry in **TCP Dynamic Ports** and click **OK**. When prompted with a warning message, click **Yes**.

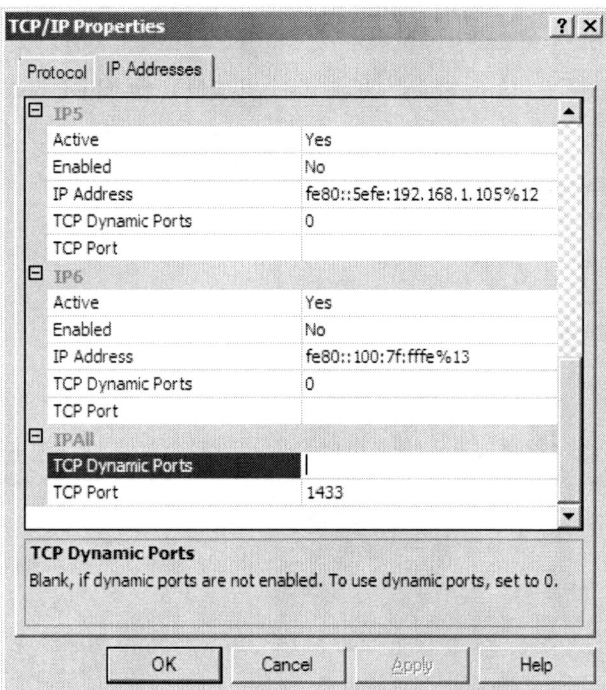

Disabling dynamic TCP ports on the secondary site SQL server.

5. Select **SQL Server Services**, right-click **SQL Server (CONFIGMGRSEC)**, and click **Restart**.
6. On **CM01**, start the **ConfigMgr console**.
7. Navigate to the **Administration** workspace, and select **Site Configuration and Sites**.
8. Select **S01 – Secondary site, Liverpool**, and on the ribbon, click **Upgrade**.

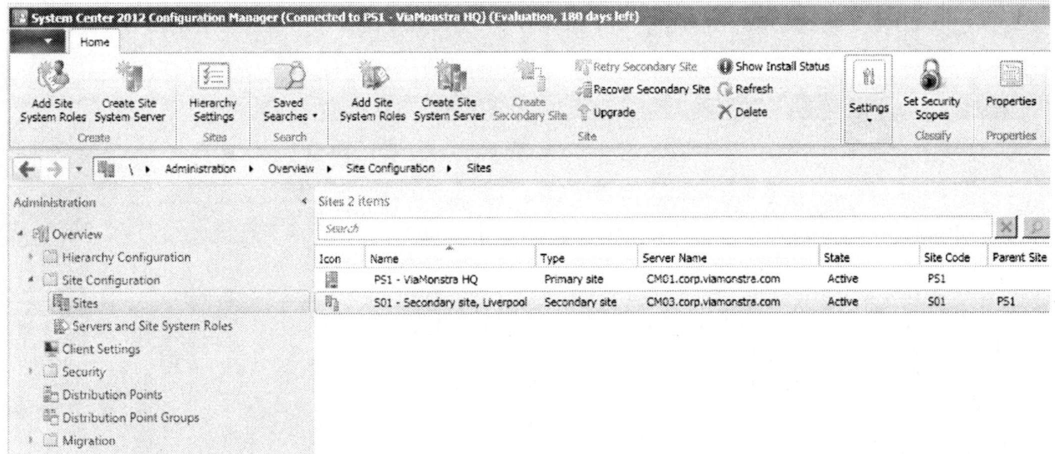

Starting the secondary site upgrade process.

9. Click **Yes** on the site upgrade warning message.
10. On the ribbon, click **Show Install status**. Click the **Refresh** button a few times to receive real-time information about the upgrade process.

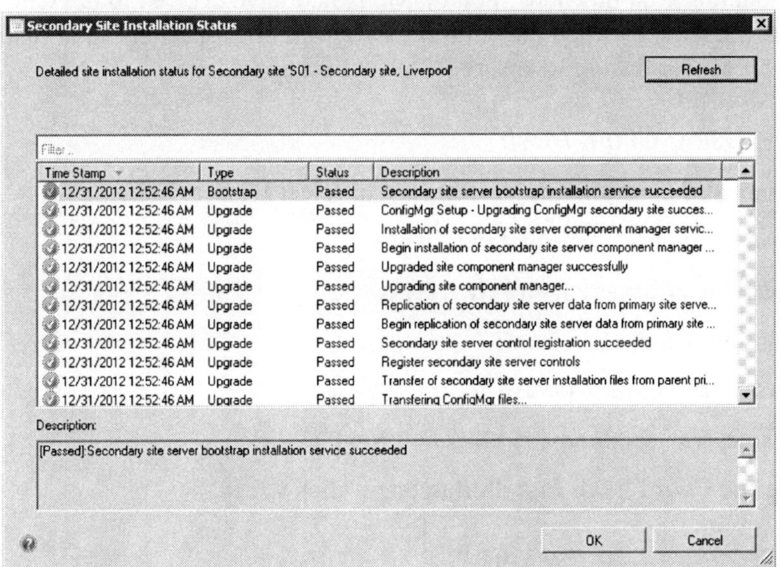

Monitoring the upgrade process.

11. Click **OK** to close the installation status.

12. Right-click the column heading bar below the Search box and select **Build Number**.

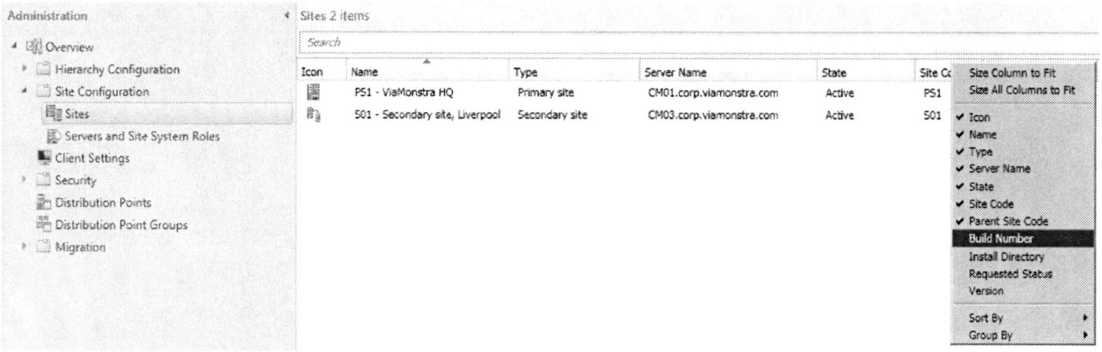

Adding Build Number information.

13. The build number for Service Pack 1 is **7804**.

Upgrade ConfigMgr Clients with Service Pack 1

All existing clients also must be upgraded to Service Pack 1. In essence, you can use any of the client installation methods mentioned in this book. For ViaMonstra, I have decided to use Client Push to perform the first test upgrade, then use the built-in ConfigMgr client package, and finally enable the Automatic Client Upgrade feature to ensure all clients are upgraded.

Upgrade the First Client Using Client Push

1. Navigate to the **Assets and Compliance** workspace and select **Devices**.
2. Select **CM01**, and on the ribbon, click **Install Client**.
3. On the first page, read the information and click **Next**.
4. Select the following setting and click **Next**:

   Always install the client software

5. On the **Summary** page, read the summary and click **Next**.
6. On the **Completing the Client Push Installation** page, click **Close**.

Upgrade Client Using Software Distribution

During the site server service pack upgrade process, ConfigMgr automatically upgrades the Configuration Manager Client package with Service Pack 1 files and also updates all the existing distribution points. You will be able to verify this by looking at the Content status for the package in the Monitoring workspace. However, there is a slight issue with that package, it doesn't have any program associated. With that in mind ViaMonstra has decided to create a new ConfigMgr Client package and deploy the package to a new collection containing all ConfigMgr 2012 RTM clients.

1. Select the **Assets and Compliance** workspace.
2. Select **Device Collections**, right-click the **Software** folder, and select **Create Device Collection**.
3. On the **General** page, enter the following details:
    a. Name: **SWD All ConfigMgr 2012 RTM Clients**
    b. Comment: **All existing ConfigMgr clients with RTM code**
    c. Limiting Collection: Click **Browse** and select **All Desktop and Server Clients**.
4. Click **Next**.
5. Click **Add Rule, Query Rule**.
6. Name the rule **All ConfigMgr RTM clients** and click **Edit Query Statement**.
7. Select the **Criteria** tab.
8. Click the **yellow icon** and click **Select** to create the criteria.
9. Select **System Resource** as the **Attribute class** and **System Resource and Client Version** as the **Attribute**.

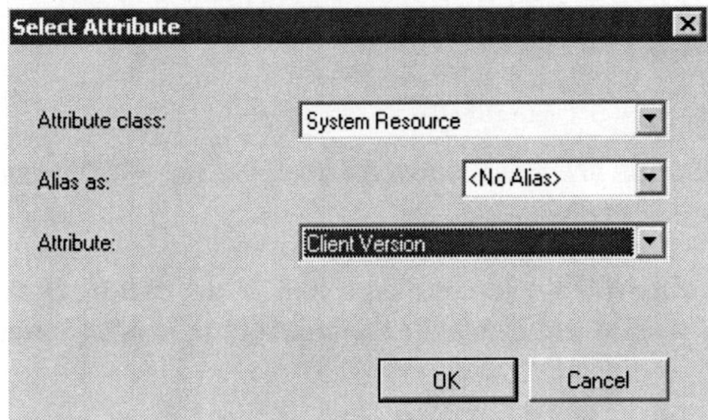

Creating a collection based on client version.

10. Click **OK** to return to the Criterion Properties dialog box.
11. In **Operator**, select **is equal to**, and in **Value**, type **5.00.7711.0000**.
12. Click **OK** three times and return to the Memberships Rules page.
13. Enable **Use incremental updates for this collection**, click **Summary**, click **Next**, and then click **Close** to close the wizard.
14. In the **Software Library** workspace, select **Application Management, Packages**.
15. On the ribbon, click **Create Package from Definition**.
16. On the **Package Definition** page, select **Configuration Manager Client Upgrade** and click **Next**.

17. On the **Source Files** page, select **Always obtain source files from a source folder** and client **Next**.
18. On the **Source Folder** page, select **Network patch (UNC name)**, type **\\cm01\sms_ps1\Client**, and click **Next**.
19. On the **Summary** page, read the summary and click **Next**.
20. On the **Completion** page, click **Close** and a new package named Configuration Manager Client Upgrade will be created.
21. Highlight the new package and select the **Programs** tab. Note the command line. By default, it will look like this: CCMSETUP.EXE /noservice SMSSITECODE=AUTO.
22. Right-click the program, open the **Program Properties**, and change the command line to **CCMSETUP.EXE /noservice SMSSITECODE=PS1**. Using SMSSitecode=Auto is only required in environments with multiple primary sites. Click **OK** to close the Program Properties.

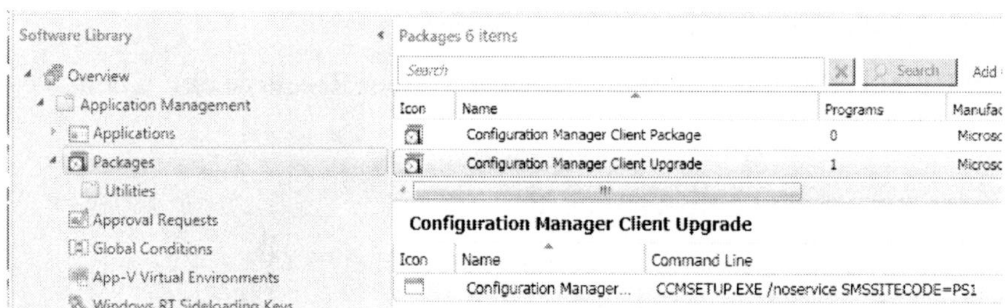

The Configuration Manager client installation program command line after the SMSSitecode change.

23. Select the **Configuration Manager Client Upgrade package**, and on the ribbon, click **Distribute Content**. Go through the wizard and distribute the content to the **All Content** Distribution Point group.
24. Select the **Configuration Manager Client Upgrade** package, and on the ribbon, click **Deploy**.
25. On the **General** page, click **Browse**, select the **SWD All ConfigMgr 2012 RTM Clients** collection, and click **Next**.
26. On the **Content** page, click **Next**.
27. On the **Deployment Settings** page, click **Next**.
28. On the **Scheduling** page, click **New**, select **Assign immediately after this event** (the setting defaults to "As soon as possible"), click **OK**, and click **Next**.
29. On the **User Experience** page, click **Next**.
30. On the **Distribution Points** page, click **Next**.
31. On the **Summary** page, read the summary and click **Next**.
32. On the **Completion** page, click **Close**.

Automatic Client Upgrade

In the old days before SMS 2.0, when upgrading the primary site with a new service pack, all clients were automatically upgraded, as well. Back then the upgrade process was somewhat uncontrolled, and all clients could end up being upgraded at the same time. In ConfigMgr 2012 SP1, the feature is different and now allows the administrator to control the number of days the process uses to upgrade the clients. With the feature enabled, all clients create a Windows scheduled task that starts the client upgrade process. The scheduled task will be created with a random date and time for each client.

1. Select the **Administration** workspace.
2. Navigate to **Site Configuration / Sites**; select **PS1** and on the ribbon, click **Hierarchy Settings**.
3. On the **Automatic Client Upgrade** tab, enable **Upgrade client automatically when new client update are available**. Read the warning message and click **OK**.
4. In **Automatically upgrade clients within days**, type **10** and click **OK**.

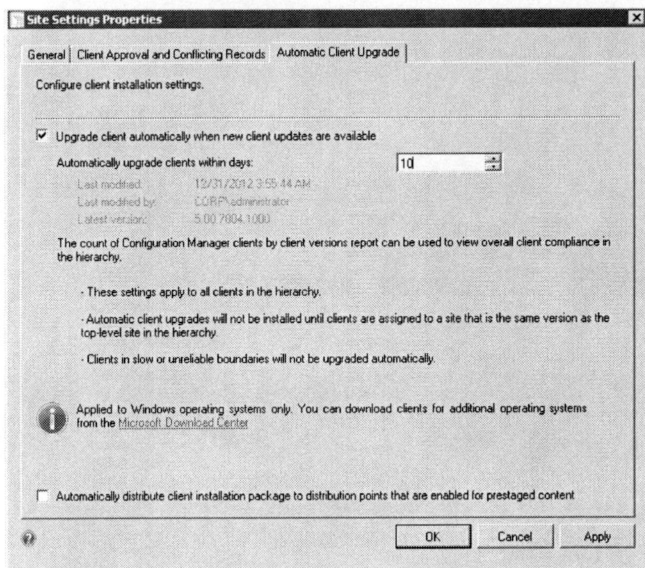

Configure automatic client upgrades.

5. A scheduled task named **Configuration Manager Client Upgrade Task** will be created next time a client downloads the ConfigMgr machine policy. To view the task, open **Control Panel**, select **System and Security**, **Administrative Tools**, and click **Schedule Task**.

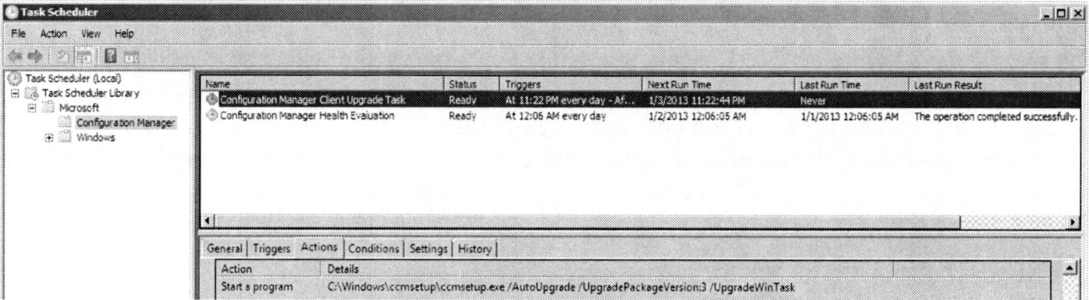

A Configuration Manager Client Upgrade Task configured to start the upgrade process January 3.

6. You can manually trigger the task to start the upgrade process. Just right-click the task and select **Run**. The task is automatically deleted after the client is upgraded. You can monitor the upgrade process by reading C:\Windows\ccmsetup\logs\ccmsetup.log.

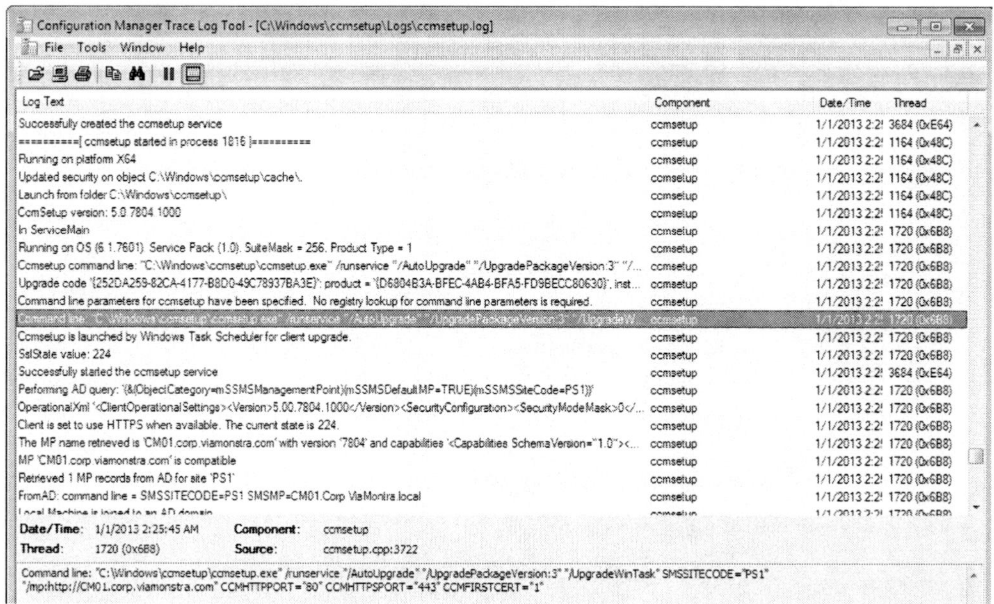

Monitoring the automatic upgrade process by reading ccmsetup.log on the client.

Upgrading to Service Pack 1 CU2

Starting with ConfigMgr 2012, Microsoft now releases hotfixes for System Center products the same way they have been doing it for SQL Server, in bundles. Those bundles are called *cumulative update* (or just CU). The benefit is that you only need to apply the latest CU to get all hotfixes installed. This a huge improvement from previous versions where you had to install each update individually. The process for installing a hotfix is not the same as it is for a service pack. Some cumulative updates have updates only for the server, whereas others also include updates for the administrator console and clients. To install the latest CU2 for Service Pack 1, follow these steps:

1. Request, download, and extract **CU2** (KB2854009) to **D:\Setup\CM2012SP1CU2**.
2. Close the **ConfigMgr console** before beginning the installation.
3. Run **CM12-SP1CU2-KB2854009-X64-ENU.exe** from **D:\Setup\CM2012SP1CU2** as **administrator**.
4. On the **Welcome** page, read the instructions and click **Next**.
5. On the **Microsoft Software License Terms** page, accept the license terms and click **Next**.
6. On the **Prerequisite Check** page, make sure that status is successful for all checks, and click **Next**.

Note: If you get a warning on the "Verifying restart is not required" prerequisite check, cancel the setup and reboot the server. Then start the setup again.

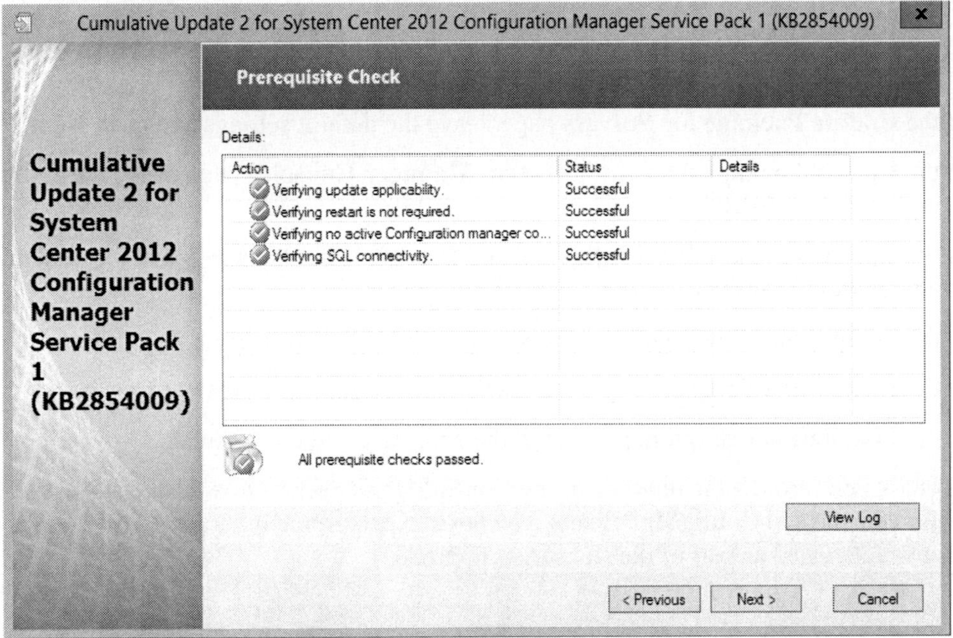

The CU2 prerequisite checker.

7. On the **Console Update Option** page, make sure the **Install the update for the Configuration Manager console** check box is selected and click **Next**.
8. On the **Database Update** page, select **Yes, update the site database** and click **Next**.
9. On the **Deployment Assistance Options** page, include all the systems in the Configuration Manager packages and click **Next**.

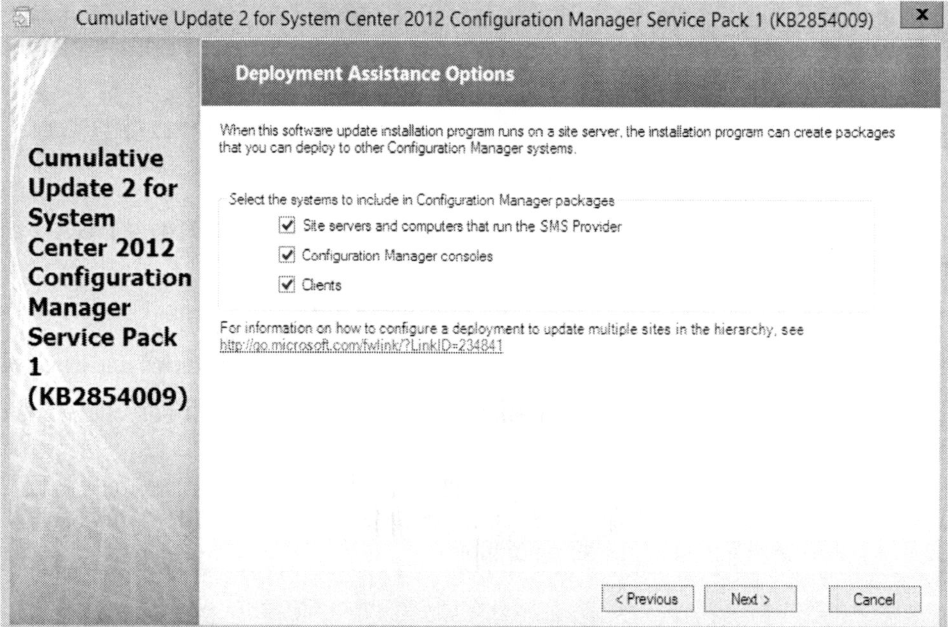

Creating CU update packages.

10. On the **Update Package for Servers** page, leave the default settings and click **Next**.
11. On the **Update Package for Configuration Manager Consoles** page, leave the default settings and click **Next.**
12. On the **Update Package for Configuration Manager Clients** page, leave the default settings and click **Next.**
13. On the **Setup Summary** page, read the summary and click **Install.**
14. On the **Installation Progress** page, read the summary and click **Next**.
15. On the **Installation Complete** page, read the summary and click **Finish.**

This process took you through the upgrade of the ConfigMgr site server and all site systems. For the ConfigMgr console and ConfigMgr clients, you have to perform another installation using the packages that were created as part of the site server upgrade.

Upgrade the ConfigMgr Consoles

A ConfigMgr package is created as part of the site server installation. You can use this package to upgrade all ConfigMgr consoles. All you need to do is create a collection with the devices where the console is installed and run the package. Notice that ConfigMgr console on the site server is upgraded as part of the CU2 installation.

1. From the **ConfigMgr console**, launch **PowerShell**.
2. To create the **collection**, type the following command:

   ```
   New-CMDeviceCollection -Name "SWD ConfigMgr 2012 Console SP1
   CU2 Install" -LimitingCollectionName "All Systems"
   ```

3. To create the **collection query**, type the following command:

   ```
   Add-CMDeviceCollectionQueryMembershipRule -CollectionName
   "SWD ConfigMgr 2012 Console SP1 CU2 Install" -RuleName "All
   computers with ConfigMgr 2012 SP1 console" -QueryExpression
   'select *  from  SMS_R_System inner join
   SMS_G_System_ADD_REMOVE_PROGRAMS on
   SMS_G_System_ADD_REMOVE_PROGRAMS.ResourceId =
   SMS_R_System.ResourceId where
   SMS_G_System_ADD_REMOVE_PROGRAMS.DisplayName like "%2012
   configuration manager console%"'
   ```

4. To distribute the content to the **All Content** distribution group, type the following command:

   ```
   Start-CMContentDistribution -PackageName "SP1 Cumulative
   update 2 - console update - PS1"
   -DistributionPointGroupName "All Content"
   ```

5. To deploy the package to the collection, type the following command

   ```
   start-CMPackageDeployment -PackageName "SP1 Cumulative
   update 2 - console update - PS1" -StandardProgramName
   "Cumulative update 2 - console update install"
   -CollectionName "SWD ConfigMgr 2012 SP1 CU2 Install"
   -ScheduleEvent AsSoonAsPossible -RerunBehavior
   RerunIfFailedPreviousAttempt -FastNetworkOption
   DownloadContentFromDistributionPointAndRunLocally
   -SlowNetworkOption DoNotRunProgram
   ```

Upgrade the ConfigMgr Clients

Just as with upgrading the ConfigMgr console, there also is a package for the X86 and X64 ConfigMgr agents. It's easy to repeat the steps from the preceding section and deploy the CU2 update as a package. The only thing you need to figure out is how to create the two collections. The rest of the process is similar to the preceding steps.

1. From the **ConfigMgr console**, launch **PowerShell**.

2. To create the **X64 collection**, type the following command:

```
New-CMDeviceCollection -Name "SWD ConfigMgr 2012 Client X64
SP1 CU2 Install" -LimitingCollectionName "All Systems"
```

3. To create the **X86 collection**, type the following command:

```
New-CMDeviceCollection -Name "SWD ConfigMgr 2012 Client X86
SP1 CU2 Install" -LimitingCollectionName "All Systems"
```

4. To create the **X64 collection query**, type the following command:

```
Add-CMDeviceCollectionQueryMembershipRule -CollectionName
"SWD ConfigMgr 2012 Client X64 SP1 CU2 Install" -RuleName
"All X64 CM12 SP1 Clients" -QueryExpression 'select *  from
SMS_R_System inner join SMS_G_System_COMPUTER_SYSTEM on
SMS_G_System_COMPUTER_SYSTEM.ResourceId =
SMS_R_System.ResourceId where
SMS_G_System_COMPUTER_SYSTEM.SystemType like "%x64%" and
SMS_R_System.ClientVersion = "5.00.7804.1202"'
```

5. To create the **X86 collection query**, type the following command:

```
Add-CMDeviceCollectionQueryMembershipRule -CollectionName
"SWD ConfigMgr 2012 Client X86 SP1 CU2 Install" -RuleName
"All X86 CM12 SP1 Clients" -QueryExpression 'select *  from
SMS_R_System inner join SMS_G_System_COMPUTER_SYSTEM on
SMS_G_System_COMPUTER_SYSTEM.ResourceId =
SMS_R_System.ResourceId where
SMS_G_System_COMPUTER_SYSTEM.SystemType like "%x86%" and
SMS_R_System.ClientVersion = "5.00.7804.1202"'
```

6. To distribute the **X64 content** to the **All Content** distribution group, type the following command:

```
Start-CMContentDistribution -PackageName "SP1 Cumulative
update 2 - x64 client update - PS1"
-DistributionPointGroupName "All Content"
```

7. To distribute the **X86 content** to the **All Content** distribution group, type the following command:

```
Start-CMContentDistribution -PackageName "SP1 Cumulative
update 2 - x86 client update - PS1" -
DistributionPointGroupName "All Content"
```

8. To deploy the **X64 package** to the collection, type the following command:

```
start-CMPackageDeployment -PackageName "SP1 Cumulative
update 2 - x64 client update - PS1" -StandardProgramName
"Cumulative update 2 - x64 client update install"
-CollectionName "SWD ConfigMgr 2012 Client X64 SP1 CU2
Install" -ScheduleEvent AsSoonAsPossible -RerunBehavior
RerunIfFailedPreviousAttempt -FastNetworkOption
DownloadContentFromDistributionPointAndRunLocally
-SlowNetworkOption DoNotRunProgram
```

9. To deploy the **X86 package** to the collection, type the following command:

```
start-CMPackageDeployment -PackageName "SP1 Cumulative
update 2 - x86 client update - PS1" -StandardProgramName
"Cumulative update 2 - x86 client update install"
-CollectionName "SWD ConfigMgr 2012 Client X86 SP1 CU2
Install" -ScheduleEvent AsSoonAsPossible -RerunBehavior
RerunIfFailedPreviousAttempt -FastNetworkOption
DownloadContentFromDistributionPointAndRunLocally
-SlowNetworkOption DoNotRunProgram
```

Use System Center Updates Publisher to Perform the Upgrade

You also can use System Center Updates Publisher to perform the cumulative upgrade. ConfigMgr automatically creates the required cab file with all the necessary information. Performing the upgrade using System Center Updates Publisher is described in Chapter 8.

The main reasons for using System Center Updates Publisher for this are:

- You do not have to create multiple query-based collections. The supplied cab file already contains the required detection rules.
- You do not have to worry about collection update schedules.
- Clients will be upgraded automatically as part of the normal software update cycles.

Appendix J

Configuring HTTPS Support

ConfigMgr 2012 adds support for HTTPS on a site system level. This means that you can have a mix of HTTP and HTTPS clients on the same primary site, but each site system role server can service only one of the protocols. As a result, you can keep your infrastructure simple even if there is a requirement to support part of the environment with certificates. There are several reasons why you might consider implementing PKI as part of a ConfigMgr 2012 solution:

- PKI is a company requirement due to the enhanced security.
- You are planning to implement support for Mac OS.
- You are planning to support Internet-based clients.

Implementing PKI

It's very important to emphasize that being a good System Center administrator doesn't automatically make you an expert on PKI. It is a service that ConfigMgr can utilize, but is a service that should never be implemented by a ConfigMgr admininstrator but only by a security specialist. In this appendix, you see how to implement PKI in a lab environment, but even if it seems easy, there's long way from a small lab environment to a real production environment.

Note: Before engaging yourself with Microsoft and PKI, I strongly recommend that you read *Windows Server 2008 PKI and Certificate Security*, by Brian Komar (Microsoft Press 2008). Note that what you see in this book is again for a lab environment only. In real life, you should never install Certificate Services on a domain controller.

Certificate Templates

Like Word documents, certificates are based on templates that contain preconfigured information and values. ConfigMgr 2012 requires that you create version 2 templates, as version 3 is currently not supported. ConfigMgr certificates are based on one of the following templates:

- Web Server
- Workstation Authentication
- Authenticated Session

ViaMonstra uses all of these templates, as described in the following sections.

Web Server

ViaMonstra has the certificate installed on the following site systems:

> Cloud-based distribution point, management point, distribution point, software update point, state migration point, enrollment point, enrollment proxy point, application catalog web service point, and application catalog website point

Workstation Authentication

ViaMonstra has the certificate installed on following site systems and all clients:

> Management point, distribution point, and state migration point

Authenticated Session

ViaMonstra has the certificate installed on the Windows Intune connector.

Workstation Authentication for Workgroups

For ViaMonstra, you use the Workstation certificate when building your reference operating system image. The rerefence image is member of a workgroup during the build and capture process. Because of this, a certificate needs to be created for workgroup clients.

Creating and Enrolling Certificates

In the following sections, you create and enroll certificates for ConfigMgr clients, Mac OS clients, site systems roles, and the distribution point.

Create and Enroll the Workstation Authentication Certificate

To create the workstation certificate, follow these steps:

1. On **DC01**, log on as **VIAMONSTRA\Administrator**; then from the **Server Manager dashboard**, select **Tools** and start **Certification Authority**.
2. Expand **ViaMonstraRootCA**, right-click **Certificate Templates**, and click **Manage**.
3. Select **Workstation Authentication** template and click **Duplicate Template**.
4. Select the **General** tab, and type **CM2012 Client Certificate** in **Template display name**.

5. Select the **Security** tab. For **Domain Computers**, select **Read**, **Enroll**, and **Autoenroll**, and then click **OK** and close the Template console.

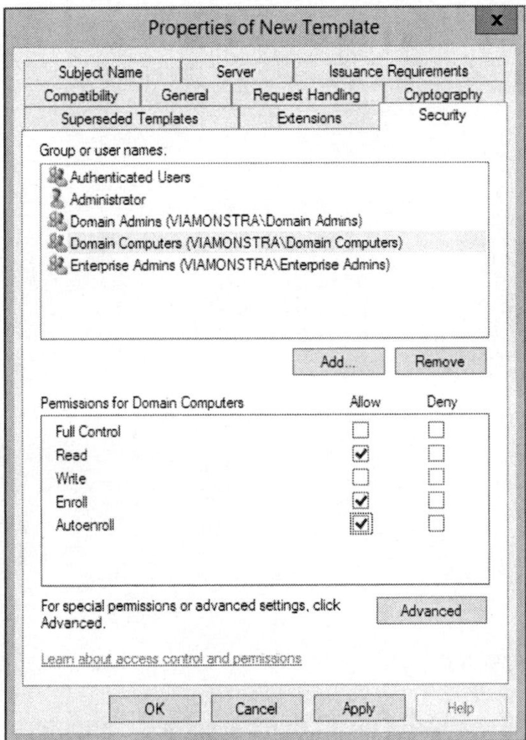

Configure certificate permissions

6. While still in the **Certification Authority console**, right-click **Certificate Template** and select **New / Certificate Template to Issue**.
7. Select the **CM2012 Client Certificate** and click **OK**.

To enroll the certificate, follow these steps:

1. On DC01, open the **Group Policy Management console**. In the **corp.viamonstra.com** domain, create a new GPO called **ConfigMgr 2012 Workstation Certificates** and click **OK**.
2. Edit the new **ConfigMgr 2012 Workstation Certificates** GPO.
3. Navigate to **Computer Configuration / Policies / Windows Settings / Security Settings / Public Key Policies**.
4. Select **Certificate Service Client - Auto-Enrollment** and open the properties.
5. In Configuration Model, select **Enabled**.

6. Enable **Renew expired certificates…** and **Update certificates….**

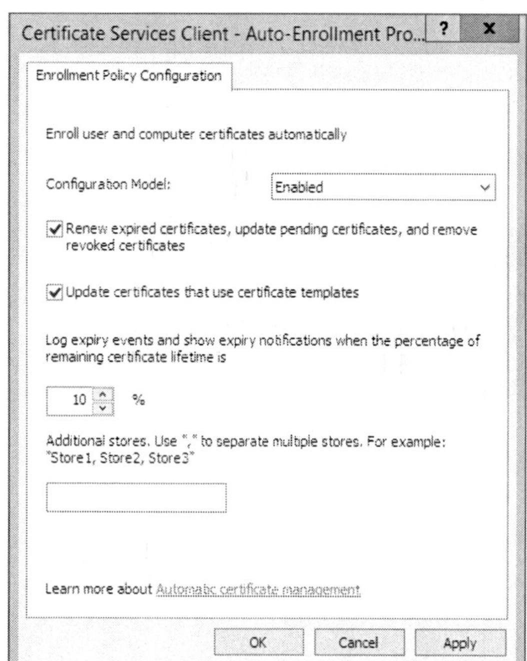

Configuring client certificate auto-enrollment policy.

7. Click **OK**. The certificates are enrolled automatically on all domain-joined computers.

Create and Enroll a Workgroup Certificate

Create and enroll the workgroup certificate following these steps:

1. On **DC01**, log on as **VIAMONSTRA\Administrator**; from the **Server Manager dashboard**, select **Tools** and start **Certification Authority**.
2. Expand **ViaMonstraRootCA**, right-click **Certificate Templates**, and click **Manage**.
3. Select the **Workstation Authentication** template and click **Duplicate Template**.

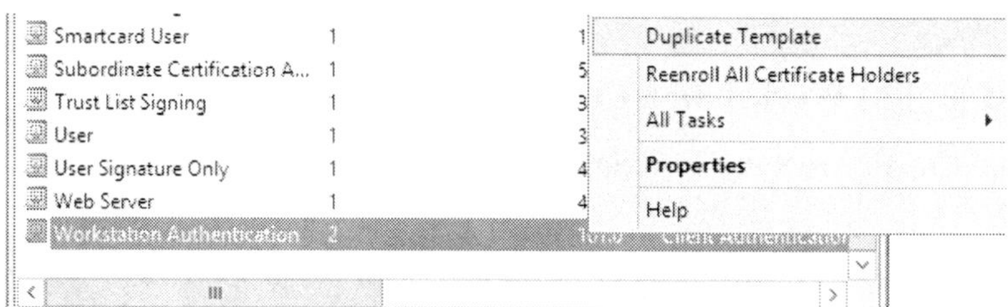

Creating the workgroup certificate

4. Select the **General** tab and type **CM2012 Workgroup Client Certificate** in **Template display name**.
5. In the **Request Handling** tab, select **Allow private key to be exported**.
6. In the **Subject Name** tab, select **Supply in the Request** and then click **OK** in the dialog box.
7. Select the **Security** tab. For **Domain Computers**, select **Read**, and then click **OK** and close the Template console.
8. While still in the **Certification Authority console**, right-click **Certificate Template**, and select **New / Certificate Template to Issue**.
9. Select the **CM2012 Workgroup Client Certificate** and click **OK.**

Issue the workgroup certificate:

1. On **PC0001**, open a management console with administrative rights. Add the **Certificate** snap-in for the **Computer account**.
2. Right-click the **Personal store**, and select **All Tasks / Request New Certificate.**
3. On the **Before you begin** page, click **Next**.
4. On the **Select Certificate Enrollment Policy** page, select **Active Directory Enrollment Policy** and click **Next**.
5. On the **Request Certificates** page, select the **CM2012 Workgroup Client Certificate** and click the link **More information is required to enroll for this computer**.
6. In the **Subject name** drop-down list, select **Common name** for **Type**, and **CM2012 Workgroup Client** for **Value**, and then click **Add**.
7. Click **OK** and **Enroll**.

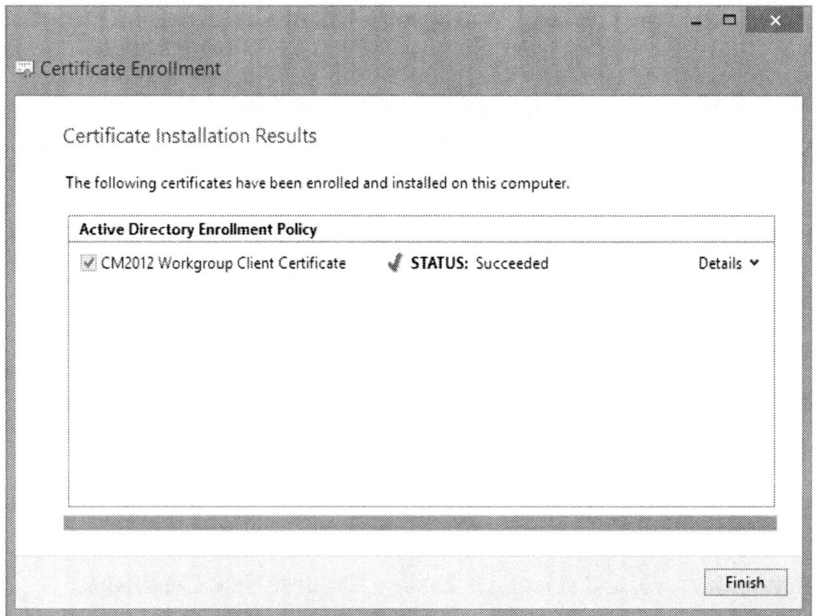

Finishing the certificate enrollment.

8. Click **Finish**.

Export the workgroup certificate:

1. On CM01, create the **D:\Setup\Certificates** folder.
2. On PC0001, while still in the management console, expand **Personal / Certificates**, right-click the **CM2012 Workgroup Client** certificate, and select **All Tasks / Export**.
3. On the **Certificate Export Wizard** page, select **Yes, export the private key** and click **Next**.
4. On the **Export File Format** page, click **Next**.
5. On the **Security** page, select **Password**, type **Password01** twice, and click **Next**.
6. Click **Next** and type **\\CM01\D$\Setup\Certificates\WGPKI.PFX** as the file name.
7. Click **Next** and finish the certificate export.

Chapter 10 explains how you use the certificate in an OSD scenario.

Create the Mac OS Certificate

Before creating the Mac certificate, you create a local security group in Active Directory named **Mac Users** in ViaMonstra / Security Groups.

To create the workstation certificate, follow these steps:

1. On **DC01**, log on as **VIAMONSTRA\Administrator**.

2. Using **Active Directory User and Computers**, in the **ViaMonstra / Security Groups** OU, create a domain local security group named **Mac Users**.
3. Using the **Server Manager dashboard**, select **Tools** and start **Certification Authority**.
4. Right-click **Certificate Templates** and click **Manage**.
5. Select **Authenticated Session Template** and click **Duplicate Template**.
6. Select the **General** tab and type **CM2012 MAC Client Certificate** in **Template display name**.
7. Click the **Subject Name** tab, select **Supply in the request**, and click **OK** to acknowledge the security risk.
8. Click the **Security** tab, and remove the **Enroll** permission from the **Domain Admins** and **Enterprise Admins** security groups.
9. Click **Add**, and specify the security group that can enroll the certificate (in this example, the **Mac Users** group). Select the **Enroll and Read** permission.

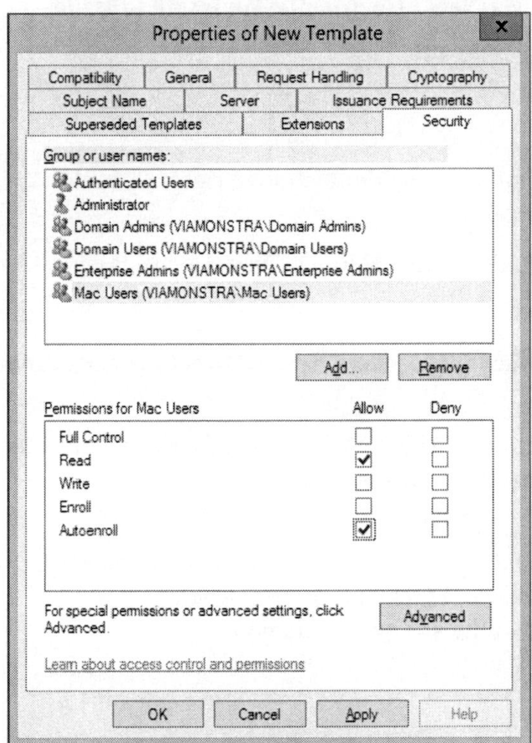

Configuring Apple Mac certificate security.

10. Click **OK** and close the Certificate Templates console.
11. Right-click **Certificate Template**, and select **New / Certificate Template to Issue**.
12. Select the **CM2012 MAC Client Certificate** certificate and click **OK**.

Create the Web Server Certificate

To create the Web server certificate, follow these steps:

1. On **DC01**, log on as **VIAMONSTRA\Administrator**; from the **Server Manager dashboard**, select **Tools** and start **Certification Authority**.
2. Right-click **Certificate Templates** and click **Manage**.
3. Select **Web Server** and click **Duplicate Template**.
4. Select the **General** tab and type **CM2012 WEB Certificate** in **Template display name**.
5. Click the **Subject Name** tab, select **Supply in the request**, and click **OK** to acknowledge the security risk.
6. Click the **Security** tab, and remove the **Enroll** permission from the **Domain Admins** and **Enterprise Admins** security groups. Add the **ConfigMgr_Servers** group (contains all CM12 servers running IIS) and add **Read** and **Enroll** permissions. Click **OK** and close the Certificate Templates console.
7. Right-click **Certificate Template** and select **New / Certificate Template to Issue.**
8. Select the **CM2012 WEB Certificate** and click **OK**.

Enroll the Web Server Certificate

1. On **CM01**, open a management console (mmc) with administrative rights. Add the **Certificate** snap-in for the **Computer account**.
2. Right-click the **Personal store** and select **All Tasks / Request New Certificate**.
3. On the **Before you begin** page, click **Next**.
4. On the **Select Certificate Enrollment Policy** page, select **Active Directory Enrollment Policy** and click **Next**.
5. One the **Request Certificates** page, select the **CM2012 WEB Certificate** and click the link **More information is required to enroll for this computer**.
6. In the **Alternative name** drop-down list, select **DNS** for **Type** and **cm01.corp.viamonstra.com** for **Value**, and then click **Add**. (cm01.corp.viamonstra.com is the name specified in the site system Internet FQDN properties, where CM01.corp.viamonstra.com is the FQDN of the site system name.)

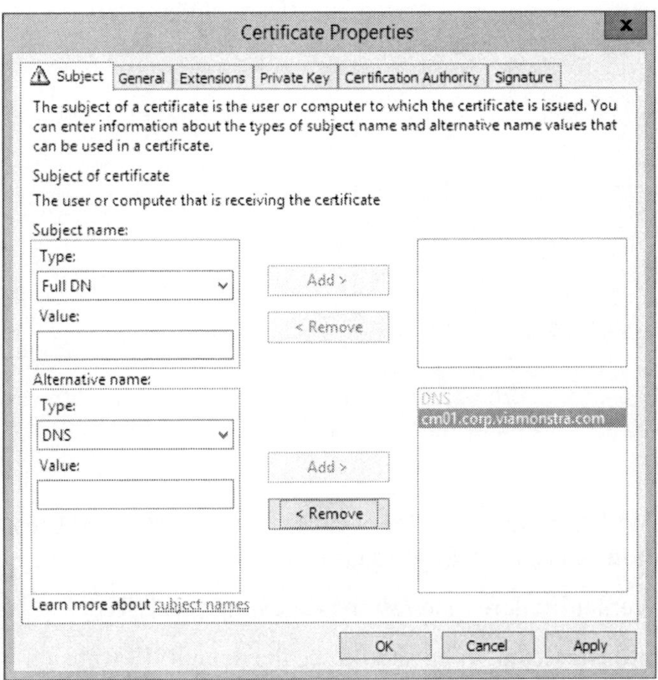

Configuring the certificate DNS name.

7. Click **OK** and **Enroll**.

Note: If you get the error "The revocation function was unable to check revocation because the revocation server was offline" when enrolling the certificate, make sure the revocation list has been published. The default publishing interval is one day, but you can do a manual publish if you don't like to wait: On DC01, in the Certification Authority console, right-click Revoked Certificates, select All Tasks / Publish, select Delta CRL only, and click OK.

8. Click **Finish.**
9. From the **Server Manager dashboard**, select **Tools** and start **Internet Information Services (IIS) Manager**.
10. Expand **CM01 / Sites**, and then right-click the **Default Web Site** and select **Edit Site Bindings**.
11. In the **Site Bindings** dialog box, select **https 443** and click **Edit**. Then, in the **Edit Site Binding** dialog box, select the certificate containing a long string of alphanumeric characters in the name (see the following screenshot) and click **OK**.

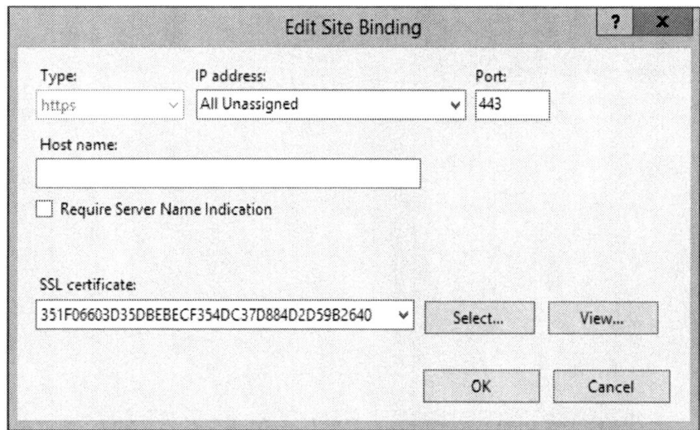

Selecting the web server certificate.

12. Repeat the same steps for the **WSUS Administration** website, but use **https 8531** instead. Then close **Internet Information Services (IIS) Manager**.
13. To test the certificates, open Internet Explorer and test the following two URLs:
    a. **http://cm01.corp.viamonstra.com**. You should see the default IIS website.
    b. **https://cm01.corp.viamonstra.com**. You should see the default IIS website.

Testing the Web Server certificate.

Create and Enroll the Distribution Point Certificate

To create the distribution point certificate, follow these steps:

1. On **DC01**, log on as as **VIAMONSTRA\Administrator**; from the **Server Manager dashboard**, select **Tools** and start **Certification Authority**.
2. Right-click **Certificate Templates** and click **Manage.**
3. Select **Workstation Authentication** template and click **Duplicate Template**.
4. Select the **General** tab and type **CM2012 DP Certificate** in **Template display name**.
5. Click the **Request Handling** tab, and select **Allow private key to be exported.**
6. Click the **Security** tab, and remove the **Enroll** permission from the **Domain Admins** and **Enterprise Admins** security groups. Add the **ConfigMgr_Servers** group (contains all ConfigMgr 2012 servers) and add **Read** and **Enroll** permissions.
   Click **OK** and close the Certificate Templates console.
7. Right-click **Certificate Template**, and select **New / Certificate Template to Issue**.
8. Select **CM2012 DP Certificate** and click **OK**.

To enroll the certificate, follow these steps:

1. On **CM01**, open a management console with administrative rights. Add the **Certificate** snap-in for the **Computer account**.
2. Right-click the **Personal store**, and select **All Tasks / Request New Certificate**.
3. On the **Select Certificate Enrollment Policy** page, select **Active Directory Enrollment Policy** and click **Next**.
4. On the **Request Certificates** page, select **CM2012 DP Certificate** and click **Enroll**.

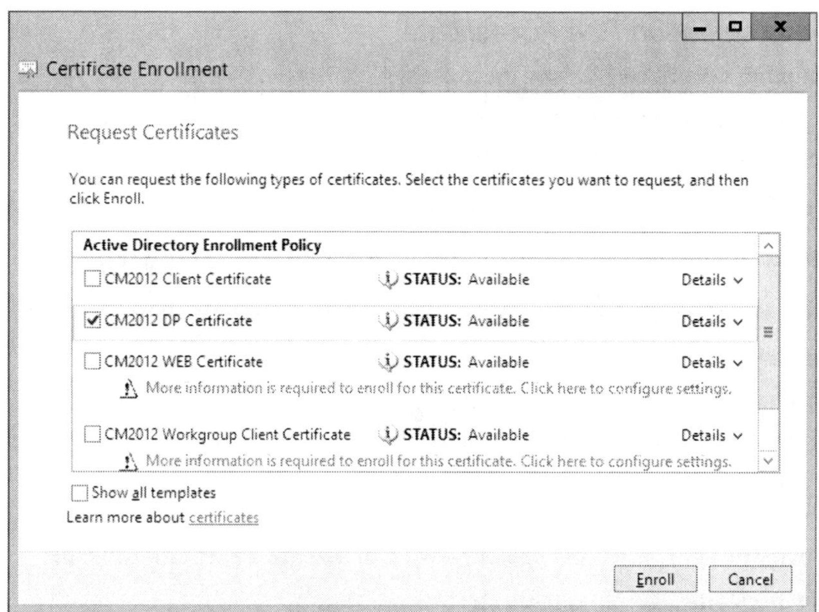

Requesting the Distribution Point certificate.

5. On the **Certificate Installation Results** page, click **Finish**.
6. The certificate must be exported for use in OSD and when creating other distribution points. In the **Personal / Certificates** node, right-click the **CM2012 DP Certificate** (scroll to the right to see the template name) and click **All Tasks / Export**.
7. On the **Welcome to the Certificates Exports Wizard** page, click **Next**.
8. On the **Export the Private Key** page, select **Yes, export the private key** and click **Next**.
9. On the **Export File Format** page, ensure **Personal Information Exchange – PKCS #12 (.PFX)** is selected and click **Next**.
10. On the **Security** page, select **Password**, type **Password01** twice, and click **Next**.
11. On the **File to Export** page, type **D:\Setup\Certificates\CM2012DP.pfx** and click **Next**.
12. On the **Completing the Certificates Export Wizard** page, click **Finish**.

Create the Cloud-Based Distribution Point Certificates

A cloud distribution point solution requires two certificates, a management certificate that you import in Windows Azure and a cloud-based distribution point service certificate. The management certificate must be exported as a .cer file and as a .pfx file. The cloud-based distribution point service certificate is used to encrypt data and authenticate the cloud-based distribution point service to the clients. This certificate must be exported as a .pfx file. You do not have to install the certificate on any clients, but the clients must trust the issuer of the certificate.

Create the Azure Management Certificate

1. On **DC01**, log on as **VIAMONSTRA\Administrator**; from the **Server Manager dashboard**, select **Tools** and **Certification Authority**.
2. Right-click **Certificate Templates** and click **Manage**.
3. Right-click the **Web Server** template and select **Duplicate Template**.
4. On the **General** tab, type **CM2012 CloudDP Management** as the **Template display name**.

Specifying the management certificate name.

5. Select the **Request Handling** tab, and select **Allow the private key to be exported**.

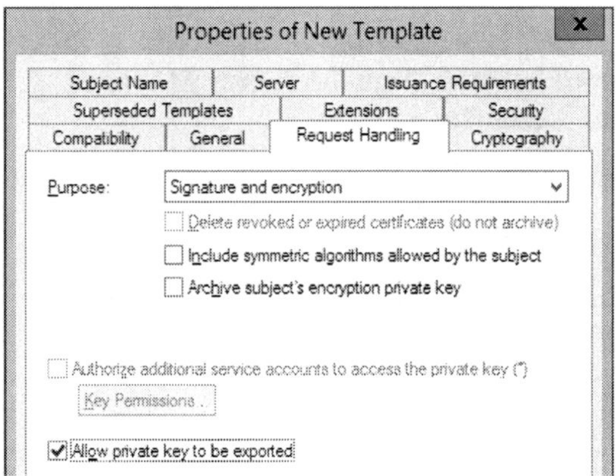

Allowing the certificate to be exported.

6. Click the **Security** tab, and remove the **Enroll** permission from the **Domain Admins** and **Enterprise Admins** security groups. Add the **ConfigMgr_Servers** group and then add **Read** and **Enroll** permissions.
7. Click **OK** and close the Certificate Templates console.
8. Right-click **Certificate Templates**, and select **New / Certificate Template to Issue**.
9. Select the **CM2012 CloudDP Management** certificate and click **OK**. This creates the certificate and makes it ready to be enrolled on the site server.

To enroll and export the certificate, follow these steps:

1. On **CM01**, open a management console with administrative rights. Add the **Certificate** snap-in for the **Computer account**.
2. Make sure **Local computer** is selected, click **Finish**, and **OK**.
3. Expand **Certificates / Personal store / Certificates**, right-click **Certificates**, and select **All Tasks / Request New certificate**.
4. On the **Before you begin** page, click **Next**.
5. On the **Select Certificate Enrollment Policy** page, select **Active Directory Enrollment Policy** and click **Next**.
6. On the **Request Certificates** page, select the **CM2012 CloudDP Management** certificate and click the link **More information is required to enroll this certificate….**
7. In **Subject name**, select **Common name** for **Type**, type **clouddp01.corp.viamonstra.com** for **Value**, and click **Add**.

8. In **Alternative name**, select **DNS** for **Type**, type **clouddp01.corp.viamonstra.com** for **Value**, and click **Add**.

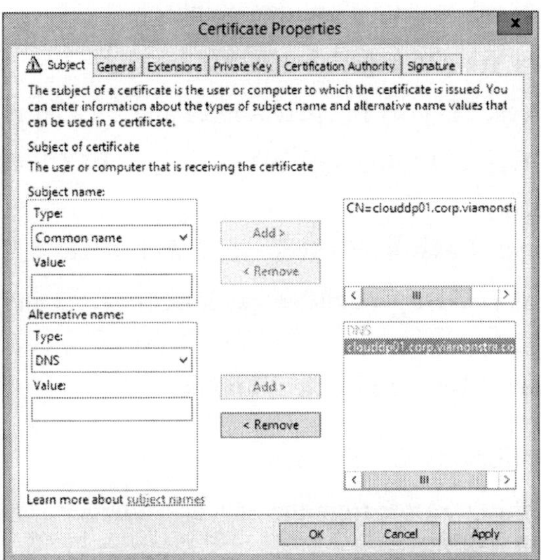

Configuring the certificate properties.

9. Click **OK**.
10. On the **Request Certificates** page, click **Enroll**.

Note: If you get the error "The revocation function was unable to check revocation because the revocation server was offline" when enrolling the certificate, make sure the revocation list has been published. On **DC01**, in the **Certification Authority console**, right-click **Revoked Certificates**, select **All Tasks / Publish**, select **Delta CRL only**, and click **OK**.

11. On the **Certificates Installations Results** page, click **Finish**.
12. While still in the **Personal certificates store**, right-click the new **clouddp01.corp.viamonstra.com** certificate and select **All Tasks / Export**. In the following steps, you need to walk through the export process twice, exporting the certificate as a .cer file and a .pfx file.
13. On the **Welcome to the Certificate Export Wizard** page, click **Next**.
14. On the **Export Private Key** page, select **No do not export the private key** and click **Next**.
15. On the **Export File Format** page, select **DER encoded binary X.509 (.CER)** and click **Next**.

Note: If the DER encoded binary X.509 (.CER) is greyed out, you did not select the "No do not export the private key" option in step 14.

16. Save the file as **D:\Setup\Certificates\clouddp01.cer** and finish the wizard.
17. Again, select **All Tasks / Export**. This time you export the certificate with the private key which is required later when creating the cloud-based distribution point.
18. On the **Welcome to the certificate Export Wizard** page, click **Next**.
19. On the **Export Private Key** page, select **Yes, I export the private key** and click **Next**.
20. On the **Export File Format** page, select **Personal Information Exchange – PKCS #12 (.PFX)** and click **Next**.
21. On the **Security** page, enable **Password,** type **Password01** twice, and click **Next**.
22. On the **File to Export** page, save the file as **D:\Setup\Certificates\clouddp01.pfx** and click **Next**.
23. On the **Completing the Certificate Export Wizard** page, click **Finish**.

Create the Cloud-Based Distribution Point Service Certificate

1. On **DC01**, log on as **VIAMONSTRA\Administrator**; from the **Server Manager dashboard**, select **Tools** and **Certification Authority**.
2. Right-click **Certificate Templates** and click **Manage**.
3. Right-click the **Web Server** template and select **Duplicate Template**.
4. On the **General** tab, type **CM2012 CloudDP Service** as the **Template display name**.

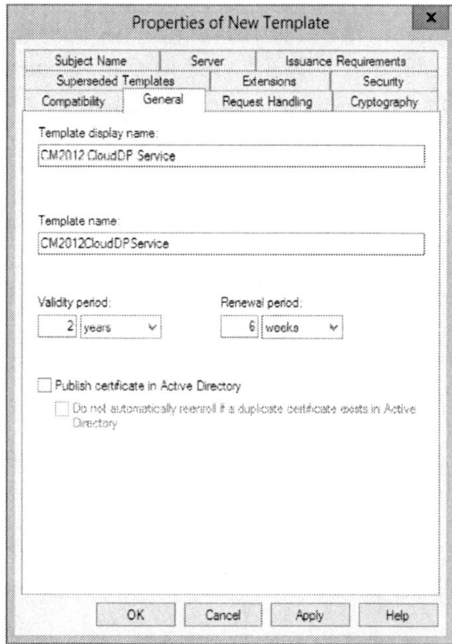

Specifying the cloud-based distribution point service certificate name.

5. Select the **Request Handling** tab and select **Allow the private key to be exported**.

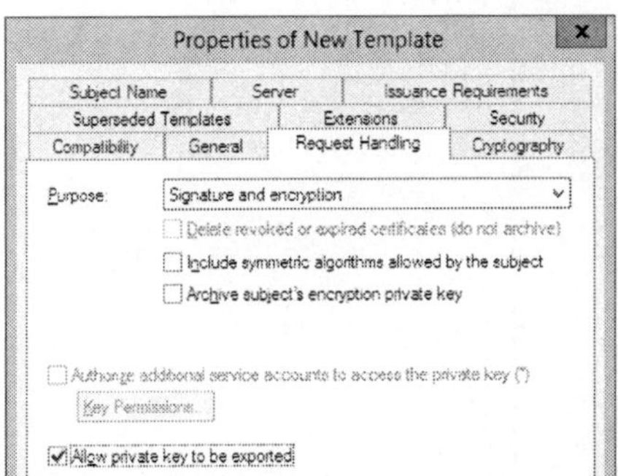

Allowing the certificate to be exported.

6. Click the **Security** tab, and remove the **Enroll** permission from the **Domain Admins** and **Enterprise Admins** security groups. Add the **ConfigMgr_Servers** group and add **Read** and **Enroll** permissions.
7. Click **OK** and close the Certificate Templates console.
8. Right-click **Certificate Templates**, and select **New / Certificate Template to Issue.**
9. Select the **CM2012 CloudDP Service** certificate and click **OK**. This creates the certificate and makes it ready to be enrolled on the site server.

To enroll the certificate, follow these steps:

1. On **CM01**, open a management console with administrative rights. Add the **Certificate** snap-in for the **Computer account**.
2. In the **Certificates snap-in** wizard, select **Computer account** and click **Next**.
3. Make sure **Local computer** is selected, and then click **Finish** and **OK**.
4. Expand **Certificates / Personal store / Certificates**, and then right-click **Certificates** and select **All Tasks / Request New certificate**.
5. On the **Before you begin** page, click **Next**.
6. On the **Select Certificate Enrollment Policy** page, select **Active Directory Enrollment Policy** and click **Next**.
7. On the **Request Certificates** page, select the **CM2012 CloudDP Service** certificate and click the link **More information is required to enroll this certificate….**

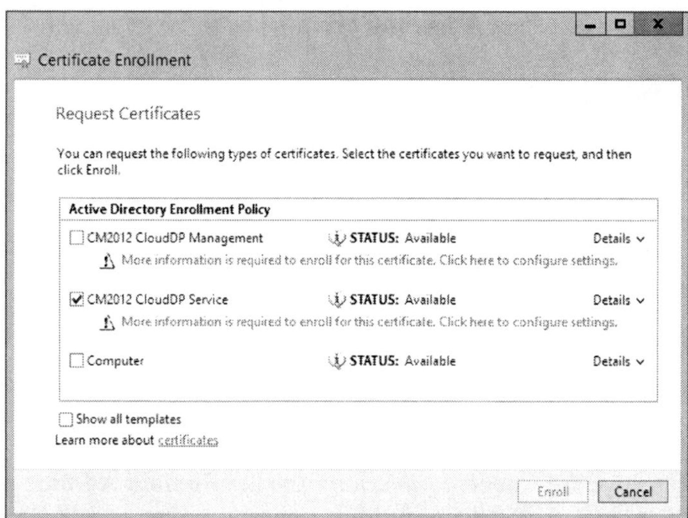

Enrolling the cloud-based service certificate.

8. In **Subject name**, select **Common name** for **Type**, type **clouddp01.corp.viamonstra.com** for **Value**, and click **Add**.
9. In **Alternative name**, select **DNS** for **Type**, type **clouddp01.corp.viamonstra.com** for **Value**, and click **Add**.

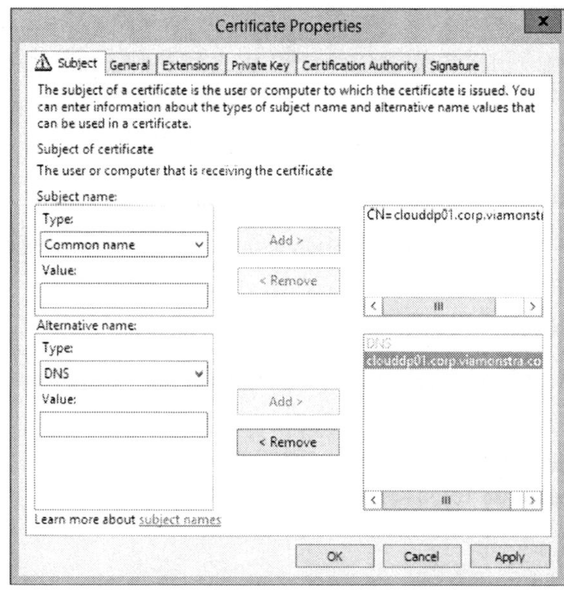

Configuring the certificate properties.

10. Click **OK**.
11. On the **Request Certificates** page, click **Enroll**.

12. On the **Certificates Installations Results** page, click **Finish**.
13. While still in the **Personal certificates store**, right-click the new **clouddp01.corp.viamonstra.com** certificate (scroll to the right and verify it's from the the CM2012 CloudDP Service), and select **All Tasks / Export**.
14. On the **Welcome to the Certificate Export Wizard** page, click **Next**.
15. On the **Export Private Key** page, select **Yes, I export the private key** and click **Next**.
16. On the **Export File Format** page, select **Personal Information Exchange – PKCS #12 (.PFX)** and click **Next**.
17. On the **Security** page, enable **Password,** type **Password01** twice, and click **Next**.
18. On the **File to Export** page, save the file as **D:\Setup\Certificates\clouddp01SRV.pfx** and click **Next**.
19. On the **Completing the Certificate Export Wizard** page, click **Finish**.

The Root CA Certificate

The root certificate must be exported for use in the site server and when creating distribution points. To export the root CA certificate, follow these steps:

1. On **CM01**, log on as **VIAMONSTRA\Administrator**, open a management console as **administrator**, and import the **Certificates** snap-in.
2. Open **Trusted Root Certification Authorities**; in **Certificates**, right-click the root certificate (**ViaMonstraRootCA**) and click **All Tasks / Export**.
3. On the **Welcome to the Certificates Exports Wizard** page, click **Next**.
4. On the **Export File Format** page, ensure **DER encoded binary X.509 (.CER)** is selected and click **Next**.
5. On the **File to Export** page, type **D:\Setup\Certificates\ViaMonstraRoot.cer** and click **Next**.
6. On the **Completing the Certificates Export Wizard** page, click **Finish**.

Configuring the Site Systems to Use HTTPS

In the following steps, you configure the site and site systems to support HTTPS:

1. On **CM01**, open the **ConfigMgr console**. In the **Administration** workspace, select **Site Configuration / Servers and Site System Roles**.
2. Select **CM01.corp.viamonstra.com**; from the **Site System Roles**, select **Management Point**; and then on the ribbon, click **Properties**.

3. In the **Client connections** area, select **HTTPS**, enable **Allow mobile devices and MAC computers to use this management point**, and click **OK**.

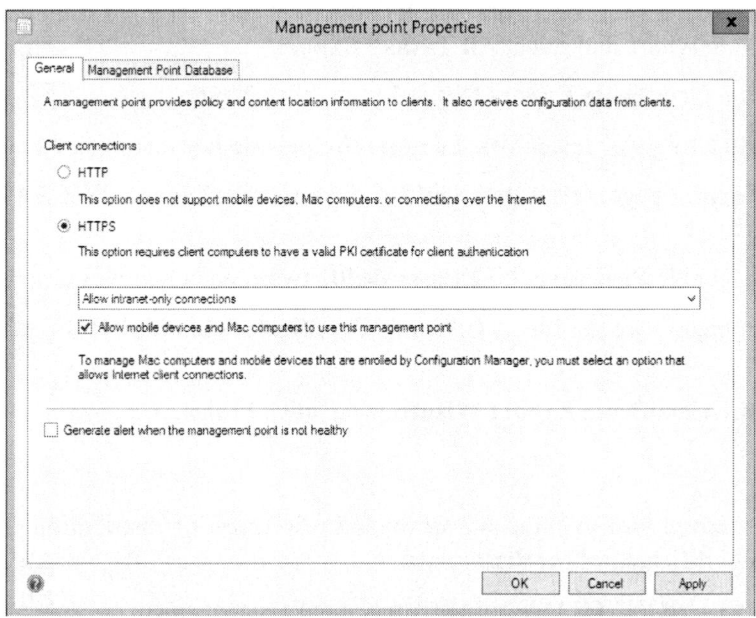

Configuring a management point to support HTTPS.

4. Open the properties for the **Software update point**, select **Require SSL communication to the WSUS server**, ensure that ports **8530** and **8531** are selected, and click **OK**.

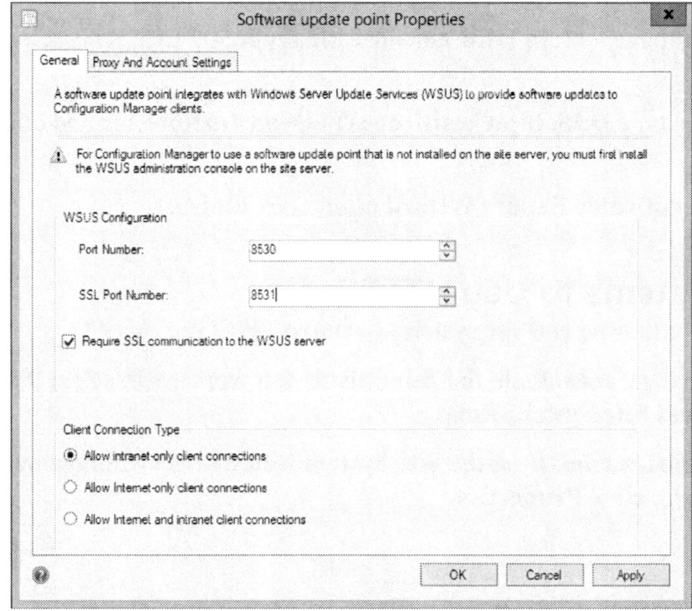

Configuring a software update point to support HTTPS.

5. Open the properties for the **Application Catalog website point**, click **HTTPS (Recommend)**, and then click **OK**.

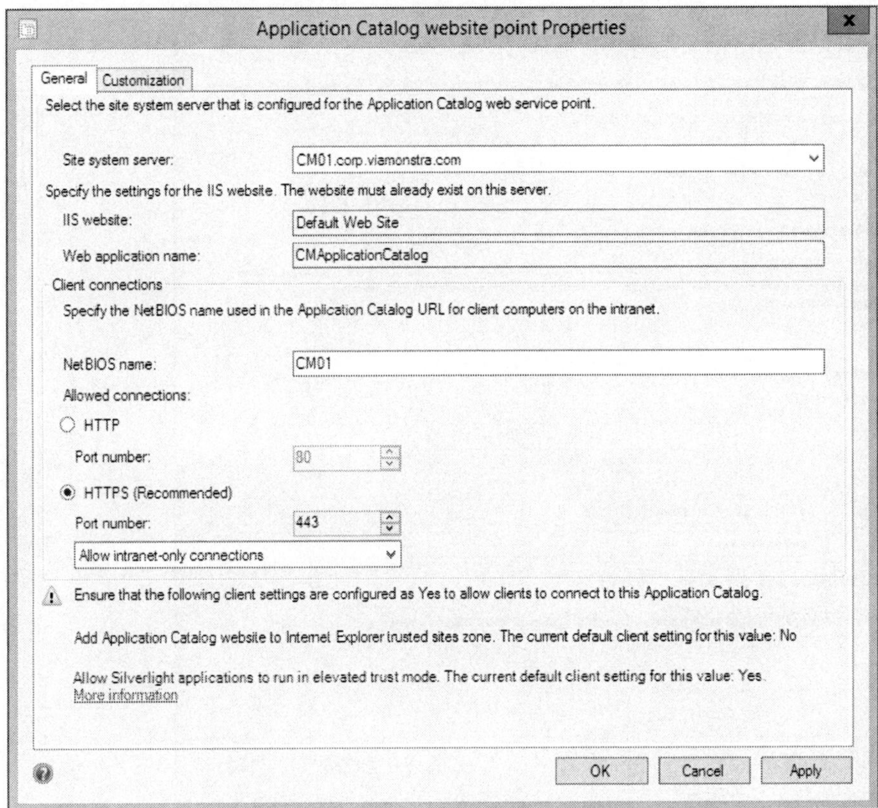

Configuring an application catalog point to support HTTPS.

6. Open the properties for the **Distribution point**, and click **HTTPS**.

7. Select **Import certificate**, click **Browse**, and select **D:\Setup\Certificates\CM2012DP.pfx**.

8. In **Password**, type **Password01** and click **OK**.

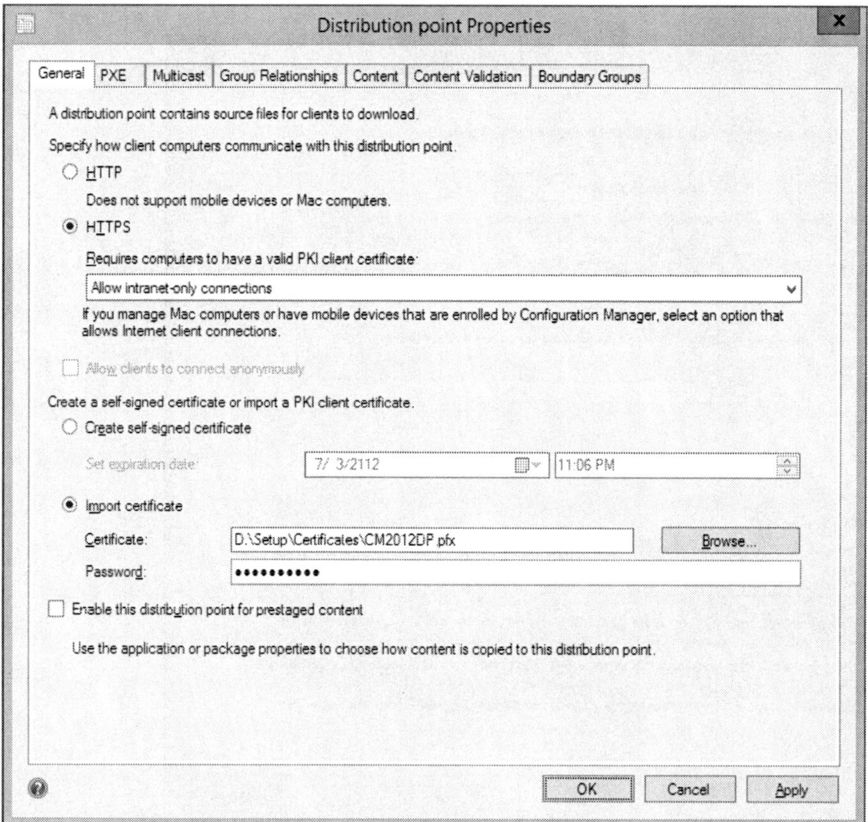

Configuring a distribution point to support HTTPS.

9. Select **Sites**, right-click **PS1 - ViaMonstra HQ**, and open the properties.
10. Select **Client Computer Communication**, and enable **Use PKI client certificate (client authentication capability) when available**.

11. Click **Set**, and verify that the **ViaMonstraRootCA** root certificate is listed.

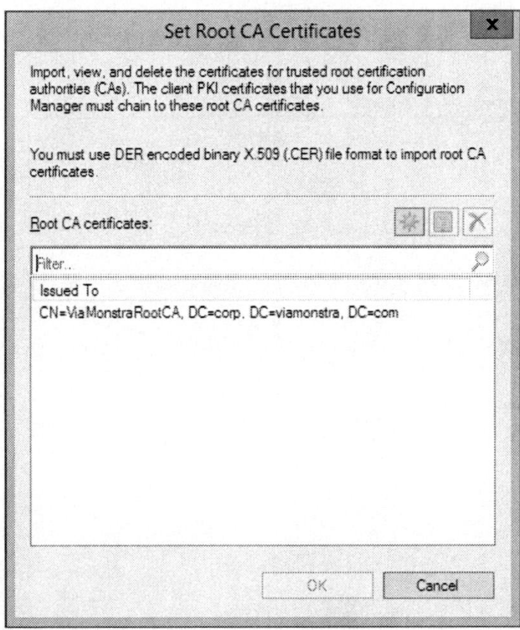

Importing the root CA certificate.

12. Clear the **Client check the certificate revocation list (CRL) for site systems** option and click **OK**.

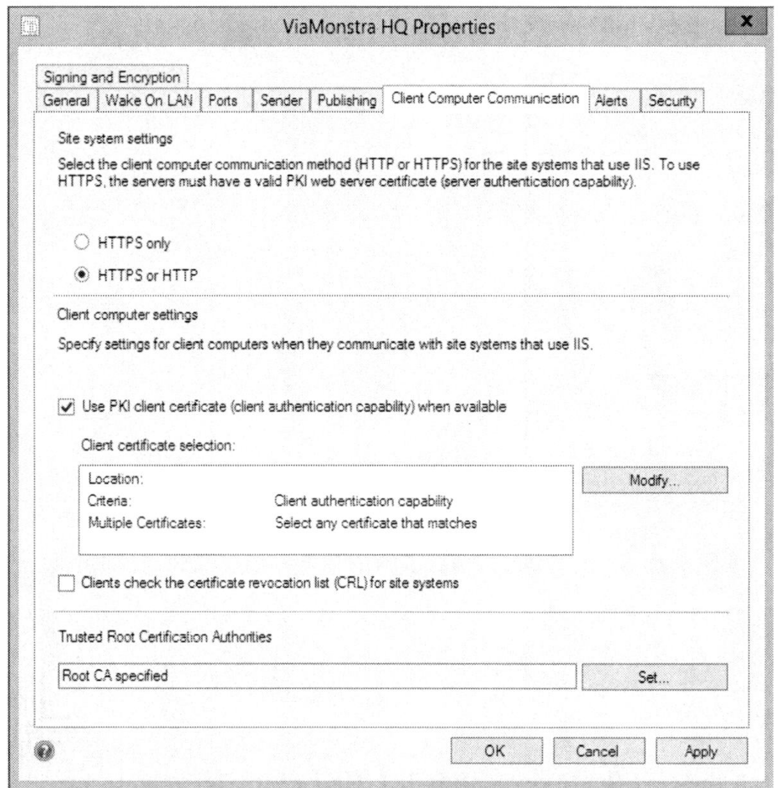

Configuring the site to support both HTTP and HTTPS.

Real World Note: In a real production environment, you normally make use of certification revocation lists (CRLs). Using certificate revocation and the certificate revocation list is beyond the scope of this book as it's external to ConfigMgr and really part of the production PKI design and implementation. That being said, enabling CRL checking in ConfigMgr is seamless but will fail if your PKI is not designed for it, and/or your Certificate Revocation List Distribution Point (CDP) is not available when clients try to use a certificate and check the CRL. For clients in the VIAMONSTRA domain this is not a problem because the default CDP in a Microsoft PKI is Active Directory, but it will be a problem for Internet-based clients not having access to it. To support Internet-based clients, you need to set up a CDP accessible from the Internet. If you want to learn more, here is a good link for ConfigMgr 2007, but the info is still valid for ConfigMgr 2012 SP1: http://tinyurl.com/mhnuzx2.

Verifying that HTTPS Is Working

There are several ways you can verify that HTTPS is working in your environment. The easiest way is to install a client using one of the command lines discussed in the following section and test the different features like application deployment, software update management, and operating system deployment. But before you start testing those features, I encourage you to verify that the infrastructure is working. The first role to check is the management point. Open the

D:\Program Files\Microsoft System Center Configuration Manager\Logs\mpcontrol.log file and verify that the certificates are okay.

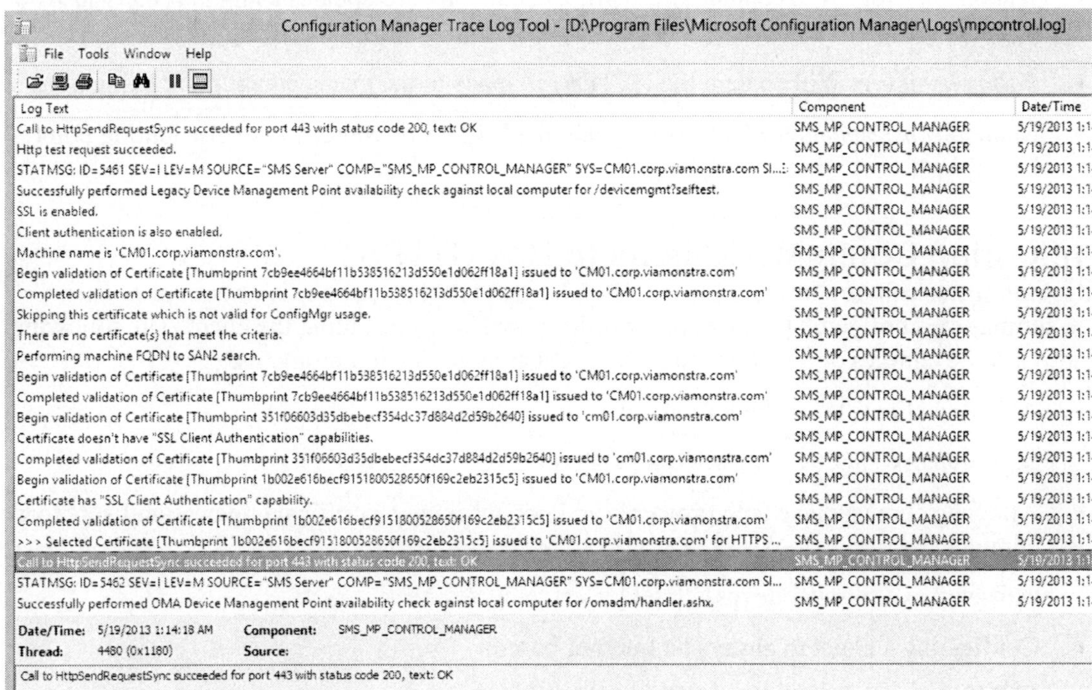

Verifying the management point.

You also can open the ConfigMgr client agent properties in Control Panel and check the client certificate. It should say PKI.

ConfigMgr Properties reporting PKI.

Other good sources on the client to check for are these log files:

- *Wuahandler.log*: Will contain information about software updates using port 8531 instead of 8530.
- *PolicyAgent.log*: Will contain the HTTPS reference to the management point being used.
- *Contenttransfermanager.log*: Will contain the HTTPS reference to the distribution point being used.

Configuring ConfigMgr Clients to Use HTTPS

ConfigMgr clients can be configured to use HTTP or HTTPS only, or a mix of both protocols. Those settings are configured by the command lines used when installing the client. The following provides a few examples of how to control the client communication protocols:

- Allowing clients to use both protocols:

  ccmsetup.exe smssitcode=ps1 /UsePkiCert

- Allowing clients to use both protocols and not checking a certificate revocation list before communicating:

  ccmsetup.exe smssitcode=ps1 /UsePkiCert /NoCRLcheck

- Configuring a client to always be Internet-based:

  CCMSetup.exe /UsePKICert CCMALWAYSINF=1 CCMHOSTNAME=cm01.viamonstra.com SMSSITECODE=PS1

- Configuring a client to select the certificate from an alternate certificate store:

  CCMSetup.exe /UsePKICert CCMCERTSTORE="ViaMonstra"

- Configuring an Internet-based client to use a hard-coded management point:

  CCMSetup.exe /UsePKICert/ CCMHOSTNAME="cm01mp.corp.viamonstra.com"

Appendix K
Configuring MDM Support

With the release of ConfigMgr 2012 Service Pack 1, mobile device management (MDM) has become a key feature. Before SP1, the only choice for managing modern mobile devices like smartphones was via the Exchange Connector. With SP1, you are now able to integrate ConfigMgr 2012 and Windows Intune through the Windows Intune connector. With Windows Intune, you have a cloud infrastructure that can be used to manage your mobile devices. Before configuring the Windows Intune Connector, let's have a look at the different kinds of mobile device management options in ConfigMgr 2012.

MDM Options Available in ConfigMgr 2012 SP1

There are three kind of mobile device management options available in ConfigMgr. The following table explains the supported devices, support features per platform, and how you can manage them with ConfigMgr.

Platform	Manage	Features
Android	Via Windows Intune connector and/or Via Exchange connector	Settings management Software distribution (only via Intune) Hardware inventory Remote wipe/retire/block
Apple IOS	Via Windows Intune connector and/or Via Exchange connector	Settings management Software distribution (only via Intune) Hardware inventory Remote wipe/retire/block
Nokia Symbian Belle	Via Exchange connector and/or Direct via client	Settings management Software distribution (only via client) Hardware inventory Remote wipe/retire/block
Windows 8 RT	Via Windows Intune connector	Settings management Software distribution Hardware inventory Remote wipe/retire/block

Platform	Manage	Features
Windows CE 5.0, 6.0, 7.0	Via Exchange connector and/or Direct via client	Settings management Software distribution (only via client) Hardware inventory Remote wipe/retire/block
Windows Mobile 6.0, 6.1, 6.5	Via Exchange connector and/or Direct via client	Settings management Hardware inventory Remote wipe/retire/block
Windows Phone 7.x	Via Exchange connector	Settings management Hardware inventory Remote wipe/retire/block
Windows Phone 8	Via Windows Intune connector and/or Via Exchange connector	Settings management Software distribution (only Intune) Hardware inventory Remote wipe/retire/block

Note: You might be thinking that Windows Intune and the Exchange connector are two competing components. Look at it this way: the Exchange connector provides you with information about all the mobile devices that are connected through ActiveSync, whereas Intune "only" gives you information from those devices that are enrolled. There can easily be a big difference in those two numbers.

Preparing Windows Intune Integration

To use the mobile device management features of ConfigMgr 2012 SP1, you need to acquire a Windows Intune subscription. If you want to test it in a lab environment, you have the option of a 30-day trial license that be acquired from www.windowsintune.com by filling in your personal or company information. You also can acquire a license through your normal volume license channels. After you have registered the Windows Intune account, you must go through these high-level steps before you can finalize the ConfigMgr integration:

1. Configure the domain name in Windows Intune.
2. Configure each user's public domain user principal name (UPN) in Active Directory and run user discovery in ConfigMgr.
3. Configure Active Directory Federated Services (ADFS). ADFS is technically not a requirement, but without ADFS, users have to manage two passwords, one for Active Directory and one for Windows Intune.
4. Configure Active Directory directory synchronization.
5. Create the Intune connector in ConfigMgr.

Configure the Domain Name in Windows Intune

Configuring your public DNS name in Windows Intune is required for enrollment redirection and to prove that you own the public domain. During the enrollment process, the device is redirected to the Windows Intune environment. Windows Intune offers the ability for you to add your own domain name, such as viamonstra.com, as explained in the following steps:

1. Log on with the account you created during the registration on www.windowsintune.com (that is, **admin@viamonstra.onmicrosoft.com**).
2. On the **Admin Overview** screen, click **Domains** and click **Add a domain**.

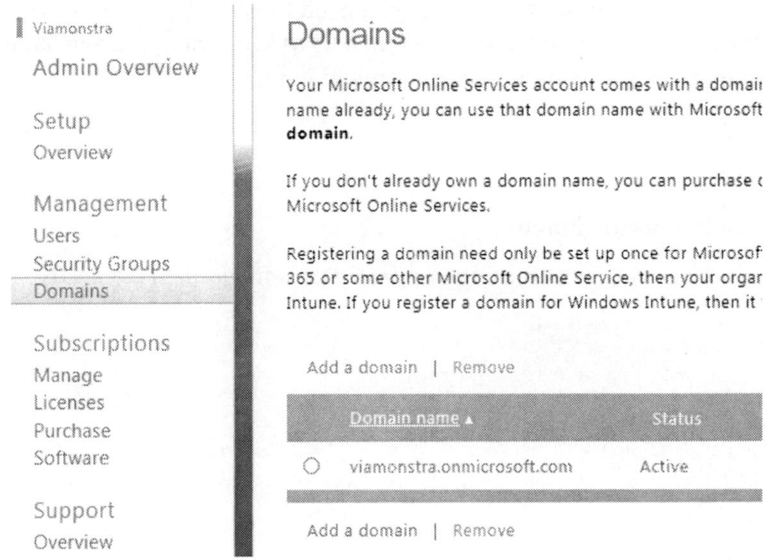

Adding a domain.

3. Type the domain name **ViaMonstra** and click **Next**.
4. Next, you need to prove that you are the owner of the domain name supplied. This can be done by adding a TXT record that is supplied to your domain or adding an MX record to the same public domain that you want to add to Windows Intune. Click **Verify** to finish adding the domain name. Microsoft Online Services automatically scan and verify your domain name.

Create a TXT record

Use the table and instructions below to create a DNS record to verify a domain that is registered at your domain name registrar. For general instructions about verifying a domain, see Verify a domain at any domain name registrar.

Host name	Text value	TTL
@	MS=ms51963782	1 Hour

Adding the TXT record to your domain.

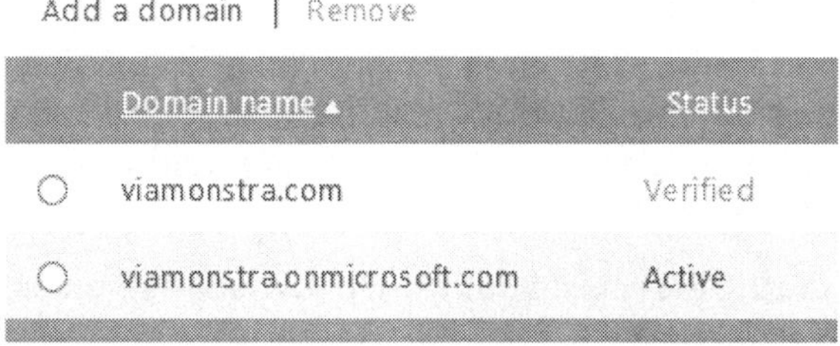

The domain name viamonstra.com is verified.

After configuring Windows Intune with your domain name, you need to add a CNAME to be able to support enrollment redirection. What you need to do is set up a CNAME (enterpriseenrollment) for your domain that targets enterpriseenrollment.manage.microsoft.com.

1. On **DC01**, launch **DNS**.
2. Add the CNAME record.
3. In **Alias name**, type **enterpriseenrollment**.
4. For **FQDN**, type **enterpriseenrollment.manage.microsoft.com**, and then click **OK**.

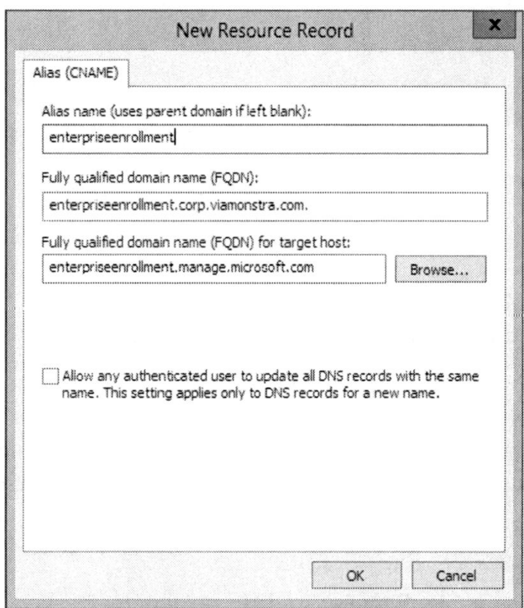

Configuring the CNAME record.

Note: The settings are almost 100 percent identical to setting up an Office 365 subscription.

Create a UPN Suffix for the Users

When working with a local domain, you need to add an alternative UPN suffix to associate the users' corporate credentials connecting to Windows Intune. A UPN suffix is the part of a UPN to the right of the @ character.

1. On **DC01**, log on as **VIAMONSTRA\Administrator**.
2. From the **Start screen**, launch **Active Directory Domains and Trusts**.
3. Right-click **Active Directory Domains and Trusts** and then click **Properties**.
4. Select the **UPN Suffixes** tab, type the alternative UPN suffix **viamonstra.com** to support Windows Intune, and then click **Add**.

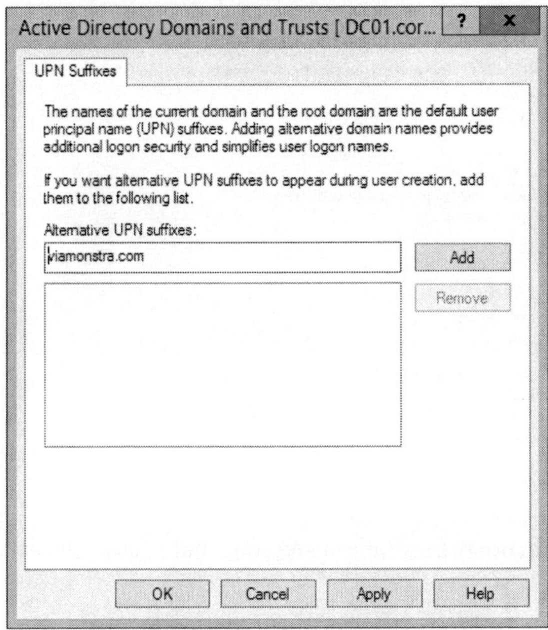

Adding the viamonstra.com UPN suffix.

5. Repeat step 4 for every additional alternative UPN suffix.
6. On **CM01**, log on as **VIAMONSTRA\Administrator** and verify that the UPNs are part of the Active Directory User Discovery. A user's UPN must be in the ConfigMgr database.

Set Up Single Sign-on and DirSync

Before you are able to set up Active Directory synchronization, you need to be sure that the following requirements are met:

- Domain viamonstra.com is set up in Windows Intune.
- The UPN viamonstra.com is set up as required.

Follow these steps to set up Active Directory synchronization:

1. Log on to the **Windows Intune Admin portal** (the web site is **account.manage.microsoft.com**).
2. Navigate to **Users** and click **Set up** (to the right of **Active Directory® synchronization**).

   This takes you to a six-step walkthrough for setting up Active Directory synchronization.

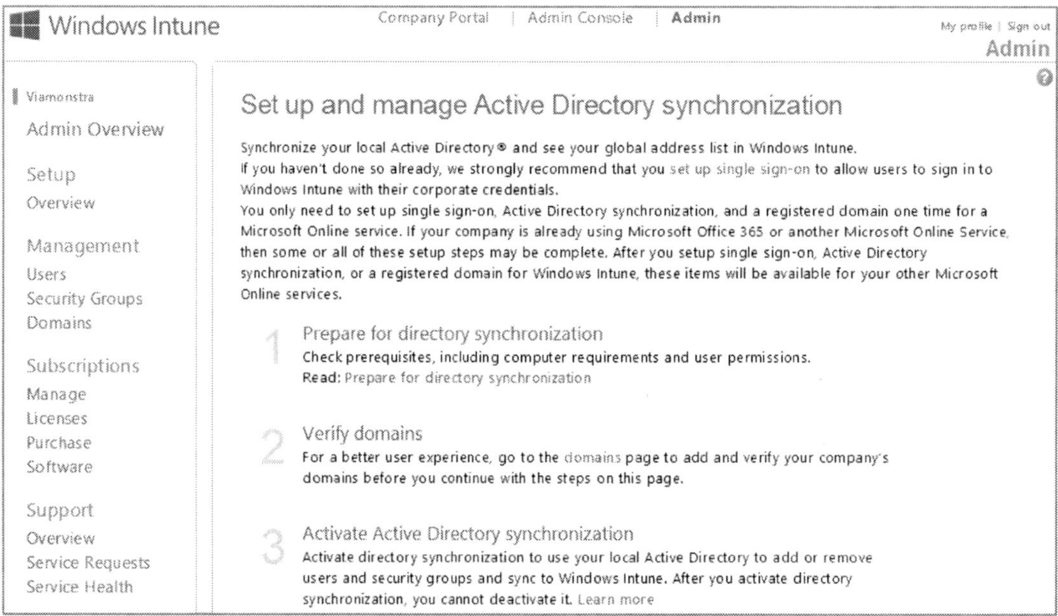

Setting up DirSync for ViaMonstra step by step.

3. Follow the **Prepare for directory synchronization** link in step one and review the information.
4. Return to the **Set up and manage Active Directory synchronization** page and activate Active Directory synchronization by clicking **Activate.**
5. After clicking Activate, download the **Directory Synchronization (DirSync)** tool.
6. Run the downloaded **dirsync.exe** file as **VIAMONSTRA\Administrator** on **CM01**, click **Next**, accept the license terms, and click **Next** again.
7. Keep the default installation directory and click **Next**. Installing the Microsoft Online Services Directory Synchronization can easily take 10 minutes.
8. After the installation is finished, click **Next**.
9. Leave the **Start Configuration Wizard** selected and click **Finish** to start the Configuration Wizard.
10. Click **Next** to start the configuration.

11. Provide the administrative account of Windows Intune (that is, **admin@viamonstra.onmicrosoft.com**), supply the password, and click **Next**.

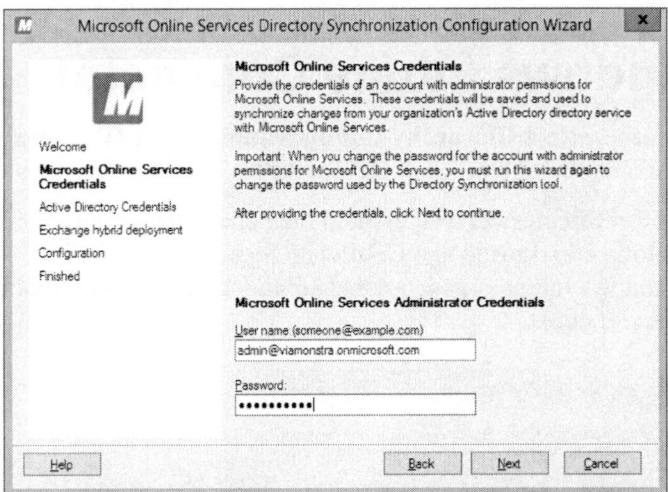

Supplying the administrative account of Windows Intune.

12. Type a domain admin account and password, and then click **Next**.

13. Click **Next** twice and then **Finish** to synchronize the directories.

Create a User Collection for Windows Intune

You can control which users can enroll mobile devices by creating a user collection and specifying that collection during the Windows Intune connector setup:

1. In the **Asset and Compliance** workspace, select **User Collection**, and then on the ribbon, click **Create User Collection**.
2. On the **General** page, enter the following details and click **Next**:
    a. Name: **All Windows Intune Users**
    b. Limiting Collection: Click **Browse** and select **All Users**.
3. On the **Membership Rules** page, click **Add Rule, Direct Rule**.
4. On the **Welcome** page, click **Next**.
5. On the **Search for Resources** page, in **Value**, type **%** and click **Next**.
6. On the **Select Resources** page, select **VIAMONSTRA\BOP, VIAMONSTRA\JAP, VIAMONSTRA\MAC** from the list and click **Next**.
7. On the **Summary** page, read the summary and click **Next**.
8. On the **Completion** page, click **Close** and return to the Membership Rules page.
9. On the **Membership Rules** page, click **Next**.

10. On the **Summary** page, read the summary and click **Next**.
11. On the **Completion** page, click **Close**.

Setting Up the Windows Intune Connector

1. In the **Administration** workspace, select **Hierarchy Configuration**, select **Windows Intune Subscriptions**, and then on the ribbon, click **Create APNs certificate request**.
2. In **File Name**, type **D:\Setup\Certificates\certreq.csr** and then click **Download**. The wizard connects to Windows Intune to download a Certificate Signing request. If necessary, log on with the Windows Intune organizational administrator account (that is, **admin@viamonstra.onmicrosoft.com**).

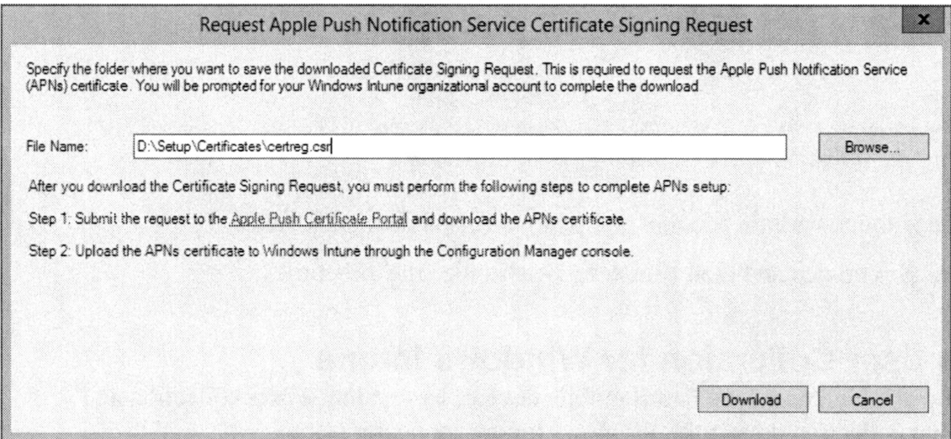

Creating the Apple certificate.

3. After the download, click **Close**.
4. On the ribbon, click **Create Windows Intune Subscription**.
5. On the **Introduction** page, click **Next**.
6. On the **Subscription** page, click **Sign In**, and sign in with your Windows Intune administrator account (that is, **admin@viamonstra.onmicrosoft.com**). After a successful sign in, you return to the Subscription page.

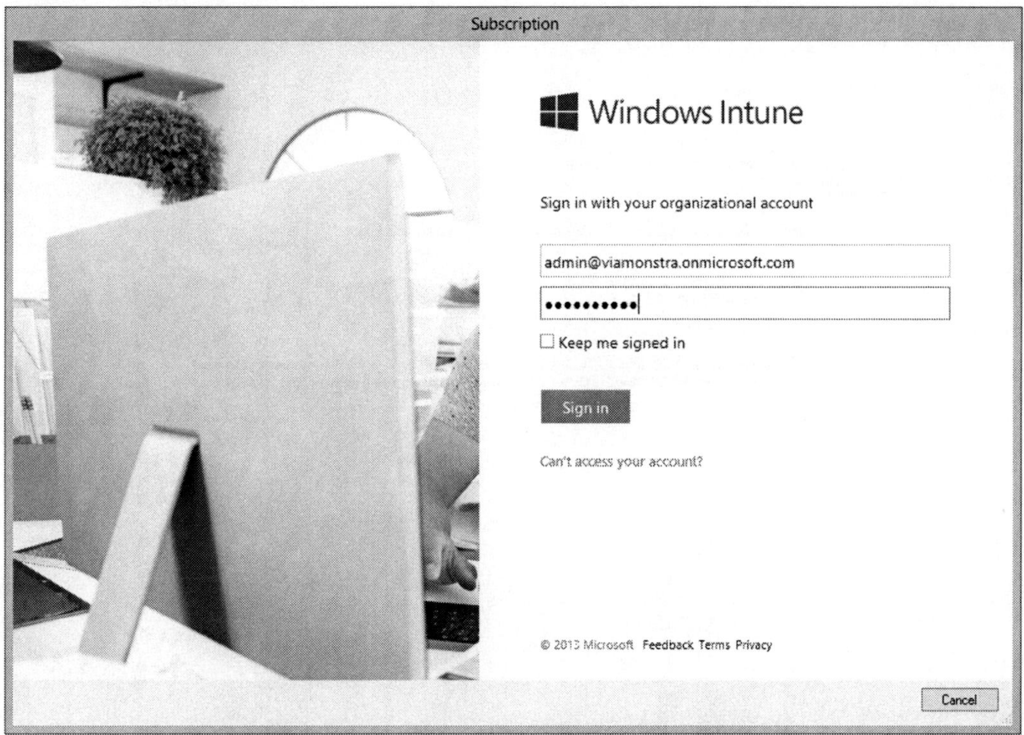

Supplying the Windows Intune organization account credentials.

7. Back on the **Subscription** page, select **Allow the Configuration Manager console to manage this subscription** and click **Next**.

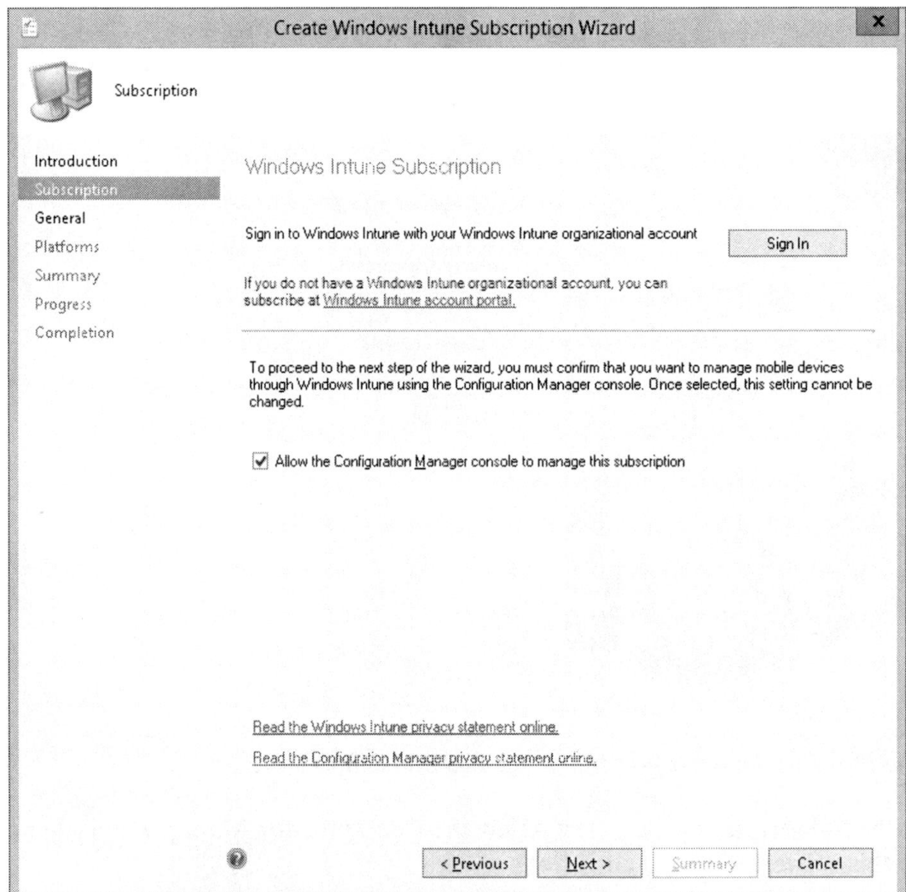

Enabling ConfigMgr to manage Windows Intune.

8. On the **General** page, configure these settings and click **Next**:

a. Collection: **All Windows Intune Users**

b. Company name: **Viamonstra**

c. URL to company privacy documentation: **http://viamonstra.com/privacy**

d. Configuration Manager site code: **PS1**

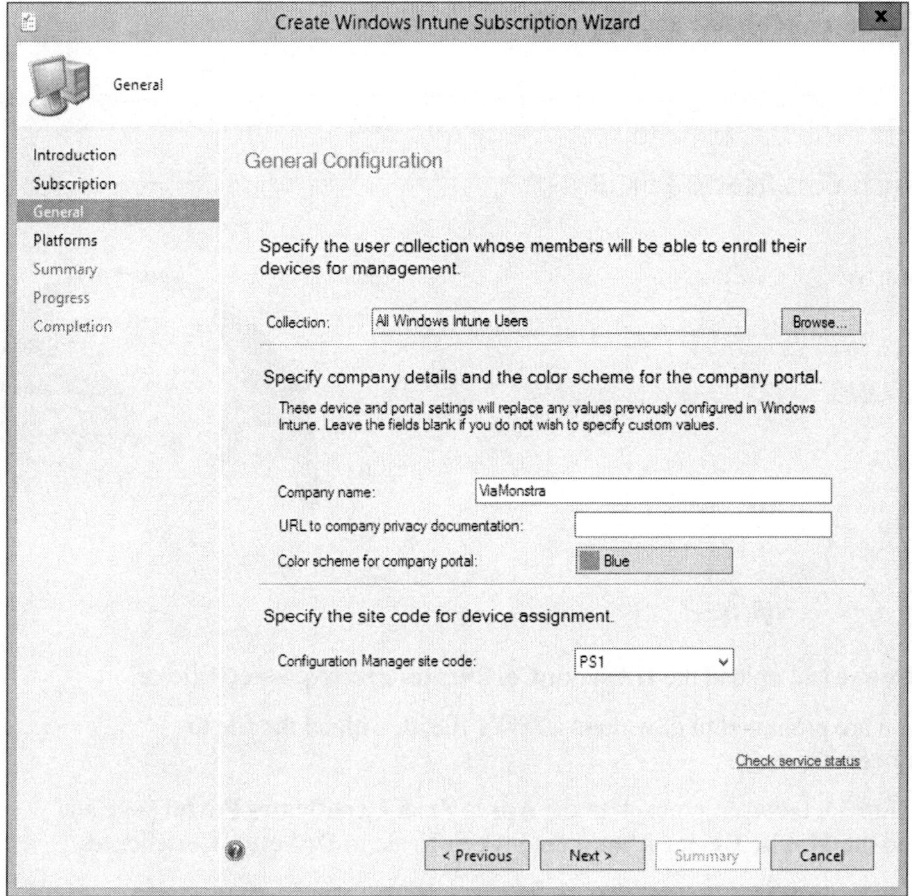

Configuring the company portal information.

9. On the **Platforms** page, select **iOS** and click **Next**. Note that you can always go back and add more platform support.
10. On the **iOS** page, click the **Apple Push Certificate Portal** link to upload the Certificate Signing request.
11. On the **Apple** website, log on with your Apple ID.

12. Click **Create a Certificate** and accept the license terms.

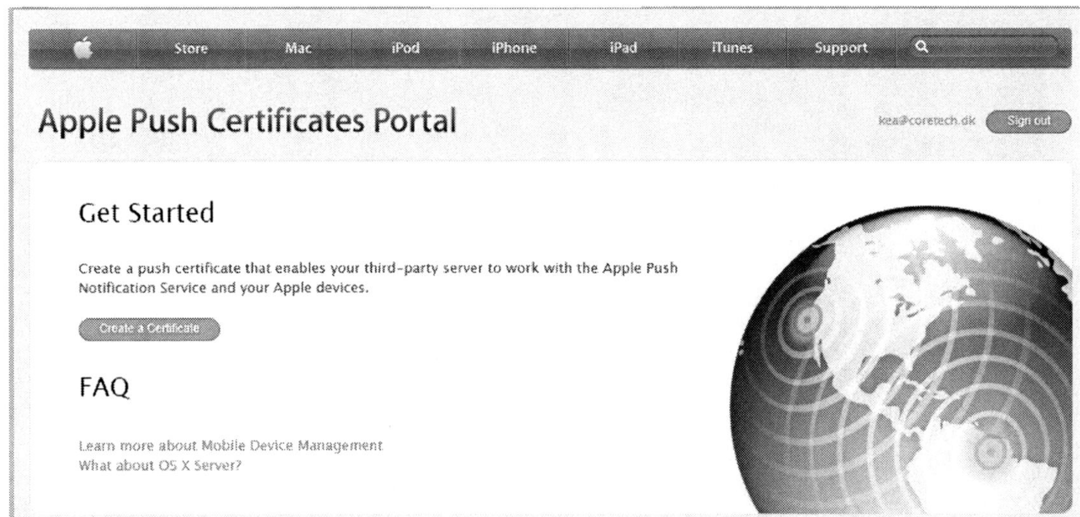

Creating the Apple certificate.

13. Click **Browse** and upload the **D:\Setup\Certificates\certreq.csr** certificate.
14. When you are prompted to download a JSON file, download the file to **D:\setup\certificates**.
15. In your Internet browser, go back to the **Apple Push Certificates Portal** page and download the **Mobile Device Management** certificate to **D:\Setup\Certificates**.

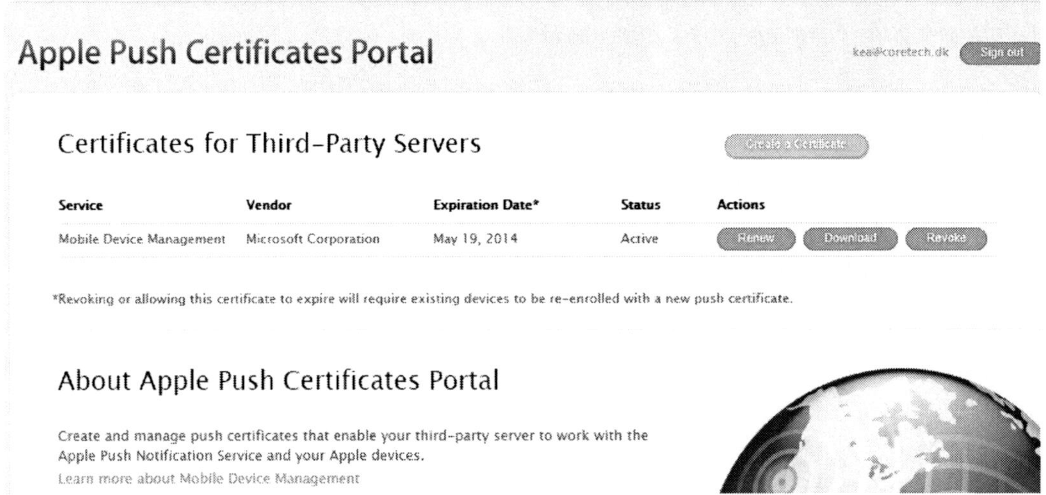

Downloading the Apple Mmobile Device Management certificate.

16. Close your browser and return to the Create Windows Intune Subscription Wizard.

17. Click **Browse** and select **D:\Setup\Certificates\MDM_ Microsoft Corporation_Certificate.pem**.
18. Finish the wizard.

In the background ConfigMgr adds a new site system role server called *manage.microsoft.com*. This is the Windows Intune distribution point. The next step in the process is to configure the Windows Intune Connector as a site system role on CM01.CORP.VIAMONSTRA.COM:

1. In the **Administration** workspace, select **Site Configuration**, **Servers and Site System Roles**, and the site server **CM01.CORP.VIAMONSTRA.COM**.
2. On the ribbon, click **Add Site System Roles**.
3. On the **General** page, click **Next**.
4. On the **Proxy** page, click **Next**.
5. On the **System Role Selection** page, select **Windows Intune Connector** and click **Next**.

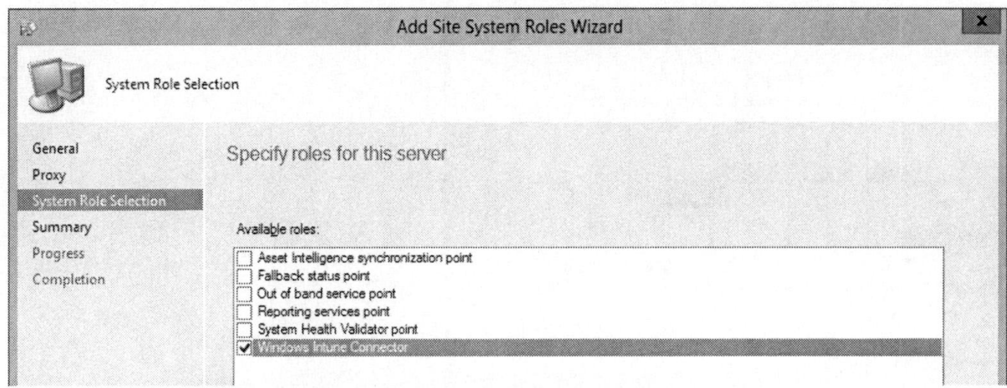

Selecting the Windows Intune Connector site role.

6. On the **Summary** page, read the summary and click **Next**.
7. On the **Completion** page, click **Close**.

Enrollment Example

The enrollment of devices is different per platform. Like many companies, ViaMonstra has a variety of mobile devices. In this example, a user, Mark Carragher (MAC), wants to enroll his iPhone device.

Enrollment Preparation

The first step of the enrollment process is to ensure that the user is allowed to enroll his device via Windows Intune. As the ConfigMgr administrator, you must add the user to the All Windows Intune Users collection:

1. In the **Asset and Compliance** workspace, select **User Collection**, select the **All Windows Intune Users** collection, and then on the ribbon, click **Add Resource**.
2. Type **MAC** in the **Name string contains** field.
3. Change **Resource type** to **User Resource** and click **Search**.

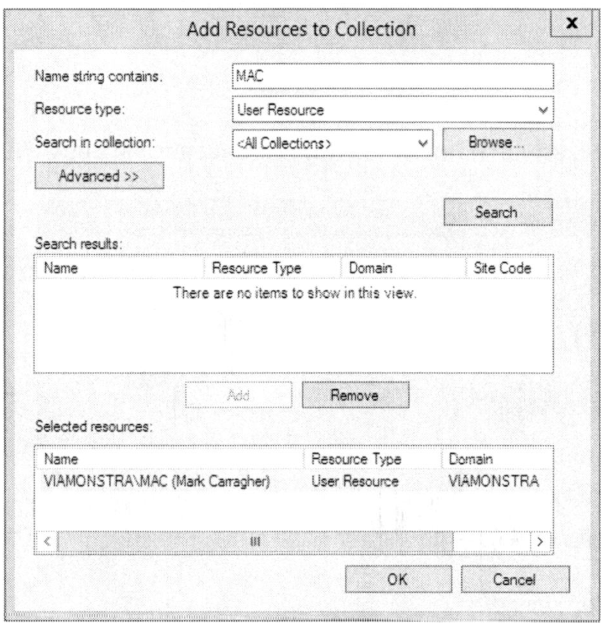

Adding the new user to the All Windows Intune Users collection.

4. Select **MAC@viamonstra.com** in the **Search results**, click **Add**, and then click **OK**.

Note: Adding users to the Intune collection automatically starts a synchronization process between ConfigMgr and Windows Intune. Use CMtrace.exe to read cloudusersync.log for detailed information.

Enroll the iPhone

Enrolling devices is a process driven by the end users. For iOS devices like iPhones and iPads, the process is fairly simple.

1. On your **iPhone**, start the Safari Internet browser and go to **https://m.manage.microsoft.com**.

2. Sign in to the **Windows Intune** portal as **mac@viamonstra.com** and complete the following enrollment process:

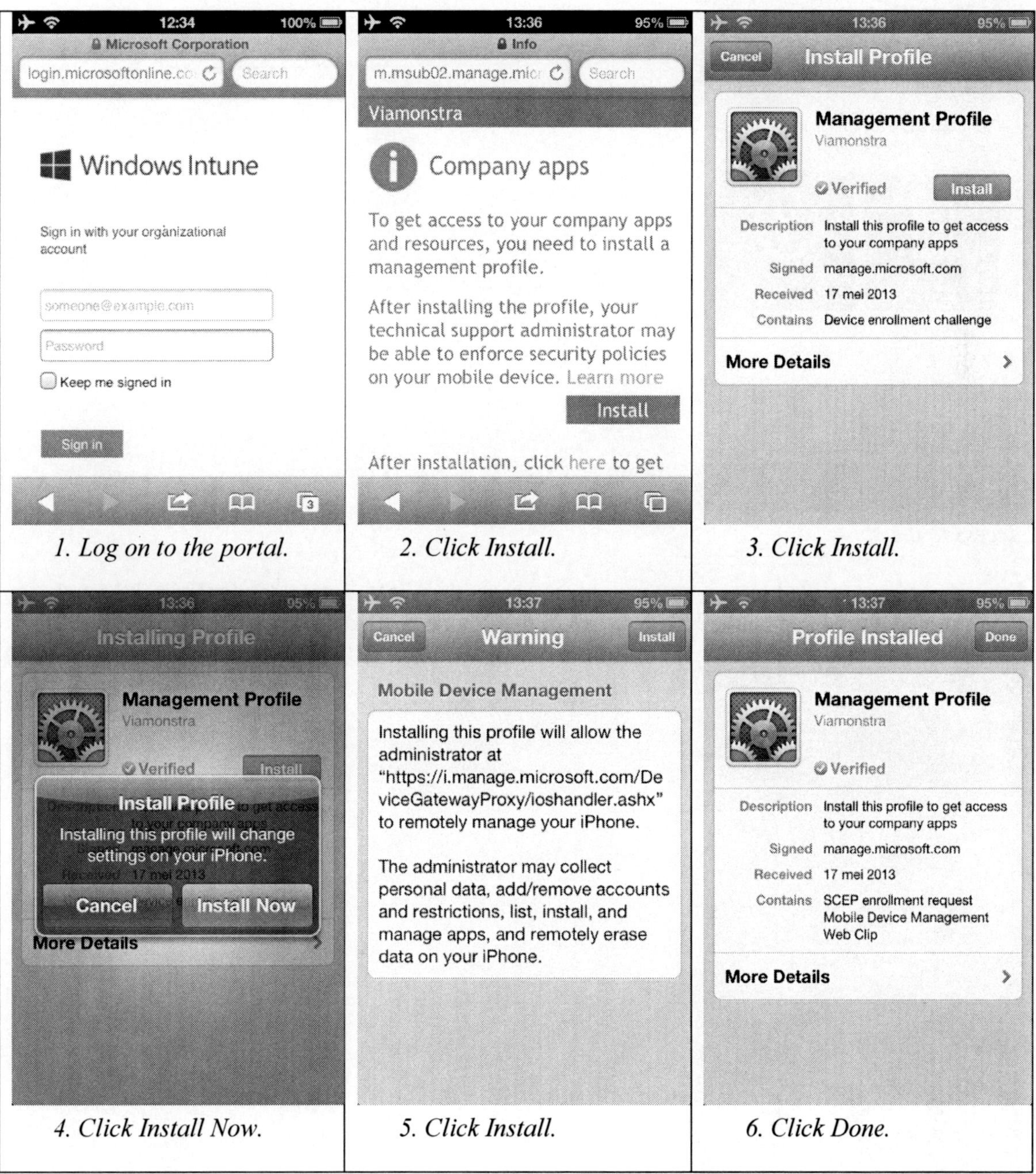

1. Log on to the portal.	*2. Click Install.*	*3. Click Install.*
4. Click Install Now.	*5. Click Install.*	*6. Click Done.*

After the enrollment process is finished you will have access to the company portal and applications.

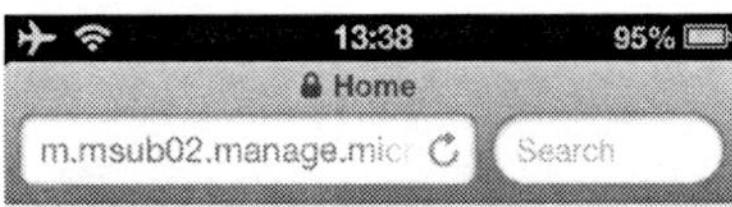

Viamonstra

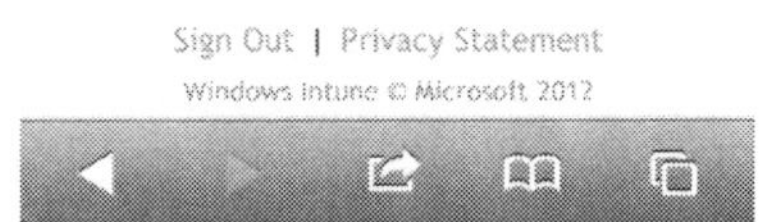

Access to the apps.

From the iPhone or iPad screen, you are able to access the ViaMonstra company portal through the Company Portal app on the Home screen of the iPhone or iPad device.

Access the apps via the Company Portal app.

Optional Federation and Single Sign-On

For domain joined devices, you either have to manage two sets of passwords or configure Active Directory Federation Services (ADFS) and Single Sign-On (SSO). It's not a requirement, but is considered to be a very good idea. For non-domain joined devices, there is no reason for you to configure ADFS and SSO.

Note: You need to plan Active Directory Federation Services carefully before installing it. For more information, please read http://technet.microsoft.com/en-us/library/jj151794 . You may need to publish federation server proxies to the Internet.

1. On **DC01**, log on as **VIAMONSTRA\Administrator** and start the **Server Manager dashboard**.
2. Click **Add Roles and Features**.
3. On the **Before You Begin** page, click **Next**.
4. On the **Server Selection** page, click **Next**.
5. On the **Server Roles** page, select **Active Directory Federation Services** and click **Add Features** in the dialog box.

Adding ADFS to support SSO.

6. Click **Next** three times and then click **Install**.
7. Click **Close** after the installation is finished.

Configure Active Directory Federation Services

For ViaMonstra, you configure the Active Directory Federation Services as described in the following steps:

1. On **DC01**, log on as **VIAMONSTRA\Administrator** and launch **AD FS Management** from the **Start screen**; select **AD FS Federation Server Configuration Wizard**.
2. Select **Create a new Federation Service** and click **Next**.
3. Select **Stand-alone federation server** and click **Next**.
4. Select the (web server) certificate that is issued to **DC01.corp.viamonstra.com** and click **Next**.

5. Review the summary and click **Next**.
6. After reviewing the results, click **Close**.

The next step (step three) in the list is downloading and installing the Microsoft Online Services Module for Windows PowerShell, but before installing it, we need to download and install the Microsoft Online Services Sign-In Assistant:

1. Download the **Microsoft Online Services Sign-In Assistant**, which you can find at **http://g.microsoftonline.com/0BX00en/501**.
2. Double-click the downloaded **msoidcli.msi** file on **DC01**, accept the license agreement, and click **Install**.
3. Click **Finish**.
4. Double-click the downloaded **AdministrationConfig-EN.MSI** file. Then click **Next**, accept the license terms, and click **Next** again.
5. Leave the installation location, click **Next** and **Install**.
6. Click **Finish** after the installation is complete.

Next, you need to set up a trust between your domain and the Active Directory for Windows Intune that is hosted in Windows Azure:

1. On **DC01**, start the **Windows Azure Active Directory Module for Windows PowerShell** from the **Start screen**.
2. In **PowerShell**, type the following command and provide the administrative account of Windows Intune (that is, **admin@viamonstra.onmicrosoft.com**):

```
$cred=Get-Credential
```

Creating a variable for the credentials and supplying the username and password.

3. In **PowerShell**, type the following command:

   ```
   Connect-MsolService -Credential $cred
   ```

4. In **PowerShell**, type the following command:

   ```
   Set-MsolAdfscontext -Computer dc01.corp.viamonstra.com
   ```

5. Since you already added the domain viamonstra.com to Windows Intune and the UPN to your local domain,you need to convert the domain to a federated domain via PowerShell. In **PowerShell**, type the following command:

   ```
   Convert-MsolDomainToFederated -DomainName
   corp.viamonstra.com
   ```

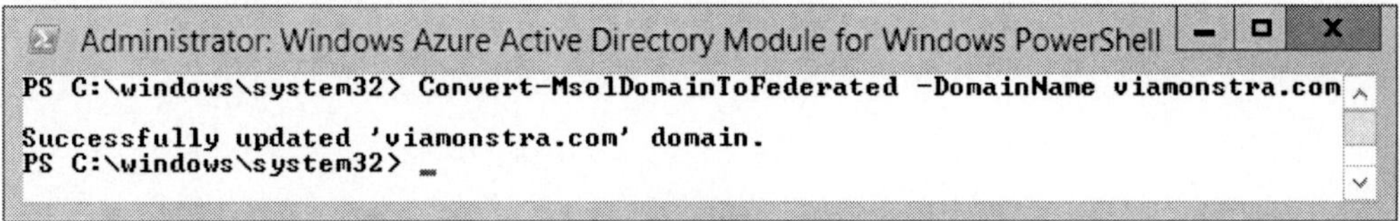

Converting the ViaMonstra domain to federated.

Note that you can use Get-MsolFederationProperty -DomainName viamonstra.com to retrieve the configuration of the federation.

Index

L

M

N

O

P

Q

R

S

T

U

V

W

Beyond the Book – Meet the Expert

If you liked the book, you will love to hear Kent in person.

Live Presentations

Kent Agerlund frequently speaks at conferences like Microsoft Management Summit (MMS) and TechEd around the world. You also can find Kent at infrastructure tours and local events like Microsoft Campus Days/TechDays, the Nordic Infrastructure Conference (NIC), and user group meetings around the globe.

For current tour dates and presentations, see http://blog.coretech.dk/kea.

Video Trainings

For video-based training, see the following sites:

- www.truesec.com
- www.deploymentartist.com

Live Instructor-led Classes

Kent Agerlund presents scheduled instructor-led classes in the US and in Europe. For current dates and locations, see the following sites:

- www.coretech.dk
- www.truesec.com
- www.labcenter.se

Lightning Source UK Ltd.
Milton Keynes UK
UKOW02f1901280813

216129UK00005B/453/P